CREATIVE INDIA

CREATIVE INDIA

FROM MOHENJO DARO TO THE AGE OF RAMAKRSNA-VIVEKANANDA

BENOY KUMAR SARKAR

GYAN

Published by

Gyan Publishing House
5, Ansari Road
Daryaganj, New Delhi-110002
Phone: 011-47034999, 9811692060
E-mail: books@gyanbooks.com

Distribution Network
gyanbooks.com
India, USA, Canada, UK, Australia, France

ISBN: 978-81-212-8574-2 (PB)
First Published, 1937

2nd Impression 2023

Printed at: Gyan Press, Delhi.

CREATIVE INDIA
Author: Benoy Kumar Sarkar

CREATIVE INDIA

FROM MOHENJO DARO TO THE AGE OF RĀMAKṚṢṆA-VIVEKĀNANDA

By

BENOY KUMAR SARKAR

Post-Graduate Departments in Economics and Commerce, Calcutta University; Hony. Professor of Economics and sometime Rector, College of Engineering and Technology, Jadabpur, Calcutta; *Gast Professor an der Technischen Hochschule*, Munich (1930-31): Member, Royal Asiatic Society (North China Branch, Shanghai), *Deutsche Morgenlandische Gesellschaft* (Leipzig), *Correspondant de la Société d'Economie Politique* (Paris), *Corrispondente al Comitato Italiano per lo Studio dei Problemi della Popolazione* (Rome), *Institut International de Sociologie* (Geneva), and Royal Economic Society (London); Correspondent, *American Sociological Review*; Editor, *Arthik Unnati* (Economic Progress)

PREFACE

The present work deals with some of the creations of the Indian peoples in personalities, ideas, institutions and movements from the Mohenjo Daro times to the age of Rāmakṛṣṇa-Vivekānanda as specimens of human energizing. It is in the light of comparative culture-history and sociology understood in the widest sense that the growth and development of the diverse regions and races in India are exhibited. The attempt is mainly selective or suggestive in regard to topics and tendencies as well as epochs and areas of the transformation of *Prakriti* (Nature) by *Puruṣa* (man) in India.

I have sought to exhibit in relief some of those phases and trends in the evolution of Indian manhood and civilization which are generally overlooked or minimized by antiquarian researchers, text-book writers on Indian history, archæology, philosophy or literature, as well as by authors of general treatises relating to the "spirit" of India or the East. The pluralistic trends of the Indian *Gestalt* of civilization or culture-complex *in motion* constitute the dynamic perspective of this investigation. Apart from the facts surveyed, no matter how circumscribed the fields, there are the viewpoints, orientations and methods of analysis such as are likely to have some meaning even to those who in India or abroad are specializing in other fields and other facts.

It is as a contribution to the realistic philosophy or inductive sociology of "values" that the work has been planned out.

The difficulties of managing a work like this might be well understood if one were to visualize a study, say, of developments in Europe from Mycenæ to the Second Five Year Plan. Evidently there is every chance of ignoring or doing injustice not only to the nooks and corners as well as pools and rivulets of life but even the broadways and avenues as well as seas and channels.

It is to be observed that the footnotes contain references also to such works as have not been used as *data* for the present publication or as differ even fundamentally from my own interpretations.

I have made it a point to make liberal use of my publications in journals or books since 1910, especially as many of them are out of print or hardly accessible in India in a convenient form, distributed, as they happen to be, in diverse culture-centres of the East and the West.

BENOY KUMAR SARKAR

CALCUTTA
December 26, 1936

CONTENTS

CHAPTER I

India as a Creator of Values

CHAPTER II

Indian Creations in Institutions

CHAPTER III

The Creations of Hindu Philosophy in Political Science

CHAPTER IV

The Literature, Art and Social Philosophy of the Indian People

CHAPTER V

The Creations of Modern India

CHAPTER I

INDIA AS A CREATOR OF VALUES

SECTION I

THE HINDUS OF HISTORY

(*c.* B. C. 3500—1935 A. C.)

The Mohenjo Daro "Hindus" represent perhaps the peak of an ascending curve in culture-history. And if their techniques, arts and sciences of material life as well as inventions of "spiritual" culture are to be assigned to the fourth millennium B. C. one will have to commence the cycle of this civilization at a much more remote antiquity. For the precursors of the Mohenjo Daro Hindus, i.e., for the primitive and rudimentary beginnings or rather the "pre-historic" origins of these "Chalcolithic" developments we have to "imagine" certain ages between, say, 3500 B. C. and some of the Palaeolithic strata of human achievements (*c.* 10,000 B. C.), such as are described, for instance, in C. H. B. Quennell's *Everyday Life in the Old Stone Age*. Evidently the Mohenjo Daro Hindus are quite recent or modern compared to those prehistoric forefathers of the Indian races.

For the present, however, in order to keep to the facts let us be somewhat modest in chronological dimensions. Today in 1935 we can be sure only of the fact that the creations of the Hindus are older than those of the Vedic ages (*c.* 1500-1000 B. C.), corresponding to or synchronous, as these latter are, with the Homeric epochs of European culture. The earliest Hindu creators of human civilization were at least as old as the Assyro-Babylonians and Egyptians. The "Hindus" of the Indus Valley (Mohenjo Daro, Harappa and other sites)[1] were perhaps not yet used to the metallurgy of iron. But they built roads 13-30 ft. wide, enjoyed hydropathic and hot air-baths and commanded the convenience of public drainage. Their agricultural technique knew the cultivation of wheat and barley, and industry the use of cotton spinning whorls. By commercial relations they came into contact with the "East" and the "West" of those days. Among their arts and crafts are to be mentioned ivory seals, dancing forms, *svastika* design, animal figures (buffalo, rhinoceros etc.), half-syllabic scripts, stone, gold, copper, bronze and silver vessels. The "Hindu" culture of this Chalcolithic period (*c.* 3500-3000 B. C.) appears to have been dominated by "cities," and the people were used to spacious dwelling houses. And in keeping with the world-forces of those days the Indus Valley "Hindus" propagated the cult of the Mother Goddess who was equally at home in Persia, Western Asia, the Aegean culture-zone, and Egypt. It is indeed possible to trace the beginnings of the tree and serpent worship, the *pipal* tree cult, the phallus-cult, as well as Śiva and Durgā of our times back to the fourth millennium B. C.

In the present study we are not interested in the continuity of this civilization of the ancient Punjab

[1] J. Marshall: *Mohenjo Daro and the Indus Civilization* (London 1931), J. Przyluski: "The Great Goddess in India and Iran" (*Indian Historical Quarterly*, Calcutta, September, 1934); A. K. Sur: "Pre-Aryan Elements in Indian Culture" (*Calcutta Review*, April, 1931, November and December 1932, *I. H. Q.* March, 1934). See also N. N. Law: "Mohenjo Daro and the Indus Valley Civilization" (*I. H. Q.*, March, 1932).

and Sindh as coming down to our own times. Nor indeed is it our chief theme to stress the antiquity of Creative India's attainments in the arts and sciences. It is from altogether other angles of vision,—sociologico-cultural rather than archaeologico-historical,—that we are examining some of the aspects and tendencies of creative India.

Let us commence with the conventional approach of orientalists to Indian civilization. If the same conventional method were applied to European civilization we should have to pick up some such data as the following from Western sociography:

In Europe even in the sixteenth and seventeenth centuries the barbers were surgeons. Even in the eighteenth century the magic touch of the king's hand was believed by the English people to have marvellous therapeutic effects. Patients suffering from scrofula and other diseases used to petition the Court in order to have the royal healing administered to them. Today in Europe and America millions of Christians still believe in immaculate conception and transubstantiation.

If an Indian were to note these and other facts of a like nature and exhibit them as specimens of modern Eur-America or mediaeval and ancient Europe it would be doing injustice to the intellect of the Occidental world. But this is just what European and American scholars of modern times have generally done with regard to India and the Orient. The little that is known of the Orient in Europe and America today is, to say the least, based on a fundamentally wrong attitude of mind and an unscientific presentation of the subject-matter.

The most prevalent notion is that Hindu literature is at best the literature of topics dealing with the "other world," the soul, the Divinity,—the themes which constitute the stock-in-trade of pessimistic metaphysics. The historic truth, however, is that metaphysical subjectivism is the least part of Hindu thought, and pessimism the farthest removed from actual Indian life and institutions. The Hindus have discussed every subject in the universe from the tamarind to the pole-star. Hindu literature and art are the literature and art of every human passion and activity from sex to salvation.[1]

The Hindus have written on "pure" mathematics; their algebra and arithmetic were in advance of those of the Greeks. The Hindus have in fact laid down the foundations of the mathematical science known to the modern world. To a certain extent they anticipated Descartes (1596-1650) in the principles of solid geometry and Newton (1642-72) in those of differential calculus. The solutions of Lagrange and Euler (1707-83) in indeterminate equations of the second degree were given by the Hindus more than one thousand years before their time.

[1] See the present author's "*Śukranīti* as a Document of Hindu Culture" (*Modern Review*, Calcutta, 1913); *The Positive Background of Hindu Sociology* (Allahabad) Vol. I. (1914), Vol. II, (1921, 1926), *Love in Hindu Literature* (Tokyo, 1916), *The Folk-Element in Hindu Culture* (London, 1917), *Hindu Achievements in Exact Science* (New York, 1918), "Democratic Ideals and Republican Institutions in India" (*American Political Science Review*, November, 1918), "The Hindu View of Life" (*Open Court*, Chicago, August, 1919), "Gilde di Mestier e Gilde Mercantili nell' India antica" (*Giornale degli Economisti e Rivista di Statistica*, Rome, April, 1920), "La Theorie de la Constitution dans la philosophie politique hindoue" (*Revue de Synthèse Historique*, Paris, August-December, 1920), *Hindu Art: Its Humanism and Modernism* (New York, 1920), *Die Lebensanschauung des Inders* (Leipzig, 1923), "Aspects politiques et économiques de la civilisation hindoue" (*Revue de S. H.* Paris, June, 1930) "Die Struktur des Volkes in der sozialwissenschaftlichen Lehre der Schukraniti" (*Koelner Vierteljahrshefte fuer Soziologie* XI, i, 1931), "Sociological Approaches to Vedic Culture" (*Prabuddha Bharata*, Calcutta, September, October and November 1935).

Hindu literature on anatomy and physiology as well as eugenics and embryology has been voluminous. The Hindus knew the exact osteology of the human body two thousand years before Vesalius (*c.* 1543) and had some rough ideas of the circulation of blood long before Harvey (1628). The internal administration of mercury, iron and other powerful metallic drugs were practised by the Hindu physicians at least one thousand years before Paracelsus (1540). And they have written extensive treatises on these subjects.

The Hindus have written on government, municipal institutions, taxation, census, jurisprudence, warfare, and the laws of nations. Their investigations bear comparison with those of Aristotle, Machiavelli and Jean Bodin. The Hindus have written on painting, literary criticism, dramaturgy, dancing, gesture, music, irrigation, navigation and town-planning.

In Europe the six notes of the gamut were invented by Guido, monk of Arezzo in Tuscany (995-1050) and the seventh was added by Le Maire of Paris in the sixteenth century. But the Hindus wrote about the full musical scale at least as early as the fifth century and they devised also a sort of musical notation, signs and symbols, which may be regarded as the analogues of the mediaeval European *neumes*.

Hindu treatises on algebra, arithmetic, astronomy, pharmacy, chemistry, medicine and surgery were not confined to India. They were translated into Chinese (and ultimately into Japanese) on the one side; and on the other, were translated into Arabic by the Moslems of Western Asia. In the Middle Ages the Moslems taught the Christians of Europe at Cordova in Spain, at Cairo in Egypt, at Damascus in Syria, and at Bagdad on the Tigris. The Europeans have thus learnt the Hindu decimal system of notation in mathematics, the use of some Hindu medicinal drugs, and Hindu metallurgy.

The musical theories of the Hindus were the same as those of the Europeans down to nearly the end of the Middle Ages, as both were based on "melody." "Harmony" is a recent European growth (seventeenth century). Similarly the theories of painting also were the same both in India and Europe. Like the Hindus, the ancients and mediaevals in Europe did not have the "perspective" with which the modern world is familiar. Hindu books on painting have, besides, influenced the art and art-criticism of China during her "Augustan Age." Europeans and Americans who are today admiring the Chinese masters are thereby indirectly paying homage, to a certain extent, to Hindu art-philosophy.

In a sense the geography of Creative India is as wide as Asia itself. It is the result of *l'aptitude colonisatrice, la faculté pour l'homme de sortir de ses frontières pour aller séjourner*, the colonizing aptitude, the capacity of man to move out of his frontiers in order to live abroad, as Lasbax would say.[1] This indeed constitutes the celebrated *Aitareya Brāhmaṇa* (VII, 15) cult of *charaiveti* (march on). Hindu thought is even now governing the Bushido morality of the Japanese soldiers. It is at the back of the philosophical writings of the neo-Confucianists (of the Sung Age) and of the mystical Taoists in China as well as of the energistic Nichirenism of the people in Japan. It runs to a certain extent through the Sufistic teachings of the Persian poets, is responsible for the Buddhism of Siam and Indo-China, and regulates the everyday life of the Central-Asian, Mongolian and Siberian rustics. And the islands of the South Seas and the Indian Ocean from the Philippines

[1] E. Lasbax: *La Cité Humaine* (Paris 1927), Vol. II, pp. 219-220.

on the East to Madagascar on the African coast bear on them indelible marks of Hindu colonial expansion, in vocabulary, literary tradition, sculpture, and architecture.

All this is a fairy tale today. But it was brought about by the most natural circumstances. For about fifteen hundred years from the close of the fourth century B. C. the Hindus maintained a "Greater India" of international commerce and culture. Creative India thus grew into the heart and brain of Asia.

It is often supposed that Hindu history is that of a people who belonged to some ante-diluvian age. It is even held in some quarters that the epoch of Hindu achievements was synchronous with the primitive Vedic age or that it was exhausted in the so-called Buddhist period. The facts are quite otherwise. The Vedic age is by no means the greatest age of the Hindus; nor is there, strictly speaking, a "Buddhist period" of Indian history.

It may be true that the Hindu ships brought muslin and indigo to the builders of the pyramids in Egypt, and jewels to Syria for the breastplate of the Hebrew high priest. It is indeed true that Hindu traders had settlements in the international quarters of the great city of Babylon, a New York of antiquity. The Mohenjo Daro culture of India goes, besides, back to *c.* 3500 B. C. But for all practical purposes the great achievements of the "ancient" Hindus should be regarded as synchronous with those of the Greeks from Pythagoras (sixth century B. C.) to Aristotle (fourth century B. C.), of the Alexandrians (Hellenists) and of the Roman Empire (*c.* A. C. 100-600).

As for the subsequent ages, it should be remembered that the "classical" races of Europe were extinct and gave the torch of civilization to the "barbarian" Teutons; whereas the Hindus continued to live and expand maintaining and furthering their race-consciousness. Down to the Renaissance of the sixteenth and seventeenth centuries, represented by Descartes, Leibniz and Newton, these new European races could not virtually distance the Hindus in any branch of science or art, theoretical or applied. And down to the "Industrial Revolution," i.e., the application of steam to manufacture and communication in the late eighteenth and early years of the nineteenth century the Hindu political, economic and social institutions were more or less on a par with those in Europe.

Liberty of the people was not then greater in the Western world than in India, women's rights were then not known in any part of the globe, mankind did not know anywhere the blessings of universal literacy, industry was everywhere limited to the cottage and domestic system, the family was tied to the village, the civilization was throughout mainly agricultural and rural, and the Hindu Louis's, Fredericks and Peters were as good or as bad "enlightened despots" as were those of Europe.

The Hindus are alleged to have been defective in organizing ability and in the capacity for administering public bodies. Epoch by epoch, however, creative India has given birth to as many heroes, both men and women, in public service, international commerce, military tactics, and government, as has any race in the Occidental world. Warfare was never monopolized by the so-called Kṣatriya or warrior caste in India, but as in Europe, gave scope to every class or grade of men to display their ability.

Hindu history is the history of as many institutions, councils, conferences, academies and congresses, as that of the Western races. The Hindus organized municipal commissions for civic life and built hospitals for the sick and wounded at least three hundred years before the Christian era. The Hindus had *pariṣats*, i.e., academies or clubs for philosophical and scientific investigation in every age of their history. They established universities for the advancement of learning and propagation of culture. And they instituted societies or associations for religious and moral purposes as well.

It is a vicious practice to try to understand Hindu characteristics or the "spirit" of independent Hindu civilization from the failures and demoralization of the Hindus in an epoch of political nothingness. It is also unscientific to forget the actual superstitions and backwardnesses of the European Middle Ages and "early modern" times while making an estimate of independent Hindu culture down to the end of the eighteenth century.

One must not in any case forget that among the last representatives of independent Hindu India we have such remarkable names as Sivāji (1627-1680) and Bāji Rāo (1720-1740) as well as Ranjit Singh (1780-1839). For the same period we have Moslem leaders like Asaf Jah (1724-1748) of Hyderabad and Haidar Ali (1722-1782) as well as Tipu Sultan (1749-1799) of Mysore.

From the Bengali and the South Indian angles of vision the lower terminus of political sovereignty exercised by the Hindu races is likely to be somewhat distorted. It is therefore very necessary to observe that Hindu states were enjoying independence down to the middle of the nineteenth century. The eighteenth century of Indian political history was dominated by the Hindus.

With the annexation of the Punjab by Raghunāth (Rāghobā) in 1758 during the Peshwaship of Balaji Baji Rao (1740-1761) the Maratha Empire extended from the Himalayas in the North to the southern extremity of the

Indian Peninsula. The Peshwa's power endured as a sovereign authority,—although territorially much reduced,—down to 1818.

Ranjit Singh (1780-1839), the "lion of the Punjab," was a contemporary of Rammohun (1772-1833). The entire Punjab (including Kashmir and Jammu) was ruled by him as an independent Hindu state. It was not until 1849 that the Punjabis lost their independence.

The part played by the Indians as creators in the nineteenth and twentieth centuries is not to be belittled. The "modern" trends in India's creations,—both at home and abroad,—are but to be organically linked up with her previous achievements in arts, sciences, law, polity and what not. The traditional cults of *śaktiyoga* (energism), *charaiveti* (march on) and *digvijaya* (conquest of the quarters) which are responsible for these creations of today are manifest in more or less the same form in the different "regions" of modern India. No matter what be the angle of vision,—Punjabi, Maratha, Madrasi, Bengali, Hindu, Moslem, or otherwise,—the sociography of contemporary India is likely to be almost uniform. Due regard will no doubt have to be paid to the "personal equations" of the observer and interpreter. Foreign reporters on contemporary India also could not possibly overlook the more or less uniform transformations of character and creative urges among the diverse Indian races. Even as "indentured labourers" or "assisted emigrants" the men and women of India have been creating values,—agricultural, industrial and commercial,—in the lands beyond the Indian seas,—especially in Africa and America,—for over a century.[1]

[1] For the "Greater India" of today see the chapter on "Americanization" in B. K. Sarkar: *The Futurism of Young Asia* (Berlin, 1922); S. A. Waiz (editor): *Indians Abroad* (Bombay), Bulletins on Kenya, South Africa, Fiji, British Guiana and Canada

For Indian men and women of the twentieth century it is but a second nature to comprehend even in the smallest intellectual unit bearing on India the achievements of the Cholas, the Vijayanagara Rayas and the Marathas of the South, as well as the Rajputs, the land of Nanak, the Bengali people, and the United Provinces. Thanks, again, to the intimate personal friendships and study-travels embracing as they do the different quarters of India it is possible for many publicists, scholars, and readers of journals to assimilate a part of India's messages from far and near. The impacts of Moslem India are accordingly no less perceptible on the mentality of the Hindus than those of Hindu India on that of the Mussalmans.

Finally, the movements and activities of the Indian men and women of today are in constant interaction and cooperation with those of the other races of mankind. In the progress of contemporary civilization, in schemes of world-reconstruction and in projects of futuristic societal planning creative India is thus continuing to function as a colleague of the other creative members of the world-system.

During the nineteenth and twentieth centuries, then, the Indian races have been exhibiting their virility in no questionable manner. Creative India's role in technocracy and culture is as much in evidence today as in the days of Mohenjo Daro.

Altogether, the place of creative India in the world of values,[1] dynamic as it is, will be found to be exten-

(1927), East Africa (1928, 1929), British Guiana (1928), etc; *The Indian Year Book* (Bombay), 1918 (pp. 523-527), 1926 (pp. 399-407), 1928 (pp. 430-441) and subsequent volumes; R. K. Mukerjee: *Migrant Asia* (Rome, 1936).

[1] C. Bouglé: *Lecons de Sociologie sur l'Evolution des Valeurs* (Paris, 1929), pp. 3-9; Ribot: *La Logique des sentiments* (Paris 1920) ch. II.

sive and varied. And the problem of the "revision of values" which has become a vital question of philosophy in post-war Eur-America is no less urgent in the science or sciences bearing on India, the Indian races and the Indian culture-systems, especially in their age-to-age orientations to the rest of the world. A new indology is a desideratum today in order to help forward the transvaluation of values demanded long ago by Nietzsche.[1]

SECTION 2

THE ROLE OF THE HINDUS IN THE DEVELOPMENT OF MATERIAL SCIENCE AND SCIENTIFIC METHODS

Investigations in radio-activity since 1896 have effected a marvellous revolution in our knowledge of Energy. The ultimate atoms of matter are now believed to possess "sufficient potential energy to supply the uttermost ambitions of the race for cosmical epochs of time."

Speaking of these new discoveries in connection with radio-activity, Soddy remarks in his *Matter and Energy*: "It is possible to look forward to a time, which may await the world, when this grimy age of fuel will seem as truly a beginning of the mastery of energy as the rude stone age of palaeolithic man now appears as the beginning of the mastery of matter."

This optimism seems almost to out-Bacon Bacon's prophecy in the *Novum Organum* (1621) relating to the wonderful achievements he expected from a "new birth

[1] For a corresponding but more elaborate work on Eur-America see H. E. Barnes: *The History of Western Civilization* (New York, 1935) 2 vols.

of science." The "new birth" was inevitable, he declared, "if any one of ripe age, unimpaired senses, and well-purged mind, apply himself anew to experience and particulars."

Becquerel's discovery of radio-active substances is thus a quarter less than three hundred years from Bacon's first advocacy of experimental and inductive methods. The "long and barren period" between the scientific activity of ancient Greece and that of modern Europe, described by Whewell as the "stationary period of science," was drawing to a close in Bacon's time. The age was, however, yet, "dark" enough to be condemned by him in the following words:

"The lectures and exercises there (at the Universities) are so ordered that to think or speculate on anything out of the common way can hardly occur to any man. Thus it happens that human knowledge, as we have it, is a mere medley and ill-digested mass, made up of much credulity and much accident, and also of childish notions which we first imbibed."

Positive science is hardly three hundred years old. It is necessary to remember this picture of the intellectual condition of Europe at the beginning of the seventeenth century in every historical survey of the "exact" sciences (whether deductive mathematical or inductive-physical) as well as in every comparative estimate of the credit for their growth and development due to the different nations of the world.

Hindu investigations in exact science, come down to about 1200 A. C.[1] Strictly speaking, they cover the

[1] Consult U. C. Dutt: *The Materia Medica of the Hindus* (Calcutta 1877, 1900), K. L. Dey: *The Indigenous Drugs of India* (Calcutta 1896), P. C. Ray: *History of Hindu Chemistry* (Calcutta), Vol. I. (1902), Vol. II. (1909) (incorporating B. N. Seal: *The*

period from the *Atharva Veda* (*c.* 800 B. C.), one of the Hindu Scriptures, to Bhāskarāchārya (*c* 1150), the mathematician; or rather to the middle of the fourteenth century, represented by Mādhavāchārya, the compiler of "The Sixteen Systems of Philosophy" (1331), Guṇaratna (1350), the logician, the "*Rasa-Ratna-Samuchchaya*," the work on chemistry, and Madanapāla, author of the *Materia Medica* (1374) named after himself.

We are living today in the midst of the discoveries and inventions of the "second industrial revolution." To the moderns, therefore, the whole science of the ancient and mediaeval Hindus discussed here belongs to what may be truly called the pre-scientific epoch of the history of science. Its worth should, however, be estimated in the light of the parallel developments among their contemporaries, the Greeks, the Chinese, the Graeco-Romans, the Saracens, and the mediaeval Europeans.

Whewell, according to whom the scientific inquiries of the ancients and mediaevals "led to no truths of real or permanent value" passes the following summary and sweeping judgment on all these nations:

"Almost the whole career of the Greek schools of

Mechanical, Physical and Chemical Theories of the Ancient Hindus); B. K. Sarkar : *The Positive Background of Hindu Sociology* (Allahabad) Vol. I. (1914) (incorporating B. N. Seal : *Hindu Ideas About Plants and Plant Life*, *Hindu Classification of Animals*, *Hindu Ideas About the Nervous System*, *Hindu Mechanics*, and *Hindu Acoustics*), P. Neogi: *Iron in Ancient India* (Calcutta, 1914), B. N. Seal : *The Positive Sciences of the Ancient Hindus* (London, 1915), B. K. Sarkar : *Hindu Achievements in Exact Science* (New York, 1918), S. R. Das : "Astronomical Instruments of the Hindus" (*Ind. Hist. Q.* June, 1928), B. Datta : "The Scope and Development of Hindu *Gaṇita*" (*I. H. Q.* Sept., 1929), M. N. Banerjee : "Iron and Steel in the Rig Vedic Age" (*I. H. Q.* Sept. 1929, June, 1932), B. Datta and A. N. Singh: *History of Hindu Mathematics* (Lahore, 1935).

philosophy, of the schoolmen of Europe in the Middle Ages, of the Arabian and Indian philosophers, shows that we may have extreme ingenuity and subtlety, invention and connection, demonstration and method; and yet out of these no physical science may be developed. We may obtain by such means logic and metaphysics, even geometry and algebra; but out of such materials we shall never form optics and mechanics, chemistry and physiology." Further, "the whole mass of Greek philosophy shrinks into an almost imperceptible compass, when viewed with reference to the progress of physical knowledge." "The sequel of the ambitious hopes, the vast schemes, the confident undertakings of the philosophers of ancient Greece was an entire failure in the physical knowledge."

While accepting for general guidance the above estimate of Whewell regarding the ancients and mediaevals, the student of culture-history would find the following noteworthy points in a survey of the world's positive sciences from the Hindu angle :

1. The "pure" mathematics of the Hindus was, on the whole, not only in advance of that of the Greeks, but anticipated in some remarkable instances the European discoveries of the sixteenth, seventeenth, and eighteenth centuries. That mathematics is the basis of the mathematical science of the moderns.

2. Like the other races, the Hindus also may be taken to have failed to make any epoch-making discoveries of fundamental "laws," planetary, inorganic, or organic, if judged by the generalizations of today. But some of their investigations were solid achievements in positive knowledge, viz., in materia medica, therapeutics, anatomy, embryology, metallurgy, chemistry, physics, and descriptive zoology. And in these also, generally speaking, Hindu inquiries were not less if not more definite,

exact, and fruitful than the Greek and mediaeval-European.

3. Hindu investigations helped forward the scientific developments of mankind through China (and Japan) on the east and the Saracens on the west of India, and this both in theoretical inquiries and industrial arts.

4. Since the publication of Gibbon's monumental history the historians of the sciences have given credit to the Saracens for their services in the development of European thought. Much of this credit, however, is really due to the Hindus. Saracen mathematics, chemistry, and medicine were to some extent direct borrowings from Hindu masters. The Greek factor in Saracen culture is known to every modern scholar; the Hindu factor remains yet to be generally recognized. That recognition would at once establish India's contributions to Europe.

5. The attempts on the part of modern scholars to trace the Hellenic or Hellenistic sources of Hindu learning have not been successful.

6. But, like every other race, the Hindus also got their art of writing from the Phoenicians. Besides, the Hindus may have derived some inspiration from Greece in astronomy as admitted by their own scientists, e.g., by Varāhamihira in *Brihat Samhitā* (II. 14)[1].

7. Hindu intellect has thus independently appreciated the dignity of objective facts, devised the methods

[1] N. B. Mitra: *Hindu Mathematics* (Calcutta, 1916), which examines the view of Kaye in *Indian Mathematics* (Calcutta 1915), S. R. Das: "Aspects of the History of Hindu Astronomy" and "Alleged Greek Influence on Hindu Astronomy" (*Indian Historical Quarterly*, December 1925, March 1928), B. Datta: "The Scope and Development of Hindu *Gaṇita*" (*I. H. Q.* September 1929).

of observation and experiment, elaborated the machinery of logical analysis and truth investigation, attacked the external universe as a system of secrets to be unravelled, and wrung out of Nature the knowledge which constitutes the foundations of science.

8. The claim of the Hindus to be regarded as some of the pioneers of science and contributors to exact, positive, and material culture rest, therefore, in all respects, on the same footing as those of the Greeks, in quality, quantity, and variety. An absolute superiority cannot be claimed for either, nor can any fundamental difference in *Weltanschauung*, mental outlook, view of life, or angle of vision be demonstrated between these two races or culture-systems.

It has been suggested above that the age of experimental and inductive science is somewhat less than three hundred years. The establishment of the Royal Society in London in 1662 may be taken as a convenient starting point for the modern epoch in "exact" science. It is this period that has established the cultural superiority of the Occident over the Orient. But this epoch of "superiority" should require to be analyzed a little more closely.

Neither the laws of motion and gravitation (of the latter half of the seventeenth century), nor the birth of the sciences of modern chemistry and electricity during the latter half of the eighteenth could or did produce the superiority in any significant sense. There was hardly any difference in materialism between Europe and Asia at the time of the French Revolution (1789). The real and only cause of the parting of ways between the East and West, nay, between the mediaeval and the modern, was the discovery of steam, or rather its application to production and transportation. The steam engine, patented by Watt in 1769, came into use in mines and iron works during 1775-85, and effected an "industrial revolution" during the first decades of the nineteenth century. It is this revolution that has later ushered in the "modernism" of themodern world in social institutions, science, and philosophy, as well as brought about the supremacy of Eur-America over Asia.

The year 1815 may be conveniently taken to be the year I of this modernism, as with the fall of Napoleon it marks also the beginning of a new era in world-politics, practically the era in which we still live. The difference between the Hindu and the Eur-American, or between the East and the West, is a real difference today. But it is not a difference in mentality or "ideals" or so-called race-genius. Neither geography nor climatography nor ethnography is required to explain this. So far as England is concerned, it is the difference of one century, the "wonderful century" in a more comprehensive sense than Wallace gives to it.[1] And so far as France, Germany and other countries of Europe are concerned, the chronological distance between them and India is much shorter, because it is not before the middle of the nineteenth century that France and Germany experienced the technocratic transformation pioneered by England. Italy's transformation came much later still.

A few general remarks may be made with regard to the cultivation of exact sciences among the Hindus:

1. Like the Greeks, as Whewell admits in his *History of the Inductive Sciences* (1858), the Hindus also "felt

[1] Mackenzie : *The Nineteenth Century* (London 1893), Price: *Political Economy in England* (London 1900); Merz : *History of European Thought in the Nineteenth Century* (London 1904), two volumes, Hauser : *Les Débuts du Capitalisme* (Paris 1931). See also Pettigrew : *Superstitions connected with the History and Practice of Medicine and Surgery* (London 1844).

the importunate curiosity with regard to the definite application of the idea of cause and effect to visible phenomena," "drew a strong line between a fabulous legend and a reason rendered," and "attempted to ascend to a natural cause by classing together phenomena of the same kind." This scientific attitude of mind, be it observed *en passant*, Whewell does not find in any non-Greek except the Hindu! He forgets altogether the claims of the Chinese.

2. Epoch by epoch, the Hindu scientific investigation was not more mixed up with metaphysics and superstitious hocus-pocus than the European. It enlisted in its service the devotion of hosts of "specialists" in succession. Their sole object was the discovery of the positive truths of the universe or the laws of nature, according to the lights of those days.

3. There thus grew up in India a vast amount of specialized scientific literature, each branch with its own technical terminology. The positive sciences of the Hindus were not mere auxiliaries or handmaids to the "architectonic" science of *nīti* or *artha* (i.e. politics, economics, and sociology). The sciences (*śāstras*) on plant and animal life, veterinary topics, metals and gems, chemistry, surgery, embryology, anatomy, symptomatology of diseases, arithmetic, algebra, astronomy, architecture, music (acoustics), etc. had independent status. Besides, like Pliny's *Natural History*, there have been scientific encyclopaedias in Sanskrit, e. g., the *Bribat Sambitā* of Varāhamihira (505-587 A. C.).

4. Scientific investigation was not confined to any particular province of India or to any race or class of the Hindu population. It was a cooperative undertaking, a process of cumulative effort in intellectual advance. Thus, among the heroes of Hindu medicine, Charaka (*c* 600 B. C.) belongs to the Punjab in the

N. W., Suśruta (*c* 100 A. C.) is claimed by the Punjab as well as Benares in the Middle West, Vāgbhata (*c* 700 A. C.) belongs to Sindh (Western India), Vrinda (900) to the Deccan (Middle-South), Chakrapāṇi (1050) to Bengal (Eastern India), Śāramgadhara (1350) to Rājputana (Further West), Viṣṇudeva (1350) to Vijayanagara (Extreme South), and Narahari (seventeenth century) is claimed by Kashmir (Extreme North) but belongs most probably to Mahārāṣṭra (South-western Coasts).

5. No one hypothesis or theory dominated Hindu thought in any age, or monopolized the researches of all investigators in successive epochs. The intellectual universe of the Hindus was "pluralistic." There were different schools criticising, correcting, and modifying one another's enquiries.

The schools of abstract philosophy grew ultimately to be sixteen in the time of Mādhavāchārya (1350), "though as a southerner," says Haraprasad Śāstri, "he omits the two Śaiva schools of Kashmir and puts the schools of Buddhist philosophy into one." There were fifteen different schools of grammar in the sixth century B. C., 10 different schools of politics and economics in the fourth century B. C., various schools of dramaturgy and dancing in the second century B. C., and also various schools of *Kāma* or sexology about the same time.

The diversity of scientific doctrines in India may be illustrated by the differences of views regarding the nature of life. According to Brajendra Nath Seal,[1] the Chārvākas (materialists and sensationalists) held "that life (as well as consciousness) is a result of peculiar combinations of dead matter (or the four elements) in organic forms, even as the intoxicating property of spirituous liquors results from the fermentation of in-

[1] *The Positive Sciences of the Ancient Hindus* (London 1915).

toxicating rice and molasses." According to a second school (the *Sāṃkhya*), life is neither a bio-mechanical force nor any mere mechanical motion resulting therefrom. It "is in reality a reflex activity, a resultant of the various *concurrent* activities of the sensori-motor, the emotional and the apperceptive reactions of the organism." A third school (the Vedantist) rejects both these doctrines. According to this, "sensations do not explain life. Life must be regarded as a separate principle, prior to the senses."

Another illustration may be given from Hindu physics as interpreted by Seal. This relates to the various hypotheses of sound phenomena. One school held that the physical basis of audible sound is the specific quality of air, and that air-particles flow in currents in all directions. A second school, e.g. that of Śabara Swāmi held that it is not air-currents but air-waves, series of conjunctions and disjunctions of the air-particles or molecules, that constitute the sound physical. A third school held that the sound-wave has its substratum not in air but in ether. Further, Praśastapāda held the hypothesis of transverse waves and was opposed by Udyotakāra who held that of longitudinal waves.

6. The story of scientific investigation among the Hindus is thus, like that among other nations, the story of a growth and development in critical inquiry, sceptical attitude, and rationalism. Historically and statistically speaking, superstition has not had a deeper and more extensive hold on the Oriental intellect than on the Occidental.

SECTION 3

BUDDHISM AS AN INSTRUMENT OF LIFE

A great impetus was imparted to social studies by the publication of the *Sacred Books of the East*. It has rendered inestimable service to the sciences of mythology and philology. But on the other hand, it is this series of books that has up till now offered the greatest impediments to the growth of a scientific comparative sociology. For it has diverted the attention of scholars from the achievements of Oriental races in exact science, mathematico-physical and physiologico-medical. It has also militated against the recognition by the Occident of the Oriental endeavours in civic administration, social service, conciliar enterprise, industrial activity, and institutional life. Today Eur-America is obsessed by the notion that Asia has stood for non-secular religiosity all through the ages.

Max Müller, the editor of the Series, is personally responsible for a great part of this modern superstition. His *India : what can it teach us* ? was published in 1883. In this book he categorically declared that the sole message of India was the "sublime" philosophy of otherworldlyism quietism, despair! This sweeping generalization is also summed up in a sentence of his *Chips from a German Workshop*. "The sense that life is a dream or a burden is, "says he," a notion which the Buddha shares with every Hindu philosopher." And Schopenhauer, the father of "modern pessimism," seems to have believed that he found allies in ancient Hindu thinkers. He therefore unequivocally stated that "the fundamental characteristics of Brahmanism and Buddhism are idealism and pessimism, which look upon life as the result of our sins and upon the existence of the world as in the nature of a dream."

Since then India has been treated in Eur-America as a synonym for mysticism or pessimism or both.[1] Now, to the outside world, India happens to be known by a single personality, Buddha, and Buddha commands also the devotion of millions in China and Japan. He is, therefore, taken to be the "light of Asia." To the laymen as well as scholars of the West there is thus but one shibboleth which explains the entire East. It is Buddhism, and Buddhism = mysticism + pessimism.

Psychologically or statistically, however, it is impossible to make out a distinction between the East and the West on the score of mysticism or pessimism. Has not mysticism of diverse denominations flourished luxuriantly on the Occidental soil? The cult of the Infinite, the Absolute and the Eternal has indeed a formidable tradition in the Eur-American world. It counts in its calendar such stalwarts as Phythagoras and Plato among the Greeks, St. Paul the Apostle, and Plotinus the neo-Platonist, St. Francis and Jacopone da Todi among the

[1] In recent works like those of Pitirim Sorokin, for instance, *Social Mobility* (New York 1927), *Contemporary Sociological Theories* (New York 1928), *Principles of Rural-Urban Sociology* (New York 1929) the conventional view about the alleged distinction between the East and the West has been ignored and the Hindu data in institutions and theories have been appraised like the data of other races and regions as factors of universal significance. For new tendencies in indology see C. Formichi: "Pensiero e Azione nell' India Antica" (*Rivista Italiana di Sociologia*, Rome, 1914), A. Hillebrandt: *Altindische Politik* (Jena 1923), A. B. Keith: *History of Sanskrit Literature* (Oxford 1928), p. 450, H. Lueders: "Indien" in *Der Orient und Wir* (Berlin 1935), H. von Glasenapp: "Lebensbejahung und Lebensverneinung bei den indischen Denkern" (*Jahrbuch der Schopenhauer-Gesellschaft*, 1935), B. K. Sarkar: "The New Indology in Lueders and von Glasenapp" (*Calcutta Review*, May 1936); *cf.* M. Winternitz: "Ethics in Brahmanical Literature" (*Prabuddha Bharata*, Calcutta, February 1936).

Italians, Ruysbroek the Flemish, and Boehme the German, Pascal and Madame Guyon of France, Bunyan and Blake among Englishmen, and the New England transcendentalists, not to mention the latter-day Rosicrucians and spiritualitarians. To this point we shall address ourselves, again, later (p. 30).

Not less is pessimism an historic trait of the Occidental mind. The Books of Job and Ecclesiastes in the *Old Testament* are saturated with it. It was a leading *motif* of Greek tragedies. Theognis, nick-named the "snow" (i.e. inanimated) has the following lines: "Best of all for all things upon earth is it not to be born, not to behold the splendour of the sun; next best to traverse as soon as possible the gates of Hades." Euripides is equally lachrymose. Socrates also is reported by Plato to have said: "Death, even if it should rob us of all consciousness, would still be a wonderful gain, inasmuch as deep dreamless sleep is by far to be preferred to every day even of the happiest life."

Jesus's message was the very cream of pessimism. "He that loveth father or mother more than Me," announced this prophet of Christendom, "is not worthy of Me;" "If man cometh unto Me and leaveth not his father and mother and wife and children, he cannot be My disciple." The *New Testament* with its emphasis on the "sins" of the "world" and the "flesh" is the most dismal literature conceivable even without a Nietzsche's help. The regime of the Church Fathers, celibacy, monasticism, and nunnery is of course the very reverse of optimism and of the sense of *joie de vivre*.

Pessimism has also attacked the general literature and poetry of the Western world. Byronic despair is proverbial. Here is a chip:

"Count o'er the joys thine hours have seen,
Count o'er thy days from anguish free,

And know, whatever thou hast been,
'Tis something better not to be."

Heine's *Weltschmerz* is a vein in the same quarry. Lamartine's *Le Désespoir* likewise has the Shelleyan burden: "Our sincerest laughter with some pain is ever fraught." De Musset belongs to the same class.

Hartmann, the philosopher of the *Unconscious*, is an inveterate woman-hater and a confirmed pessimist. His pupil, Mainlaender, in the *Philosophy of Redemption*, has outdone the master. According to him the movement of all being is not the will to live but "the will to die." The guide to them both, Schopenhauer, had pronounced "the denial of the will to live."

It is impossible to maintain, in the face of these facts, that pessimistic philosophy is the product exclusively or distinctively of the Orient.

Probably Buddhism is the theme on which, among all Asian topics, the greatest amount of scholarship has been bestowed by Eur-American scholars. But its place in the scheme of Oriental life and thought remains yet to be understood. In fact, it is the most misinterpreted of all phenomena in the East. Let us try to understand Buddhism in actual history.

In the first place, Buddhism as a cult, of which Buddha is the God, is not the religion or morality founded by the ascetic or monk Śākya called the Buddha, i.e., the "awakened" or enlightened (B. C. 563-483). The distinction[1] between Śākyaism and Buddhism is the same as that between teachings of Jesus the Jew and the teachings of St. Paul about Jesus the Christ, who is a god.

[1] This distinction is the *Leitmotif* of the present author's *Chinese Religion through Hindu Eyes* (Shanghai 1916).

The Buddha-cult was formulated by Aśvaghoṣa and came into existence as a distinct faith about the first century A. C. during the reign of the Indo-Tartar emperor Kāṇiṣka. The religion, also called Mahāyānism (the Greater Vehicle), was theologically much allied to, and did not really differ in ritual and mythology from, the contemporary Jaina and the Puranic-Hindu "isms." It is difficult to distinguish the image of an Avalokiteśvara of this Buddhist pantheon from that of a Jaina Tīrthamkara or a Hindu Viṣṇu. The Buddhism that is professed in China and Japan is this latter-day creed of gods and goddesses.

What now about the teachings of the man Sākya himself? Even granting for the moment that these were pessimistic, it need be realized that they were not the sole source of light in the India of the fifth and sixth centuries B. C. Sākya lived in an age when the "stormers and stressers" were legion. There were eminent physicians, surgeons, grammarians, logicians, pedagogues and psychologists; and there were systems of each of these classes of intellectuals. Sākya had no monopoly as a theologian or moralist or spiritual doctor in that "pluralistic universe."

Of course, Sākya, the son of the president or archon (*rājan*) of the Sakiya republic, had become an ascetic. He fled the world, indeed, but did he ever become a recluse? No, he remained a propagandist, a dynamic force, a "going concern" all his life. He founded, no doubt, an order (*Samgha*) of monks, but he taught also the world of husbands and wives, of diplomats, consuls, merchants and governors. The confederacy of the Vajjians in Eastern India looked up to him as adviser on critical occasions in national politics.

Nor were the monks of Sākya mere meditators. They were, as a rule, energists. Quietism or non-action is not the principle on which his *Samgha* was organized. The first hospitals of the world were built by his disciples, at least as early as the third century B. C. Schools, academies and rest-houses were the handiwork of the Śākyan monks.

It is the custom to mention Emperor Asoka the Great (B. C. 270-230) as the most distinguished follower of Śākya. He is generally known as the "Constantine of Buddhism." But, strictly speaking, as has been noted above, there was no "Buddhism" in the third century B.C. Besides, in what sense can it be said that Śākyaism was a a "state religion" in Asoka's time? The citizens of India under his administration were not all followers of Śākya. No article of faith was imposed by the monarch upon the officers. Toleration was as a rule the declared policy in matters of conscience, although not in ritual. Nor can the famous edicts of the emperor be regarded as manifestos in favour of Śākyaism. His own cult of *Dharma* or Duty, again, was distinct from, though perhaps based on, Śākya's tenets as well as those of other "remakers" of mankind.

Asoka's time to time announcements to the people were really the ordinances of an "enlightened", benevolent despot. The paternal solicitation and moralizing of the monarch are manifest in the Kalinga edict. "All men," as we read, "are my children, and just as for my children I desire they should enjoy all happiness and prosperity, both in this world, and in the next, so, for all men I desire the like happiness and prosperity."

Asoka's cares and efforts were thoroughly humanistic. He did not play the quietist, seeking a "denial of the will to live." He did not regard the sweets of life as curses to be shunned. He was the keenest of internationalists. Like Śākya and other great men of India Asoka was an embodiment of *charaiveti*, "march on"

(*Aitareya Brāhmaṇa* VII, 15). He sent his own son to proselytize Ceylon. It was his embassies that brought Western Asia, Egypt, Greece, Macedon, Epirus, and Kyrene within the sphere of Hindu influence. His secular activity in civic life was the most pronounced. Altogether he is one of the greatest Caesars of all ages.

And as for the regular monks and ascetics of the Buddhist organizations, they also did not keep wholly aloof from politics. They knew how to take part in intrigues and promote revolutions. They were tried as seditionists by some rulers and worshipped as "king-makers" by others. They would band themselves into military orders in order to be qualified as partisans in civil wars. They were adepts in Jesuitical casuistry, too. During the seventh and eighth centuries, e.g., under Harṣa-vardhana, Śaśāṃka, Dharmapāla and others the political interferences of monk-generals were constantly in evidence. The mediaeval history of China and Japan also affords instances of warfare conducted by Buddhist monks as politico-military divines.

After all, it must be admitted, however, that Sākya's *Weltanschauung* or view of life was certainly "not of this world." But his *Nirvāṇism*, i.e., doctrine of annihilation did not imply the "denial of the will to live." It tended rather to emphasize the annihilation of evil and the removal of misery and pain.[1] Its trend was systematically "amelioristic." Activism was thus the very keynote of his propaganda. Sakyaism or Buddhism is fundamentally an instrument of life.

The idea of *appamāda* (i.e. vigilance, earnestness,

[1] Consult N. Dutt: *Early History of the Spread of Buddhism* (Calcutta 1925), and *Mahāyāna Buddhism in relation to Hīnayāna* (London 1930). See also L. de la Vallée Poussin: *Nirvana* (Paris, 1926) and T. Stcherbatsky: *The Conception of Buddhist Nirvana* (Leningrad, 1927).

strenuousness) or energism was the cardinal element in Sākya's pedagogy of the moral self.

His educational creed may be gathered from some of his sayings in the *Dhammapada*. Thus we read :

"By rousing himself, by earnestness, by restraint and control the wise man may make for himself an island that no flood can overwhelm.

"Earnest among the thoughtless, awake among the sleepers, the wise man advances like a racer leaving behind the hack.

"By earnestness (energizing) did Indra rise to lordship of the gods. People praise earnestness; thoughtlessness is blamed.

"A mendicant who delights in earnestness and looks with fear on thoughtlessness, moves about like fire, burning all his fetters, small or large.

"He who does not rouse himself when it is time to rise, who though young and strong, is full of sloth, whose will and thought are weak, that lazy and idle man will never find the way to knowledge."

According to Sākya the wise man is thus an energist, a moral and intellectual gymnast, a fighter. There is no place for non-action, passivity, stationariness, cowardly retreat or *status quo* in the Sākyan system of self-discipline. The follower of the Buddha must "advance like a racer" and "move about like fire." It is nothing but the traditional Vedic cult of world-conquest, moving on from point to point,—*charaiveti* that Sākya and the Sakyans represent.

The same energism was strongly inculcated by Asoka also. We read in his Minor Rock Edicts (No. 1) as follows :

"Even the small man can, if he choose, by

exertion, win for himself much heavenly bliss.

"For this purpose has been proclaimed this precept; viz., 'Let small and great exert themselves to this end'.

"My neighbours, too, should learn this lesson, and may such exertion long endure."

Is all this the metaphysics of *Weltschmerz* and *désespoir*, or rather the ethics of the "perfection of character by effort"? Whatever be the superstition of Eur-American scholars regarding Asia, Sākya, the republican, and Asoka, the imperator, are two of the most successful apostles of secular endeavour and humanistic energizing in Hindu, Chinese, Japanese, nay, Asian estimation.

And yet it has often been said that Europeans and Americans cannot understand the Hindu or the Asian mind. Oriental viewpoints and ideals are supposed to be fundamentally different from Occidental!

But it is extremely difficult to point to any characteristic Oriental way of looking at things. Let us go back to the item of mysticism or the cult of the Eternal and Hereafter. There have been in Europe also mystics or "seers" of the Infinite, as many and as great as in Asia, from the earliest times till today, as we have already mentioned above (p. 24). The very first speculations of Hellas were embodied in the teachings of Pythagoras. He believed in the transmigration of the soul and preached the esoteric doctrine of numbers. He was a vegetarian and believed in general abstinence and ascetic mortification of the flesh. Plato's "idealism" also was mystical as much as was the monism of the contemporary *Upaniṣadists* of India and Taoists of China.

No world-teacher has been a greater occultist than Jesus. He declared: "My kingdom is not of this world." His other-worldliness and pessimism are undeniable. Indeed, the greatest passivist and submissionist among the world's teachers has been this Syrian Saviour of Europe and America. His political slogan was "Render unto Caesar the things that are Caesar's." Such extreme "non-resistance" was probably never preached in India.

Plotinus (third century A. C.), the greatest neo-Platonist, was a mystical pantheist. He actually practised Yogic exercises by which he hoped to attain union with the "ultimate principle," the highest God of all. The monasticism, celibacy, nunnery, and notions about "the world, the flesh, and the devil," the "seven deadly sins," etc. of Christianity have been practically universal in the Western world. They have had too long a sway to be explained away as accidental, or adventitious, or imported, or unassimilated over-growths. Spiritualistic "self-realization" was the creed of many a transcendentalist denomination in Europe during the Middle Ages. To the English Puritans, even music and sports were taboo. The painters of the "romantic movement" in Germany, e.g., Cornelius, Overbeck and others fought shy of women and preached that all artists should be monks. The race of Jacopone da Todis, Rosicrucians, Ruysbroecks, and Boehmes is not yet a thing of the past in Eur-America. And now that Bergson, the philosopher of the *élan vital*, has enunciated his doctrine of "intuition", mysticism is perhaps going to have a fresh lease of life.

Thus the psychology of the "soul" and the metaphysics of the infinite life and permanent verities, are as good and orthodox Occidental commodities as Oriental. Even in the conception of the universe as a living being the tradition of the Occident has been as long as that of India.

According to Plato in his *Phaedo* this universe is a

living creature in very truth, possessing soul and reason by the providence of God. Virgil in his *Aeneid* (Book VI, 96 ff.) writes:

"First Heaven and Earth and Ocean's liquid plains,
The Moon's bright globe and planets of the pole,
One mind, infused through every part, sustains;
One universal animating soul
Quickens, unites, and mingles with the whole.
Hence man proceeds, and beasts and birds of air,
And monsters that in marble ocean roll;
And fiery energy divine they share."

Similarly the Earth-Spirit, conceived by Goethe, is a personification of the active, vital forces of nature, the principle of change and growth within the universe.

This doctrine makes Plato, Virgil and Goethe virtually Hindu Vedantists. How, then, does European mentality differ from Hindu? According to the Vedantists, the world originates out of Brahma (Self), the absolute Reality, the absolute Intelligence, the absolute Bliss.

To the same group belongs also Browning with his message of immortality of soul or continuity of life-energy, thus:

"Fool! all that is, at all,
Lasts ever, past recall;
Earth changes, but thy soul and God stand sure:
What entered into thee
That was, is, and shall be:
Time's wheel runs back or stops: Potter and clay endure."

The whole stanza can be bodily transferred into a section of the Hindu *Gītā*. The Emersons of America also disprove the notion that "transcendentalism" is an Oriental monopoly.

For one thing, it must be clearly understood that in India the state was never theocratic. No religion dominated the policy of governments. The statecraft was not regulated by the personal faith of the rulers. Hindu politics was, as a rule, thoroughly, secular, i.e. Lutheran and Machiavellian.

Neither the vegetarianism of a sect nor the *ahimsā* (non-killing) of a cult could successfully counteract the military ambitions of the people. The national or racial desire for a "place in the sun" was never held inconsistent with even the most other-worldly and Godward tendencies in certain schools of thought.

The real Bible of the Hindu state was not to be found in any theological "ism" but in *nīti-śāstra* or political science. It laid down the ideals of man as a "political animal" in the comprehensive Aristotelian sense. Hindu *nīti-śāstra* was the science of *Staatsraeson* (reasons or logic of the state).[1] On the one hand, it pointed out the duties of rulers to the people, and on the other, it taught the people how to resist the tyranny of the ruler and expel or execute him for "misconduct." It placed a high premium on the fighting capacity of human beings. It was the perennial fountain of inspiration to soldiers.

Sākya the Buddha's monasticism did not enervate the people of his time. His contemporaries as well as the generations that followed him kept on the even tenor of their militarism. The political history of India does not appear to have ever been modified by his or

[1] F. Meinecke : *Die Idee der Staatsraeson* (Berlin, 1925); B. K. Sarkar : "Kauṭalya in Buddhist Perspectives" (*Calcutta Review*, July, 1935). See also P. Masson-Oursel: *L'Inde Antique et la Civilisation Indienne* (Paris, 1933), pp. xi-xii, 99-101, 128-129 as well as the present author's "Secularization of Hindu Politics in French Indology" (*Calcutta Review*, March, 1936).

any other preacher's Quakerish pacifism. Within about a century after Śākya's death Chandragupta Maurya founded the most extensive of all the empires realized in India up till now. The Bismarck of this nation-builder is by tradition believed to be have been Kauṭalya, the finance minister. There is hardly any trace of Śākyan teachings in his *Artha-śāstra*, the code according to which the empire is said to have been consolidated.[1] It is as un-Śākyan or un-Buddhist as Machiavelli's *Prince* or Treitschke's *Politik* is un-Christian. It is indeed conceived in the atmosphere of *Staatsraeson*, i.e. the "requirements" of "public" life.

A glimpse into the military India of the third and fourth centuries B. C. would indicate that there was a direct cooperation of the sexes in militarism such as has been conceived only yesterday by the war-lords of modern Eur-America and that Hindu wars were no mere skirmishes of savages (*Artha* X, iii).

Western scholars have stated that the Hindus were weak as a nation of fighters because of their caste system. It is alleged that the Hindus delegated the entire war-work to the Kṣatriya (warrior) caste on the principle of "division of labour" and that they did not learn how to utilize the total man-power of the country.

This is a fallacy like other fallacies about India started during the nineteenth century. It has no foundation in facts, it is utterly unhistorical. Even so late as the seventeenth century Śivāji the Great, the Frederick the Great of India, the greatest Hindu of all ages, and one of the profoundest remakers of mankind, electrified the non-Kṣatriya low-class Mawalis into the "Maratha Peril" of the Great Moghul.

[1] See the present author's "Kautalya and His Boswell" (*Calcutta Review*, August, 1935).

Besides, the very opposite is the idea inculcated in all Hindu political and military text-books. "My teacher says," as we read in the *Artha-śāstra* (IX, ii), "that of the armies composed of Brāhmaṇas (priests), Kṣatriyas (warriors), Vaiśyas (merchants), or Sūdras (lower orders), that which is mentioned first on account of bravery is better to be enlisted than the one subsequently mentioned. "No," says Kauṭalya, "the enemy may win over to himself the army of Brāhmaṇas by means of prostration. Hence the army of Kṣatriyas trained in the art of wielding weapons is better; or the army of Vaiśyas or Śūdras having greater numerical strength."

The discussion indicates that army service was not the "preserve" of a special caste. There was nothing against the Brāhmaṇa class *as such* being drafted for the regiments. The whole nation could be drilled at need.

Śukra-nīti is a later work than *Artha-śāstra*. And what are its teachings? "Even Brāhmaṇas should fight if there have been aggressions on women or if there has been a killing of cows (held inviolable according to Hindu religion) by the enemy. The life of even the Brāhmaṇa who fights when attacked is praised by the people" (IV, vii, lines 595 etc.).

The general *Bushido* morality of the Hindus is reflected in the following lines of the same work (IV, vii, lines 620 etc.):

"People should not regret the death of the brave man who is killed in battles. The man is purged and delivered of all sins and attains heaven.

"The fairies of the other world vie with one other in reaching the warrior who is killed at the front in the hope that he be their husband.

"The great position that is attained by the sages

after long and tedious penances is immediately reached by warriors who meet death in warfare.

"Two classes of men can go beyond the solar spheres, i.e., into heaven, the austere missionary and the man who is killed at the front in a fight."

The cult that has actually obtained in the land of Sākya the Buddha is thus the exact antipodes of quietism and pacifism[1]. The alleged pessimism of the Hindus is an *idola* of modern Eur-America. The Occident has by holding to this attitude been responsible for mankind's greatest single fallacy in the study of culture-history. The removal of this error is the most fundamental of all the desiderata of sociology. Not until this *idola* has been overthrown can there be a reformation and rebirth of social science.

SECTION 4

RELIGION, MORALITY AND LAW IN INDIAN THOUGHT

Let us now watch how the Hindu mind was functioning in "societal" domains in an important epoch of Indian history, say, from Kauṭalya to Varāhamihira, i.e., for nearly nine hundred years from B. C. 300 to 600 A. C. By the third or fourth century A. C., i.e., towards the second half of this extensive period a new India had already made its appearance, the India of the Guptas. We witness a new stage, new actors, and what is more, a new outlook. Extensive diplomatic relations with foreign powers, military renown of *digvijaya* (world-conquest) at home, overthrow of the "barbarians" on

[1] See the present author's *I Dati Secolari e Sociologici nella Letteratura Buddistica Pali* (International Congress of Orientalists, Rome, September, 1935).

the western borderland, international trade, maritime activity, expansion of the motherland, missionising abroad, the blending of races by which the flesh and blood of the population was almost renewed, and social transformation as epoch-making as the first Aryanization itself,—all these ushered in during the fourth and fifth centuries of the Christian era a thorough rejuvenation and complete over-hauling of the old order of things in Hindustan.

This is one aspect of what we may for certain purposes describe as the age of Kālidāsa. A consideration of equal if not greater significance about Kālidāsa has also to be noted. With the establishment of the Guptas at Pātaliputra we enter "modern India." The currency of thought, the conventions and technique of life obtaining in the age of the *Raghuvamśa* are almost the same as today. But the Hindus of the age of the *Artha-śāstra* (*c* 300 B. C.) or even of Aśvaghoṣa's *Awakening of Faith in the Mahāyāna* (*c* 100 A. C.) thought in other terms and lived in other spheres.

And in the message of Kālidāsa's *Raghuvamśa* we have a "Hegelian" synthesis of opposites,—the Machiavellian Kauṭalya shaking hands with the Nirvāṇist Sākyasimha,—*Staatsraeson* in *rapprochement* with *Dharma* or *Sittlichkeit* (i.e., justice, morality etc.). Here are secularism and other-worldlyism welded together into one artistic whole, a full harmony of comprehensive life (*Infra*, p. 65).

A great deal of the Pali texts—the *Piṭakas* and the *Jātakas*—belongs to the period between the Mauryas and the Guptas (*c* B. C. 325—A. C. 550).[1] The economic, political, juridical and social data of this vast literature

[1] B. C. Law : *History of Pali Literature*, Vol. II. (London, 1933) pp. 518, 548.

constitute some solid foundations of Hindu positivism for about eight to nine hundred years.

Two important works in Pali deserve special mention in this connection. They are the Ceylonese chronicles, namely:

1. The *Dīpavamśa* (Chronicle of the Island of Ceylon) in verse in Pali (*c* 300 A. C.)
2. The *Mahāvamśa* (*c* 500 A. C.), a reconstruction of the *Dīpavamśa*.

Mahāyāna Humanism

The Buddhist *milieu* of this period, extensive as it is, has to be seen also in the tremendous amount of literature produced in Sanskrit. Students of Hindu politics as well as of Sanskrit language and literature as a rule have bestowed but a stepmotherly attention on this mass of Sanskrit Buddhist texts.

For the purpose of studies in secular life and institutions these texts are exceedingly valuable. They are mostly in the form of biographies, legends or legendary biographies and biographical legends bearing on Śākya, who in most of this literature is not a mere man or monk or prophet, but a veritable god, the Buddha. These stories of "new" or rather the only Buddhism, i.e., the Buddha-cult strictly so called, are as important in Indian social and moral thought as the *Jātakas*, the stories of Śākyaism, i.e., of old Buddhism (*Hīnayāna*).

Although some of these texts bearing on the new Buddhism (*Mahāyāna*) possess psychological and purely theological interest most of them are ethical, addressed to the great problem of the remaking of man.

Some of the more important of the Sanskrit Buddhist texts and their authors are being enumerated below :[1]

1. The *Mahāvastu* (the Book of Great Events), the Life of Buddha in "mixed Sanskrit" (*c* B. C. 150—*c* A. C. 300).

2. *Avadānaśataka* (*c* 150 B. C.)

3. *Karmaśataka* (*c* 150 B. C.)

4. Aśvaghoṣa (*c* 100 A. C.), a contemporary of Kāṇiṣka, and founder of *Mahāyāna* Buddhism.

   i. *Buddhacharita*, a poem
   ii. *Saundarananda*, a poem
   iii. *Sūtrālaṃkāra*, legends in prose and verse based on the *Jātakas* and the *Avadānas*.

5. Nāgārjuna (*c* 150 A. C.), another founder of *Mahāyāna* :

   i. *Mādhyamikasūtra*
   ii. *Mādhyamikakārikā*
   iii. *Dharmasaṃgraha*

6. The *Divyāvadāna* (*c* 200 A.C.), which contains the *Aśokāvadāna* in Chs. XXVI-XXIX.

7. The *Saddharmapuṇḍarīka* (Lotus of the Good Law), in prose and *gāthā* (verse) in "mixed Sanskrit" (*c* 200 A. C.)

8. The *Karaṇḍavyūha* (*c* 200 A.C.) of the Bodhisattva, available in two recensions, prose and verse.

9. The *Sukhāvatīvyūha* (The Land of Bliss), *c* 200 A. C.

10. Āryadeva (*c* 250 A. C.), described as a great master of *Mahāyāna* by Yuan Chwang and Itsing.

[1] G. K. Nariman : *Literary History of Sanskrit Buddhism* (Bombay, 1923) pp. 18, 28-36, 41-75, 92-97, 100.

i. *Śataka chatuśataka*

ii. *Śatakaśāstra*

11. Vasuvandhu Asaṃga (*c* 350 A. C.)

i. *Abhidharmakoṣa* in *Sūtras* and *Kārikās*

ii. *Gāthāsaṃgraha*

iii. *Paramārtha Saptati*

12. Āryasūra (*c* 350 A. C.), *Jāṭakamālā* (*Bodhisattva Avadānamālā*).

13. The *Lalitavistara* (Life of Buddha) (*c* 400 A. C.)

14. The *Laṃkāvatāra* (*c* 550 A. C.).

15. Śāntideva (*c* 650 A. C.)

i. *Sikṣāsamuchchaya*

ii. *Sūtrasamuchchaya*

iii. *Bodhicharyāvatāra*

As usual, most of the dates are questionable. The relative chronology also is not to be depended upon.

It is this Buddhist Sanskrit literature that furnishes the spiritual inspiration for the peoples of Central Asia, China, Korea, Japan, and Tibet. It is to these texts that the "Greater India" movement of the epoch of the first six or seven centuries of the Christian era owed its *raison d'être*.

In the history of Hindu positivism no documents are more valuable than these Sanskrit Buddhist texts. The *Mahāyāna* mentality is the most profoundly humanist mentality, the *Weltanschauung* of service to mankind and martyrdom in the interest of the oppressed and the suppressed, the lowliest and the miserablest.

On the one hand, we have in these documents the most glorious Bibles of selfless social service. On the other hand, they contain the most optimistic messages of unending hope, of eternal possibilities of perfection (*pāramitā*), and of the diverse pragmatic ways to salvation for the meanest creature on earth. It is in the atmosphere of these humane and humanitarian stories, legends, ideals and fancies that the energism of men and women for whom the *Artha*, *Nīti* and other technically socio-political *Śāstras* were composed.

In Śāntideva's *Sikṣāsamuchchaya* we have a passage describing the ten things by which a Bodhisattva acquires power. The passage is quoted by the author from a work entitled *Tathāgataguhya-sūtra*[1]. "How, O Great King," it is asked, "a Bodhisattva gives up his body and life, but he does not give up the Good Religion? He bows before all beings and does not allow his pride to rise. He has patience with the feeble beings and does not put any difficulties in their way. He gives up the best excellent food to the beings who are suffering from hunger. He gives security to those beings who fear. He is full of zeal for the complete healing of the sick. He satisfies the poor with riches. He repairs the shrines of the Tathāgata by lumps of plaster. He brings glad tidings to the beings. He shares his possessions with the poor and the unfortunate. He bears the burden of those who are weary and exhausted."

The Positivism of the Jaina Siddhānta

To the two classes of Buddhist texts, Pali and Sanskrit, have to be added the Prākrit texts of Jainism. The Jaina canon known as the *Siddhānta* was "written down" in the present form about 550 A. C. We are to understand, however, that the Jaina social philosophy was a formative force in the intellectual and cultural

[1] M. Winternitz: "Notes on the *Guhya Samāja Tantra* and the Age of the *Tantras*" in the *Indian Historical Quarterly*, Calcutta, March, 1933, Haraprasad Memorial Volume.

world of India under the Mauryas, Āndhras, Kuṣāns, Vākātakas, Bhāraśivas and the Guptas.

The Jaina *Aṃgas* and *Dasāos* are like the Buddhist texts full of anecdotes and stories. The psychological and ethical discussions or commands in this Prakrit literature are brought out in and through extremely realistic and secular descriptions of villages, cities as well as economic, political and social life. Works like the *Uvasagadasāo*[1] (The Religious Profession of an Uvasaga), the *Antagada-dasāo*, the *Anuttaro vavai-dasāo* and the like are quite rich in the data of secular life and worldly interests, although meant to be treatises for monks and ascetics. For certain purposes these *Dasāo* may be treated like the *Panchatantra*, the *Kathāsaritsāgara*, etc. Certainly, they deserve recognition by students of the *Dharma-Artha-Kāma*-complex as contributions from the angle of Jaina idealists or Utopists.

The positivism of the Jainas is embodied in the doctrine of four gifts,—(*āhārābhayabhaiṣajyaśāstradāna*)[2]. In the remaking of personality the Jaina social philosophy's contribution consists in emphasising the supreme need of service to others. The first service is the gift of food (*āhāra*), the second that of *abhaya*, i.e., courage (non-fear or protection), the third that of *bhaiṣajya* (medicine), and the fourth that of *śāstra* (learning).

The *Siddhānta* comprises 45 texts grouped as follows :[3]

[1] A. F. R. Hoernle's translation of the *Uvasaga dasāo* (Bibliotheca Indica Series, Calcutta 1888); L. D. Barnett's translation of the *Antagadadasāo* and *Anuttarovavaiya-dasāo* (Oriental Translation Fund, London 1907).

[2] Inscription in Banasamkari temple at Udri in Sorab, Shimoga District, Mysore, cited in R. Shamsastry: *Evolution of Indian Polity* (Calcutta 1920) p. 101.

[3] *Weber's Sacred Literature of the Jains*, transl. by H. W. Smith for the *Indian Antiquary* (Bombay) October, 1888, p. 285.

1. *Aṃgas* : 11 or 12 (one missing)
2. *Upāṃgas* : 12
3. P*ainnas* : 10
4. *Chheda sūtras* : 6
5. *Sūtras* : i *Nandī*
   ii. *Anuyogadvāra*
6. *Mūla sūtras* : 4

In the Jaina as in the Buddhist atmosphere the gods do not play a prominent part. Nay, in Vedic and post-Vedic Brahmanism also the role of the gods, strictly speaking, is rather subordinate. Positivism is the fundamental feature of all the Indian systems.

In the system of the Vedic *Brāhmaṇas* it is on account of the efficacy of the sacrifice that the gods are compelled to capitulate (*les dieux se voient obligés de capituler*) and the sacrificer rises to the celestial world and is assured a definite place for the future.[1] Man is made super-human. It is man and his energy that are really adored through the sacrifices. The *milieu* is humanistic and secular.

This philosophy of the sacrifice pervades not only the *Upaniṣads* but Buddhism and Jainism also in spite of the prejudice of the last two systems against sacrifice. The concept of the *Riṣi*, who without the help of the gods and often against their will (*sans l'aide des dieux et souvent contre leur gré*) discovers by the sole force of his intelligence the ritual or the formula which assures the success, is the immediate precursor of the Buddhas and the Jinas who discover the way to salvation by direct intuition and spontaneous enlightenment. It is not by chance that the sacred words of the *Arhat* and the

[1] S. Lévi; *La Doctrine du Sacrifice dans les Brāhmaṇas* (Paris, 1898) pp. 9-12.

Buddha figure already in the *Brāhmaṇas*. The very dogmas which these words symbolise reside also there in germ and already in the process of growth. It is the touch of humanism and positivism that makes the diverse Indian systems kin.

Dharmaśāstras (Smritis)[1]

The compilers of the leading *Dharma Sūtras* (*Sāstras*) during the epoch from Kauṭalya to Varāhmihira were as follows :

1. Viṣṇu (*c* 250 A. C.)
2. Saṃkha (*c* 300 A. C.)
3. Yājnavalkya (*c* 350 A. C.)
4. Nārada (*c* 500 A. C.)
5. Brihaspati (*c* 550 A. C.)
6. Kātyāyana (*c* 550 A. C.)

The political (*Artha*) tradition was kept up by the *Dharmaśāstras* during this period as before. It is to be observed that the *Dharma* or *Smriti* treatises are mainly books on "private" law (i.e. the law of family and property) while the *Artha* and *Nīti* treatises are books on "public" law (i.e. constitution or polity).[2]

We shall now see a bit of the private law as expounded by Nārada, a leading jurist of the Gupta Empire. Nārada's exposition of private law commanded authority as well as a considerable degree of popularity in mediaeval India. A large part of his doctrines was incorporated, sometimes without acknowledgment, in

[1] P. V. Kane: *History of Dharmasastras*, Vol. I. (Poona, 1930) pp. 59, 69, 79, 148, 187, 205, 210, 218, Winternitz : *Geschichte der Indischen Literatur*, III, 482, 498, 500.

[2] See the chapter on "the concept of law" in A. K. Sen : *Studies in Hindu Political Thought* (Calcutta, 1926) pp. 85-134.

the works of subsequent writers on both civil and criminal law, while commentators ascribed to him all sorts of important texts bearing on legal institutions. Definitely secular and legalistic in his approach, Nārada emphasized the rule of reason as a source of law and maintained that where the sacred precept was at variance with custom, the latter should prevail.

Nārada's code of law deals in the introductory chapter with legal procedure, complaints and courts of justice. Then the law is classified under eighteen titles similar to those of Manu, except the minor differences and the fact that Nārada eschews entirely the social and religious items contained in the former's encyclopaedic treatise. Nārada's classification includes debt, deposits, partnership, breach of labour contracts, boundary disputes, marital relations, inheritance, and heinous offences. Like Manu and Yājnavalkya he is liberal and sympathetic in his treatment of the rights of illegitimates, permitting an illegitimate son to inherit his maternal grandfather's property (xiii : 18). But he differs substantially from these authorities in that he holds that even the youngest son, "if able," may govern the family and manage its property (xiii : 5), and allows a father to distribute the property among his sons in whatever proportion he desires (xiii : 4, 15). In his system the widow may inherit part of her husband's property, *while unmarried daughters may share in their father's* estate (xiii : 3, 12, 13). The right to divorce and re-marriage is allowed to women on many grounds (xii : 96-101). Books xii and xiii of the *Nārada-smriti* are the embodiments of "modernism" in ancient Hindu conceptions of property and marriage. As the exponent of a secular and realistic view of the law Nārada appears to be as prominent a figure in comparative jurisprudence as is Sukra in comparative politics.

SECTION 5

THE ANTI-IDEALISTIC SYSTEMS OF INDIAN PHILOSOPHY IN THEIR BEARINGS ON ECONOMICS AND POLITICS

Political philosophy is, as the very title implies, a branch of philosophy. It may not, indeed, have to discuss the theory of perception or the nature of reality with which the philosophies technically so called have to deal. But both in category as well as in substance the intercourse between political philosophy and these other philosophies is intimate.

How do the political philosophers of the Hindus, e.g., those of the Śukra cycle, stand in relation to the philosophical systems of their days? A question like this may not be inappropriate to ask in connection with the economic, social and political categories of the *Śukranīti*.[1] The problem is to ascertain the real value of the "materialism" such as was propagated by the Kauṭalyan or Śukra authors in the light of the prevailing bodies of knowledge in other fields.

We are aware that the world in which the authors were discussing their special problems, namely, those bearing on the *saptāmga*, was a richly diversified one in point of the number of *vidyās*. Their name is legion, so to say, the Sukra authors have informed us (IV, iii, line 45); and more precisely, we are told, there are thirty-two primary branches of learning (IV, iii, lines 51-128).

So far as the so-called philosophies (*darśanas*) are concerned, the Śukra authors know them to be perhaps more than six. It is clear, at any rate, that the

[1] The references to the *Śukranīti* are always to the lines and not to the *slokas*. See the present author's translation in the *Sacred Books of the Hindus* (Allahabad), Vol. XIII.

conventional six are quite well known to them. But it is interesting to note that the six have not been mentioned by them "as a group" (IV. iii. lines 55-56).

This is a curious item, and, incidentally, may possess some value in the question of chronology. The relevant passages in the *Sukranīti* cannot certainly be as old as the times when the philosophies were not yet known to be six. These must have to be accorded a date posterior, say, to Haribhadra's *Ṣaḍdarśana-samuchchaya-sūtra.*

But how far posterior? The fact that the authors do not call the philosophies six in number in the same breath as they describe the *vidyās* as thirty-two, seems to point to a period in which the figure, six, as indicating the number of philosophical systems has lost its special significance. Can we, then, take it that the intellectual atmosphere is oriented to the conditions which gave rise to Mādhavāchārya's *Sarvadarśana-Saṁgraha* (1331)? But of this more, later.

The impact of all these sciences, and especially of the six philosophies, on the *Sukranīti* may be postulated as a matter of course. That the authors were working *en rapport* with the professors of other academies is evident from the chapters on minerals, plants, animals, architecture, sculpture, painting, etc. These chapters may, indeed, be regarded as almost wholesale incorporations from specialized treatises on the subjects dealt with.

But in regard to some of the philosophies, at any rate, the impact seems to be not so much one of assimilation as of antipathy and repulsion. The authors are quite explicit on the question of their intellectual *credo.* They are thoroughly convinced that their own science (*nītiśāstra*) is more important than every other science (I, 20-24). For, what food is in the physical organism of an individual, that the *nīti-śāstra* is in the body politic.

The authors do not certainly disparage by name all the sciences outside of their own field. They have singled out only four, namely, grammar, logic, *Mīmāmsā* and *Vedānta* (I, 14-20). We are told, for instance, that one can master a language even without studying grammar. In the same manner, treatises on logic may be dispensed with by persons who are bent on the pursuit of truth. Similarly, one does not have to memorize Jaimini's lectures in order to master the rituals necessary in Vedic performances. Nor is it an absolute necessity to study the Vedantic disquisitions in order to be convinced of the frailties and littlenesses of the "world and the flesh."

The comparative insignificance of these four *vidyās* is further exhibited from another angle of vision. Not every human being on earth, we are to understand, is likely to be in need of these sciences. And as these sciences have no utility outside of their circumscribed horizons, they can be useful to a very limited number of persons, to the "specialists." But what can the teeming millions do with these specialized branches of knowledge,—the men and women of the work-a-day world who have to pursue their common-place round of duties?

The position of the Sukra authors has been most categorically declared at the very commencement of their work. "Other sciences," say they, "are but *kriyaikadeśabodhi*, i.e., have, for their subject matter, certain limited interests of mankind." These must certainly yield the palm to *nītiśāstra* which does not deal with *ekadeśa* (one aspect or domain) of human affairs (*kriyā*), but is, on the contrary, *sarvopajīvaka*, i.e., helpful to all, aye, an instrument in, or, so to say, a pivot of, the social order. Verily, Kauṭalya (Book I, ch. II) had caught the right Śukra tradition, when he stated that there is but one *vidyā* on earth, namely, political science, in the estimation of Śukra and his scholars.

Such being the value of their science in their own eyes, the materialism that the Śukra authors preach is self-conscious and aggressive. The doses are quite strong and are not diluted with solutions of non-*nīti* thought.

They have not cared to indicate by bibliographical references the kind of philosophical symposium they used to enjoy. But the manner in which they have analyzed the economic foundations of the *saptāmga* does not fail to betray the company they kept. From top to bottom they are interested in the investigations into the utilities and the ways and means of human welfare. Their sole gospel is furnished by social service, *loka-hita* (I, 4-5), or utilitarianism.

To use another modern term, it is not in the "idealistic" strands of thought that the Śukra authors are interested. The philosophies of Berkeley and Hume which seek to eliminate the external world and posit the exclusive existence of the mind, converting the universe into nothing but a system of mental states, would have left no impress upon the brains of the writers of the *Śukranīti*. And, of course, they would have had nothing to do with the Hegelian "absolute" soul as the only entity, should it have been adumbrated in their *goṣṭhi* (club) or *pariṣat* (academy) by certain professors of "the other sciences."

On the contrary, should it have been necessary for them to declare their philosophical or metaphysical article of faith they would have sought their natural allies among one or other system of "realism."[1] The distinction between idealism and realism is an eternal item in human thought. The philosophical *milieu* of the Śukra authors was fully aware of it. And it was up to them to choose which system to follow.

It is not necessary to read literally the ideas of "modern" idealism (Hegelian and Anglo-Hegelian) or "neo-idealism" (Crocean) and the realism and pragmatism of American professors or the neo-realism of Bertrand Russell's *Analysis of Mind* in the metaphysical controversies of ancient and mediaeval India. But that the world was a pluralistic one and that the scholars as well as laymen had to decide for themselves, consciously or unconsciously, between one or other "ism," is evident on all hands.

In what academies or *Kutūhalaśālās* (halls for curio-seekers, knowledge-hunters or truth-investigators) the Śukra economists sought affiliations in order to equip themselves with an adequate *Weltanschauung* (world-view) it is not difficult to discover. One interesting story, coming, as it does, from the Buddhist tradition, may serve as a specimen for the point in question.

Sākya the Buddha is said to have been abroad lecturing on the impermanence and unsubstantiality of body, sensation, perception and so forth. This sort of idealistic annihilation of the world of external objects was not to go unchallenged from the side of those who believed that body, sensation, etc. were not items to be trifled with. Sākya, therefore, had to encounter opposition of various shades from the "stormers and stressers" of his times.

The *Chulasachchaka Sūtta* of the *Majjhima Nikāya*

[1] See the chapter on "Realism" in W. E. Hocking: *Types of Philosophy* (New York, 1929), pp. 325-326, 329-30.

narrates how one of the great high-brows of the day, Sachchaka Nighaṇṭaputta, invites Sākya to an open debate[1]. Sachchaka's thesis was quite a chip of naturalism. He propounded the supreme value of the Mother Earth in the world of nature as well as in the world of man.

"Whatsoever seeds and plants grow and expand and come to maturity," thus argued Sachchaka, "do so all in dependence upon the earth, and, firm based upon the earth, and thus come to maturity." It is this solid earth of mud and stones that furnishes equally the basis of all human endeavours. Sachchaka went on in his argument vehemently emphasising the point that "whatever deeds that require strength are all done in dependence upon the earth, and firm-based upon the earth," and that these deeds cannot be done in any other way.

The analogy of the earth was then exploited by Sachchaka in order to substantiate his thesis of the dignity of body, the dignity of sensation etc. What the earth is to plants and human beings, said he, that the body is to the individual. "By body is this individual man, and firm-based upon body does he bring forth deeds good or evil." The argument is carried forward in regard to sensation, perception, etc.

Sachchaka is evidently an uncompromising champion

[1] Bhikku Silachara's *First Fifty Discourses*, Vol. II. pp. 84-88 in Nalinaksha Dutt's *Early History of the Spread of Buddhism* (Calcutta, 1925), pp. 60-63. See also *Mahati-sutta*, and *Bri-jala-sutta*, etc. in Rhys-Davids: *Dialogues of Buddha* for some of the other *vitaṇḍās* (discussions) bearing on realism. *Cf.* H. von Glasenapp: *Brahma und Buddha* (Berlin, 1926), pp. 113, 115, 298, "Die Lehre Vallabhācharyas" (*Zeitschrift fuer Indologie und Iranistik*, Leipzig 1934, Bd. 9, Heft 3), and "Lebensbejahung und Lebens verneinung bei den indischen Denkern" (*Jahrbuch der Schopenhauer Gesellschaft*) for diversities in Indian thought-systems.

of the doctrine of the physical basis of life. And, yet, one will have to admit that this exaltation of the body, sensation, etc., this glorification, in one word, of materialism, does not rise to the pitch such as is embodied in the dogma of "economic determinism" or "materialistic interpretation of history," strictly so called, with which Marxism is identified. For, Sachchaka's world-view, materialistic as it is, does not assert that life, mind, culture, or law, religion, philosophy, science and fine arts are but the reflexes of the physical foundations. The "causal" relation is wanting in Sachchaka's philosophy, but it is this causal concatenation that furnishes the keynote to "modern" materialism.[1]

The controversy between Śākya and Sachchaka is but typical of the philosophical conflicts (*vitaṇḍās*) in old Hindu thought. And Śukra's materialism, as manifest in the analysis of the territory and finance, two of the seven limbs of the state, is ideologically in tune with the ideas of Sachchaka. According to the authors of the *Śukranīti*, the external world is not to be explained away as but a unit of mental states. The physical objects are, in their estimation, solid pragmatic realities.

The story of Śākya *vs.* Sachchaka has incidentally brought out another feature of intellectual polarity which will help to throw fresh light on the materialism of the Śukra philosophers. The dialectic of the one is the exact opposite of that of the other. And we are reminded at once of one of Karl Marx's statements in the *Kritik der politischen Oekonomie*. "With Hegel," says he, "the mind or the absolute (the world-reason) is

[1] R. Michels : *Corso di Sociologia Politica* (Milan, 1927), pp. 25-31, 47-52, discusses the limitations within which "economic interpretation" can be valid. See also the criticism in P. Sorokin: *Contemporary Sociological Theories* (New York, 1928), pp. 527-536, etc.

the creator of the real. With me is the process quite otherwise. I consider the ideal to be nothing else but the material established in the human brain." The logic of modern materialism is thus a direct antithesis to Hegelianism, i.e., idealism *par excellence.* It is only reasonable to find that in its philosophical affiliations the materialism of the *Śukranīti* was oriented to a mentality or mentalities the farthest removed from the Śākyan.

Sachchaka, as contemporary of Śākya, the Buddha, is certainly too "old" for the *Śukranīti* in the form in which we have it to-day. But the anti-Hegelian spirit, to employ a modern term with a retrospective effect, such as Sachchaka's story reveals, has always been a living force in the Indian philosophical world. And the Śukra authors, no matter to how many successive ages the cycle may belong, have always had the opportunities to fraternize with the Sachchakas of their days and exploit the findings of the latter group in the interest of their own investigations.

Take, for instance, the six philosophies (*darśanas*) of the "older tradition." These in their developed form are certainly younger than the thoughts recorded in the *Dialogues of the Buddha.* Now, if the very environment in which Śākya the Buddha preached could not fail to furnish a philosophical stimulus to the economic realism of the Śukra authors, they would have found an equally congenial atmosphere in the *vitaṇḍā* or discussions of the *darśana*-academies.

At first sight it might appear, indeed, that these "six systems" on account of their alleged pre-occupation with "salvation" would repel the Śukra economists. But this can, at least, be only a superficial view. For, at least three of them, namely, the *Sāṃkhya*, the *Vaiśeṣika*, and the *Nyāya* deal with the facts and phenomena of physics or natural philosophy rather than with the mental and moral philosophy proper. Thus they happen to furnish just the scientific foundations of materialism such as an economic or political system demands for its theoretical groundwork.[1]

No system of thought could be more serviceable to an economist than the *Sāṃkhya*, for instance, which constitutes the very antithesis of Vedantic mysticism. By establishing a rigid dualism, almost in the manner of Immanuel Kant, it effectively segregates the spiritual from the material. And its "material" alone is powerful enough to be the *cause* of everything that happens in the non-spiritual world.

The "matter" of the *Sāṃkhya* is not only real. It is eternal and indestructible at the same time. And the material world, self-evolving as it is, does not need the postulate of a God or a divine machinery.

The very possibilities of a secular science, material or moral, are then to be sought in the *Sāṃkhya* philosophy, furnished, as it is, with its purely naturalistic rationalism.[2] Nor is this realistic agnosticism the exclusive characteristic of the Sāṃkhyans. However much the professors of the *Vaiśeṣika* and *Nyāya* systems might differ from the Sāṃkhyans in the theories concerning the constitution of matter, the method of approach to

[1] The physico-chemical and mechanical theories of the "philosophical schools" have been analyzed at length in Brajendra Nath Seal's *Positive Sciences of the Ancient Hindus* (London, 1915). See also S. N. Das Gupta: *History of Indian Philosophy* (Cambridge), Vol. I. (1922), Vol. II. (1932), for the leading systems as well as for Ayurvedic positivism.

[2] Garbe: *Sānkhya Philosophie eine Darstellung des indischen Rationalismus* (Leipzig, 1894), pp. 130, 137, 207, 232, 237-238. *Cf.* A. M. Pizzagalli: *Cārvāka Nāstika e Lokāyatika* (Pisa, 1907), pp. 74-77; B. K. Sarkar: "Hindu Politics in Italian" (*Indian Historical Quarterly*, Calcutta, September, 1925-April, 1926).

the problems of the universe was identical. Even *buddhi* (intelligence?) is grouped by the *Nyāya* philosophers in the same category as earth, water, air and other material substances.

As long as the *Sāṃkhya*, the *Nyāya* and the *Vaiśeṣika* were there, the Hindu students of mental, moral and social phenomena never had to feel that their feet were off the ground. The idealism of the *Vedānta*, such as in its extreme form might interfere with an objective investigation of the pluralities of the universe on the alleged ground that the many do not exist or that the only reality is the *Brahman*, mind, soul or whatever else it may mean, could be always challenged or rectified with the weapons forged in the other schools.

The Sukra materialists, then, were not alone in the field. They had but to draw upon the experience of other intellectuals who were oriented to the world in their own way. Their colleagues in different branches of materialism were many, and *Nītiśāstra* could flow on smoothly along the well-established currents of thought.

It seems that during the more recent phases of its development the *Sukranīti* cycle was being enriched with the findings of a new school of philosophical materialists. This school has been described by the Sukra authors as *Nāstika-matam* or system of the *Nāstikas* (IV, iii, 108-109). In their estimation the *Nāstikas* are important enough to be described as representing one of the thirty-two branches of learning.

Now, whom do the Sukra authors call *Nāstika*? Three characteristics are described by them as marking this system. First, we are told that "reason" is the chief feature in the *Nāstika* theory. In the second place, the *Nāstikas* are said to explain the origin of all things by reference to "Nature." And thirdly, they do not believe in the existence of the *Vedas*.

They are thus sceptics, but not necessarily atheists.

Whatever be the characteristics of *Nāstika* philosophy, it is evident that the Śukra authors consider it to be quite a "respectable" system of thought. They enumerate it in the same dispassionate, colourless, scientific manner as they enumerate the *Vedas*, *Upavedas*, *Darśanas* etc. And here, *en passant*, we touch another aspect of the chronological problems.

The word *Nāstika* has been traced by Pizzagalli in his brochure *Cārvāka Nāstika e Lokāyatika* as far back as the *Maitarāyaṇīya-Upaniṣad* (3, 5), one of the latest *Upaniṣads*. It occurs several times in the *Mahābhārata* (XII, 181, 1-6; XII, 322,16, XII, 121, 38). Manu also knows the term (II, 10-11, III 150, IV, 163; XI, 66-67).

But in none of these instances does the word describe the representative of a "system" of thought. It conveys simply the derogatory sense of a general character. By using *Nāstika* the writers want us to understand a negator, one not abiding by the *Vedas* and *Smritis*, etc. or perhaps, very often, an "ill-mannered," "uncultivated" boor, even a vicious sinner, and so forth. Down to Manu nobody could think of mentioning a *matam* (body of knowledge, doctrine, or system of thought) as being the handiwork of a school of *Nāstikas*, not to speak of listing it in a schedule of the sciences along with the conventional *matas* of historic tradition[1].

The Śukra authors, however, are bold enough to do so. Shall we say that this boldness is but an

[1] Pizzagalli pp. 24, 28, 32. According to this Italian scholar *artha* and *nīti* literature embodies the most genuine expression of Hindu materialism; *cf.* B. M. Barua: *A History of Pre-Buddhistic Indian Philosophy* (Calcutta, 1921) for some of the anti-idealistic and allied trends.

expression of their "liberalism"? Is it that they are tolerant or catholic enough, being students of materialism, to invite the "reason-worshipping" philosophers into the fold of the established convention? Or shall we say that this boldness points to the comparative lateness or "modernism" of the passage in which the expression occurs? Perhaps we may take it in both ways. The Śukra authors or, at any rate, those of their cycle, responsible for the incorporation of the list of the thirty-two *vidyās*, are at once liberal and modern.

We know as a positive fact that it is in Mādhava's "compendium of all the philosophies," known as the *Sarvadarśana-samgraha* (1331) that the *nāstika* philosophy is, for the first time, presented as a *mata*, a system of thought. It is described as *Brihaspatimata*, also as *Lokāyatika*[1]. The Chārvākas, who are generally known to be professors of *Nāstika* doctrines, have derived their inspiration, according to the tradition recorded by Mādhava, from Brihaspati, the *purohita* (priest) of Vedic gods. And this Brihaspati, we are assured further, is none than the traditional father of *nītiśāstra* and *arthaśāstra*.

Mādhava, as the follower of Śaṃkarāchārya, is, of course, a Vedantist, i.e., the farthest removed from the disciples of Brihaspati. But he is objective enough to give the Devil his due, and include the system of the Chārvākas in his examination of the "sixteen systems" prevailing in his time. Indeed, he accords this system the very place of honour in his book, although, no doubt, as may be guessed, for dialectical reasons. Mādhava's mission is to establish the supremacy of the *Vedānta*. And, in order to do this, he has to proceed

[1] D. R. Sastri: "The Lokāyatikas and the Kāpālikas" in the *Proceedings of the Sixth Oriental Conference*, Patna, 1933.

in a climbing series,—demolishing the systems one by one at each step. Naturally, the least Vedantic or rather the most anti-Vedantic system conceivable is the Brihaspatian philosophy, the *Nāstika-matam*. So Mādhava's book has to commence with his very antithesis, namely, Brihaspati.

The Śukra authors, however, have no special axe to grind, so far as this *matam* is concerned. They can afford to be genuinely objective and mention it as a fact of the philosophical universe. It is then very probable, chronologically speaking, that the *Sarva-darśana-saṃgraha* is responsible for the place of the *Nāstika* theory in the Śukran list or that both belong to the same intellectual complex.

Śukra's description of the *Nāstikas* agrees in "general features" with that given by Mādhava. The Chārvākas, says this Vedantist author, are used to denying *pāralaukikam artham* (other-worldly interests). According to them, everything exists through its own *svabhāva* (nature). Their logic recognises no *anumāna* (inference), but is based solely on *pratyakṣa* (observation or perception). They believe that the soul is identical with the body. The pursuit of pleasure is the sole teaching of their ethics. And so on[1].

The definition of *Nāstika-matam* in the *Śukranīti* is not, as a matter of course, as elaborate as in the *Sarva-darśana-saṃgraha*. But it is precise enough to lead one to believe that this compendium of the sixteen systems was not unknown to the Śukra authors. To this extent, perhaps, an aspect of the chronological question may be taken to be solved.

[1] Cowell: *Sarva-darśana-samgraha* (London, 1894); Muir's article on Indian materialists in the *Journal of the Royal Asiatic Society* (1862), Hopkins's *Great Epic of India* (New York); Pizzagalli, pp. 52-53, 56.

But for the present, we are interested in the philosophical orientations of the Sukra economists. The account rendered of the Chārvākas by Mādhava possesses, as one can notice, certain characteristics which would appeal very powerfully to the mentality of the Sukra philosophers. Whether the Sukra authors be prepared to deny the existence of the *Vedas* or not, there is no doubt that the "rationalism" and *svabhāva* theory (naturalism) of the Chārvākas would fit in quite well with their general trend of thought. The logical and psychological affiliations of the *Sukranīti* with *Nāstika-matam* may be considered to have been intimate.

Then there is an historical affinity as well. Mādhava says, as we have seen above, that the founder of *Nāstika matam* is identical with the founder of *nīti-śāstra* and *arthaśāstra*. That common founder is known, indeed, to be Brihaspati, who, as priest of the gods, is bound to be the sworn enemy of Sukra, the preceptor of the *Asuras* (demons). It is not quite clear, therefore, how the name of Brihaspati would have sounded in the ears of the professors of the Sukra cycle. But, perhaps, by the fourteenth century the old feuds between the Vedic gods and demons, Brihaspati and Sukra, had retired into the limbo of oblivion. And the Sukra investigators of *artha* and *nīti* would have found no difficulty in accosting as comrades, and holding *tête-à-têtes* with their colleagues of the Brihaspati cycle in one and the same *goṣṭhī* or *pariṣat*.

It is not necessary to identify the Sukra professors of economics, politics and allied sciences with the Sachchakas of the Buddhist tradition, or with the *Nyāya-Vaiśeṣika-Sāṃkhyans* or, finally, with the *Nāstika-Chārvāka-Lokāyatikas*. Only one point has been sought to be established. It is that the anti-Vedantic, anti-Hegelian, anti-idealistic trends of thought, were varied enough all through the ages to furnish the positive foundations on which a materialistic scheme of *loka-hita* (utilitarianism) can be built up.

SECTION 6

THE HINDU SYNTHESIS OF THE POSITIVE AND THE TRANSCENDENTAL

The transcendental and other-worldly aspects of Hindu life and thought have been too much of. It has been supposed and believed during the last century that Hindu civilization is essentially non-industrial and non-political, and of course pre-industrial and pre-political, and that its sole feature is ultra-asceticism and over-religiosity which delight in condemning the "World, the Flesh and Devil"!

Nothing can be farther from the truth. The Hindu has no doubt often placed the transcendental in the foreground of his life's scheme, but the positive background he has never forgotten or ignored. Rather, it is in and through the positive, the secular, and the material that the transcendental, the spiritual and the metaphysical have been allowed to display themselves in Indian culture-history. The *Upaniṣads*, the *Vedānta* and the *Gītā* were not the works of imbeciles and weaklings brought up in an asylum of incapables and a hospital of incurables.

The Hindu has never been a "scorner of the ground," but always "true to the kindred points of heaven and home," has been solicitous to enjoy the good things of this earthly earth and beautify this "orb of green." The literature, fine arts, religious consciousness, industrial life, political organization, educational system, social economy, etc. of the Hindus—all have sought to realise this synthesis and harmony between the eternal antitheses and polarities of the universe: the worldly and other-worldly, the positive and transcendental, the many and the one, the form and the spirit, culture and faith, science and religion, caste disunions and Vedantic oneness, image-worship and the realization of the Infinite (*Brahman*).

The ideal of realizing the infinite in the finite, the transcendental in the positive, manifested itself also in the educational system of Hindu India[1]. One may ask, Was that system essentially monastic and ascetic, and did it kill all secular and social instincts of the learners? Did the *Brahmachārins* come out from the preceptors' homes merely as monks, missionaries and *sanyāsins*? Could they not satisfy the diverse material wants of men? Did they not know how to provide for the necessaries, comforts and decencies of life? Was the education absolutely non-political? Did not the students learn how to help in the administration of the state? Were not social and political sciences, plant-life and dissection of animals, physical phenomena and chemical manipulations among the courses of instruction? Answers to such questions may be given in another question, namely, How else can we account for the remarkable progress of the nation in architecture, sculpture, medicine, dyeing, weaving, ship building, navigation, military tactics and implements and all such aspects of socio-economic and economico-political life as have to depend on the help of physical and natural sciences?

The graduates trained under the "domestic system" of the *Gurukulas* or preceptors' homes were competent

[1] *See* the present author's "Pedagogy of the Hindus" (The *Collegian*, Calcutta, 1912), and "Oriental Culture in Modern Pedagogics" (*School and Society*, New York, April, 1917).

enough to found and administer states, undertake industrial and commercial enterprises; they were builders of empires and organisers of business concerns. It was because of this all-round and manly culture that the people of India could organise vast schemes of colonization and conquest, and not content with being simply confined within the limits of mother India, could build up a Greater India beyond the seas, and spread culture, religion and humanity among the subject and hospitable races.

It was under the influence of this system of education, again, that the ideal Hindu king "protected himself, but not through fear; followed the dictates of duty, but not through remorse; realized revenues, but not through greed, and enjoyed happiness, but not through attachment". That system certainly cannot be dismissed as inexpansive, inert and unfit to survive that could produce *Riṣis* from Vaśiṣṭha and Viśvāmitra to Rāmaprasāda and Rāmakrishna Paramahamsa, scholars from Charaka, Pāṇiṇi and Chāṇakya to Chandrakānta Tarkālaṃkāra—a race of eminent women from Maitreyī to Ahalyā Bāi and Rāṇī Bhavānī, monarchs from Chandragupta Maurya to Śivāji and Ranjit Singh and has continuously kept up the genial stream of national culture and civilization through diverse forms and agencies by giving rise to hosts of thinkers and actors capable of solving different problems in different ages.

It is because the secular achievements of Hindu civilization have not been accorded by scholars the attention they deserve, and a proper estimate of the positive background of Hindu socio-economic and socio-political life has not been framed, that the distorted picture of a race of metaphysicians, airy philosophers, and transcendental speculators has been drawn regarding

Indian peoples to excite the pity of the go-ahead pushing Occident and pander to the foolish, unthinking vanity of the present-day fallen Orient. The *Upaniṣads*, the *Vedānta*, the *Bhakti Śāstras*, the *Darśanas*, the *Gītā* and the whole body of Hindu transcendental literature in which people may find, in the words of Schopenhauer, "the solace of their life" as well as the "solace of their death," cannot, however, be fully appreciated and interpreted in the true light until and unless we bring to bear upon them the results of investigations regarding the social, economic, political, international and other human institutions and ideals, in the midst of which this literature has flourished and that have actually governed the life and activity of Hindus. This mass of metaphysical lore requires, in fact, to be regarded as the "criticism," as Matthew Arnold would say, of Indian "life" and its problems and achievements. The transcendental speculation has to be understood and explained with reference to the *milieu* according to the philosophico-comparative methods followed in the schools of literary studies founded by such critics as Taine, Edmond Scherer, Sainte-Beuve, Dowden, Brandes and Kuno Francke. This should really be looked upon not as the sole but simply as *one* of the various features in the organic growth and historic evolution of Indian literature, institutions, civics, arts and industries.

The principal correctives of the one-sided, partial and erroneous view about Hindu life and ideals, in addition to what we have already stated, are thus two:—(1) a more searching and detailed inquiry into the economic, political and art history of India, and (2) a study, according to the canons of scientific literary criticism, of the whole literature of Hindustan, Sanskritic, and Dravidian, Prakrit and Vernacular, in both its metaphysical and realistic or secular branches.

So far as the secular branches of Sanskrit literature are concerned, it would not be too much to remark that the adequate parallax for modifying and correcting the false notions about the Hindu genius can be supplied if the *Kāvyas*, *Nātyas*, *Kathās*, *Purāṇas*, *Tantras*, *Itihāsas*, *Vāstuvidyās*, *Silpaśāstras*, *Arthaśāstras*, *Nītiśāstras*, *Dharmaśāstras* and *Smritis* were critically investigated as documents of Indian historico-sociological development. These alone cannot fail to impress upon the inquirer to what great extent the eternal verities of the universe and the highest problems of life enunciated and discussed in the *Upaniṣads*, *Darśanas*, *Gītā* etc. have influenced and governed the ordinary pursuits of human life in India, and been embodied in its thousand and one usages, institutions and festivals; to what enormous proportions the transcendental culture-lore of the Hindus has been humanized, secularized, and popularized by being translated and adapted into the commonplace folk-lore;—to what depth the Hindu ideal of realizing the one in the many, the ideal in the real, the transcendental in the positive, has been done into the actual life and work,—the *Realpolitik*,—of the people. It will be evident to every close student of this literature that the synthesis of the world's permanent polarities has been concretely demonstrated and manifested in the ever-moving gradations of the social polity known as *Varṇāśrama*, the hymeneal rites and marriage rules, the joint family, the cottage industry, the autonomous system of co-operative village commonwealths, the *Āchāryakulas*, the *Pariṣats*, the elastic theological apparatus and religious paraphernalias, the institution of kingship, and the doctrine of *maṇḍala* (sphere of international activity) that constitute of complex web of Indian life.

To take only one instance,—the *Raghuvamśa* of

Kālidāsa, the immortal epic of Hindu India. It is impossible to study it from cover to cover without noticing how powerfully the greatest poet of Hindustan has sought to depict this Hindu ideal of synthesis and harmony between the positive and the transcendental, the *bhoga* (enjoyment) and the *tyāga* (renunciation). *Raghuvamśa* is the embodiment of Hindu India in the same sense that *Paradise Lost* is the embodiment of Puritan England. The grand ambitions of the Vikramādityan era, its colossal energies, its thorough mastery over the things of this world, its all-round economic prosperity and brilliant political position, its Alexandrian sweep, its proud and stately outlook, its vigorous and robust taste are all graphically painted in this national epic, together with the "devotion to something afar from the sphere of our sorrow," "the light that never was on sea or land," the *sanyāsa*, *vairāgya*, *ahiṃsā*, *yoga*, preparation for the other world, the idea of transitoriness of this world and the desire for *mukti* or perpetual freedom from bondage. (*Supra*, p. 37)

This antithesis, polarity or duality has not, however, been revealed to us as a hotch-potch of hurly-burly and pell-mell conflicts and struggles, but presented in a serene, sober and well-adjusted system of harmony and synthesis which gives the "World, the Flesh and the Devil" their due, which recognises the importance and dignity of the secular, the worldly and the positive, and which establishes the transcendental, *not to the exclusion of*, but only above as well as in and through the civic, social and economic achievements[1].

The greatest example of the Hindu ideal of

[1] The ultra-religious interpretations of Hindu culture as furnished by E. Sénart in *Les Castes dans l'Inde* (Paris, 1897), and by Max Weber, in *Gesammelte Aufsaetze zur Religionssoziologie* (Tuebingen, 1922-23) are not borne out by the facts of Indian history.

synthesis and hence perhaps of the world's highest ideal, is to be found in the picture where Kalidāsa beggars his hero, the Indian Napoleon, the conqueror of the four quarters, at the end of his proud *digvijaya* and 'triumph' by making him perform the *Viśwajit* sacrifice, which necessitates the giving away of the whole of his earthly belongings. Truly, the greatest artist of Hindustan has sung of the synthetic ideals of the one in the many, the infinite in the finite, the transcendental in the positive as the sole motto of the House of Raghu.

The same Vikramādityan grasp of this mundane sphere, the same vigour in attacking the problems of secular life, the same human, practical and positive outlook, the same solicitude for the discharge of the 'lowliest duties' that characterize the heroes of Kālidāsa, whose natural ambition was no meaner than that of swaying not only the lithosphere from sea to sea, but also the atmosphere and the skies, confront us at every step throughout the *Smriti*, *Nīti*, *Artha*, *Silpa* and *Vāstu* literature. Like other *Nīti* works, the lectures of Sukra, the master of social philosophy and legislation, to his disciples, the Asuras and Daityas, constitute one of the most important documents of this literature, and, as such, socio-economically and economico-politically illustrate the Kālidasan ideals of harmony between the positive and transcendental or realization of the transcendental in and through the positive.

The historical data about Hindu positivism have been ignored by such one-sided indologists as Max Mueller in works like *India What can it Teach us?* and *Chips from a German Workshop*. Besides, exponents of monistic "religious interpretation" among the sociologists like Max Weber in *Gesammelte Aufsaetze zur Religions-sociologie* have propagated the traditional indology on a large scale. Hindu culture has been side-tracked into monistic and fallacious interpretations coming as they do from indologists, sociologists, geographers, climatologists, ethnologists, regionalists, political philosophers and economists.

A specialization in the positivistic, secular, humanistic, scientific, rationalistic, and energistic data or factors of Hindu culture is therefore a desideratum. But it should not, therefore, be misunderstood as emphasizing or accentuating them to the exclusion of the idealistic, spiritual, religious and allied facts and ideas. It is not as an illustration of the monistic "historical materialism" or "economic interpretation" that has taken a final shape at the hands of Karl Marx or Achille Loria that the positivistic interpretations of Hindu culture ought to be listed.

Dualism or rather pluralism is, on the contrary, the key to the appropriate methodology in the interpretation of *viśva-śakti* or world-forces. The position of Pareto in his *Trattato di Sociologia Generale*[1] in this regard is acceptable. In his judgment historical materialism marked a noteworthy scientific progress in so far as it placed in clear light the contingential character of certain phenomena, namely, the moral and the religious, to which an absolute character was ascribed and is still ascribed by many. Further, it has, says he, certainly a part of truth because it asserts the inter-dependence of economic and all other social phenomena. But the error lies in changing this inter-dependence into a relation of cause and effect.

Equally acceptable is another Paretian viewpoint to the effect that the "economic man" is no more the

[1] Florence, 1916, Vol. I. p. 426, Vol. II. pp. 276-277; also *Manuel d'Economie Politique* (Paris, 1909) pp. 18-19. R. Michels: *Corso di Sociologia Politica* (Milan, 1927), pp. 14-16, 25.

whole man than is the "religious man," the "ethical man" etc. Extra-economic actions cannot be ignored in the examination of the complete personality. In regard to scientific purposes, again, says, Pareto, it is possible to be "analytical" but *la pratica è essenzialmente sintetica* (practice is essentially synthetic).

It is the synthetic view that one ought to stand for, and as one can claim, is the factual reality of Indian history and Hindu culture. Perhaps it is possible to connect the general scientific orientations of Hindu religious development with those of the German philosopher Fichte in his *Reden an die Deutsche Nation* (1808), Address VIII.

The Apostles and the early Christians, says he, placed their faith in Heaven in such an extraordinary manner as to be entirely indifferent to the things of life, the state, *irdisches Vaterland*, the earthly fatherland, and nation. This attitude is appraised by Fichte as an unnatural condition, as something outside the rule of the world-process, indeed, as a rare exception. It is, further, says he, a very abnormal or perverse use (*verkehrter Gebrauch*) of religion, such as has been very often made in Christendom and other faiths, which, without reference to the existing circumstances, recommends this retreating from the interests of the state and the nation as real religious disposition (*Zurueckziehung von den Angelegenheiten des Staates und der Nation als wahre religioese Gesinnung*). In the regular order of things, however, earthly life itself is to be regarded really as life (*soll das irdische Leben selber wahrhaftig Leben sein*), in which one can feel happy and which, naturally in expectation of something higher (*freilich in Erwartung eines hoeheren*), one can gratefully enjoy.

In Fichte's analysis, it is of course true that religion

is the consolation of unjustly oppressed slaves. But it is still because of the religious sense, above all, that people try to protect themselves against slavery and thus prevent religion from degenerating into a mere consolation of the prisoners. It fits the tyrant quite well, says Fichte, to preach religious resignation (*Den Tyrannen steht es wohl an, religioese Ergebung zu predigen*) and to direct to Heaven those whom he does not wish to accord any nook or corner on Earth (*und die denen er auf Erden kein Plaetzchen gestatten will an den Himmel zu verweisen*). In Fichte's words, we others should make it a point not to run after assimilating this concept of religion, and if we can we ought rather to prevent the conversion of the Earth into a Hell and thereby awaken a greater longing for Heaven. Fichte considers the natural drive of man,—such as only in a condition of real necessity may be given up—to consist in discovering the Heaven on this Earth and the eternally enduring things in his earthly day's work, in planting the imperishable and the immortal even in the temporal, and in teaching in a manner that can be seen by the mortal eyes.

Hindu culture, as it has historically grown through the ages and in diverse regions of India as well as "Greater India," bears testimony to this Fichtean *natuerliche Trieb des Menschen* (natural impulse or drive of man) and *regelmaessige Ordnung der Dinge* (regular order of things). All the activities and ideas of the Hindus in regard to the *irdisches Vaterland* (earthly fatherland), the establishment of Heaven on Earth (*Himmel auf dieser Erde*) and the discovery of the eternal in the ephemeral or the transient are so many phases of Hindu positivism.

And in this position we can agree with Giorgio del

Vecchio,[1] whose analysis leaves no doubt about the supreme value of each element in the personality. In his examination the orientations derived from the self are as "real" as those from the "not-self:" *Cotesta dualità resta insopprimibile come legge immanente del nostro essere* (This duality remains irreducible as the immanent law of our being). The two terms, fundamental but antithetic, are equally (*egualmente*) legitimate and valid, says he. The entire reality is to be referred equally (*egualmente*) to both these principles. Each one dominates and embraces the other, does not definitely eliminate it, because in its turn is dominated by and comprised in the other. Such idealism as is pragmatic enough to recognize the equal validity of diverse factors or elements in our *coscienza* (conscience) and *azioni* (actions), as does not consider any single motive by itself to be sufficient for human life and refuses to recognise in this or that particular tendency the intimate essence or supreme law of human nature can rescue the philosophical mind from the fallacy of a monistic "religious interpretation" of culture.

In this attitude we meet indeed Immanuel Kant in another way. This philosopher's attitude to the universe is epoch-making. As is well-known, he postulated the thorough-going distinction between Nature (*Prakriti?*) and Man (*Puruṣa?*) or rather the complete independence of the sense-world from the moral world, according to each a dignity and law of its own. It is the Kantian dualism[2] in a new guise that can render unto Religion the things that are Religion's and unto the other forces the things that naturally belong to them. Without

[1] "Etica, Diritto e Stato" in *Rivista Internazionale di Filosofia del Diritto* (Rome, 1934).

[2] J. Dewey: *German Philosophy and Politics* (New York, 1915) pp. 29-30.

necessarily holding the brief for Spengler in other items we are prepared to cry with him for "Back to Kant," so far as our general orientations in regard to positivism in philosophy are concerned.

SECTION 7

THE INTERNATIONAL CULTURE-CONTACTS OF THE INDIAN PEOPLE

All through the ages the peoples of India have had active intercourse with the other peoples of the world. Since the days of Mohenjo Daro culture (*c.* 3500 B. C.) the Hindus have never lived in an alleged "splendid isolation." Creative India has always had her mettle tested by the single world-standards of merit-measurement.

It is generally assumed that internationalism or cosmopolitanism is a very recent phenomenon in human affairs. As a matter of fact, however, culture has ever been international. Lendings and borrowings, imports and exports, colonizations and migrations characterize even the most primitive stages in the history of human evolution. On the one hand, Hindu culture, like every other culture, bears the stamp of the more universal world-forces; and on the other hand, not only Asia, but the Western world also exhibits features which have been directly or indirectly influenced by the Hindus. India has always been a necessary link in the chain of a growing series of human values.

The dawn of human civilization finds the Hindus (Dravidians and Aryans) as captains of industry and *entrepreneurs* of commerce. They were in touch with the Pharaohs of Egypt. The mummies of the Egyptians were wrapped in muslin which was imported from India.

Hindu trade gave to the land of the Nile ivory, gold tamarind-wood, sandal-wood, monkeys, and other characteristic Indian plants and animals. It is also believed that the textile craftsmen of Egypt dyed their cloth with Hindu indigo. Hindu ships brought the Indian commodities to the Arabian ports, or to the land of Punt on the Egyptian side; and from there these were transported to Luxor, Karnak and Memphis.

Excavations and discoveries in the Aegean islands, especially in Crete, have pushed backward the limits of Hellenic antiquity. Homer is today not so much the first of the Hellenes as the last of the Minoans, or Mycenaeans, or Aegeans. This Aegean civilization was the connecting link between Egypt and the "isles of Greece." It is interesting to observe that the Hindus (Dravidians) were in touch, probably indirect, with this primitive culture also. Hellenic-European civilization and proto-Indian civilization (Mohenjo Daro, Harappa and other sites) thus came to have certain elements in common.

It is perhaps still difficult to connect India with the Mediterranean area of culture by archaeological evidences. The intercourse is suggested by certain decorative *motifs* of folk-art common to the two regions, e.g., the deer with four bodies and a single head, two lions with one head, the lion with three bodies and one head, animal processions, animal combats, and so forth. These designs belong probably to a common "Early-Asian" tradition, which has influenced the Aegean as well as Hindu culture-areas.

Hindu commerce with the land of the Euphrates was more intimate and direct. As early as about 3000 B. C. the Hindus supplied the Chaldaean city of Ur on the Euphrates with teak-wood. The Assyrians also, like the Egyptians, got their muslin from India. In fact, vegetable-"wool", i.e., cotton, and wool-producing plants have been some of the earliest gifts of Hindu merchants to the world. From the tenth to the sixth century B. C. the Assyro-Babylonian trade of the Hindus seems to have been very brisk. Hindus brought with them apes, elephants, cedar, teak, peacocks, rice, ivory and other articles to Babylon, the Rome of Western Asia. It was through this Indo-Mesopotamian trade that the Athenians of the sixth century B. C. came to know of rice and peacocks.

This expansion of Hindu activity influenced the literature of the time, e.g., the *Vedas* and *Jātakas*. A cylinder seal of about 2000 B. C. bearing cuneiform inscriptions and images of Chaldaean deities has been unearthed in Central India. In Southern India has been found a Babylonian sarcophagus. Perhaps the Hindus owe their script to this West-Asian intercourse. The present-day characters of the Indian alphabet are derived from Brāhmī and earlier Kharoṣṭhi. Both of these are said to be Semitic in origin. These the Hindus may have learnt from the Phoenicians about 1000-800 B. C. through the international settlements of the Mesopotamian cities. Babylon was like modern New York the melting-pot of races. Besides, some of the astronomical conceptions of the Hindus may have to be traced to the land of the Euphrates, - until the Mohenjo Daro archaeology is placed on positive foundations in this item.

One of the eight dialects in which the famous inscriptions of Boghozkoi are written is Indian. Hindu numerals like *eka*, *tri*, *pancha*, *sapta* and *nava*, have been found in the same inscriptions of the Hittites in their exact Sanskrit form. The names of gods almost identical with those of the Hindus such as Mitrasil, Arunasil, Indra and Nasattijanna (twins) occur in the explorations from the Mitani kingdom which was situated between the Kur River and the Caspian Sea. Sureja is likewise another god of the Kur Valley in which a Hindu replica may be suspected. India's intercourse with Kurdistan, and Asia Minor, or for that matter, with the geography of Hittite culture is more and more coming to be established as a fact of ancient Asian history.

Hindu trade with the Hebrews also was considerable. Solomon (1015 B. C.), King of Judaea, was a great internationalist. In order to promote the trade of his land he set up a port at the head of the right arm of the Red Sea. He made his race the medium of intercourse between Phoenicians and Hindus. The port of Ophir (in Southern India or Arabia?) is famous in Hebrew literature for its trade in gold under Solomon. The Books of *Genesis*, *Kings* and *Ezekiel* indicate the nature and amount of Hindu contact with Asia Minor. It is held by Biblical scholars that the stones in the breast plate of the high priest may have come from India. The Hindus supplied also the demand of Syria for ivory and ebony. The Hebrew word, *tuki* (peacock), is derived from Tamil (South Indian) *tokei*, and *ahalin* (aloe) from *aghil*.

This Hindu-Hebrew commerce was a principal channel through which the nations of the Mediterranean became connected with India and the Far East. Long before the Greeks had any direct communication with the Hindus, they thus came to know of the latter, first, through Babyon and, secondly, through Judaea.

The Persians overthrew the Babylonian Empire in 540 B. C. Their territory extended into Thrace in Europe and into the Indian frontiers on the east. Northwestern India was for some time a satrapy of this Iranian (Persian) empire. The Persians got their gold from the Hindus who conducted extensive mining operations in the Punjab and elsewhere in India. Hindu soldiers joined the ranks of their Iranian fellow-subjects when Xerxes led the memorable expedition against Greece (480 B. C.), and the bones of many a Hindu may have been mixed with the dusts of Europe at Thermopylae. This was probably the first contact between the Hindu and the Greek.

During this period Persia was Zoroastrian in socio-religious life, and it may be that the teachings of the Prophet of Iran had some influence over the Vedists of India. There are stories in Persia which claim the conversion of the Hindu philosopher "Cangraghacah" to the lore of the *Zend Avesta* after being defeated by Zoroaster himself in intellectual debate. On the other hand, Hindu influence on Iranians may also have been a fact. At any rate the Persians probably taught the Hindus the use of stone in architecture in the place of wood and brick. The "winged lions" as motives of Hindu art may also have to be traced to Iran.

Hindu genius for manufacture and commerce was thus of service to every race of antiquity that did anything for mankind. And when Alexander's deliberate internationalism (336-323 B. C.) ushered in the epoch of Eurasian culture-hybrids in Greece, Egypt, the overthrown Persian Empire, and the frontiers of India, the Hindus actively co-operated with the other races in bringing about the new conditions of the Hellenistic world.

Chandragupta Maurya (321-298 B. C.), the first Hindu Emperor of a United India, defeated the Hellenistic-Syrian invader, Seleukos, and compelled him to give him his daughter in marriage. Hindu-Greek marriages became perhaps common occurrences, Greek sculptors and merchants lived at Pātaliputra (site of modern Patna), on the Ganges, Greek ambassadors were taken care of by the Foreign Office of the Hindu state, and Greek professors might have been invited to the Hindu capital to lecture on the Greek language.

In international politics the Maurya Emperors were the "allies" of the Hellenistic rulers of Western Asia, Europe, and Africa. To withstand the all-seizing ambition of the Roman conquerors the Greeks naturally sought the help of the Hindu rulers. Once or twice thus did the Hindus meet the Romans as foes (third century B. C.). Elephant-corps were probably despatched from India to help Pyrrhus of Epirus and Antiochus I of Syria against their enemies.

Hindu embassies visited the Hellenistic kings of Syria, Egypt, Macedonia, Epirus, and Kyrene on religious, cultural, and diplomatic missions. Sanskrit lore was taught at Antioch, Tarsus, and Alexandria. Platonists, Aristotelians and Stoics exchanged notes with the Hindu logicians, philologists, Upaniṣadists, Buddhists, and Jainas. Hebrew, Hellenic, and Hindu factors combined to hold the Christ-cult in an eclectic metaphysico-theological solution.

During the first two centuries of the Christian era, the Kuṣāṇs of Northern India promoted trade with the Roman Empire by land, and the Āndhras of Southern India had touch with Rome by sea. Roman mercenaries were in the army of the Hindu monarchs. Roman citizens lived in India, Roman coins circulated in the Indian markets. Embassies from the Indian States went to congratulate Augustus, the first Roman Emperor, on his accession. Trajan also received a Hindu embassy (100 A. C.). Spices, perfumes, muslins, cosmetics, pearls, aromatics and other luxuries and novelties "made in India" commanded an extensive sale in the bazars of the Roman Empire. The balance of trade was in favour of the Hindus, leading to considerable "drain" of gold from Rome to India.

The Indo-Roman intercourse was deep and long enough to influence the general eclectic character of those times. Hindu philosophy was assimilated by the Greeks of Alexandria and became a formative agency in the development of Neo-platonism under Plotinus (third century A. C.). On the other hand, Ptolemaic astronomy may have been absorbed by the Hindus. The Kuṣāṇ Emperor struck coins according to the Roman models. The vast extent of Hindu commerce was indicated by the international elements in the currency. The obverse had the Hindu Emperor in Tartar dress, a Persian fire-altar, and Greek inscription; the reverse had the Hindu god Śiva as well as Greek, Persian and Tartar deities. Hindu-Hellenistic or Graeco-Buddhist (Gāndhāra) sculptures of North-western India and Central Asia, also, were the products of a cosmopolitan imagination fostered by the mingling of races. That art has been to a certain extent the parent of sculptures in China, Korea and Japan.

The Kuṣāṇs were Scythians or Tartars of Central Asia naturalized on Indian soil. Through them the northern frontiers of India were extended almost as far as Siberia. Along with this territorial expansion, Hindu missionizing activity was greatly enlarged owing to direct political sovereignty or spheres of influence. Central Asia was dotted over with temples, monasteries, hospitals, schools, museums and libraries.

It was through this "Greater India" on the land side that China, the land of Confucius and Laotsze, came within the sphere of influence of Hindu culture. The Hindu-Chinese intercourse, begun through the Tartar intermediaries, continued for about one thousand years. Hindu activity in China was promoted by sea also through Indian navigators, colonizers, and merchant marine. This maritime enterprise gave to India the cultural hegemony ultimately over Burma, Siam, Annam, Java and Japan.

China received Mahāyānic Buddhism and Sanskrit texts from the Central-Asian provinces of India in 67 A. C. After that China became Hinduized not only in theology and metaphysics, but in every department of thought and activity. Thousands of Hindus lived in Chinese cities, e. g., at Changan in the N. W. and at Canton on the sea, as priests, teachers, merchants, physicians, sculptors and "interpreters." The name of Chinese tourists, students, philosophers, and translators, also, in India is legion. The Chinese founded their drama on Hindu precedents, imported musical instruments (stringed) from India, and introduced even some of the acrobatic feats, dances and sports prevalent among the Hindus.

During his Indian tour the great Itsing (634-712) mastered Hindu medicine at the University of Nālandā. Hindu mathematics and logic were cultivated among the intellectuals of China; Sanskrit treatises on painting and art criticism, e. g., *Ṣaḍaṃga* (six limbs of painting) in Vātsāyana's *Kāmasūtra* (erotics), *Chitralakṣaṇa* (marks of painting), etc. furnished the canons of Chinese art during its greatest epoch (Tang and Sung Dynasties, 600-1250); and the traditional Confucianism had to be reinterpreted, e. g., by Chu-Hsi (1130-1200), in the light of the imported Hindu philosophy. China became a part of "Greater India" in poetry, aesthetics, folk-festivals, morals, manners, and sentiments. The "Augustan Age" of Chinese culture, the age of the mighty Tangs and brilliant Sungs, was the direct outcome of the "holy alliance" for centuries between India and China.

Nobody can understand and appreciate China's paintings, literature, and achievements in humanism without feeling at the same time what humanity owes to Hindu culture. And as for Japan, she was always an appendix to Indo-Sinic civilization. From chop-sticks and *No*-dance to Nichirenism, *Zen*-(meditation)-philosophy, *Bushido* (militarism), Sesshiu's landscapes, and Basho's *Hokku*-versicles, the Japanese derived almost every bit of their life and institutions from India or China or from Hindu centres in China.

India was the heart and brain of Asia during the Middle Ages. While the Far East was being Hinduized, the age-long intercourse with the peoples of Western Asia and beyond was not neglected by the Hindus. The epoch of Roman Imperialism and Graeco-Roman culture had passed away. But the Gupta-Vikramādityan Napoleons of India in the fifth century welcomed the Chinese scholar-tourists with one hand and the Egyptian (Alexandrian) and Arabian traders with the other. One Sassanian Emperor deputed his physician to India to translate Hindu folk-tales into Persian. Every school-child in Europe and America knows them to-day as the so-called Aesop's *Fables*. Another Persian monarch sent an embassy to the court of the South-Indian Emperor in the middle of the seventh century. The game of chess so popular in the western world to-day came from Hindus through the Sassanians.

Then came the days of Mohammed's converts, the Saracens, and the Caliphates, which Islamized the world, deeply or superficially, from Canton in China to Cordova in Spain. On the one hand, the Saracens kept alive the intellectual tradition of Hellenic antiquity in the Dark Ages of Europe, and on the other, they became the connecting link between the East and the West. The thirteenth century Renaissance of Europe, represented by Roger Bacon, was an offshoot of the Saracen contributions. On this Saracen culture

Hindu influence was almost as great as on the Chinese.

Hindu professors of algebra, medicine, alchemy, logic, and folk-lore taught the Moslems of the educational institutions at Bagdad. Hindu physicians practised at the capital of the Caliphate, and were in charge of the Imperial Hospital. Mansur (753-74) sent a deputation to Sindh (in Western India), which had come under his political influence, for Hindu astronomical tables. Harun Alrashid (786-808) and Mamun (813-33), the Charlemagnes of the Abbasside Saracens, encouraged by all means the propagation of Hindu culture among the Moslems. Sanskrit texts were translated into Arabic under the auspices of the State. The pre-Moslem Persian versions of Hindu literature were also used. Besides, advanced scholars came to India to study the Hindu sciences at first hand.

The great Harun was cured of a severe illness by Mankh, a Hindu physician. This fact gave a great fillip to the cultivation of Hindu medical science throughout the Saracen Empire. Mankh translated into Arabic a Sanskrit work on medicinal plants. Sanak, another Hindu scientist, wrote an Arabic book on poisons according to the Indian toxicologists. Many drugs were imported into Persia from India, e.g., pepper, lac, nard, myrrh, red sandal, cinnamon, calotropis, myrobalan, occimum sanctum and others.

The Moslems read with their Hindu teachers the standard medical literature in Sanskrit, e.g., *Charaka*, *Suśruta*, and *Vāgbhaṭa*, the treatises on leeches and on poisons, and studied also the diseases of women. They are specially indebted to the Hindus for a knowledge of the internal administration of iron, oxides of arsenic, mercury and other metals. From the Saracens the Christian nations assimilated these Hindu discoveries. The later Greek physicians became acquainted with the Hindu system and availed themselves of the Indian medicaments. Not before Paracelsus (1493-1541), however, and then in the teeth of great opposition from reactionaries, did these bold and dangerous Hindu practices become common in Europe.

The Saracens learnt the decimal system of notation from the Hindus and passed it ultimately on to the Europeans. They learnt also the Hindu science which has since been wrongly called algebra after them. They learnt similarly their Manzil or division of the sky into twenty-eight lunar asterisms from the same source. They enriched themselves with Hindu geometry also. Thus they learnt the correct value of the π, and also how to find the area of the circle.

To understand the contributions of the Saracens to Europe, e. g., of Musa in mathematics, and of Rases and Avicenna in medicine, alchemy and physiology, one need consider the part played by the Hindu brain in mediaeval science. The founders of the first Universities of Europe got their inspiration from the centres of Moslem learning, e. g., at Cordova and Bagdad. These had in their turn been to a considerable extent nurtured on Hindu culture.

We watched the Hindu navigators of hoary antiquity conveying their merchandise to minister to the wants of the builders of the Pyramids. We have now come down to the era of the Crusades (11th-13th century). The forefathers of the modern Christian nations were then busy withstanding the "expansion of Asia" in Europe. They were at the same time picking up a knowledge of the superior arts and sciences of the Asians. All these five millenniums the Hindus had maintained a cosmopolitan outlook in commerce and culture. Thus in the sixth century A. C. a Hindu scientist Varāhamihira honestly admitted India's indebtedness to the Greeks in astronomy in the following words (*Brihat Samhitā*, II. 14): "The Yavanas (Ionians, i.e., Greeks) are indeed *mlechchhas*, i.e., barbarians, but amongst them this science of astronomy is firmly established; hence they are honoured as though they were *Riṣis*, i.e. holy sages." This has been the historic attitude of the Hindu mind with regard to the world. Hindu culture has influenced and been influenced by the leading culture-systems of mankind.

Since the thirteenth century India has been Moslem as well as Hindu. During the later Middle Ages it was, first, through the Arabs that the Indians were in touch with the mercantile commonwealths of Venice, Florence, and other Italian cities, as well as with the Hanseatic League of Northern Germany. Secondly, the Buddhist Tartars of China overran the whole of Russia and carried the western frontiers of Asia almost to the Carpathian mountains. They introduced the Europeans to the Chinese discoveries, e.g., printing, gunpowder, mariners' compass, etc. and also to the heritage of Hindu thought in Central Asia and China. Further orientalization of the Occident was promoted by the establishment of Turkey as a first class power in the Southeast of Europe during the fifteenth and sixteenth centuries. The more momentous consequences of this event have been the Renaissance, the discoveries, the expansion of Europe, the birth of America, and the "Commercial Revolution."

The Hindus and Moslems of India under the Great Moguls during the sixteenth and seventeenth centuries were in intimate touch with Persia and Western Asia. India was enriched by the naturalization of new fruit-bearing plants from abroad. Some of the best treasures of Persian literature were made available to the people in translations. A new language, the Indo-Persian Urdu was improvised to be the medium of the new joint aspirations of the original inhabitants and Indianized newcomers. Poets, scholars, architects, painters and musicians were invited from Western Asia to settle in India.

On the whole, Persia has left an indelible impression on Hindu culture. For the past three hundred years the social etiquette and fine arts of India, poetry, painting, architecture, and music, both Hindu and Moslem, have been consciously or unconsciously influenced by the canons of Persian masters. On the other hand, Sanskrit literature and philosophy were rendered into Persian. It need be remarked that the Latin versions of the Persian translations of Sanskrit originals have had some influence on European minds also, e.g., on Herder, the inspirer of the romantic movement and prophet of world-culture, and Schopenhauer.

It was during this period of Indo-Persian or Hindu-Islamic Renaissance that the European merchants came into direct contact with India. The merchants and sea-going vessels of India were then continuing the tradition of their best periods. The Indian mercantile craft was larger, more durable and more elegant than the Portuguese, French, and English ships, according to the estimation of the European experts. India was an "industrial power" still, and her market was Europe.

The year of the first French Revolution (1789) was also the year of the presentation of the first Sanskrit work, *Sakuntalā*, a drama by Kālidāsa, the Hindu Shakespeare (fifth cent. A. C.), in a modern European language. Goethe's raptures over it are well known And as "imitation is sincerest flattery," he took a hint from the Hindu dramatist.

India's contribution to the Industrial Revolution of the early nineteenth century has been, first, a vast market for the industrial powers of the Western world, and secondly, a land of raw materials. She has thus been in touch with the modern cultural forces, viz., the steam engine and democracy, and has served to help forward the development of technocracy and the "world-economy."

SECTION 8

THE CHARAIVETI (MARCH ON) OF CREATIVE INDIA IN SIAM, CHAMPA, INDONESIA, TIBET, CHINA AND MOSLEM ASIA

The values created by the Hindus in life and thought did not remain confined to the Indian motherland. The *Aitareya Brāhmaṇa* (VII. 15) cult of *charaiveti* (march on) impelled the Hindus not only to move from region to region within the Indian boundaries in order to "colonize," Aryanize, civilize or humanize the diverse races of this South-Asian subcontinent but also to move out of India with the object of "conquering and to conquer" extra-Indian races and regions. Thus was established in the course of centuries an extensive "Greater India" throughout Central, Northern and Eastern as well as Western Asia including the Indo-Pacific Archipelagoes.[1] A short account of this *exubérance de vitalité* or expansion of Hindu culture is being furnished below.

Buddhism is known to have reached Siam through Cambodia early in the fifth century (422 A. C.). Burma also played some part in the propagation of Buddhism in Siam. Along with Buddhism came the entire Pali literature, furnished as it is with the elements of positivism and the morality of strenuous and energistic life.

[1] R. K. Mookerji: *History of Indian Shipping* (London, 1910); L. Finot: "Hindu Kingdoms in Indo-China" (*I.H.Q.*, Calcutta, 1925).

It is to be remembered that in the early centuries of the Christian era Siam had no independent existence, being but a province of Camboja. Whatever is known about the establishment of "Greater India" in Camboja during this period may refer therefore equally to Siam also. From the earliest inscriptions of Camboja, e.g., those from the sixth to the ninth century A. C., be they in Khmer or in Sanskrit, we understand the prevalence of Hindu gods, Brahmā, Viṣṇu and Śiva alongside of Buddha.

It was during the period in question that Siam also came to be annexed to the sphere of Hindu positivism. The earlier beginnings of the Hinduization of this country are not yet clear. But early in the thirteenth century when the first royal dynasty of Siam was established (1218 A. C.) it had already a Hindu name. The first historical king is known to have been Śrī Indrāditya and his successors also had Hindu names. The name of the capital of this dynasty was also Hindu or rather Indian, namely, Sukhodaya.

The third king Rāma Rāja (1283) bore on his very name the influence of the *Rāmāyaṇa*. He was a Buddhist by faith. The inscription (1293)[1] issued by him describes temples with the image of Buddha as well as monks and a *Mahāthera* (head priest) well-versed in the *Tripiṭaka*. The Siamese alphabet that was invented by him (1284) was modelled on the Cambojian which is well-known to be Sanskritic.

[1] Fournereau : *Le Siam Ancien* (1895), 2 Vols., Bradley: "The Oldest Known Writing in Siam" in the *Journal of the Siam Society* (1909) and "The Proximate Source of the Siamese Alphabet" in the *J. S. S.* (1913); all cited in P. N. Bose : *The Indian Colony of Siam* (Lahore, 1927). See also W. Credner : *Siam das Land der Tai* (Stuttgart, 1935), pp. 330, 333, 339, 343, 347, 348, 357.

The titles of ministers of the state council as well as of the principal officials are found to be Hindu. The *montree*, the *parohita* (*purohita*), the *mahāsenāpati*, the *rājakoṣādhipati*, the *amancha* (*amātya*) etc. are all of Indian categories. The five Hindu symbols of royalty are in use. The civil and criminal law of the *Manu Samhitā* has furnished the basis of Siamese law. The influence of the *Mahābhārata* also as of the *Rāmāyaṇa* is no less patent.

The influence of Hindu positivism in the history of Champā from the seventh to the thirteenth century is patent in the royal dynasties of the period, of which each one of the fifty rulers bears a Sanskrit name. And most of these names end in "Varman", no matter how varied be the dynasties[1].

A Sanskrit inscription of King Prakāśadharma Vikrāntavarman I (655-690) has a fine verse on *śakti* (prowess) in which *daṇḍa* (punishment) and *bheda* (disunion), two of the important categories of Hindu *Nītiśāstra*, are utilized in the right eulogistic manner of Hariṣeṇa and other Indian *praśasti-kāras*.

Another inscription of his shows familiarity with the *Rāmāyaṇa*. Familiarity with the ideology of the *Manu Samhitā* can be seen in the inscription of Vikrāntavarman II (710-730), Indravarman I (799), Indravarman II. (875). The atmosphere is throughout one of the promotion of *dharma* (law and duty) as the function of the king who is "a god in human form."

Familiarity with the *Mahābhārata* is evident in an inscription of Rudravarman III (*c* 908-917) and with the *Artha-Purāṇaśāstra* in an inscription of Jaya Harivarman I (*c* 800-820).

[1] R. C. Majumdar: *Ancient Indian Colonies in the Far East*, Vol. I. *Champa* (Lahore, 1927), Book III.

In Harivarman IV's inscription (1081) which is partly in Sanskrit verse and partly in Cham prose, the portion in Cham has reference to *sāma*, *dāna*, *bheda* and *daṇḍa*.

An inscription entirely in Cham of 1088 describes Śrī Jaya Indravarmadeva V as virtually an embodiment of all the good things to be found in the Hindu *Nītiśāstras*. In this description we are told that the eighteen titles of law prescribed by Manu were followed by him and that he knew also the *ṣādguṇya* (the six military attitudes). The inscription makes use of the categories, *trivarga*, *artha*, *dharma*, *kāma*, *sāma*, *dāna*, *bheda*, *upapradāna* (bribery), *krodha*, *lobha*, *moha*, *mada*, *mātsarya*, *yoga*, *dhyāna*, *samādhi* etc. among others.

The *Dharmaśāstras*, especially the *Nāradīya* and the *Bhārgavīya*, are referred to in the inscription (in Cham) of Jaya Indravarman VII (1180-1190). These and other inscriptions of Champā may indeed be regarded for certain purposes as exquisite and concrete illustrations (some of them in fine Sanskrit verse) of the principles or theories adumbrated in the texts of political philosophy created on Indian soil.

It may not be difficult to connect the architecture and sculpture of Champā with those of India. The matter of the figures, of course, is Hindu and their forms also could not but be derived in the main and originally from Indian executions. As regards the buildings, the temples also, in spite of great difference in details their forms may be described as having some family likeness with the Hindu temples, e.g., of South India and of Buddhist *vihāras*. The influence of the *Silpaśāstras* may then have to be detected in Champā art also.

The *Brahmāṇḍa Purāṇa* of Bali is older than the tenth century and can be traced to the fifth or the sixth.[1] In this treatise a Kṣatriya dynasty of Indonesia has been linked up with the Indian sage Pulaha.

It is possible to suspect also the existence of the Indian *Viṣṇu Purāṇa* in Bali during this period since some of its stories are found to have influenced the Balinese *Brahmāṇḍa Purāṇa* and other works.

In the twelfth and thirteenth centuries the Indian *Tantras* also were powerfully influencing the literature of the Indonesians. The frequent use of Sanskrit verses in these texts is a noteworthy feature. It is interesting to observe that the peoples of Java and Bali used to offer salutations in verse to the Panchakanyā (five ladies), Ahalyā, Dropadī, Sītā, Dārā, and Mandodarī in the same manner as the Hindus of those days as well as of today.

Vyāsa's *Nītipraya* is said to have been written for a prince. It deals with what Indian *Smriti* and *Nītiśāstras* call *rājadharma* or duties of kings. Another Balinese work, the *Nītiśāstra Kawi* is in the same strain. Incidentally it may be observed that Viṣṇugupta Kauṭalya is referred to in a Balinese inscription of 1041.

The earliest law-book of the Javanese appears to be the *Sivaśāsana* which in title as well as in substance is Indian. And this is taken to have been composed in the tenth century (991 A. C.). Another Javanese law-book is entitled *Āgama*, a work probably of the thirteenth century (*c* 1273), which likewise is Indian in title. Indeed, it is the *Manu Samhitā* Indonesianized although not without local influence. Between the eleventh and thirteenth centuries the Indian Manu was the virtual dictator of legal practices to the people writing in Kawi. Treatises like the *Ādigāma*, *Pūrvā-*

[1] H. B. Sarkar : *Indian Influences on the Literature of Java and Bali* (Calcutta, 1934).

dhigāma, *Devādhigāma*, *Svara-jambu*, *Devadanda* or *Dharma-vichāra*, *Sārasamuchchaya* and others composed in this language, interspersed as they are with original Sanskrit texts, testify to the *digvijaya* of Manu and Indian positivism in Insulindia during the period from Harṣa to Hemādri.

The Indian *Rāmāyaṇa* furnished the *motif* of extensive bas-reliefs in the temple-architecture of Java. The oldest *Rāma*-bas reliefs are to be seen in the Prambanan group, presumably of the ninth century.

The *Rāmāyaṇa-Kākāwin* was composed in Old Javanese sometime during the tenth or eleventh century (*c* 1100 ?). The author has an Indian name, namely, Rājakusuma, Kusuma-vichitra and Yogīśvara. This *Kawi-Rāmāyaṇa* follows, in the main although in a much abridged form, the original story as given by the Indian Vālmīki.

The temple of Angkor Vat was constructed in the twelfth century (*c* 1112-1180) during the reign of Sūryavarman II and the architect is said to have been his spiritual preceptor, Divākara.

The *Ādiparvan* of the Sanskrit *Mahābhārata* was available in *Kawi* prose (Old Javanese) by the tenth century. Some of the other *Parvans* were likewise available in Old Javanese in the eleventh century. These books of the Indonesian *Mahābhārata* are in prose. Sanskrit verses occur in these *Kawi* texts although often in corrupted and incomplete forms.

The Indonesian *Bhāratayuddha*, although based on the *Mahābhārata*, is not one of its *Parvans*. It is an independent *Kawi* work dealing with the war between the Kauravas and the Pāṇḍavas. It was important enough to eclipse the Indonesian *Bhīṣmaparvan* which was a regular section of the *Mahābhārata*.

To the middle of the twelfth century (1157) belongs the *Kawi* poetical work, the *Bhārata Yuddha* by Mpu Sedah who exhibits intimate familiarity with Sanskrit prosody, reminding one of Aśvaghoṣa and Kālidāsa. The *Kawi* word for medical science is *Uṣado* (Sanskrit *Auṣadha*, medicine) and the treatises betray Hindu as well as Buddhist among other influences.

The translations and adaptations of the *Rāmāyaṇa* and the *Mahābhārata* in the diverse languages of "Greater India" during the period from the tenth to the thirteenth century are to be treated as forerunners of the translations of the same Sanskrit epics during the period from the fourteenth to the sixteenth or seventeenth century in the diverse languages of India itself. Students of Hindu positivism will have to treat Yogīśvara, the author of the Indonesian *Rāmāyaṇa* in *Kawi*, as occupying the same place in the history of civilisation as *Krittivāsa*, the author of the Bengali *Rāmāyaṇa*, and Tulsīdāsa of the Hindi.

During the period from Harṣa to Hemādri the Bay of Bengal was but a Hindu Lake. The territories on all sides,—Bengal at the apex to the north, the territories on the Western shores, namely, the South Indian regions and Ceylon, the territories on the Eastern shores, namely, the whole of Greater India extending up to Yunnan in China on the north and to Siam, Champā and Cambodia in the farthest East, and finally, the Islands of the Southern seas comprising Sumatra, Java, Bali and Borneo, representing as they do, the gates to the Pacific and the bridges of India for contact with the Philippines and Japan,—were engaged in one and the same work, namely, the propagation of Hindu culture among the diverse races of mankind, Indian and non-Indian. The story of all these extra-Indian races for whom the Hindu arts and sciences were being adapted belongs, so far as this particular period is concerned, to the history of India as an integral part. Hinduism has always proved to be a proselytising religion and culture embodying the *Aitareya Brāhmaṇa* (VII, 15) spirit of *charaiveti* (march on). It has always been on the go, conquering and to conquer fresh regions and races. From the seventh to the thirteenth century Hindu culture was making converts not only within the still un-Hindu nooks and corners of continental India but also among the most heterogeneous peoples of Greater India.

The Himalayan mountains were no more a barrier to the infiltration of Indian arts and sciences in extra-Indian regions than was the Bay of Bengal. Tibet, for example, appeared in the Middle Ages to be but an appendix to the North-Indian system of civilization. And this Indianizing of Tibet was consummated independently of the Indian missionary work in China. The relations between the Tibetan people and Hindu culture were direct. And like the Chinese the Tibetans imported from India not only the rites and ceremonies, the religious texts and philosophical disquisitions directly associated with Buddhism but many items of life and thought such as had no bearings on religion and philosophy. Indeed, to the Tibetans as to the Chinese almost anything and everything associated with India and the Indian people appeared to be Buddhistic.

During the tenth century Tibet was a great field for the proselytising activity of Hindu culture. For one thing, the Indian *Silpaśāstras*, especially in their practical aspects, have left an indelible impression on the architecture, sculpture and painting of the Tibetan people. A Tibetan treatise dealing with the parts of a *chaitya* (*mc'od rten*) entitled *Chaitya-samvibhāga* is to be found in a section of *bs Tanagyur*.[1] It contains precise indications relating to the diverse parts of which a *chaitya* is composed as well as the proportions to be observed while constructing it. The architectural terminology was derived by the Tibetans entirely from Indian sources. The eight fundamental types of *mc'od rten* described in Tibetan treatises correspond to the models of *chaityas* existing in India.

An Indian treatise on the marks of painting, the *Chitralakṣaṇa*[2] comes from the Tanjur collection of Tibetan literature. A work on the marks of *stūpas* or *chaityas* was translated by the *Lotsava* (saint) Buston and is to be found in the *bs Tan agyur di Co* collection.

About 1000 A. C. flourished the Tibetan *Lotsava*, Rin c'en bzan po[3] who translated the *Prajnā-pāramitā*. A veritable renaissance of Buddhism is ascribed by Tibetans to the many-sided propaganda carried on by this monk-scholar-saint. He may aptly be described as the Itsing or rather the Yuan-Chwang of Tibet and is by all means one of the most remarkable personalities of medieval Eur-Asia. It is to the new spirit embodied in Rin cen bzan po that the missionizing activities of the Bengali Atīśa and the Kashmiri Somanātha in Tibet are to be credited.

He was a great translator and organizer of translations. *Sūtras* and *Tantras* like the *Laghusamvaratantra*, *Mahāparinirvāṇasūtra* etc., commentaries on the *Tantras*

[1] G. Tucci : *Mc'od rten e Tsa Tsa nel Tibet Indiano ed Occidentale* (Rome, 1932).

[2] The German translation of the Tibetan translation of the original Sanskrit was done by B. Laufer in *Das Chitralaksana* (Leipzig, 1920).

[3] G. Tucci : *Rin cen bzan po e la Rinascita del Buddhismo nel Tibet intorno al Mille* (Rome, 1933). See the present author's summary of this Italian work in the *Ind. His. Q.* for June, 1934.

like the *Vajra-Yoginī-stotra*, the *Ṣaḍaṃgayogatīkā* etc. were Tibetanized. Tradition ascribes to his initiative the translation of over 150 Sanskrit texts. Among them are to be found also medical works like the *Aṣṭāṃga hridaya* and veterinary treatises relating to horses, e.g., the *Sālihotrīya*.

Seventy-five *Paṇḍits* are known to have been invited from India by his royal patron, the King of Guge, on account of his interest in Hindu culture. The translation bureau established by him had on the staff such Indian names as follows:

1. Dīpaṃkaraśrījnāna. 2. Śraddhākaravarman. 3. Padmākaravarman. 4. Kamalagupta. 5. Dharmaśrībhadra. 6. Subhāṣita. 7. Gangādhara. 8. Buddhabhadra. 9. Janārdana. 10. Atīsa. 11. Buddhaśrīśānti. 12. Buddhakaravarman. 13. Prajnāśrīgupta. 14. Vīryabhadra. 15. Tathāgatarakṣita. 16. Vijayaśridhara. 17. Devakara. 18. Subhūtiśrīchadra. 19. Kanakavarman.

Rin cen bzan po was not only a literary man. He was an architect and a great builder too. Tradition ascribes to him the construction of 108 temples and other buildings. His temples and *stūpas* are rich in frescoes and wooden carvings and sculpture. Artists were invited under his inspiration from Nepal, Bengal as well as Kashmir.

The Indian tradition was preserved and continued in Tibet at a time when in India itself Buddhism was in decline. Since, at any rate, the tenth and eleventh centuries, entire Tibet has had the appearance, in external form as well as in spirit, of India as she is likely to have been in the heyday of Mahāyānism, i.e., under the sway, say, of the gods of Northern Buddhism.[1]

[1] Getty: *The Gods of Northern Buddhism* (Oxford, 1914). See

Tibet during the entire Middle Ages can therefore be aptly regarded like Afghanistan and Central Asia during certain periods, say, up to the seventh or eighth centuries A. C., as but an expansion of Hindustan beyond the Himalayas. Lamaist Tibet is but a province of Buddhist India, nay, of Hindu India too, in so far, as the Mahāyāna-Lamaist-Tantric gods and rituals are virtually but duplicates and analogues of the Puranic-Tantric Neo-Hindu gods and rituals. What is generally known about the Indianization of China and Japan applies equally if not more appropriately to the Indianization of Tibet also.

The frescoes in the monastery at Luk illustrate Amitābha, Vairochana, medicine-gods, the thousand-handed and thousand-eyed Avalokiteśvara, and scenes in the life of Buddha. In the temple at Gumphug one comes across fine specimens of indigenous Tibetan art. Chinese influence can hardly be detected here. But, on the other hand, the direct imitation of Tantric *paṭas* of India is in evidence. Manuscripts of medical treatises bear illustrations of gods or masters of medicine. Indian *Āyurveda* also seems to be represented in Tibetan culture.

The *maṇḍala* type of architecture is represented by the largest temple at Toling. The form might have been borrowed from the temple at Somapura near Pahaḍpur in North Bengal. It is the *Vajradhātu maṇḍala* of the Tantric cycle that is reproduced in this temple. Vairochana is in the centre, Akṣobhya is placed in the

also "Sino-Japanese Buddhism and Neo-Hinduism," "The Alleged Extinction of Buddhism in India," "The Bodhisattva-cult in China, Japan and India," "The Buddhism of China and Japan Euphemism for Śaivā-cum-Śāktaism," "Neo-Hinduism in Trans-Himalayan Asia" and "Modern Hinduism" in B. K. Sarkar: *Chinese Religion through Hindu Eyes* (Shanghai, 1916) pp. 281-303.

east, Ratnasambhava in the south, and then come Amitābha and Amoghasiddhi. The entire Mahāyānic pantheon is visible here, especially the one connected with the Sarvavid, Vairochana, Guhyasamāja and Samvaratantra.

The chapels surrounding the great temple are twenty in number. In the company of Vairochana, Vajrapāṇi, Samvara, Sākyamuni, Lokapāla, etc. are found very often the eight gods of medicine. Vijaya, Sitāpatra, Tārā, Prajnāpāramitā are the conspicuous figures in the "white temple."

At Tsaparang a temple is dedicated to Vairochana. As the centre of Vajradhātumaṇḍala the figure of Vairochana is the special favourite of the sect founded by Rin cen bzan po. Statues of Maitreya in gilded bronze and of Bhairava with five heads of which the central is that of a buffalo are likewise to be met with in some of the temples of Tsaparang.

Lamaism is the joint product of the labours of Tibetan devotees who had been to India aspiring after spiritual perfection as well as of Indian sages who were invited by the Tibetans as their guides or who were forced to leave their fatherland on account of hostile attacks. Tibet is literally dotted over with bits of Hindu culture in religion, literature and fine arts[1].

Emperor Harṣavardhana's (606-647) Chinese contemporary was the Tang Napoleon Tai-tsung (627-650) and the contact between the two was established by Yuan-Chwang, the Max Mueller of those days, who visited India in 629 and returned to his native country in 645. The travels of another great Chinese scholar-

[1] *Cronaca della Missione Scientifica Tucci nel Tibet Occidentale* (1933) by G. Tucci and E. Ghersi (Rome 1934), summarized by the present author in the *I. H. Q.* for June 1935.

saint, Itsing, perhaps more learned than Yuan-Chwang, the "organizer," and Fa Hien, the devotee or man of *bhakti* (faith), were also undertaken (671-695) under the Tangs (618-905). The seventh and eighth centuries witnessed the Indianization of Chinese culture on a magnificent scale such as had not been attempted before.

The conquest of Tibet by Tang Tai-tsung (627-650) brought India into contact with China by a new land-route. During the rule of this Tang Napoleon there were in Loyang more than three thousand Indian monks and ten thousand Indian families. It was through Indian "culture-contacts" that Chinese ideographs were furnished with phonetic values. As a result the Japanese alphabet was also created in the eighth century.[1]

The dramatic art of the Chinese was likewise influenced to a certain extent by Hindu pantomimic dances and acrobatic performances, etc., as Bazin suggests in *Le Theatre Chinois*.

During the eighth century the scholar Itsing on his return from travels and researches in India could count among his collaborators a large number of Indians settled in China. Some of them may be mentioned as follows :

1. Anijana, a priest from Northern India. 2. Dharma-ratna, a priest from Tukhara. 3. Dharmānanda, a priest from Kabul. 4. Śringīśa, a layman from Eastern India. 5. Gotamavajra, likewise a layman from Eastern India. 6. Harimati. 7. Arjuna, Prince of Kashmir.

The mighty Tangs were followed by the brilliant Sung dynasty which ruled the entire Empire from 960 to 1127, and later, only South China down to 1279. Under the Sungs the fortunes of Hindu culture were

[1] K. Okakura : *Ideals of the East* (London 1905).

no less prosperous than under the Tangs. Indeed by the twelfth and thirteenth centuries not only Taoism but even Confucianism had been thoroughly transformed under Indian influence. The result was a reinterpreted Confucian cult or Neo-Confucianism.[1]

This was the epoch of Chu-hsi (1130-1200) *par excellence* who commanded the intellect and morals of Young China. And it is the neo-Confucianism as propounded by this philosopher of Sung times under the influence of Buddhist or Indian ideology that has ruled China and Japan since. The story of Hindu humanism from Harṣa to Hemādri is the story of a world-process which embraced virtually three-fourths of Asia in its endevours at remaking.

The ancient and medieval Chinese were strong in historiography. In catalogue-making also they were past-masters. The progress of Indianization in China can be followed step by step in and through the catalogues of Buddhist *sūtras*. In Chinese the treatises bearing names which end in "*lou*" may conveniently be taken for catalogues.

In *Litai san pao ki*[2], a catalogue compiled in 597, there is a list of 24 previous catalogues of Buddhist works, the oldest of which is by tradition ascribed to the epoch of the first Chinese Emperor Tsin Shi-hwangti (*c* B. C. 246-200). But none of these catalogues were seen by Fei Tchang-fang, the compiler of the *Li tai san pao ki*.

The catalogues of Buddhist *Sūtras* such as could be used by Fei Tchang-fang in 597 were three in number. By 730 three more catalogues were compiled. Down

[1] Edkins : *Chinese Buddhism* (London 1893) ch. XX.

[2] P. C. Bagchi : *Le Canon Bouddhique* (Paris 1927) pp. xxxii-lii.

to the end of the thirteenth century sixteen catalogues were prepared and all these are available today.

The *charaiveti* of Hindu culture was not confined to those Asian regions which accepted the Indian faiths as their own. Moslem Asia also was considerably Hinduized in culture. During the period from Harṣa to Hemādri Greater India was thus flourishing in the Saracen Empire in Western Asia as in Central, Northern, Eastern and South-eastern Asia including the Islands of the Indian Archipelago.

The *Panchatantra* was translated first into Persian. From Persian it was rendered into Arabic as *Kalila and Dimna*. The medical work of Charaka likewise passed through Persian version into Arabic. Practically all the other Arabic versions of Hindu texts were made direct from the original.[1]

The astronomical (mathematical) works of Brahmagupta, namely, the *Brahmasiddhānta* (called *Sindhind* in Arabic) and the *Khaṇḍa-khādyaka* (Arkand) were translated into Arabic by Alfazari and Yakub Ibn Tarik during the reign of Mansur (753-774).

Under Harun Alrashid (786-808) the ministers, belonging as they did to the Barmak family, were Buddhists converted to Islam. It was under their auspices that Hindu scholars were invited to Bagdad and Sanskrit works on medicine, pharmacology, toxicology, philosophy, astrology and other subjects were translated into Arabic.

At this time the son of Dhanya or Dhanin was the director of the hospital at Bagdad. A Hindu physician named Kanka was also practising there. Atri's work on drinkables was introduced to the people. Vedavyāsa's

[1] E. C. Sachau: *Alberuni's India* (London 1910), pp. xxvii-xl.

work on wisdom or philosophy, allied perhaps to Bādarāyana's *Vedānta* philosophy, was likewise to be found among the Sanskrit texts known in the Saracen capital. This may have had some part in the formation of Arabian Sufism. A *Jātaka* by Satyavarman perhaps belonged also to the Indian literature imported into the Saracen Empire under Harun. Vyāghra's book on the signs of swords and a work on astrology attributed to S N G H L, a name which it is difficult to decipher, are likewise mentioned. The Buddhist story, adapted in Christian literature under the title of *Joasaph and Barlaam*, as well as some of the fables of Buddhaghoṣa relating to the cunning of women were also rendered available in Arabic during this period.

Treatises on *Sarpavidyā* (science of snakes), on *Viṣavidyā* (science of poison), auguring, talismans, veterinary art, sex-lore, logic, ethics, politics, war, and general philosophy are known to have been translated by the Saracens. The Moslem authors wrote also commentaries, adaptations and summaries etc. of the Hindu books.

At home in Khiva Alberuni (979-1048) was in a position to study the *Brahmasiddhānta*, the *Khaṇḍakhādyaka*, the *Charaka Samhitā* and the *Panchatantra* in Arabic versions. An Arabic translation of Vitteśvara's *Karaṇasāra* could likewise be used by him. There were in existence also certain Arabic treatises on astronomy and chronology in which the knowledge of Hindu mathematics was implied.

While in India (1017-30 ?) he wrote his work on India in which in addition to his special subjects, namely, astronomy and mathematics, philosophy, literature, general culture etc. are introduced. The sub-title of the book is "An accurate description of all categories of Hindu thought, as well those which are admissible as those which must be rejected." Besides, during the same period he produced a number of independent treatises. These are being enumerated below:

1. A treatise on the determination of the *nakṣatras* or lunar stations.

2. The *Khayal-alkusufaini* in which among other items the theory of *Yoga* is described.

3. The Arabic *Khaṇḍa Khādyaka*, more or less similar in contents to No. 2.

4. A book in which the *Karaṇas* are described.

5. A treatise on the various systems of numeration in use among different nations including the Indian.

6. The Key of Astronomy.

7. Treatises on the methods for the computation of longitude.

Two works of Varāhamihira were translated into Arabic by Alberuni. The one was the *Brihatsamhitā* and the other the *Laghujātaka*. A Sanskrit treatise on loathsome diseases owes its Arabic rendering to him. Among philosophical works he is responsible for the translation of Kapila's *Sāṃkhya* and Patanjali's treatise on *Yoga* as well as of the *Gītā*.

Translations from the *Viṣṇudharmottara Purāṇa*, *Viṣṇu Purāṇa*, *Matsya Purāṇa*, *Vāyu-Purāṇa* and the *Āditya-Purāṇa* are to be found in Alberuni's work on India.

As for the works on astronomy, mathematics etc. his book exhibits knowledge of (1) Brahmagupta's *Puliśa-siddhānta*, *Brahmasiddhānta*, *Khaṇḍakhādyaka*, and *Uttara-khaṇḍakhādyaka*, of which the first three were translated by himself into Arabic, (2) Balabhadra's commentary on the *Khaṇḍakhādyaka*, (3) Varāhamihira's *Panchaśiddhāntikā* and *Brihatjātakam* in addition to the two other works translated by himself, (4) Utpala's commentary on the *Brihatsamhitā*, (5) a book by Āryabhata II., (6) Vitteśvara's *Karaṇasāra*, (7) Vijayanandin's *Karaṇatilaka*, (8) *Srīpāla*, (9) *Book of the Riṣi Bhuvanakoṣa*, (10) *Book of the Brāhman Bhattila*, (11) *Book of Durlabha*, (12) *Book of Jīvaśarman*, (13) *Book of Samaya*, (14) *Book of Auliatta*, (15) *Panchāla Minor Mānasa*, (16) Mahādeva Chandrabīja's *Sarvadhara*, (17) a calendar from Kashmir.

Among other Hindu books that went to the making of Alberuni's *India* may be mentioned (1) Haribhaṭa's dictionary, (2) a treatise on the medicine of elephants, (3) the *Mahābhārata*, (4) the *Rāmāyaṇa*, (5) Manu's *Dharmaśāstra*, and last but not least, (6) the *Gītā*.

Previous to the composition of the work on India Alberuni had translated two Sanskrit books into Arabic, as he says in the preface (Vol. 1. p. 8), one about the *origines* and a description of all created beings called *Sāṃkhya*, and another about the emancipation of the soul from the fetters of the body called *Pātanjali*. According to this eleventh century Moslem "indologist" "these two books contain most of the elements of the belief of the Hindus." He hoped that the work on India would "enable the reader to dispense with these two earlier ones, and with other books of the same kind."

Alberuni was convinced that "misrepresentation" (Vol. I. p. 5) was "much in fashion among those who undertake the task of giving an account of religious and philosophical systems from which they slightly differ or to which they are entirely opposed." While examining the manner in which he classifies the "misreporters" and liars about other nations we are easily reminded of another great Moslem scholar, Abul Fazl, who nearly six centuries later, analysed the causes of intolerance and prejudices of races against one another. It is interesting that two of the greatest intellectuals of the Moslem world were inspired by the self-same ideal, namely, the love of truth as well as the desire to rescue the Moslem conception about Hindu culture from hearsay as well as second-hand information. Not less significant is the fact that in attempting to be "objective" narrators of a "simple historic record of facts" both have exhibited definite pro-Hindu leanings, although, of course, Alberuni's propaganda in favour of the Hindu achievements does not verge on the almost hundred per cent identification of Abul Fazl, the "Hindusthani Shaikh", with the fortunes of his Hindu countrymen.

In regard to Hindu religion and philosophy Alberuni makes it a point to distinguish between the educated and the uneducated classes. This distinction is with him eternal. In the case of the Arabs and Greeks also he observes that the ideas of men and women differ according as they are cultivated or not.

"It is well known," says he, "that the popular mind leans towards the sensible world and has an aversion to the world of abstract thought which is only understood by highly educated people, of whom in every time and every place there are only few." He is therefore not surprised that among the Hindus "idols are erected only for uneducated low-class people of little understanding and that the Hindu never made an idol of any supernatural being, much less of God." (Vol. I p. 122). In the sixteenth century (1598) Abul Fazl also took the same liberal view about Hindu images.

Alberuni describes the "educated people" among the Hindus as calling God *Iśvara*, i.e., self-sufficing and beneficent who gives without receiving. They consider the unity of God as absolute (Vol. I. p. 31). Then passing "from the ideas of the educated people among the Hindus to those of the common people," he observes, "that they present a great variety and that "some of them are simply abominable."

But Alberuni is faithful to the Koranic gospel of "speaking the truth even if it were against yourselves" (*Sura*, 4, 134). It is therefore quite in keeping with his love of truth to admit at once that "similar errors also occur in other religions. Nay, even in Islam we must decidedly disapprove, e.g., of the anthropomorphic doctrines, the teachings of the Jabriyya sect, the prohibition of the discussion of religious topics and such like."

The Hindu culture that was assimilated by Alberuni was presented by him to his readers in the perspective of Greek thought. It is very noteworthy that the manner in which we moderns try to institute parallels or identities between the Hindu and the Hellenic ideologies can be traced back to this Afghan-Moslem scientist and philosopher of the eleventh century. In his work on India the Moslems found Plato, Proclus, Aristotle, Grammaticus, Alexander of Aphrodosias, Apollonius of Tyana, Porphyry, Ammonius, Aratus, Galenus, Ptolemy and Pseudo-Kallisthenes rubbing shoulders with the authors of the *Sāṃkhya*, *Yoga*, the *Gītā* and other systems (Vol. I. pp. xlii, xxlii). Nor is this all. His comparative method served to bring in the Hindu ideas into the *milieu* of Zoroastrian, Christian, Jewish, Manichaean, and Sufi sources.

Arabic culture was in those days the connecting link between Asia and Europe. Alberuni was thus functioning in Moslem Asia and beyond, indeed in the entire Christian world, in much the same manner as his great Chinese predecessors of the seventh century,

Yuan Chwang and Itsing, in China and Japan, so far as the propagation of Hindu culture is concerned. This Moslem mathematician of Khiva is an important landmark and agent in the establishment of Greater India. His services to the *charaiveti*, the dynamic march of Creative India are immense. Not the least paradoxical feature in this evolution consists in the fact that while his masters of the Ghazni House were laying the foundations of a Moslem *raj* in India his scientific and philosophical researches in Hindu culture were contributing to the Hinduization of the Moslem world and, through the Moslems, of the culture of Europe in exactly the same friendly spirit as had been shown by the Barmak ministry and others during the days "of good Harun Alrashid."

SECTION 9

INDIAN IMPACTS ON MODERN EUR-AMERICA

Modern civilization may be said to begin in 1776 with the publication of Adam Smith's *Wealth of Nations*. Its formative period may be taken to have closed with 1815, when the fall of the Napoleonic empire, on the one hand, and the almost assured success of the "Industrial Revolution" on the other were laying the foundations of a new interpolitical system and a new socio-economic order throughout the world. Ever since the year No. 1 of this new culture India has been in intimate touch with the West; for by the Regulating Act of 1772, the year of the partition of Poland, England took charge of the administration of the eastern provinces of the present British India.

It goes without saying that the achievements of the Occidental world in industry, science, philosophy and the fine arts during the nineteenth century have profoundly influenced the thoughts and activities of the people of India, as of other regions in Asia. But what is most likely to be missed by the student of culture-history is the fact that even the ancient and medieval civilization of the Hindus has been one of the feeders of this modern civilization itself, i.e., that the cultural movements in Europe and America since 1776 have been affected to an appreciable extent by the achievements of free India down to that period.

Naval Architecture

In the days of the sailing ships and oaken vessels, the naval engineering of the Hindus was efficient and advanced enough to be drawn upon with confidence for European shipping. At Madapollum, for example, on the Madras coast, many English merchants used to have their vessels yearly built. The Hindu ship architects could ingeniously perform all sorts of iron works, e.g., spikes, bolts, anchors etc. "Very expert master-builders there are several here," says the English traveller, Thomas Bowrey in his *Geographical Account of Countries Round the Bay of Bengal* (1669-1675); "they build very well, and launch with as much discretion as I have seen in any part of the world. They have an excellent way of making shrouds, stays, or any other riggings for ships."

Writing even as late as 1789, on the eve of the Industrial Revolution in Europe, Solvyns, the French traveller, could still recommend, in his *Les Hindous* (Vol. III., 1811), the Hindu method of uniting the planks as "not unworthy of the imitation of Europeans" He says, "In ancient times the Hindus excelled in the art of constructing vessels, and the present Hindus can in this respect still offer models to Europe."

In the building of a boat the Hindus began by choosing a large piece of timber which they bent as they pleased. To the two ends of this they attached another piece thicker than it, and covered this simple frame with planks; "but they have a particular manner of joining these planks to each other, by flat cramps with two points which enter the boards to be joined, and use common nails only to join the planks to the knee. For the sides of the boat they have pieces of wood which outpass the planks. This method is as solid as it is simple."

Some of the Hindu methods were actually assimilated by the Europeans. Thus, as the French writer observes: "The English, attentive to everything which relates to naval architecture, have borrowed from the Hindus many improvements which they have adopted with success to their own shipping." Further, the Portuguese "imitated" the pointed prow in their India-ships. This was a characteristic feature of the grab, a Hindu ship with three masts.

The industrial and material culture of Old India was thus sufficiently vital to influence contemporary Europe at the threshold of the nineteenth century civilization. The tradition is reported also by old American sea-captains that fishing boats like the sloop, yawl, cutter, etc. so common in the United States waters were modelled in the "colonial period" on Hindu patterns.

The So-called Bell-Lancasterian Pedagogics

During the formative period of the modern educational systems in Europe and America, the pedagogy of the Hindus, especially on its elementary side, has played an important part.

It is well-known that primary education was grossly neglected in America during the first half-century of her independence. In England even so late as 1843,

32 per cent of men and 49 per cent of women had to sign their names on the marriage register with a cross. Illiteracy was the rule in France also at the time of the Revolution, as Arthur Young observed. Guizot's Education Commission (1833) found that "the ignorance was general" and that "all the teachers did not know how to write."

In an age of paucity of "public schools" private educational efforts naturally elicited the people's admiration. And none drew more sympathy and support than Andrew Bell's (1753-1823) "mutual-tuition" or "pupil-teacher" or "monitorial" system of school management. His first school was founded in England in 1798, but in less than a dozen years 1000 schools were opened to teach 200,000 children. This "mutual instruction" was a craze in France also under the Restoration. The same system, known in America after Lancaster (1778-1838), the English rival of Dr. Bell in theology, was in vogue in the New England States during the first quarter of the nineteenth century. It could become so universal simply because of its cheapness as it did not involve the appointment of teachers. And as to its educational value, Bell was so enthusiastic as to declare, after visiting Pestalozzi's school at Yverdun in 1815, that in another twelve years mutual instruction would be adopted by the whole world and Pestalozzi's method would be forgotten.

What, now, is the origin of this much-applauded mutual instruction or monitorial system, the so-called Bell-Lancasterian "discovery" in pedagogy? Historians of education are familiar with the fact that the plan of making one boy teach others has been indigenous to India for centuries. Bell, himself, in his *Mutual Tuition* (Pt. I. ch. I, V) describes how in Madras he came into contact with a school conducted by a single master or superintendent through the medium of the scholars themselves.

And, in fact, in England the monitorial system or the method of making every boy at once a master and a scholar is known as the "Madras system."

England's debt to India in pedagogics has been fitly acknowledged in the tablet in Westminster Abbey, which describes Andrew Bell as "the eminent founder of the Madras System of Education, which has been adopted within the British empire, as the national system of education for the children of the poor."

Śakuntalā and the Romantic Movement

The romantic movement in Germany and England, with its aftermath, the English pre-Raphaelite movement, has been one of the greatest forces in Europe's modern letters and art. The poetry of Old India has furnished an impetus to this current also of nineteenth century thought.

The *Śakuntalā* of Kālidāsa, the Hindu dramatist of the fifth century A. C., was Englished by Jones in 1789. Foster's German rendering (1791) of it from the English version at once drew the notice of Herder (1744-1803), the great champion of comparative methodology and *Weltliteratur*. And Herder introduced it to Goethe on whom the effect was as tremendous as that of the discovery of America on geographers and of Neptune on students of astronomy. Goethe's ecstasy expressed itself in the ultra-enthusiastic lines :

"Wilt thou the blossoms of the spring, the fruits of late autumn,
Wilt thou what charms and enraptures,
Wilt thou what satisfies and nourishes,
Wilt thou in one name conceive heaven and earth,
I name, Śakuntala, thee, and in that is everything said."

These are the words of a man who in 1771 had dramatized the narrative of Goetz, a medieval bandit. The sentiment in favour of the Rousseauesque "state of nature," the love of "ancient reliques," the Bolshevist revolt against the *status quo* of art, the subversion of classic restraint, the lyric abandon to the promptings of the imagination, the awakening of the sense of wonder, and the craving of the soul for the unknown, the mystery —a great deal of all that was later to be associated with Scott, Shelley, Schiller, and Lamartine had been anticipated and focused in that drama of *Sturm und Drang* (storm and stress). It is not strange, therefore, that the great "futurist" of the eighteenth century, the father of modernism in European literature, should have welcomed the Hindu Shakespeare as warmly as he did the Elizabethan. For in Goethe's eyes wistfully looking for more light, more spontaneity, more freedom, both shed the "light that never was on sea or land," the one as the star of the Middle Ages, the other as the sun of a hitherto unknown world.

Śakuntalā left an indelible impression upon the literary activity of this pioneer of romanticism. It is the story of a woman with child deserted by her lover. The Gretchen-episode in the tragedy of *Faust* may thus have been inspired by the dramatist of India. At any rate, German critics have pointed out that the conversation between the poet, the manager and the Merry Andrew in the prelude to *Faust* is modelled upon that in Kalidāsa's play, in which the manager and one of the actresses talk as to the kind of performance they are to give. *Śakuntalā* occupied a great place in the dramatic and lyrical imagination of Schiller also, in whose *Thalia* Germans are familiar with his Indian reminiscences. It is well known, besides, how the *schoene Weiblichkeit* which he failed to discover in the Greek classics he found at last in the Hindu drama.

The *Śakuntalā furore* has lasted till almost today. One of the noblest "overtures" in European music is the *Śakuntalā* overture of the Hungarian composer Goldmark (1830-1915).

The Gītā in Eur-America

Another force that Old India has contributed to the life and thought of the modern world is the profound optimism of the *Gītā* (ca. B. C. 600-200?), a section of the *Mahābhārata* (the Great Epic). The *Gītā* was translated into English in 1785. It was popularized in Germany by Herder and Humboldt. Since then its *Leitmotif* has been absorbed by the sponge-like minds of the greatest thinkers of Eur-America. It may be said to be held in solution in almost every great "poetical philosophy" or "philosophical poetry" of our times down to Bergsonian "intuition."

In the first place, the *Gītā* is the philosophy of duty and *niṣkāma karma* (work for its own sake), of the "categorical imperative." In the second place, it tries to solve the mystery of death, which is but an aspect of the larger and more comprehensive problem of the evil. The solution is reached in the conceptions of the immortality of the soul, the infinite goodness of God, the nothingness of death, and the virtual denial of the existence of evil. Such postulates are of the deepest significance as much to the lover who seeks an "eternal" union of hearts, as to the warrior who must bid adieu to the body in order to save the soul. This Bible of Old India has therefore influenced not only the *Imitation of Christ* by Thomas á Kempis but also Tennyson's *In Memoriam* and Browning's *La Saisiaz*, both inspired by the death of friends.

The "obstinate questionings" in Browning's poetry are the same as those of Arjuna in the *Gītā*, viz :

"Does the soul survive the body?
Is there God's self—no or yes?"

The answer in both *La Saisiaz* and the *Gītā* is in the emphatic affirmative. It is a message of hope to suffering humanity. Men and women in distress can brace their hearts up if they are assured that somehow through God's mysterious dispensation the good persists in and through the evils that are apparent. This Hindu optimism is voiced also by Walt Whitman, the voracious student of world-thought, in the following words :

"Roaming in thought over the Universe
I saw the little that is Good steadily hastening towards immortality,
And the vast all that is called Evil,
I saw hastening to merge itself and become lost and dead."

Tennyson had made only a tentative and halting statement to the same effect, namely,

"Oh, yet we trust that *somehow* good
Will be the final goal of ill."

But the paean of the Upaniṣadic *ānanda* (or bliss) and *āmrita* (or immortality) rises clearly forth in Browning, thus :

"Why rushed the discord in, but that harmony should be prized?"

Further,

"The evil is null, is nought; is silence, implying sound;
On the earth the broken arcs ; in the heavens, "a perfect round."

The syllogism of the *Gītā* leads, indeed, on such-like arguments, to the more drastic conclusion:

"Up then! and conquer! in thy might arise!

Fear not to slay the soul, for the soul never dies".

Even militarism and man-killing are thus not evils in Hindu optimism. No wonder that the *Gītā* should have been a source of inspiration to the most diverse minds seeking comfort and strength. It could not fail to be a trumpet to the prophets of Duty, and such prophets were Carlyle, the sage of Chelsea, and Mazzini, the political mystic of the Italian regeneration.

With the memorable words, "Close thy Byron, open thy Goethe," Carlyle sent forth his *Sartor Resartus* to the English people, as the manifesto of an al-round Germanism. This German *Kultur* was the idealism of Kant, Lessing, Fichte, Schelling and Hegel, the nearest European ally of Hindu monism. It opened the Anglo-Saxon mind to the sense of the infinite, of the majesty of the spiritual self, and electrified the soul to the recognition of the "duties that lie nearest thee." The gospel that taught to "make thy numerator zero in order that the quotient may be infinite" converted the Bostonians of the trans-Atlantic world from Lockites into metaphysicians. This "new thought" of the day was worshipped by Parker and Emerson around the *Dial*. The New England Transcendentalists thus became kinsmen of the Hindus (*Infra*, p. 115).

Manu as the Inspirer of Nietzsche

Nietzsche's Dionysian cult is one of the latest great forces in world-culture. The web of recent Eur-American life is being supremely invigorated by the warp of the Nietzschean *Will to Power*. It is interesting to observe that almost the whole of this new cult is reared on Hindu humanism and energism. Old India has contributed its hoary Manu as the master-builder in order to boss the supermen who are to architecture the Occident of the twentieth century.

Nietzsche, like the "futurists" of all ages, believes that the world is in need of a thorough-going "transvaluation of values." How is that to be effected? The means to the re-humanizing of humanity have been devised, says he, by the Hindus. "Close thy Bible, open thy Code of Manu" is his prescription. And why? Because Manu is the propounder of an "affirmative" religion,—the religion of the "deification of power," whereas Christianity is the creed of the slave, the pariah, the *chandāla* (*The Will* etc., Vol. I, ii. p. 126). Says Nietzsche:

"One breathes more freely, after stepping out of the Christian atmosphere of hospitals and poisons into this more salubrious, loftier and more spacious world. What a wretched thing the *New Testament* is beside Manu, what an evil odour hangs around it!" (*The Twilight of Idols*, p. 46)

In Nietzsche's estimation Manu is also a better because more frank teacher of political science than the philosophers, insincere as they are, of the Western world. Thus, "Manu's words again are simple and dignified; virtue could hardly rely on her own strength alone. Really it is only the fear of punishment that keeps men in their limits and leaves every one in peaceful possession of his own" (*The Will* etc., II, iv, p. 184).

In international politics Hindu theory since the days of Kauṭalya (fourth century B. C.), generally considered in Germany to be the Bismarck of the first Hindu empire, has been candidly Machiavellian. Nietzsche finds greater truth in the mercilessly correct view of international relations given by the Hindus than in the hypocritical statements of Occidental statesmen whose actions belie their words." In Nietzsche's language (*The Will*, II, iv. p. 183),

"Rather what Manu says is probably truer: we must conceive of all the states on our own frontier, and their allies, as being hostile, and for the same reason, we must consider all of their neighbours as being friendly to us."

This is the celebrated doctrine of *maṇḍala* ("geopolitical" sphere of states) fully described in Kauṭalya's *Artha-śastra* and Kāmandaka's *Nīti*, both treatises on politics.

The fundamental reason for Nietzsche's sympathy with, and advocacy of, Hindu culture is to be found in the fact that the Hindus were keenly alive to the animality in human life and interests, and that their *Weltanschauung* embodied the joy of living in its entirety. As Nietzsche observes, Manu has "organized the highest possible means of making life flourish." Further,

"The fact that, in Christianity, 'holy' ends are entirely absent, constitutes my objection to the means it enjoys......My feelings are quite the reverse when I read the Lawbook of Manu,.........an incomparably intellectual and superior work......... It is replete with noble values, it is filled with a feeling of perfection, with a saying of yea to life, and a triumphant sense of well-being in regard to itself and to life, the sun shines upon the whole book. All those things which Christianity smothers with its bottomless vulgarity, procreation, woman, marriage, are here treated with earnestness, with reverence, with love and confidence" (*The Antichrist*, pp. 214-215).

It is this secular outlook, this positive standpoint, this humanism that, according to Nietzsche, has given a sanctity to life in Hindu thought. "I know of no book," says he, "in which so many delicate and kindly things are said to woman, as in the Lawbook of Manu; these old gray-beards and saints have a manner of being gallant to women which perhaps cannot be surpassed. 'The breath of a woman,' says Manu, on one occasion, 'the breast of a maiden, the prayer of a child, and the smoke of the sacrifice are always pure.' Elsewhere he says; 'There is nothing purer than the light of the sun, the shadow cast by the cow, air, water, fire and the breath of a maiden' (*The Antichrist*, p. 215).

Hindu Culture in America

America is generally supposed to be outside the sphere of influence of Hindu culture. But the facts are quite otherwise. The beginnings of the Yale University at New Haven were laid with the money that had been earned in Southern India. American architects and town-planners while discussing the old "colonial" style of their buildings take care to point out that the forms of these bungalows were borrowed by their fathers from the villas of Bengal. These were the eighteenth century conditions.

During the first half of the nineteenth century the Transcendentalists of Boston were at home as much in the new idealism of Kant, Fichte and Hegel as in the *Upaniṣads* and *Gītā* of India. Thoreau, Parker and Emerson were propagating the cult of *Vedānta*, as suggested above (p. 112), through their organ, the *Dial*.

The great energist and democrat, Walt Whitman, found the inspiration for his epoch-making *Leaves of Grass* not only in the activities of the American "pioneers" but in the soul-enfranchising thoughts culled from Hindu literature as well.

From Abraham Lincoln to Roosevelt American industry, commerce and finance have been almost daily oriented to the problems of Indian cotton and silver. And on the other hand the American Universities and Academies have been establishing chair after chair for Indic studies. Lanman's *Harvard Oriental Series* is a model of researches in indology. Bloomfield's Vedic investigations, Hopkins's *Mahābhārata* studies, Ryder's treatment of *Kālidāsa*, Jackson's contributions to Iranic scholarship are but a few of the many substantial works that the American men and women have used to enrich their life and thought with "Hindu" data.

It is this pro-Indian trend of American idealism and humanistic approach to culture that was responsible for the tremendous reception accorded to our Vivekānanda in 1893. For the last thirty years, i.e., since 1905 the American people has been extending its welcome to Indian ideas and enterprises in a most remarkable manner. Indian travellers, students, businessmen, scholars, publicists, missionaries,—men and women of every description have found hearty reception in American homes, clubs, workshops, schools, and parties. Today the American mind is as open, as receptive, as cordial to "Hindu" ideals and activities as it ever was, and is indeed fostering the growth of a spiritual "Greater India" in the New Hemisphere.

India in Western Literature, Universities and Movies

During the romantic period while Shelley was singing of "*champak* odours," Schiller was trying to adapt *Sakuntalā* to the German stage and Heine was discovering the "*schoensten Ort*" on the banks of the Ganges. The latter's "*Die Lotosblume aengstigt*" has subsequently been set to music by Schumann.

French romanticism was perhaps fed more on Mohammedan than on Hindu sources, e.g. the *Orientales* of Victor Hugo (1829) and of Lamartine (1834). Le Conte de Lisle (1820-94) is known to have travelled "in the Indies." Victor Cousin (1792-1862) had not, however, failed, eclectic as he was, to make use of the Hindu contributions brought to light in his days. In his *Histoire de la philosophie* as in Janet's *Histoire de la science politique* the Western will find the Hegelian interpretation of the Hindu "spirit." Besides, the misery of the "untouchable classes" in Indian population had evoked a powerful French tragedy, *Le Paria* (1821) by Delavigne, which at the "*Comédie Française*"[1] Theatre served to give a fillip to the spirit of social equality that had been fostered by the "ideas of 1789."

Sanskrit poetry has been quite lucky in its European translators. Griffith's exquisite English verse has popularized the *Rāmāyaṇa*, the *Raghuvamśa* and other epics and lyrics. In French the translations by Bergaigne, Victor Henry, Hérold and others are well known. The *Indische Liebeslyrik* by Rueckert (1788-1866), a poet and scholar, master as he was of diction, has enriched German poetry with love songs from Kālidāsa, Bhāravī, Bhartrihari and Jayadeva. The *Ritusamhāra* and the *Gītā* can be read in Italian on account of Pizzagalli.

During the nineteenth century, especially in its latter half and since, the Universities of Eur-America have almost vied with one another in introducing Indic subjects, *indianisme*, or indology in their curricula. The result is well known to savants who are interested in the publications of the Royal Asiatic Society through its Branches, the *Société Asiatique*, the *Deutsche Morgenlan-*

[1] A. F. Hérold: *L'Inde à la Comédie Française et à la Comédie Italienne en* 1770 (Paris, 1911).

dische Gesellschaft, the Kern Institute (of Holland), the American Oriental Society, the International Congress of Orientalists and so forth. The investigations of these learned societies may be said to be chiefly, if not exclusively, oriented to theologico-metaphysical scholarship, to archaeology, and to philology, especially to the grammar of the "dead" languages. The kind of work that has been done in this direction can be easily sampled out from Sylvain Lévi's account of French indology (with bibliography) in a chapter of *La Science Française* (Vol. II 1915), C. Brockelman's *Die morgenlaendischen Studien in Deutschland* in the *Zeitschrift der D. M. G.* (1922)[1] and G. Gabrieli's *Bibliografia degli Studi Orientalistici in Italia dal* 1912 *al* 1934 (1935).

Modern India has remained a taboo in these learned societies until almost today. But as the interest in the living Indian languages is already evident in the scholarly work of Grierson in England and Jules Bloch (*La Formation de langue marathie*, 1914) in France it is not perhaps to be doubted that contemporary India is likely soon to be attacked by orientalists,—from the philological angle at any rate. The School of Oriental Studies in London may be said to have set the example (1912) (p. 126).

But while the "upper ten thousands" in the field of science have neglected the present-day life and institutions of India, consuls, diplomats, governors, missionaries, merchants and travellers have tried to furnish Anglo-American, French and German literature with reports of what is going on in the South-Asian dependency. Contemporary Eur-American fiction and drama are therefore in a position to exploit Indian themes for modern art. The

[1] E. Windisch: *Geschichte der Sanskritphilologie und Indischen Altertumskunde*, Vol. I. (Strasburg 1917) and Vol. II (Berlin 1920).

Western "masses" derive their knowledge about India and the East from these sources,—and more especially perhaps from the cinemas and moving picture theatres which either seek to dramatize the extant storyliterature or otherwise attempt to objectify the impressions of their own agents who are deputed to the spot in order to collect first-hand information.

The India that has thus passed current in the lay mind of Eur-America can be visualized in one of the master-pieces of contemporary German drama, the *Spiegel-Mensch* (Mirror-Man) of Werfel (1920), which has been described as a "second *Faust*" in *La Nouvelle Revue Française* of Paris. All the important incidents in this play take place in the East which is exhibited with its snakes and magic, its alleged pessimism and superstition.

The Indian references in Sudermann likewise are anything but flattering. The Hindu hermits are brought in in his *Es lebe das Leben*. In his *Die Ehre* the dramatist shows not only the tropics with their palms, oranges, parrots and monkeys, the Sumatra tobaccos and spices, the regions of Central Asia, the Tibetan grandee, and the custom prevailing in Tibet of entertaining the guest with one's wife, but also India with its hot climate, its water-pipes, shawls, light blue sapphires, and its golden image of Gaṇeṣa, the god of success, riding a rat.

Such specimens of *indianisme* abound in the Eur-American letters of the present-day. These are in fact acquiring a wide notoriety through the interest that has been recently popularized in mysticism and "Hindu philosophy" or the so-called Hindu "point of view." The success of "Hindu" lectures on *yoga* in Eur-America, the inroads of theosophy upon contemporary "new thoughters," and last but not least, the Tagore-cult, which the Nobel-prize has served to establish for mankind since 1913—all these have been tending somewhat to divert Western attention from the India of flesh and blood, the India of human interests and ambitions to the India of phantasy and romance. But fortunately during the same period the thousand and one constructive and materialistic activities of Young India have succeeded in creating a reaction in the Occidental estimate of the Indian spirit.

In the young but sturdy republic of Czechoslovakia there are today novelists and poets whose creative imagination can cover in its sympathetic sweep the activities and sentiments of the men and women on the banks of the Ganges. Attention may be invited to the romance entitled *A Palace on the Banks of the Ganges* by A. Czech-Czechenherz published at Prague in 1934. The same author's work, *Shiva : Divine Dancer*, came out in 1935.[1]

It is interesting to observe that even before Czechoslovakia was born as an independent sovereign state Czech (Bohemian) thinkers used to discuss the problems of social life and cultural development almost in the same manner as their colleagues in far-off India. The ideals and methods preached in 1894, for instance, by one who is none other than the octogenarian President Masaryk of today, in his book, *The Czech Question*, might virtually word for word be found in the *Swadeshī Samāj* (Indigenous Society) of our Rabindranath Tagore published in 1904. The lines of thought were so uniform.

Verily, in the Czech soul there is something which makes the Slavic men and women akin to the people of

[1] For the translation of the main contents of these Czech works I am indebted to the Czechoslovak Consul in Calcutta, Dr. J. Lusk.

India. And it is of this affinity of spirit between India and Czechoslovakia that we are further convinced in the essay on "Awakened India" by Prof. Lesny, which is used as a preface to Czech-Czechenherz's romance.

One must not ignore the important part that the India-section of the museums in Great Britain or the Fine Arts Museums of New York, Boston, Cleveland and other American cities, the *Musée Guimet* of Paris, the *Museum fuer Voelkerkunde* in Berlin and Munich or the Tretiatov Gallery in Moscow have played in contributing not only to the studies in comparative art-history and art-technique but also to the enrichment of modern Western plastic arts by furnishing hints and suggestions. In Vincent Van Gogh the Dutch master's *Letters of a Post-Impressionist* the student of painting is familiar with the *motifs à la japonaise* which were being introduced in Europe about the middle of the last century. India's part in the technique of post-impressionist art will be apparent to observers of the new "artistic" anatomies exhibited by the "moderns" since Cezanne.

Sanskritic Culture and the "Comparative" Sciences

The greatest *differentium* between the modern civilization and all that the world witnessed between the Mohenjo Daro or Chaldaean ages and the industrial revolution is the phenomenal expansion of the human mind. This has brought in its train a catholicity of interests and toleration of divergent views. In this emancipation of the intellect from the thraldom of parochial and racial outlook Old India's contribution has probably been the most helpful and significant. The reason is not far to seek. The "discovery of Sanskrit" by the European scholars of the eighteenth century opened the portals to the series of sciences called "comparative." And it is this that has rendered possible the recognition, though not complete yet, of the fundamental uniformity in the reactions of man to the stimuli of the universe.

The trend of latter-day scholarship is to detect, through the ages of history, the close parallelism and pragmatic identity between Hindustan and Europe not only in theology and god-lore, but in rationalism, positive science, civic life, legal sense, democratic ideals, militarism, morals, manners, and what not. The evidences from the Hindu angle are being supplemented in recent years by the findings of Egyptology, Assyriology, and Sinology, i.e., the sciences dealing with extra-"Aryan" culture-zones.[1] The establishment of a comparative psychology of the races, past and present, Oriental and Occidental, is thus being looked for as the greatest work of anthropological researches in the twentieth century. The data are already varied and extensive enough to employ the energies of a "new Montesquieu" such as Myres expects in his *Influence of Anthropology upon the Course of Political Science* (1916). The sociological investigations of the Russian-American scholar Pitirim Sorokin, e.g., those published in *Social Mobility* (1927), *Contemporary Sociological Theories* (1928), and *Principles of Rural-Urban Sociology* (1929) furnish instances of new orientations in which the conventional postulates about the East and its alleged distinctions from the West have been proven to be unsound.

The first fruit of the discovery was "comparative philology." Jones founded the Asiatic Society of Bengal at Calcutta in 1784, and in 1786 hit upon the hypothesis

[1] H. Goetz : *Epochen der indischen Kultur* (Leipzig 1929); H. Piper : *Die Gesetze der Weltgeschichte* (Leipzig) : *Der gesetzmaessige Lebenslauf der Voelker Chinas und Japans* (1929), *Indien* (1931), *Aegypten* (1933).

of a common source of Sanskrit, Greek, Latin, Gothic, Celtic and Persian. The linguistic survey was pursued more systematically by the poet Schlegel, who, in his *Die Weisheit der Indier* (1808, *The Language and Wisdom of the Indians*) announced that the languages of India, Persia, Greece, Italy, Germany and Slavonia were the daughters of the same mother and heirs of the same wealth of words and flections. Comparative philology was scientifically established by Bopp's *Das Conjugations system* (1816) and *Comparative Grammar* (completed in parts between 1833 and 1852).

Once the unity of the Indo-Aryan or Indo-Germanic languages was realized, the road was opened to the interpretation of ideas, ideals, rituals, customs, superstitions, folk-lore, etc. on a more or less universal basis. This has ushered in the sciences of comparative mythology and comparative religion, for which Max Mueller's *Sacred Books of the East* series is chiefly responsible. The investigation has not stopped at this point. Secular, economic, political and juristic institutions and theories have been attacked by the methodology of comparative science, and the result has been works like Gibelin's *Etudes sur le droit civil des Hindous* (1846), Maine's *Village Communities* (1871), *Ancient Law*, and *Early History of Institutions* (1876), Salvatore Cognetti de Martiis's *Socialismo Antico* (1889), and Gomme's *Primitive Folkmoots* (1886) and *Folklore as an Historical Science* (1908), Max Weber's *Gesammelte Aufsaetze zur Religionssoziologie* (1923). More "intensive" studies have indeed compelled a modification of the conclusions of the pioneers. For instance, Formichi's *Salus Populi* (1908) and Hillebrandt's *Altindische Politik* (1923) can be cited as instances of the "new indology." In any case, in the field of social science Sanskritic culture has been demanding a gradually enlarging space.

Modern Indian Languages in European Scholarship

In modern times Indians have made it a point to study, at least for scientific purposes, Chinese, Japanese, Tibetan, Burmese, Javanese, Siamese, Cambodian on the one hand as well as French, German, Italian, Dutch, Russian, Portuguese, Spanish etc. on the other. English, of course is being taken for granted.

The cultivation of foreign languages in Europe is no doubt much older and of course more extensive. From Greek and Latin the scholars of England, France, Germany, Italy and Russia, in all branches of arts and sciences as well as their philologists have come to the study of modern European languages. In regard to modern Indian languages the output of scientific investigations in Europe is not yet considerable. But it is already very substantial and is growing in dimensions.

The study of modern Indian languages by Europeans is at least as old as the sixteenth century and is older than their study of Sanskrit. It is the Portuguese missionaries —the Catholic Fathers—who in the interest of propaganda not only learnt but also promoted the living languages of India.[1] Konkanese in Bombay, Canarese and Tamil in South India, Bengali in East Bengal are some of the first to have commanded the attention of these missionaries. Some of the oldest specimens of Bengali prose are to be found in the missionizing activities of the Portuguese of the seventeenth century. They were printed in Lisbon in Roman character. Two of them have been recently published by the Calcutta University.

[1] S. K. Chatterjee's lecture on "European Researchers in Modern Indian Languages" at the "*Āntarjātik Banga*" *Parishat* ("International Bengal" Institute), reported in the *Amrita Bazar Patrika*, Calcutta, for September 20, 1935.

Interest of the European missionaries in modern Indian languages remained steady throughout the next centuries. It is well known that the beginnings of modern Hindi, Bengali, Urdu and other Indian literatures, early in the nineteenth century, were due to missionary efforts.

The scientific interests of the Europeans in Indian philology were however confined to Sanskrit in the first half of the nineteenth century. This was a part of their general movement in regard to the study of the classical antiquities. But gradually their interest began to be transferred to the living languages of Europe, their own mother-tongues. Along with this change in their attitude the living languages of the Orient also began to be studied philologically. Molesworth's *Marathi Dictionary*, the German philologist Trumpp's studies in Sindhi and Punjabi, Caldwell's *Grammar of the Dravidian Languages*,—these are some of the first signs of this new orientation.

The beginnings of the scientific study of modern Indian languages were laid in the 70's of the last century. The philological investigations conducted by Beames chiefly in the fields of Hindi and Urdu may be regarded as an important landmark. Hoernle's studies in Hindi roots also belong to the same period. Among the founders of this branch of linguistics is to be mentioned an Indian, namely, R. G. Bhandarkar, whose Wilson Lectures at the Bombay University constitute the synthesis of up-to-date researches as well as the starting point of new lines of inquiry.

By the beginning of the present century the study of modern Indian languages assumed new forms and proportions on account of the publications of the Linguistic Survey organized by the Government of India. The scholar under whose directions the survey was conducted is Grierson. These publications have enabled philologists to follow the variations in sounds, grammatical construction, vocabulary etc. from district to district, nay, sub-division to sub-division. Grierson's work is a monument of descriptive linguistics (p. 118).

The French scholar Jules Bloch has specialized in Marathi, as we have noticed above. His study on the formation of the Marathi language is universally considered to be an epoch-making contribution to linguistics. His latest publication is a work on the Indo-Aryan languages from the Vedic to the present times.

The British philologist Turner made his *début* as Sanskritist. But he is now known as a principal worker in the domain of modern Indian languages. One of his latest publications is the Nepali Dictionary. On Gujarati and Sindhi phonology he is perhaps the pioneer.

The German philologist Reinhard Wagner is the teacher of Bengali at the University of Berlin. He approaches Bengali language from the standpoint of culture and is interested in translations from Bengali into German. Among German orientalists von Glasenapp may be described as somewhat of a "modernist" in so far as he takes interest in Bengali and Hindi as sources for present-day developments in India.

Not less mentionable is the Italian orientalist Tucci's knowledge of Bengali, Hindi and Urdu.

SECTION 10

RACE-MIXTURE AND CASTE-FUSION IN INDIAN SOCIAL POLITY

Certain considerations of a general character bearing on what Toennies, Richard, Simmel, Ross, von Wiese and Bouglé would call the doctrine of social relations or social processes[1] emerge from a bare chronology of the leading state-systems of India, from the Mohenjo Daro period (c 3500 B. C.) down to 1818 A. C. The politics of the "Hindus"—i.e., the so-called Dravidians, the so-called Aryans, and the Aryo-Dravidians,—were not the politics of the Hindus in isolation. "Culture-contact" was a leading formative force in the evolution of Hindu states. International as well as inter-racial relations, the politics of the boundaries, the "geopolitics" constituted the anatomy of India's political history as that of Europe's political history through the ages. These contacts between the races such as have contributed to the making of political India were of the most diverse character. No less heterogeneous than those in Europe were the contacts of the indigenous Indian tribes, races or nations with the non-Indian tribes, races or nations. These extra-Indian peoples may be somewhat chronologically enumerated as follows:

(1) Assyro-Babylonian, (2) Iranian-Persian, (3) Hellenists, (4) Parthians, (5) Scythian—Yuechi—Sakas (Tartars), (6) Huns, (7) Tibetans, (8) Chinese, (9) Arabs (Islamized), (10) Turks (Islamized), (11) Moghuls (Islamized), (12) Europeans.

In certain instances the Indian peoples had to submit to these non-Indian peoples (excepting perhaps the Chinese) as subject races. In other instances the independent Indian states had to carry on their activities

[1] F. Toennies: *Gemeinschaft und Gesellschaft* (1887, eighth edition, 1935); G. Richard : *La Sociologie générale et les lois sociologiques* (Paris 1912); Spykman : *The Social Theory of Georg Simmel* (Chicago, 1925). On Toennies and Simmel see B. K. Sarkar: *The Political Philosophies Since* 1905 (Madras, 1928) pp. 95, 121, 284, 273. For v. Wiese see his *Systematic Sociology* (New York, 1932). See also footnote on p. 133.

in a system of *maṇḍala* or geopolitical "sphere," which comprised both Indian and non-Indian states. This is an important consideration the value of which cannot be overlooked in a survey not only of political literature like the *Nītiśāstras* but of every Hindu *Vidyā* and *Kalā*, science and art, philosophy and religion. India's debt to non-Indian races is no less an historic reality than her contributions to their progress.

Our attention is invited by the chronology of the Indian state-systems to another set of "geopolitical" forces. We are led to witness the incessant dynastic expansions, contractions and dissolutions, the ups and downs in the fortunes of families, as well as the constant activities of soldiers and generals on the go. During the five thousand years or so exhibited here the Indian peoples seemed all the time to carry out in life the *Aitareya-Brāhmaṇa* (VII, 15) ideal of being ever on the move, "*charaiveti*," "*charaiveti*" (go on, march on, etc.) and functioned, so to say, as the living embodiments of "social mobility," both horizontal and vertical[1]. All these movements from region to region and family to family could not but set in motion strong demographic "convection-currents" leading very often to rearrangements in or transformations of social stratification,—the fall of the high and the heightening of the low (p. 148).

It is an interesting fact that the origins of not only some Rajput dynasties but of several other ruling families in Indian history through the ages are dark and shrouded in mystery. Another interesting item that we come across rather often in regard to the establishment of the Indian dynasties is, as the analysis of inscriptions leaves no doubt, that subsequent generations

[1] P. Sorokin: *Social Mobility* (New York 1927), Ch. VIII. "The Channels of Vertical Circulation."

tried to get their forefathers or founders recognized either as Kṣatriyas or somehow related by blood to certain well-known royal families. We are forced to suspect that the originators of many ruling dynasties in India were not born with blue blood in their veins but came from the ranks and may have been perhaps "natural-born." Not all of them rose indeed from the very lowest of the low, but certainly very many of them are likely to have been born in the lower strata of society. From the "heroic ages" of the Vedic complex, the *Purāṇas* and the Epics down to the Mauryas, Pālas, Senas, and the Rājputs of all grades the story of origins is more or less uniform in being somewhat indefinite.

The statistical analysis of the stories regarding the origins of Indian ruling dynasties as derived from literature as well as from inscriptions, ought to be valuable as the subject of monographs. It will throw light not only on race-intermixture and caste-fusion but also on the importance of the *vis*, the "folk" and the demos in societal remaking. Sociologically, the place of bastards in the establishment of the world's influential families demands careful investigation. Among the manufacturers of states and the makers of epochs in the history of mankind the role of "base origin" and illegitimate birth cannot by any means be overlooked.

The presumptions in this regard are perfectly legitimate. It is the personal qualifications, the proficiency in the use of arms as well as the diplomatic handling of situations—that accounted for the ascendency of many lowly individuals to the position of generals and premiers and finally to kingship. The demand for military skill and diplomatic tact was perennial in the Indian society here and there and everywhere. In India as elsewhere the army has functioned as a great "ladder."

And as the dynasties were changing, the boundaries of states were moving in season and out of season, the adventurers from every nook and corner were in a position to exploit the conditions and build up their social, economic and political fortunes.[1] Individuals of lower castes could thereby get themselves admitted as Kṣatriyas, Brāhmaṇas and what not. The Indian aristocracies of all denominations were very often the instances of social mobility of the vertical type. This aspect of "geopolitics" was as common in India as in Europe.

For, the world submits inevitably to the man, who whatever be his origin, is audacious enough to take up the ambitious messages of the *Atharva Veda* as the guiding principles of life and actually venture upon carrying them out. In this *Veda* (XII, i, 54) *Puruṣa* (man) is made to declare to the Earth as follows :

Aham asmi sahamāna
Uttaro nāma bhūmiām
Abhīṣāḍasmi viśvāṣāḍ
Āśām āśām viṣāsahi

"Mighty am I, Superior by name, upon the earth, conquering am I, all-conquering, completely conquering every region."

The respect for personality and individual valour, the Buddhist *viriya*, the *parākrama* of the Gupta inscriptions, that finds expression in this and similar passages of the *Atharva Veda* and other Vedic texts furnished the atmosphere of energists and enabled them to look for chances wherever there was a muddle. And in the sphere of energism and individualism the *Sūdra* and the

[1] "Caste System and Military History" in the present author's *Chinese Religion Through Hindu Eyes* (Shanghai, 1916).

Vrātya found the world as wide for themselves as the *Ārya*.

And here we encounter a new form of race contacts in political evolution. These consisted in blood-fusion between the diverse tribes, races or nations within the boundaries of India herself. These contacts were engendered as much by migrations as by military marches, conquests, and settlements, and by economic necessity. The alleged inferior, despicable, "fallen," depressed and similar orders of the Indian population found in these stirs and turmoils the chances for self-assertion. Another class of people likewise got opportunities of elevation in this kind of dynamic unrest. These were all those groups or communities which somehow or other did not happen to belong to but rested outside the groups representing the culture, wealth or political influence of the region. A very common name for both these classes,—the "fallen" and the "outsiders,"—was *Vrātya* in certain periods.[1]

But because of this kind of mobilization the *Vrātya* and others of the same standing came to acquire or conquer for themselves positions of dignity in the social structure. The demographic make-up of the state-systems of five thousand years or so in diverse regions of India was marked by *varṇa-saṃkara*, miscegenation, confusion of castes, elevation of the fallen, Aryanization of the non-Aryans, Hinduization of the non-Hindus. The role of the *Vrātya* as a creative factor in Indian demography is fundamental. Equally fundamental is the place of *varṇa-saṃkara* (caste-mixture) as well as *anuloma* and *pratiloma* marriage (union of the "higher" with the lower castes) in the social system of the Hindus.

[1] J. W. Hauer: *Der Vratya*, Vol. I (Stuttgart 1927) pp. 223-240, 334-335.

The "legal fiction" or "pious wish" of caste restrictions was positively broken in upon by the *Realpolitik* of race-mixture and inter-caste marriage, i.e., *varṇa-saṃkara*. The purity of stocks was thus as much a myth in India as in Europe. The intermingling between castes or races implied a veritable democratization of Indian society and culture. The *Vrātya* and the *varṇa-saṃkara* were some of the "folk elements" which served to enrich and strengthen the foundations of Hindu civilization.[1]

The impact of the *Vrātya* and *varṇasaṃkara* on Indian culture has had important bearings on the origin and character of the *Nītiśāstras* as of all the other theoretical disciplines and practical arts and crafts. Not the least important feature of this aspect of Indian as of European "geopolitics" consists in the fact that castes and races might rise and fall or disappear but that civilization went on for ever from precedent to precedent,—nay, perhaps more liberalized and more democratized.[2]

The normal data of Indian political history yield then the following results: Culture-contact as an element in social mobility or social mobility as an element in culture-contact was responsible in India as elsewhere for "internationalism" as understood in the sense of impacts of geographically extra-Indian peoples on the

[1] B. K. Sarkar: *The Folk-Element in Hindu Culture* (London 1917); *cf.* in this connection the analysis of problems in the relations between the higher and the lower classes in P. Sorokin : *Social Mobility* (New York, 1927) chs. x, xi, xii; and *Contemporary Sociological Theories* (New York, 1928) pp. 547-551.

[2] In regard to the question of alleged "superior" and "inferior" races see F. Hankins: *The Racial Basis of Civilization* (New York, 1924) which critically examines the doctrines embodied in Aryanism, Anglo-Saxonism, Nordicism etc.

Indian and *vice versa*. Then there arose transformations in economic, social and political stratification within the Indian boundaries in every region as well as every age. Thirdly, the mingling of races, Indian as well as extra-Indian, in flesh and blood was a constant determinant in the entire process of family, community or society-making through the ages. The fusion of castes may be taken for certain purposes as but an aspect of the mingling of races. In other respects also inter-caste marital alliances constituted the basic factors in the social organization. And last but not least, the alleged "lower" races or castes and the alleged "outsiders", i.e., non-Aryans, non-Hindus and what not were getting access to the "upper ten thousands" in blood, ritual, wealth and political power. In the *śāstras* on law, politics and social *mores* one will have to read the influence of all these aspects of "social interactions," "social processes", "social relations," or *Beziehungen* as prevalent in contemporary sociology.[1]

Here the facts of Hindu culture and politics find themselves in general agreement with the doctrines of the Italian sociologist Pareto in *Les Systèmes Socialistes* (1902) and *Trattato di Sociologia Generale* (1916). No society has ever existed without dominant classes, the "*élites*," says he. The distinction between the upper and the lower socio-economic orders furnishes the fundamental basis of all societal organizations. But the *élites*, says Pareto, have a tendency to degenerate, decay and disappear. The dissolution of the upper classes is not only moral but physical as well. They are ulti-

[1] G. Tarde: *Les Lois de l'Imitation* (Paris, 1890), *L'Opposition universelle* (Paris, 1897), *Les Lois Sociales* (Paris, 1898); E. Durkheim: *De la Division du Travail Social* (Paris, 1893), E. A. Ross: *Principles of Sociology* (New York, 1923), E. S. Bogardus : *Fundamentals of Social Psychology* (New York, 1924). See also footnote on p. 127.

mately replaced by new dominant classes such as emerge out of the people. Sociologically, Pareto never detects the government of societies in a democratic manner. The course is from aristocracy to aristocracy. Only, the aristocracies rise, have their day, cease to be, and give place to new aristocracies. In his doctrine of the "circulation of the *élites*" there is much that Indian history as the history of other countries can offer corroborative data.

We need not, however, be hundred per cent Paretian and admit that the *élites* of one generation or culture are *entirely* replaced by those of the next. The emergence of new elements from the lower orders is a reality. For one thing, the army, as we have indicated above, has been one of the greatest "social ladders." These new elements have, because of military, political, economic, sexual and other circumstances, many chances of getting admitted into and fused or mixed up with the already existing dominant classes. A new "metabolism" is all the time in action giving rise to a new *Gestalt*, form or complex in social relationships. It is these intermixtures that enable the transition from generation to generation of *élites* to appear not as an abrupt breach with the past or the total replacement of old social "physiognomy" by the new, but as a generally steady although often revolutionary process of societal transformation. Thus considered, the historical movements, the social mobilities, the dynamic processes, the *charaiveti* activities ought really to be described as the continuous democratizations of world-culture through the rise of the lower and their absorption into the *élites* rather than as marches from aristocracy to aristocracy.[1]

[1] *Cf.* the section on "Social Forces in Mediæval Indian Poetry." *Infra.* See the present author's *Les Races, les Classes et les Forces*

Transformatrices au point de vue du Métabolisme Social (International Congress of Sociology, Brussels, August, 1935), as well as some of the data in N. K. Bose: "Caste as a Social Phenomenon," "Caste through the Ages," and "The Contact of Cultures" (*Calcutta Review*, August and September 1934, January-March 1935), and B. N. Datta: "Das indische Kastensystem" (*Anthropos*, Vienna, Vol. XXII, 1927); "Traces of Totemism in Some Tribes and Castes of North-Eastern India," a paper at the Indian Science Congress, 1933 (*Man in India*, Vol. XIII, 1933), "Anthropological Notes on Some West Bengal Castes" (*Man in India*, 1934), "Races of India" (*Journal of the Department of Letters*, Calcutta University, 1935). Attention is invited also to the following papers at the "*Āntarjātik Banga*" *Parishat* ("International Bengal" Institute): "The Aboriginals of West Bengal" by H. Palit (*Amirta Bazar Patrika*, May 3, 1934), "The Castes of Bengal" by B. N. Datta (*Advance*, 12 December, 1935).

See likewise D. R. Bhandarkar: "Foreign Elements in the Hindu Population" (*Indian Antiquary*, Bombay, 1910); S. Lévi: *Préaryen et Prédravidien* (Paris, 1923), Eng. transl. by P. Bagchi; P. Mitra: *Pre-historic India* (Calcutta, 1927); N. R. Ray: "Some Additional Notes on Foreign Elements in the Hindu Population" (*Indian Historical Quarterly*, Calcutta, 1928); N. N. Ghose: *Indo-Aryan Literature and Culture* (Calcutta, 1934); R. K. Mookerji: *Hindu Civilization* (London, 1936).

CHAPTER II

INDIAN CREATIONS IN INSTITUTIONS

SECTION I

THE "GROUP-PERSONS" IN INDIAN PUBLIC LIFE AND RELIGION

Indian culture-history is marked by the growth and development of a large number of institutions, each with its characteristic name. These institutions have flourished in all spheres of life, cultural, political and economic. The creative activity of the Hindus is responsible for a great deal of this institutional *viriya* or energism and organized efforts in public life.

One institution at least of creative India is known to orientalists. This is the *saṃgha* or church of Buddhist Asia. Necessarily it is perhaps as old as Sākya the Buddha (B. C. 623-543). It has really had a longer history, since in Pāṇiṇi the philologist's time (B. C. 650) *saṃgha* was the "generic" term for any public body, incorporated association or corporation (III, 3, 42; V. 3, 112-114). Its social significance was roughly equivalent to that of the Greek *polis* (lit. city) as popularized by the political philosophers of Hellas. The different organized bodies of the seventh century B. C. were known as *saṃghas* of different species.

Thus there was the *pūga* characterized as the *saṃgha* of a special denomination. It was a corporation of men (i) belonging to different social groups (*nānā-jātiyāḥ*), (ii) practising diverse (no regular or fixed) professions (*aniyata-vrittayah*), but (iii) distinguished from other *saṃghas* by having a preponderance of economic or secular interests (*artha-kāma-pradhānāh*). Such an association was either a rural commune or a municipium.

A second *saṃgha* of the day was the *vrāta*. It was similar to the *pūga* in having the first two "properties." But its *differentium* was indicated by the concept of *utsedha jīvinah*, i.e., the profession of blackmailing, brigandage or hooliganism as a regular means of livelihood. The European counterpart of the Hindu *vrāta* was the order of *Ritter* or "Knights" whose exploits have received a romantic treatment in Goethe's *Goetz* and Schiller's *Raeuber*. The modern Bengali novelist Bankim Chandra Chatterji's *Ānanda Maṭha* (The Abbey of Bliss) is likewise an idealization of a similar corporation.

The *āyudha-jīvi saṃgha* was a third organized body of Pāṇini's days. As the name implies, it was an association of men who "lived by the profession of arms". Men proficient in military tactics used evidently to incorporate themselves into bands, and were available most probably for mercenary service. This *saṃgha* was therefore distinct from the *vrāta*.

The world into which Śākya was born was thus familiar with several incorporated associations. It was only a commonplace floating term of the period that Buddhist *Vinaya* (discipline, organization, government) literature of the fourth century B. C. adopted as the name of an ecclesiastical polity.

But the secular significance of the term continued to prevail as current as ever. For, about the same time the school of politics associated with the name of Kauṭalya (XI, i.) described all corporate bodies by Pāṇini's term. In the Kauṭalyan category there were at least two classes of *saṃgha*. One class consisted of those who "lived by the science of economics" *vārttā-śāstropajīvinah*), i.e., were engaged in farming, industry, commerce or banking. To the other class belonged those with whom the "epithet of *rājā* or king was a source of social existence," i.e., who were rulers by profession. In Kauṭalya's days, therefore, the ordinary *śreṇī* or gild was as good a *saṃgha* as the republic or non-monarchical body of people among whom "every person is a *rājā*."

During the period that closed with Alexander's failure in India and Chandragupta Maurya's expulsion of Hellenistic Greeks from Afghanistan Hindus were used to at least six classes of public association, viz. the *pūga*, the *vrāta*, the *āyudha-jīvi*, the *śreṇī*, the *rājā*, and the *vihāra* (monastery or church). While the first four would have been usually known by their special names, the common term *saṃgha* would have denoted the republics of the Lichchhavikas, Vrijjikas and others as well as the ecclesiastical organization of Buddhist monks.

In the later literature of political institutions the term *saṃgha* seems to have dropped out of general use. The most "generic" term for *polis* with the authors of the *Smritiśāstras*, at any rate, is *samūha*. In the third or fourth century A. C. Yājnavalkya (II, 192) used it generically for any corporation. *Samūhas* were known to be divided into various classes differing from one another according to the nature of objects for which the association was instituted or the kind of persons organizing themselves into a *polis*. One of these was the *śreṇī*, i.e., gild, a second was the *naigama* (also *nigama*) or body of traders (the "gild merchant"), and a third was the *pāṣaṇḍi*, or group of socio-religious heretics and dissenters, e.g., Buddhists, Jainas and other denominations; and *gaṇa* (town) was the fourth.

The use of *samūha* as a "genus" is to be noticed in Mitra-Miśra's *Vīra-mitrodaya* (*c* 17th century), a commentary on Yājnavalkya. For, according to him the *pūga* is a particular class of *samūha*. It was made up of those who "lived at the same place," but belonged to different social orders, the so-called castes, and followed different professions. It was thus a territorial concept, the term for a village or town, having the same connotation as in the grammar of Pāṇiṇi. In Vijnāneśvara, also, another, older commentator, of Yājnavalkya, *samūha* is generic, for he defines *gaṇa* to be a division of *samūha* and considers *grāma* (village) and other settled areas as belonging to this species. The same use of *samūha* is to be seen in Kātyāyana, a jurist cited by Mitra-Miśra, still older than Vijnaneśvara. The *milieu* that produced the *dharma* or *smriti śāstras* (law-books) was therefore one in which at least four or five institutions, the *śreṇī*, the *naigama*, the *pāṣaṇḍi*, the *gaṇa* were centres of public life. The common name for all of these bodies was *samūha*.

But it would appear that people were using some of these terms interchangeably. The same institution was being described by different names, and the same name was being given to different institutions. We have just noticed that Vijnāneśvara used *gaṇa* where Mitra-Miśra employs *pūga* to denote the identical "group-person." Both commentators were right because their common authority Yājnavalkya (II, 8, 187-192, 361) himself was responsible for the confusion, as he had used *gaṇa* in the sense of a town-corporation. Nārada (450 A. C.), another jurist who preceded these scholiasts, had also done the same. Indeed, the same confusion is to be noticed in all writings on *smriti* (tradition) and *dharma* (law) (cf. Manu III, 164, IV, 209, Sukra, IV, v, 59-62). Kātyāyana similarly identifies *gaṇa* with *pūga* when he defines it as a *samūha* of *kulas* or families.

During the early centuries of the Christian era, the term *gaṇa* appears to have been elevated one flight up in the series of "communities." From its status as the name of a *grāma*, and *pura*, the *domus* and *civitas* of mediaeval European jurisdictions, it came to imply also the *regnum* of a whole people, thus giving rise to another confusion in language. In the eulogies on military triumphs or other meritorious deeds inscribed by poets of the period we find the term being used to describe the association of "self-rulers," i.e., of "polyarchal" peoples organized on the principle of *sva-rāj*. Republican nationalities of the Yaudheyas, Malavas and others are thus known as *gaṇas* in the coins and inscriptions of the Āndhra-Kuṣāṇ and Gupta times. The poets of the *Mahābhārata* also described the states in which "all were equal" by the same epithet.

Neither *samūha* nor *gaṇa* seems ever to have acquired the comprehensive connotation of *saṃgha*. But the diversity of Gierke's "group-persons" in Hindu public life through the ages is self-evident. The attempt on the part of grammarians, logicians, political theorists and lawyers to analyse the concept of a public body and differentiate its various species is also significant. The story of Hindu public life has therefore partially to be sought in the development of *saṃghas*, *samūhas* and *gaṇas*, the different categories of what may be called the Asian *polis*.

As specimens of Hindu energism in group-activity let us begin with organization in social service or welfare work. In Europe the hospital was unknown until Emperor Constantine (306-337) founded it for the first time in the fourth century A. C. But in India the first hospitals both for animals and human beings were founded at least as early as the third century B. C. by Asoka the Great (Rock Edict II). And about 400 A. C.

among the institutions that drew the notice of Fa Hien, the Chinese scholar-saint, at Pātaliputra, the capital of the Gupta Empire, we are told of the free hospitals founded by the respectable nobles and landowners of the country. These were resorted to by "the poor of all countries, the destitute, cripples and the diseased" and every kind of requisite help was offered gratuitously.

Similarly Hindu public life can count in its manifold experience the founding and maintenance of *pariṣats* (academies) for the prosecution of research in the arts and sciences, as well as of educational institutions of ambitious scope and encyclopædic character. It was in the hands of scholars who graduated from such centres of learning that the administration of government was entrusted. One such institution was the University at Nālandā in Eastern India (Bihar), founded by Emperor Narasimha-gupta Bālāditya (*c* 469-473). Itsing, the Chinese scholar, was an *alumnus* of this University for ten years (675-685) in the departments of medicine and logic. The number of residents at Nālandā exceeded 3000, was perhaps between 3500 and 5000, at that time. The lands possessed by the University comprised more than 2000 villages, the gifts of kings for several generations. Itsing mentions eight halls and three hundred apartments among the buildings of the institution.

The Nālandā corporation was a residential-teaching University like the later *El Azhar* at Cairo and gave instruction, room,- board and medicine free of any cost whatsoever. Yuan Chwang, who preceded Itsing as "post-graduate" scholar from China at Nālandā, was very much impressed by its architectural magnificence (629-645). "The richly adorned towers," as we read in his Chinese biography, "and the fairy-like turrets, like pointed hill-tops, are congregated together. The observatories seem to be lost in the vapors of the morning and the upper rooms tower above the clouds." This was the institution that inspired in subsequent years the monastery-college at Horiyuji near Nārā in Japan. And it is on record that the Afghan scholar Vīra-deva was elected Chancellor here in the ninth century, then enjoying the patronage of Deva-pāla, the Bengali *sārvabhauma* of Eastern India. It is obvious that for several centuries after their establishment the Universities of Bologna, Paris, and Oxford would certainly have envied the material endowments and international reputation enjoyed by the presidents and faculties of Nālandā for about seven hundred years (*c* 500-1200). The long story of this University bears undoubted testimony to the continuous and cumulative organizing ability of the race in which it flourished.

A very interesting *sāhitya pariṣat* (literary academy) of Southern India was the *Saṃgam* of the Tamils at Madura. Early in the Christian era in this Pandyan city a body of censors formed themselves into an institution to correct the abuses of literature. The third of these *Saṃgams* was in existence in the second century. Forty-nine critics and poets were members of this association, which thus anticipated by about fifteen hundred years the *Académie Française* founded by Richelieu (1637) in its aim at checking the growth of literary weeds. The *Saṃgam* enjoyed the patronage of the state for several generations. Its influence on the people may be gathered from the fact that the celebrated Tamil classic, the *Kural* of Tiruvalluvar, received the imprimatur of the Academy before king Ugra-Peruvalludhi. It is interesting to note that the author himself was not a member of the association. Similarly the two other master-pieces of the Augustan age of Tamil literature, the *Epic of the Anklet* and the *Jewel-Belt*, were submitted to the examination of this body of connoisseurs.

Pariṣats or academies, whether stationary or peripatetic, have indeed existed in India since time immemorial. Medicine, grammar, logic, chemistry, mathematics, political science, jurisprudence, almost every branch of learning has grown up in India through the clubbing of intellects. Cooperative researches have been the tradition of intellectual life among Hindus. As a result of these corporate investigations we know today only of "schools" or "systems" of thought, very rarely of the individuals who built them up through the ages. Most of the names in the annals of science and philosophy in India are those of masters, pioneers or patrons and organizers, and these, again, are very often but pseudonyms associated with the patronymic saints or gods, the Prometheuses and Apollos of Hindu culture.

It is this collective or *pariṣadic* origin that explains why the treatises on arts and sciences in Sanskrit literature have in general the title of *Samhitā*, i.e., compilation. Mostly encyclopaedic works, as these are, they bear internal evidence of the collaboration and cumulative experience of many minds.

Individualistic ideals and ends are as a rule associated with moral, religious, and spiritual affairs in India. Yet even in this field the capacity for cooperation has been equally evident as in other spheres. Every twelve years Hindus have had a Council of Trent, so to speak, since the earliest times. These congresses of spiritual leaders, the *sanyásins*, monks and hermits, are called *Kumbha-Melā* after the planetary conjunction (of Kumbha) which recurs periodically. The present-day survivals of these institutions are tremendous vitalizing forces; their delegates number about 75,000 and the audience or visitors millions.

Some of the inscriptions of the ancient Gujaratis throw an interesting sidelight on the Hindu legal sense and institutionalism. India's appreciation of corporate energism will be evident from the measures that General Uṣavadāta adopted to perpetuate the benefits from his charities. This great philanthropist of the Āndhara Deccan had the terms of his endowments registered by the *nigama-sabhā* (town-corporation) of Govardhana (Nasik). And these were then inscribed on the door of the monastery. Gifts for public purposes used thus to be looked after by public bodies.

As embodiments of Hindu institutional life we have to mention also the *vihāras* or monasteries of ancient and mediaeval India. These were *samūhas*, i.e., public bodies and were bound by definite rules and regulations as to election, quorum, voting, and business procedure. Students of European polity are aware that on various occasions in the West the church and the state have borrowed from each other the methods of internal administration. It would appear that in the Orient also common principles of organization have been followed by religious associations and secular institutions alike. The ecclesiastical bodies of Buddhist Asia should have thus to be treated as quasi-political corporations, even independently of the fact that in certain regions, e.g., in Tibet and Mongolia, as in Catholic Europe, the spiritual head has claimed also temporal dominion over his flock.

The origins of all this institutionalism are of course to be sought in the publicity work and propaganda methods of Sākya the Buddha himself (B. C. 623-543). Sākya's father and brother were *rājās* or archons, i.e., presidents of the Sākiya Republic in Eastern India. It was natural, therefore, that when he fled the world and founded a *Saṃgha* (Order) of monks, the only constitution that he could conceive for it was that with which he had been familiar at home and in his own state. And as a matter of course, he made no distinction between his own ecclesiastical order, the *Saṃgha*, and the contemporary republican Confederacy of the Vijjian States, when called upon to enunciate the "seven conditions of welfare for a community."

Of these seven conditions three may be regarded as directly constitutional or political. "So long, O mendicants" said Sākya, "as the brethren meet together in full and frequent assemblies,—so long as they meet together in concord and rise in concord, and carry out in concord the duties of the Order, *** so long as the brethren honour and esteem and revere and support the elders of experience and long standing, and hold it a point of duty to hearken to their words,—so long may the brethren be expected not to decline but to prosper" (*Mahāparinivvāna-sutta*, I, 6.)

In this Sākyan constitution, defining, as it did, the type as much of an ecclesiastical society as of a secular state, e.g. a clan-republic, there are emphasized, as we see, the importance of the assembly, the need of unity, and the authority of age and experience. This last feature is such as was embodied in the primitive Indo-Aryan, Teutonic and Hellenic polities or is in....... evidence today in the Japanese *Genro* ("elder statesmen"). These and other principles of Sākya's politics have all been codified in the *Chulla-vagga* and the *Mahā-vagga*, both of which treatises may be regarded as statute-books laying down the fundamental laws and constitutions (*Vinaya*) of Asian ecclesiastical bodies.

The following is a typical picture of the method of deliberations generally observed in the Buddhist monasteries and conferences of ancient India: "Then

10

the venerable Mahā Kassapa laid the resolution before the *Saṃgha*: 'Let the venerable *Saṃgha* hear me. If the time seems meet to the *Saṃgha*, let the *Saṃgha* appoint that these five hundred *bhikkhus* (monks) take up their residence during the rainy season at Rājagaha. **This is the resolution. Let the *Saṃgha* hear. The *Saṃgha* appoints accordingly. Whosoever of the venerable ones approves thereof, let him keep silence. Whosoever approves not thereof, let him speak. The *Saṃgha* has appointed accordingly. Therefore is it silent. Thus do I understand" (*Chullavagga*, XI, i, 4).

An important feature of these monastic institutions was that no business was held valid without quorum. "If an official act, O *bhikkhus*", as we read Sākya saying in the *Mahāvagga* (IX, iii, 2), "is performed unlawfully by an incomplete congregation, it is no real act and ought not to be performed." Along with this caution against incomplete congregations went the injunction against "unlawful acts." In the following extract the *Mahāvagga* (IX, ii, 1) mentions some of those acts that have to be ruled out as unconstitutional. "They performed unlawful acts", we are told, "before an incomplete congregation; they performed unlawful acts before a complete congregation; they performed seemingly lawful acts before an incomplete congregation; they performed seemingly lawful acts before a complete congregation; a single *bhikkhu* pronounced expulsion against a single one; a single *bhikkhu* pronounced expulsion against two, a single *bhikkhu* pronounced expulsion against a number of *bhikkhus*; a single *bhikkhu* pronounced expulsion against a *Saṃgha*." As no unlawful acts were to be permitted within the church or among the church members, Sākya definitely laid down the rule: "Therefore, O *bhikkhus*, you ought to train yourself thus: Lawful acts which are performed by complete congregations,—such acts we will perform" (*Mahāvagga* IX, ii, 4).

A breach of this ruling appears to have been committed by the monks at Vesali in 443 B. C. about a century after the death of Sākya. They ordained, for instance, that it is permitted to a *Saṃgha* which is not sufficiently numerous to accomplish an ecclesiastical act by saying "we will make the other *bhikkhus* consent when they come." This ruling called *anumati-kappa* was challenged as illegal by the *bhikkhus* of other centres, and the case was submitted to a jury for trial. The jury decided against it.

In order to ascertain the opinions of the members in regard to the topics discussed the ecclesiastical organizations made use of coloured *salākās* (or pins) of wood. These were the voting tickets. A *salākā-gāhaka* ("taker" or collector of pins) or teller was appointed by the association to explain the significance of the colours to the voters and then take the votes. In the *Chulla-vagga* (IV, xiv, 26) we find Sākya describing the ballot and other kinds of voting. "I enjoin upon you, *bhikkhus*," says he, "three ways of taking votes, ** the secret method, the whispering method, and the open method." The secret method of taking votes is then described. "The *bhikkhu* who is teller of the votes is to take the voting tickets of different colors, and as each *bhikkhu* comes up to him he is to say to him thus, 'This is the ticket for the man of such an opinion, this the ticket for the man of such an opinion. Take whichever you like.' When he has chosen (he is to add), 'Do not show it to anybody.' " The *Chulla-vagga* (IV, x) enumerates also ten cases of "invalid" voting.

As conflict of opinions is inevitable in democratic deliberations, the rule of the majority was accepted by the *Saṃgha* as the regular procedure. "By that *bhikkhu*, the taker of the voting tickets," we read in the *Chulla-vagga* (IV, xiv, 24), "are the votes to be collected. And according as the larger number of the *bhikkhus* shall speak, so shall the case be decided."

All this points to the highly developed institutional sense and corporate consciousness among Hindus. And these principles of *samūha* (or public associations and corporations) were not the patents of Buddhist, Jaina or any other religious bodies but were held in solution in the general socio-economic and civic life of ancient and mediaeval India. These quasi-political institutions were only drawing upon and contributing to the same stream of national experience as did the economic *śreṇīs* (gilds) and the political *gaṇas* (republics) or constitutional *sabhās* and *samitis* (assemblies)[1].

SECTION 2

THE STATE-SYSTEMS OF INDIA

In regard to the types of political organization[2] we have to realize, first, that Hindu states were thoroughly

[1] Consult E. Gibelin : *Étude sur le Droit Civil des Hindous* (Pondichery, 1846), 2 vols., R. Fick : *Die sociale Gliederung im nordoestlichen Indien zu Buddhas Zeit* (Kiel, 1897, Eng. transl. by S. K. Maitra, Calcutta, 1920), Mrs. C. A. Rhys Davids: "Economic Condition in Ancient India" (*Economic Journal*, London, September, 1901), K. P. Jayaswal: "Introduction to Hindu Polity" (*Modern Review*, Calcutta, May-July, 1913), R. C. Majumdar : *Corporate Life in Ancient India*, (Calcutta, 1919), R. K. Mookerji : *Local Government in Ancient India* (Oxford, 1919), the present author's "Gilde di Mestier e Gilde Mercantili nell' India antica" (*Giornale degli Economistie Rivista di Statistica*, Rome, April, 1920), and "The Economics of Hindu Guilds" (*Journal of the Indian Economic Society*, Poona, 1921).

[2] The following historical works may be consulted for dates, events and political maps:

secular. In India, paradoxical as it may seem to preconceived notions, religion is not known to have often dominated political history or philosophy. Politics were invariably independent of theology; nor did priests interfere in the civil administration as a matter of right, temporal or spiritual. In short, with the exception of the quasi-religious statal organization of the Sikhs in the seventeenth century and after Hindustan knows of no "theocracies" strictly so-called. Even under Asoka the

V. A. Smith: *The Oxford History of India* (1919), H. C. Ray: *The Dynastic History of Northern India* 2 Vols. (Calcutta, 1932, 1936), S. K. Aiyangar: *Ancient India* (Madras, 1911), L. Renou: *Bibliographie Védique* (Paris, 1931), D. R. Bhandarkar: *Ancient History of India* (Calcutta, 1919), R. G. Basak: *History of North Eastern India* (Calcutta, 1934), H. C. Roy-Chaudhuri: The *Political History of Ancient India* (Calcutta, 1932), C. V. Vaidya: *History of Mediaeval Hindu India*, 3 Vols. (Poona, 1921-26), K. P. Jayaswal: *History of India* 150-350 A. C. (Patna, 1933), R. D. Banerji: *History of Orissa* (Calcutta, 1931), A. C. Altekar: *The Rāṣṭrakūtas and their Times* (Poona, 1934), H. K. Trevaskis: *The Land of the Five Rivers* (Oxford, 1928), R. K. Mookerji: *Harsha* (London, 1926), H. K. Sarda: *Mahārāṇa Kumbh* (Ajmer, 1917), B. A. Saletore: *Social and Political Life in the Vijayanagara Empire* (Madras, 1934), 2 vols, K. P. P. Menon: *History of Karala* (Ernakulam, 1933), 3 vols, Kincaid and Parasnis: *History of the Maratha People* (London, 1918), G.S. Sardesai: *Main Currents in Maratha History* (Patna, 1933), J. D. Cunningham: *History of the Sikhs* (London, 1918), De la Valleé Poussin: *Indo-européens et Indo-iraniens: L'Inde jusque vers 300 av. J. C.* (Paris, 1924), *L'Inde aux temps des Mauryas* (Paris, 1930), *Dynasties et Histoire de l'Inde depuis Kanishka jusqu'aux invasions musulmanes* (Paris, 1935), V. R. R. Dikshitar: *The Maurya Polity* (Madras, 1932), K. A. Nilakantha Sastri: *Studies in Chola History and Administration* (Madras, 1932), S. N. Sen: *The Administrative System of the Marathas* (Calcutta, 1923) and *The Military System of the Marathas* (Calcutta, 1928), G. T. Date: *The Art of War in Ancient India* (London, 1929), P. Masson-Oursel's paper in *L'Inde Antique etla Civilisation Indienne* (Paris, 1933).

Great, Harṣa-vardhana, and Dharma-pāla, the supreme dignity of the empire as a worldly organism was not sacrificed to the personal religiosity of the crowned heads. Consequently, the struggle for "Caesaro-papism" among the so-called "Byzantine" emperors, the long-drawn-out conflict between the Papacy and the Holy Roman Empire, the rivalry with regard to the custodianship of the "twain keys" to heaven, the temporal sovereignty of spiritual heads, the political influence exerted by the Pope through his cardinals, legates and pardoners over the internal politics of states in Western Europe,—these and other facts that contribute to the complexity of occidental history are not matched in Hindu political development.

Hindu monarchs with non-Hindu officers, non-Hindu princes with Hindu ministers and generals have been the norm in India's history. The functions of priests were confined to the private religious life of the royal families and the people. Their place on state councils was relegated to the administration of social and national festivals. And the dictates of religious scriptures were placed before the mind's eye of rulers and statesmen, if at all, solely as principles of moral guidance. These may be taken to have been checks and restraints on the possible autocracy and high-handedness of the powers that be. Nothing analogous to the Church as an institution of "public law" was ever attempted by the priest-craft of the Hindu, Buddhist, Jaina and Moslem faiths, notwithstanding the efficiency of their ecclesiastical organization and occasional military activities.

With these general remarks we shall tabulate here the principal landmarks in the history of Hindu politics. Let us exclude from our consideration the Mohenjo Daro (*c* 3500 B. C.) and the Vedic (*c* 1000 B. C.) epochs and begin with the Maurya Empire (B. C. 323-185). Its capital was located at Pātaliputra (site of modern Bankipore) on the Ganges in Eastern India. Under Asoka the Great the empire included the regions covered at present by Afghanistan and Baluchistan, the whole of Northern India, the Deccan, and Southern India excluding the extreme south (Chola, Pāṇḍya, Kerala, Satyaputra and Ceylon). The area and pretensions of the undivided Roman Empire at its zenith were thus anticipated by this first *sārva-bhauma* (universal) empire of the Hindus by about five hundred years.

It should be pointed out, however, that this was the only Hindu state with jurisdiction over all India. For subsequent periods in pre-Moslem times the fortunes of the south were to all intents and purposes separate from those of the north, exactly as in Europe the story of the Eastern (or "Byzantine") empire ran independently of that of the Western. In spite of Samudra-gupta's *dig-vijaya* or conquest of the quarters (A. C. 330-350), embracing some of the southern territories in its Alexandrine sweep, and the Rāṣṭrakuṭa (Deccan) intervention (*c* 914-916) in northern Indian politics as well as Rājendra-chola the *Gangāikonda's* (1013-1042) victories on the banks of the Ganges northerners and southerners never again came to be held together by a single administrative and military system.

Three states acquired prominence in three different parts of India after the extinction of the Mauryas. The first was the empire of the Suṃgas (B. C. 183-63). It served virtually to keep up the continuity of the Maurya Empire in the eastern provinces. The capital remained unchanged. Puṣya-mitra, the founder of this House, inflicted a decisive defeat on Menander, the Hellenistic invader of India (B. C. 153). The second was the empire of the Āndhras (*c* B. C. 120-A. C. 250). They were rulers of the Deccan from sea to sea with eastern and western capitals[1]. These southern emperors maintained commercial intercourse with western Asia, Greece, Rome, Egypt and China. Gotamī-putra (109-135) and Yajna-śrī (173-202) are two of their most aggressive monarchs. Their rivals in the north were the Indo-Tartars or Kuṣāṇs (A. C. 15-226) with capital at Puruṣa-pura (modern Peshawar). This northern and north-western power was in relations of commerce and diplomacy with the Han Empire of China and with the Roman Empire during its period of greatest extent. Kāṇiṣka (A. C. 78-123) of this House was the contemporary of Trajan and Hadrian. Through the Kuṣāṇ empire the Indian sphere of influence, political and cultural, was extended over Central Asia. Excavations have brought to light an underground "Greater India" from among the "ruins of Desert Cathay."[2]

For the time being the Bhāraśiva achievements in state-making need not detain us in this brief survey. But the next important scene reveals in the Gangetic Valley the India of the Vikramādityan Guptas (A. C. 320-350) with capital at Pātaliputra through whom Hindu culture commenced to become a world-power;[3] as subsequently it served to help forward the Chinese renaissance of the Tang-period (618-905) and thus indirectly sponsor the emergence of Japan as a civilized

[1] D. R. Bhandarkar : "Dekkan of the Sātavāhana Period" in the *Indian Antiquary*, 1918 which must be studied, however, in the light of the new material placed by V. S. Sukthankar in the R. G. *Bhandarkar Commemoration Volumes*.

[2] M. A. Stein: *Ruins of Desert Cathay* (London, 1912), Vol. I. pp. viii, x, 469-496.

[3] The present author's *Chinese Religion Through Hindu Eyes* (Shanghai, 1916), pp. 184-229.

state. The epoch of Gupta Imperial glories was synchronous with that of the dismemberment of the Western Roman Empire, but was paralleled by the period of consolidation in the Byzantine Empire from Constantine to Justinian. The age of the Guptas is, in India's literary history, the age of Kālidāsa (*c* 400-460), the Virgil of the Hindu *Aeneid*, the *Raghu-vamśa* ("The House of Raghu"), and is as famous in popular tradition as that of Alexander or Charlemagne in Europe. In the language of this poet of Imperial nationalism the Vikramādityas were idealized as

> "Lords of the lithosphere from sea to sea,
> Commanding the skies by chariots of air."

The Gupta Empire was followed by what may be described as a diarchy like that of Āndhra-Kuṣāṇ India. The Empire of the Vardhanas (606-647) in Northern India had its capital at Kanauj on the Ganges in the middle-west. Emperor Harṣa had deplomatic touch with the Chinese Napoleon, Tang Tai-tsung. The empire of the Chālukyas (550-753) in the Deccan had its capital at Vātāpi (modern Badami in Bijapur) and Nasik. Pulakeśī II was paramount sovereign over India south of the Narmadā and reciprocated embassies with Khusru II, the Sassanian monarch of Persia.

During the seventh and eighth centuries India witnessed the formation of myriads of states similar to those in Europe. In various quarters the effort to achieve hegemony gradually led to the operation of centripetal tendencies. Out of a veritable *mātsya-nyāya* ("logic of the fish") or Hobbesian "state of nature" there eventually arose the condition of what may for ordinary purposes be characterized as a pentarchy. India's destiny remained for several centuries in the hands of five chief nationalities. (1) The Bengalis of the Gangetic Valley became a great power under the

Pāla and Sena Emperors (730-1200). Dharma-pāla (795-830) and Lakṣmaṇa-sena (1119-1170) are the Charlemagnes of Bengal. (2) The Gurjara-Pratīhāras, the so-called Rajputs (816-1194), of Upper India and Rājputana, celebrated in Rājaśekhara's *Karpūramanjarī* as "world-monarchs" had their capital at Kanauj. A *digvijaya* (conquest of the quarters) was successfully undertaken by Mihira Bhoja (*c* 840-890) of this dynasty. (3) The Rāṣṭrakūṭas (750-973) of the Deccan with capital at Malkhed became a power by dispossessing the Chālukyas of their dominions. Govinda III was the *sārvabhauma* ("world-ruler") of the South. The Rāṣṭrakūṭas were replaced by the Chālukyas (973-1190) who in their turn were expelled by the Hoysālās of Dvāra-samudra and the Yādavas of Devagiri. (4) The Cholas (850-1310) of Southern India militated against the Chālukyas of the Deccan and also came to measure their strength with the Pālas of Bengal. Rāja-rāja (985-1018) and Kulottūnga I (1070-1118) are the most celebrated monarchs of this House. (5) The kingdom of Kashmir (*c* 650-1339) had a more or less isolated career in the extreme north. The Gurjara-Pratīhāras submitted to Mohammedans in 1194, the Senas in 1200, the Hoysālās, Yādavas and Cholas in 1310, and Kashmir in 1339.

The history of India for about sixteen hundred years from the time of the Mauryas exhibits the picture of a gradually growing and expanding political consciousness as well as scientific and cultural development. The Hindu Alexanders, Caesars, Constantines, Charlemagnes and Frederick Barbarossas could easily challenge competition with their Western peers on their own terms of *śakti-yoga* or *Machtpolitik*. It is, moreover, only fair to note that for one Justinian in Europe there were a dozen Maurices, for one Charles the Great the name of Charles the Fats was legion, and for a

Frederick II, the "wonder of the world," there were myriads of Adolfuses and Wenceslauses.

Not altogether extinct, however, was the sovereignty of the Hindus with the advent of Islam. Excluding the isolated enterprise of the Bengali Danujamardana (*c* 1417), devoted to Kālī, the patron-goddess of energists, there were at least four state-systems embodying independent Hindu power during the period when portions of the Indian sub-continent were members of consolidated Mussalman empires or lesser Mussalman states. Inevitably the first to come in touch with the new factor in Indian politics were the kingdoms of the Rajputs in the Middle-west. Beginning in the ninth and tenth centuries these "cognates" and "agnates" of the Gurjara-Pratīhāras have continued their existence until today. The empire of Vijayanagara (1336-1565) in the extreme south was necessarily the last to feel the Moslem pressure.

By the middle of the seventeenth century two important Hindu reactions were provocated by the firm establishment of the Moslem as a paramount power. In the Deccan the bulwark of Hindu independence was built up by Śivāji the Great (1627-1680), the Frederick the Great of India, in his empire of the Marathas. This was continued during the eighteenth century under the Peshwas or ministers (1714-1818). Fragments of Maratha states still exist more or less as "feudatories" or "subordinate allies" of Great Britain, no matter what be the *de jure* relation.

The second great reaction against political Islam manifested itself almost simultaneously in the militant nationalism of the Sikhs in the Punjab. From Guru Govind (1675-1708), organizer of the Khalsa polity, down to Ranjit Singh (1780-1839), monarch of a united Punjab including Kashmir, nay, down to 1849, it was the Hindus (Sikhs) who held Northern and North-western India. It is worthwhile to emphasize that Ranjit Singh, the contemporary of the Bengali Rammohun (1772-1833), was the sovereign ruler of a powerful state[1].

The administrative genius of Ranjit Singh (1780-1839), the Sikh, preserved in the Punjab during the early nineteenth century the tradition of Indian positivism. He was thus a great contemporary, junior of course, rather a distinguished successor, of the Marathas of the Deccan and Tipu Sultan (1749-1799) of Mysore. He was already imbued with the modern spirit in so far as the translation of French and English works into Punjabi found in him a thoughtful patron. In this he was but carrying out the same principles as inspired his contemporary Rammohun (1772-1833) in Bengal who had to live under different political conditions. Among Ranjit's political achievements are to be listed his resuscitation of the institutions of rural democracy.[2]

Some of the Sikh kingdoms maintain themselves today in "subordinate alliance" with the British power.

During this period of tug-of-war between the Hindus and Islam no part of India came to be subject to a "foreign power." The Mussalmans were as much the children of the soil as the original inhabitants. Neither the Sultanate of Delhi (1200-1526) nor the Moghul monarchy that replaced it was in any sense the "government of one people by another." The Moghuls are celebrated chiefly through such world-

[1] L. Griffin: *Ranjit Singh* (Oxford, 1898), H. K. Trevaskis: *The Land of the Five Rivers* (Oxford, 1928), K. Singh: *History and Philosophy of the Sikh Religion* (Lahore, 1914), Part I.

[2] Lectures at the Ranjit Singh Birth Anniversary, Lahore (November, 1935) by Sardar Sewa Ram Singh, Sardar Man Singh, Sardar Kissan Singh Thapar and others.

figures as Akbar, Shah Jahan and Aurangzeb (sixteenth and seventeenth centuries). The Moghul period of Indian history is one of the most creative epochs of civilization. For the people of India, it was an era of prosperity, material and intellectual. The epoch, known generally as the age of Indo-Saracenic Renaissance, looms therefore as large in the consciousness of the Young India of today as does the age of the Vikramādityan *sārva-bhaumas*. The policy of the Moslem states was generally secular and the personal bigotry and intolerance of some of the rulers were not more frequent than were the fanaticism and inquisitionism of Christian monarchs of contemporary Europe[1]. From Prithvīrāja and Mohammed Ghori of the twelfth century to Bāji Rāo (1720-40) and Haider Ali (1761-82) of the eighteenth, Hindu and Moslem India can exhibit therefore as many Charleses, Gustavus, Adolfuses, Louis XIVs, Fredericks and Peters as can the western half of Eur-Asia.

To make the foregoing account complete, notice has to be taken of the autonomous city-sovereignties and independent clan-commonwealths of the Hindus. They were in existence off and on during the extensive ages that gave birth to Vedic literature, the *Jātakas*, the early Jaina and Buddhist books and the *Mahābharata*, down to the beginnings of the Gupta Empire (*c* 350 A. C.). Some of them are described in the Greek and Latin literature on India and Alexander. These nation-

[1] For Moorish-toleration in Europe during the epoch of Christian fanaticism, see Mc Cabe's *Peter Abelard* (New York, 1901), pp. 227-229. Turkish liberalism was appreciated by Bodin in his days (*vide* Bluntschli's *Geschichte der neueren Staatswissenschaft* (Munich, 1881), *cf.* also Toynbee's *Nationality and the War* (London, 1915), p. 415, and Macdonald's *Turkey and the Eastern Question* (London, 1913), p. 34, *Vide* Voltaire's *Lettres Philosophiques* (1734.)

alities were republican in type, more or less aristocratic or oligarchic in character, and thus resembled in general features the states of ancient Greece and Rome as well as the mercantile towns of medieval Italy and of the Hanseatic League.

It is clear that political development in India was not a continuous growth in the strictest sense of the term. Students of history will not find in it the simplicity and unity that characterise, generally speaking, the dynastic history of Japan or, still better, of China from the days of Tsin Shi-hwang-ti (B. C. 222). We have here all the complications and intricacies of the Byzantine Empire and the Caliphate.[1] The inextricable cobwebs of diplomatic intercourse that Europe witnessed in the Middle Ages owing to the rivalry among the Christian empires and kingdoms on the one hand, and their relations of intrigue with the competing Moslem nationalities on the other, repeated themselves in the military annals of the Hindus also and subsequently of the Hindus and the Mussalmans. Nay, from the standpoint of the political centre of gravity and *status quo*, the picture of India's state-systems is as bewilderingly varied and diversified as is that of the Western world from the armageddon of the Homeric epics down to the order brought into being by the Versailles treaty (1919). Nothing short of the kaleidoscopic changes in Freeman's *Historical Geography of Europe* can therefore fitly portray the multitudinous ups and downs of "races" and "classes" in India through the ages.

The fallacy of sociologists from Bodin to Buckle, Montesquieu to Maine, and Hegel to Huntington, equipped as this last is with "energy-charts" and "maps of

[1] J. B. Bury: *History of the Later Roman Empire* (London, 1889) Vol. II, p. 510-511.

civilization", as well as of indologists from Max Mueller to Vincent Smith and Sénart has, however, been broadening down "from precedent to precedent." Fundamentally, it consists in their not recognizing this essential parallelism and pragmatic identity in the development of *Realpolitik* in the East and the West. As a rule, they are obsessed by the postulate of Eur-American "superiority" to, or at any rate, difference from, the oriental races. The shortcomings of Hindu politics, such as they happen to be, are thus assumed by them to be "characteristic" of India.

But anybody with the sense of historical perspective must have to admit that none of the alleged failings of Hindu culture, e.g., weakness of military organization, lack of patriotism, absence of national solidarity, and so forth,—temporary and occasional although they be,—are the attributes exclusively of Indian, or for that matter, of Asian *Weltanschauung*. The "southern" and "subtropical" climate of India or any denomination of "regionalism" and the caste-system of the Hindus cannot be rationally invoked to explain socio-political and socio-economic phenomena that are almost universal and world-wide in their range. Genuine "comparative history" is the only solvent of false explanations and unscientific hypotheses.

While not prepared to be a "monist" or "absolutist" in the conception of *Kultur-geschichte* we may accept with certain limitations the general thesis as to what Bagehot would call the influence of "physics" upon "politics." But an extreme geographical interpretation of history is to be seen in Huntington's *Pulse of Asia* (1907, Ch. XVIII). It will be noticed that the philosophical analysis attempted by "physicists" is invariably based on too many assumptions in regard to the historical data themselves, especially to those bearing on the Orient. The hemispheroidal generalizations are therefore reared on erroneous premises. Some of the worst specimens of the mal-application of the comparative method so far as the selection of sociological facts is concerned are furnished in the writings of Huntington. In the *Pusle of Asia* this neo-climatologist and radical "regionalist" takes for granted in the newspaper style that "Mohammedanism favors immorality" and that Persians are "prone to lying". The postulate of the "white man's burthen" is, moreover, the pervading philosophy of this book (p. 323) as also of his *Civilization and Climate* (1915). His appreciation of Japan in the latter volume is accordingly explained by a corollary to the same logic, viz., that "nothing succeeds like success." From the obverse side the identical *idola* is illustrated in the chapter on the "Problem of Turkey" in his "*World Power and Evolution* (1919), which *en passant* is inspired more by political propagandism than devotion to science.[1]

The Hellenes, notwithstanding the temperate zone of their "isles of Greece," were not more remarkable for unity than were the Hindus of the time of Alexander. Nor did their character display any enviable patriotism when put to the test of Macedonian gold[2] and arms. The crushing defeat inflicted on Seleukos and Menander

[1] A short but comprehensive criticism of the prevailing fallacies in comparative culture-history is set forth in the present author's "Futurism of Young Asia" in the *International Journal of Ethics* (Chicago for July, 1918). See also the section on "Asians *vs.* Latins and Slavs" in his paper on "Americanization from the viewpoint of Young Asia" in the *Journal of International Relations* (Worcester, Mass. U. S. A., July, 1919) for an examination of the alleged social and cultural distinction between the Oriental and European labourers in regard to their assimilability to American conditions.

[2] I. B. Bury : *History of Greece* Vol. II, pp. 303, 305-306.

by Chandragupta Maurya (B. C. 303) and Puṣyamitra Suṃga (B. C. 153) respectively was not less decisive a feat of Hindu *viriya* or *parākrama* (i.e. energism) which served to keep European military power away from India than were the victories of the Greeks over the Persians at Marathon and Salamis which saved Hellas from the "expansion of Asia." The failure of Hindu nationalities before hordes of Scythians, Tartars or Huns was no worse specimen of military incompetency, social disintegration, moral corruption and political instability than was the disruption of the Roman empire by the "barbarians."[1]

The process by which during the seventh and eighth centuries the Saracens[2] made themselves masters of Sicily, Southern Italy, Spain and south-western France and converted the Mediterranean Sea into an Asian lake do not by any means prove that the organizing ability of the Christians, although they had no caste restrictions, was appreciably superior to that of the Gurjara-Pratīhāras who fell equally before other inroads of Islam. Nor did East-Europeans exhibit extraordinary physical vigour and martial qualities because of the physiography of Russian snows when in the thirteenth century they had to capitulate to the avalanche of Buddhist-Shamanist Mongols[3] of Central Asia inch by inch as far to the interior of Europe as the Carpathian

[1] S. Dill : *Roman Society of the Last Century of the Western Empire* (New York, 1899) pp. 303-345; Bury : *Later Roman Empire*, Vol. I, pp. 25-36; G. F. Young: *East and West through Fifteen Centuries* (B. C. 44-1453) (London 1916) Vol. II, pp. 131-137.

[2] S. P. Scott: *History of the Moorish Empire in Europe* (Philadelphia, 1904), Vol. II, pp. 35-37; Young, Vol. II, pp. 567-570; *Cambridge Mediaeval History*, Vol. II (1913), pp. 379-385.

[3] Howorth: *History of the Mongols* (London, 1876-88) Vol. I, pp. ix, xi. vol. II. (*The So-called Tartars of Russia*) pp. 25-183; H. Yule: *Book of Ser Marco Polo*, Vol. I (London, 1903) pp. xl, xlii.

Mountains. In the fifteenth and sixteenth centuries, again, the Christians of the Balkans, Greece, Italy, and Spain persisted in their antagonistic relations even in the face of Ottoman invasions. Certainly they did not appear to be more alive to the fact of the common danger, and failed not less ignominiously to present a united front against the peril from "Greater Asia" than did the Hindus and Mohammedans in the eighteenth century while confronting the menace from the "expansion of Europe."

The facts of defeat and decay are so widely "distributed" in the history of the world's races of men that scientific students of social development should take care not to dogmatize about the degeneracy or downfall of a particular people as an isolated or characteristic phenomenon of civilization. And those scholars who would try to explain or account for such decays and declines by single categories like region, climate, social habits, caste, religion, dietary, demographic trends, etc. would only demonstrate that they have command over little facts and less logic. The monistic sociology of the declines and falls of Hindu states as of the Roman Empire or other states is as unhistorical in data as illogical in reasoning.

The first important sociological *datum* is to be found in the consideration that decline, degeneracy, fall, extinction and what not are not the exclusive marks of Hindu civilization but are to be encountered under other than Indian regions, climates, diets, gods, *mores* and so forth. In the second place, objective sociology has to grapple with the great historic reality that the decline and fall among the Hindus have been, as observed before, temporary and occasional, i.e., followed and preceded by rise, growth, development and expansion. This cyclical character of Hindu *élan vital* is to be observed not only during the thousands of years from the Mohenjo Daro epochs down to the eighteenth century but also in modern times. We must always have to consider the fact that under virtually the same conditions of geography, race, caste, religion, food etc. as during the seventeenth and eighteenth centuries the Hindus of the nineteenth century, especially of the twentieth have been exhibiting signs of rejuvenation and re-making on the most diverse fronts of individual and social life.[1] These "fluctuations" of vital energism from epoch to epoch belong to some of the most fundamental problems of "social mobility" such as cannot be interpreted in terms exclusively of region, race, religion etc.

Be that as it may, comparative sociology will have to declare that the political annals of mediaeval India do not offer greater insecurity and worse absence of peace than such as were exhibited by the Welsh, Irish and Scotch wars of England, the Hundred Year's War between France and England, the wars of the Hapsburgs, the wars of the innumerable German baronies,

[1] From the standpoint of general sociology the "geographical interpretation of history" has been found to be wrong by C. Vallaux: *La Mer* (Paris 1908) and *Le Sol et l' Etat* (Paris 1911). More recent criticisms of Le Play, Huntington and others are to be seen in P. Sorokin: *Social Mobility* (New York 1927), *Contemporary Sociological Theories* (New York 1928) and *Principles of Rural-Urban Sociology* (New York 1929). Jean Brunhes's *La Géographie humaine* which is a standard work of the anti-geographist or anti-regionalist sociology is available in English translation as *Human Geography* (Chicago). Vidal de la Blache likewise opposes the doctrine of geographical determinism. His own doctrine of *possibilisme* establishes the thesis that nothing comes out of the "necessities" but that "everywhere are to be found the possibilities." There is no "law of islands" and no "law of rivers." The same regions have the most varied destinies. See E. Lasbax: *La Cité Humaine* Vol. II. (Paris 1927), Chapter on *Le Géographisme historique*.

the wars of the Italian kingdoms and cities, the English Civil War, the French wars of the Fronde, the meteoric acquisitions of Sweden's Gustavus Adolphus and of the Polish Kingdom, the expansion of Turkey to the gates of Vienna, the courting of Moslem alliance by Christian monarchs against brother-Christians, the annexations of Peter and Frederick, and the steady decline and fall of the Holy Roman Empire. In regard, specifically, to the relations between Moslem states and original Hindu states or between Moslem empires and their Hindu citizens or between Hindu empires and Moslem citizens, it is questionable if one can prove, item by item, that the picture was in any way weaker than was the story of the contest between Roman Catholics and Protestants culminating in the horrors of the Thirty Year's War.

So far as the ancient period is concerned, the historian has to observe that the records of Hindu imperial power are not usually marked by the accession and disappearance of dozens of puppet emperors such as were chosen and slain by the army in Rome. No generation was without its *sārva-bhauma*, *chakravarti*, or *chāturanta*, i.e., "world-ruler," whose regime was signalized by peace and security for the people. This *pax sārva-bhaumica* (peace of the world empire) was the result of a well regulated administrative machinery, and was helped forward to no small extent by remarkably long reigns, two or three of which sometimes covered a whole century. In any case no Eur-American scientist can legitimately congratulate himself on the superiority of the trend of occidental history if only he remembers a mediaeval statement cited in Engelbert's *De Ortu et Fine Romani Imperii.*[1] "The Roman Empire", ran the opinion,

[1] C. N. S. Woolf: *Bartolus of Sassooferato* (Cambridge, 1913), p. 286.

"was and is always troubled by wars and rebellions", hardly ever were the gates of the temple of Janus shut; the greater number of Roman emperors have died violent deaths; and the Roman Empire has been the cause rather of disorder than of peace."

This must not be summarily dismissed as only the view of a radical anti-imperial propagandist. For, the duration and geographical extent of peace given by the "Romans" were not really of a remarkable order. From the Oriental platform, besides, the claim may be advanced that not more than once did European history exhibit the formation of a "unitary" state (of an "inorganic" character, of course, to use Seeley's phrase) with the size and area of the Maurya Empire (third century B. C.). This was the Roman Empire at its height during the second and third centuries A. C. Even the less extensive Gupta Empire of the fifth century, the Vardhana Empire of the seventh century, and the Chola Empire of the eleventh century were barely approached by the Franco-German Empire of Charlemagne, or by the haphazard European possessions of the Spanish Emperor Charles V, or by the ephemeral conquests of Napoleon.

While, therefore, for purposes of comparative politics it is necessary to conclude that *pax sārva-bhaumica* or *fédération de l'empire* is at least as conspicuous an achievement of Hindu statesmanship as *pax Romana* of Occidental, it is on the other hand to be admitted on scientific grounds that the political unity of India is, historically speaking, as great a myth as is the political unity of Europe. India furnishes but another illustration of the universal sway of the *mātsya-nyāya* (logic of the fish), the Hobbesian "state of nature," which can lead but to pluralism, whether anarchic or well-ordered. The East has reproduced the same *Naturprozess* of

Gumplowicz's *Der Rassenkampf* (Ch. IV) as has the West.

The facts of Hindu political evolution and culture-history like those of the historic races in the diverse regions of the world should but lead to the conclusion to which the exponents of a new science, namely, *Geopolitik* (Geopolitics) have been arriving at under the leadership of Karl Haushofer.[1] According to Wuest a world-view such as can actually transcend the limitations of space is impossible both as a concept and as a fact. The so-called "higher unit" which is alleged to be established by the break-up of a previous world-view of a different character through assimilation, absorption, transformation etc. is very questionable and in the long run is liable to disruption. In his analysis it is impossible to emancipate the world-view from its space-limitations. The attempts to establish artificial world-languages, e.g., Esperanto, Ido, Novial, Volapuek, have not been able, we are told, to advance beyond their crude beginnings. According to this philosophy, Coudenove-Kalergi's Pan-Europa movement is like the League of Nations idea a still-born phenomenon. The abolition of the Caliphate by Kemal Pasha is regarded as but the last item in an inevitable development, namely, the disappearance of an unnatural Pan-Islam. By enunciating the doctrine that every world-view is by nature nothing but national or territorial although it can to a certain extent transform the space and even transcend it Wuest has exposed the philosophical bankruptcy of internationalism as a cult. It is demonstrated by other writers that neither religion nor art, nor language, nor technocracy, nor economic deve-

[1] *Raumueberwindende Maechte* (Leipzig 1934) pp. 167, 170-178, 195, 207, 230-232, 259, 272-273, 277, 340-341, 351-352; *Geopolitik der Pan-Ideen* (Berlin 1931).

lopments, nor colonialism nor imperialism can in the last analysis lead to the genuine transcending of space or region. All the so-called international or internationalizing endeavours are essentially *raumgebunden* (space-limited and space-conditioned).

There is no mysticism or metaphysics in Haushofer's social philosophy. In the midst of all internationalizing ideologies his geopolitics teaches the world to remain awake to the one great reality of life, namely, that it is nothing but nationalism that rules mankind and that the eternal problem of today is, as our *Mahābhārata* has taught for all ages, to study the science and art of *Macht*, i.e., *śakti* or power. In geopolitics the student of Hindu societal theories will thus come across such dicta of Somadeva's *Nītivākyāmrita* as *na hi kulagatā kasyāpi bhūmih* (no body's territory is derived from his family) and *vīrabhogyā vasundharā* (it is by the powerful that the Earth can be enjoyed).

Finally, in the state-systems of the Hindus for over half a millennium the sociologist will have to see but a verification of the law enunciated by Jacques de Morgan in *Préhistoire Orientale* (p. 216) that history knows nothing but *précipiter les masses humaines les unes contre les autres* (hurling the human groups against one another). This is what he calls the "perpetual renewal or renovation in which history consists." The Hindu state-systems have likewise exhibited the same *perpétual combat contre la mort* (eternal struggle against death) and the same solicitude for *la paix dont la possession, en fin de compte, n'est reservée qu'aux justes qui sont forts* (peace, the possession of which, in the last balance sheet, is reserved only for those righteous who are strong), such as, in Lasbax's analysis of the new social forces since the last Great War (1914-18), are today inspiring the nations of the world to remain equipped with "defensive patriotism" and with "collective health" in view of the wars that are going to break out tomorrow (*des guerres surgiront encore*).[1]

SECTION 3

THE FINANCIAL ORGANIZATION AND ECONOMIC POLICY OF THE CHOLAS AND THE MAURYAS

Budget-making is an essentially modern institution. It is only since the time of Napoleon that regular estimates of receipts and expenditures have been yearly prepared in France.[2] And in spite of the comparative abundance of reliable data no ingenuity of modern research has been able to reconstruct the shect of liabilities and assets for any period of the Roman Empire. But the administrative history of Hindu India is yet in its beginnings. It is out of the question therefore to attempt such wide guesses about the annual expenses even of the Maurya Empire (B. C. 322-185) for which information is more plentiful than for others as have been done in regard to the Athenian state by Boekh[3] or about the total revenues as have been done in regard to the Roman Empire by Gibbon and Guizot[4]. Nor of course is it possible to test the fiscal policy of Hindu states by the modern canons of taxation, especially on the complicated questions of justice, faculty, i.e. ability to pay, or equality of assessment.

[1] E. Lasbax : *La Cité Humaine* (Paris) Vol. II. (1927) pp. 352-357.

[2] Palgrave: *Dictionary of Political Economy* (Art. on "Finances-France") Vol. II. p. 68, Leroy-Beaulieu: *Traité de la science des finances* (Paris, 1912), Vol. II. pp. 11, 12.

[3] Schoemann : *Antiquities of Greece* (London, 1880) p. 445.

[4] Ramsay and Lancian: *Roman Antiquities* (London, 1898), p. 28?.

A contemporary account of the finances of the Vardhana Empire (A. C. 606-647) is furnished by Yuan Chwang, the Chinese state-guest (A. C. 629-645) of Harṣa's. It is said that forced labour was not exacted by the government. When the public works required it, labour was exacted and paid for in strict proportion to work. Those who cultivated the royal estates paid a sixth of the produce as the share for the state. The river passages and the road barriers were open on payment of a small toll. In regard to public expenditure there are said to have been four charges on the private demesnes of the Crown. The first charge was of course the management of the affairs of state and the provision for sacrificial offerings. The second was for providing subsidies for the ministers and chief officers of state. Honorariums for men of distinguished ability constituted the third charge, and the fourth was religious charity. Altogether, in the Chinese scholar-pilgrim's opinion, the taxes on the people were light, and personal service required of them was moderate.[1] Evidently we have here the material for a very elementary balance-sheet much too naive for an imperial organization, based as it was on the triumphs of *dig-vijaya* (conquest of the quarters) and military aggression no less than on the victories of peace. The reporter was a layman and naturally failed to notice the "sinews of war" that operated the administrative machinery of *pax-sārva-bhaumica* (peace of the world-state). It is on such facile statements about "light taxes" and "religious charities," however, that students of comparative politics in the nineteenth century were used to founding their estimate of the Hindu political systems. In the publications on finance, as in the treatises on legislation and jurisprudence it has been the custom, therefore, to summarily

[1] *Si Yu-ki* (Beal's transl. London, 1885), Vol. I. pp. 87, 88.

dismiss the Oriental monarchies as primitive polities of the "patrimonial" type. Today the states of Old Asia are treated by scholars more or less in the same light as the feudal kingdoms of mediaeval Europe, i.e., as organizations modelled on a private household, the domestic establishment of the ruler.[1]

South Indian Revenues (*c* 900-1300)

But let us examine the imperialism of Hindu *sārva-bhaumas* ("world-rulers") on the basis of their own charters, decrees and promulgations (*śāsanas*) that have been rendered accessible by the archæological investigations of recent years. The statesmen of the Chola Empire (900-1300) would appear to have been at their wits' end in devising new forms of revenue. No complete list of all the heads of government income is available for this South Indian (Madras and Mysore) state. But several Tamil inscriptions[2] described the immunities from dues to the government enjoyed by certain villages through the grant of royal charters. From the schedule of these "privileges" we can automatically see a great part of the other side of the shield, viz., the normal contributions to the Imperial treasury for which each village was ordinarily liable. Not all the items are, however, fully intelligible.

The available list indicates only the revenue from villages or village-unions. But it is questionable if we are justified in treating it exclusively as what should technically be a branch of "local finance." The village through its *panchayat* was indeed responsible as a unit

[1] Article on Finance in the *Encyclopaedia Britannica.*

[2] H. Krishna Shastri : "Fiscal Administration under Early Cholas" in the *R. G. Bhandarkar Commemorative Essays* (Poona, 1917).

for the realization of all public income within its area.[1] But the heads of income do not seem to have been classified and specifically ear-marked as local and national. We need not, besides, attempt here a classification of the Chola revenues according to one or other of the accepted taxonomies. They can easily be brought down to the tripartite division into taxes, fees and prices.[2]

(*a*) *Sources other than Land.* In the first place, there was a "tax in money".[3] It is not clear as to what should be meant by this item. It may have been a direct tax *per capita* like the poll tax of 1377-1380 in England during the Hundred Years' War or the *tributum* in Rome.

Something like "general property tax" has to be seen in several imposts. Like the horses and cattle taxed by mediaeval German States[4] "animals" were counted to contribute to the Chola exchequer. The furniture, clothing, and ornaments are not enumerated in the schedule of taxes on "personalty". But "movable" property as contrasted with the real estate was assessed in the form of "fixed capital" like looms and oil-mills. Tanks also were included in the list of property-dues.

A tax was realized on weights, whatever it might imply. But some light may be thrown on this item from the legislation in the *Arthaśāstra* of Kauṭalya

[1] Aiyangar : *Ancient India* (Madras, 1911) pp. 161, 163, 164.

[2] Plehn : *Introduction to Public Finance* (New York, 1896) pp. 76-79, 92-100; Seligman : *Essays in Taxation* (New York, 1913), pp. 430, 431.

[3] The list can be seen conveniently in Aiyangar, pp. 165, 166, 180-182.

[4] Seligman : *Essays* p. 39, cf. N. P. Aghnides : *Mohammedan Theories of Finance* (New York, 1916), pp. 526, 527.

(fourth century B. C.) where we read that no trader was allowed to have his weights and measures. Every day the businessmen had to have their scales and weights stamped afresh by the government.[1] The authorities realized a revenue from the stamps. Now if this custom of the first Hindu empire, that of the Mauryas, or rather of Kauṭalya were followed by the Tamil *sārva-bhaumas*, we may consider this business tax on weights to be another property tax. The rate may have been small, but the total receipts of the empire under this head must have shown a high figure, as the number of taxable individuals including the pettiest retailer was obviously large.

It is doubtful if the business or license tax paid by the Tamil goldsmith should not be scheduled as a charge on property. But "unripe fruit" in the *Kartigai* month, though a levy in kind, must be regarded as such. Stocks, bonds and mortgages that are so prominent in modern economic life and necessarily occupy an important place in the taxation of property are not naturally to be looked for in Hindu finances of the eleventh, twelfth and thirteenth centuries. But it is interesting to note that the "sonship" was assessed among certain social classes, e.g. the "right hand" and "left hand" orders. The public income from the sonship dues was identical with that accruing from inheritance tax or on the transfer of property from the dead to the living.

None of these property dues were of course prices charged by the government for economic or other services rendered to the people. They were all deduced from the power of the state to obtain revenue by

[1] Shamasastry's article on "Chanakya's Land and Revenue Policy" in the *Indian Antiquary*, 1905, pp. 50, 51. *Re* Kauṭalya's age and personality, see the present author's "Kauṭalya and His Boswell" in the *Calcutta Review* for August, 1935.

"compulsory dues and charges upon its subjects," i.e., taxes in the strictest sense of the term. None of them can moreover be regarded as income from "state property" and "state monopolies," the two sources that long contributed about 25 per cent of French revenues.[1]

Taxes on comsumption were, besides, not neglected by the Chola Empire. There was a tax on bazars. The levy of tolls was common. The tax on trade or sales like the Athenian and Roman excise of 1 per cent[2] was another regular feature of the financial system. As taxes on the necessaries of life these excise duties could not but touch the community at every grade. They served, therefore, economically speaking, as real poll taxes though of an "indirect" denomination. We do not know if salt was a state monopoly as under the Roman republic[3] or as in Maurya India (or rather the Kauṭalya State). But the French *gabelle*[4] was not to be forgotten by the Tamils who were too mindful of their revenues to overlook tapping this neccssity of life that is bound to obey the law of "inelastic demand." We shall have details about Hindu salt tax in connection with Kauṭalya finance.

A rent or license tax was realized from the fishers. Taxes on the collection of rents also are mentioned. Tax-"farming" may thus have been a fact in certain directions. Furthermore, the "penal power" of the state was effectively made use of to co-operate with its finance department. We do not have a long list of fines demanded of the delinquents by the Tamil Empire. It is known only that apothecaries were fined for "rotten

[1] Palgrave, Vol. II, p. 69.

[2] Schoemann, p. 449.

[3] Ramsay, p. 277.

[4] Brissaud : *History of French Public Law* (Garner's transl. Boston, 1915), p. 505.

drugs." An income of minor character is obvious in Kulottūṃga's legislation (1070-1118) by which the state charged a seigniorage upon coining.[1]

Income from the "services" of the state is mentioned in three connections. First, the villagers had to contribute their mite to maintain the watchman who was placed over the *vettis* (paths). This was for obvious reasons a regular rate or cess, though local, for one of the minimum functions of government. Secondly, the state seems to have supplied the *karman* to measure the paddy of the cultivators. He had to be paid for by the rural commune at a certain rate. Lastly, a water-rate or "tax on water-courses" for irrigation was an inevitable charge upon every peasant.

Mines, though they must certainly have been important sources of Chola revenues, are not mentioned in the inscriptions. Nor are the customs duties referred to. Of course neither of these could form part of the regular dues of a village to the government. But we are in a position to realize that when all these dues and others not enumerated in the inscriptions that happen to have been found are considered in their totality the income of the Tamil Empire would rise to a considerable amount.

(*b*) *Collections from Land.* We have now to add the revenue from property *par excellence*, the "real estate" as it is called. Not only in primitive communities but in Rome also even under the Empire land revenue was the mainstay of the government. And this land revenue was essentially a rent from "Crown-land," *ager publicus*, i.e., public domain. It took the Romans long to get used to the idea of a non-land revenue. Taxes like the *tributum* were considered by the republic as "forced

[1] Aiyangar, pp. 149, 150.

loans" to be repaid out of the loot of conquest, and these were resorted to only when the proceeds of the "domain" proved inadequate to meet the extraordinary expenses[1].

Under the Tamils also South India's financial backbone must have been furnished by the realizations from land. The rate was not low. The Early Roman Empire used to levy land revenue at the rate of 1/10th of the produce[2]. But in Chola India the government demand was 1/6th. The high rate was indeed the normal *bhāga* or share of the government in land-produce according to the stereotyped "pious wish" of the *dharma-śāstras* (law books) and *nīti-śāstras* (political science). And yet in *Realpolitik* this conventional norm was but a fiscal camouflage that may deceive the academic student of financial history but did not fail to press the tax-payers themselves. For in Chola legislation the additional imposts on land, besides, the tolls and octrois, were clearly defined as being 1/10th of the yield. The total revenue from land was thus 4/15ths or more than 25 per cent of the gross outturn in Rājādhirāja's time (1035-1053)[3].

An interesting theoretical study in connection with the Chola revenue from real property would be that bearing on its precise character as to whether it was rent or tax. Incidentally it may be pointed out that communism in landownership is practically unknown in Hindu law-books[4]. The trend of ancient thought on

[1] Seligman : *Essays* p. 35. The same Roman views are expressed in the sixteenth century by the French political philosopher Bodin in his *Les six livres de la république* (Bk. VI. Ch. ii. *Des Finances*).

[2] Ramsay, p. 276.

[3] Aiyangar, pp. 181-182.

[4] Hopkins : *India* (Land Tenure) pp. 221, 225, 229. Mac-

land-tenure is to regard it as individual concern. But in Tamil inscriptions, while the individualistic tenure (the *ryotwari*, to use the British Indian term) is easily to be inferred, communal property in certain lands is also assured to village *panchayats* by the legislation of Rāja-rāja the Great (985-1018)[1]. We may take it that so far as the Chola Empire is concerned, land was owned both in severalty as well as in common.

This does not, however, settle the question as to how far, if at all the Crown was the legal proprietor of land, i.e., how far the "village community" (wherever it may have existed) or the individual cultivators were but "tenants" of the state-landlord (paying "economic" rents for the usufruct of public property) and how far their dues were "direct taxes" paid on their own immovable possessions. It is the tendency of modern indologists to postulate all lands as state property and the income from land necessarily as Crown rent. But it is hardly possible to maintain this position on the strength of actual proprietary documents, *śāsanas* (laws or charters) and epigraphic records. For all practical purposes the presumption rather should be that Hindu India did not know of state-landlordism, i.e., land-nationalization[2] except of course in very limited areas. The land revenue of Hindu states was therefore, generally speaking, a tax. But, as Giffen[3] explains away the distinction between rent and tax, "the fact of a government levying so general a charge may be held *ipso facto* to convert charge into a tax having much the same

donell and Keith : *Vedic Index* (London, 1912) Vol. I. pp. 245, 246.

[1] Aiyangar, pp. 161, 163, 164.

[2] See the discussion on "public lands" in Rau's *Finanzwissenschaft* (Leipzig, 1864), pp. 127-133, cf. Bodin, pp. 623-634.

[3] "Taxation" in the *Enc. Brit.*

economic effects and consequences as a tax." For in strict theory, "where the government makes a charge, it levies a tax." The features of monopoly and compulsion on the tax-payers associated with all forms of land-revenue "make the charges difficult to distinguish logically from other taxes."

(*c*) *The "Modern" Character of Tamil Finance.* On the whole, the Chola revenues were bulky in dimensions and the people of Southern India heavily taxed. Only one ruler is spoken of as having slightly reduced the amount of the people's dues. Kulottūmga's name became a household word in Madras of the eleventh and twelfth centuries, for in 1086, the year of the British Domesday Book, he abolished the tolls[1] after the completion of cadastral survey,—the second such survey of the Chola Empire. But the general story of *les nerfs de la république*, the nerves of the state, as Bodin puts it, under the Cholas was uniform. Like the governments of Europe in the days of Adam Smith[2] the South Indian monarchs knew how to exact as much as they could, "only desirous of finding the easiest means of doing so." The one redeeming feature seems to be that the Empire was conscious of the high price at which *pax sārva-bhaumika* was being enjoyed by the people. Rāja-rāja accordingly expressly instructed the finance officers to be elastic in the collection of revenues[3]. But no figures are available as to any of the heads of government income, and there is no means of making an estimate as to the probable national income. It is naturally impossible to form an idea as to the taxable capacity or "faculty" of the people. Nor is it convenient to hazard a conjecture as to the actual "burden

[1] Aiyangar, pp. 149, 150.
[2] *Enc. Brit.* (Taxation)
[3] Aiyangar, p. 182.

of taxation," i.e., the proportion of the aggregate wealth of the people that the state demanded for all its functions and services.

Taxation as such was unknown in France previous to 1300[1]. As a function of the state and as an institution of "public law" it virtually ceased to exist with the destruction of the Roman Empire by the Teutons. In its place was substituted the "private claim" of customary dues, fines or tolls by landlords and barons[2]. The transition from this "feudal" to "modern" finance was a lengthy process in England[3]. It was not before the rise of nation-states in the fifteenth and sixteenth centuries that the right of government to levy "taxes" became established or rather re-established in the Western world. But, for the purpose of comparative economics and politics it is necessary to note that the Chola finances do not exhibit the features of the disintegrated feudal polity of mediaeval Europe. The revenues of the Chola Empire possessed the same variety in form as the Roman-Imperial and the modern French. They may be classified by students of *Finanzwissenschaft*, if required, according to the Latin *patrimonium*, *tributum* and *vectigalium*, or the more popular *domaine*, *contributions directes*, and *contributions indirectes* of modern French science. And of course the right of taxation was firmly planted in the political consciousness of Chola India.

The Consumption-Schedule of Hindu States

It is not difficult to explain why the Imperial structures of the Hindus should have been heavily

[1] Brissaud, pp. 487-491, Leroy-Beaulieu, Vol. II, pp. 6, 7.
[2] *Enc. Brit.* (Finance).
[3] *Ibid.* (article on "English Finance").

assessed organizations. The reasons are to be sought in the great variety and quantity of state's "consumption." They are essentially identical with what economists like Nitti and Leroy-Beaulieu[1] have traced in the growth of public expenditures in modern times. The functions of Hindu governments were manifold. Consciously or unconsciously, whether backed by a definite theory of *nīti* (state-craft) like the late German empire or not, every state in India was a *Kulturstaat*. The invariable end of all Hindu polities was the protection and development of *dharma*. Like *Kultur* and Arnoldian "culture" *dharma* is a very comprehensive category. Exceedingly elastic in its significance, again, like the English term "law" the concept of *dharma* is the basis of distinction, the *fundamentum divisionis* between man and the brute. *Dharmeṇa hīnāḥ*, says the *Gītā*, *paśubhiḥ samānāḥ*. In *dharma*, the analogue of the "virtue" in Plato's *Republic*, is to be found the *differentium* between the human world and that of *paśu*, or "beasts and birds," as Hobbes would have it. An agency for the promotion of humanism, i.e., for the advancement of all that lets "the ape and tiger die" and develops the people's material and moral interests, of anything, in short, that is conducive to national well-being was necessarily a multifunctional corporate organism. The *Dharma-staaten* of India had therefore before them an almost unlimited range of what in scientific parlance is known as "developmental" activity. Not of an Arcadian character could thus be the "appropriations" of the Hindu empires.

We need not enumerate the duties of government as stated in the *nīti-śāstras*. Let us note only the functions of the historic state-systems that may be gathered from

[1] *Traité*, Vol. II., pp. 171-181.

the inscriptions and contemporary reports. The economic development of the country was undertaken by the Maurya, Gupta, Kashmiran, Tamil and Ceylonese governments. Their care for irrigation[1] in different parts of the empire is a solid testimony to their recognition of the secular interests of the state. The construction of magnificent roads was another function along the same line[2]. The beautifying of cities and measures for street-cleaning, sanitation, etc. were important items of state business in Chola territories[3]. The promotion of aesthetic as well as "productive" arts and crafts was a normal function of almost every Hindu state. The encouragement or "protection" of skilled workmen, the steady maintenance of shipbuilders and naval architects, and state employment of miners and other industrial artisans were among the duties of the Maurya civil service. Shipbuilding[4] and manufacture of arms and ammunitions were in reality Crown monopolies. Wood-cutting, carpentry and smithery works came naturally therefore under state control. All governments undertook to lay out parks and grounds for recreation and pastime. Pharmaceutical gardens were treated as public necessities. Palaces and public halls were likewise some of the "useful magnificences" that no state could dispense with. The Pāṇḍya rulers (*c* 100-300 A. C.) were patrons of *pariṣats* or academies

[1] *Epigrafia Indica* 1905-1906, pp. 46-49; *Gupta Inscriptions*, pp. 56-65; Kalhana, Bk. V. 68-117; Venkayya: "Irrigation in Southern India" in the *Archaeological Survey of India Annual Report* 1903-1904, Deakin : *Irrigated India and Ceylon* (London, 1893), pp. 239-242.

[2] Mc. Crindle : *Ancient India* (Meg. XXXIV), p. 86, Arrian, III; Law: *Studies in Ancient Hindu Polity* (London, 1914), pp. 68-75.

[3] Ayyar : *Town Planning in the Ancient Deccan* (Madras, 1916), pp. 42, 44, 51.

[4] Mc. Crindle : *Anc. Ind.*, p. 86; Strabo. XV, 46.

of literature[1]. The Guptas[2] and the Palas[3] considered universities among important charges on the Imperial Exchequer. Temples and *vihāras* or monasteries were built at government expense both by the Vardhana and Chālukya emperors of the seventh century[4], indeed by all ruling houses. Not the conventional religion and morality of the time alone found an asylum in these institutions. The financial authorities must have regarded them as schools of higher learning as well. From the cultural standpoint these were at once the art-galleries and museums of the people. And as resorts for relief of the sick, the distressed and the poor the ostensibly religious buildings discharged an important economic function like the Catholic institutions of mediaeval Europe. Add to all this the minimum functions of every state as state, viz., the protection of person and property, or national defence by army and navy as well as internal policing by adequate executive and judicial staff. The extent of these minimum functions can be realized from the fact that in the Maurya Empire or rather the Kauṭalyan state the appropriations on this head absorbed 25 per cent of the total revenues[5].

It is not necessary to compare the functions of Hindu states, item by item, as regards quantity and variety, with the long list of modern state activities, expanding daily as they have been under the impact of socialism, especially under its latest form of "economic planning" or "planned economy." The socialistic trend of *dharma*-states is apparent enough. One must not

[1] Aiyangar, pp. 70, 337, 359, 360, 379-382.

[2] Itsing : *Record of the Buddhist Religion* (671-695) (Takakusu's transl. Oxford, 1896), pp. 65, 154, 177.

[3] *Ind. Ant.*, 1888, pp. 308-311.

[4] *Si Yu-ki*. Vols. I and II.

[5] *Ind. Ant.*, 1909, p. 263.

surmise, however, that every public work among Hindus was the undertaking of the state. For, private effort, i.e., the patriotism of citizens was responsible in every age for the founding and maintenance of useful institutions. In Gupta India hospitals[1] were built and endowed by the public-spirited townsfolk of Pātaliputra, the Rome of the Hindus. Rudra-dāmana (*c* A. C. 150), a satrap of Gujarat, repaired the Sudarśana reservoir at his own expense, the ministers having refused to supply funds from the government treasury[2]. General Uṣavadāta's (*c* A. C. 100) endowment in the Āndhra Deccan may serve as a standing example of the manner in which the people co-operated with the state and supplemented its activity along developmental or cultural lines.

One of the hill caves in Govardhana (Nasik District in the Bombay Presidency) was excavated at Uṣavadāta's expense[3]. Among his numerous benefactions we read of the gift of 300,000 cows, the construction of the flights of steps on a river and the giving away of sixteen villages for religious purposes. This philanthropist used to maintain 100,000 scholars and priests with board. He bore the marriage expenses of eight Brāhmaṇas at Somnāth in Gujarat. His quadrangles, public halls and halting places as well as gardens, tanks and wells were spread over the country from Broach and Bassein, the ports on the Arabian Sea coast, to Daśapura in Malwa, far inland in Upper India. Ferry boats were placed by him over six rivers in northern Bombay. Both sides of these rivers were also furnished with rest houses and equipped with arrangements for

[1] Fa Hien : *Fo Kuo-ki* (Beal's transl., Boston, 1885), p. 107.
[2] *Ep. Ind.*, 1905-1906, *loc. cit.*
[3] *Nasik Inscr.* No. 17, R. G. Bhandarkar : *Early History of the Dekkan*, sec. iv.

the distribution of water to travellers. Moreover, he founded certain benefactions for the support of several academies of Vedic learning in various parts of the Maratha country.

Such private endowments for public purposes were undoubtedly numerous in every epoch of Hindu history. But none the less the financial burden of public administration weighed heavy upon the "pillars of the state." The government could not afford to depend solely upon local patriotism and voluntary contributions. The expenses of national house-keeping had to be met regularly from the resources of the empire. The finance department had therefore to raise the necessary revenue by hook or by crook.

Census was an important institution of the Mauryas. It was used by the municipal corporation of Pataliputra as well as by the Imperial Civil Service. The *gopa* or village magistrate, the *sthānika* or district magistrate, as well as the *nāgaraka* or mayor of the city were alive to the importance of vital statistics. The numbering of persons, houses and cattle, as well as the measurement of lands, pastures and gardens furnished the *samāhartā* or collector-general with definite data for the valuation and assessment of the people's wealth[1]. The cadastral surveys organized by the Cholas[2] in 986 and 1086 were also calculated to ensure the same end. Both these instruments tended to bring about centralization and consolidation of the public revenues and were indeed together with the war office, the judiciary and the executive service the most effective means of establishing *pax sārvabhaumica* (peace of the world-empire). The financial organization aimed at by the Hindu

[1] *Ind. Ant.*, 1905, p. 5.
[2] Aiyangar, 144, 149, 150, 175-177

empires was thus akin to the "integration" of national outlays and revenues that has been the steady achievement of modern Europe since the fifteenth and sixteenth centuries. And in classical times it is the system of the Roman Empire with its official tax-collectors who replaced the *publicani* or revenue "farmers" of the republic that should be kept before the mind's eye while appraising the public expenditure, national resources or heads of income, and financial administration of Hindu India, say, from B. C. 322 to A. C. 1300.

Kauṭalyan Finances (*c* 300 B. C.)

We shall now proceed to analyze the revenues of the Maurya Empire, or rather of the Kauṭalyan *Arthaśāstra*. One of the functions of the *gopa*, the officer at the lowest rung of the executive hierarchy, was to register the probable dues of the villagers in "working men"[1] along with taxes, tolls and fines. It is not clear if we are to understand that the empire used to receive contributions in "services" like the Roman republic in its earlier stages,—such, for instance, as is recommended by Viṣṇu (III, 32), Manu (VII, 138), or Sukra (IV, ii, line 241). In Megasthenes's *Indika*, again, we read that one of the objects of the vital statistics kept by the census officials of the municipal corporation of Pātaliputra was the levy of a tax. If some particular tax is to be singled out because of this statement it was evidently a poll-tax on the citizens per head.

The financial authorities themselves classified the revenues into seven principal groups according to the kind of resource tapped by them. "Fortified cities" constituted the first revenue jurisdiction. The *rāṣṭra*

[1] *Ind. Ant. loc. cit.*

or "country" districts constituted the second. Mines were treated as a distinct source of public income. Gardens and forests also formed two independent groups. Quadrupeds like cows, buffaloes, sheep, goats, asses, camels, horses, and mules likewise contributed their quota. The seventh head was traffic both by land and water.

Each of these sources is described in detail in the *Artha-śāstra*[1]. The several items of income from the "country," the second in the above grouping, comprised six heads. Crown-lands yielded the first revenue that was known as *sītā*. The second head was *bhāga* (share) or revenue in kind realized from private landlords. A special tax, *bali*, was demanded for religious purposes corresponding to the dues realized by Athens for the festivities. Sundry collections known as *kara* were made in money. *Tara* was the toll realized on boats, ferries and ships. The sixth item consisted of various dues, *vartanī* (road-cess), *śulka* (toll), etc. and was levied as a rate on all traffic.

The fortified cities contributed to the Imperial exchequer under twenty different heads. These were toll, fines, weights and measures, jails, currency, passports, excise, slaughter-houses, oil, *ghi* (clarified butter), salt, goldsmiths, commerce, courtesans, gambling, house-building, artisans, gate-dues, and religious institutions. There were special taxes on a people called Bāhārikas. They appear to have been mercenary soldiers or some wealthy community living at Nālandā, the famous University town of later ages. Like the Jews in Europe this race was considered by the Maurya empire or rather by Kauṭalya to be a good victim for fleecing.

[1] *Ind. Ant.*, 1905, p. 47.

Altogether, there were at least fifty different names under which revenues flowed into the treasury. For our present purpose we shall classify them into eight modern categories: (1) land revenue, including the income from forests and gardens, (2) customs duties, (3) excise on sales, (4) "direct" property taxes of various denominations, (5) fines as the penalties for all sorts of offence, (6) economic "earnings" or profits from the commercial undertakings of the naval department, (7) income from the Crown monopolies in extractive (mine, salt, etc.) and other industries, (8) miscellaneous collections like port-dues, etc.

(*a*) *Land Revenue.* As with the Roman Empire[1] the chief source of Maurya or Kauṭalyan income was the receipt from land. In the West the process of fiscal reorganization from Hadrian to Diocletian led up to the system of assessment for fifteen years. But in regard to the Kauṭalyan polity no information is available as to the period for which the valuations were made.

In Athens land belonged to the state. In Kauṭalyan India certain passages of the *Artha-śāstra* may lend colour to the hypothesis as to the "public ownership" of the chief "agent of production." If Kauṭalya's statement (II, i, vi) may be taken as "positive law" on the subject, both land and water belonged to the government. The people could exercise their proprietary right in regard to all other species of property excepting these two[2]. But, on the other hand, this position will appear to be inconsistent with the fact noted above that two

[1] W. T. Arnold : *Roman System of Provincial Administration* (Oxford, 1914), pp. 203, 204, Ramsay, 275-281, *Enc. Brit.* (Finance).

[2] Cf. the Mohammedan theory of public domain in Aghnides, pp. 500-521. Note the conditions of land tenure in Japan, K. Asakawa : *Early Institutional Life of Japan* (A. C. 645), Tokyo, 1903, p. 73.

distinct items were enumerated as land-revenue from the *rāṣtra* or country districts of the empire. The *sītā* was the income from the Crown-lands, and was therefore rent. The other realization was specially known as *bhāga*, the "share" of the state in the "produce" of the people's lands. The private proprietors were known as *svavīryopajīvinah*. Besides, the right of private property in real estate was clearly recognized in the law of sales. According to the legislation in the *Artha-śāstra*,[1] village lands were to be sold in the presence of forty neighbours who owned land in the vicinity. The state could demand only the legitimate excise on the sale. The same proprietary right is to be inferred from, though also limited by, the ruling that lands could be sold by cultivators only to cultivators, and that persons enjoying revenue-free lands could sell them only to persons who already possessed such lands. The distinction between Crown-lands and private lands is also to be noted in the law of escheat. By the general law on the subject the rights of ownership over houses, fields, gardens, tanks and temples were forfeited if proprietors took no cognizance for a continuous period of five years.[2]

In the budget of the Maurya (Kauṭalyan) Empire as in that of the Roman we have therefore to look for two entries, theoretically considered, under land revenue. The first was rent paid by the *ryot* or tenant to the state-landlord, the second was a "direct tax" paid by the citizen to the government. The Imperial (Kauṭalyan) demand from land was very high, higher even than what we have seen under the Cholas. For the land alone,[3] where irrigation was carried on by hands the

[1] *Ind. Ant.*, 1905, p. 10; Law, pp. 161, 162.
[2] *Ind. Ant.*, 1905, pp. 9, 105, 113, 114.
[3] *Ibid*, p. 110. Note the 50 per cent in Islamic theory, Aghnides, p. 529.

due was 1/5th of the yield; where irrigation was carried on by conveying water on shoulders or through water raised from tanks, lakes and streamlets the due was 1/4th; and where irrigation was carried on by pumping (*sroto-yantra*) water from rivers, the due was 1/3rd. An additional *udaka-bhāga* or water-rate was charged by the government at 1/4th or 1/5th of the produce. The total rates ranged therefore from 2/5ths or 40 per cent to 7/12ths or about 57 per cent of the gross outturn. Provisions for the remission of taxes are recorded. But it was not done on any *doctrinaire* principle. Abatements were graduated according to the difficulties and cost of improvement effected by cultivators. Gardens were assessed at the same rates as cultivated lands. An additional one-sixth or 16-2/3 per cent had to be paid as excise on sales.

(*b*) *Taxes on Consumption.* Important taxes of the Kauṭalyan system were two-fold: customs and excise. Along with land revenue these constitute the mainstay of this finance. In Athens[1] under Pericles the policy of free trade appears to have been adopted, as the city depended for its food supply on external sources. Its normal customs duty was therefore as low as 2 per cent. The Roman *portoria* (customs dues) were higher, the earliest maximum being 5 per cent. The extreme maximum under Constantine was 12-1/2 per cent. But the Maurya tariff was high enough to verge on, if it did not actually establish, an economic "protection." Thus in regard to imported salt the empire demanded, in the first place, one sixth or 16-2/3 per cent of the entire commodity, and in the second place a 5 per cent as trade or sale tax on the remaining 5/6ths. Similarly

[1] *Enc. Brit.* (Finance); for a detailed account of Athenian finances see Schoemann, pp. 432-464.

foreign liquors, wines and intoxicants had to bear heavy import duties which varied from one-fifteenth or 6-2/3 per cent to one-tenth or 10 per cent of their value.[1] In both cases in addition to the tariff the government charged an extra duty in order to compensate the loss in the sale of local produce. The total maximum may have approached the British customs rate, which though down to 1700 not generally higher than 5 per cent rose to 25 per cent by 1759.[2]

The normal Kauṭalyan (Maurya) duty on foreign goods was one-fifth of their value, i.e., 20 per cent. One-sixth, i.e. 16-2/3 per cent was realized from fresh fruits, vegetables, pepper, dried fish, flesh and other perishable goods. The rates on conches, diamonds, pearls, etc. were to be fixed at the custom house by experts. Silk garments, arsenic oxide, skins, carpets etc. were charged *ad valorem* from 6 to 10 per cent. The minimum rates on the tariff schedule were 4 to 5 per cent. In order to be consistent, of course, the Empire severely dealt with all cases of smuggling. The highest fine of 3,000 *paṇas* or $750 was the punishment prescribed for this offence by the penal code. This was nothing extraordinary considering that the penalty for smuggling according to the latest law in the United States is a fine of $ 5,000 or imprisonment for two years or both. No figures are available as to the gross customs receipts. But it may be surmised that the 27 per cent of the total German Imperial revenues as accruing from customs alone would not have been envied by the Kauṭalyan chancellor.[3]

[1] *Ind. Ant.* 1905, pp. 53, 55.

[2] S. Dowell : *History of Taxation and Taxes in England* (London, 1884), Vol. I, pp. 82-88, 145, 146, 163-167, 211-223, Vol. II. p. 37.

[3] *Ind. Ant.*, 1905 pp. 49, 50; J. H. Higginson : *Tariffs at Work* (London, 1913), p. 112; Plehn, 184.

It might seem as if the Empire intended almost to place an embargo on foreign import. But there were certain tendencies in the fiscal policy of Kauṭalya in regard to international trade that should indicate a different character of the tariff. The protective duties were high indeed but they were not intended to be "prohibitive." Rather, on the other hand, there was a deliberate attempt on the part of the authorities to encourage foreign imports. They regulated the prices[1] in such a manner that a reasonable profit was assured to the dealer in imported goods. And if necessary, special instructions were issued to the proper officials to accord concessions in certain particulars to foreign merchants. Under these conditions it is doubtful if the Kauṭalyan tariff should be considered as "protective" in any significant sense. In any case its character as a measure for revenue purposes is unquestionable.

The duty of 1 per cent on all sales was a regular tax of the Roman Empire. Such an impost, call it market due, toll or octroi, was, as we have noted, prevalent in Athens also. The rates in the Kauṭalyan system were much higher. Commodities sold by cubical measure were charged 6-1/4 per cent, those by weighing 5 per cent, and those by computation 9-1/11 per cent *ad valorem*. This tax, known by the generic name of excise or inland trade revenue, was assessed by Kauṭalya in two ways. In certain lines, e.g., salt, precious metals, etc. he retained the monopoly of manufacture and sale for the government. But the general method of assess-

[1] *Ind. Ant.*, 1905, p. 57. Note the seven distinct expenses of marketing, *śulka* (toll), *vartanī* (road-cess), *ativāhika* (conveyance-cess), *gulma-deya* (duty payable at military stations), *tāra-deya* (ferry charge), *bhakta* (porter's wage) and *bhāga* (share of the state), that were calculated by the customs officials in fixing the price of the imported commodities.

ment was the grant of a license to the vendor or manufacturer.

The excise branch of the revenues was thoroughly centralized. The licensing procedure was most efficiently observed. Nobody was permitted to sell the goods at the places of growth or manufacture, e.g., fields, gardens, forests and mines. All commodities had to be brought to the customs house or toll office near the city gate. These were then marked with the state stamp called *abhijnāna-mudrā* (mark of identification) in *sindura* (vermilion). The tax was levied, however, only after sale. The law was strict, as evasion of the excise was a capital offence. False statements to the officials made by merchants in regard to amount or price were moreover punished as cases of theft, i.e., by fine, mutilation or even death (*Artha*, II, xxi.).

It is evident that the customs and excise receipts of the Kauṭalyan state were much more voluminous than those of the Roman Empire. Analogues for this aspect of Hindu finance have to be sought in modern states like England, France, and Czarist Russia, where half of the national revenues is made up of the returns from customs duties and excise, or the United States where virtually the whole of "federal" revenues is derived from these two elements in the consumption taxes.

Recent authorities on the "shifting" of taxation are for practical considerations inclined to do away with the formal or verbal distinction that economists have long drawn between the taxes on consumption (like customs and excise) and the taxes on property or income.[1] But using the conventional nomenclature we

[1] Giffen's art. on Taxation in the *Enc. Brit.* (*The Different Kinds of Taxes*), Seligman : *Shifting and Incidence of Taxation* (New York, 1902), pp. 310, 311.

have to mention that in addition to customs and excise, the so-called "indirect" taxes, the Kauṭalyan Empire levied "direct" taxes as well. It has already been pointed out, of course, that a great part of the land revenue was a direct tax on real estate in so far as land was the private property of citizens. The taxes on personality or movable property have now to be enumerated.

(*c*) *Direct Taxes*. In Kauṭalya's list we do not have the taxes on looms, oil-mills, etc. that are mentioned in the Chola inscriptions. Nor do the Tamil taxes on "sonship" or inheritance and succession appear in the *Arthaśāstra*. But, as we have seen, weights and measures were taxed.[1] Gamblers had to pay license. Dramatists, players, singers, and musicians were charged 5 *paṇas* ($1.25). This figure does not, however, explain the rate. A tax was levied from prostitutes as in Athens[2] and in Rome under Caligula.[3] As a rule, cattle were not taxed *per capita*. They figured in the *samāhartā*'s (collector-general's) book only in connection with the excise on sale. But under abnormal conditions, when an emergency finance was the problem, a special due was charged on domestic quadrupeds.[4] The same circumstances brought painters, sculptors, and artists generally within the tax-collector's grip.

It seems, on the whole, however, that Kauṭalya considered the taxes on property rather as a safety-valve to fall back on in dire necessity than as a normal source of regular Imperial revenues. And when the necessity arose (e.g., through war conditions) the Empire did not

[1] *Ind. Ant.*, 1905, pp. 50, 51, 58.
[2] Schoemann, p. 449.
[3] Seligman : *Essays*, pp. 36, 37.
[4] *Ind. Ant.*, 1905, pp. 59, 114.

hesitate to levy what were virtually "super-taxes" on both immovable and movable properties of the wealthier classes. In the first place, the rates of land tax were enhanced (*Artha*, V, ii). But regions barren or difficult to cultivate were exempted from this emergency taxation. And persons engaged in the "key" or "essential industries," e.g. in agriculture, forestry, and elephant-training, were likewise granted a privilege. In the second place, contributions in "services" were levied from "lack-landers," especially from culprits and bad characters. The government in co-operation with the *samāhartā* and the superintendent of agriculture was to improvise "war-farms" and "war-gardens," and induct such able-bodied persons into the work of cultivation (*Artha*, V, ii.).

In the third place, persons rearing pigs and cocks had to contribute 50 per cent of their stocks. Those who had sheep and goat farms were taxed 16-2/3 per cent, and herdsmen who reared cows and buffaloes 10 per cent. In the fourth place, a special levy of 500 *paṇas* ($ 125) was raised from merchants in diamonds, horses, and elephants. Dealers in cotton goods had to pay 400 *paṇas*, dealers in grains and liquids 300, traders in glass and glassware 200, artisans and carpenters 100, and dealers in mud-pots, inn-keepers and small retailers 50. In the fifth place, dramatists (and theatre managers?) as well as prostitutes had to surrender half their annual earnings. And lastly as in Athens, the government exacted extraordinary donations and gifts from temples and religious establishments. The process might almost be described as a legalized looting of ecclesiastical property by the secular authorities.

Some of the war-taxes were described by Kauṭalya euphemistically as *praṇaya* or "love"-gifts.[1] The

[1] Cf. "benevolences" in British fiscal history, Dowell, Vol. I. pp. 155-157, 202, 203, 243 etc.

Empire used to pose as "beggar" and appeal to the "patriotism" of the citizens for "voluntary" subscriptions. And in order that the "modernism" of Kauṭalyan finance may be appreciated still further it has to be pointed out that titles of honour were conferred by the government on the patriotic contributors. Subscribers to the "liberty fund" were honoured, for instance, with a rank in the court, an umbrella, or a turban or some ornaments in return for their gold. Moreover, the government took special steps to advertise and give publicity to the donations of the patriots in order to create a spirit of rivalry among the rich in the acts of self-sacrifice (*Artha*, V, ii.).

It was not with an alleged Machiavellian wickedness but in quite the scientific methods of "high finance" that Kauṭalya approached the problem of financing a war or meeting an emergency. The financial experts of the civil service knew how to cause the rich to "vomit" (*vamana*) their accumulated wealth or otherwise deplete and drain (*karṣaṇa*) them of their property (*Artha*, IV, iii.) Exploitation of "gold-lords" by the state was a process of expropriation that the *Artha-śāstra* does not hesitate to pronounce as the objective of the "ways and means" committee. Like the "liturgies" and *eisphora* of the Athenian city state[1] high imposts of various denominations were therefore borne by people of large incomes in the Kauṭalyan state. And the impact of war or emergency finance must have tended to make the demands of the government even in normal times "progressive" in spirit, if not mathematically so.

(*d*) *Fines.* We shall now consider the "non-tax" revenues of Kauṭalya. These were principally of two classes: one derived from the penal (*daṇḍa*-inflicting)

[1] *Enc. Brit.* (Finance).

power of the state, the other from the economic activities of the government. The Empire as *daṇḍa-dhara*, i.e., "sanction"-exercising organization must have realized an enormous amount from fines, as these were the usual penalties inflicted by the courts of justice. The list of "crimes" was lengthy. The arms of law could reach almost any individual. Dealers in foreign goods had as many chances of transgressing the *śāsanas* (commands of the state) as the butchers in municipal areas. The number of offences against sanitary laws was as large as that against the prescribed hours and places of fording rivers. Persons committing nuisance on roads and other specified spots were fined one *paṇa* (twenty-five cents). Travellers without passports (bearing government stamps) had to pay a fine of 12 *paṇas*. Bearers of false or forged passes were fined 1000 *paṇas*. No foreigners were admitted into the country without permit. Delinquents had to pay a fine of 3000 *paṇas* the highest fine sanctioned in Kauṭalyan legislation. This was the fine also meted out to those who tried to smuggle foreign goods in evasion of customs duties. Negligence in having the day's government stamp fixed on weights and scales was fined 27-1/4 *paṇas*. A fine of 600 *paṇas* was inflicted on the merchant who having imported foreign salt failed to compensate the government for the loss it might incur in not finding customers for its own salt.

(*e*) *Economic Earnings.* The second head of non-tax revenue comprises the items of income that the Empire derived from its economic enterprises. Shipping lines with fleets of boats for passengers and goods were operated by the state. The traffic by sea was large enough to render the undertaking a lucrative proposition. The Empire carried on another business under the supervision of the naval department. State boats were let out on hire by the *nāvadhyakṣa* or port commissioner for purposes of pearl fishery and the fishing of conch shells. The ferry charges on rivers must also be considered in connection with the government's commercial ventures. These were regulated according to the size of rivers and the amount of freight carried[1]. Any load of commodities whether for sale or not was charged four *māṣās* (about six cents). One *māṣā* was paid by a traveller with a minor quadruped carrying some load. Two *māṣās* were demanded for a load carried on the head or on the shoulders, a cow or a horse. Double was the rate for transporting a camel or a buffalo. The ferry charge for a small cart was five *māṣās*, for one of medium size drawn by bulls six *māṣās*, and for a big cart seven *māṣās*. The ferry dues on large rivers were twice the respective rates.

But by far more important than these quasi-political commercial undertakings as sources of "sinews of war" or "roots of the army" were the industries owned and run or controlled by the government. Altogether three state-monopolies are mentioned in the Kauṭalyan schedule. The first monopoly was oil. The oil seeds were all brought to the government granary and pressed and made into oil by the state mills. The administration of tobacco monopoly in France since the time of Colbert (1674) furnishes a modern analogue. The next monopoly was salt, as we have mentioned above. In order to "protect" this government industry the Empire legislated that purchasers of foreign salts must have to pay compensation to cover the loss sustained by the state. Evidently foreign salt was not excluded altogether from the territory. There was, besides, the system of granting license by which private capitalists could manufacture and sell the commodity. In addition

[1] *Ind. Ant.*, 1905, pp. 53, 111, 112, Sixteen *māṣās* make one *paṇa*.

to the economic "profits" from the salt industry the government thus came to realize a large revenue from the customs, excise, and licenses.

The realization of salt *gabelle* was three-fold. First, the importing merchant had to pay the regular 16-2/3 per cent as customs *plus* the 5 per cent on the remainder as excise. Secondly, the indigenous manufacturer purchased license from the government on the same terms. There was thus no economic discrimination against foreign salt. The effects of a countervailing excise duty were brought in operation, indicating the "fiscal" character of the tariff. And thirdly, it appears that the government charged 13-1/8 per cent as premium on the money that it received as price for the salt collected from the importer and the home manufacturer.

The most important monopoly of the Kauṭalyan system was the mines and minerals. Indeed the manufacture of salt was scheduled in the *Artha-śāstra* under the category of mining. As defined by Kauṭalya mining was a comprehensive term, including as in mediaeval British law "wreck of the sea and royal fish[1]." There were therefore two branches of mining according to Kauṭalya: (1) ocean mining, i.e., pearl fishery, the fishing of conch shells and corals, and manufacture of salt, and (2) land mining. The revenues from land mining were described as those accruing from gold mines, silver mines, mines of rubies, and metals such as iron, copper etc[2].

In ancient and mediaeval legislation or custom mines were "public" everywhere[3]. The silver mines at

[1] Palgrave, Vol. II. p. 765.
[2] Law : *Hindu Polity*, pp. 5-10.
[3] For a general discussion on "state mines" see C. F. Bastable: *Public Finance* (London, 1903), pp. 174-176.

Laurium were owned by Athens. Mines were state property under the Roman Empire. Down to 1688 all English mines belonged to the Crown. In 1568 the Exchequer Chamber stated the theory that the "king shall have the whole of the base metal."[1] According to Kauṭalya also both land and ocean mines as well as the essaying of ores, coining, and commerce in minerals were *jura regalia*, or Crown rights *sui generis*. But the mines were not worked by the government except when the operations needed small outlay. Modern advocates of modified *laissez faire*, i.e., partial public ownership may quote the Kauṭalyan precedent as an instance of the "individualistic minimum" of state intervention in industry. As a rule, the Empire let out the mines on royalty basis to private enterprise. The royalty included nine distinct items. As usual, the rates were high. The rental for the Laurium mines was only 4-1/6 per cent. The French mines yielded 10 per cent. The English rate on copper was 12-1/2 per cent to the state *plus* 11-1/9 per cent to the landlord. But Kauṭalya demanded 16/2/3 to 20 per cent as *vibhāga*, i.e., the government's "share" in the yield. In addition the capitalists had to pay 13-1/8 per cent *plus* 5 per cent as sundry charges[2].

There may have been some other industries similarly undertaken or let out on license with a view to augmenting the public income. The shipbuilding and munitions industries were of course state monopolies, as has been mentioned above. But obviously they are to be considered not so much from the standpoint of finance as of national defence.

[1] Palgrave, loc. cit.

[2] *Ind. Ant.* 1905, p. 113, Schoemann, p. 448. Brissaud, p. 487, Palgrave, *loc. lit.*, *Ind. Ant. loc. cit.* Islamic law has 20 per cent, *cf.* Aghnides, 528.

(*f*) *Miscellaneous Collections.* Several miscellaneous taxes remain to be discussed as minor sources of income. The port duties[1] realized by the *nāvadhyakṣa* were distinct from both customs and excise. Villages on sea shores and on the banks of rivers and lakes were assessed at certain rates. The fishing license demanded by the state was one-sixth or 16-2/3 per cent of the actual haul. Merchants had to pay the customary tax of port towns. Another group of minor collections came from currency. A premium of 13-1/8 per cent was regularly charged on coins of private or foreign mintage[2]. Besides, the same amount was realized by the government on every occasion that anybody had to pay fine in cash[3]. Finally, we have to mention the escheats. Houses, fields, gardens, tanks and temples lapsed to the state, as we have seen, if the proprietors neglected to exercise their rights of ownership for five years (*cf*, Manu VIII, 30). Similarly the Empire was the heir of prostitutes' property in the absence of daughters.

No conceivable resource of the people appears thus to have been left untapped by Kauṭalya. The all-reaching tentacles of Hindu finance lie on the surface. And if, as Adam Smith remarks, there be "nothing in which governments are so prone to learn of one another as in the matter of new taxes, the Hindu empires of pre-Moslem India can still give points to the latest specialists in public finance. For, the methods and principles of statesmen from Kauṭalya to Kulottūṃga were eminently matter-of-fact and realistic. Indeed, with the exception of stamp duties, national debt, postal receipts and a few others characteristically modern, the assets

[1] R. K. Mookerji : *Indian Shipping* (London, 1911), p. 106.
[2] *Ind. Ant.* 1905, p. 53.
[3] *Ibid.* pp. 9, 54, 57.

schedule of the first class powers of today can hardly exhibit any taxes and non-tax revenues in addition to what the Hindu statesman-philosopher Kauṭalya hit upon pragmatically in the third and fourth centuries B. C.

The Ability to Pay

A study of the finances provokes naturally the correlated investigation into the general economic condition of the empire. But as yet it is hardly allowable to attempt a wide solution as to the "ability" of the people to meet the diverse demands of the government. In the first place, a great rise in prices may be postulated because of the high rate of customs and excise. This was sure to be felt by the entire community as consumers. In the second place, the normal land tax of 40 to 57 per cent, though it may not have shorn the landowning or agricultural classes to the skin, was certainly not a moderate levy. In the third place, the traders and the intellectual middle classes could not get scot-free from the Imperial demand as the property tax was mercilessly applied to them especially in emergencies. And in the fourth place, the moneyed aristocracy, bankers, gilds and other wealthy groups had to "vomit" out their gold at the call of the empire.

Economically speaking, then, we have no grounds for believing that there was any class-discrimination of the type to which France, for instance, was a victim during the *ancien régime*. Kauṭalya maintained no privileged class on anything like an appreciable scale. Nor would the government demands, though heavy, appear to have been oppressive or likely to sap the economic foundations of the society. On the contrary, there were certain distinctive services by which the state sought to develop the "staying power" and taxable capacity of the *prakriti* (subject). We have spoken above of the socialistic trend of Hindu states as *Dharmastaaten*, in so far as the sphere of their activity was co-extensive with the range of human interests. It is necessary now to add that the same tendency is noticeable in two other directions.

First, the Kauṭalyan Empire owned several industries and controlled the production of wealth in certain lines. Government supervision of some sort or other brought the economic functions of the people within the compass of partial "public ownership." The consequent abolition of *entrepreneurs* or middlemen in a few channels of business was a positive advantage to the community. Secondly, the Empire sought to regulate by legislation the more important branch of the nation's economic life, viz., distribution and exchange, i.e., value. The maximum rate of interest was determined by the government[1]. The market was protected from the ravages of "profiteers." Reasonable prices and fair profits were fixed by official experts after calculating the legitimate expenses of production including the cost of marketing. The government scheduled likewise the rates of wages and fees for laundrymen, painters, dramatists, singers, and artists.

Such an Imperial intervention in the *prakriti*'s economic activity or what is the same thing, such "state socialism" under "enlightened despots" must have been appreciated at least by the common labourer. The rate of wages in Kauṭalyan India was 5 *paṇas* a month or 15 dollars a year. It is interesting to observe that in Chola India in the eleventh and twelfth centuries a

[1] The rate was 15 per cent per year (Law : *Hind. Pol.* pp. 171-177). The usual rate at Athens was 12 to 18 per cent (Schoemann, p. 435).

temple janitor earned 8-1/3 Rupees per month, i.e., $ 30 a year.[1] These rates, however low by the present day Eur-American, standard, should appear to have been quite above the rates determined by the Ricardian "iron law of wages" when compared with the current prices and the purchasing power of money during the two periods.[2]

And as for the salaries paid by the government (*Artha*, V, iii.) they were liberal enough to satisfy the officers' appetite. They were, indeed, humanly speaking, calculated to prevent the desire for "squeeze." The common soldier of the Kauṭalyan Empire received 500 *paṇas* ($ 125) per year. The highest salary in the third and fourth centuries B. C., e.g., that for the generalissimo was 48,000 *paṇas* ($ 12,000) a year. The *samāhartā* (collector-general) was paid at half this rate. The earning of a middle class man, e.g., of an accountant in Southern India under the Cholas was 16-2/3 Rupees per month, i.e., 60 dollars a year.[3] Payments were either in kind or in money. The Cholas used to pay even handicraftsmen often in land for customary work. Under Kauṭalya payment in gold might be commuted for that in kind at fixed rates.[4]

We are not concerned here with "index numbers" or the statistics of wages and prices nor with the manner in which the tariff, if it was really protective to some

[1] *Ind. Ant.*, 1905, pp. 53, 55-57, 59.

[2] *Ind. Ant.*, 1905, p. 53. One Rupee in Kauṭalyan India bought 49 *sers* (Madras) of rice. In British India one Rupee today buys not more than 8 *sers*. Cf. Aiyangar, p. 183. These comparisons must not be taken too literally, however.

[3] Aiyangar, p. 181.

[4] *Ind. Ant.*, 1909, p. 264; 1905, p. 53. For 5 *paṇas* one obtained 165 *sers* (Madras) about the beginning of the present century.

extent, may have affected the course of investments, commerce and industries. The stray figures for the third and fourth centuries B. C. and the eleventh and twelfth centuries A. C. may be taken for what they are worth. Only, it is necessary to bear in mind that in British India today the average *per capita* income is Rs. 42 or 14 dollars *per annum*. On the whole, then, it may reasonably be concluded that the financial burden[1] of *pax sārva-bhaumica* (peace of the world-empire), howsoever heavy it might be whether absolutely or relatively, was easily borne by a contended peasantry and working class, a prosperous industrial and commercial aristocracy, and last but not least, a well-paid civil service and army.

SECTION 4

AGRICULTURE, MANUFACTURE AND COMMERCE IN INDIAN ECONOMY

The River-Economy

The country of the authors of the Sukra cycle is not only a land of hills but it is also a land of rivers. The suggestion that the capital should be built at a

[1] For price-schedules see Pran Nath: *A Study in the Economic Condition of Ancient India* (London, 1929) and Kauṭalyan finance, B. Breloer : *Kauṭalya-Studien* III. *Staatsverwaltung im alten Indien Erster Band* (Leipzig, 1934), as well as the present author's "Kauṭalya, Economic Planning and Climatology" in the *Indian Historical Quarterly* (Calcutta), for June, 1935. For general considerations of finance see his *Positive Background of Hindu Sociology* Vol. II. Part I (Allahabad, 1921) as well as U. N. Ghoshal : *Agrarian Systems in Ancient India* (Calcutta, 1930) and *Contributions to the History of Hindu Revenue Systems* (Calcutta, 1930), K. V. R. Aiyangar: *Aspects of Ancient Indian Economic Thought* (Benares, 1934). See also the last footnote to the next section as well as footnote 1 to the section on "Treatises of Hindu Economics."

place that is bestirred by the movements of boats indicates the importance given to rivers by Sukra in his description of an ideal economico-political organisation. That the authors were very familar with rivers would be evident from the political application that naturally suggested itself to them in the matter of diplomatic relations. Thus in advising rulers to bow down to powerful enemies Sukrāchāryya illustrates his point by the mention of the fact that the 'cloud never moves against the current of the wind' and that 'the rivers never leave the downward course.' A common natural phenomenon has been here pressed into service to explain what in terms of modern statesmanship would be called 'moving along the line of least resistance.' So also in advising the king to restrain passions and try cases or administer *Vyavahāras* according to *Dharma*, the author mentions that the subjects follow the king who does this "as the rivers the ocean." The fact that Sukrāchāryya has to lay down the humane rule that if a "bound-down" or *asiddha* person violates the limitations imposed upon him when swimming a river, &c., he is not guilty (and should not be punished) is also an evidence in point. The rule that "anybody who can save somebody's wealth from absolute destruction owing to the ravages of water of deluge (from rivers, &c.) has right to one-tenth" points to the same adaptation of juristic ideas to the physical features of the country (IV, v, lines 601-2).[1]

Rivers are no negligible features in the topography of the country for which Sukrāchāryya's code has been designed. The fact that rivers are very changeful and constantly shift their beds was well-known (III, 283-84). And the advice that one should not cross the

[1] The references to the *Śukranīti* are to lines and not to *ślokas*; See the English translation by the present author (Allahabad, 1914).

rivers by arms or get into a boat that is likely to give way, indicates the familiarity of the authors with rivers. These are to be wisely used, says he, in the interests of the state's commerce. Means must be adopted to make them highways of water-traffic, as also the impediments presented by them to land-communication must be removed. That rivers should not be allowed to remain barriers to intercourse, as naturally they are, is sufficiently suggested in the following advice: "Bridges should be constructed over rivers. There should also be boats and water-conveyances for crossing the rivers." "Roads are to be provided with bridges" (IV, iv, 125-129).

But rivers have been mentioned in the *Sukranīti* specially in connection with agriculture and land-revenue, and the inferences that can be made from accounts of the natural resources of the state do also point to the importance of rivers as sources of the country's national wealth. The observation of Herodotus that 'Egypt is the gift of the Nile' is in the Hindu sage's language expressed by saying that the lands are the 'daughters' of rivers, or rivers are the 'mothers' of soils. But rivers are not the sole irrigators of lands. There are other mothers of lands also, e.g., rain, tanks, wells, &c. In the assessment of lands the ruler is advised to make a distinction between land and land on the basis of the nature of the source of water-supply. Thus "the king should realise one-third, one-fourth, or one-half from places which are irrigated by tanks, canals and wells,. by rain and by rivers respectively." The equity of this diversity of assessment lies in the fact that where rivers are irrigators the cultivation is certain, and hence the Government demand is heaviest. But Sukrāchāryya is also aware of the fact that though rivers are superior to all other sources of irrigation in point of certainty, the moisture yielded by them, however, is not copious,—and do in fact yield the palm to clouds which, though precarious and uncertain, give abundant water when they do pour down their contents. The difference between rivers and clouds is like that between ordinary well-to-do men and sovereigns in the matter of riches. And the analogy that naturally suggests itself is expressed in the following lines: "Can the nourishment that is due to the rain-water from clouds be derived from the water of rivers &c.? So also the promotion of the people's weal depends on the property of the king. Can this accrue from the wealth of the rich folk"? (III, 552-554, IV, ii, 227-229).

From the above account of rivers it would have been sufficiently clear that the authors of the Sukra cycle were well-acquainted with the importance of rivers in politics, commerce, agriculture and public finance, and that the general aspect of the country is that of a plain intersected by rivers rather than that of rugged mountainous defiles and precipices.

Mining, Metallurgy and Smithery

The following is the list of metals known to Vedic technocracy : *Ayas* (bronze, iron),[1] *Kārṣṇāyasa* (iron), *Chandra* (gold), *Jātarūpa* (gold), *Trapu* (tin), *Rajata* (silver), *Loha* (copper), *Lohāyasa*, *Lohitāyasa*, *Śyāma* (iron), *Śyāmāyasa*, *Sīsa* (lead), *Suvarṇa* (gold), *Harita* (gold), *Hiraṇya* (gold).

Rudra is described as shining with brilliant golden ornaments. The Aświns are also adorned with golden ornaments. The Asuras had plenty of gold and jewels.

[1] P. Neogi : *Iron in Ancient India* (Calcutta, 1915), M. Banerji: "Metals and Metallurgy in Ancient India" (*Indian Historical Quarterly*), March and December, 1927, also June, 1930, June, 1932.

"Blacksmiths made spears, swords, hatchets, needles, awls, iron legs for those who had lost their natural ones, iron-forts etc. Goldsmiths melted gold and fashioned bright jewels."

In India as described in the Kauṭalyan *Arthaśāstra* there were two classes of mines, viz. (1) ocean-mines and (2) land-mines. The duty of the Superintendent of ocean-mines was to look after the collection of diamonds, and other precious stones, pearls, corals &c. The Superintendent of land-mines had to perform the difficult work of prospecting and discovering new mines on plains and mountain slopes. Silver ores are those which have the colour of *śaṃkha* and do not emit much foam and smoke. Similarly, we find mentioned the properties of the ores of gold, bitumen, copper, lead, tin, iron &c. Incidentally it is interesting to observe that the Brāhmaṇa who committed heinous offence might be condemned to the mines.

Megasthenes relates in his *Indika* that, whilst the land on its surface bears all kinds of cultivated fruits, it has underneath numerous veins of all sorts of metals, for it is in possession of much gold and silver, and not a little copper and iron, yea, even tin and other metals which are used in the manufacture of useful articles and ornaments, as well as implements of war. He further says that Taprobane (Ceylon) produces more gold and more large pearls than the continent of India and that the people's raiment is interwoven with gold and ornamented with gems.

Broadly speaking, there were, in Seal's analysis, three great discoveries in applied chemistry to which India owed her capture of the world-markets : (1) the preparation of fast dyes for textile fabrics by the treatment of natural dyes like *manjiṣṭha* with alum and other chemicals; (2) the extraction of the principle of indigotin from the indigo plant by a process, which, however crude, is essentially an anticipation of modern chemical methods; and (3) the tempering of steel in a manner worthy of advanced metallurgy, a process to which the mediaeval world owed its Damascus swords.

According to authors of the Sukra cycle, as to all Hindu writers, the Earth is full of wealth, and Kuvera is the deity presiding over it. They appreciate *Kuveratā* or the possession of wealth more than many other qualifications, though, of course, it is inferior to *Iśatā* or overlordship, i.e., sovereignty. They would therefore enjoy the good things of this world and advise others to do so.

In this pursuit of wealth they do not scruple to disembowel the "unsunned" treasure of the underground universe and search its entrails wide and deep. It is because of this that we have the very old European tradition about the 'wealth of Ind' in the gorgeous East which "with richest hand showers on her kings barbaric pearls and gold." Mining becomes thus one of the occupations of the people, and the rulers have a right to its yield. Among other functions the *Sumantra* or Finance Minister of the state has to study the amount of revenue realised through mines. This income from the mines is described as *itara* or other than *pārthiva* (i.e. terrestrial), according to the public finance of the Sukra statesmen. "Duties, fines, royalties on mines, prices and contributions, etc. are known to constitute non-terrestrial income according to writers and specialists." The mention of mines among the regions of *sulka* or duty which is the king's share from the buyer and the seller points also to the importance of mining as an item that feeds the income-schedule of the state budget. So we read (*Sukra*, IV, ii, 233-235): "The king should realise from minerals at the following rates: half of gold, one-third of silver, one-fourth of copper, one-sixth of iron, tin and lead, half of gems, half of alkalis; after the expenses have been met." The ruler is also advised to appoint miners to their proper works and store by minerals carefully for emergency or other purposes (II, 404-405).

In Hindu economics not only the miners, but goldsmiths, coppersmiths and other metal-workers as well require patronage and "protection" of the State. The *Sukranīti* (IV, iv, 85-87) advises that "the king should always keep in his kingdom the tools and implements of the metal-workers after inspecting them" and find occupation for "those who make lighter machines, gunpowder, arrows, cannon-balls, and swords, and construct various tools and implements, arms and weapons, bows and quivers, etc.; those who prepare ornaments of gold, jewels, etc., builders of chariots, stone-carvers, blacksmiths, and those who enamel metals."

This enumeration of the industries connected with metallurgy to be encouraged by the king involves also a good deal of legislation on the subject. Thus among the laws to be promulgated among the people one is that "falsehood must not be practised by anyone with regard to the standard of weights and measurements, currency, some kinds of metals etc." (I. 587-592). So also "the man who adulterates metals deserves double the punishment" (IV, v. 660). State intervention in industry cannot be one-sided. If it is the duty of the ruler to maintain the artists and artisans and thus "protect" them with work and wages, it is also his look-out to see that the people should be protected from them. Hence guardianship of the state must be exercised against the dangers of false and counterfeit coinage and the passing of base metals for genuine and high class commodities.

An account of the fabrication of imitation-jewellery in Hindu India has been preserved in the dramatic literature of the 1st cent. B. C. In the *Mrichchhakatika* (*Troy Cart*) of Śūdraka a question is raised about the identity of certain ornaments produced in a court of justice, and the discussion is as follows:

"*Judge*—Do you know these ornaments?

Mother—Have I not said? They may be different though like. I cannot say more; they may be imitations made by some skilful artists.

Judge—It is true. Provost, examine them; they may be different though like; the dexterity of the artists is no doubt very great, and they readily fabricate imitations of ornaments they have once seen, in such a manner that the difference shall scarcely be discernible."

The examination of metals as to their genuineness and worth thus becomes an important function of the state as well as people. The Sukra statesmen know very well that metals may be made to acquire artificial character, and have mentioned the preparation of artificial gold as an art or one of the sixty-four *kalās* (IV, iii, 178-180). The testing of minerals must therefore be an important branch of learning and is referred to as a *kalā*. And the wise men are those who know how to determine their value by carefully examining them. One test is given in the following lines: "If two pieces of a metal—one pure and the other suspected as alloy—be successively passed through the same hole, and threads of equal length be drawn out of them and weighed, and if the weights of both are equal, then the metal is unalloyed, otherwise not" (IV, ii. 178-179).

We have already referred to some of the industries connected with metal work. The use and manufacture of seals and emblems are mentioned in the *Sukranīti* at several places (II, 490-91, 739-40). Thus, "one should put on the clothes, uniforms and emblems granted by the King;" "they should put down their seals over it at the end of the writing;" "the king should give to each cultivator the deed of rent having his own mark (seal)." These and other manufactures are suggested also in the enumeration of the *kalās*, e.g., (1) melting, powdering, incineration etc., of metals, (2) the knowledge of the mixtures of metals and herbs of medicinal plants, (3) analysis and synthesis of metals, (4) preparation of alloys, (5) alkalis and salts, (6) cleansing and polishing, (7) dyeing of stone and metal vessels, (8) making of ornaments, (9) enamelling, (10) preparation of tools and implements, etc.[1]

Besides the important part played in commercial, social, religious, and literary lives of the people of India, the metals and gems have had their influence on Indian art also. The architecture as well as sculpture of Hindustan bear abundant testimony to the treatment of *dhātus* and *ratnas* by artists. In their historical works Fergusson, Rajendralal Mitra, Havell, Smith, and Manomohan Ganguly have sufficiently noted the manipulation of metals and gems in Hindu art. The tenth chapter of Smith's work, that on Hindu minor arts, deals among other things with the following topics relevant to the points discussed here: (1) coinage, (2) gems, seals and jade, (3) jewellery, (4) reliquaries and gold images, (5) silver patera and bowels, (6) copper-vessels.

The use of metals for the fabrication of domestic vessels is as old as Vedic India. The *Rig-Veda* alludes

[1] A. Venkatasubbiyah : *The Kalās* (Madras 1911).

to golden cups. The *Sūtras* and the *Mahābhārata* frequently refer to vessels of other than gold and clay. Tvastra, the Vulcan of the Hindu pantheon, was the most celebrated artificer of metallic arms, but the Ribhus greatly excelled him in the formation of sacrificial vessels of wood and metal.

Plant Industry and Trade

The *Periplus* mentions, among other articles of trade that passed through the ports on the Arabian and Bengal coasts in the first century B.C., pepper, betel, spice, wine, wheat, sandal, aghil (kind of black aromatic wood). These uses of flora as commercial merchandise, i.e. articles of trade or as raw materials for the thousand and one arts and industries in secular life demand our attention here. The mention of or allusion to these industrial arts in the *Sukranīti*[1] is to be noticed mainly in the sections dealing with the 64 *kalās* and with the list of artisans to be maintained by the state, but should also be sought here and there and everywhere in the treatise. References to constructions of bridges, boats, cars, chariots, war-implements, arms and weapons, wooden images, temples, palaces, forts, ploughs etc. as well as other processes and products that point to the utilisation of timber and the art of the carpenter, are instances in point, and bespeak the existence of timber-merchants as well as various grades of wood-carvers and carpenters connected with domestic, religious, architectural, military and agricultural arts.

We have to note the Ayurvedic preparations from the vegetable drugs of the country mentioned in *Sukra-*

[1] G. P. Majumdar : *Upavana-Vinoda* (a Sanskrit Treatise on Arbori-horticulture), Calcutta 1935, which makes use of *Śukranīti* and other texts in the introduction.

nīti, as well as the trade in medicinal herbs, suggested by various passages in it. The mention of honey as a floral produce is interesting.

Other *kalās* or industries connected with plants are (1) cleansing, polishing, dyeing, etc. of wooden vessels, (2) preparation of boats, chariots and conveyances, (3) preparation of threads and ropes, (4) weaving of fabrics by various threads, (5) extraction of oil from seeds, (6) climbing of trees, (7) preparation of vessels with bamboo, straws, etc. and (8) making and preservation of betels.

The means of livelihood enumerated in the *Śukranīti* (I. 311-312) are: (1) learned professions—art of teaching etc., (2) service, (3) heroism (soldier's art), (4) agriculture, (5) usury, (6) commerce, shop-keeping, (7) industries and arts, (8) begging.

Agriculture is one of the four subjects dealt with in the science of *Vārttā*. "In *Vārttā* are discussed (1) interest, (2) agriculture, (3) commerce, and (4) breeding of cows. The man who is well up in *Vārttā* need not be anxious for earnings." About the occupation of agriculture Śukrāchāryya's general idea is (1) that it is superior to that of the Vaiśyas, i.e. commerce, and the menial service of the Śūdras; and (2) that it is too important to be left to a proxy (III. 552-54).

Even Brāhmaṇas can take to agriculture according to Manu, says Śukrāchāryya (III. 364-67).

Among the 64 *kalās* we have only one connected with agriculture, viz. that of drawing the plough (IV, iii, 37). It would thus appear that agriculture was not probably regarded as a *kalā*. Besides, it may be remarked that the country of Śukrāchāryya was not purely an agricultural one, but industrial as well.

In agriculture, as in shop-keeping and other occupations, women are to be assistants of males, says Śukra (IV, iv. 54).

Agriculture is also one of the occupations which should be patronised by the state (IV, iv, 54).

The equitable law of Śukra statesmen exempts agriculturists in the harvest seasons from liability to give evidence (IV, iv, 85-87). Another law with regard to the peasant class is that, like the artists, ascetics, etc. the cultivators should have their disputes decided "according to the usages of their guild," because "it is impossible to detect them through others' help" (IV, v,206-207). The truth and evidences are to be found out with the help of persons born of (i.e. connected with) them. Śukra legislators have mentioned a third law relating to the peasants. This is about joint-stock enterprise which "applies equally to commerce and agriculture" (IV, v, 35-37). The law is stated below:

"Those who deal in gold, grain and liquid (collectively) will have earnings according to the amount of their share, greater, equal or less." (IV, v, 614-617).

It is to be noticed that all these secular laws apply to the Mlechchhas also, though they may follow "other masters in religious beliefs and practices."

About agricultural tools and implements the *Śukranīti* is not a good source of information. We have noticed the plough already. About agricultural livestock we have the following rule:

Brāhmaṇas	should	have	16	cows to	their ploughs.
Kṣatriyas	"	"	12	"	"
Vaiśyas	"	"	8	"	"
Sūdras	"	"	4	"	"
Antyajas	"	"	2	"	"

There are various kinds of soils with varying degrees of fertility and access to market. The Sukra financiers recognise the consequent variation in agricultural returns and have apportioned the land revenue in an equitable manner. The following land-laws are what we get about rents, revenues, tenures, etc. affecting the agricultural population of the country:

(1) The king should receive rent from the peasant in such a way that the latter be not destroyed. It is to be realized in the fashion of the weaver of the garland who, in plucking flowers from plants, takes care that the stock be not exhausted, and not of the charcoal or fuel merchant who destroys the wood altogether (IV, ii, 222-23; I, 418-19; II, 345-346).

(2) That agriculture is successful which yields a profit twice the expenditure (including Government demand) after duly considering variations in actual produce (IV, ii, 224-26).

(3) The king should realise (*a*) one-third from places irrigated by tanks, canals and wells, (*b*) one-fourth from places irrigated by rains, (*c*) one-half from riparian soils, and (*d*) one-sixth from barren and rocky soils (IV, ii, 227-30).

(4) If people cultivate new land and dig tanks, canals, wells, etc. for their good, the king should not demand anything of them till they have realized profit twice the expenditure (IV, ii, 242-44).

(5) Income of the state from land or land revenue is called *Pārthiva* (terrestrial) Income. This is various according to the sources, e.g., natural waters, artificial waters, villages, cities etc. (II, 668-70).

(6) The king should give to each cultivator the deed of rent having his own mark or seal (IV, ii, 247).

(7) The apportionment and realisation of land-

revenue are to be managed in the following way (IV, ii, 248-252):

(*a*) Having determined the land-revenue of the village the king should receive it from one rich man in advance, or accept a guarantee for the payment of that in monthly or periodical instalments;

(*b*) Or the king should appoint officers, called *grāmapas*, by paying one-sixteenth, one-twelfth, or one-eighth of his own receipts.

(8) If necessary, the king should set apart lands for houses to be built by peasants (I, 423-24).

(9) It is one of the functions of the *Sumantra* or Finance Minister to study the amounts of land, in cultivation and out of cultivation, to know the realisers of rent and the amount realized etc. (II, 204-10).

Cattle-breeding and Animal Industries

Milk is one of the most important products of the animal world. Among the 64 *kalās* we have two connected with this, viz., milking and churning (IV, ii, 182). Similarly, ghee is also mentioned in the *Sukranīti* as an article of great economic importance. One of the important items of state interference in Indian industry and commerce seems to have been the prevention of adulteration in food-stuffs. We find Sukrāchāryya combating this evil. The regulation is given in the following lines: "Falsehoods must not be practised by any one with regard to ghee, honey, milk, fat etc." (I, 590-2). Sukrāchāryya's state is a guardian of the people's health and wealth, according to what moderns would call the "socialistic principle."

Not these innocent industries only,—but even the more cruel and untouchable ones are noticed in the *Sukranīti*. Thus in addition to the above two *kalās* we have three more connected with animal life in the list of 64 arts, namely,

(1) Softening of leathers (IV, iii, 180).
(2) Flaying of skins from the bodies of beasts (IV, iii, 181).
(3) Extraction of oil from flesh (fats) (IV, iii, 187).

It is to be understood, as a matter of course, that the chemical and mechanical processes allied or auxiliary to the above industries must also have been well known.

Commerce and industry in leather must have been important enough. We do not find any reference to fishermen as a class or fishing as an occupation. But we read of bird-catchers and leather merchants among other classes of persons who deserve state encouragement (II. 407).

And at least one product of the leather-industry was in demand, viz., shoes. Thus, among the general rules of morality to be observed by both people and princes, we have the following: "One should always bear medicinal substances in jewels, etc. consecrated by *mantras*, have umbrellas and shoes, and walk in the streets with eyes fixed on the straight path only" (III, 8-9). Here we have the ideal of material life that a gentleman of the Śukra days was expected to follow; and shoes form an item in what would have been regarded as the 'proper' or decent dress of a householder. That the use of shoes was rather common would be evident from the following happy adage of Śukrāchāryya also: "It is better to cover feet with shoes than try to cover the whole earth with leather" (III, 574).

Flesh or meat as a diet is known to the Śukra authors, but, like fishing, meat-eating is a purely local custom confined, as it is, to the artisans and artists of Madhyadeśa.

Worms and insects as destroyers of grains are known to Sukra authors (III. 574). They have advised the king not to accumulate for future use those that have been thus attacked by pests. Among the presents brought by princes and potentates of various parts of India to king Yudhiṣṭhira, referred to in the *Sabhāparva* of the *Mahābhārata*, various skins are mentioned. The skins of animals that lie in holes, and of wild cats, i.e. the furs of varieties of martin and weasel families, were brought by the Kāmbojas of the Hindu Kush; blankets by the Ābhiras of Gujarat; clothes of the wool of sheep and goats or thread spun by worms (silks) by the Scythians, Tukharas and Kankas; housings for elephants by princes of the Eastern tribes, lower Bengal, Midnapur, and Ganjam. Pāṇini, also, has not only given words for wool, cotton, weaving, cloth, turbans, sewing, etc. but also gives a special rule (IV, iii, 42). Woollen stuffs and furs as well as silks are mentioned by Vālmīki among the constituents of Sītā's trousseau (*Rāmāyaṇa*, I, 74). It may also be added that animal products, e.g., the hair of yak, gour, gayal and other bovine animals living in hills were used in the manufacture of one species of *chāmaras*, or flying flappers, described in the *Yuktikalpataru* as one of the most important insignia of royalty. Some idea of economic zoology may be formed from the fact that the author mentions the Meru, Himālaya, Kailāsa, Malaya, Vindhya, Gandhamādana and other mountains as the habitats of the animals yielding the requisite hairs of various kinds.

We know the tender story of Bharata's placing a pair of Rāma's slippers on the vacant throne of Ayodhyā to officiate for him during his exile. Mediaeval Sanskrit authors allude to shoes pretty frequently. The *Viṣṇu Purāṇa* enjoins all who wish to protect their person never to be without leather shoes. Manu forbids the use of others' shoes (IV, 66), as Sukra considers the use of others' gold and jewels, etc. as a *chhala* or social offence. The *Purāṇas* recommend the use of shoes in thorny places and on hot sand. Arrian notices the Indian shoes made of white leather, which, according to the description given, may be identified with the Oriya shoes of to-day. According to Mitra the material for these boots and shoes was bovine leather, and even the hide of sacrificed cattle. Āśwalāyana quotes Sānvatya (IV, ix, 24) to mention the fact that the hide of cattle sacrificed in Sulgava ceremony is fit to be converted into shoes and other useful articles. So also hog-skin is a fit material for shoes according to a Vedic verse quoted by Savara Swāmi in his commentary on the *Mīmāmsā* aphorisms. We hear also of leather bottles, leather jars (*dritis* in Manu), leather straps, strings and bands, leather sails etc.

The *Arthaśāstra* of Kauṭalya can give an idea of the economic entomology or agricultural zoology of the Hindus. Measures for the extermination of pests were undertaken by Government. These pests generally included rats, locusts, injurious birds, insects and tigers. To destroy rats, cats and mungooses were let loose; some varieties of poison were also used for the purpose. To kill tigers, several kinds of poison were in use.

Tamil sources can be used for South Indian life of the early Christian era. Among the woollens we find mention of manufactures from the wool of rat which was regarded as particularly warm. There are 30 varieties of silk mentioned, each with a distinctive appellation of its own, as distinguished from the imported silks of China which had a separate name.

The Italian traveller Marco Polo (1202) describes Cambay as a port with "great trade in hides, which are very well-dressed."

According to the *Dharma-Sūtra* of Baudhāyana (i. 2. 4), traffic in wool and in animals with two rows of teeth (horses, mules etc.) is a forbidden practice in the Dravidian districts,—the *locale* of this work according to Buehler—but is common among the "Northerners" (i.e. Western and North-western India according to the geographical terminology of those days recorded by Yuan Chwang also).

There are several *Jātakas* in which we are told explicitly of a successful, if sporadic, deal in birds between Babylon and Benares, and of horses imported by hundreds from the North and from Sindh. *Tandulanali Jātaka*, *Suhanu Jātaka*, *Kundaka-Kucchi-Sindhava-Jātaka*, *Bhojajajanuya-Jātaka* and *Ajanna-Jātaka* may be referred to. In the days of Solomon also Indian peacocks etc. found customers in Syria. The *Baveru-Jātaka* furnishes evidence in this regard. Peacocks were first taken to Babylon by Indian sea-going merchants in the 6th cent. B. C.[1]

[1] R. Mitra : *Indo-Aryans* (London 1881), Watt : *Dictionary of the Economic Products of India* (1889-96), R. Fick: *Die sociale Gliederung im nordoestlichen Indien zu Buddhas Zeit* (Kiel 1897), Mrs. Rhys-Davids: "Economic Condition in Ancient India" in the *Economic Journal* (London, September 1901), P. C. Ray : *History of Hindu Chemistry* (Calcutta 1902, 1909), R. K. Mookerji : *History of Indian Shipping* (London 1911), Schoff : *The Periplus of the Erythraean Sea* (London 1912), L. D. Barnett : *Antiquities of India* (London 1913), B. K. Sarkar : *The Positive Background of Hindu Sociology*, Vol. I. (Allahabad 1914), J. N. Samaddar : *Economic Condition in Ancient India* (Calcutta 1922), N. C. Bandyopadhyaya: *Economic Life and Progress in Ancient India*, Vol. I. (Calcutta 1925), P. T. S. Iyengar: "The Trade of India from the Earliest Period up to the Second Century A. D." (*Ind. His. Q.*, Dec. 1925, March-Sept. 1926), B. Breloer : *Kautaliya Studien*, Vol. I (Bonn. 1927), Vol. II. (Bonn. 1928), Vol. III. Pt. i. (Leipzig 1934), S. K. Das : *Economic History of Ancient India* (Calcutta 1928), Pran Nath : *A Study in the Economic Condition of Ancient India* (London 1929), R. Ganguli : "Cultivation in Ancient India" (*Ind.*

SECTION 5

THE ECONOMIC ASSOCIATIONS OF INDIAN PEASANTS, ARTISANS AND MERCHANTS

It is well known that the "chartered liberties" enjoyed by mediaeval towns, e.g., those of the Hanseatic League, have been great formative forces in the evolution of modern states in Europe. An analysis of the municipal privileges, the *liber burgus* as they were called, brings us invariably down to the basic economic factors, viz., the gild merchant and the craft organization. Probably these units were not identical with the boroughs. Nor do they seem to have exclusively represented the vital principle of borough life. But there are no grounds for doubting that these industrial and commercial nuclei were some of the chief "characteristic elements of the municipal constitution." It was these economic fraternities that had the lion's share in the government of the greatest cities like London, Paris, Cologne, Ghent and Florence[1].

The Orient was not poor in such economic centres of civic vitalities in ancient and mediaeval times. Students of commercial history are generally familiar with

His. Q., Dec. 1930, and March 1931), L. Renou: *Bibliographie Védique* (Paris 1931), P. Masson-Oursel : *L'Inde Antique etla Civilisation Indienne* (Paris 1933), A. K. Bose : "Agriculture" (*Ind. Hist. Q.*, June 1934), B. Bhargava : *Indigenous Banking in Ancient and Mediaeval India* (Bombay 1935), G. P. Majumdar : "Food (Man's Indebtedness to Plants)" in *Indian Culture*, Calcutta, January 1935, A. Geiger: *Die indoarische Gesellschaftsordnung* (Tuebingen 1935). See also the last footnote to the previous section, and footnote 1 to the section on "Treatises of Hindu Economics."

[1] C. Gross : *Gild Merchant* (Oxford 1890), Vol. I. pp. 92, 105, 159-162; G. Unwin : *The Gilds and Companies of London* (London 1908), pp. 61, 89; Brissaud : *History of French Public Law* (Garner's translation from French), Boston, 1915, p. 253. See the first footnote to Section 1.

old Chinese gilds. But it is not so well known that in India as in China almost every economic function from agriculture to money-lending and banking was organized into a gild.

Epigraphic evidences in regard to the gild of peasants are practically nil for the time being. Cultivators' unions have only to be inferred from the general laws on the subject of "companies." Gautama, XI, 21 (*c* 550 B. C.), Manu, VIII, 40 (*c* 150 A. C.), Brihaspati, I. (*c* 650), Sukra (IV, v, 35-36), all writers mention the association of agriculturists in their schedule of *śreṇīs*. The association of shepherds, however, is not unknown in the inscriptions. In the eleventh century, under Rājendra Chola, the shepherds of a village in Southern India agreed to become surety for one Eran Sattan, a fellow shepherd "who had received 90 ewes of this temple in order to supply *ghee* (clarified butter) for burning one perpetual lamp." If he died, absconded, or got into prison, fetters, or chains, the fraternity bound themsleves to discharge his duties. The responsibility was thus considered to be a joint one by the members.

In regard to the gild merchant more inscriptions may be drawn upon. In Madras of the twelfth century under Vikrama Chola (1118), the hero of an historical Tamil poem, there was a traders' gild with a membership of 500. Its activities and interests were co-extensive with the South Indian Empire. In Gupta India during the fourth and fifth centuries bankers (*śreṣṭhins*), traders (*sārtthavāhas*) and merchants (*kulikas*) used to close their business correspondence with clay seals. The *nigama* or corporation of these commercial interests, with headquarters probably at Pātaliputra, was something like a modern chamber of commerce. Such bodies working, as they did, in concert (*sambhūya*) were notorious in the fourth century B. C. owing to their attempts to "corner" the market. The problem of "profiteering" had to be tackled by the Maurya Empire especially because the union of merchants tried to raise prices so high as to yield a cent per cent profit.

The gild merchant must have been in existence in the sixth century B. C. as Gautama's *Dharma-Sūtra* mentions it as one of the law-"making" or law-"declaring" bodies. Still, as the *Valahassa*, *Chullakaseṭṭhi*, *Supparaka* and other *Jātakas* or Buddhist "Birth Stories" narrate, maritime and land commerce used to be undertaken on the joint stock principle by companies of "five hundred trading folk," "seven hundred merchants" etc. India's experience in commercial unions is therefore at least as old as China's.

The story of Hindu craft gilds may be told with more details and greater confidence. Unions of industrial experts or workingmen's gilds were conspicuous institutions of the Gupta Empire. In 465, under Skandagupta, a gild of oil-men at the city of Indrapura presided over by Jīvanta was entrusted with an endowment out of the interest of which a temple lamp was to be maintained. The terms of the deed stipulated that the removal of the corporation from its present head-quarters would not invalidate its jurisdiction over the property. Nullification of the trust might ensue only from the dissolution of the gild (or secession of some of its members). In Kumāragupta's time (413-455) a gild of silk weavers was formed at the city of Daśapura. They had migrated from Central Gujarat, but part of their comrades took up other pursuits, e.g. archery and fighting, astronomical studies, and asceticism, at their new place of domicile. Incidentally it appears that the change of hereditary or caste occupations was not rare in Gupta India.

Among Gujaratis of the early Christian era under Āndhra Emperors, there were gilds of weavers, druggists (*gāndhikas*), corn-dealers (*dhānyaka śreṇīs*), and oil-manufacturers. Like the gilds of the Gupta Empire the Āndhra gilds also discharged the functions of banks. Money and real estates were received by them in perpetuity as a deposit or trust fund. For the use of this property they paid to the beneficiary named in the grants interest varying from 9 to 12 per cent. In 120 A. C. two gilds of weavers at Govardhana (Nasik) were entrusted by General Uṣavadāta with 2,000 and 1,000 *kārṣāpaṇas*. In the third century several other gilds of the same city, viz., those of potters, *odayāntrikas* (workers fabricating hydraulic engines or water-clocks), and oil-millers, became trustees of a permanent endowment to provide medicines for the monks of a *Samgha*. The planting of wayside trees was one of the objects for which a gild was similarly endowed with the income of two fields.

Like the gild merchant the craft gild also must have been prominent in Maurya times. Kauṭalya's scheme of fleecing the "gold-lords" for the public treasury has reference most probably to the gild of goldsmiths. His *Artha-śāstra* suggests besides that certain wards of the city should be set apart for the corporations of artisans. And one of the functions of the Imperial superindendent of accounts was to record all about the customs, professions and transactions of the associations, whether of traders or workmen, rural or urban.

Kauṭalya's idea about the establishment of gilds in the different wards of a city was but a reflex of the actual civic life of his own and previous times. For in the *Silavanga* and other *Jātakas* streets (*vīthis*) are sometimes named from a particular class of artisans living in them. Even an entire village of 1,000 families was often monopolized by a single industry, e.g. smithery or timber-work.

Gilds were then prominent institutions among Hindus as early as the sixth and seventh centuries B. C.; and epigraphy traces them down to the Chola Empire. The Buddhist story-books open up to us an economic India in which the various orders of manual and skilled workers were organized on the corporate basis. There were gilds of sailors, muslin-weavers, leather-workers, painters, goldsmiths, workers in war-implements, stone-carvers, and so forth. In addition to the conventional "eighteen gilds" there must be mentioned also the unions or companies of traders and commercial men. For all subsequent periods since then, therefore, the law books could not but devote special attention to the gilds as economic institutions of the land. Gautama's *Dharma-sūtra* was composed or compiled in the *milieu* of gilds of peasants, herdsmen, traders, money-lenders, and artisans. Gilds held a high place in the Kauṭalyan theory of finance as important sources of public income. Authors of the third century A. C., e.g., those responsible for the compilation of Viṣṇu's law-book were living in an age when the gilds of metal workers, especially goldsmiths and silversmiths, were well in evidence in social life. Not only Manu, VIII, 5,219 (*c* 150) and Yājnavalkya, II, 15,187,192 (*c* 350) but all jurists down to Nārada, X, 5 (*c* 500) and Brihaspati, XVII, 19 (*c* 650) had consequently to reckon gilds among the subjects of "private law". These public bodies were expressly mentioned in connection with crimes and punishments to which all individuals were liable according to the laws of the state. The violation (*vyatikrama*) of *sambids* (gild compacts or agreements) was accordingly important enough to demand special treatment along with the general law of contract.

But not all unions, companies or associations are "corporations." How far, therefore, it may be asked, were these *śreṇīs* (often identified with *gaṇas* and *pūgas*) of the Indian socio-economic system real gilds? To what extent did these *samūha* organizations come to be conceived and recognized by Hindus themselves as "artificial civic bodies," i.e. "aggregate individuals" with "natural corporate existence"? The book of Brihaspati (Ch. XVII) furnishes an answer to these queries. The juridical concept of a corporate person or one-in-the-many as pertaining to *śreṇīs* is quite manifest in the particulars he lays down regarding the constitution and rights and duties of *samūhas*. The older Yājnavalkya and his mediaeval commentators also leave no doubt on the point.

Gilds were governed by boards of two, three or five persons. They conducted their business in a *sabhā*, i.e., public assembly. As corporate bodies they could make *samaya* or compact with private individuals as well as among themselves, and the state had to see to it that gild compacts were enforced like all other compacts in the land (Nārada, X, 1-2).

The "power of attorney" could be conferred by them on the some of their members, and these agents represented the associations in law courts or other public offices. Accordingly the funds donated by the government to a single member had to be deposited with the joint stock of the *samūha* (Brihaspati XVII, 22, 24). In Yājnavalkya's code (II, 180) anything acquired by a member of the gild while on gild business was to become common property. Eleven times the value of the acquisition was the penalty for wilful violation of this ruling. According to Brihaspati (XVII, 15) any member who injured the joint stock might be punished with deportation.

The agreement entered into by a gild was binding on each and all of the members. Anybody failing to perform the duties implied thereby was liable to be banished and have his property confiscated (Brihaspati XVII, 13). All expenditures were treated as common charges. Responsibility for loans contracted by a member on behalf of the association was also common. Lastly, *śreṇīs* had the "right of joint action" in relation to the state, as we have noticed in the agreement of the South Indian shepherds, one of the privileges for which the European craft used to fight.

According to Kātyāyana, an authority later than Brihaspati, cited in Mitra-Miśra's *Vīra-mitrodaya* (16th century) and Chaṇḍeśvara's *Virāda-ratnākara* (14th century), two commentaries on Yājnavalkya and on other jurists new members were entitled to share equally with the old the properties of the established gild. Debts of the *samūha* were likewise to be shared by them as a matter of course. Nay, the spiritual merit, as says Mitra-Miśra, accruing from charities and religious services that the gild may have undertaken in the past was believed to be beneficial to persons who were elected to membership long after the deeds had been performed. The usual mode of co-option was *sarva-sammati*, i.e., unanimous approval.

Nothing illustrates better the "legal fiction" of corporations as "immortal persons" than these latter-day ideas in regard to *gaṇa*, *śreṇī* and *varga*. It is clear, therefore, that Hindu *samūhas*, whether of capitalists, working men or peasants, and trade unions or commercial fraternities had the distinctive characteristics of a homogeneous "community" with common rights and common obligations,—the "real group-persons" of Gierke and Figgis.

We shall now analyze the constitutional, political

or civic immunities and liberties enjoyed by the gilds of ancient and mediaeval India. This will throw light on the amount of decentralization achieved in Hindu polity. No governmental documents are available however. The only authorities are literary.

In the first place, *śreṇīs* were monopolistic organizations anxious to maintain intact their economic autonomy. We learn from Nārada that the gilds were indeed open to more than one socio-religious group or caste. But generally speaking, their regulations were as exclusive in spirit as the ordinances, say, of the English hatters' craft in the fourteenth century. They sought to regulate the number of apprentices and also the hours of labour. On festive occasions, in street processions and at social gatherings each *śreṇī* was represented by its own banners and buntings bearing on them the implements and emblems of the respective crafts.

In the second place, the *jeṭṭhaka* (alderman) and *seṭṭhi*, i.e., the heads of corporations were treated by kings as representatives of the people functionally divided as artisans, merchants and peasants. In pre-Maurya times, i.e., previous to the third quarter of the fourth century B. C. it was through their gilds that the people were summoned by the king on important occasions. *Sreṇīs* appear thus to have played an important part in the public finance. The taxes to be paid by traders and other inhabitants of the town were agreed upon by the ruler "in consultation with the heads of the gilds."

Necessarily, therefore, in the third place, *mukhyas*, i.e., heads, presidents or representatives of the corporations constituted, like councillors of the king, an important "estate" of the realm. At the coronation of kings, e.g., in the *Rāmāyaṇa*, gilds had the right to the sprinkling or anointing ritual. Sometimes gild members occupied high state offices, as we know from the

Jātakas. Socially, on the whole, they were "peers" of the king. As poets of the *Mahābhārata* have declared the royal ideal of manliness, kings were ashamed to return to their homeland if they were defeated in battles. For, "what would the elders of the gilds say to me," argued the kings, "and what should I speak to them in reply?" The moral control exercised by gilds on state policies may be presumed to have been of a high order. Undisputed, therefore, was their influence on public opinion.

In the fourth place, leaving aside the fact that men following the soldier's profession were often organized on the gild principle (*śreṇi-vala* or gild corps e.g., the Kṣatriya gilds of Gujarat described by Kauṭalya), the ordinary industrial and commercial *śreṇīs* had great military importance as well. The chief reason of course was their power over the purse or the sinews of war.

Political theorists, therefore, considered it a part of the statecraft to pacify the gilds of one's own state and try to win over the elders of the enemy's gilds. The methods suggested in the *Mahābhārata* are the well known ways and means of *Realpolitik*, such as were appreciated by Philip of Macedon, Machiavelli the Italian, Walpole the Englishman, and Guizot the Frenchman. These are the corrupt practices of bribery and the sowing of dissensions among the members of corporations. Or perhaps in the language of Bolshevik economics these should partially be described as the traditional tactic of capitalism which is said to be "international" enough to seek allies even among enemy bankers.

Again, *śreṇīs* had their own judicial tribunals. The craftsmen had thus the privilege of being tried by the jury of their own peers. In the matter of legal decisions, if we may take Brihaspati as a narrator of actual facts, even court practice had to yield to the opinion of gilds. Corporations were "invested with the power to decide law suits" and their meetings were declared to be "resorts for the passing of a sentence." As such, gild courts may have had jurisdiction over cases affecting the community at large and not solely over their own disputes. But it is to be observed that the judicial system of the Maurya Empire for which alone we have some reliable evidence does not have a place for gilds as public tribunals.

Of equal importance was the legislative or law-making power of *śreṇīs*. The gilds "made" or "declared" their own laws and had their own usages binding upon them. As a rule, the state could not institute any regulations overriding these gild customs. We learn from Manu, Brihaspati and other codifiers of laws or customs that "rules of their own profession" were recognized by the state for cultivators or peasants and farmers, artisans such as carpenters or others, artists, money-lenders, companies of tradesmen, dancers, persons wearing the token of a religious order such as the Pāśupatas, and even robbers. Gautama also, the earliest of the writers, observes that peasants, traders, herdsmen, money-lenders, and artisans have authority to lay down rules for their respective classes. And in the suits brought before the state judiciary in appeal from gild tribunals, the royal judges were expected to learn the facts and rules "from those who in each class had authority to speak". The king's officers were to give decisions "in accordance with what were declared to be the rules in the *śreṇī*."

Last but not least, the administrative *sva-rāj* or "self-determination" of *śreṇīs* was practically unconditioned. They could exercise their governmental power as almost sovereign units, as *imperia in imperio*, i.e., without depending on the sanction of the state.

The right of the *samūha* to punish even the *mukhya* or president is stated by Kātyāyana as well as by Mitra-Miśra who cites him while interpreting Yājnavalkya's opinion on the question. In Brihaspati's law also the gild-*sabhā* could normally punish one of the guilty members, ostracize or even banish him, as has been pointed out above. Only, if in boycotting him the gild were "actuated by hatred" might the state "restrain" the corporation. The ultra-democratic constitution of Chinese gilds was all but outdone by the *samūhas* of India.

The executive, judicial and legislative autonomies of *śreṇīs*, or the *laissez faire* enjoyed by these "local" bodies must have been considerably restricted and circumscribed by the "centralizing" exploits of successful empire-builders or "nation"-makers. But archaeological researches have not as yet unearthed any evidence as to the adverse effects, inevitable as they must have been, of the *śāsanas* (i.e. legislative enactments or statutes and ordinances) of *sārvabhaumas* ("universal monarchs") on the immunities of gild-soviets. It is apparent however, that, on the whole, the *sva-rāj* of Hindu *śreṇīs*, i.e., the "functional" sovereignty of India's old economic associations was essentially an analogue if not a replica of the *liber burgus* of mediaeval Europe in so far as this latter was achieved by and dependent on gilds and crafts.

CHAPTER III

THE CREATIONS OF HINDU PHILOSOPHY IN POLITICAL SCIENCE

SECTION I

THE GEOMETRY OF POLITICAL RELATIONS IN THE DHARMA AND ARTHA SASTRAS

In Eur-America it has been the tradition of scholarship for historians of philosophy to devote attention to political (economic, social and legal) speculations along with the speculations on man, nature, knowledge, mind, truth, good, God etc. No account of Greek philosophy is held to be complete which overlooks the contributions of the Greek moralists or philosophers to political and social thought. Similarly in the studies relating to the beginnings of "modern" philosophy, say, the philosophy, of Kant, Fichte, Hegel etc. the politics, economics, jurisprudence and sociology of the thinkers in question are accorded an appropriate place. To mention a few works published in the nineteenth century, interest in political philosophy is manifest as much in Victor Cousin's *Histoire de la philosophie*, Lewes's *Biographical History of Philosophy*, and Zeller's *Geschichte der griechischen Philosophie* as in Leslie Stephen's *English Thought in the Nineteenth Century*, Merz's *History of European Thought in the Nineteenth Century*, and Lévy-Bruhl's *Histoire de la philosophie moderne en France.* And in treatises like Janet's *Histoire de la science politique dans ses relations avec la morale* or Bonar's *Philosophy and Political*

Economy one can detect the attempts to bring economics and politics into contact with general philosophy.

In the field of indology, however, scholars, both Indian and non-Indian, have up till now as a rule fought shy of economics, politics or sociology in their studies relating to the history of "Hindu" philosophy. Works dealing with the ideas of ancient or medieval Indian thinkers on body, mind, soul, universe, reasoning, intuition, meditation etc. have been systematically practising non-cooperation with the Hindu ideas of property, state, society and law. This absence of the comprehensive treatment of Hindu philosophy is one of the main reasons for a one-sided and therefore fallacious and misleading interpretation of the Hindu mind and its creations. No survey of Hindu civilization or culture-history can be adequate which ignores or is indifferent to the achievements of the Indian people in political, economic and social institutions as well as political, economic and social thought[1].

So far as the ideologies are concerned, we have to observe that the specialized treatises or *Śāstras*[2] on politics, economics and sociology in Hindu literature are numerous. To be very brief, they are to be encountered, generally speaking, under two groups: (1)

[1] The contributions of Hindu philosophy to political categories were first discussed by the present author in the *American Political Science Review* (November 1918, August 1919), the *Political Science Quarterly* (New York, December 1918, March 1921), the *International Journal of Ethics* (Chicago, April 1920), *Revue de Synthèse Historique* (Paris, August-December 1920), *Séances et Travaux de l' Académie des Sciences Morales et Politiques* (Paris, August 1921) and the *Deutsche Rundschau* (Berlin, March 1922).

[2] P. V. Kane : *History of Dharmasastras* (Poona) Vol. I. (1931). the present author's "Kauṭalya and His Boswell" (*Calcutta Review*, August 1935), J. J. Meyer : *Ueber das Wesen der altindischen Rechtsschriften und ihr Verhaeltnis zu Einander und zu Kauṭilya* (Leipzig 1927).

Dharma (and *Smriti*) *Śāstras* and (2) *Artha* (and *Nīti*) *Śāstras*. As a full-fledged treatise, the oldest *Dharmaśāstra* is perhaps the *Dharma-sūtra* of Gautama (*c* 550 B. C.?), and the oldest *Arthaśāstra* perhaps that associated with the name of Kauṭalya (*c* 330 B. C.?). Excluding the vernacular and English paraphrases or translations of the old Sanskrit treatises in the nineteenth and twentieth centuries the last *Smritiśāstra* of the Hindu tradition is perhaps the commentary on Vijnāneśvara's *Mitākṣarā* by the Maratha jurist Bālambhatta (1740-1830?) or the Bengali jurist Jagannātha Tarkapanchānana's (1695-1806?) *Vivādabhamgārṇava*. And in the line of *Nītiśāstras* the last work is perhaps the *Rājanīti*[1] in Marathi language (*c* 1810), based on Sanskrit texts, by the Maratha scholar Malhar Ramrao Chitnis.

We have to face here a literature which has a more or less continuous history of nearly two thousand five hundred years. And this literature from beginning to end is essentially analytical in its contents. The Hindu speculations have given rise to a number of categories and we find that the philosophers are engaged in defining and analyzing them. The topic may be constitutional, legal, economic, financial, social or international. But we notice that in the treatment by these authors one is led to feel that society, polity or economy is nothing but a system of relationships, contacts, *liaisons*, attitudes, dealings, *rapports*, *Beziehungen*. In the Hindu philosophy of *Dharma*, *Smriti*, *Artha* or *Nīti* mankind is presented in the form of an individual *visàvis* individuals or groups, or of groups *visàvis* groups or individuals.

[1] Edited by K. N. Sane for the *Kāvyetihāsa Samgraha Series* No. 23 (Poona, 1887). See the present author's "Maratha Political Ideas of the Eighteenth Century" (*Ind. Hist. Q.*, Calcutta, March 1936).

Some of these attitudes, relations or contacts are described under the complex of *saptāmga*, the seven-limbed organism (*Kauṭalya*, VI, i, VIII, i; Viṣṇu III, 33; Śukra, I, lines 121-124, V, 1-2, Kāmandaka I, 16, IV, 1). Here we are presented with the theory of the constitution involving as it does the analysis of the *svāmin* (ruler), the *amātya* (minister or councillor), the *suhrit* (ally), the *koṣa* (treasure), the *rāṣṭra* (territory), the *durga* (fort) and the *vala* (army). The analysis of these seven categories is not the only topic of Hindu philosophy in political science. Then there are the problems, among others, of *aiśvarya* (sovereignty) which have also demanded the attention of the theorist. And here we encounter the Hindu theory of the state. In this analysis, likewise, the authors have given currency to a number of characteristic categories.

The state (*rājya*) as an entity is grounded in the phenomenon of *aiśvarya* or *svāmitva*, i.e., sovereignty. The theory of the state, therefore, is fundamentally the philosophy of sovereignty. It may be exercised by the one or the few or the many. It may be vested in the long run in the legislature or the executive or the judiciary. It may be identical with the despotism of custom or the rule of positive law. It may manifest itself in and through a single organ as the *primum mobile* embracing all organized spheres or exhibited simultaneously in several coexistent co-ordinate corporations of a pluralistic universe. And finally, it may happen to be the monopoly of the bourgeoisie or of the proletariat. In any case, it is *aiśvarya* that ushers into being the phenomena called politics in societal existence. In political speculation the central problem obviously is the analysis of the great *śakti* (force) that constitutes the core of "political" relations, i.e., the *élan* of *samūha* (organized)life.

"What is sovereignty" is then the moot question to be attacked by all political philosophers. Let us proceed to examine how the problem was grasped by the *Dharma* (*Smriti*) and *Artha* (*Nīti*) theorists of India. It is to be remembered, however, that we are here concerned with the thought which prevailed in the world ages before the ideas discussed in Preuss's *Gemeinde, Staat und Reich als Gebietskoerperschaften* (1889), Leroy-Beaulieu's *L'Etat moderne et es fonctions* (1890), Novicow's *Les Luttes entres sociétés humaines et leurs phases successives* (1893), Lecky's *Democracy and Liberty* (1896), Michel's *L'Idee de l'Etat* (1898), Merriam's *History of the Theory of Sovereignty since Rousseau* (1900), Scherger's *Evolution of Modern Liberty* (1904), Joseph-Barthélemy's *Role du Pouvoir executif dans les républiques modernes* (1906), Duguit's *Le Droit social, le droit individuel et la transformation de l'etat* (1908), Hobhouse's *Social Erolution and Political Theory* (1911), Barker's *Political Thought in England from Spencer to the Present Day* 1914), Lenin's *State and Revolution* (1917), Laski's *Studies in the Problem of Sovereignty* (1918), Joseph-Barthélemy's *Problème de la Competence dans la démocratie* (1918), Watson's *State in Peace and War* (1919), Spann's *Der Wahre Staat* (1921), Dewey's *Human Nature and Conduct* (1922), Hitler's *Mein Kampf* (1924), Sorokin's *Sociology of Revolution* (1925), Meinecke's *Idee der Staatsraeson* (1925), Hocking's *Man and the State* (1926), Redano's *Lo Stato Etico* (1927), Masaryk's *Making of a State* (1927), Karl Haushofer's *Geopolitik der Pan-Ideen* (1931) and *Raumüeberwindende Maechte* (1934, essays by sereal authors), Bouglé's *Socialismes Français* (1933) and *Koellreutter's Grundriss der Allgemeinen Staatslehre* (1933). The development of political philosophy in the world since the American War of Independence and the first industrial revolution should, as a rule, be left out of the consideration while examining the categories of thought created by the

Indian pilosophers from Gautama and Kauṭalya to Jagannātha and Chitnis.[1]

The "analytical" treatment of political phenomena, —bearing on the constitution or on sovereignty,—is a prominent feature of Hindu thinking. The conviction is forced upon us under the guidance of the *Dharma* and the *Artha Śāstras* that man in politics is fundamentally a bundle or complex of social relationships. These treatises do not seem to be interested in this or that particular state. Neither the Maurya Empire nor the Chola Empire nor indeed any state of Hindu history has engaged their attention. Their topic for discussion is the state *ueberhaupt*, i.e., the state as "the thing in itself," so to say. Be it observed that we are not attaching to this phrase any metaphysical implications. No treatment can be more objective, concrete and human than what we find in these works. To these authors a state is a human association and therefore is nothing but a system of relations and orientations. Altogether, we are presented by the Hindu philosophers with the very pattern, form, geometry, so to say, of human relations. Whatever be the content of the state, howsoever varied be the races that constitute its membership, wheresoever located it be, the relations between the members of the state are eternal. Examined in this light, the creations of the Hindu philosophers in and through the *Dharma* and *Artha Śāstras* would appear to be fine logical contributions to what is being described as "pure," "analytical" or formal sociology in contemporary Eur-America.

This kind of sociology is called by Leopold von

[1] See the present author's *Political Philosophies Since 1905* (Madras 1928).

Wiese[1] the leading exponent, as *die Lehre von den sozialen Beziehungen und den sozialen Gebilden*, i.e., the science of social relations or processes (competition, boycott, exploitation etc.) and social "forms" (such as the group, mass, state, people, nation, class etc.). It is sometimes shortly named the *Beziehungslehre* or science of relations. And the special feature of this science of relations consists in the fact that it deals not with historical or time-conditioned categories but with the categories such as are "above" or indifferent to time (*ueberzeitlich*) and somewhat eternal (*quasi-ewig*). These categories relate to such relations or processes of "to" and "away from" (*Zu-und Auseinander*) as prevailed, are prevailing and will prevail as long as there are men.

This "formal" or "analytical" sociology is claimed by von Wiese to be new and very recent. Starting as it did with Toennies's *Gemeinschaft und Gesellschaft* in 1887 it is said not to have assumed a definite form until 1908 with the publication of Simmel's *Soziologie: Untersuchungen ueber die Formen der Vergesellschaftung* (Sociology: Researches into the Forms of Society-making). But in the present author's treatment the entire Hindu literature of *Dharma*, *Smriti*, *Artha*, and *Nīti Śāstras* is rich in the analysis of social forms and social relationships or processes. In other words, the "new sociology" must have to be regarded methodologically, at any rate, as very old, at least as old as Gautama and Kauṭalya, nay, much older still, because even Gautama and Kauṭalya had their predecessors.

[1] *Soziologie* (Berlin, 1931) pp. 34, 47, 117, 120-124, 131-133 and *System der Allgemeinen Soziologie* (Munich, 1933, second edition). The position maintained for Hindu thought in the present treatise has a parallel in A. Menzel's standpoint as exhibited in his *Griechische Soziologie*, a monograph on Greek Sociology published in the *Sitzungsberichte der Akademie der Wissenschaften* (Vienna, 1936).

And here it should be reasonable to agree with Sorokin,[1] who holds that its "founders were all law-givers who formulated the first rules of social relations, and especially all jurisconsults and theorizers of law."

Sociology is much too popular a category in present-day world-culture. Unluckily, however, this category has as many contents as there are sociologists. And it is very interesting that the category was unknown until 1842 when Comte used it in his *Cours de Philosophie Positive*, Vol. IV. Up till then he had been using instead the category "*physique sociale*" (social physics). But in view of the fact that the Belgian statistician Quetelet employed it to describe the researches in anthropology and demography Comte considered it prudent to replace it by a new word, "sociology."

But since Comte's days the subject-matter of sociology has changed so much and so often with researchers that today it is almost impossible to describe what this discipline is and what this is not. For instance, the "classical sociologists," Comte, Spencer and Schaeffle, three of the founders of this science, however much they differ in methods and messages, belong to what the Italian sociologist Carli in *Le Toerie Sociologiche* (Padua 1925) calls the historico-encyclopædic school. They seek to explain history, point out the processes of evolution, and suggest the future lines of advance. On the other hand, the founders of "new sociology," Toennies, Tarde, Durkheim and Simmel, for example, among the continentals are interested in the analysis of forces, facts, groups and relations. The American and British sociologists like Small, Ross, McDougall, Wallas, Cooley, Ellwood, and others belong to this

[1] *Contemporary Sociological Theories* (New York, 1928) pp. 495-498.

class which, as we have seen, is generally known as the school of "analytical" or "formal" sociology.[1] The first or the classical school may also be aptly described as culture-sociology.

To understand a bit of this diversity in the concepts of sociology let us take Toennies, whom von Wiese calls the pioneer of contemporary German sociology. In 1887 Toennies published his *Gemeinschaft und Gesellschaft* (Community and Society).[2] A student of classical, encyclopædic, historical or cultural sociology would perhaps hardly recognize any sociology in Toennies's work. Here we are introduced to an examination of all those human connections or relations with one another which are cementing forces and to the conclusion that they fall inevitably into two groups. First, they are derived from the "natural," "instinctive" and allied activities of man. In contrast with such activities can be discovered, secondly, those which are due to the artificial attempts to pursue or serve some ends although the natural feelings may be opposed to such activities. The community is based on the natural, the society on the artificial cementing bonds. There is privacy, personal intimacy in the community (family, village, tribe, folk, gild, *śreṇī*, faith, religion, custom, conscience etc.) In the society (city, state, exchange, commerce, trans-

[1] L. von Wiese : *Soziologie* (Berlin, 1931) pp. 45-49, 109.

[2] G. Richard : *La Sociologie Générale* (Paris, 1912) pp. 21-32; *Revue Internationale de Sociologie* (Paris, July 1935), pp. 89-92. Rumpf: "Von reinformaler zur typologisch-enpirischer Sociologie" in *Schmollers Jahrbuch Leipzig*, 1924.

Some of the more representative works of Toennies are indicated below:
Gemeinschaft und Gesellschaft (Leipzig, 8th edition, 1935), *Die Sitte* (Frankfurt, 1909), *Kritik der oeffentlichen Meinung* (Berlin, 1922), *Einfuehrung in die Soziologie* (Stuttgart 1931) and *Geist der Neuzeit* (Leipzig, 1935).

portation, "public opinion," fashion, reason, contract etc.), on the other hand, the predominant atmosphere is that of business, law, public life. This distinction between natural and artificial group-persons, between feeling and intellect among social forces, between "culture" and "civilization" is but one of the many new topics with which this science has been enriched in recent years. But, on the other hand, the encyclopædic, historical, evolutionary or cultural sociology has not all disappeared.

In any case, while going through the following survey of the categories of Hindu philosophy in political science the problem of the "eternal" and the "universals," the truths independent of time and space as well as of epochs and races, the "constants" and the permanent factors cannot be got rid of. Meinecke in his *Idee der Staatsraeson* (1925, p. 452) has come to the conclusion that during nearly two thousand years certain leading thinkers were expressing essentially the same ideas. "Cicero, Aquinas and Frederick the Great could have understood one another," says he, "because all three spoke the easily comprehensible language of "natural law."" This German work is, besides, a testimony to the profound ideological reality that from Machiavelli to Treitschke European political philosophy has traded in two fundamental categories. One has reference to *Staatsraeson*, which we may call *śaktiyoga*, i.e., *Machtpolitik*, the doctrine of power or force and *daṇḍa* (punishment, sanction etc.), the other points to *Sittlichkeit* (morality), *Rechtlichkeit* (law), corresponding to the Hindu doctrine of *dharma*, i.e., law, justice, etc. It is the permutation and combination of these two eternal polarities, marked often by the emphasis on one to the exclusion of the other, that constitutes virtually the entire encyclopædia of political philosophy as exhibited in this work. This is a very instructive and eminently acceptable generalization. We understand that changes in space and time do not after all engender any profound variations in the theories of the state, law, diplomacy, societal organization etc.

The existence of social "constants" can be borne out in other fields, for instance, in the domain of law. The Italian jurist Giorgio del Vecchio[1] invites our attention to the fact that the organism of law became enriched through new inventions such as the printing press. New institutions were created by the press. But the preceding structure of law remained entire, and no new laws were expressly formulated. Similarly in our times, says he, new branches of law have been created on account of numerous transformations of living conditions and modes of activity. But the main trunk remains substantially unchanged. The structure has been amplified and perfected but its fundamental unity is to be found intact.

This problem of "constants" in social progress can be referred to certain universal considerations. However undeniable and incontestable be the objective signs of amelioration or progress enjoyed by a society the individual men and women cannot see or feel in them any grounds for feeling happy. It is this paradox of civilisation to which the Italian sociologist Alfredo Niceforo is led as a result of his investigations *sull' importanza dello studio della distribuzione dei caratteri mentali* (on the importance of studying the distribution of mental characters, Catania 1913).

An explanation of the impossibility of feeling happy is found by Niceforo in the circumstances that two

[1] "The Crisis of the Science of Law" in the *Tulane Law Review* (New Orleans, 1934) p. 334.

distinct elements are to be discovered in the social facts, one of which is superficial and variable and the other profound and invariable. The external part is variable. But the part which does not change is internal and is the fundamental element.[1] These are the *résidus sociaux*, the social residues or *résidus constants*, the constant i.e. permanent residues and they remain always hidden under all apparent variations of forms. The ideas of equality, liberty etc., the optimistic and humanitarian ideologies, the conceptions of altruism and so forth are considered by Niceforo to be the external and variable elements of social facts. But they are misleading because it is under them that lies hidden the desire to dominate on the part of the minorities, i.e., of the most qualified or the fit. And this desire for domination constitutes the profound and secret motive of all action in social groups.

It will be noticed that, from the stand-point of content or substance, most of the categories of Hindu political philosophy are analogues of those of European and that it may be reasonable to connect even modern and contemporary theories with the findings of the old Hindus. In so far as political and social phenomena, and, for that matter, all mental and moral or human phenomena are universal and eternal, it is possible to detect Platonic, Aristotelian, Patristic or Macchiavellian strands even in the philosophical discussions of contemporary problems. Besides, some of the economic and social institutions of today can be traced back to the Middle Ages for their crude and even semi-doveloped beginnings. It is from this angle of vision that we can appreciate the attempts of Sorokin (*Contemporary Sociological Theories*) to trace virtually every "ism" of

[1] A. Niceforo : *Les Indices numériques de la Civilisation et du Progrès* (Paris, 1921), pp. 201-205.

today back not only to medieval literary documents but to the most primitive records of human thought.

But in a strictly scientific way of looking at things the theories that have grown around democracy and socialism, technocracy and world-economy, *le marché mondial*, constitutional liberty and class-struggle are essentially the products of the nineteenth and twentieth centuries, the epochs of the first and the second industrial revolutions. These phenomena were unknown as facts of "large dimensions" in the previous epochs.[1] It would be psychologically untenable, therefore, to bring in the philosophies of Europe from, say, Plato's *Republic* to Frederick the Great's *Anti-Machiavel* (1736) and *Das Politische Testament* (1768) into the atmosphere of present-day ideologies.

For instance, so far as a "modern" thinker like Hobbes or Bossuet and a still more modern thinker like Hegel was unused to the grammar of trade unions, syndicates, class-struggle, international proletariat and so forth, the "absolutism" or monistic idealism that is associated with their political theories can hardly be invoked to interpret what may be described as the "neo-absolutism" of today, namely, that prevalent among the thinkers of Soviet Russia, Fascist Italy and Nazi Germany. One must by no means overlook the very important consideration that it is on the generation-long experience of parliamentary liberties, labour organization, democratic procedure and international camaraderies that these professedly anti-parliamentary, anti-democratic, and anti-socialistic systems of neo-capitalistic *Duce*-states or *Fuehrerstaaten*, i.e.

[1]On the question of modernistic economy in medieval Europe· see H. Hauser : *Les Origines Historiques des Problèmes Economiques Actuels* (Paris, 1930), pp. 3-9, *Les Débuts du Capitalisme* (Paris, 1931), 16, 31, 42.

leader-polities and dictatorships have been reared.

When one is adequately oriented to the diversities in the institutional and other factual experiences of economic and social life one should be careful in establishing equations of the ancient and mediæval Hindu categories as of the ancient and medieval European with those prevailing in the nineteenth and twentieth centuries. Naturally, therefore, the question of the Hindus or of the Europeans of yore as having "anticipated" the "moderns" should not generally be raised. For comparative politics we are likely to be within scientific limits if we read the *Dharma* and the *Artha Śāstras* in the main as embodying the ideologies of European thought down to the beginnings of the industrial revolution.

SECTION 2

THE DOCTRINE OF MĀTSYA-NYĀYA

(*The Logic of the Fish*)

At the back of political thinking in India there was the process of dichotomy at work. Hindu thinkers tried to understand the state by differentiating it from the non-state. Their method was logical as well as historical. That is, in the first place, they tried to investigate in what particulars the state analytically differs from the non-state; and in the second place, they tried to picture to themselves as to how the pre-statal condition developed into the statal, i.e., how the state grew out of the non-state. The chief solution of both these problems they found in the doctrine of *mātsya-nyāya* or the logic of the fish.

What, now, is the non-state according to Hindus? The same question was asked by the philosophers of

Europe thus: "What is the state of Nature?" And the Hindu answer was identical with the European.

According to Hooker (1554-1600) in the *Ecclesiastical Polity* the state of nature is a state of strife. The *Leviathan* of Hobbes (1588-1670) declares similarly that the state of nature is a state of war and of no rights. In Spinoza's (1632-77) opinion also, in the *Tractatus Theologico-Politicus*, the state of nature is a state of war and a state of the right of might. The non-state is thus conceived to be a war of "all against all," an "anarchy of birds and beasts," or a regime of vultures and harpies, as John Stuart Mill would have remarked.

It is interesting to observe that in China also the state of nature was analyzed by Moh-ti (*c.* 500-420 B.C.) in almost self-same terms. In the non-state, as Su Hu explains it in *The Development of Logic in Ancient China*, "each man has his own notion of right. Therefore one man has one notion of right, two men have two notions of right, and ten men have ten notions of right. The more men there are, the more conceptions of right will there be. Consequently each approves his own notion of right and denounces every other man's. So they denounce one another."

This Hobbesian "law of beasts and birds" or the *Naturprozess* of Gumplowicz is the logic (*nyāya*) of the fish (*matsya*) in India[1]. Should there be no ruler to wield punishment on earth, says the *Mahābhārata* (*Sāntiparva*, LXVII, 16-17, LXVIII, 11-12), "the strong would devour the weak like fishes in water. It is

[1]The history of the theory of *mātsya-nyāya* in European sociology from Heracleitus to Gumplowicz may be seen in Barnes's article on "The struggle of races and social groups" in the *Journal of Race Development* U. S. A. (April, 1919), pp. 394-400. For Protagoras's conception of the origin of the state after primeval chaos *vide* Barker's *Plato* (London, 1918) p. 130.

related that in days of yore people were ruined through sovereignlessness, devouring one another like the stronger fishes preying upon the feebler". In the *Manu Samhitā* (VII,20) likewise we are told that "the strong would devour the weak like fishes" if there be a virtual reversion to the non-state (if, for example, the king is not vigilant enough in meting out punishments to those that should be punished). The *Rāmāyaṇa* (*Ayodhyākāṇḍa*, LXVII,31) also describes the non-state region as one in which "people ever devour one another likes fishes". And a few details about the conditions in this non-state are furnished in the *Matsya Purāṇa* (CCXXV,9). "The child, the old, the sick, the ascetic, the priest, the woman and the widow would be preyed upon", as we read, "according to the logic of the fish" (should *daṇḍa* or punishment fail to be operative at the proper time).

The idea of the fish-like struggle for existence or self-assertion was thus a generally accepted notion in the "floating literature" of Hindustan. It found an important place in the exclusively political treatises also. It was utilized as early as the latter half of the fourth century B.C. by Kauṭalya,[1] one of the first among the historical names in political science. According to him in the *Artha-śāstra* (I, 4) the logic of the fish prevails while the state is unformed. "In the absence of the wielder of punishment the powerful swallows the powerless". And Kāmandaka also, who several centuries later (*c* 500 A.C.) generally follows Kauṭalya, writes in his *Nīti-Sāra* (Digest of Politics), II, 40, that in the absence of punishment (*daṇḍa*) the destructive or ruinous logic of the fish operates through mutual animosities of the people and leads to the disruption of the world.

[1] Re date and personality see "Kauṭalya and His Boswell" by the present author in the *Calcutta Review* (August, 1935).

Nor was the doctrine confined within the circle of academicians and theorizers. We find it prevalent even among diplomatists and practical statesmen, e.g. of the ninth century. In the declarations of the Bengali emperor Dharmapāla[1] we are informed that his illustrious dynasty owed its origin to an "election" by the people. We are told further that it was "in order to escape from the logic of the fish", i.e., in order to escape from being absorbed into another kingdom, or to avoid being swallowed like a fish that the people of Bengal "made his father Gopāla accept the sovereignty". The mediæval Hindu monarch was here using almost the same metaphor as has been employed in the nineteenth century by I. S. Mill in his essay on *Liberty* when he explains how "in order to prevent the weaker members of the community from being preyed upon by innumerable vultures it was needful that there should be an animal of prey stronger than the rest, commissioned to keep them down".

This theory of the non-state or the state of nature has had important bearings on other doctrines of Hindu political philosophy. For the present we have only to note that in India political speculation was not divorced from the general intellectual currents in the society. The political philosophers tried to keep abreast of the contemporary thought in other branches of inquiry. The logical apparatus and dialectical machinery used in political discussions were familiar instruments in the cultural *milieu* of the scientific world.

Mātsya-nyāya, for instance, is an expressive technical term in India's legal phraseology. In Raghunātha's (fifteenth century) *Laukika-Nyāya-Samgraha*[2]

[1] R. D. Banerji : *Banglar Itihasa* (History of Bengal) Calcutta, Vol. I. (1915) pp. 147-149.

[2] K. L. Sarkar: *Rules of Interpretation in Hindu Law* Lecture VI.

(compilation of popular legal maxims) we find the "logic of the fish" coupled with the "logic of the monsters". The logic of the monsters is known as *Sundopasunda-Nyāya*. Sunda and Upasunda are two monster-brothers, like Pyrochles and Cymochles in Spenser's *Faerie Queene*. They are said to have quarrelled over the nymph Tilottamā and destroyed each other in the contest. Thus when two contradictory facts are equally strong, they neutralize each other. But when they are of unequal strength, i.e., when one can overpower the other, there is generated a field for the operation of the logic of the fish and the survival of the fitter.

The logic of the fish arises, as Raghu-nātha explains it, under a double set of conditions. First, there must have to be a conflict between a powerful and a comparatively powerless unit. And secondly, the latter must have been crushed and obliterated by the former. It is frequently referred to, says he, in the *Itihāsas* (treatises on History) and the *Purāṇas*, and he quotes the following passage from Vaśiṣṭha[1]: "By this time that *Rasātala* region had become extremely sovereignless, i.e., an anarchic non-state, characterized by the ignoble logic of the fish". Vaśiṣṭha's verse is elucidated by Raghu-nātha with the gloss that "strong fishes began to make an end of the weaker ones".

The non-state is then a state of anarchy, one in which the "tyranny of robbers" has full play, "justice is non-existent" and the "people prey upon one another". It is "the greatest evil" (*Mahā*, *Sānti*, LXVII, 1-3, 12-15). "Enjoyment of wealth and wives is impossible" under it. Only the robber is then happy. Even his happiness is precarious, because "the one

[1] A. K. Maitra : *Gauḍa-lekha-mālā* (Inscriptions of the Bengali Imperial Dynasty) in Bengali, 1912, p. 19.

is deprived of his loot by two, the two are robbed of theirs by several combined". A "free man is made a slave" and "women are raped".

The psychology of men in the state of nature is brought out in the Book on *Santi* (peace), LIX, 15-21, of the *Mahābhārata* according to the following causal nexus: "Then foolishness or stupidity (*moha*) seized their minds. Their intelligence being thus eclipsed, the sense of justice (*dharma*) was lost. Cupidity or temptation (*lobha*) overpowered them next. Thus arose the desire (*kāma*) for possessing things not yet possessed. And this led to their being subjugated by an affection (*rāga*) under which they began to ignore the distinction between what should and what should not be done. Consequently there appeared sexual license, libertinism in speech and diet, and indifference to morals. When such a revolution set in among men, Brahman (the idea of Godhead) disappeared, and with it, law (*dharma*)".

It is thus with the negation of morals and manners, the nullification of property, the very antithesis of law and justice that the non-state is identified. And this appears to have been the fundamental position of Hindu theorists on the state. From this negative analysis it requires but a logical "conversion" according to the law of "contraries" to establish positively the philosophy of the state. To this we shall now address ourselves.

SECTION 3

THE DOCTRINE OF DAṆḌA

(*Punishment*, *Coercion*, *Sanction*)

Two "inseparable accidents" of the Hindu theory of the state, are, first, the doctrine of *mamatva* ("mine-ness") or *svatva* (*suum*), i.e., "one's own"-ness, *proprium*, *Eigentum* or property, and secondly, the doctrine of *dharma* (i.e., law, justice and duty). And behind them both lies the doctrine of *daṇḍa* (punishment, restraint, or sanction). Herein is to be sought the nucleus of the whole philosophy of sovereignty.

A state is a state, argue Hindu philosophers, because it can coerce, restrain, compel. Eliminate control or the coercive element from social (*samūha*) or organized life, and the state as an entity vanishes. *Daṇḍa* is *ueberhaupt* the very essence of statal relations. No *daṇḍa*, no state. A *daṇḍa*-less i.e., sanctionless state is a contradiction in terms. In Koellreutter's language *Staat ohne Macht ist undenkbar* (state without command is unthinkable).

We have noticed above that the absence of *daṇḍa* is tantamount to *mātsya-nyāya* or the state of nature. It is clear also that property and *dharma* do not exist in that non-state. These entities can have their roots only in the state. The theory thus consists of two formulae:

I. No *danda*, no state;

II. (a) No state, no *dharma*, and

(b) No state, no property.

What, then, is the *rationale* of this *daṇḍa*?[1] What is it that makes coercion the *sine qua non* of the state? Why is it that the very idea of government should imply a restraint, a check, a control, a sanction? In Hindu political philosophy the answer to these questions is to be found in the "original nature of man".

[1]In regard to *daṇḍa* see the section on the "psychological premises of Hindu politics" in the *Pos. Back.* Vol. II. (Allahabad, 1921), pp. 31-34; cf. O. Koellreutter: *Grundriss der allgemeinen Staatslehre* (Tuebingen, 1933), chapter on *Macht und Autoritaet*, pp. 54-57.

The phenomena of government are founded on the data of the human psychology. And in regard to them the general trend of thought all the world over seems to have been the same. In ancient China Hsun Tze (B.C. 305-235?) strongly condemned the doctrine of Mencius (B.C. 373-289) who had postulated the "original goodness" of human nature. For, according to his counter-theory (Book XXIII) "man is by nature wicked, his goodness is the result of nurture". A curved twig, to cite again from Su Hu's work (VI, iii), needs straightening and heating and bending in order to become straight.** And man who is by nature wicked needs teaching and discipline in order to be right and requires the influence of *Li* and *Yi* (*Sittlichkeit*) in order to be good. The ancient rulers understood the native viciousness of man,** and therefore created morals, laws and institutions in order that human instincts and impulses might be disciplined and transformed."

Let us now turn to the Western world. Seneca, the Stoic philosopher of the first century A.C., "looked upon the institutions of society as being the results of vice, of the corruption of human nature. They are conventional institutions made necessary by the actual defects of human nature." The philosophical "anarchists " of modern times will not, however, accept this doctrine. Men indeed had known a previous period of innocence; but after a time, according to this Roman thinker, they became avaricious. "Avarice rent the first happy society asunder. It resulted that even those who were made wealthy became poor, for desiring to possess things for their own, they ceased to possess all things. The rulers grew dissatisfied with their paternal rule; the lust of authority seized upon them"[1]

[1] A.J. and R.W. Carlyle: *Mediæval Political Theory in the West* (London), Vol. I. (1903) pp. 24, 129.

This doctrine of human depravity and the natural wickedness of man was entertained by the Church Fathers also. St. Irenaeus (second century A.C.) in discussing the causes which have made government necessary holds the view that "men departed from God and hated their fellow men, and fell into confusion and disorder of every kind; and so God set men over each other imposing the fear of man upon man, and subjecting men to the authority of men, that by this means they might be compelled to some measure of righteousness and just dealing".

The idea that "the institution of government was made necessary by sin and is a divinely appointed remedy for sin" was continued and developed by St. Augustine and St. Gregory the Great. It was "emphatically restated by the ecclesiastical and political writers" of the period from the ninth to the thirteenth century and found a champion in Pope Hildebrand, Gregory VII. (1073-1085)[1].

The verdict of Hindu thinkers on the nature of man is identical. According to Kāmandaka (II, 42), men are by nature subject to passions and are covetous of one anothers' wealth and wives. "Rare", says Manu (VII, 21-24), "is the man pure or sinless" (by nature). *Durlabho hi śuchirnaraḥ.* The lower ones tend to usurp the places of the higher. People are prone to interfering with the rights of others and violating morals and manners.

Not that there was no Saturnian golden age of pristine purity and bliss. For, says the *Mahābhārata* (*Śānti*, LIX,14) anticipating over a millennium the dogmas of Father Lactantius and others, "at first there was neither state nor ruler, neither punishment

[1] *Ibid* Vol. II, 143-146, Vol. III, 97, 105, 187.

not anybody to exercise it. The people used to protect one another through innate righteousness (*dharma*) and sense of justice". But, as among Stoics and Canonists, the "fall" of mankind is accounted for by the Hindus also on the basis of a postulate of sin, loss of true religion, *moha*, stupidity and what not.

On the whole, therefore, it is not a roseate, romantic conception of human tendencies and instincts that the *Mahābhārata* offers. The dictum, "spare the rod, and spoil the child", proverbial in Western pedagogics, might be dittoed by the Hindu thinkers. For, as we read in the Book on *Śānti* (LXVIII,8-22), by nature "men tend to overthrow one another. Left to itself the "whole world would be in a mess" like a devil's workshop. As a rule, men are used to behaving like the "creatures that cannot see one another when the sun and the moon do not shine", or like the "fishes in the shallow waters", or "birds in places safe from molestation where they can fly at one another's throats in a suicidal strife".

Men, we are told, normally acknowledge only one right and that is the right of might. Those who do not part with their property for the asking run the risk of being killed. (LXVIII,14) . Wives , children and food of the weak are liable to be seized perforce by the strong. "Murder, confinement and persecution constitute the eternal lot of the propertied classes". The very phrase, "This is mine" (*Mamedam*), may be lost from the vocabulary, and *mamatva* or property become "extinct",—an ideal which was being feverishly pursued in the Utopia of Soviet Russia during 1918-21 previous to the inauguration of Lenin's "New Economic Policy" (1922).

The natural tendency of human relations, again, is toward sexual promiscuity (*yonidoṣa*), LXVIII,22.

The formation of marriage alliances or of stable societies is not instinctively prompted to man as he is. And if possible, he would shirk even agriculture, commerce, and other means of livelihood, preferring a state of slothful ease and "primrose path of dalliance".

Such is the man natural, or man as Nature made him, in the political anthropology of the *Mahābhārata*. This state of license is the farthest removed not only from a Wordsworthian "Nature's holy plan" but also from the picture of original man governed by a law of "reason" as exhibited in Locke's treatises on *Civil Government*. Nor is it anything but antipodal to the Rousseauesque faith in man's natural impulses and idealization of the "human heart by which we live". Instead, therefore, of postulating with the writer of the *Emile* that "all things are good as their Author made them, but everything degenerates in the hands of man", or finding "reason to complain what man has made of man", the Hindu students of political theory set a high premium on the institutions and coventions that make up the artificial thing called civilization. In fact it is to "educate" man out of the deplorable mire of primitive license and beastly freedom that government has been instituted, say they. The state is designed to correct human vices or restrain them and open out the avenues to a fuller and higher life. And all this is possible only because of *daṇḍa*.

In all discussions of political theory, therefore, the doctrine of *daṇḍa* occupies a foremost place. Some writers have even called their treatises on politics and statecraft *daṇḍa-nīti* (Laws of Sanction, or Science of *Daṇḍa*). In the *Manu Samhitā* (VII, 14-23), at any rate, no other category is calculated to command greater attention. For, is not *daṇḍa* "divine, God's own son, the protector of all beings, and as powerful as law itself?" Indeed, it keeps all created beings to their respective duties (*sva-dharma*), the "virtue" of Plato or the "functions" of Bradley[1] and other neo-Hegelians like Bosanquet and the Italian philosopher Croce,—and makes the diverse men and women cooperate to the enjoyment (*bhoga*) or happiness of all mankind. The *division du travail* of which Durkheim speaks is brought about by *daṇḍa* according to Manu. Nay, it is in reality "the king, the male (compared with which all other things are female), the manager of affairs, the ruler, the surety for the four orders pursuing their own duties in life. Further, it governs, protects, watches; and last but not least, is identical with law. To crown all, the whole world is rectified by *daṇḍa* and even the gods and demigods are subject to its authority.

Daṇḍa, as interpreted by Manu, is obviously the very principle of omnipotence, comparable to the *majestas* of Bodin or the *summa potestas* of Grotius. It is the abstraction of that power whose concrete embodiment is *aiśvarya*, *svāmitva* or sovereignty in a state, which is explained by Figgis as the real "divine right" of kings. It is absolute, with jurisdiction over all, uncontrolled by any entity. To use a very recent category, *daṇḍa* is the most signal feature of *Staatsraeson* (reason of the state), an expression of *Machtpolitik*, and marked by *autolimitazione* (self-limitation) in the sense of Jellinek and Redano[2].

A ruler *in office* personifies this *daṇḍa* but the ruler as a person is subject to it as every other individual

[1] H.W. Carr: *Philosophy of Benedotto Croce* (London, 1917), p. 127, etc., B. Bosanquet: *Some Suggestions in Ethics* (London, 1918) pp. 43-44, 64-65, also the present author's *Pos. Back.* vol. II. (1921) p. 28.

[2] F. Meinecke: *Die Idee der Staatsraeson* (Munich, 1925), pp. 349-354, U. Redano: *Lo Stato Etico* (Florence, 1927), pp. 207-210.

is. Hence the inevitable dilemma of kingship in the Hindu theory of the state. It is by wielding this terrible weapon that the king is to preside over and regulate the state. He is the *daṇḍa-dhara*, i.e., holder or bearer of the instrument of sovereignty, the *Macht-traeger*, but he is himself liable to be scorched by it, may be one of its first victims for he is not "infallible".

In Hindu political thought, therefore, *daṇḍa* is a two-handed engine and cuts both ways. On the one hand, it is a terror to the people and is corrective of social abuses. It is a moralizer, purifier, and civilizing agent. As Kāmandaka (II,40-42) observes, it is by the administration of *daṇḍa* that the state can be saved from a reversion to the logic of the fish and utter annihilation, as well as the people set right. It is through fear of punishment, according to the *Śukra-nīti* (IV, i, lines 92-102), that people become "virtuous" and refrain from committing aggression or indulging in untruths. *Daṇḍa* is efficacious, moreover, in causing the cruel to become mild, the wicked to give up wickedness, and the garrulous to beware of loquacity. It can subdue even beasts, and of course it frightens the thieves and terrifies the enemies into submission as tributaries, demoralizing all those that are wayward. Nay, it is good also for preceptors and can bring them to their senses, should they happen to be addicted to an extra dose of vanity or unmindful of their own avocations. Finally, it is the foundation of civic life, being the "great stay of all virtues"; and all the "methods and means of statecraft" would be fruitless without a judicious exercise of *daṇḍa*. Its uses as a beneficent agency in social life are, therefore, unequivocally recommended by Śukra.

But, on the other hand, *daṇḍa* is also a most potent instrument of danger to the ruler himself, to the powers that be. For, "uneasy lies the head that wears the crown", in more sense than one. The mal-administration of *daṇḍa*, says Kāmandaka (II,39) leads to the fall of the ruler. If the ruler is wise enough to manipulate it carefully, as Manu observes (VII, 19), it is surely conducive to the greatest good of the people. But what is the guarantee that the holder of the weapon would not bungle with it and handle it thoughtlessly or arbitrarily? Should that be the case, the *daṇḍa* would lead to the ruin of the state. And would the office-bearer, the king, got scot-free? By no means. Manu (VII, 28-30) is an advocate of regicide. He does not hesitate to declare that *daṇḍa* would smite the king who deviates from his duty, from his "station in life". It would smite his relatives too together with his castles, territories and possessions. The common weal depends, therefore, on the proper exercise of the *summa potestas*, the *aiśvarya*, the *Staatsraeson*.

Daṇḍa thus carries with it its own nemesis, and we are at once reminded of Mill who says in his *Liberty* that "as the king of the vultures would be no less bent upon preying on the flock than any of the minor harpies it was indispensable to be in a perpetual attitude of defence against his beak and claws". It is a like bulwark of people's rights as against the ruler that is furnished by the Hindu doctrine of *daṇḍa* in so far as its efficacy is attributed to the careful handling of it. In the first place, Manu would not allow any ill-disciplined man to be the administrator of the *daṇḍa*. In the second place, the "greatest amount of wisdom" e.g., that accruing from the "help of councillors and others" is held to be the essential pre-condition for the handling of this instrument. And here is available the logical check on the eventual absolutism of the *daṇḍa-dhara* (*Machttraeger*) in the Hindu theory of sovereignty.

By the doctrine of *daṇḍa*, then, the state is conceived as a pedagogic institution or moral laboratory, so to speak, not necessarily a Lycurgan barrack, of course. In Redano's language Manu would say that *lo Stato si fa educatore del popolo suo*,[1] i.e. the state makes itself the educator of its own people. It is an organization in and through which men's natural vices are purged, and it thereby becomes an effective means to the general uplifting of mankind. It is nothing but *lo Stato etico* (the ethical state) that is recognized by Manu. Hindu theorists therefore consider the state to be an institution "necessary" to the human race if it is not to grovel in the condition of *mātsya-nyāya* ruled by the law of beasts. Man, if he is to be man, i.e., possess *dharma*, virtue, liberty, justice etc. cannot do without political organization. He must have a state, and must submit to sanction, coercion and punishment,—in a word, to *daṇḍa*.

In the two-handed engine of the *daṇḍa*, then, we encounter, on the one side, *Staatsraeson* (interests of the state), and on the other, *Sittlichkeit* (i.e. morality, virtue, *dharma*, etc.). The conception of this eternal polarity in societal existence is one of the profoundest contributions of Hindu philosophy to human thought.

[1]U. Redano: *Lo Stato Etico* (Florence, 1927), pp. 276-278, 278-282. The German "idealist" Jellinek's political philosophy has been rendered into Italian in this text of what may be described as the Fascist theory of the state. It is interesting to observe how the Italian interpreter is combating one German idealist, Hegel, and establishing his own thesis by virtually paraphrasing another German idealist, Jellinek; pp. 207 214, 270-271.

SECTION 4

THE DOCTRINE OF MAMATVA (PROPERTY)

According to the *Mahābhārata*, *Manu Samhitā*, *Śukranīti* and other texts of Hindu political theory, government is by nature coercive because man is by nature vicious. The state can thus be born only in and through *daṇḍa*, i.e., punishment or sanction. It is out of a condition of the "logic of the fish" (*mātsya-nyāya*) or the Hobbesian and Spinozistic "state of nature", that *daṇḍa* brings into existence a well-regulated civil society called the state (Manu VII, 20, Kauṭalya, I. iv). In Aristotelian terminology *daṇḍa* would be the "efficient cause" of the state.

What, now, are the marks of the state? How does it declare its existence? What are its functions? In what manner does it make itself felt among the people? In Hindu theory the state, as soon as it crystallizes itself into shape, conjures up, first, *mamatva* ("mine"-ness, *Eigentum*, *proprium*) or *svatva* (*suum*), i.e., property, and secondly, *dharma* (law, *Sittlichkeit*, justice and duty) out of primitive chaos or socioplasmic anarchy. Both these institutions are creations of the state. The state functions by generating them, and people recognize it in its activities fostering their nurture. *Mamatva* and *dharma* are therefore two fundamental categories in the political speculation of the Hindus.

According to the *Śāntiparva* (LXVIII, 8-19) of the *Mahābhārata* property does not exist in the non-state (*mātsya-nyāya*) i.e., in the condition of men left to the pursuit of their "own sweet will". In the non-state, of course, men can possess or enjoy, but they do not "own". Property, however, is not mere *bhoga*, i.e., enjoying or possessing, its essence consists in *mamatva* or *svatva*, i.e., ownership. It is "one's own"-

ness that underlies the "magic of property". To be able to say *mamedam* (This is mine) about something constitutes the very soul of owning or appropriation.

This proprietary consciousness is created in men for the first time by the state through its sanction, the *daṇḍa*. For it enjoins that vehicles, apparel, ornaments, and jewels must be "enjoyed by those to whom they belong", and that one's wife, children, and food "must not be encroached upon by others". And it is only through *bhaya* or fear of the state that the people observe these injunctions, and the sanctity of property is kept entire.

A distinction is here brought out between mere *bhoga* and *mamatva* as the basis of the difference between the non-state and the state. In Europe the identical discrimination has been made by Rousseau in his *Social Contract*. "In the state of nature", says he, "there is but possession which is only the effect of the force or right of the first occupant"; whereas "ownership which is founded only upon a positive title" is an incident of "civil society".

Property (*bhoga* plus *mamatva*), then, is a *differentium* between the non-state and the state. And juridically speaking, the property taken cognizance of by the state is *laukika*, i.e., worldly, material, or secular, as the *Mitākṣarā*, the *Sarasvatī-vilāsa*, and other law-books make it clear[1]. Thus considered it is necessarily also a *differentium* between the state and the extra-state, e.g., a *Sukhāvatī*, the transcendental Land of Bliss in Buddhist metaphysical lore[2]. For, in that super-sen-

[1] Jolly: *Recht und Sitte* (Strassburg, 1896), p. 91. *Svatvam laukikam (das Eigentum ist weltlich)*; *Sarasvativilas "geht vielleicht am weitesten in dieser Richtung" in dem es die Entstehung des Eigentums aus rein weltlichen Akten betont"*.

[2] *Buddhist Mahayana Texts* (Sacred Books of the East Series) vol. XLIX. Part II, pp. 13, 43, 55.

sual region "beings are not born with any idea of property even with regard to their own body". Besides, according to the *Gītā*, property is not to be acquired by ascetics and monks who desire to live, like the Senecan "wise man" or the Catholic Capuchin, an extra-statal or super-political life, in which, as the proverb goes, man is either a beast or a god.

We are not concerned here, however, with property, *laukika* as it is, in its bearings as a legal institution. The Hindu analysis of the distinction between real and personal property or discussion of the right to use, destroy, transfer, bequeath and sell each species of property, need not therefore detain us. We are interested for the present in the concept of property as a political category only, i.e., as influencing the theory of the state. But it may be remarked, in passing, that it is the state backed by *daṇḍa* that gives validity to the "seven modes" (Manu X, 115) of acquiring property and to its "three titles" (Vaśiṣṭha XVI, 10) as well as to other legal incidents.[1]

Nor does it fall within our scope to discuss the concept of property as an economic entity. Obviously, of course, the property generated by the state is Aristotelian in its exclusiveness, as the phrase *mamedam* signifies. It does not contemplate the communism of Plato or of More. "A field", says Manu (IX, 44) "belongs to him who cleared away the forests, and a deer to him who first wounded it". This is individualistic tenure and jurisdiction in their primitive form.[2] But no matter whether held in common or private, it is pertinent to observe that the sacredness of property can be established only by the state through its *daṇḍa*.

[1] Jolly, pp. 90-92.

[2] C.J.M. Letourneau : *Property: Its Origin and Development* (London, 1907), p. 72.

Two miraculous changes are effected in social life, once private property is thus ushered into existence. First, people can sleep at night without anxiety "with doors open". And secondly, women decked with ornaments may walk without fear though "unattended by men" (*Mahā, Śānti*, LXVIII, 30-32). Property is in Hindu philosophy, thus considered, not the cause but the effect of the state. The position is entirely opposite to that of the Marxian "economic interpretation of history".

This sense of security as regards property is therefore the first great achievement in the humanization of Caliban. This is the first item in the civilizing of man by *daṇḍa* out of the *mātsya-nyāya*, or "law of beasts and birds". One can, therefore, discover in *daṇḍa* the very foundation of human liberty and progress. And this is the standpoint of Hindu political philosophy as of modern "idealism" in European philosophy.[1]

SECTION 5

THE DOCTRINE OF DHARMA

(*Law, Justice and Duty*)

Property is the first acquisition of man through the state. His second acquisition is *dharma*. The doctrine of *dharma* is like the doctrine of *mamatva* an essential factor in the theory of the state, and both have their foundations in the doctrine of *daṇḍa*.

There is no *dharma* in the non-state, i.e., in the condition of men left to themselves. It comes into existence with the state. *Dharma* is created by the state or rather by its sanction, *daṇḍa* (Manu VII, 14,

[1] U. Redano: *Lo Stato Etico* (Florence, 1927), pp. 278-282.

15, 18). No state, no *dharma*. *Dharma* does not flourish where "politics" is not, it flourishes only as long as there is the state. In other words, *dharma* appears as *mātsya-nyāya* disappears, and *dharma* ceases to exist with the extinction of the state. Logically, therefore, a people can have no *dharma* when its statal life is abolished, e.g., through loss of freedom, revolution or anarchy.

We shall now proceed to analyze this *dharma*. What is that category in Hindu philosophy which, besides property, serves to differentiate the state from the non-state ? What is that characteristic, shorn of which, as shorn of *mamatva*, the state would revert to the condition of *mātsya-nyāya*? The answer to these questions lies in the doctrine of *dharma*.

Dharma is a very elastic term. Like *jus*, *Recht*, *droit*, *diritto*, it has more than one meaning. It really admits of almost all the ambiguities associated with the term "law" as analyzed by Holland in his *Jurisprudence*. Thus there are at least five senses in which *dharma* can be used both in scientific treatises as well as in common parlance, viz,

1. religion, a category of theology, e.g., Confucian *dharma*, Mohammedan *dharma*, Christian *dharma*, Hindu *dharma* etc.
2. virtue, as opposed to vice or sin, a category of ethics,
3. law, as a category of jurisprudence,
4. justice,
5. duty.

For purposes of political theory we need not attend to 1 and 2 for the time being and may confine ourselves to the import of *dharma* as law, justice, and duty, as somewhat new values of life. The doctrine of *dharma* then enunciates three propositions:—first, that the state differs from the non-state as a law-giving institution; secondly, that the state differs from the non-state as a justice-dispensing institution; and thirdly, that the state differs from the non-state as a duty-enforcing institution.

In the *mātsya-nyāya* there is no law, no justice, no duty. The state is the originator of law, justice and duty.

A. *Dharma* as Law.

Dharma (law) is the creation of the state, and the state, as such, has the sanction of *daṇḍa*. Theoretically, therefore, every *dharma*, if it is nothing but *dharma*, is *ipso facto* what should be called "positive" in the Austinian sense. *Dharma* is obeyed as *dharma*, only because of the coercive might of the state. All *dharma-śāstras*, i.e., the legal text books, e.g., those of Manu, Yājnavalkya, Nārada, Brihaspati and others, would thus automatically acquire the character of "statute"-books simply because their validity, provided they have any validity, depends on the authority of the state. The Yājnavalkyas and Manus would obviously have no "sanction" in a condition of *mātsya-nyāya*.

But probably, so far as actual practice is concerned, the *dharma-śāstras* of India had no greater sanctity than as treatises embodying the "positive morality" of the different ages. Let us, therefore, examine how the nature of *dharma* (as law) was understood by the theorists themselves. As is well-known, law as a category of jurisprudence has passed through two stages in European thought. The same two concepts we notice in Hindu political philosophy also.

In ancient European theory law is the embodiment of eternal justice. Thus according to Demosthenes (fourth century B.C.) laws are the gifts of the gods and the discovery of the sages. In Aristotle's conception law is the rule of God and reason. Stoics like Cicero and Seneca believed that law lies in the hearts of all men.

The doctrine of "natural law", of law as the "king of all things", was maintained by the jurists such as Gaius and others whose views are codified in the *Digest* of Justinian. It was the theory also of Celsus and other Church Fathers. In medieval European (Teutonic) theory,[1] so far as there was any theory independent of the tradition of Roman jurisprudence, law was not something "made" or created at all, but something which existed as a part of the national, or local, or tribal life.

The modern theory of law in Europe may be said to have originated in the sixteenth and seventeenth centuries with Bodin and Hobbes in their analysis of sovereignty. It has since become classical, however, as the handiwork of Austin, the father of analytical jurisprudence (Lecture VI). According to this view, law is the command of the sovereign enforced by a sanction.

Thus there are two theories of law,—first, law as uncreated or original, existing either as a part of the universal human conscience, taught by "natural reason", or as a custom among the people; and secondly, law as created by the fiat of a law-maker, as something which is to be obeyed not because it is just, good or eternal, but because it has been enacted by the state. Both these conceptions are to be found among the speculations of Hindu political philosophers. The

[1]Carlyle, Vol. I. p. 235; T. Mackenzie: *Studies in Roman Law* (Edinburgh, 1862), G.L. Gomme: *Folklore as an Historical Science* (London, 1908), pp. 84-100.

distinction between positive law and ethics is clearly set forth by Vijnāneśvara (eleventh century) in his notes on the text of Yājnavalkya[1] in regard to the judicial duties of the king.

The ethical conception of law as the dictate of conscience i.e., as *jus naturale* has a long tradition in Hindu thought. In the *Brihadāraṇyakopaniṣat* (I, 4, 14) law is identical with truth and as powerful as king. It is of course the creation of God. Brahman (God), we are told, "was not strong enough". So he "created still further the most excellent *dharma*. * * * * * There is nothing higher than law. Thenceforth even a weak man rules a stronger with the help of the law, as with the help of a king. Thus the law is what is called the true. And if a man declares what is truth, they say he declares the law; and if he declares the law, they say he declares what is true. Thus both are the same."

According to Āpastamba (I, 7, 20, 8), law is what is "unanimously approved in all countries by men of the Aryan society, who have been properly obedient to their teachers, who are aged, of subdued senses, neither given to avarice, nor hypocrites". In the *Manu Samhitā* (II, 1), again, law is whatever is practised and cherished at heart by the virtuous and the learned, who are devoid of prejudices and passions. Vaśiṣṭha (I, 5, 6) and Baudhāyana (I, 1, 1, 4-6) also hold the view that law is the practice of the *śiṣṭas*, i.e. those whose hearts are free from "desire." The *śiṣṭas* or *riṣis*, i.e., passionless and unavaricious persons of India are obviously the "sages" of Demosthenes.

And in Yājnavalkya's Code (I, 1, i, Introduction, 7),

[1] T. N. Mitra: *Law Relating to Hindu Widow* (Calcutta, 1881) pp. 32-33. K.L. Sarkar: *Rules of Interpretation in Hindu Law* (Calcutta) Lect. IX. p. 116.

according to which law is *sadāchāra*, i.e., the "practice or conduct of good men", what "seems pleasant or good to one's self", and the "desire that springs from mature consideration", as well as in the *Vyavahāra Darpaṇa*, where law is described as something "eternal and self-existent, the king of kings", far "more powerful and right" than they, we have once more the Oriental counterpart of Greek, Stoic, Roman and Patristic conceptions of law as morality.

In Hindu analysis *dharma* came to be defined as positive law also. The conception of law as *rājnām-ājnā* in Kauṭalya's language, i.e., as command enforced by sanction, finds clear expression in the writings of Nārada, Śukra, Jaimini and his commentator Sabara Svāmi. In Nārada's *Smriti* (Introduction, 1, 2) we are informed that the performance of duty having fallen into disuse, positive law (*vyavahāra*) has been introduced, and that the king as superintending the law is known as *daṇḍa-dhara* or wielder of *daṇḍa* (the power to punish). The sanction is definitely mentioned in the *Śukra-nīti* (I, lines 623-624) according to which the sovereign should categorically state in his command that he would "surely destroy by severe punishment those offenders who after having heard these his decrees would act contrary to them."

In order that the law may be seriously recognized as command Śukra stipulates that the greatest amount of publicity should be given to it. For instance, it is the duty of the sovereign to have the laws announced by the state drum (I, 625-626) or have them inscribed in esplanades as written notices. The documents embodying these commands (*śāsana-patra*) are to bear the king's signature, date, etc. (II, 607, 608). Laws thus being the promulgations of the state, we read further in the *Śukra-nīti* (IV, i, lines 116-119) that the king is the "maker of the age", the "cause of time," and of the good and evil practices, and that since the ruler is the dictator of virtues and vices, people make it a point to practise that by which he is satisfied. Besides, as law is upheld by sanction we can easily understand why Śukra advises the sovereign to make use of his terrible weapon (I, 120) in order to maintain the people each in his proper sphere.

The same idea of positive law is expressed by Jaimini in the very definition of *dharma*. The *Mīmāmsā-sūtra* declares *chodanālakṣaṇohrtho dharmah.*[1] *Dharma* is that desired-for object (*artha*) which is characterized by command (*chodanā*). Jaimini has also examined the reason as to why that which is determined by a command should be obligatory. He analyzes the reason as lying in the fact that "the relation between the word of command and the purpose to which it is directed is eternally efficacious."[2]

The doctrine of *dharma* as law introduces into the theory of the state the cardinal element of *aiśvarya* or *svāmitva* i.e., sovereignty. Whether *dharma* be taken as equivalent to the dictates of a moral sense, or as the observance of a tribal or some other established usage, or as the deliberate order issued by an authority with threat of punishment in case of violation, it is clear enough that *dharma* is like *daṇḍa* the most awe-inspiring fact in the state's life. *Daṇḍa* and *dharma* are indeed the two faces of the political Janus, so to speak, the one looking to the failures, the other to the triumphs. Or, to express the same thing in a different way, *daṇḍa* is the root of a tree which flowers in *dharma*. The state can be recognized

[1] G. Jha: "Shabara Swami's Commentary on Jaimini's *Mīmāmsā*" in *Indian Thought* for 1910.

[2] K.L. Sarkar, Lect. I. pp. 23-24.

positively by *dharma* which is in evidence while *daṇḍa* maintains its vitality from behind.

B. *Dharma* as Justice.

We have now to understand the doctrine of *dharma* as justice in its bearing on the theory of the state. Justice does not exist in the *mātsya-nyāya*; if therefore a reversion to *mātsya nyāya* is to be avoided, i.e., if the state is to be maintained, justice must not be tampered with. Justice is necessarily as integral a limb of sovereignty in Hindu conception as law.

The dignity of justice has been declared by Manu (VIII, 15) in the following terms: "If justice is violated, it destroys the state, if preserved, it maintains the state. Therefore justice must not be destroyed". Such sentiments in the *Manu Samhitā* could be bodily incorporated in the writings of a Jonas or an Alcuin of the ninth century and other mediaeval European theorists[1] with whom the maintenance of justice is *sine qua non* of the state and kingship.

But what is justice ? It is a most practical or pragmatic definition that Hindu theorists offer. According to Manu (VIII, 3) justice consists in the application of law to the cases arising between the members of the state. And that law is to be known from the customs and from the *Institutes*, e.g., those of Gautama, Yājnavalkya and others.

Justice, as interpreted by *Sukra* (IV, v, lines 7-11) consists of two elements. First, it consists in a discrimination of the good from the bad (of course, according to the laws). Secondly, it has a utilitarian basis inasmuch as it is calculated to minister to the virtues of the rulers and the ruled and promote the common weal.

[1] Carlyle III, 109.

The doctrine of *dharma* as justice is thus organically connected with the theory of the state as contrasted with the non-state.

C. *Dharma* as Duty.

Mātsya-nyāya is a condition in which duties are nil. According to the *Śāntiparva* (LXVIII, 16) men left to themselves tend even to persecute their mothers, fathers, the aged, the teachers, the guests and the preceptors. It is the fear of *daṇḍa* that brings about an order among men, each man minding his own duty (*sva-dharma*) (*Śānti.* LXVIII, 8, *Manu* VII, 21, 22, 24, *Sukra* I., lines 45-51). The doctrine of *dharma* as duty is thus like that of *dharma* as justice naturally a doctrine of the conservation of the state. It is only from this standpoint that the theory of duties has a bearing on the theory of the state.

The doctrine of duty as stated in the *Gītā* (Ch. III) runs thus: "One's own duty, though defective, is better than another's duty well performed. Death in peforming one's duty is preferable; the performance of the duties of others is dangerous."[1]

The passage here has no mere metaphysical significance. This theory of *sva-dharma* (one's own duty) or "My Station and its Duties", as Bradley would define it, has a political significance as well. It has the sanction of the state behind it; for, says Manu (VIII, 335), "neither a father, nor a teacher, nor a friend, nor a mother, nor a wife, nor a son, nor a domestic priest must be left unpunished if they do not keep within their duty." According to Sukra (I, line 120, IV, iii. l 15) also the people should be kept each in his proper sphere

[1] B. Bosanquet: *Philosophical Theory of the State* (London, 1899), pp. 204-207. Barker: *Plato and His Predecessors* (London, 1918), p. 176.

by a "terrible use" of the weapon of sovereignty.

Duties are thus enforced by *daṇḍa*, which also backs the laws. Indeed from the angle of the *prajā* or *prakriti* (the people in the state), *dharma* as duty is but the obverse of *dharma* as law. What the state calls "laws" are recognized as "duties" by its members as a matter of course. The doctrine of duty is thus identical with that of law turned inside out.

Altogether, then, the doctrine of *dharma* in its entirety imparts to the state the character of an institution for the advancement of *la civiltà*, *Kultur*, "culture". The state elevates man out of the law of beasts by instituting legislation, adjudication, and enforcement of duties. The functions of the state are thus in keeping with the ideas involved in the doctrine of *daṇḍa*. The state as a pedagogic or purgatorial or moral-training institution is not merely a *mamatva*-insuring instrument, i.e., a property-securing agency, but a *dharma*-promoting *samūha* (public association), *lo stato etico* of Redano, the *Rechtsstaat* of Jellinek, i.e., the *Kultur-staat* of Fichte and Hegel, or the "virtue-state" of Plato. And herein the Hindu theory meets Aristotle's conception of the state as the means to the furtherance of the "highest good" of man.

SECTION 6

THE DOCTRINE OF VARNĀŚRAMA

(*Classes and Stages*)

Out of *mātsya-nyāya* evolves *dharma* through the fiat of *daṇḍa*. Now *dharma* has need to be embodied, i.e. *lo stato etico*, *l'organismo spirituale*, the *Rechtsstaat*, *Kultur-Staat* must have to materialize in space and time. This is accomplished in the *rāṣṭra*, which provides *aiśvarya* (sovereignty) with "a local habitation and a name". It is in and for the *rāṣṭra* that the state institutes *mamatva* and *dharma*. Property, law, justice and duty are concretely realized through this medium. The doctrine of *rāṣṭra* thus furnishes the crowning arch in the Hindu theory of the state.

What is this *rāṣṭra*? It signifies "the country". According to Śukra (IV, iii, line 2) both "movable and immovable things" are indicated by the term. It is a territorial concept comprehending an aggregate of human beings and material possessions and thus constitutes the "physical basis" of the state. It may be taken almost as equivalent to *res publica*. The doctrine of *rāṣṭra* would therefore naturally consist of two parts: (1) the doctrine of property and (2) the doctrine of *prajā*, *prakriti* or population. The doctrine of property has already been investigated. Let us now examine the doctrine of population in its bearing on the theory of the state.

In the *mātsya-nyāya* condition there is the people, but no state, because there is no *daṇḍa* to enforce *dharma*. If the *prajā* is not to remain *ad infinitum* an amorphous mass of *selb-staendig* atoms, it must have to follow *sva-dharma*, i.e., the members of the society must perform their respective "duties" which, as we have seen, are really "laws" turned inside out. The observance of these duties would necessarily imply the organization of the people into a unified state, a *samūha* or a *polis*.

Now, organisationally speaking, the *prakriti* or members of a society naturally fall into economic and professional groups, classes or orders, the *groupements professionnels*, the so-called "castes" of India. The alleged classification of a society into four occupational groups, e.g., Brāhmana, Kṣatriya, etc. is however a conventional myth, at best a legal fiction. Students of *Realpolitik* like Śukra (IV, iii, lines 22-23) are aware that the actual number of these orders or castes is "unlimited". The reason, as may be guessed, is stated in the *Śukra-nīti* to be the "intermixture of blood through marriages". These orders of *prajā* or classes of members of the state are known as *varṇas* i.e., colours, probably designated after some typical (or hypothetical?) ethnic complexion. Further, from the standpoint of the individual, we have to notice that people pass through well-marked metabolistic or rather physiological stages, e.g., infancy, adolescence etc. These stages or periods of life in every person are called the *āśramas*. They are arbitrarily known to be four in the span of human existence.

The total population with all its interests and problems of all the different periods of life is then comprehended by the two categories, *varṇas* (classes) and *āśramas* (stages) (Kāmandaka, II, 18-35). If therefore the people is to constitute a state, every member of each of the *varṇas* (no matter what their number and what their occupations) must have to observe the *Ordnung*, system or discipline, i.e. perform the duties (*sva-dharma*) of his "station" at each of the four *āśramaṣ* or periods of life. Thus, the soldier at the front must "do or die", the young man while at school must not marry, the king must keep to the coronation oath, and so forth. This is the doctrine of *varṇāśrama*, the counterpart of the Platonic correlation of "virtue" and status (*Republic*, II, III, IV)[1].

Incidentally we may refer[2] to what a contempo-

[1] See the present author's *Pos. Back.* Vol. II. (1921) p. 90, and "Die Struktur des Volkes in der sozialwissenschaftlichen Lehre der Schukraniti" (*Koelner Vierteljahrshefte fuer Soziologie*, Cologne, 1931).

[2] A. Joussain: "Introduction à la psychologie des Masses" (*Revue Internationale de sociologie*, Paris, May-June 1935).

rary French author analyzing the conception of the "masses" as equivalent to "the peoples" has to say about the existence of "castes" in European social polity. He maintains that *l'état social* of peoples such as have "attained to certain degree of civilisation" comprises not only the "*classes definissables par leur genre de vie, leur education, leurs manières, leurs occupations*" etc. (classes distinguishable according to their mode of living, education, manners, occupations etc. etc.) but also "*des castes, classes héréditaires et assez fermes* (castes, i.e., hereditary and very closed classes). Instances of such castes or "hereditary and very closed classes" are furnished by this writer from *la noblesse sous l'ancien regime* (the French aristocracy previous to the revolution of 1789-93) and the Roman patriciate. These are characterized, says he, "as in India" by the "community of professional occupations and religious observances", even by a "certain community of race". And these European castes are in his judgment at the same time professional groups, religious groups and ethnic groups.

We are not for the time being interested in the question of the universality of "castes" in addition to that of "classes". We would stress only that in the Hindu philosophy of social anatomy and social physiology it is necessary to observe the fiat of the political factor, the state. Students of the "new sociology" ought to note that the doctrine of social stratification, order and discipline is essentially political. This indeed is a substantial contribution of Hindu thought to the study of human relations.

As soon, then, as the *prajā* is organized into a state, be it in any part of the world or in any epoch of history, a *varṇāśrama* spontaneously emerges into being. It is inconceivable, in this theory, that there should be a state and yet no *varṇāśrama*. To say that the state has been born and yet the various orders or classes of the people do not follow *dharma* would indeed be a contradiction in terms, a logical absurdity. *Sva-dharma* (*Recht*) leads inevitably to *varṇāśrama* (*Ordnung*). The two are "relative" terms. In Koellreutter's terminology[1] *der Rechtsstaat* is at the same time *der Ordnungsstaat*. They indicate coexistent phenomena in the social world. In others words, the doctrine of *varṇāśrama* is a corollary to that of *dharma*, is but *sva-dharma* "writ large".

The non-existence of *varṇāśrama* is possible only under conditions of non-performance of duty. Suppose the *varṇas* do not follow *dharma*, e.g., the soldier flies from the enemy in a cowardly manner, the husband does not maintain the wife, the judge encourages the fabrication of false evidence, the king violates the *samaya* or compact with the *prakriti* and so forth. According to Śukra (VI, iv, lines 6, 82-83.) the offenders are to be rectified by the *daṇḍa* of the state. This is the supreme moment for the exercise of *aiśvarya* (sovereignty) and *Staatsraeson* (interests or reasons of the state). Why, even the king is not immune from penalty. Rather, as Manu (VIII, 336) declares "the settled rule", where "a common man would be fined one *kārṣāpaṇa* the king shall be fined one thousand". Really, a state is no state unless it can enforce as duty the *dharma* that it has enacted as law. This should be postulated in the irreducible minimum of the state's functions. One can, therefore, easily understand with Kāmandaka (II, 34) why if *dharma* is violated by the members of the state there is bound to be a *pralaya*

[1] *Deutsches Verfassungsrecht* (Berlin, 1935), pp. 11-15, see also O. Koellreutter: *Grundriss der allgemeinen Staatslehre* (Tuebingen, 1933), chapter on *Der Rechtsstaat*, pp. 106-109.

or dissolution of the world. Verily, with the extinction of *varṇāśrama* there is a reversion to *mātsya-nyāya*. The violation of *sva-dharma* and of *varṇāśrama* brings back the "state of nature", and the state automatically ceases to exist.

Varṇāśrama, though obviously an ethnico-economic and a socio-pedagogic term, is thus fundamentally a political concept. It is an indispensable category in an organic theory of the state. It is identical with *rāṣṭra* from the demographic (*prajā* or population) aspect. The doctrine of *varṇāśrama* is therefore the doctrine of *rāṣṭra minus* the doctrine of property; and further, the doctrine of *dharma* (as law and duty) applied to the total *prakriti* (or members of the state) coincides with the doctrine of classes and stages. The doctrine of *varṇāśrama* then is clearly an integral part in a consistent philosophy of politics.

From the standpoint of the *soziale Beziehungen*, social relations, and social interests, such as are being studied by the "new sociology" in Eur-America since the publication of Toennies's *Gemeinschaft und Gesellschaft* (1887) it may be pointed out that the Hindu category of classes and stages as embodied in the doctrine of *Varṇāśrama* is one of the most scientific and psychologically sound formulae in regard to the understanding of the "geometry" or "formal" anatomy and physiology of society. Without reference to the actual social conditions prevailing in India through the ages we should be inclined to appraise this doctrine as the greatest single contribution of Hindu philosophy to societal science.

SECTION 7

THE DOCTRINE OF MANḌALA

(*Geopolitical Sphere*)

The conception of "external" *aiśvarya* (sovereignty) was well established in the Hindu philosophy of the state. The Hindu thinkers not only analyzed sovereignty with regard to the constituent elements in a single state. They realized also that sovereignty is not complete unless it is external as well as internal, that is, unless the state can exercise its internal authority unobstructed by, and independently of, other states.

"Great misery", says Śukra, "comes of dependence on others. There is no greater happiness than that from self-rule". This is one of the maxims of the *Śukra-nīti* (III, line 646) bearing on the freedom of the *rāṣṭra*, or the land and the people in a state. Kauṭalya also in his remarks on "foreign rule" expresses the same idea in a negative manner. Under it, we are told in his *Artha-śāstra* (VIII, ii),[1] the country is not treated as one's own land, it is impoverished, its wealth carried off, or it is treated "as a commercial article". The description is suggestive of John Stuart Mill's metaphor of the "cattle farm" applied to the "government of one people by another".

The doctrine of independence (*svārājya*, *aparādhīnatva*) implied in this conception of external sovereignty was obviously the foundation of the theory of the state in relation with other states. And it gave rise to certain categories of *droit des gens* or *jus gentium*

[1] *Indian Antiquary*, 1910, p. 83. For older uses of the concept of *sva-rāj* (self-rule) *vide* the *Atharvaveda*, XVII, i. 22, 23; cf. Macdonell and Keith: *Vedic Index*, Vol. II, p. 494.

which normally influenced Hindu political thinking from at least the fourth century B.C. These concepts can more or less be grouped under the doctrine of *maṇḍala*, that is, sphere or circle (of influence, interests, ambitions, enterprise, and what not). Using the expression of Karl Haushofer, one can describe this *maṇḍala* as a complex of "geopolitical" relations,[1] i.e., all those situations relating to boundaries and the contacts with foreign races such as every statesman must carefully attend to.

This doctrine of *maṇḍala*, underlying as it does the Hindu ideas of the "balance of power" pervades the entire speculation on the subject of international relations. It is hinted at by Śukra (IV. i, lines 39-43) and referred to by Manu (VII, 154, 156, 204). Kāmandaka has devoted a whole chapter (VIII) to the topic. It has been exhaustively treated by Kauṭalya (VI, ii.) We are not concerned here with the doctrine as such, we shall only study it in its bearing on the theory of sovereignty.

In the first place, the doctrine of *maṇḍala* is essentially the doctrine of *vijigīṣu* (aspirant to conquest), of *Siegfried*. It is the cult of expansion. Now, the *Mahābhārata* (XII, lvi, 15, V, cxxvii, 19-20, cxxxiv, 39)[2] inculcates the ethics of "manliness as the highest thing" and characterizes it as consisting in a ceaseless "upward striving". The same aspiration to "press only up" and "bend not" or "elect glory even at the cost of life" can influence each and all of

[1] K. Haushofer: *Geopolitik der Pan-Ideen* (Berlin, 1931), K. Haushofer (editor): *Raumueberwindende Maechte* (Leipzig, 1934); Hennig: *Geopolitik* (Leipzig, 1931), B. K. Sarkar: "Haushofer's Cult of Geopolitik" (*Calcutta Review*, April 1934).

[2] Hopkins: "The position of the ruling caste etc." in the *Journal of the American Oriental Society*, 1889, pp. 156, 187-189.

the states on earth. The doctrine becomes necessarily a spur to the struggle for existence, self-assertion and world-domination among the *Siegfrieds*. The conception is thus altogether a dynamic factor calculated to disturb the equilibrium and *status quo* of international politics.

First, then, in regard to the doctrine of *vijigīṣu*. According to Kauṭalya[1] it is the ambition of each state to acquire "strength and happiness" for the people. The *élan vital* of a ruler in Kāmandaka's conception also lies in the "aspiration to conquer" (VIII, 1, 3, 6). The king, says he, should establish in himself the *nābhi* (or centre of gravity) of a system. He should become the lord of a *maṇḍala*. It is part of his duty to try to have "a full sphere around him" just as the "moon is encircled by a complete orb". The "full sphere" is, of course, the circle of states related to the *Siegfried* as allies, enemies and neutrals. Perpetual "preparedness" must therefore be the first postulate of *Realpolitik* in Hindu theory. "One should be ever ready with *daṇḍa*" (the "mailed fist"), declares Manu (VII, 102, 107) quite seriously, "should always have one's might in evidence and policies well-guarded, as well as be ever on the look out for the enemy's holes". Further, one should "bring to subjection all those elements that are obstacles to the career of triumph".

The *rationale* of this preparedness is very simple indeed. It is as elemental as human blood itself. It goes without question in the *Sukranīti* (IV, i, lines 15-17) that "all rulers are unfriendly", nay, they are "secret enemies to those who are rising, vigorous, virtuous and powerful". This position of Śukra's

[1] *Ind. Ant.* 1909, p. 184.

was maintained by Fichte[1] in 1807 and is identical with that of Carl Schmitt (in *Der Begriff des Politischen*, 1927) and of Oswald Spengler (in *Jahre der Entscheidung*, 1933), both of whom hold that in the war-relation or war-situation is to be found the proper political situation (*der eigentliche politische Zustand*).[2] According to them, further, as in Hindu political philosophy, the essence of foreign politics lies only in the conflicting relations or rivalries of the peoples. "What wonder in this?" asks Śukra, and his solution is given in another query, which, "geopolitical" as it is, carries its own answer: viz., "Are not the rulers covetous of territory?" Such being the data of international psychology, Kāmandaka (VIII, 58, 67) frankly suggests that "in order to do away with one's enemies their kith and kin should be employed" whenever possible. For, is not poison outdone by poison, diamond cut by diamond, and the elephant subdued by the elephant? "Fishes, again, swallow fishes, similarly relatives, relatives." The *Rāmāyaṇa* is cited in the *Kāmandakīnīti* for a corresponding precedent in diplomatic tactics. The fact is well known that in order to overthrow Rāvaṇa his brother Vibhīṣaṇa was exploited by Rāma.

The *vijigīṣu*, then, cannot by any means afford to indulge in "pious wishes" or have faith in the utopian statecraft of idealistic dreamers. What under these conditions are likely to be the relations between the hypothetical Siegfrieds of the *nīti-śāstras*? These firebrands are normally endowed with a war-menta-

[1] F. Meinecke: *Die Idee der Staatsraeson* (Munich, 1925), pp. 462-463.

[2] O. Koellreutter: *Deutsches Verfassungsrecht* (Berlin, 1935), p. 4. The ideas of Schmitt and Spengler are combated by this author while offering the "national-socialistic" viewpoint of politics.

lity and a bellicose attitude. The world in their eyes is a theatre of warfare and equipment for warfare, as it has really been since the Chinese philosopher Sun Tzu wrote his *Art of War*; and they proceed on the assumption that nothing can be unfair in war. The student of political science must therefore have to make almost the same remarks about the "aspirants" of Hindu political speculation as as those of Grotius in the prolegomena to his epoch-making *Law of War and Peace* (1625). "I saw prevailing throughout the Christian world", writes the father of international law in regard to the European international politics of the early seventeenth century, "a license in making war of which even barbarous nations would have been ashamed. Recourse was had to arms for slight reason or no reason, and when arms were taken up, all reverence for divine and human law thrown away, just as if men were henceforth authorized to commit all crimes without restraint".

The *vijigīṣu* would think like Maude of the British War-office that the "surest means of keeping the peace is war", or like Stockton, the American militarist, that "the army and the navy is not a burden during peace, but if properly maintained is but a paying business proposition." He can also have the idealism of a Hegel in order to support his *sādhanā* or *Streben* to win the place in the sun, and if necessary may as well induct the ancient Greek sophists in his service to prove that might is right.

The theorists who propounded the cult of *vijigīṣu* would have been in good company with the philosophers of ancient Greece. In Aristotle's postulate of "natural" slaves, "natural" masters, "natural" wars, and so forth, the writers of *nīti-śāstras* could easily find a place for the "natural" aspirations, "natural" allies, and "natural" enemies of their doctrine of *maṇḍala*. The *Politica* assumes that the "barbarians" or non-Greeks, were intended by nature to be slaves (I, ii, vi) and ruled by the Greeks. And since slaves are "property" like "other things", warfare with the object of making slaves and thus acquiring wealth is a legitimate and "naturally just" occupation (I, viii). This Aristotelian justification of warfare can be easily recognized as forming the theoretical basis and psychological background of all wars from the conquests of Alexander and the Roman Cæsars down to the Thirty Years' War.[1] Furthermore, the methods and tactics of the Christian *vijigīṣus* who are responsible for the expansion of Europe in Asia, Africa and America down to Italy's exploits in Abyssinia (1936), can all be traced to the *dicta* of the father of political science, though as a rule moralists are apt to associate them with the teachings of Machiavelli's *Prince* (1513).

The opinions adumbrated in the *nīti-śāstras* are in any case neither exclusively oriental nor exclusively medieval or primitive. Nor need they be dubbed exclusively Machiavellian. For, has not the *Prince* furnished the fundamental logic of statesmen from the Athenian Pericles and Macedonian Philip down to the Meternichs, Bismarcks and Cavours of modern times? "Also it must be recognized", as Figgis, justifying the methodology of Machiavelli, says in his volume on political theory *From Gerson to Grotius* (1907, p. 101) "that in a state of things like international politics, where there is no recognized superior, and even Inter-

[1] T. J. Lawrence: *Essays on Modern International Law* (Cambridge, 1885), IV; Machiavelli: *Discourses*, Bk. II, xxi, W. S. Lilly: *First Principles in Politics* (London, 1907), p. 56, Hobhouse: *Metaphysical Theory of the State* (London, 1918), pp. 100-103, R. Stockton: *Peace Insurance* (Chicago, 1915), p. 203.

national Law is but the voice of public opinion, the condition of affairs is very much more nearly akin to the state of nature as imagined by Hobbes than it is in the relation of individuals". It is on such considerations that, like Machiavellism, the doctrine of *vijigīṣu* maintains its legitimate place in a theory of international relations. It provides an unvarnished statement of the only hypothesis, namely, that of *Staatsraeson*, which can satisfactorily explain the innate militarism that the human world inherits from "beasts and birds".

Let us now examine the other aspects of the doctrine of *maṇḍala*, that of the struggle for existence and "place in the sun" among the states. To a *vijigīṣu*, as Bhīṣma (*Mahā* II, lxix, 15) declares, "right is that which a strong man understands to be right", and the international *mores* of the *Mahābhārata*[1] is summed up in the dictum that "victory is the root of right", just as its creed of life for the individual appraises "death as better than lack of fame". How, then, is this quest of fame, victory or world-domination to be regulated by each state in competition with the others ? Are there any rules or methods by which the competing states may guide themselves in this conflict of aspirations? These constitute in substance a natural corollary to the doctrine of *vijigīṣu.*

The "proper study" of the *vijigīṣu*, is, according to the *Manu Samhitā* (VII, 154), his own and his enemy's spheres, his *geopolitische Lage*, i.e., the politics of his boundaries. And how are these spheres located in his imagination? Sukra (IV , i, lines 39-41) gives a brief summary of the Siegfried's investigations as to the "balance of forces" or "conjuncture of circumstances" with a view to the "Next War." We are told that the enemies diminish in importance according as they are remote

[1] Hopkins in *J.A.O.S.* 1889, pp. 187-189

from the "centre of the sphere." First to be dreaded by the *vijigīṣu* are those who are situated around or very near to his own state, than those who live farther away and so on. With the remoteness of location, enmity, hatred or rivalry naturally declines. Whether a state is to be treated as inimical, indifferent or friendly depends *per se* on its propinquity or distance. The geographical distribution of states influences their psychology in regard to their neighbours as a matter of course in such an order that the positive antipathy of the nearest dwindles into the tolerable apathy of the next and gives way to the active sympathy and even friendliness of the farthest distant. This, however, is not the only possible grouping of powers in a *vijigīṣu*'s political estimation or diplomatic "planning". The *Śukra-Nīti* (IV, i, lines 42-43) gives another order in which the states may be distributed. According to this computation, first are situated the enemies, then come the friends, next the neutrals, and the most remote on all sides are the enemies again.

These are the elementary principles of international dealings of which elaborate accounts are given in the writings of Kauṭalya and Kāmandaka. The theory holds that there is a hypothetical tug-of-war always being fought between the *vijigīṣu* and his *ari* (the enemy). These two are the combatants or belligerents. Along with these are to be counted another two states in order to furnish a logical completeness to the hypothesis. The *quadrivium* consists of the following members (Manu, VII, 156,-Kāmandaka, VIII, 20)[1]:

[1]*Artha*, Book VI, Ch. II, in the *Ind. Ant.* for 1909, p. 183. For a fuller account of the Kauṭalyan *Maṇḍala* see N. N. Law: *Inter-state Relations in Ancient India* (Calcutta, 1921).

For *madhyama* and *udāsīna* see also the present author's "Nīlakaṇṭha and Mitra-Miśra, Two Hindu Political Philosophers of the Seventeenth century" (*Calcutta Review*, August, 1935).

1. The *vijigīṣu*: the aspirant, e.g., an Alexander "mewing his might" bent on "conquering and to conquer."

2. The *ari* (the enemy): the one that is situated anywhere immediately on the circumference of the aspirant's territory.

3. The *madhyama* (the mediatory, middling or medium power state): the one (located close to the aspirant and his enemy) capable of helping both the belligerents, whether united or disunited, or of resisting either of them individually.

4. The *udāsīna* (the towering or the highest state): the one (situated beyond 1, 2, and 3) very powerful and capable of helping the aspirant, the enemy and the *madhyama*, together or individually, or resisting any of them individually.

These four states, then, constitute the smallest unit of international grouping, the "geopolitical" complex, so to say. From the standpoint of the *vijigīṣu* all other states are either his own allies or the allies of his enemy. Such states are held to be eight in number according to the hypothesis. How, now, is the "aspirant" to pick up his own allies from the crowd? He need only study the geographical position of these states with reference to the belligerents, i.e., to himself and to his enemy.

The *madhyama* (the middling) and the *udāsīna* (the highest) may be neglected by the Siegfried, for the time being, in his calculation of the possible array of forces directly allied or inimical to his career of conquest. The two belligerents, with the eight others (divided in equal proportion as their allies *in potentia*) are then located in the following order of *entente cordiale* by Kāmandaka (VIII, 16, 17) and Kauṭalya (VI, ii).

The "aspirant" occupies, of course, the hypothetical centre. Next to his front is the "enemy". Now we have to calculate frontwards and rearwards: next to the "enemy" is situated (1) the aspirant's ally, next to that is (2) the enemy's ally, next (3) the ally of the aspirant's ally, and last (4) the ally of the enemy's ally. Rearwards from the aspirant: First is situated (1) the rearward enemy, next is (2) the rearward ally, then comes (3) the ally of the rearward enemy, and last (4) the ally of the rearward ally. In this scheme we have the geometry or "formal" morphology of *soziale Beziehungen* from the international standpoint.

It is to be observed that the doctrine of *maṇḍala* as developed by the Hindu philosophers is "geopolitically" too naive and elementary because the only factor that has been considered is the geographical propinquity or distance. They have considered neither the race (or blood) question nor the religious, linguistic or other cultural forces, nor of course the economic factors. And yet this almost puerile-looking, one-sided "geometry" of diplomatic planning possesses a profound importance in political speculation as well as applied politics.

There is nothing queer, archaic or unworkable in this conception of international relations. A simple illustration would show how humanly the political theorists of India approached the foreign policy of nations and analyzed their "geopolitics." Thus, for instance, according to the Kauṭalyan doctrine of *maṇḍala*, the "natural enemies" of France engaged in studying the *modus operandi* for "the next war" would be Spain, England and Germany, and her "natural allies" Portugal, Scotland, Ireland and Russia. A French *vijigīṣu*, i.e., a Napoleon, embarking on a war with Germany, should begin by taking steps to keep his "rear safe". With this object he should have Spain attacked by Portugal, and manage to play off the anti-English forces in Ireland and Scotland in such a manner that England may be preoccupied at home and unable to attack France in support of Germany. As Germany, on the other hand, is likely to have China as her natural ally (supposing there is no other state between Russia and the Far East), the French *vijigīṣu* should set Russia against China, and so on. It is obvious that the diplomatic feats conceived by the Hindu political philosophers could be verified almost to the letter by numerous instances in European and Asian history, especially in ancient and medieval times when Eur-Asia was divided into numberless nationalities.

Nay, the principle of Kauṭalyan *maṇḍala* is in operation even now in the numerous states carved out of the old Germanistic empires by the Versailles and other Treaties of 1918-19. For instance, the manner in which Poland was being bolstered up in post-War years by France against Germany, on the one hand, and Soviet Russia, on the other, is in keeping with the adumbrations of the old Asian Richelieu. Italy's pro-Hungarian sentiments as against Jugoslavia are also explicable quite easily by the *nīti* theory of "geopolitics".

In the recent Italo-Abyssinian war of 1935-36, for instance, France had to be sure of cooperation from her "natural" ally Russia as against Germany, the natural enemy of both, before she could decide to take a definite action. Every shrewd observer of the *geopolitische Lage* of any region can still proceed on the elemental foundations of Kauṭalyan *maṇḍala*. Only, one will have to introduce modifications into the "natural" relations created by geography or distance on account of special conditions engendered by the problems of raw material and food stuff, race-affinities, cultural sympathies etc. Kauṭalya will then be found to be valid even for today and tomorrow. The doctrine of *maṇḍala* may then be regarded as another profound creation of Hindu political philosophy and one of the most fruitful contributions of India to the enrichment of human thought.

Be this as it may, we have to observe that the group of ten states or a *decennium* constitutes one complete *maṇḍala*. The *vijigīṣu* is the centre of gravity of this sphere. Now each state can have the same legitimate aspiration, that is, each can be fired by the same ambition to form and figure out a sphere of its own. The inevitable result is a conflict of interests, a pandemonium of Siegfrieds united in discord. The problem of statesmen in each state is to find out the methods of neutralizing the policies of others by exploiting the enemies of its rivals in its own interests (*Staatsraeson*). The doctrine of *maṇḍala* thus makes of *nīti-śāstra* or political science essentially a science of enmity, hatred, espionage and intrigue,—as understood by Schmitt and Spengler—and an art of the thousand and one methods of preparedness for "the next war".

We need not go into the details of the *Machtpolitik* conceived in Kauṭalya's *Artha-śāstra* or in the sections on warfare in the *Sukranīti*. But it is already clear that the doctrine of *maṇḍala* has launched us at last into *mātsya-nyāya*, the logic of the fish, the Hobbesian law of beasts, anarchy.[1] The doctrine assumes and is prepared for a world of eternally warring states. While "internal" sovereignty dawns as the "logic of the fish" sets, "external" sovereignty postulates the

[1] Kāuṭalya, I. iv; Kāmandaka, II, 40

existence of the same logic as a fact in international relations. In one instance *daṇḍa*[1] or punishment, that is, "sanction" of the state, is exercised to crush anarchy but it is apparently in order to maintain a world-wide anarchy that *daṇḍa* or *Faust-recht* is employed by one state against another. The theory of the state is thus reared on two diametrically opposite conceptions:

1. The doctrine of *daṇḍa* which puts an end to *mātsya-nyāya* among the *prajā* or members of a single state;

2. The doctrine of *maṇḍala*, which maintains an international *mātsya-nyāya* or the civil war of races in the human family.

From one anarchy, then, the state emerges only to plunge headlong into another. This is the dilemma that pervades the political philosophy of the Hindus. This dilemma of Hindu philosophy is present in Vierkandt who in *Staat und Gesellschaft der Gegenwart* (1921, p.10) admits that every state has two faces, one towards the internal affairs, and the other towards the external. It is the *Rechtsstaat* (law-state), *Ordnungsstaat* (state of social order), *lo stato etico* (ethical state) etc. so far as home-politics are concerned. But in regard to foreign relations,—the politics of boundaries,—it is by nature a *Machtsstaat* (force-state) governed by considerations of *Staatnotrecht* (law of state necessity), *Staatsraeson* (reasons or requirements of the state).

[1] Manu, VII, 20; Sukra I. line 45.

SECTION 8

THE DOCTRINE OF SĀRVA-BHAUMA

(*World-Sovereign*)

The Hindu theory of sovereignty did not stop, however, at the doctrine of a universal *mātsya-nyāya*, that is, of a world in which each state is at war with all. It generated also the concept of universal peace through the establishment of a *Weltherrschaft* as in the French chauvinist[1] Pierre Dubois's *De Recuperazione Terre Sancte* (1307) or the Italian mystic-patriot Dante's *De Monarchia* (I, iv, viii, x). The doctrine of *maṇḍala* as centrifugal force was counteracted by the centripetal tendencies of the doctrine of *sārva-bhauma* (the ruler over the whole earth). With this theory of the world-state and *Pax Sārvabhaumica* we shall conclude our present study.

In Europe the idea or ideal of a universal empire took most definite shape towards the beginning of the fourteenth century "exactly when the actual development of the modern nationalities was rendering it practically impossible"[2]. This crisis and this transition in Western political thought are best represented in Bartolus (1314-1357),[3] the "prince of jurists", for he began by seeing a single universal empire, but he ended by recognizing a miniature empire in every *de facto* independent power. The same conception of a world sovereignty or a *fédération de l'émpire* is

[1] F. J. C. Hearnshaw (editor); *The Social and Political Ideas of Some Great Thinkers of the Middle Ages* (London).

[2] A. J. Carlyle, vol. III (London 1915), p. 179. But the concept of the Dantesque universal monarchy is as old as Cicero. See F. Atger: *Histoire des Doctrines du contrat social* (Nimes 1906) p. 26.

[3] C. N. S. Woolf: *Bartolus of Sassooferato* (Cambridge 1913), pp. 45, 109, 196.

however as old in India as the political philosophers of the earliest Vedic period.

"Monarchy at its highest", we read in the *Aitareya Brāhmaṇa* (VIII, iv, 1) "should have an empire extending right up to the natural boundaries, it should be territorially all-embracing, up to the very ends uninterrupted, and should constitute and establish one state and administration up to the seas". In their "geopolitical" planning the ancient theorists were evidently thinking of the Indian continent as identical with the entire world. The achievement of a pan-Indian nationality was in their eyes the equivalent of the world-federation just as in medieval European theory the unification of Western Christendom was tantamount to the constitution of one state for all mankind, or as in the Eur-American world-peace movements of today "the world" is postulated to be the territories inhabited by the albinoes or white races, and "saving the civilization" is understood to be the expansion of albinocracy at the cost of Asian and African races.

This theory of a world-nationalism (or, what is the same thing, a United Indianism) exercised a powerful influence on the political speculations of the Hindus. It gave rise to set formulae and slogans that fired the imaginations of the Alexanders, Charlemagnes and Fredericks of India through the ages. The *Aitareya Brāhmaṇa* (VIII, i, 39) records some of the ambitions and ideals of the young India of the sixth century B.C. and beyond. "I want to attain to lordship over all rulers," proclaims one aspirant, "I want to achieve the conquest of both space and time......I want to be *sārva-bhauma*......and be the *eka-rāt* (sole monarch) of the earth up to the skies".

Hindu political thought produced several other

categories to express the same idea of the world-state or universal sovereignty. We have, first, the doctrine of *chakravarttī*. It indicates that the *chakra* or wheel of the state-chariot rolls everywhere without obstruction. The wheel is the symbol of sovereignty. Or, if *chakra*[1] be taken as denoting a country from sea to sea, the *chakravarttī* would be the ruler of a state from sea to sea (i.e. extending to the farthest limits). It is this conception of a political "dominion", of a secular overlordship, that is employed metaphorically with a spiritual significance in the conception of the Lord Buddha as *Chakravarttī*. "A king I am, Sela," says Buddha[2] using the language of his contemporary imperialists, "the king supreme of righteousness. The royal chariot-wheel in righteousness do I set rolling on,—that wheel that no one can turn back again."

Secondly, we have the doctrine of *sārva-bhauma* expressed in the more popular and conventional conception of *samrāt*. The *Mahābhārata*, for instance, uses this category in order to convey the idea of a world dominion. "There are *rājās* (kings) in every home (state) doing what they like", we read in the Book on *Sabhā* (XV, 2), "but they have not attained to the rank of *samrāt*; for that title is hard to win". And this rank is at last won by Yudhiṣṭhira in the epic. Yudhiṣṭhira would thus be the *Veltro* of Dante's *Divine Comedy*, so to say.

Another category in which the doctrine of *sārva-bhauma* is manifest is that of *chāturanta*, of which *Kauṭalya* (I, v, vii) availed himself in order to establish his ideal of imperial nationalism. The *chāturanta* state is that whose authority extends up to the remotest

[1] Monier Williams's Dictionary.

[2] *Sela-sutta* in *Sutta-nipata* III, 7,7; R. S. Hardy: *Manual of Buddhism* (London 1880), p. 126.

antas (limits) of the *chatur* (four) quarters. The ruler of such a state *ananyām prithivīm bhumkte*, i.e., enjoys the whole earth with none to challenge his might. In the *Artha-śāstra*, he is known also as *chakravarttī* for the territory of such a *chāturanta* is called *chakravartti-kṣetra* (dominion of a *chakravarttī*).

The *sārva-bhauma*, *chakravarttī*, *samrāt*, or *chāturanta* of Hindu political theory is identical with the *dominus omnium*, or lord of *universitas quaedum* in Bartolus's terminology,[1] the *hwangti* of the Chinese[2]. He is "the monarch of all I survey." He rules a state whose limits extend from sea to sea (*āsamudra-kṣitīśa*) and his chariots have free passage up to the skies (*ānāka-ratha-vartma*), as Kālidāsa, the Virgil of India, puts it in his *Raghu-vamśa* (" The House of Raghu"). The pretensions of the doctrine of *sārva-bhauma* thus bear close analogy with the universal authority claimed by Pope Hildebrand (*c.* 1075) for the Papacy, or with that rival conception of his opponents, the Ghibelline imperialism of the German Hohenstaufens. Herein is to be perceived the Hindu counterpart of the doctrine, albeit from the monarchical angle, of a single state for entire humanity, the futurist version of which has embodied itself from time to time in diverse forms,—in the visions of "permanent peace" or in the pious wishes for a "parliament of man" or for the "League of Nations", or for its antithesis, the communist "Third International" of the proletarian world.

The doctrine of *sārva-bhauma* does not stand alone in Hindu political philosophy. It is backed up by several other concepts which may be regarded as its logical feeders. First is the concept of the gradation of rulers in the scale of *aiśvarya* (sovereignty). The *Rig Veda*

[1] Woolf. pp. 22, 196.
[2] Hardy, p. 126.

(IV, xxi, 1), the *Satapatha Brāhmaṇa* (XI, iii, 2,1,6) and other ancient documents recognize a hierarchy or graded rank of states from the lowest unit up. According to the *Aitareya Brāhmaṇa* (VIII, iv, 1) the smallest nationality is a *rājya*. From this rung the ladder gradually takes us through higher or larger "powers" like the *sāmrājya svarājya*, *vairājya* and *mahārājya* up to the greatest power, known as the *ādhipatya*.

Another scale of small nationalities, medium states, and great powers is furnished in the following schedule of the *Sukra-nīti* (I, lines 365-374):[1]

	Title		*Annual Income in silver karṣa*
1.	*Sāmanta*	...	1 to 3 hundred thousand
2.	*Māṇḍalika*	...	3 hundred thousand to 1 million
3.	*Rājā*	...	1 million to 2 million
4.	*Mahārāja*	...	2 million to 5 million
5.	*Svarāt*	...	5 million to 10 million
6.	*Samrāt*	...	10 million to 100 million
7.	*Virāt*	...	100 million to 500 million
8.	*Sārva-bhauma*	...	500 million and up.

The *sārva-bhauma* is further described as being the ruler "to whom the earth with its seven islands is ever bound".

This concept of a scale of nationalities or a rank of states, as "first class powers" or "great powers" and "small nations" or the like, according to income and title, is essentially linked up in Hindu theory with the concept of political *yajnas*, sacrifices and rituals, which are fully described in the *Brāhmaṇas*. The *Gopatha Brāhmaṇa*[2] says that Prajāpati became *rājā* by

[1] A little more than 25 cents in the present United States currency, or roughly approximating to a shilling.

[2] Part I. pp. 77, 78, in the *Bibliotheca Indica* series.

rājasūya sacrifice, *samrāt* by *vājapeya*, *svarāt* by *aśvamedha*, *virāt* by *puruṣamedha*, and so forth. We need not go into the details of these rituals. We have only to note that not every ruler is entitled to perform any and every sacrifice. Each sacrifice has its own value or mark of sovereignty attached to it; the dignity, might and rank of states being dependent on the character of the sacrifice performed.

According to the *Śatapatha Brāhmaṇa* (V, i, 1, 13) again, the office of the king is the lower and that of the emperor is higher, and therefore one becomes king by offering the *rājasūya*, and by the *vājapeya* one becomes emperor. But the *rājasūya* is known to be the highest sacrifice in the *Taittirīya Brāhmaṇa*[1], for according to this work, it can be performed only by universal monarchs exercising sovereignty over a large number of princes as the lord of an imperial federation. The *Aitareya Brāhmaṇa* (VIII, 21-23) also says that by virtue of the *rājasūya*, Janamejya, Saryāta and ten other rulers "subdued the earth" and became "paramount sovereigns". In the *Āpastamaba Śrauta Sūtra* (XX, i, 1), however, *aśvamedha* (horse-killing) sacrifice possesses the greatest dignity, for it can be performed by a *sārvabhauma* (the ruler of the whole earth).

It is obvious that authorities differ as to the relative importance of the political sacrifices, but all are united in the concept that the rituals have a state-value on their face, and that it is the greatest power or the largest nationality alone that is entitled to the highest sacrifice (be it the *rājasūya* or the *aśvamedha*, or what not). The concept of *yajna* like that of the scale of the states, is therefore an important element in the theory

[1] R. L. Mitra; *Indo-Aryans* (London 1881) vol. II, pp. 2, 3.

of *Weltherrschaft*, world-monarchy, or federated universe embodied in the doctrine of *sārva-bhauma*.

Last but not least in importance as a foundation for the doctrine of *sārva-bhauma* is the concept of *dig-vigaya* (or conquest of the quarters) of which the *Aitareya Brāhmaṇa* speaks (VIII, iv 1). It implies that there is no longer a mere *vijigīṣu* or aspirant, awaiting his chance, mewing his might, or watching the conjuncture for "the next war". The Siegfried has already conquered the quarters of the globe, he has factually realized his highest ambitions. The wheel of his chariot has rolled to the very extremities of the world, and there is none to question his power and prestige. All rival states have been subdued by him. He has brought them to subjection almost in the manner that Napoleon wished when he said in 1804: "There will be no rest in Europe until it is under a single chief, an emperor who shall have kings for officers, who shall distribute kingdoms to his lieutenants and shall make this one king of Italy, that one of Bavaria; this one ruler of Switzerland, that one governor of Holland, each having an office of honour in the imperial household". *Dig-vijaya* has conferred on the *vijigīṣu* the chiefship of such a Napoleonic league of nations.

It is under these conditions of a "conquest of the quarters" that the hero of the *Raghu-vamśa* is authorized to celebrate the *viśva-jit* (indicating world-subjugation) sacrifice at the end of his Alexandrine exploits. *Dig-vijaya* brings about a situation in which there is absolutely no scope for the doctrine of *maṇḍala* or international *mātsya-nyāya* i.e., geopolitical planning. The world is at peace under the undisputed sway of the lord of the *universitas quaedum*, the *sārva-bhauma*. The unstable equilibrium of a *vijigīṣu's* hypothetical *maṇḍala* and survey of the *geopolitische Lage* (geopolitical situation) has given way to the *pax sārva-bhaumica* established by the *de facto* as well as *dejure* monopoly of world-control through *dig-vijaya.*

A natural concomitant of the concept of *dig-vijaya* is the idea that the *sārva-bhauma* has all the other rulers related to him not as to the *vijigīṣu* of a *maṇḍala*, that is, not as to the ambitious storm-centre of an international complex of geopolitical relations, but bound as to a *rāja-rāja* or king of kings, to whom allegiance is due as overlord. With the rise of the *sārva-bhauma*, the *maṇḍala* necessarily disappears. The old order of the "enemy" and the other states has vanished, the new order of the world-state has arisen. An epoch of universal peace has replaced the age of warring nationalities, conflicting *ententes*, armed neutralities, militant attitudes, and geopolitically "planned economies". The doctrine of *sārva-bhauma*, as the concept of federal nationalism, imperial federation, or the universe-state, is thus the keystone in the arch of the Hindu theory of sovereignty. The message of *pax sārva-bhaumica*, in other words, the doctrine of world-unity and international concord, is the final contribution of the *Nīti-śāstras* to the understanding of the state and of Hindu philosophy to the political science of mankind.

CHAPTER IV

THE LITERATURE, ART AND SOCIAL PHILOSOPHY OF THE INDIAN PEOPLE

SECTION I

HINDU LITERARY NORMS

Mohenjo Daro Monuments Visàvis Vedic Texts

The Homeric antiquity of Greece lost its prestige about half a century ago on account of the discoveries in Crete. Homer was then found to be not so much the first of a new series as the last of an old. The same "misfortune" has befallen Vedic India today owing to the "inconvenient "discoveries of the Mohenjo Daro—Harappa culture. In the perspective of the "Hindus" who were responsible for the technocracy and spiritual life of that civilization the Vedic *Riṣis* are found to be much too "flat, jejune, modern". Once more has Vedic civilization grown into a regular "problem" of world-culture. This question has bearings not only on the old issues relating to the so-called Indo-Aryan complex but on the new ones also relating to the origins of civilization itself. And the problems are as much anthropologico-geographical as chronologico-ḥistorical.

The relations, both statical and dynamic, as well as formal and contentual, between the Vedas and the "Indus valley" happen for the time being to be quite mysterious. One reason for this mystery is perhaps to be found in the data themselves. The monuments of Mohenjo Daro complex are as yet non-literary. They speak to us only through "stocks and stones", so to say. On the other hand, the language of the Vedas is almost exclusively literary. The "stocks and stones" should appear to be almost unknown to the Vedic *milieu*. On the face of it there is hardly any intellectual nexus between the two complexes. The mind operating behind or through the one set of human creations does not seem to have any affinity with that behind the other.

One thing, however, is clear. The "stocks and stones" created by the men and women of Mohenjo Daro have their bearings on the life systems to the East of the Indus, i.e., to India Proper no less than on those to the West, i.e., to Persia, Asia Minor, Egypt and so forth. Janus-like they are double-faced in their forms and contents. Archaeology will perhaps have to wait for quite a few decades, before the exact orientations of these finds to the East and the West are deciphered.

But in the meantime it may not be entirely out of the question for the students of social science to attempt reading some meaning into the diverse art forms, architectural, sculptural, etc., such as have been unearthed in plenty. The language of art, the "geometry" of forms, is universal. The "stocks and stones" also can be eloquent especially because they have their cognates and agnates. Some of the "stocks and stones" to which the "Hindus" of modern India are used, no matter how diverse their cranial types and howsoever removed from the Indus Valley they may happen to be, are the family likenesses of just those "antique" specimens which have rendered the creations of Vedic *Riṣis* but the phenomena of yesterday. A psychological affinity between those Indians of 3500 B.C. and the Indians of today as registered in the *élan vital* or creative urge behind many of the art-forms may be considered to be fairly plausible. This is one side of the story.

From another standpoint, we may have to believe in no distant future that the Vedic *Ṛiṣis* were not without culture-contacts with the *Ṛiṣis* of Mohenjo Daro. May be, some of the items of the Mohenjo Daro complex are actually to be found in certain Vedic strands. Perhaps it may be established somewhat that during certain periods of this culture-contact the Mohenjo Daro monuments and the Vedic texts supplemented each other. In other words, the archaeology of the Mohenjo Daro finds may have a part of its literary background in the Vedas, while the archaeological monuments corresponding to Vedic literature may have in part to be detected in the finds of Mohenjo Daro, Harappa and allied regions. The antiquity of Vedic life and thought may altogether have to be pushed farther back towards the third or fourth millennium B.C.

All this guess-work is to be treated for the present as nothing but conjecture pure and undefiled. But that the history of the achievements of Hindu culture finds itself today in the most complicated melting point there is no doubt. The beginnings of a new indology are already in sight.[1]

[1] W. Wuest: "Ueber die neuesten Ausgrabungen im nordwestlichen Indien" (*Zeitschrift der Deutschen morgenlaendischen Gesellschaft* Vol. LXXXI.)-

R. Chanda; Survival of the Prehistoric Civilisation of the Indus Valley (*Memoirs of the Archaeological Survey of India*, Calcutta 1929).

B. Svarup; "Harappa Seals and the Antiquity of Writing in India" (*Journal of the Bihar and Orissa Research Society*, Patna, vol. IX.)

S. V. Venkatesvara; "Vedic Iconography" (*Rupam*, Calcutta, April-October, 1930).

The Vedas

Among the earliest literary creations of India we find sentiments like the following:

"Mighty am I, Superior by name, upon the earth, conquering am I, all-conquering, completely conquering every region". This is the emphatic proclamation of *Puruṣa* (Man) to the Earth in a section of the earliest Hindu literature. Thus sang the poets of the *Atharva Veda* (XII, 1, 54).

The all-round desire for conquest manifested itself with equal force in the avocations of daily life. "In the villages and in the wilderness, in the assembly halls that are upon the earth, in the gatherings and in the meetings" the people of Vedic India were eager to "hold forth". This wish to shine and flourish is the perpetual burden of the songs in the *Vedas*. As long as we do not know anything definite about the literary records of the Mohenjo Daro epoch or epochs the Vedic desire for world-conquest may be regarded as one of the very first spiritual urges of creative India.

The composers of Vedic poetry took part in the "election" of the king in the communal *agora*. The following is a bit of the political folk-songs associated with such functions: "Thee let the people choose unto kingship, thee these five divine directions" (*Atharva* III, 4).

It was an age of government by discussion. Vedic poetry reflects the democratic harangues of the public speakers. An orator addressed the audience thus: "Be your design the same, your hearts the same, your mind the same that it may be well for you together" (*Atharva*, VI, 64).

Vitalism, i.e., the philosophy of a life in the here

L. Renou; *Bibliographie Védique* (Paris, 1931).

and the now, is the clear message of the *Vedas*. The best method of *misunderstanding* the authors of the Vedic cycle is to approach them from the angle of theology and god-lore. The main body of this literature consists indeed of hymns, prayers and sermons. But its essential *motif* is secular, the distinctive feature is its pre-eminently martial character.

The *Vedas* held the mirror up to the social life of the time. And what was it but the life of fighters and colonizers, of the Cuchulains, Volsungs and Theseuses? The *Riṣis* who pioneered the settlements were not laying out cities and states in the "other world". Their vision was concentred in this earth. They knew that their mission was to enrich it with the Promethean fire.

The poetry of the *Rig Veda* would be meaningless unless we take it as a grand saga of the quest of fire. It was not without struggle that fire was annexed to civilization in order to promote the development of technocracy. The Vedic poets are aware of this struggle and have sung of its various stages until the final victory of man's creative endeavours in India.

Fire hid itself "in secret like a thief with an animal which he had stolen" (*Rig Veda*, I, 65). A vigorous search had to be instituted to take possession of it. "Having taken in his hand all manly powers, he has made the gods fear, when sitting down in his hiding place. There the thoughtful men find him" (*Rig* I, 67). It was "looked and longed for in heaven" and "looked and longed for on earth" (*Rig* I, 98).

When once the energy has been harnessed to human needs, what do the Vedic poets want it to do? The following is a typical ode to fire:

"Burn, O Agni, the nearer enemies, burn the curse of the distant evil-doer. Burn the unseen ones. May thy never-ageing, never-tiring flames spread out.

"Bestow mighty vigour on those who toil for thee, bright luck and welfare, O Agni, on the Viśvāmitras" (*Rig* III, 18, 2, 4).

A prosperous territory and a happy home, success over the enemy and expansion of dominions,—this is what the Hindus wanted in the Vedic age. Their literature portrays, therefore, the worldly interests of men and women. We read in it songs in praise of cattle, grain, and *soma* drink; it is pervaded by the spirit of carnivals, merrymakings, and Theocritean pastorals; it is the poetry of hearty send-offs to the soldiers going to the front, or of war-chants in honour of triumphant generals "at home". We read in it, further, of the romantic love between the damsel Urvasī and Pururavas (*Rig*, X). Centuries later this would furnish the plot of Kālidāsa's drama. The Vedic woman is made of the same flesh and blood as the modern woman. And we see her shifts to win and fix a man's love against a rival (*Atharva VII*, 38, 113).

The Upaniṣads, the Dhammapada and the Gītā

Man does not live by bread alone. So we have the *Upaniṣads* singing of the soul and the Infinite. Here is a specimen (*Brihadāraṇyaka*, I, iii, 28):

> "From the non-existent (i.e., transitory, unreal) me to the ever-existent (i.e., permanent truth, reality) lead;
> From darkness (i.e., ignorance)
> me to light (i.e., knowledge) lead;
> From death me to immortality lead."

It does not require a specially Oriental mind to appreciate this desire for "more light" of the ancient Hindu poets.

Self-control, restraint of passions, contemplation etc, constitute the theme of a portion of Hindu literature. The authors who followed the lectures of Sãkya the Buddha and other moralists were specialists in this branch. But the poetry of *Dhammapada* which contains the sayings of Buddha seeks mainly to rouse the *élan vital*, the creative will and intelligence of human beings. It harps on *appamāda*, i.e., a life of vigilance, strenuousness, and activity. Buddhism is essentially dynamic. The Buddhist is a proselyte by nature; his cult is social service and alleviation of the sufferings of men and animals.

Dhyāna, *yoga*, meditation, and silent "communion", are some of the topics of Hindu authors. They have preached sometimes a keen solicitude for the "higher self" and an indifference to the mundane affairs. Such non-secularism is the characteristic of a type of mentality all over the world. In the *Old Testament* this indifferentism is represented by Ezekiel. According to him there are aspects of life which are higher than the ordinary political interests. Emphasis on lonesome meditation and a life of seclusion from publicity is a prominent feature of the teachings of the Greek philosopher Zeno and his school. The "wise man" of the Roman thinker Seneca (*De Otio*, III, IV, *Ad Serenum*, VIII, etc.) does not differ from the Riṣis, Buddhas, Bhikṣus, and Yogins of India. And the *New Testament* with its contempt of the "the world and the flesh" is the gospel of non-political other-worldlyism.

The poets of India have emphasized the conception of progress of the world through revolutions. The Hindu masses are thus ever expectant for a change in the *status quo*. Herein lies the bed-rock of their never-failing optimism. The greatest Bible of hope

20

in India is the *Gītā* (c. sixth-second cent. B.C.), a section of the Great Epic, the *Mahābhārata*. The declarations of Lord Krisṇa to the warrior Arjuna teach the peasant and the prince to prepare the way for a Messiah in every age. Perhaps there is hardly any Hindu today anywhere in India who does not know the following verse:

"Whensoever into order corruption creeps in, Bharata,
And customs bad ascendant be, then myself do I embody.
For the protection of the good and miscreants to overthrow,
And for setting up the order do I appear age by age."

In this doctrine of *Yugāntara* (transformation of the time-spirit) we have a characteristic literary product of creative India.

The Tamil Classics

A South Indian classic of the early Christian era (*c* 200 A.C. ?), which may be compared to the finest romance of Sanskrit literature and which enables us to feel a bit of the secular interests of Hindu India, is the Tamil work, the *Manimekhalāi*. The kind of Buddhism propagated in and through it appears to have no reference to the *Mahāyāna* system associated with Āryadeva or Nāgārjuna. The romance is evidently *Hīnayāna* in general features.

South Indian culture was Brahmanized, Piṭakized and Jainized in succession. The Sanskritization of Tamil culture proceeded step by step.[1]

[1] S. K. Aiyangar ; *Some Contributions of South India to Indian Culture* (Calcutta 1923), "The Buddhism of Manimekhalai" in *Buddhistic Studies* (Calcutta 1931), C. Srinivasachari; "Some Poli-

A prosperous epoch of Tamil literature in Southern India may be taken to have been synchronous with the Empire of the Guptas in Northern India, i.e., the age of Kālidāsa, the *Purāṇas* and the *Mahābhārata*. A Tamil classic, the *Kurāl*, by Teruvallu (*c* 300 A.C. ?) which, in certain sections, reads almost like the *Gītā* may be referred to this era. This work, recognized as it was by the third Tamil *Samgam*, deserves a careful analysis by students of social philosophy.

People have detected the ideas of the *Amgas* and the *Āgamas*, i.e., Jainism in the *Kurāl*. On the other hand, it exhibits indebtedness to the Kauṭalyan *Artha-Śāstra*, coincidences with the *Kāmandakī-nīti*, *Manu Samhitā*, and the *Mahābhārata* (*Bhīṣma Parva*). Be this as it may, this book of verses, complete as it is in 1330 aphoristic stanzas, is divided into three parts according to *trivarga*, i.e., *dharma*, *artha*, and *kāma*. We can then establish to a certain extent a psychological affinity between this South Indian moralist and Bhartrihari, the author of three *Śatakas* or centuries of verses, namely, *Śringāra-śataka* (on love) *Vairāgya-śataka* (on dispassion), and *Nīti-śataka* (on morals and propriety) (p. 311). And in any case the student of positivism can find in this eclectic work a clue to some of the solid foundations of Hindu social life in Southern India in the early centuries of the Christian era. It is worth while to observe that *porul* which corresponds to *artha* commands greater attention of the author than the other two interests. Indeed,

tical Ideals in the *Kural*" (*Ind. Hist. Q.* March 1933), S. Vipulananda; "The Development of Tamilian Teligious Thought" (*Annamalai University Journal* vol. I. 2)., R. A. Nilkanṭha Sastri; "Education in the Tamil Country" (*Indian Culture*, Calcutta, July 1934), V. V. S. Aiyar; *The Kural or the Maxims of Tiruvalluvar* (Shermadevi, 1935). See also G. U. Pope: *The Sacred Kural* (transl. London, 1886).

we may take it almost as a *Kāmandakī-nīti* in Tamil.

Poetry, Drama, and Stories

Secularism, *le joie de vivre*, has been the one grand theme of Hindu *belles letters*. Political incidents and movements were worked upon by all the leading poets and dramatists. Those who study Hindu poetry, drama, fables and stories hardly require to read the *Dharma*, *Artha* or *Nīti Śāstras* separately. The social philosophy of Kauṭalya and Manu is to be found in this creative literature in an artistic form.

Among the poets and dramatists who dealt with *Nīti* topics are to be enumerated in a somewhat chronological order the following for the Gupta period, which may be conveniently described as the age of Kālidāsa[1] :

1. Bhāsa (*c* 350 A.C.): *Avimāraka*
2. Sūdraka (*c* 400 A.C.): *Mrichchhakatika*
3. Kālidāsa (390-460): *Raghuvamśa*
4. Bhāravī (*c* 550 A.C.): *Kirātārjunīya*
5. Dandin (*c* 550 A.C.): *Daśakumāracharita*
6. Visākhadatta (*c* 550 A.C. ?): *Mudrārākṣasa*

To the same category as the Sanskrit Buddhist legends but more oriented to *Nīti* or political and social thought are the story-books of "Hindu India." Some of them are being named below:[2]

[1] Winternitz: *Geschichte der Indischen Literatur* (Leipzig 1921), pp.37, 45, 47: Keith: *History of Sanskrit Literature* (Oxford 1928) pp.82, 297: see also the present author's *Love in Hindu Literature* (Tokyo, 1916).

[2] A. Hillebrandt; "Zur Kritik des Mudrārākṣasa" (*Nachrichten der koeniglichen Gesellschaft der Wissenschaften*, Goettingen 1905), *Ueber das Kautiliyaśāstra und Verwandtes* (Breslau 1908), "Nīti und Mudrārākṣasa" and "Visākhadatta" (*Jahresbericht der Saechsischen Gesellschaft fuer Vaterlaendische Kultur*, Breslau, 1908). Hillebrandt is one of the very few Western indologists who have tried to study Sanskrit

1. The *Tantrākhyāyika* (*c* 350 A.C.)
2. The *Panchatantra* (*c* 400 A.C.)
3. The *Brihatkathā* (*c* 450 A.C.)
4. The *Hitopadeśa* (*c* 500 A.C.)

Two master-passions have made man here and there and everywhere both in the East and the West. These are, first, love, and second, war, or first, war, and second, love. The literature of the Hindus from the age of the Maurya emperors (third and fourth centuries B.C.) to the age of the Gupta Napoleons (fourth and fifth centuries A.C.) is the literature of war and love.

Bhāsa, the dramatist of the second century A.C. (?) writes: "How different, in operation, from other nooses, is the noose of sweetheart's arms? Fastened about the neck, it imparts life; loosened, it produces death."

The *Purāṇas*, embodying as they do older tradition, acquired their final form during the period from the second to the fifth century A.C. Their principal theme is the titanic conflict between the gods and the Asuras; the scene that appeals most powerfully to the folk-imagination is the cataclysmal churning of the ocean; and the most popular hero is Viśvāmitra, the embodiment of Satanic pride and energy, who would create other worlds and have a place in the sun.

Kālidāsa (fifth century A.C.), the Hindu Virgil, is the author of *Raghuvamśa* and describes the

texts in an humanistic manner (cf. his *Kālidāsa: Ein Versuch zu seiner literarischen Wuerdigung*). His *Rituallitcratur* (in the Grundriss der Indo-Arischen Philologie) which deals with the Vedic and post-Vedic *mores* is well founded on comparative anthropology. See also his *Altindische Politik* (Jena 1923) and *Aus Alt-und Neu-Indien* (Breslau 1933).

fully developed personality of his countrymen thus:

"Lords of the lithosphere from sea to sea,
Commanding the skies by air chariots,
Who adopted the life of silent sages when old,
And passed away at last through yoga's aid".

We may take a bit of natural sentiment from *Kādambarī*, a Sanskrit novel in prose, of the seventh century; as follows:

"Next day the two Gandharva kings came with their queens, and the festivities were increased thousandfold. Chitraratha, however, said; 'why, when we have places of our own, do we feast in the forest? Moreover, though marriage resting only on mutual love is lawful amongst us, yet let us follow the custom of the world'. 'Nay', replied Tārāpiḍa, "where a man hath known the greatest happiness there is his home, even if it be a forest. And where also have I known such joy as here"? (Ridding's version).

The following "thanks to the human heart by which we live" is from the *Karpūra-manjarī*, a drama in Prakrit language (A.C. 900) by Rāja-śekhra: "What need of the performance of song and dance? And what need of strong drink? What need of incense and aloes? And what need of saffron? On all the earth in daintiness naught can equal man's tender passion". And again, "The consort of an emperor and the wife of a common man, in the matter ot love there is not even a grain of distinction between them to be found, methinks, even, if a certain difference in outward splendor is effected by rubies and decorations and garments and saffron." (Lanman's version).

It is but this Hindu conception of love's omnipotence, even though unadorned, that finds expression in the following lines of Rossetti's *House of Life*:

> "Some ladies love the jewels in Love's zone
> ... ...
> And some that listen to his lute's soft tone;
> ... ...
> Some prize his blindfold sight; ....
> My Lady only loves the heart of Love:
> Therefore Love's heart, my lady, hath for thee
> His bower of unimagined flower and tree."

It should be observed *en passant* that Bhartrihari (*c.*800), a poet, who like all other Indian authors is apt to be misunderstood, was quite comprehensive in his treatment of the *rasas* (emotions). In his synthetic imagination there was a place not only for a century of verses on renunciation, but also for another two centuries, one of which was given over to love and the second to morals (p. 307). Besides, even in the treatment of sex in the *Sringāra-Śataka* (stanzas 51-52, 99-100), the poet did not forget the duality or polarism of human personality. He was conscious as much of the spiritual in man as of the sexual. His "whole duty of man" was oriented not only to the sensuous elements in life but also to the moral or social obligations as well as to the super-sensual.

The same all-round view of the aesthetic *psyche* is accordingly mirrored forth in Indian treatises on poetics. In *Daśa-rūpa*, a treatise of the sixth century on ten forms of drama, it is expressly stated that the themes of art are almost unnumbered, because *rasa* or sentiment can be conveyed among mankind by almost any and every treatment (IV, 90). It is implied that dramatists do not have to observe any taboo in the treatment of manners and emotions. Creative India's imagination and intelligence could not but be multiform and all-embracing.

The Purāṇas, Epics and Tantras

Each one of the eighteen *Purāṇas* is an *Encyclopaedia Indica.* Economics, politics, law, social philosophy, and morals constitute therefore a great part of this literature. A very substantial portion of these texts may be taken to have come into shape by the time of the Guptas.[1]

The *Matsya Purāṇa* brings the dynastic history to the fall of the Āndhras about 236 A.C. In the *Vāyu*, *Brahmāṇḍa*, *Viṣṇu* and *Bhāgavat Purāṇas* the narrative is carried down to the exploits of the Guptas previous to the *digvijaya* (world-conquest) by Samundragupta, say, 335 A.C. As the original authority for the *Matsya* and the *Vāyu* is known to be the *Bhavisya Purāṇa*, this last is considered to be the foundation of the entire *Purāṇic* tradition. The *Bhavisya* must have been in existence by 250 A.C.

The *Bhavisya Purāṇa* is, it is said, the oldest only in so far as the dynastic lists are concerned. But many of the other *Purāṇas* "must be considerably older." The *Purāṇas* in the form of definite texts existed in the days of Kauṭalya, i.e., the fourth century B.C. as authoritative works.[2]

Some of the *Purāṇas*, traces of which are not to be found today must have been known to Gautama (*c* 550 B.C.) and Āpastamba (*c* 450 B.C.) authors or compilers of *Dharmaśāstras.*[3]

[1] G. S. Bose; *Purāṇa-Praveśa* (Calcutta, 1934).

[2] F. E. Pargiter; *The Purana Text of the Dynasties of the Kali Age* (London, 1913), *Ancient Indian Historical Tradition* (London, 1922).

[3] Winternitz: *Geschichte der Indischen Literatur*, vol. I. (Leipzig, 1909) pp. 441, 445, 451-480.

The more important *Purāṇas* came into their present shape by the beginning of the sixth century A.C. They may have been brought together for the first time a few centuries earlier. And of course, the traditions contained in the *Purāṇas* could be older by *many* centuries.

The order in which the eighteen *Purāṇas* are almost uniformly mentioned is given below: 1. *Brahma*, 2. *Padma*, 3. *Viṣṇu*, 4. *Vāyu*, 5. *Bhāgavat*, 6. *Nārada*, 7. *Mārkaṇḍeya*, 8. *Agni*, 9. *Bhaviṣya*, 10. *Brahmavaivarta*, 11. *Limga*, 12. *Varāha*, 13. *Skanda*, 14. *Vāmana*, 15. *Kūrma*, 16. *Matsya*, 17. *Garuḍa*, 18. *Brahmāṇḍa*.

The most important single event of Hindu culture under the Gupta Empire or in the age of Kālidāsa is the recasting, reinterpretation and final redaction of most of the great *Purāṇas*. These are the same texts which for over fifteen hundred years have remained virtually the Bibles of the people for social ethics and civic sense. It is to be understood that like the *Dharmaśāstras*, the *Purāṇa* also have been worked upon from generation to generation. It is impossible to establish a single date for an entire *Purāṇa*. Every chapter, sometimes every section will have to be dated on its own internal and external evidences.

It is during this period that the two great epics, the *Mahābhārata*[1] and the *Rāmāyaṇa*, were compiled in the final form. Their value in politics, law, eco-

[1] The *Ādiparvam* of the *Mahābhārata* has been for the first time critically edited by V. S. Sukthankar for the Bhandarkar Oriental Research Institute (Poona 1933), with the cooperation of Shrimant Balasaheb Pant Pratinidhi, R. D. Karmarkar, A. B. Paranjpye, V. R. Rajavade, N. B. Utgikar, P. L. Vaidya, V. P. Vaidya, M. Winternitz, R. Zimmermann and others.

nomics, and morals etc. is immense.[1] Nothing is more characteristic of the literature, art and social philosophy of hydra-headed creative India than these two epical encyclopaedias.

Some of the Hindu creations in poetry have reference to the goddesses as inspirers of courage and hope. From the Great Mother or Mother Goddess of the Indus Valley epochs (*c* 3500-3000 B.C.) down to our own Durgā-cult and Kālī-cult of today the tradition of the Hindu race as the inventor of such female divinities or as the creator of the Eternal Feminine as the Mother Divine is a constant feature in aesthetics and social psychology. During certain periods these creations constituted the speciality of the *Tantra* literature.[2] A Tantric invocation for strength to the Diety as Female principle would show that Mother-cult is in Hindu poetry a euphemism for energism, the worship of *Śakti*. One of the prayers is worded as follows (Avalon's version):

"May Thy sword glittering in Thy hands,
Besmear'd with the blood and fat of Asuras
(Titans) as with mire,

[1] E. W. Hopkins: "The Social and Military Position of the Ruling Caste in Ancient India as Represented by the Sanskrit Epic" (*Journal of the American Oriental Society*, 1889); *The Great Epic of India* (New Haven, 1920); J.J. Meyer: *Das Weib im altindischen Epos* (Leipzig, 1915). Like Hillebrandt, Meyer also is a humanist. See his *Daśakumāracharita* (1903) and *Das altindische Buch vom Welt-und Staatsleben* (1926). To the same group belongs C. Formichi: *Gl'Indiani e la loro scienza politica* (Bologna 1899), *Salus Populi* (Turin 1908), "Pensiero e Azione nell'India antica" (*Rivista Italiana di Sociologia*, Rome, 1914).

[2] Avalon; *Tantra of the Great Liberation* (transl. from Sanskrit, London), *Hymns to the Goddess* (London, 1913), *Principles of Tantra* (London), Vol. I. (1914) Vol. II. (1916).

Be for us welfare:
Oh, Chandikā ! to thee we bow.
Oh, Mother, who hast shown Thyself in many forms,
Who else than Thee is able to achieve
That destruction of the great Asuras,
Enemies of righteousness,
Which Thou hast wrought today ?

... ...

Queen of the Universe art Thou and its guardian;
In the form of the universe art Thou its maintainer;
By the Lords of the universe art Thou worshipped,
They its supporters have great devotion to Thee.
Oh, Devī be gracious;
Ever protect us from the fear of enemies,
As Thou hast just now saved us by the slaughter of the Asuras.
Make cease at once the sins of the whole world
And the great dangers which come of all portents."

Verily, life is a grand war in Indian estimation. And yet this conception of the "armageddon" of life is not a Hindu patent. "Thus we half-men struggle", says Robert Browning. And the Siegfrieds of the *Nibelungenlied*, e.g., of Hebbel's plays and Wagner's operas, are Browningite in their obstinately aggressive individuality. Whitman also sings :

"Knowest thou not there is but one theme for ever-enduring bards,
And that is the theme of war, the fortune of battles,
The making of perfect soldiers?"

Nor in Hindu works of literary criticism, e.g., in Viśvanātha's *Sāhitya Darpaṇa* (Mirror of Literature) will the reader of Clark's *European Theories of the Drama* find something characteristically Oriental. The difinitions of poetry, for instance, as discussed by the

Indian rhetorician will appear to be but chips from the block quite assimilable to those with which the West was familiar from Plato to Sidney. The doctrine that in poetry pain is transmuted into pleasure, as, for instance, in the "tragedy" of the *Rāmāyaṇa*, indicates at least that in the analysis of *rasas* the Hindu psychologists were not following a scientific willow-the-wisp.[1]

Altogether, in these *motifs* and ideals of creative India what else do we see except the "phrases" in a continuous "thematic" development, to use an expression from modern music, of the yearning after fire, energy, life? And is this fire-hunger, energy-hunger exclusively Hindu? This is "human, all-too human," as Nietzsche would remark.

Rāmaprasāda and Rāmakṛṣṇa

Not every Mother-worshipper or Tantrist sings in the strain described above. There was Rāmaprasāda in the eighteenth century in whose "Mālsī" songs addressed to Kālī we encounter the genuine devotee's concentration on the "inner self," the purification of thoughts and actions. Rituals, pilgrimages and all the external paraphernalia of religious life are held as of hardly any worth in this kind of thought. It is this type of positivism as embodied in attention to individual character that is the most marked feature of Hindu folk-morality.

A modern Tantrist, Rāmakṛṣṇa (1836-86), devotee as he is of the Divine Mother, strikes quite another note in his messages.[2] "As the same sugar", says he (No.690), "may be made into various figures of birds

[1] Mitra: *Sāhitya Darpaṇa*, pp. 43-44.

[2] *The Teachings of Sri Ramakrishna* (Advaita Ashrama, Mayavati and Calcutta, 1934).

and beasts, so one sweet Divine Mother is worshipped in various climes and ages under various names and forms. Different creeds are but different paths to reach her."

It is to be understood that indifferentism to externals as well as the appreciation of other faiths, in one word, the toleration of every form, positive or negative, in matters religious and spiritual, have come down from the earliest times to our own days. This explains why it is extremely difficult for the exponents of new faiths to conquer Hindu India with messages alleged to be unknown to the Hindus. In spite of the thousand and one rites and ceremonies attended with the folk-religion or folk-religions of the Hindus the unity of the Godhead furnishes the bed-rock of popular intelligence and "collective conscience" as understood by Durkheim, Lévy-Bruhl and Bouglé.

The positivism of Rāmaprasāda is continued by Rāmakṛṣṇa also. "Travel to all the four quarters of the earth", says this Master of the middle of the nineteenth century in a categorical manner (No.663), "you will find nothing (no true religion) anywhere. Whatever there is, is here (he said, pointing to his heart)".

It is wrong to believe that all this is much too high a philosophy or metaphysics for the people who are used to the folk-gods, folk-rituals and folk-festivals. Should religious reform or social reform be said to imply insistence less on the forms of religion, images, conventions, etc. and more on its spirit, such reforms have been propagated in India all through the ages for the folk in folk-language and by the persons born and bred among the folk. Rāmaprasāda and Rāmakṛṣṇa are but two of the modern exponents of this norm-*cum*-reform in Hindu folk-spirituality.

SECTION 2.

THE FINE ARTS AND ART-TECHNIQUES OF INDIA

Kālidāsa as Art-Critic

In Kālidāsa's play, *Śakuntalā* (fifth century A.C.), we have among the *dramatis personae* Anusūyā, a damsel of the hermitage, who is skilled in painting. Besides, a considerable portion of Act VI. Sc. II is a study in art criticism. It introduces us to some of the themes of the Hindu painters, their methods of execution, and the aesthetic taste of the spectators.

King Duṣyanta has through inadvertence dismissed his wife Śakuntalā from the palace. He soon perceives his mistake and becomes lovesick. A picture of Śakuntalā is then painted. The king hopes to derive some relief from this likeness.

"(*Enter a maid with a tablet*)

Maid. Your Majesty, here is the picture of our lady.

(*She produces the tablet*)

King (*gazing at it*). It is a beautiful picture. See.

A graceful arch of brows above great eyes;
Lips bathed in darting, smiling light that flies
Reflected from white teeth; a mouth as red
As red *karkandhu*-fruit; love's brightness shed
O'er all her face in bursts of liquid charm—
The picture speaks, with living beauty warm.

Clown (*looking at it*). The sketch is full of sweet meaning.

My eyes seem to stumble over its uneven surface. What more can I say? I expect to see it come to life, and I feel like speaking to it.

Miśrakeśī. The king is a clever painter. I seem to

see the dear girl before me.

King. My friend,

> What in the picture is not fair,
> Is badly done;
>
> Yet something of her beauty there,
> I feel, is won.
>
> ... ...

(*Sighing*)

I treated her with scorn and loathing ever;
Now o'er her pictured charms my heart will burst.

... ...

Clown. There are three figures in the picture, and they are all beautiful.

Which one is the lady Śakuntalā?

King. Which one do you think?

Clown (*observing closely*). I think it is the one, leaning against the creeper which she has just sprinkled. Her face is hot and the flowers are dropping from her hair; for the ribbon is loosened. Her arms droop like weary branches; she has loosened her girdle, and she seems a little fatigued. This, I think, is the lady Śakuntalā; the others are her friends.

King. You are good at guessing. Besides, here are proofs of my love.

> See where discolorations faint
> Of loving handling tell;
> And here the swelling of the paint
> Shows where my sad tears fell.

Chaturikā, I have not finished the background. Go, get the brushes.

... ...

Clown. What are you going to add?

Miśrakeśī. Surely, every spot that the dear girl loved.

King. Listen, my friend.

The stream of Mālinī, and on its sands
The swan-pairs resting; holy foot-hill lands
Of great Himalaya's sacred ranges, where
The yaks are seen; and under trees that bear
Bark hermit-dresses on their branches high,
A doe that on the buck's horn rubs her eye.
... ...

And another ornament that Śakuntalā loved I have forgotten to paint.

... ...

The *Siris*-blossom, fastened o'er her ear,
Whose stamens brush her cheek;
The lotus-chain like autumn moonlight soft
Upon her bosom meek.

Clown. But why does she cover her face with fingers lovely as the pink water-lily?

She seems frightened. (*He looks more closely*).

I see. Here is a bold, bad bee. He steals honey, and so he flies to her lotus-face.

... ...

King. Sting that dear lip, O bee, with cruel power,
And you shall be imprisoned in a flower.

Clown. Well, he doesn't seem afraid of your dreadful punishment.

King. Will he not go, though I warn him?

... ...

Clown. (*aloud*) It is only a picture, man."

(Ryder's version.)

There is no touch of pessimism, idealism, or

subjectivism in all these remarks and suggestions. A modern lover examining the photo or oil-painting of his darling could not be more realistic.

Does this conversation open up to us a society of ascetics or *Yogins* waiting for Divine illumination to evolve *śilpa* (art) out of the neo-Platonic "meditation" or the Hindu *Dhyāna*? or does it make the India of the fifth century a cognate of the modern world in its matter-of-fact grasp of the realities of flesh and blood?

It is really a specimen of creative India's positivism that Kālidāsa, the Shakespeare or Goethe of Hindu literature, has furnished in this bit of discussion in pictorial art. We feel how profound humanists the Hindu audiences were in their outlook, how non-mystical in their views and criticism in regard to *Chitra-lakṣaṇa* (i.e. "marks" of a painting).

The Perspectives of World-Art

And yet European and American scholars as well as their Asian paraphrasers have tried to discover and demonstrate an alleged "Oriental" pessimism in the arts and crafts of creative India. It is generaly held that the inspiration of Hindu painters and sculptors is totally different from that of the Western. The images and pictures executed by the artists of India are believed to have been the products of *Yoga*, of an ultra-meditative consciousness. They are said to reveal a much-too subjective or idealistic temperament. Further, they are all alleged to be religious or mythological in theme.

Comparative art-history would indicate, however, that Hindu plastic art or drawing, designing, colour-composition etc. has not been the handmaid of theology to a far greater extent than the classical and medieval works of Europe. We may at once ask the following questions: Is it not Greek mythology that we see embodied in the sculptures of Phidias? Similarly are not the Catholic and Russian paintings mere aids to the popularization of the Bible stories? Indeed, art has long been more or less "illustrative" of history, legends, traditions, and myths both in the East and the West.

The world does not know much of the Greek paintings. But we know the legends in the drawings on the Greek vases of the fifth century B.C. In one the serpent is being strangled by Heracles, almost as if the hydra Kāliya is being quelled by Krisṇa. In another Theseus is fighting the Amazons; and in a third Gorgon is pursuing Perseus or Kadmos killing the dragon. What else are the themes of the medieval *Purāṇa*-painters? And Hindus whose infancy is nurtured on the stories and paintings of the *Rāmāyaṇa* will easily remember familiar scenes in the coloured *terra cottas* of Hellas which portray, for instance, a Paris in the act of leading away Helen, or the parting of Hector and Andromache.

It may be confidently asserted, besides, that the spiritual atmosphere of the Gothic cathedrals of the thirteenth century with their soul-inspiring sculptures in alabaster and bronze has not been surpassed in the architecture of the East. The pillars at Chartres with *bas* reliefs of images and flowers could be bodily transported to the best religious edifices of Hindustan. The elongated virgin at the Cathedral *Notre Dame* of Paris is almost as conventionalized as a Korean Kwannon. The representation of virtues and vices on the portal of the Saviour at the Amiens Cathedral suggests the moralising in woodwork on the walls of Nikko in Japan. And scenes from the passion on the tympanum at Strassburg or from the Last Judgment on the tympanum of the north door in the Cathedral at Paris are oriented to the same psychological background as the *bas* reliefs depicting incidents in the holy career of Buddha with which the *Stūpas* (mounds) of Central India make us familiar, or of the Dalai Lama on the surface of the marble pagoda at Peking.

Further, it may be asked, can any Classicist rationally declare that the Greek Apollos are not the creations of subjective, the so-called *yogic* or meditative experience? In what respects are the figures of the the Hindu Buddhas and Śivas more idealistic? Polykleitos, for instance, dealt with abstract humanity, ideals, or "airy nothings" in the same sense as the artists of the Gupta period (A.C.300-600) or Dhīmān and Vītapāla of the Pāla period (780-1175) in India. Nowhere has a sculptured image, *bas* relief, or coloured drawing been completely "photographic". Art as such is bound to be interpretive or rather originative; and identification of the artist's self with his theme is the *sine qua non* of all creative *élan*, in science as in art.

We have to recognize, moreover, that saints and divinities are not the exclusive themes of art work in India. Hindu art has flourished in still life, social (*genre*), natural, plant, and animal studies as well. The avoidance of the nude in the early Christian art of Europe has its replica in the East. Physical beauty was not more often a taboo in Hindu art-psychology than in the Western. The dignity of the flesh has left its stamp on India's water colours, gouache paintings, and stone and bronze.

Even the figures of the Hindu gods and goddesses are to be perceived as projections of the human personality. The medieval Rājput paintings of the Rādhā-Krisṇa cycle and the Śiva-Durgā cycle can have but one secular appeal to all mankind. Accordingly we are not surprised to find in Dhananjaya the medieval dramaturgist's *Daśa-rūpa* the dictum that anything and everything can be the theme of art (IV. 90, Haas's transl.)

Lastly, can one forget that the conditions of life that produced the Byzantine and Italian masterpieces were almost similar to the *milieu* (economic and socio-religious including court patronage and guild control) under which flourished the celebrated Ajantā painters and Bhārhut sculptors? For, in the Middle Ages in Asia as in Europe the church, the temple or the *vihāra* (monastery) was the school, the art-gallery, and the museum; the priests and monks were painters, poets, calligraphists and pedagogues; and the Scriptures constituted the whole encyclopaedia. And if today it is possible for the Western mind to appreciate Fra Angelico, Massaccio, and Giotto, it cannot honestly ignore the great masters of the Hindu styles, especially in view of the fact that the works of the Oriental medievals are not more "imperfect" in technique according to modern ideas than those of their Occidental fellow-artists.

The fundamental identity of artistic inspiration between the East and the West, allowing for the differences in schools and epochs in each, is incidentally borne out by coincidences in social life for which art-work is responsible. Thus, the interior, nave and aisles of the Buddhist cave temples do not impress an observer with any feelings different from those evoked by the early Christian churches and Norman Cathedrals. The towers and contours of the twelfth century Romanesque Cathedral at Ely and the sixteenth century Gothic structure at Orleans have the *ensemble*, so to say, of the *gopurams* of Southern India. And the Gothic tapestries representing the hunting scenes of a Duke of Burgundy suggest at the very first sight the aspects of medieval Hindu castles and the figures and head-dresses of the Indo-Saracenic Moghul styles.

It may sometimes be difficult for a non-Hindu fully to appreciate the images and paintings of India because their conventions and *motifs* are so peculiarly Hindu. Exactly the same difficulty arises with regard to Western art. Who but a Christian can find inspiration in a *Last Supper* or a *Holy Family* or a *God dividing light from darkness*? For that matter, even the *Aeneid* would be unintelligible to the modern Eur-American lovers of poetry unless they made it a point to study Roman history. Nay, a well-educated Jew may naturally fail to respond to the sentiments in the *Divine Comedy* or Signorelli's *Scenes from Dante*. All these difficulties refer to the subject matter, the theme, the legend, the history.

But the difficulties of appreciation by foreigners do not make an art-work necessarily "local" or racial. It may still be universal in its appeal and thoroughly humanistic. There are hardly any people who in modern times can enter into the spirit of the *Ka* statues which stand by the sarcophagi in the cave tombs of the Pharaohs. And yet how essentially akin to modern mankind were the Egyptians if we can depend on the evidences of their letters! A *Ka* is described in one of the inscriptions thus: "He was an exceptional man; wise, learned, displaying true moderation of mind, distinguishing the wise man from the fool; a father to the unfortunate, a mother to the motherless, the terror to the cruel, the protector of the disinherited, the defender of the oppressed, the husband of the widow, the refuge of the orphan." There is no gap in fundamental humanity between the men and women of today and the race that could write such an epitaph, in spite of the fact that many of its conventions and usages seem entirely meaningless at the present time.

The student of foreign literature has specially to qualify himself in order that he may understand the unfamiliar idioms of its language and the peculiar turns of expression. No other qualification is demanded in modern men and women for an appreciation of the old and distant carvings, statuettes, drawings, figures, *bas* reliefs etc. The chief *desideratum* is really an honest patience with the racial modes and paraphernalia of foreign art.

With this elementry preparation the Occidental connoisseur should be able to say about Hindu sculptures and paintings what Max Weber, the American "futurist," writes about all antiques in his essay on "Tradition and Now." "Whether we have changed or not," says he, "I believe, in spite of all the manifestos to the contrary, in whatever tongue they be written or spoken, that the antiques will live as long as the sun shines, as long as there is mother and child, as long as there are seasons and climes, as long as there is life and death, sorrow and joy" (*Essays on Art*).

Painting in Sanskrit Literature

In *Śukra-nīti*, a Hindu sociological treatise, we read a few injunctions against the construction of human images. We are told that "the images of gods, even if deformed, are for the good of men. But the images of men, even if well formed, are never for human good." Sukra's generally recognized dictum seems to be that "the images of gods yield happiness to men, and lead to heaven; but those of men lead away from heaven and yield grief." (Ch. IV. Sec. iv lines 154-158).

Verses of a similar import from the *Śilpa-śāstras* (treatises on arts and crafts) may be used as texts by those who want to prove the wholly non-secular character of Hindu art. But such art-critics would commit the same fallacy as those psychologists who formulate the race-ideal of the entire Hindu population of all ages on the strength of a few sayings of Śākya the Buddha and other moralists. In spite of Śukra, Hindus have had sculptures of human beings in the streets and public places, *bas* reliefs of warrior-kings on coins, and paintings of men and women on the walls of their houses, palaces and art galleries. Secular art was an integral part of their common life. Imagery and similes from the worldly paintings and sculptures are some of the stock-in-trade embellishments of every literary work, e.g., poetry, fiction, drama, in India.

We have already seen Kālidāsa's Duṣyanta as a painter of his lady. In Subandhu's prose romance, *Vāsavadattā* (sixth century A.C.), there is a description of the Vindhya mountain. One of the objects mentioned is the lion "with his sinewy frame, and now rising high behind and now before." And the author is at once led to think of the scene as a possible theme of painting. Thus (in Gray's version)

> "His ears erect, in sudden onslaught skilled,
> His mane astart, and jaws all hideous,
> His stiffened tail high-waving in the breeze,—
> No artist could portray this awful beast
> What time he croucheth on the mighty brow
> Of some great elephant, shrill trumpeting
> Adown the lonely dells of Vindhya's mount."

Painting was an accomplishment of the literary women. The box of paints, canvas, pencil, tapestry, and picture-frames are referred to in *Chārudatta*, *Clay Cart*, *Raghu-vamśa*, *Uttara-rāma-charita* and *Kādambarī*. All these references apply to mundane paintings. In *Vāsavdattā*, again, Pātaliputra (Patna) is described as a city of which the conspicuous objects are the statues, which adorn the white-washed houses.

It is almost a convention with the heroes and heroines of Hindu literature to speak of the faces of their beloved as "pictures fixed on the walls of the heart." This conceit occurs even in Kriṣṇamiśra's morality play, *Prabodha-chandrodaya* (eleventh century).

In Subandhu's romance the heroine Vāsavdattā is seen by Kandarapaketu in a dream. She "was a picture, as it were, on the wall of life. And when he awoke he embraced the sky, and with outstretched arms cried to his beloved, as if she were painted in in the heavens, graven on his eyes, and carven on his heart." Kandarpaketu goes to sleep "looking on that most dear one as if limned by the pencil of fancy on the tablet of his heart."

Similarly Vāsavadattā thinks of Kandarpaketu "as if he were carven on her heart .... as if he were engraved there, inlaid, riveted." She exclaims to one of her maidens: "Trace in a picture the thief of my thoughts." And "over and over thinking thus, as if he were painted on the quarters and subquarters (of the sky), as if he were engraved on the cloud, as if he were reflected in her eye, she painted him in a picture as if he had been seen before."

The joy of life in all its manifestations is the one grand theme of all Hindu art. It is futile to approach the sculptors and painters of India with the notion of finding a typically Hindu message in them. The proper method should be to watch how far and in what manner the artist has achieved his ends as artist; i.e. as manipulator of forms and colors, as creator." Interpretation of life, or "criticism of life" may be postulated of every great worker in ink, bronze, or clay, whether in the East or in the West. The only test of a masterpiece, however, is ultimately furnished by the questions: "Is it consistent in itself? Does this handiwork of man add to the known types of the universe? Has it extended the bounds of creation?"[1]

Human ideals are the same all the world over. One piece of art in India may be superior to another in Europe, and *vice versa*. But this superiority is not necessarily a superiority in art-ideal or race-genius. It has to be credited to the individual gifts of the master in workmanship, or perhaps to the group-psychology of a creative epoch. There is but one world-measure for all human energy. And since neither the Eastern nor the Western evolution can be summed up in single shibboleths, types, or schools, it would be absurd to try to appraise Indian experience solely in terms of the aesthetics that found one of its most powerful expressions in the art-theory of the Young Germany as represented by Cornelius, Overbeck, Schiller and others (cf. Schiller's *Use of the Chorus*).

Moghul Portraits

Till recently Moghul painting had been regarded as Persian painting, imported into India by Moghul rulers.[2] But critical researches have shown the folly

[1] See the present author's "Aesthetics of Young India," "Social philosophy in Aesthetics," and "A German Annual of Asian Art" in *Rupam* (Calcutta, 1922, 1924 and 1927).

[2] Adapted from O. C. Gangoly's lecture at Patna, reported in the *Amrita Bazar Patrika*, Calcutta, 25 September 1935.

of that belief. No doubt, in the beginning, Indian artists imitated the Persian style of painting, but they had too much of individuality to remain long under that influence. They soon asserted a style of their own, and established a school which was quite different from Persian painting in temper and outlook. The Persian style was more decorative than realistic; it was conventional in line and background, and flat in treatment. The Indian school was more realistic and comparatively free from artificiality.

It is not accurate to assert that the Indo-Persian school of painting was initiated during the Moghul period. There are paintings which show that Indian artists had contact with Persian artists a few centuries earlier than the reign of Akbar. Yet such examples are very rare, and a systematic development of Moghul painting can be traced from the reign of Akbar, before whom there had been no strong organization of painters. It is Akbar who founded the imperial studio, and brought together the artists of the two schools, Eastern and Western. The former flourished in Gwalior, Nand Gwalior being the prominent artist of this school, and the latter in Gujarat, the prominent among the artists of this school being Bhim Gujarati and Shankar Gujarati. But whatever the origin of these artists, there is no doubt that they left a large number of illustrated books. The most important of the paintings of these days were: "*The March of Babar after the battle of Panipat*," "*The Birth Celebration of Humayun*," "*The Siege of Chitor*" "*A Scene from Hitopadeśa*," which had been rendered into Persian.

Portraiture was the most distinguishing feature of Moghul painting. At the beginning it was imitated from Bokharah, but Indian artists soon established a school of their own. Persian painting had been little interested in individuality, and therefore, portraiture had not been encouraged. But the artists of the Moghul period were mainly interested in portraying princes, their hunts and courts. Thus Moghul painting came to acquire a highly historical value.

The school founded by Akbar did not attain perfection in his own reign but in the reign of Jahangir. One very notable thing was that there were 41 Hindu artists, and seven Mohammedans, and all of them rendered contemporary life with remarkable faithfulness. The most interesting pictures of the period were the portraits of Malik Anwar and of Raja Man Singh. Zoological painting was taken up by Mansur whose fine artistic sense inspired many others to imitate him. The pictures of ducks, cranes, camel fights and elephant fights served the purpose of artistic refinement as also of records of history, showing that the princes took interest in camel fight and elephant fight just as the Spanish emperors took interest in bull fight.

At this point Moghul painting had passed its meridian. Some new traits were introduced. The paintings of court scenes not only manifested charm and elegance, but also ornament and grandeur. *Khushkhat* (calligraphy and drawing) attained perfection in this period and animal painting also maintained its reputation.

With Aurangzeb's accession to the throne Moghul painting began to decline, but it did not die altogether. In spite of his puritanical prejudices, Aurangzeb employed a very skilled artist to paint the weekly condition of Prince Morad, whom the king had imprisoned in Gwalior jail. It was, however, in this reign that art began to be decentralised. The fashion set by the Imperial court was imitated by chiefs and kings, ramifications existing in Hyderabad, Bijapur and other provinces.

Owing to strict *purdah* the *harem* was inaccessible to the artists. Actual portraits were, therefore, rare. There was, however, one lady artist who executed some pictures. There were yet portraits of queens, princesses, and dancing girls, most of which, though imaginary, showed that at least some of the painters had intimate acquaintance with *harem* life, which they depicted, as one of ease, luxury, and idleness.

Moghul painting also commingled with Rajput painting. The latter was quite different in temper and inspiration. Moghul painting was secular and interpreted individual life. It was not interested in the idealisation of life. It gave a refined representation of life, which was splendid but superficial; yet in portraiture it was a success. The figures in Rajput miniature, of the period after this contact, were not actual, but idealised pictures. For instance, the *Papiharagini* was suggestive of mystery, a work entirely removed from the senses. The dress and background indicated Moghul influence, while the decorative trees were reminiscent of Persian style.

Moghul painting was not idealistic nor was it romantic. It was confined to the lives of the princes, and was far away from the general culture of the people. It recorded passing events, never took deep root in the soil of Indian thought, and only remained on the verge of it. Yet it furnished a cinematographic representation of the events of the Moghul period, and was also a brilliant episode in the history of Indian painting.

Indian Art-Principles in the Interpretations by Rodin, Van Gogh and Gaugin

"Modern" is the term that seems to have been monopolized by the artists who claim Cezanne as their inspirer. And yet in this modernism Old India's paintings and sculptures have been a stimulating force.

The plastic art-creations at Bhārhut and the frescoes at Ajantā constitute in stone and colour, as we have indicated, the poetry of the whole gamut of human emotions from "the ape and tiger" to the "god-in-man." The encyclopaedic humanism of Hindu art is indeed comparable only to the comprehensive secularism in the painted *bas* reliefs of ancient Egyptian hill-caves and the stately *kakemonos* of the Chinese masters. While the message of the artists and craftsmen of India is thus universal as the man of flesh and blood, they developed certain peculiarities in the technique and mode of expression which "he that runs may read".

The most prominent characteristic of Hindu sculptures and paintings is what may be called the "dance-form". We see the figures, e.g., Śiva, the prince of dancers, or Kriṣṇa the flute-player, in action, doing something, in the supple movement of limbs. Lines of graceful motion, the play of geometric contours, the ripple of forms, the flowing rhythm of bends and and joints in space would arrest the eye of every observer of the bronzes, water-colors, and gouache works in India. Another characteristic that cannot fail to be noticed is the elimination of details, the suppression of minuter individualities, on the one hand, and on the other, the occasional elongation of limbs, the exaggeration of features, etc. All this is brought about by the conscious improvising of a new "artistic anatomy" out of the natural anatomy known to the exact science of *Āyurveda* (medicine). In the swollen breasts, narrowed waists, bulky hips etc. of Late Minoan or Cretan (*c.* 1500 B.C.) works which bridged the gulf between the Pharaonic and the primitive

Hellenic arts we can see the analogues or replicas of some of the Hindu conventions.

Leaving aside other characteristics, e.g., the absence of perspective, the grouping of color-masses, the free *laissez faire* treatment of sentiments, and so forth, one can easily pick up the Hindu elements from modern French creations, for instance, the Cezannesque paintings and Rodin's sculptures and drawings.

Let us listen first to Rodin lecturing on the beauties of *Venus of Melos*. In the synthesis of the work of art, says he, the arms, the legs, count only when they meet in accordance with the planes that associate them in a same effect; and it is thus in nature, who cares not for our analytical description. The great artists proceed as nature composes and not as anatomy decrees. They never sculpture any muscle, any nerve, and bone for itself; it is the whole at which they aim and which they express. It is this theorizing on sculpture that virtually underlies Hindu art work.

Similarly, Vincent Van Gogh (1830-1890), the Dutch painter, who, if not in execution like Cezanne, has, at least in ideal, pioneered the new art movement of today, seems almost to have given the theory of Hindu art from the side of painting. Says he:[1] "I should despair if my figures were correct; .... I think Michaelangelo's figures magnificent, even though the legs are certainly too long and the hips and the pelvis bones a little too broad. ...... It is my most fervent desire to know how one can achieve such deviations from reality, such inaccuracies and such transfigurations, that come about by chance. Well, if you like, they are lies, but they are more valuable than the real values."

[1] A. M. Ludovici: *The Letters of a Post-Impressionist.*

Rodin was charged with the crime of being an "innovator" in art, for he introduced movement and action in statuary. His *St. Jean Baptiste* (1880) is a specimen in point, as also the interlaced figures like the *Hand of God* holding man and woman in embrace, *Cupid* and *Psyche*, *Triton and Nereid*, etc. In regard to this "new technique," the representation of activity, we are told by Van Gogh that the "ancients did not feel this need." "To render the peasant form at work is," as he reiterates, "the peculiar feature, the very heart of modern art, and that is something which was done neither by the Renaissance painters nor the Dutch masters, nor by the Greeks."

It is thus clear why the theory and practice that seek "movement" in art-form, appreciate an "incorrect" anatomy, and look upon arbitrary proportions not as distortions but rather as "restorations," should find an affinity with the work of the Hindu masters. And the psychology of this "post-impressionist" art-*credo* is perfectly natural, because like the previous pre-Raphaelitism and the still earlier romanticism, the new art-movement is essentially a revolt. It is a reaction against the academicians' rule of thumb. It is born of a Bolshevistic desire to search for truth and beauty from far and old.

This latest revolution against the *status quo* of art was brought about when Gaugin, the French master, conceived "the truth that the modern European and his like all over the globe could not and must not be the type of the future. Anything rather than that! Even black men and women were better than that,—cannibals, idolators, savages, anything!"

Such being their article of faith, the contemporary artists of Eur-America have been seized by *Wanderlust*. Today they draw their inspiration from the ancient Mexicans, Mayans, and other American-Indians, from the Negro art of the Congo regions, from Karnak and Nineveh, from the Tanagras of Greece and the "primitives" of Italy. And they roll their eyes from "China to Peru." Consequently the Buddhist, Śaiva, Vaiṣṇava, Moghul, and Rājput arts of the Hindus could not but have been requisitioned to enlarge the list of the new Ossians and Percy's *Reliques* as whetters of the "futuristic" imagination in the Western world.

And the creative art endeavours of Young India's futurists are neither mere calls for "Back to the Past" nor harangues inciting to "Down with the West," as superficial observers or professional spiritualitarians would seem to read in the literary proclamations of the school. These are but the initial surgings of a dynamic *śakti* (energy) that had been pent up for a century or so,—in its *sādhanā* (effort) towards achieving the assimilation of this cosmic neo-eclecticism of the modern world; so that a synthetic stage of cultural *svarāj* (self-determination) may ultimately evolve, on which Asia will be enabled, as of old, freely to move and to strive, to un-make and to make, boldly to borrow and to lend as an independent unit in the *bourse* of spiritual exchange, unhampered to struggle, to experience, to live.

Consult: A. K. Coomaraswamy : *Mediaeval Sinhalese Art* (London, 1908), *Indian Craftsman* (London, 1910), E. B. Havell: *Indian Sculpture and Painting* (London, 1908), *Indian Architecture* (London, 1926), V. A. Smith: *A History of Fine Art in India and Ceylon* (Oxford, 1911), H. Goetz: *Epochen der Indischen Kultur* (Leipzig, 1929), R. Grousset: *Histoire de l'Extrême-Orient* (Paris, 1929), Ph. Stern: "L'Art del'Inde" in *L'Inde Antique et la Civilisation Indienne* (Paris, 1933); P. K. Acharya: "The Origin of the Hindu Temple" and "The Aspect and Orientation in Hindu Architecture" (*Indian Culture*, Calcutta, July 1934, January 1935).

SECTION 3

SOCIAL FORCES IN MEDIEVAL INDIAN POETRY

Hindu Impacts on Islam

During the period from the beginnings of the fourteenth to the end of the eighteenth century Hindu culture has to orient itself to two sets of foreign cultural agencies. The first are furnished by the Moslem *milieu*, and the second by the European, especially, the Portuguese, Dutch, French and British. The seventeenth century may be taken to be the starting point of the influences from the European side. The virility of Hindu positivism is as manifest in these two *milieux* or under these two sets of "culture-contacts" as in the previous ones.

The *Aitareya Brāhmaṇa* (VII. 15) philosophy of *charaiveti* (march on) corresponding to *l'aptitude colonisatrice* of Lasbax's *La Cité Humaine* (Vol. II. p. 219) should appear to have continued unhampered even in the epoch of Moslem intercourse with the Hindus. The tenacity of Hindu positivism made itself felt in Islamic circles. And if there were no converts to formal Hinduism among the Mussalmans there were at any rate signs of spiritual assimilation by them of the gifts of Hindu culture. The impacts of Hindu arts and sciences on the Mussalmans was considerable.[1]

It is not perhaps possible to say in this instance as in many others that "captive Greece captured Rome". But there is no doubt that a large section of the Mussalmans,—rulers, scholars, authors, and the public,—came to be Hinduized in morals, manners and sentiments.

[1] See the section on Alberuni's *India* (c 1030), *supra*, pp. 96-102.

Indianized Persian or Persianized Hindi evolved as Urdu in the fourteenth or even in the thirteenth century. Perhaps one of the first Urdu writers is Amir Khusru who flourished under the Khiljis (1290-1320) and is known to have died in 1325.

The translation of Sanskrit works into Persian is at least as old as Sultan Firoz Shah Tughlak (1351-1388). It was on the strength of such translations that the Hindu physical sciences had a place in *Dalail-i-Firuz Shahi*[1], a lengthy poem by Izzul-din Khalid.

While, on the one hand, Sanskrit texts were being rendered into Persian and mainly through Moslem interest and under Moslem auspices it is significant to observe that Sanskrit works were being rendered into the spoken languages of the Indian people, — the vernaculars,—and this also through Moslem interest. The first translation of the Sanskrit *Mahābhārata* into Bengali, for instance, was accomplished under the order of king Nasir Shah (1282-1325).

The translation of the *Bhāgavata Purāṇa* into Bengali by Mālādhar Basu was done under the orders of Husain Shah (1493-1518). Parāgal Khān, a general of this ruler, as well as Parāgal's son, Chhuṭi Khān, are famous in Bengal as inspirers of the Bengali translation of portions of the *Mahābhārata* by Kavīndra Parameśvara and Śrī Karaṇa Nandi.[2]

Hindu-Moslem *rapprochement* was thus in evidence in pre-Moghul India. The movement got a fillip

[1] *Maathirul-Umara* vol. II. p. 190, in M. Z. Siddiqi: "The Services of the Muslims to Sanskrit Literature" (*Calcutta Review*, February 1933).

[2] D. C. Sen: *History of Bengali Language and Literature* (Calcutta, 1911) pp. 10-12, 14; N. N. Law: *The Promotion of Learning in India during Muhammadan Rule by Muhammadans* (London, 1916) pp. 107-111, 185-186.

under the Moghuls. The translation bureau of Akbar the Great published Persian renderings of the *Mahābhārata*, the *Rāmāyaṇa*, the *Gītā*, the *Atharva Veda*, the *Yogavāśiṣṭha*, the *Maheśamahānanda*, the *Harivamśa* and other Sanskrit works. Hindu texts had another great Moslem patron in Prince Dārā Shikoh (1614-1659), the eldest brother of Aurangzib or rather the eldest son of Shah Jahan (1628-1659). The translation and in certain instances the retranslation of the *Vedas* into Persian was undertaken on account of the interest of Dārā Shikoh.

With the help of Benares Paṇḍits Dārā Shikoh is known to have translated several Hindu philosophical works into Persian. In 1657 was ready *Sirr-ul-Asrar* (The Secret of Secrets). This is the title of his rendering of the *Upaniṣads*. He was the translator also of the *Gītā*, the *Yogavāśiṣṭha*, the *Rāmāyaṇa* etc. His attempt to reconcile Sufism and Hindu pantheism found shape in the work *Majima-ul Bahrain* (1654).

Interest in Hindu prosody, *Kāmaśāstra*, *Alamkāra*, music, physiognomy, etc. was keen among the Mussalmans in the time of Aurangzib (1659-1707) also. It was for his grandson Prince Jahandar Shah, that these Hindu *Vidyās* were incorporated in a Persian text book entitled *Tuhfatul-Hind*.

Hindu-Moslem cultural cooperation was manifest in the eighteenth century in the establishment, in 1724 at Delhi under Muhammad Shah's orders, of an observatory by Jai Singh, the Hindu astronomer and ruler of Ambar (Jaipur).

The Humanism of Nāmadeva, Kabīr, Nānak Chaitanya and Vemana

In the thirteenth and fourteenth centuries the *charaiveti* (march on), *l'exubérance de vitalité* or expansion of Hindu culture was likewise in evidence in the new Indian (vernacular) literatures. It was going on in Marathi-speaking regions through the development of the *abhangs* or folk-songs of *bhakti* in honour of Viṣṇu. The *Gītā* was thereby rendered accessible to the people in their spoken language by poets like Jnāneśvara (*c* 1300) and Nāmadeva (1270-1350). The democratization of the *Gītā* is an achievement of first-rate importance as furnishing the folk with the gospel of life's duties.

By the beginning of the fifteenth century the Bengali translation of the *Rāmāyaṇa* by Krittivāsa was available to the people of Bengal as a fountain of daily philosophy. The work was inspired by the cult of *bhakti* (faith or devotion), an attitude of life such as become a passion with Chaitanya (1485-1533), two generations later.

The egalitarian philosophy which sought to abolish the distinctions between the castes was a prominent characteristic of Hindu societal thinking in the fourteenth and fifteenth centuries,—with Nāmadeva as with Chaitanya. A founder of this movement is the Southerner Rāmānanda (*c* 1400?) who derived his cult of *bhakti* from another Southerner, Rāmānuja. Although a Southerner, he was a maker of Hindi language and in point of social liberalism or radicalism was distanced by one of his *chelās* or followers, namely Kabīr (1470-1518?), a Mussalman weaver of Benares. It is well-known that Kabīr called himself the child of both Āllāh and Rāma. The annihilation of the distinction between Hinduism and Islam was the *Leitmotif* of his preachings and verses. Kabīr was by all means a pre-Moghul personality.

Another pre-Moghul personality in whom socio-religious radicalism ran to greater extremes than even in Kabīr and, who indeed was a *chelā* of the latter, was Nānak (1469-1538), the founder of Sikhism. Secular occupation was not discounted by Nānak. In his conception the state of a householder was no less acceptable to Hari (God) than retirement from the world.[1] He did not consider secular business to be an obstacle to the attainment of final emancipation. He preached likewise that emancipation was not confined to the higher castes but accessible to all men, including the Chaṇḍāl, the *pariar*. All men were received by him as disciples and the foundation of a popular religion was thereby laid. He taught that it is the duty of the disciple to destroy the enemies of his faith and to help in the diffusion of the Sikh religion. Besides, the disciple is strictly to obey the order of the *Guru* and never to forsake him; he is also to minister to his brother Sikhs. He is to pay taxes, if demanded by the *Guru*.

In the fourteenth and fifteenth centuries Hindu positivism was strong enough to express itself in the different regions of India in a manner such as might enable the people to energize in a spirit of hopefulness. The old texts were reinterpreted to assimilate new races, castes and creeds. Hinduism proved to be a "going concern" even under the conditions of the first two or three centuries of Moslem politics. And in the sixteenth and seventeenth centuries Hindu positivism was once more in a flourishing condition. The age of Kavikamkana, the Bengali poet who wrote the *Chaṇḍī-mangala* in 1589, and of Tulsidās (1532-1624), who completed the Hindi *Rāmāyaṇa* about the same time, is, as an era of the expansion and democratization of Hindu culture, not to be beaten by any epoch

[1] Nand Lal: *Rohitnāmā* (Rules ot Conduct) pp. 9, 80, in E. Trumpp: *Ādi Granth* (London, 1877), CXV, CXVI.

of Indian societal achievements, previous or subsequent. Along with these two senior contemporaries in Northern India Tukārām (1608-1649), the Mārāthā writer of *abhangs* constituted a triumvirate of extraordinary importance in the annals of Hindu humanism during the period of Indo-Moghul Renaissance.

It is as an expression of the traditional democratic or socialistic strands in Hindu culture such as we have seen even in the earliest Vedic and post-Vedic *milieux* that we have likewise to assess the works of the great Telugu poet of the seventeenth century, namely, Vemana. The devotional or *bhakti* egalitarianism of the Tamil *Kural* is carried forward in Vemana's verses to a pitch verging on revolution. In his sarcasm on the inequalities of material possession he is no less radical and realistic than in his invectives against the disabilities engendered by caste distinctions.

On one occasion we encounter this Telugu poet of equality and fraternity declaiming as follows:[1]

"Why should he constantly revile the Pariar? Are not his flesh and blood the same as those of our men? And of what caste is He who pervades the Pariar as well as all other men? Why should you plunge in water to purify yourself if a Pariar touches you?"

Again, "call not him an outcaste who possesses a good disposition. Did not the hermit Vaśiṣṭha take a Pariar wife? How can he be called Brāhman whose qualities are those of a Pariar?"

In the same strain are the following lines: "If a man still has in his heart the principles of a Pariar, and

[1]*Verses* III, 227-229 (Brown) in B. A. Saletore: *Social and Political Life in the Vijayanagara Empire* (1346-1646), vol. II. (Madras, 1934), pp.8, 54, 58.

yet scorns Pariars, how should he become twice-born, while devoid of any good quality?"

Vemana's condemnation of socio-economic inequalities is no less emphatic. "If one be possessed of wealth," says he, "they look upon him as the god of love; but if he falls into poverty, and is unable to rise and help himself, be he as Cupid himself, they look upon him as a Pariar."

The problem of the Pariar, of the untouchables, and of the distinctions between the higher and the lower castes found in Vemana a powerful exponent. His place in Hindu positivism is of the same rank as that of Kabīr, Chaitanya and the others, if not even higher.

Democratic Strands in Hindu Social Thought

It has been the custom to treat the social reform movements among the Hindus from the fourteenth to the eighteenth century as due to the impacts of Islam, monotheistic and democratic as it is. Sociologically, however, it is necessary to dive deeper into the phenomena. For one thing, it is patent to every student of the Hindu institutions and ideologies that both monotheism and democracy are coeval with the Hindu mind itself. Historically speaking, the concepts of the unity of Godhead and the equality of classes have never been absent in the Indian socio-religious and socio-economic tradition. The processes by which the non-Indians, non-Aryans, non-Brāhmaṇas, the Vrātyas, the Śūdras, the "wild tribes" and what not have got themselves Indianized, Aryanized, Brāhmaṇized constitute the most solid realities of race-history and cultural development in every nook and corner of India and in every epoch of India's growth, since, at any rate, the Vedic times of which we have literary records. In other words, it is not so much the *Varṇāśrama* as the protests against the *Varṇāśrama*, not so much the law and order, as the violations of law and order, not so much the alleged pure races or castes as the *varṇa-samkaras*, the "mixed colours", fusions of ethnic elements,—or rather the simultaneous operation of these two sets of forces that constitute the norm of Hindu cultural evolution. In the socialistic or democratic movements of Hindu India in the Moslem *milieu* we have but to read the continuations of the eternal society-making process, the social "metabolism," that has led to the vertical mobilization of groups from the lower to the higher strata. The very category, "expansion of Hindu culture," implies nothing but this democratization, or rather the impact of the "masses" upon the main stock of Hindu institutions and ideals.

Thus considered, the history of Hindu societal evolution can furnish evidences of socialism and democracy, understood in a general sense, such as have been analyzed by the Italian sociologist Salvatore Cognetti de Martiis in his *Socialismo Antico* (1889).[1] The study of "economic ideals" as distinguished from economic realities is the subject-matter of this treatise. And India is exhibited from the standpoint of the ideas of "social utopia" which came to evolve in its literature and folk tradition.

He does not consider the struggle between the old and the new aristocracies to be a special phenomenon of any particular race-history, say, that of the Phoenicians. It is in his judgment a universal fact of civilization in the old and the new worlds,—in Egypt,

[1] See the present author's "Hindu Politics in Italian" in the *Indian Historical Quarterly*, September 1925—April 1926.

Greece and Rome as much as in India, China and Peru. The protests against private property, and glorifications of equality, fraternity, justice, peace and happiness are to be encountered, for instance, in the literature of every country.

Already even the Rig Vedic tradition of Yama (IX, 113, 8, X, 14, 13, X, 58, 1, X, 17, 1) introduces us to conditions of bliss such as existed in some golden age, after which therefore the social reformers of the day are aspiring. The Buddhist conception of equality and fraternity does not disappear with the so-called Buddhist ages. It reappears in the Vaiṣṇava *milieu* . The *Viṣṇu Purāṇa* accords great importance to the Śūdras. The democratic spirit associated with Rāmānandism exercises a beneficial influence on the souls of the popular classes, leading to the energetic manifestation of the consciousness of self-importance. Viṣṇudās Kavi's *Svargārohaṇa* (Ascent to Heaven) dwells at length on the merits of the oppressed classes to the exclusion of the upper ten thousands who are exhibited in the worst colour. We are, therefore, in a position to assert that from the *Vrātya* Book of the *Atharva Veda* to the *Svargārohaṇa* of the Vaiṣṇava poet the Hindu democratic or egalitarian tradition has broadened down from precedent to precedent.[1] And so far as the Moslem atmosphere is concerned, we should be prepared to admit that it did not kill the traditional Hindu spirit of expansion as promoted by race-fusion or culture-contacts.

Telugu Folk-Poetry

In the imagination of the Hindus the Vijayanagra

[1] See the discussion of the Paretian doctrine of the "circulation of the *élites*" in the section on "Race-Mixture and Caste-Fusion in Indian Social polity." *Supra*, pp. 131—132.

Empire (1346-1646) was like the subsequent Maratha Empire a bulwark of Hindu culture established against the avalanche of Islam. The founders of these Empires were therefore esteemed as veritable *avatāras* or incarnations of Lord Kriṣṇa. Bukka I. (1343-76), the virtual founder of the Vijayanagara State is described in an inscription as one in whom God "reappeared" to deliver the world of the Mlechchhas. This account embodies the famous declaration of Lord Kriṣṇa in the *Gītā* to the effect that it is whenever *dharma* finds itself in jeopardy that He appears age by age.

Folk-poetry as that embodied in the *Madhurā-vijayam* associated the exploits of the Hindus with the interventions of the gods. The manner in which the magic sword of the prospective deliverer of the Hindus from the thraldom of the Moslems came into his hands is described in this Telugu poem[1] in the mystical manner of the Irish poet Yeats. "O Sovereign, once upon a time the divine Viśvakarmā, gathering the splinters from the weapons of all the Devas (gods) and melting them together," says a strange woman to the son of Bukka I, "shaped this strange sword and presented it to Parameśvara for gaining victory over the *Daityas* (demons)." The fortunes of this magic sword, like that of the one in the Arthurian legend, are then narrated briefly. The young prince is finally presented with it with the following words: "By wielding this weapon," says the strange woman, "you will attain unabating vigour and the weapons of the enemy will become powerless against you. Just as Kriṣṇa slew Kamsa in Madhurā in olden times, O king!

[1] B. A. Saletore: *Social and Political Life in the Vijayanagara Empire* (Madras, 1934) vol. I. pp. 8—10. vol. II. pp.1, 5, 272, 273.

do you proceed now to the southern Madhurā and slaughter the Mussalman king, the enemy of the world."

Equally deified in folk-imagination was Kriṣṇa Deva Rāya the Great (1509-20) under whom the Vijayanagara Empire witnessed the zenith of its expansion. In the *Vyāsayoga charitam* the poet Somanātha describes the monarch's death as the departure of Lord Kriṣṇa from the ken of mankind at the end of His *avatāra-hood*.

A private Tamil inscription of 1380 has as its chief item of prayer the exercise of "universal sovereignty" by Bukka Rāya. "Universal dominion" is sought for Deva Rāya in an inscription of 1428 associated with merchants.

We are to understand that the positivism of creative India popularized in folk-tradition the doctrine of political deliverers or "world-conquerors" as being none other than *Yugāvatāras* or Gods in human form. The secularization of alleged religious texts or rather the interpretation of alleged godlore in terms of worldly personalities and human exploits was in the very blood of the Hindu masses and classes. The records from Vijayanagara as from the Maratha annals should furnish concrete illustrations as to how a scientific and critical student of Hindu social institutions and theories ought to interpret them. Those who would follow the folk-tradition of India through the ages are not likely to be shunted off into misleading tracks by mere names of gods and goddesses and the atmosphere of religious ritualism or metaphysical speculations. It is the things "human, all-too human" that they would encounter in Hindu institutions and theories. Hindu religion is nothing if it is not in the main a handmaid to worldly progress and material prosperity.

Bengali Positivism in Literature

Writings on the history of Bengali literature as on that of other Indian literature have been vitiated by a fundamental fallacy. In the story of a thousand years' literary development, for instance, scholars have managed to watch only the struggle for supremacy among the various orders of gods and socio-religious systems.[1] According to the methodology of literary historiography and art-criticism prevalent in and about Bengal or, for that matter, All-India, the *Aeneid*, the great national epic of the Romans would have no significance except what may be gathered from the ultimate triumph of Venus over Juno in the life-history of Aeneas. The method is not uninteresting, but when art appreciation is obsessed by such a religio-theological "interpretation" the result is likely to be misleading, and unsatisfactory as in the case of Max Weber's *Gesammelte Aufsaetze zur Religionssoziologie*, or of Durkheim's *Les Formes Elèmentaires de la Vie Religieuse*.

As an expression of this ultra-religiosity in the interpretation of literature and art is to be mentioned the attempt to exhibit the creations of poets, painters and sculptors in terms of *dhyāna* (meditation), *yoga* (communion with God), and so on. Love between man and woman has likewise been attacked by this method and presented as nothing but an allegory of the union between God and the soul. Other "values" in the societal complex have been virtually ignored.

[1] D. C. Sen: *History of Bengali Language and Literature* (Calcutta, 1911). For general sociological orientations see C. Bouglé: *Lecons de sociologie sur l'evolution des valeurs* (Paris, 1929), pp. 6-8; see especially the chapters on *Les valeurs religieuses et valeurs morales* and *Les valeurs esthètiques*, pp.127-129, 153-155, 246-252.

The successive stages in the evolution of Hindu literature,—in Bengali, Hindi, Marathi, Gujarati, Tamil, Telugu, etc. have been labelled with the hallmark of one or other of the metaphysico-religious systems, e.g., Vedic, Upaniṣadic, Śaiva, Buddhist, Tantric, Vaiṣṇava, Jaina, Śākta, etc. The entire literary material of India is generally presented to the world as the handmaid of creeds, dogmas and rituals.

The absurdity would be evident if one were to treat the whole course of Western literature as nothing but Hellenic and Roman paganism, Oriental Christianity, Roman Catholicism, Lutheranism, Pilgrim Fathers, Oxford Movement, Unitarianism, Christian Science and so forth in succession. Students of world literature who are obsessed by the influence of religious ideas on human achievements would read in the *Aeneid* only a *Purāṇa* of Latin mythology, in the *Divine Comedy* only an encyclopaedia of mediaeval Christianity, and in the *Paradise Lost* just a Bible of the Puritans. Or where in modern literature and art they find the treatment of subjects from Hellenic mythology they would be inclined to interpret it as "Back to paganism!"

It is necessary to cry halt to this sort of ultra-religious or metaphysical appraisals as has been done by the present author in *Love in Hindu Literature* (Tokyo 1916). A sober interpretation of the facts of Hindu literature is a desideratum. We have to get used to the concept of new values in the making of human personality. Even where the setting or scaffolding is religious or mythological and the *dramatis personae* divine or semi-divine one need not be tempted to mean by the texts "more than what meets the ear."

Most of what has been passing in India for other-worldly literature and art is in reality the literature and art of human passions, human ideals, human interests and conflicts. To be more definite, it may be said that folk-life and sex-life have been the two chief *motifs* of a considerable portion of Indian literature and art. The medieval writings like the Rādhā-Krisṇa songs (*Padāvalī*) of Vidyāpati (*c* 1450), the *Kavikamkana-Chaṇḍī* (1580) etc. of Bengal ought to be approached as one approaches the literary creations of Eur-America with the methodology of modern art-criticism.

Under the title of *Bāra-māsyā* or the "twelvemonth" story of men and women an extensive literature grew up in Bengal. Generally it was incorporated as a section in large works, the titles of which end as a rule with *Mangala* (welfare or blessings). In the *Chaṇḍī*, by Mādhava of East Bengal, available in manuscript, one comes across a narrative of the joys and sorrows of the year. Such calendars of human vicissitudes constituted a stock in trade, so to say, of the poetry of creative Bengal.

These stories are not always the stories of opulence and happiness. The hunter-girl Fullarā, for instance, in the *Kavikamkana-Chaṇḍī* (pp. 199-202) describes her own *Bāramāsyā*, which is nothing but a tale of woes, both physical and economic.

Perhaps after the *Rāmāyaṇa* of Krittivāsa (*c* 1450) no Bengali poetical work is more popular than Mukundarāma's *Kavikamkaṇa-Chaṇḍī* (*c* 1589). This work *pro-forma* should appear to be a treatise on *Chaṇḍī* the Mother, and therefore something like a contribution to religious poetry. But one has only to open the work, available in print, at any page and be convinced that no literary work in any language is more profane, secular and worldly than this Bengali composition written as it was with the object of propagating the cult of Kālī. Every line in it breathes the spirit of living human beings, their daily exploits and ambitions, their hatreds and quarrels, their joys and sorrows. Mukundarāma is the poet *par excellence* of man's mastery over the things of this Earth, and the prophet born to accord an "Everlasting Yea" to life. It is of life and the world that he sings, of men and women in action and in struggle. He has furnished the Bengali masses with the well of *śaktiyoga* (energism), pure and undefiled. It is for a dose of inspiration in human endeavours and for the sunny atmosphere of human humour that one turns to this apostle of humanism in the sixteenth century.

The establishment of a town by Kālketu belonging to the lowly and untouchable caste of *Vyādha* (hunter or fowler) is an important item in this work. And this furnishes the poet with an occasion for describing the diverse races and classes of population, the occupational structure of the people,—the milkmen, the Kāyasthas, the Brāhmanas etc.—and the different wards of the city. The Moslems also come in for treatment and their manners and customs, marriage ceremony, and other social institutions have commanded the author's attention. In this realistic account given over to the Moslem *mores* the Mollahs (Moslem priests) are described as officiating in the *jabāi* (i.e. ceremonial sacrifice) of hens and of she-goats for the Moslem householder.[1] The poet is objective enough to mention that the fee obtained by the Moslem priest in connection with the hen-"sacrifice" is 40 cowries (= 0-0-6 pies approximately) and that that for the she-goat-"sacrifice" is the head of the animal *plus* 120 cowries

[1] *Kavikamkana-Chaṇḍī* (Calcutta, 1924), vol. I., pp. 258-261; J. N. Das Gupta : *Bengal in the Sixteenth Century A.D.* (Calcutta, 1914), pp. 57-95.

(= 0-1-6 pies approximately). It is interesting sociologically to observe that in sixteenth century Bengal the Moslem householders are described in a manner which we of today should consider similar to the *āchāra* or practice of the Hindus in so far as the services of a priest in regard to the *jubāi* or sacrifice of animals, are being requisitioned. The socio-religious *rapprochement* between Hindus and Moslems is a phenomenon that strikingly arrests our notice.

The animal world of Bengal has been the subject matter of a special section (pp.99-101). The diverse animals are described in their relations with one another. And these relations are found to be identical with those obtaining in the human society. The king and his officers, priests, medical men, school masters, etc. are all brought together in this survey.

The movements and activities in which Mukundarāma is interested in this *Chaṇḍī* are not all confined to the home and the village. He knows the larger world too,—the cities, the merchants, law courts, battles, pilgrimages, boat life, social intrigues, and what not. Nay, a considerable part of his poetry is given over to foreign lands, trade with distant countries,—Ceylon, for instance, and the exchange of goods (p. 814). The result of all this "world-sense," of wear and tear among diverse men and movements is noteworthy. The merchant, Dhanapati, is quite a reasonable man in whom sobriety has been engendered because of the experiences of life. While his wife Khullanā's character is being publicly impeached in his own gild he knows how to keep his head high. He is realistic enough to remember the stories of the *Mahābhārata* in which the morals such as can be questioned by the conventional standard have even been glorified. Nay, he tries to dissuade Khullanā herself from the determination to submit to the fire-test famous in the Sitā-story of the *Rāmāyaṇa* (pp. 582-585). The author of the *Kavikamkana-Chaṇḍī* is a chastened man. He knows of all the excesses and vices of the *Kali Yuga* (pp. 992-996). But he does not get inspired to moralize over them. He is a fine story-teller, an objective dramatizer, so to say, and endowed with the Chaucerian outfit.

Moralizations do not belong to the grain of this poet's temperament. He is too human to be upset by the indiscretions of life, however grave they be. It is the sweet milk of human kindness that he administers to the people. His spiritual patents are very democratic, simple, naive. Just the use of the divine name of Hari is enough to save anybody and everybody (p. 997), he believes.

Dvija Rāmachandra is the poet-singer of the narrative poem, *Ambikā-Mangala*, a work which is still in manuscript.[1] Much of the material contained in this work resembles the contents of the *Kavikamkaṇa-Chaṇḍī*. In point of literary excellence it should appear to be of at least the same merit as this famous *Chaṇḍī* which happens to command the attention of the reading public perhaps on account of the sheer accident of being available in print.

At one point of the *Ambikā-Mangala* we have the description of the marriage ceremony of the heroine *Rambhāvatī*. Among the festivities are described the musical entertainments, dances by female dancers, etc.

[1] It is accessible in the Calcutta University collection of Bengali manuscripts. The information is derived from Sj. Haridas Palit, author of *Ādyer Gambhīrā*, a treatise on the socio-religious history of Bengal, who is connected with this Department.

At another point the merchant's wife Khullanā is being assisted by the maid Durvalā in the kitchen. The description of cooking points to the diverse items of household economy such as is prevalent in Bengal even today. One finds here among other things the jack-fruit seeds, pulse-cakes, sprawn, *chitol* fish and *mān-kachu* so characteristic of Bengali dietary.

The literature of creative Bengal has contributed untold springs of action for social energism. It is not surprising that a most remarkable emphasis on the dignity of man should be associated with the Vaiṣṇava poetry of Chandīdāsa (*c* 1350). No two lines in the entire range of the world's classics can possibly vie with the following from this great poet of Bengal consecrated as they are to the apotheosis of man:

"*Savār upare mānuṣ satya*
Tāhār upare nāi."

(Above all is man the truth, Beyond him is nothing).

Thus sings Chaṇḍīdāsa of man as the greatest of all truths. This poet can rank among the greatest *avatāras* of humanism and benefactors of mankind. And this is a bit of Bengāli mind in the fourteenth century.

Nothing short of an "Earthly Paradise" is furnished by Vidyāpati (*c* 1450) in his *Padāvalī*,[1] thus:

"Drunken are the honey-bees in honey-season
With the honey of the honey-flowers:
In Honey-Brindaban resides
The Honey-Lord of Honey-Love.
Amid the companies of honey-maids
Is honey-honey-dalliance:
Honeyed are the blissful instruments of music.

[1] Englished by A. K. Coomaraswamy as *The Songs of Vidyapati* (London, 1915). See the present author's *Love in Hindu Literature* (Tokyo, 1916).

Honeyed hands are beating honey-measures.
Honeyed is the dance's sway,
Honeyed are the movements of the dancers,
Honeyed are their happy songs,
And honeyed are the words of Vidyāpati."

Pessimism and other-worldliness are the farthest removed from this mentality. The *sociologie des valeurs* is profoundly enriched by the discovery of such quarries in the avowedly "religious" literature.

A specimen of "dalliance in spring" is furnished below:

"The new young maidens, maddened with new longings,
Are hurrying to the groves.
For ever and for ever new diversions such as these
Delight the heart of Vidyāpati."

These are some of the delights with which Vidyāpati, the Bengali-Maithil or Maithil-Bengali poet of the fifteenth century, enriches the Bengali households from the lowest upto the highest. Indeed, in the Chaṇḍīdāsa-Vidyāpati complex as in the *Chaṇḍī*-poems it is the masses that speak. We encounter here the direct delineations of the diverse incidents in the life that is actually lived by the folk,—the fowlers, the milkmen, the cowherds, the traders, the boatmen, the cultivators. Bengali poetry is nothing if it is not democratic. It is life's urges, the *élan de la vie* in its thousand and one forms, that furnish the Bengali poets with the light and warmth of Bengal's villages and towns.

While dealing with the Vaiṣṇava love poetry of the Bengali people it is appropriate to observe that humanism in India as in classical Hellas and in the modern West has ever been an expression of all-round secularism or positivism. And of this humanism sex-interest has naturally been a great part. The sex-element is as important a factor in Hindu culture as the folk-element. Instead of starting with the hypothesis of Vaiṣṇava poetry as being the metaphysics or allegory of God and the soul it should be more reasonable to begin with the objective anthropological foundations of daily sex-life among the cowherds, cultivators and other teeming millions.

The Rādhā-Kriṣṇa songs or what may in general be described as the sex-hymns of Vidyāpati have a background or context sufficiently wide and varied not only in India's art and literature but also in the incidents of her daily existence. They constitute indeed some of the specimens of actual folk-life or folklore elevated to the status of "dignified" culture-lore. The worship of *limga* or phallus as the creative male element is too deeprooted in Bengali and other Hindu consciousness to be treated as an aberration. Nor is the male sex deified only in its generative function. Śiva, "the Great God," stands for the thousand and one functions and aspects of the male principle, both beneficent and malevolent. If the Bengali and other Hindus know one Kriṣṇa to be a lover and a sweetheart they know another Kriṣṇa as a statesman and a warrior. And there are the ideal husband, the ideal father, the ideal brother, the ideal ruler and so forth of the Rāma stories.

None the less prominent in Bengali and other Indian poetry is the deification or extollation of the female element. If Rādhā is a sweet-heart and a darling, Kālī, Chaṇḍī, Ambikā, Annadā, Bhavānī, etc. is the inspirer of a Perseus the Deliverer, of an Andreas Hofer, so to say, e.g., of a Pratāpāditya of Bengal or of a Śivāji the Maratha. If Rādhā enlivens maidenhood and young age, Sītā and Sāvitrī are the idols of the *Hausfrau's* daily life. The female sex as the embodiment of *śakti* or energy has been really accorded the highest and most comprehensive place in Bengali societal polity.

Bengali positivism expressed itself also in democratic and socialistic forms. The *bhakti* (faith or devotion) movement associated with Chaitanya (1485-1533), which led somewhat to the annihilation of barriers between the castes as well as those between the Hindus and the Moslems, has been no less powerful in the pluralistic make-up of the Bengali mind then the cult of *śakti* which has come down to Rāmaprasāda (1718-75) and Rāmakriṣṇa in the nineteenth century (1836-86).[1]

Agnostic Tendencies and Invention of Deities

While in the atmosphere of the Bengali poetry of *śakti* and *bhakti* it is desirable to observe once more that the external paraphernalia of gods and goddesses, rituals and ceremonies, i.e., the apparently religious or mythological scaffolding should not blind one to the genuine literary qualities of these productions. The authors are real artists, i.e., creators of characters and situations. Indeed, the gods and goddesses themselves are to be treated as but the "creations" or "inventions" of these poets, representing as they do the folk-consciousness, the *conscience collective*, to use an expression of Durkheim, or rather the constructive

[1] H. M. Mukhopadhyaya: *Bangabhāshār Lekhaka* or "Writers in Bengali" (Calcutta 1904), pp. 210-227; The present author's *Folk-Element in Hindu Culture* (London 1917), pp. 258-262; which is based in the main on H. Palit's Bengali work *Ādyer Gambhīrā*; S. K. De: *History of Bengali Literature in the Nineteenth Century* 1800-1825 (Calcutta 1919) pp. 35-38, 412-419; J. N. Sarkar: *Chaitanya's Life and Teachings* (Calcutta 1922); *The Life of Sri Ramakrishna* (Advaita Ashrama, Calcutta, 1929).

capacities of the folk-imagination. The Hindu god-lore is essentially an item in the creative achievements of the human brain,—and hence an aspect of positivism in the most profound sense of the term.

The Bengali *Śūnya-Purāṇa* (*c* 1050?) has created the semi-Buddhistic gods and goddesses of all sorts. Rāmāi Paṇḍit's *Dharma-Pūjā-Paddhati* is likewise cast in the mould of folk-Buddhism. In the *Dharma-mangala* of Ghanarāma (*c* 1350?), Maṇik Gānguli and others, again, is encountered the *rapprochement* of folk-Hinduism and folk-Buddhism on a common Tantric foundation. Among the other folk-deities prevalent in medieval Bengal may be mentioned *Śītalā*, the goddess to propitiate against small pox, and *Manasā*, the goddess against snakes. Many of these are directly or indirectly associated with the Śiva and Kālī (Chaṇḍī, Tārā, Ādyā) complex.

No matter what be the name, and what the formal affiliation of these gods and goddesses to the leading pantheons their sociological significance is self-evident. The inventions or creations of these deities by medieval Folk-Bengal are calculated to annihilate the enemies and difficulties, both natural and human. In the second place, these are some of the agencies that are invoked to promote health, wealth, success in life, and general prosperity. In Bengali folk-consciousness the gods and goddesses are but hand-maids to human welfare. They are the instruments of man in the achievement of worldly success.

One type of gods and goddesses is exhibited as incorporating *śakti* or energy. A second type of divinities was created by Folk-Bengal to furnish the masses with "Great Exemplars" from whom might be learnt the duties and obligations of life, individual, domestic and social. It is in and through this group of gods and goddesses that the people are instructed in the ideal relations between parent and offspring, husband and wife, brother and brother, ruler and subject and so on. The literature through which such gods and goddesses become the instruments of positive morality has its chief *forte* in *bhakti*, the emotional element in human personality. It is to love, faith and hope that this *bhakti*, devotional or emotional poetry appeals rather than to the practices of intellectual gymnastics and ratiocinative argumentation. Krittivāsa's *Rāmāyaṇa* has furnished the Bengali people with positive morality in and through the stories of Rāma and his consort Śītā as well as the ancestors and allies of the great hero. It is by this Bengali epic that Folk-Bengal is introduced to the "whole duty of man." The rôle of man as the creator of gods, goddesses and God has nowhere been so prominent as in Hindu Bengal, nay, in Hindustan through the ages. And this is an aspect of world-culture that has not yet been assimilated to the investigations into the universal currents in positive philosophy. Bengali creativeness *visávis* gods and goddesses furnishes sociology with such "values" as have been hardly suspected in the world of science bearing on the "spirit" of India.

It may be said that the Folk-Bengal of the nineteenth century has not cared much to inquire into the Sanskrit *Vedas*, *Samhitās*, *Purāṇas*, *Tantras* etc. for the origins and legends of its faith and devotion, but has sought for thę "whole duty of man" in Bengali treatises like Krittivāsa's *Rāmāyaṇa*, Vidyapāti and Chaṇḍīdāsa's *Vaiṣṇava Padāvalī*, and the *Kālī*-Songs of Mukundarāma and Rāmaprasāda. Through all this literature there has been a steady increase in the number of gods and goddesses, saints and *avatāras*. In some cases a new interpretation has been imparted to the older deities and heroes, who have thereby acquired an altogether fresh significance in the people's thought and activity. There has been no generation of Bengali history without its own mythology, hagiology and anthology. It is not the Environment or the Society-cult of Durkheim that has dominated the Hindu life-systems. To use Lasbax's expression, creative Bengal has attempted through all its arts and cults to be *l'auteur de son caractére et de sa renovation* (the maker of its own character and internal renovation).[1] This is perfectly natural: because the Hindu is fundamentally an agnostic, i.e., has never believed in the possibility of human intelligence ever to unravel the mysterious eternal truths of the universe, or to understand, except perhaps negatively, the nature and attributes of God; and therefore he has ever felt to be at complete "liberty" to *imagine* and invent whatsoever God or Gods he chooses to adore. He has not feared to conceive the Divinity as He, She, It or They. He has worshipped his Deity as father, mother, brother, sister, sweetheart, lover, friend, and what not; and he has endowed his own creation or invention with any attributes he likes for the time being. He has borrowed his god-lore from the Mongols, he has taken his god-lore from the hill-tribes, he has imbibed his god-lore from the speechless message of sunshine and snows, and he has evolved his god-lore out of his own head and heart. His monotheistic polytheism or heinotheism is based essentially on his agnosticism.

An expression of this profound agnosticism and human creativeness in regard to the Divinity or Divinities is to be found in the intimacy and man-to-man familiarity with which Rāmakṛṣṇa (1836-86), a modern saint, wants the peoples of the world to attitudinize

[1] E. Lasbax : *La Cité Humaine*, Vol. II. (Paris 1927),pp. 48-50.

themselves to God. "Why do you dwell so much upon the glories of God?" asks Rāmakṛṣṇā.[1] "Does a son when with his father think of his father's possessions,—his houses, gardens, horses and cattle? On the contrary, he thinks of his father's love. He knows that it is proper for a father to maintain his children and look out for their welfare. We are all children of God. So what is there to wonder at in His paternal care of us?"

According to Rāmakṛṣṇa the "real devotee never thinks about these things. He looks upon God as his very own—his nearest and dearest—and says boldly, "Thou must fulfil my desires—must reveal thyself to me." "If you dwell so much upon His glories, you cannot think of Him as your own," says Rāmakṛṣṇa, "nor can you feel intimate with Him. You are awed by His Majesty. He is no longer near. No, no, you must think of Him as your nearest and dearest. Then only can you realize Him."

The Hindu tendency to deify the energies, Nature-Forces or personal attributes and emotions has constructed all the gods and goddesses of India, practically speaking, as so many embodiments of the various phases of the Country itself and of the Culture it has developed through the ages. And the invention of deities has not yet ceased.

Rabindranath Tagore, probably an iconoclast in socio-religious opinions, has been, however, pre-eminently an idolator, nay, a polytheist, in and through his art. His celebrated hymn (*c* 1895) to Mother India is in the right orthodox strain which is noticeable in the psalms and songs in eulogy of Sarasvatī (Goddess of Learning), Lakṣmī (Goddess

[1] *Life of Sri Ramakrishna* (Calcutta 1929), p. 310.

of Wealth), Durgā, Jagaddhātrī and other goddesses. With Tagore we sing as follows:

"O Thou, who charmest all mankind!
O Thou, whose lands are ever bright
With ray serene of pure sun-light!
Mother of fathers and mothers!

With the blue deep's waters thy feet ever wash'd
Thy scarf of green ever waving in breeze,
Sky-kiss'd on high thine Himalayan brow,
Crown'd white thy head with tiara of snows.

First in thy firmament appeared the dawn,
First rose *Sāma*-chants in thy holy groves,
First were revealed in thy forest-abodes
Wisdom and virtue and poesy's self.

Ever beneficent! glory to Thee!
From Thee flows food to countries far and wide;
Jāhnavī and Jumna, streams of thy love;
Giver of sweet sacred milk, O Mother!"

It is, again, the traditional folk-imagination, saturated with the monism of Vedantic thought, that has inspired the following verses of Tagore:

"O Thou Dust of my Motherland!
Down to Thee alone do I bend my head.
Upon Thee is the mantle spread
Of Universe-bodied Mother Divine!"

The same deification of the Country is evident in the following outburst (1905) of Dwijendralal Roy:

"Goddess mine! Meditation's Aim!
Country mine! O Heaven on earth!"

But the man who has started them all in this modern Bengali *Bhakti*-literature is Bankimchandra Chatterji. According to him the ten-armed Durgā (consort of Śiva) with her whole family and retinue, the most popular goddess of Hindu Bengal in the nineteenth century and after, who was, historically considered, one of the *Tārās* (Energies) of Avalokiteśvara Bodhisattva in mediaeval Mahāyānic India and still receives worship as Tārā in Buddhist China and Buddhist Japan, nay, can perhaps be traced back to the Mother Goddess of the Mohenjo Daro epochs, is none other than Motherland itself with all its resources and forces in natural agents and human arts. This synthetic interpretation, crystallized in the song *Vande Mātaram* (*c* 1885) is bound to remain the greatest hymn of Folk-India during the twentieth century. Bengal, and with her All-India, sings as follows:

"Hail! Motherland!
Vande Mātaram!

Thou art my muse, Thyself my creed;
In Thee my heart and soul,
And in my limbs the spirit Thou!

In mine arm Thou art strength (*śakti*);
Thyself heart's devotion (*bhakti*);
Thine the images bodied forth
In temples one and all, Mother!"

To worship Durgā is to worship Motherland, or to worship Motherland is to worship Durgā. This is the cult that in diverse forms has been invented by the brain and soul of creative India from the Vedic age of the adoration of World-Forces,—or rather, as just indicated, from the epochs of the Indus Valley culture (*c* B.C. 3500) down to the present epoch of neo-Tantrism represented by Bankimchandra and Rāmakriṣṇa-Vivekānanda.[1] The sociology of values

[1] Max Mueller: *Ramkrishna: His Life and Teachings* (New York 1890); Advaita Ashrama: *Life of Sri Ramakrishna* (Cal-

remains yet to be oriented to these aspects and trends of creative thought.

SECTION 4

TREATISES OF ECONOMICS IN INDIAN LANGUAGES

We shall now deal with a type of literature such as is generally overlooked in studies relating to Hindu culture. These are the economic treatises dealing, as they do, with the diverse branches of material life. We shall begin with the *Bribat Sambitā* of Varāhamihira (*c* 505-587 A.C.) which is an *Encyclopaedia Indica* although of no huge dimensions. It furnishes information as much about climatology and astronomy, architecture and town-planning as about the seven-limbed organism, the state. It is a landmark of Hindu scientific thought, as Pliny's *Natural History* is of Roman. We may indeed describe the period of nine hundred years from *c* B.C. 300 to 600 A.C. as that of scientific growth and development from Pāṇini to Varāhamihira.

"Treatises" on applied economics known as *Vārttāśāstras* can perhaps be not yet traced back to the Gupta period (*c* 320-550 A.C.). But the literature on farming, cattle-breeding, commerce and banking (interest) is to be found in the *Purāṇas*, the Epics, as well as in the *Bribat Sambitā*. The same remark applies to the *Śilpaśāstras* (treatises on arts and crafts). No record of Gupta positivism can be complete without

cutta 1929); *The Teachings of Sri Ramakrishna* (Advaita Ashrama, Calcutta 1934); *The Life of Swami Vivekananda* By His Eastern and Western Disciples (Calcutta 1933) 2 vols., *The Complete Works of Swami Vivekananda* (Calcutta, 1931), 7 vols.; Romain Rolland: *Ramakrishna the Man-God and the Universal Gospel of Vivekananda* (Calcutta), 2 vols.

due orientations to the secular and "exact" sciences, as many of the *Vārttā* and *Silpa* books are. The subject deserves more than an incidental notice.

Vārttā is known to the *Kautaliya Arthaśāstra* (Book I.) as agriculture, animal husbandry and commerce. The same three professions constitute *Vārttā* in Somadeva's *Nītivākyāmrita* (VI, 1) also (*c* 950 A.C.). In such a late compilation as the *Śukranīti* (I. lines 305-312) it comprises a fourth item, namely, interest or banking. Of course the subject matter comprehended in *Vārttā*, even banking as incidental to commerce, is as old as the Vedic culture-complex, nay, the Mohenjo Daro epochs. But specialized treatises on *Vārttā* or any of its diverse topics can hardly be traced back even to such recent times as the great age of literary reconstructions, compilations, codifications and redactions, namely, the Gupta Epoch. The beginnings of *Vārttā* lore as independent discipline in the thousand and one crafts and industries, occupations and professions, in one word, in the topics of applied economics may however be sought during the period covered by the Vardhanas, Chālukyas, Pālas, Senas, Gurjara-Pratīhāras, Rāṣṭrakūṭas, and Cholas (600-1300). Many of the handbooks on *Vārttā* mentioned among the Sanskrit manuscripts in Aufrecht's *Catalogus Catalogorum* as well as some of the printed texts on this branch of socio-economic science were made use of in the *Positive Background of Hindu Sociology* (1914).

Indeed, a substantial portion of Vol. I. of that work, as executed in those days, was based on *Vārttā* treatises and constitutes, as such, a contribution to Hindu *Vārttā* or applied economics. The chapters dealing with the data of Hindu mineralogy, Hindu botany (including *vrikṣāyurveda*) and Hindu zoology (including *aśvaśastra* and *gajaśāstra*) and, along with them, of Hindu medicine (*āyurveda*) are essentially studies in the *Vārttā* positivism of the Hindus. The English translation of the *Śukranīti* served to invite the attention of indologists and sociologists to the different branches of Hindu applied economics from town-planning to veterinary science.

As usual, it is not possible even in 1936 to place many of these works in the proper chronological perspective. Perhaps most of them will have to be placed somewhere between 1300 and 1700. But in Indian literary history every document has its "unwritten" or rather unsystematized and uncompiled or unedited beginnings. The economic (*Vārttā*) treatises of the Hindus also, whether described as *Vidyā* (science) or *Kalā* (practical art) may, perhaps be traced back to the age of Harṣavardhana (606-647). Varāhamihira's (*c* 506-585) *Brihat Samhitā* leaves no doubt about the existence of *Vārttā* materials in the age of the Guptas. It has, besides, to be observed that many of the economic topics dealt with in the treatises of *Vārttāśāstra* are to be found in the *Mahābhārata* and the *Purāṇas* as well as in the *Dharma*-and especially in the *Artha*-and *Nīti-śāstras* whether in connection with the discussions on public finance, functions of the state, demographic structure, social classes, or professional groups.[1]

[1] For the topics of *vārttā* (economics) see the notes in the present author's English translation of the *Śukranīti* (Allahabad 1914), "Economic Foundations of the State in Śukra's Political Theory" (*Modern Review*, Calcutta, 1921), which may be conveniently consulted in the *The Positive Background* etc. Vol. II. pt. I. (Allahabad 1921), "Economics in Hindu Thought" (*Indian Historical Quarterly* Calcutta 1926). Consult likewise Balkrishna : "Economics in Ancient India" (*Indian Journal of Economics*, 1918), and "Hindu Taxation System" (*I.H.Q.*), N. N. Law: "*Vārttā* or Hindu Economics" (*Indian Antiquary*, 1918),

While introducing the *Vārttāśāstra* we should perhaps at once enter the domain of *Śilpaśāstra*, either as one of the branches of the former or perhaps as almost a twin in the Indian intellectual system. As a category, *Śilpaśāstra* possesses by all means an independent status. It deals with the arts and crafts, especially those bearing on architecture, sculpture and painting as well as town-planning. But as belonging to applied economics we may name both *Vārttāśāstra* (farming, cattle-breeding, trade and banking) and *Śilpaśāstra* (housebuilding and the fine arts) in one and the same breath. It is interesting to observe that in the *Nītiśāstras*, e.g., in the *Śukranīti*[1] the place of *Śilpaśāstra* is no less important than that of *Vārttāśāstra*. Apart from the fact that the Agni, Matsya,

which may be conveniently seen in *Studies in Indian History and Culture* (Calcutta 1925), J. N. C. Ganguly: "Principles of Hindu Taxation" (*I.H.Q.* December 1925).

See also the last footnotes to the sections on "Hindu Agriculture, Manfacture and Commerce" and the "Financial Organization and Economic Policy of Hindu States."

[1] The material of the *Śukranīti* has been extensively utilized in B. B. Dutt: *Townplanning in Ancient India* (Calcutta 1925) and P. N. Bose: *Principles of Indian Silpasastras* (Lahore 1926). The English translation of the *Sukranīti* has been made use of by students of all sorts of economic, political, aesthetic, and social topics during the last quarter of the present century. One is convinced that while the *Kauṭaliya Arthaśāstra* has given rise to researches with special reference to politics the angles from which the *Śukranīti* have been attacked, thanks to the encyclopaedic character of its contents, have been more extensive and varied. It is possible to assert that in certain fields recent indology has been virtually dominated by Kauṭalya and Śukra. It is worth mentioning and curious at the same time that although the *Kāmandakīnīti* was rendered avaliable in English in 1896 it has failed as yet to evoke considerable interest among scholars.

See the chapter on "The Arthasastra of Kauṭilya and the Nitisastra of Sukra" in A. K. Sen; *Studies in Hindu Political Thought* (Calcutta 1926) pp.135-179.

Viṣṇudharmottara, and other *Purāṇas* deal with the topics of *Śilpaśāstras* as much as they do with the *Vārttā-śāstras*, the independent literature on housebuilding as well as temples, images, paintings, etc. is exceedingly large. The problem of dating in connection with the *Śilpaśāstras* is identical with that in connection with the *Vārttāśastras*. As in the case of the latter, the materials of the *Śilpaśāstra* can be traced in well developed forms at least to the Gupta age, e.g., to the *Brihat Samhitā* (*c* 550 A.C.). Nay, in so far as town-planning, the establishment of villages and towns, the erection of buildings, dams etc. and the construction of roads belongs to the *Kautaliya Arthaśāstra*, the *Śilpaśāstras* like the *Vārttāśāstras* can to this extent be seen even in that *milieu*.[1]

Vārttāśāstras

We shall now enumerate some of the *Vārttā* documents in manuscript or in print. Be it observed at once that no reference to absolute or relative chronology is at the present moment possible. They are being mentioned at random as embodiments of Hindu interest in economic life and economic literature.

Let us take a more or less generic work first. In the South Indian work in Mālayalam entitled *Manavala-Nārāyaṇa-śatakam*[2] there is a verse on the honour of merchants (*vaisiyar perumai*). The merchants are

[1] K. Rangachari: "Town-planning and House-building in Ancient India." (*I.H.Q.* Dec. 1927, March 1928), P. K. Acharya: *Mānasāra* (transl.) 3 vols. (Oxford 1933-34).

[2] W. Taylor: *A Catalogue Raisonnée of Oriental Manuscripts in the Library of the late College of Fort St. George* (Madras 1857), vol. III, p.15. A list of the mss. and printed works on *Vārttā* and *Śilpa Śāstras* is to be found in N. N. Law: *Studies in Indian History and Culture* (London 1925) pp. 384-401.

advised to conduct their business skilfully. They should not hanker after high rates of profit. An even and correct balance is to be used in connection with every customer. No loans are to be offered to the dishonest even if they should offer a collateral. On the other hand, loans on personal security may be offered to the honest. In book-keeping not even the eighth part of a mustard seed should be allowed by way of mistake. Public measures ought to be assisted by merchants even to the extent of a crore (of the monetary unit).

A separate stanza is given over to the *vellarber perumai* (honour of agriculturists). The agricultural work done by the *vellarber* (farmers) is to maintain the prayers of Brāhmaṇas, the strength of kings, the profits of merchants and the welfare of all. Charity, donations, the enjoyments of domestic life, connubial happiness, homage to the gods, the *Sāstras*, the *Vedas*, the *Purāṇas* and all other books, truth, reputation, renown, the very being of the Gods, things of good report or integrity, the good order of castes, manual skill,—all these things come to pass by the merit or efficacy of the *vellarber's* plough. This sort of what, to use a Marxist category, may be described as the "agricultural interpretation of history" can be traced back to the *Atharva Veda's* hymns on the cow, the draft-ox, etc. (IV, 11). We must not, however, read into Indian texts the monistic determinism of Marxist economics or sociology. Hindus, used as they are to heinotheism, are fundamentally pluralists in as much as they can appreciate, admire and deify any and every force for the time being as a supreme influence in life and thought.

We shall now deal with the specialized *Sāstras* on different branches of *Vārttā*. Several treatises on *loha*, iron and other (?) metals, are to be found among the manscripts in Sanskrit[1]. One is known as *Loharatnākara* (Ocean of Metals), another as *Lohārṇava* (Ocean of Metals), and a third as *Lohaśāstra* (Science of Metals).

A South-Indian Sanskrit treatise on gems and their qualities found in Tanjore is the *Ratnaparīkṣā*[2]. Agastya's *Maṇiparīkṣā*[3] (Testing of precious stones), the *Ratnasamuchchaya*[4], Paśupati's *Ratnamālā*[5] and others may be singled out. The section on gems in the *Yuktikalpataru* has also to be noted.

Parāśara's *Krișisamgraha* (agriculture) is available in print[6]. A treatise named *Krișivișaya*[7] is described as a guide to agriculture. The first few verses quoted in the catalogue are identical with those of *Parāśara's Krisisamgraha* published at Calcutta in 1915. But there is a discrepancy towards the end. A South-Indian Sanskrit work on agriculture is *Saśyānanda*.[8]

Horticulturial treatises[9] are plentiful in Southern-India, for instance, *Pādapavirakṣā* (Nourishment of

[1] Aufrecht : *Catalogus Catalogorum*, part I. (Leipzig, 1891) p. 546.

[2] A. C. Burnell: *Classified Index to the Sanskrit Manuscripts in the Palace of Tanjore prepared for the Madras Government* (1880), p. 141.

[3] Aufrecht: *Catalogus*, part I. p. 420.

[4] Ibid, part. I. p. 464.

[5] R. L. Mitra; *Notices of Sanskrit Manuscripts* (Calcutta, 1871), vol. I.

[6] L. D. Barnett: *A Supplementary Catalogue of Sanskrit, Pali and Prakrit Books in the Library of the British Museum* (acquired during 1892-1906), London.

[7] R. L. Mitra: *Notices of Sanskrit Manuscripts* (Calcutta, 1871) vol. I. p. 179.

[8] Oppert: *List of Sanskrit Manuscripts in the Private Libraries of South India, Vol.* II. p. 371.

[9] Oppert: *List of Sanskrit Mss.* (Madras) vol. II. pp. 223, 371.

plants), *Vrikṣadohada* (Treatment of plants), *Vrikṣāyurveda* (Treatment of plant diseases).

Gangārām Mahadakar's *Ārāmādi-pratiṣṭhāpaddhati*[1] is a treatise on gardens.

Nārada's *Mayūra Chitraka*[2], (*Meghamālā* or *Ratna mālā* gives indications of coming rains, famine or plenty from the appearance of the atmosphere.

On cattle we come across treatises like *Gosūtra* and *Gośānti*[3] etc. *Gośāstra*, a treatise on cattle, and *Govaidyaśāstra* (on cattle disease or veterinary topics) are also mentioned.

That the manuscripts or printed works mentioned here belong to a period previous to the thirteenth century is not beyond doubt. Most probably many of them do not. But they are being given here as suggestive specimens relating to the formative and early periods of these sciences.

Silpaśāstras and Vāstuśāstras

We shall now see a bit of the *Silpaśāstras* in the same manner.

Viśvakarmā, the divine architect or Vulcan, is an eponymous hero like Manu, and is encountered as an author, founder or patron-saint in connection with the arts, sciences or crafts called *śilpa* and the *Silpaśāstras*, i.e., treatises bearing on the *śilpas*. We know of a *Viśvakarmīya-śilpam*[4] which is described as a trea-

[1] Aufrecht: *Catalogus Catalogorum*, part I. (Leipzig, 1891) p. 53.

[2] Aufrecht: *Catalogus Catalogorum* part I. (Leipzig, 1891) p. 432.

[3] Aufrecht: *Catalogus Catalogorum*, part I. (Leipzig, 1891) p. 169. Oppert: *List of Sanskrit Mss. in the Private Libraries of Southern India* (Madras) vol. I. p. 533.

[4] R. L. Mitra: *Notices of Sanskrit Manuscripts* (Calcutta 1871), vol. II. p. 142.

tise on the manual arts attributed to Viśvakarman. The contents comprise such items as the origin of *Viśvakarman* and the derivation of terms like *takṣaka* (carpenter), *vardhakī* (sculptor), and so forth. The human stature of diverse *yugas* (Hindu epochs), wood and stone as material for sculpture, sacraments for sculptors and carpenters, proportions bearing on the images of planets and lingams, consecration of cars, etc. are to be found among the topics. The forms of Brāhmī, Maheśvarī and other goddesses have found a place in the discussion.

Attention has been devoted to sacrificial or Brahmaṇical thread, the sacrificial threads of gold, silver and *munja* fibre, the qualities of a special stone called *hemaśilā* (golden stone) to be found to the south of the Meru Mountain. Then there are discussions on crowns, crests and other head ornaments, movable and fixed thrones for images, etc. The proportions of doors of temples for *limgams*, the proportions of doors for other temples, the temples for Vighneśa, and allied topics belong to the table of contents.

The *Mayamata*[1] is a treatise on architecture available in print and deals with the following among other topics: 1. examination of the ground, 2. measurement, 3. ascertainment of the points of the compass, 4. rules for laying out villages and towns, 5. plinth, base and pillars, 6. stone work, cementation, 7. spires, 8. one, two, three and four storied houses, 9. *gopuras* or gates, 10. *mandapas*, 11. out-offices, barns, treasuries etc.

All the topics bearing on architecture are discussed in *Mayamatam*. According to the editor Gaṇapati Sāstrī it appears to be the oldest among the extent

[1] Trivandrum Sanskrit Series, 1919.

treatises in Sanskrit on the subject. An old Tamil translation is available in manuscript. The work is complete in 38 chapters, of which four are missing. The treatise is in verse.

The *Samarāngaṇa Sūtradhāra*[1] (Architect of human dwellings) is a peculiar name for a work on *Vāstuśāstra.* It has been published in two huge volumes comprising altogether 63 chapters. The two tables of contents alone cover 54 pages. Architecture has been taken in a very wide sense. The construction of machines (*yantra vidhāna*), for instance, occupies a significant part of this work (ch.XXXI). There is a chapter on painting (*chitroddeśa*) also (ch. LXXI.)

The work contains also discussions on *rasa*, literary "flavour," statues made of gold, silver etc., *patākā* (flag) and so on. Certain machines have interesting names such as *gajayantra* (elephant machine), *vyomachārī vihamgayantra* (wooden bird-machine travelling in the sky), *ākāśagāmī dārumaya vimānayantra* (wooden *vimāna* machine flying in air), *dvārapāla yantra* (door keeper machine), etc. The chief topics of the work are furnished by the construction of cities, palaces, and mansions of the most diverse classes. It should be observed that the entire treatise is in verse.

There is a treatise in Tamil entitled *Silpaśāstra*[2] which is said to have been originally composed in Sanskrit.

Vāsavāchārya's *Viśvavidyābharaṇa*[3] deals with the duties of artisans.

A treatise on shipbuilding and navigation is *Nāva-*

[1] Baroda, vol. I. (1924), vol. II, (1925), Editor T. Gaṇapati Sastri, see the two prefaces.

[2] Meyer in the *Indian Antiquary* for 1876.

[3] Aufrecht: *Catalogus*, part II. (Leipzig, 1896) p. 139.

śāstram also known as *Kappal Śāstram*[1]. An unnamed work deals with navigation as well as housebuilding and other topics taught in 36 works which are enumerated[2].

Kalyāna Sivanārāyaṇa's *Śilpaśāstra-samgraha* deals with architecture[3]. The author was an inhabitant of Surat.

Viśvakarman's name is associated with *Viśvakarma-prakāśa* (architecture)[4].

The most universal topic of *Śilpaśāstras* is housebuilding. But it deals with many other topics directly or indirectly allied to edifices, for instance, furniture, decorations and ornaments, etc. Besides, the topics of sculpture as well as painting are also discussed in *Śilpaśāstras*. There are chapters on sculpture and painting in the *Agni* and *Matsya Purāṇas*. The *Viṣṇudharmottara Purāṇa*, for instance, has a chapter on *chitra* (paintings).

A very common name for treatises on building is *Vāstuvidyā* or *Vāstuśāstra*. They may be said to specialize in architecture, although sculpture also comes in for treatment. Very often *Vāstuśāstra* and *Śilpaśāstra* have to be taken almost as convertible terms. Perhaps, in any case, we should treat the *Śilpasāstras* as somewhat wider in scope and more generic in nature.

The name of treatises on *Vāstu* (building or archi-

[1] W. Taylor: *A Catalogue Raisonnée of Oriental Mss. in the Library of the late College of Fort St. George* (Madras 1857), vol. III. p. 6.

[2] *Ibid*, vol. III. p. 350.

[3] Edited with a Gujarati transl. by Kalyanadas Bhunabhai Gujjar, Rajnagar, 1898.

[4] Edited with Hindi transl. by Saktidhara Sukula, Lucknow, 1896.

tecture) is legion. Jeva Nath Jotiṣhi's *Vāsturatnāvalī*[1], Śyāmācharaṇa's *Vāstusaukhya*[2], which is an extract from *Todarānanda*, Viśvakarman's *Vāstuvichāra*[3], Sūtradharamaṇḍana's *Vāstusāra*[4] may be mentioned. Gaṇapati Śāstri's edition of *Vāstuvidyā* (Trivandrum Sanskrit series, 1913) has rendered accessible the contents of a work attributed to Viśvakarman.

The *Vāstuvidyā* is entirely in verse and complete in 16 chapters. The last chapter deals with earth and tile making. Building materials, ground and other things connected with house construction constitute the subject matter.

Gangādhara's *Śilpadīpakā*[5] is a metrical treatise on architecture in five sections. Bhoja Vikramāditya's *Samarāmgaṇasūtradhāra*[6] is perhaps to be taken as one of the oldest treatises on architecture (*c* 1050). His *Yuktikalpataru* which is generally mentioned in connection with the *Nītiśāstras* is to be noted in the present context also.

Sudhākara Dvivedi's *Vāstava-chandra-śringonnati* is a work on architecture[7].

It is to be understood that *Silpaśāstras* are by all means treatises on aesthetics or rather applied aesthetics. They deal chiefly with the problem of form (*rūpam*). But in the present context we are interested in them exclusively as documents of exact science, mathematical measurements, calculations of proportions etc. bearing on

[1] Burnell: *Classified Index* (Madras 1880).
[2] Sudhākara Dvivedi : *Catalogue of Sanskrit Manuscripts in the N.W.P.* part IX. (1885), p. 56.
[3] *Ibid*, p. 56.
[4] Aufrecht, pt. I. p. 569.
[5] Barnett: *Supplementary Catalogue* 1892-1906, London.
[6] Trivandrum Sanskrit Series, 1924.
[7] Bombay Venkatesvara Press.

Nature and man. It is as furnishing fresh evidences of Hindu command over the things of this earthly earth and of their preoccupation with non-transcendental, unmetaphysical and matter of fact realities as well as the human world of daily secular interests that the *Silpaśāstras* are being introduced as twins of the *Vārttāśāstras*. Be it observed once more that none of the texts in manuscripts or print such as have been mentioned for the period from *c* 600 to 1300 may belong to this period at all. But it is presumed that the *chitralakṣaṇa*, *pratimālakṣaṇa*, (i.e. marks or characteristics of paintings, images etc.) were known during those centuries and earlier and of course the principles were practised by the painters, sculptors and architects.

Like the eighteen *Purāṇas*, eighteen *Upa-Purāṇas*, eighteen *Smritis* and eighteen *Upa-Smritis* the eighteen masters of *Vāstu-vidyā* became traditional in Hindu culture. The *Matsya-Purāṇa* (XXVIII) enumerates them as follows[1]:

1. Bhrigu
2. Atri
3. Vaśiṣtha
4. Viśvakarmā
5. Maya
6. Nārada
7. Naganjit
8. Viśālākṣa
9. Purandara
10. Brahmā
11. Kumāra
12. Nandīśa
13. Saunaka
14. Garga
15. Vāstudeva
16. Aniruddha
17. Sukra
18. Vrihaspati.

Most of the *Silpasastras* available in manuscript or in print belong really to the seventeenth and eighteenth centuries. A few are being enumerated in the following statement.

[1] P. N. Bose : *Principles of Indian Silpasastra with the Text of Mayaśāstra* (Lahore, 1926) p. 65.

Maṇḍana (*c* 1525) wrote *Rājavallabha maṇḍana* (architecture)[1]. The author was an inhabitant of Udaypur.

By the sixteenth century the masters of *Vāstuvidyā* were known to be more numerous than the eighteen of the *Matsya-Purāṇa* as indicated in the period from Harṣa to Hemādri. The *Todarānanda* mentions the following authorities[2] :

1. Varāhamihira
2. Chyavana
3. Kāsyapa
4. Vriddhagarga
5. Utpala
6. Māṇḍavya
7. Bharadvāja,
8. Vridhhavaśiṣṭha,
9. Lalla.

Srīkumāra's *Silparatna* is a systematic and comprehensive treatise of large size in Sanskrit verse dealing not only with the construction of houses, villages and other allied things but also with iconography and things connected therewith. The last chapter deals with painting. The author was an inhabitant of Kerala in South India and may have flourished in the sixteenth century, as suggested by Gaṇapati Sastri, the editor of the text[3].

The author of the *Manuṣyālayachandrikā*[4] was likewise an inhabitant of Kerala. He acknowledges his debt to Nārāyaṇa's *Tantrasamuchchaya* (*c* 1450). The first chapter deals with the examination of the

[1] Edited, with Gujarati translation, by Narayan Bharati Yasavanta, Bharabi, Baroda, 1891.

[2] B. B. Dutt : *Town-planning in Ancient India* (Calcutta 1925) p. 17.

[3] Trivandrum Sanskrit Series, 1922.

[4] Trivandrum Sanskrit Series, 1917.

soil, the second with the auspicious days, etc., the third with measurements, the fourth with classes of buildings and rooms. Outhouses, wells and tanks also have been discussed in the treatise which is entirely in verse.

Viśvakarmā wrote *Bhūvanapradīpa*[1]. The text is partly in Sanskrit verse and partly in Oriya prose. It deals with temple architecture.

In the printed edition use has been made of five manuscripts in Sanskrit, which happen to be different recensions of *Bhūvanapradīpa*[2]. The two other manuscripts used are copies of a book, entitled *Silpipothi* in Oriya, which deals with the erection of thatched huts. Certain general matters regarding the selection of building sites, the classification of soils etc., are common to both the treatises. But the *Bhūvanapradīpa* specializes in the architecture of temples. All the manuscripts appear to be quite recent in language and style.

An Oriya treatise entitled *Silpaśāstra*[3] is already in print. The author is supposed to have been Bauri Mahārāṇā.

Among the works attributed to Viśvakarman is to be found in Gujarat the manuscript of the *Aparājita Vāstuśāstra*[4], an architectural treatise.

The treatise dealing with aviaries as well as houses is the *Pakṣīmanusyālayalakṣaṇa*[5].

[1] N. K. Bose: *Canons of Orissan Architecture* (Calcutta, 1932).
[2] Ibid, p. 5.
[3] Published by Mohan Sahu (Cuttack, fourth edition, 1923).
[4] *Catalogue of Sanskrit Mss. contained in the Private Libraries of Gujarat, Kathiawad, Kach, Sind and Khandesh* edited by G. Buehler, (Bombay, 1872) p. 276.
[5] *List of Sanskrit Mss. in the Private Libraries of South India* edited by G. Oppert, Vol. II, p. 371.

A treatise on tanks and wells is the *Kupādijalasthānalakṣaṇa*, of which a manuscript is available in Travancore.

A treatise on painting is the *Chitrasūtra*[1]. Another work on the same subject is called *Chitrabhārata*[2].

A work on scuplture is known as *Tārālakṣaṇa*, another as *Mūrtti-dhyāna*.[3]

Treatises on gems and precious stones are to be found under various names[4], e.g.

1. *Ratnalakṣaṇa*
2. *Ratnaparīkṣā*
3. *Navaratnaparīkṣā*
4. *Ratnadīpikā* by Chaṇḍeśvara.

The tradition of Hindu positive thinking in regard to the arts and crafts has then come down to our own times.

SECTION 5

THE AIN-I-AKBARI AS A SEMI-MOSLEM AND SEMI-HINU ARTHA-SASTRA

A very important document of the sixteenth century, which is indeed a most remarkable product of creative India's literary endeavours in the domain of politics is the semi-Hindu, semi-Moslem treatise in Persian entitled the *Ain-i-Akbari*[5] by Abul Fazl

[1] Aufrecht : *Catalogus Catalogorum* (Leipzig) Vol. I. p. 187.

[2] Monier-Williams : *Sanskrit Dictionary*.

[3] Aufrecht, Vol. I. pp. 229, 464.

[4] Oppert, Vol. I, p. 478, Vol. II. p. 320; Aufrecht, Vol. I., p. 281, Vol. II, pp. 26, 138.

[5] Blochmann : The *Ain-i-Akbari* (Calcutta 1873), Vol. I. p. xxx. See also Gladwin's translation (*Ayeen Akbari*).

(1551-1602). It was composed about 1596-1597.

A glance at the table of contents of the *Ain-i-Akbari* exhibits its rough similarity in formal features with a Hindu *Nītiśāstra*. We may call it the *Akbar-nīti*, so to say. The contents are in short as follows:

I. The Household, The Treasury, The Mint, The Method of separating the silver from the gold, Illuminations, The Kitchen, The Days of Abstinence, Writing and painting, The Arsenal, Elephants, Horses, Camels, Cow-stables, Buildings, Building materials, etc.

II. The Army, The Civil Services, Salaries, Donations, Feasts, Regulations regarding marriages, Regulations regarding education, The Admiralty.

III. The Eras (Hindu and other), Revenues, Measurements, The Executive, The Judiciary, Nineteen Years' Rates of Revenue.

IV. The Twelve Subahs or provinces, The Assessment of Land.

V. A Description of Hindustan, The Character of the Hindus, Their Astronomy and Geography, The Nine Philosophies, The Eighteen *Vidyās*, The Eighteen *Purāṇas*, The Eighteen *Smritis*, Music, *Rājanīti* (politics), *Vyavahāra* (Law), Marriages, Festivals, etc.

VI. Moral sentences, Epigrams, Rules of Wisdom emanating from the Emperor, etc.

The *Ain-i-Akbari* is generally considered to be an Imperial Gazetteer of Moghul India. But it is not quite correct to describe it as a Gazetteer in the strictest sense of the term. The descriptive and statistical data bearing on Akbar's times, especially on the

Subahs or provinces, are certainly to be found in this treatise. But the author is not all an historian or statistician. He has his interpretations, messages, and moral ideas to propagate and they do not appear to be in any way subsidiary to something else. Abul Fazl is indeed a student of ethics, spirituality, life's mission and so forth. He is a philosopher.

Many passages and paragraphs, nay, chapters of the *Ain-i-Akbari* cannot be taken as contribution to objective history or records of actual facts. Even in regard to the land revenue settlements and figures relating thereto as given by Abul Fazl one is not quite clear as to whether we always and everywhere have the things actually in force, or come across the general scheme of financial administration such as served as the basis for executive action. These features of Abul Fazl's treatise become apparent by the side of another great Persian work, the *Seir Mutaqherin*[1] (View of Modern Times), the history of India after Aurangzeb, composed by Gholam Hussain of Bengal in 1780. This work of the eighteenth century is more objective as history, although no doubt it is furnished with its personal equation as every historical composition is bound to be. A comparison with such formally historical treatises enables us to feel that the *Ain-i-Akbari's* place in the history of political, economic and financial literature cannot be limited to its realistic historicity alone. The work has been conceived by the author as much more than an historical treatise. It is an account in which the messages, norms, ideals, etc. play as prominent a rôle as the objective book-keeping and compilation of registers.

[1] Eng. transl. by M. Raymond (Calcutta, 1902), four volumes.

The *Khatima* (supplement) to the *Mirat-i-Ahmadi*[1] (History of Gujarat) in Persian by Ali Muhammad Khan, which was composed between 1750 and 1760 and is somewhat contemporaneous with the *Seir Mutaqherin*, is likewise another work with which it should be considered generally irrelevant to compare the *Ain-i-Akbari*. The author of this *Khatima*, although influenced in scholarship by Abul Fazl, has produced nothing but a descriptive work, almost a guide-book, so to say, to the shrines of the saints, Hindu temples, etc. as well as a register of the Government officials and departments, the Sarkars paying tribute, and so forth. A work like this may be drawn upon by the researchers of today as a source-book for the economic, administrative and socio-religious facts and institutions of Gujarat in the eighteenth century without even a word of criticism. There is nothing else in the *Khatima* to occupy the reader's interest or intellect. The atmosphere of the *Ain-i-Akbari* is far otherwise.

In the preface to the Book which is given over to Hindu civilisation Abul Fazl enables us to see something of his inner springs of action. The "love of his native country," Hindustan, is referred to by himself in so many words as one of the motives impelling him to write this history. He is one of the first "patriots" of modern India. We are also told that the desire to remove the strife and animosity between the diverse races of India (Hindus and Moslems) is also an urge in this literary endeavour. He wants to function as a bridge between the two great religions, to be a peace-maker. The ambition of establishing peace and unanimity is a burning passion with him.

[1] English translation by Nawab Syed Ali and C. N. Seddon (Baroda, 1924).

This introduction gives us seven reasons for the origin of conflict among persons of diverse religions. In his treatment of the subject we come into contact with a brain which is not only modern in its make-up but which it is almost impossible to improve upon. He is discussing, of course, the problems of other religions, especially Islam *visàvis* Hinduism. But in his analysis are to be found the profoundest considerations of comparative sociology with reference to the race-questions. As an essay in toleration this Introduction can be used even today anywhere on earth. His logic is unchallengable in theory and fruitful in practice. We are reminded in this context of another great Moslem scholar, Alberuni[1].

The comparative method is a remarkable trait of Abul Fazl's logic. This manifests itself not only in the discussion of the questions relating to the conflicts arising from the diversity of faiths but also in the manner in which he deals with the arts and sciences of the Hindus. At important points he turns to the Greeks,—and this also in the manner of Alberuni,—and places Hindu achievements by the side of those of the former. In astronomy he finds analogy with Ptolemy and remembers the Persian, the Egyptian and the Greek philosophers. The references to Greek culture constitute the general perspective, so to say, of his researches in "indology." As one of the modern founders of comparative methodology in world-culture this Indian Mussalman of the sixteenth century deserves his rightful place in the history of science and philosophy and is by all means a great precursor of the Hindu Rammohun Roy of the end of the eighteenth and the early nineteenth centuries.

[1] E.C. Sachau : *Alberuni's India* (London, 1910), two volumes. See the section dealing with Greater India in Moslem Asia, *supra*.

Abul Fazl's ideals are definite and precise. It is the moral and social philosophy that concerns him the most. History, economics, statistics, biography, the personality of Akbar are to him but the pegs on which to hang his moralizings, ideals and spiritual propaganda. There is hardly any chapter of importance, especially in the first two Books in which we do not again and again come into contact with this great key to his life. He is writing about Akbar's India or rather about Akbar himself but all the time with an eye to the illustration of his own spiritual ideals. To him Akbar should appear to be an interesting character simply because it is this monarch who happens to embody all that he himself considers to be great and divine in personal and public life.

Throughout the *Ain-i-Akbari* we encounter but one problem. To the author it is a moral problem and a political problem in one. He is never tired of discussing it or referring to it and has therefore succeeded in imparting to the treatise a lofty tone such as is associated with the greatest political masterpieces of the world.

And what is the life-blood of the ideal preached in season and out of season in the *Ain-i-Akbari*? It is the category of the "just king" (pp. viii, ix, 12). This is the doctrine that occupies the central place in Abul Fazl's political philosophy. And it is here that we see how profoundly he assimilated the eternal problem of Hindu politics, namely, the *Rājarṣi-vrittam* (the conduct of the philosopher-king or royal sage) of our old Kauṭalyan tradition.

In the first edition of the *Positive Background of Hindu Sociology* (1914) the *Ain-i-Akbari* was quoted simply as an evidence of the persistence of the Hindu political ideology in the sixteenth century. The passages are reproduced below.

The political literature of the Hindus was known to Abul Fazl, who in *Ayeen Akbari* has given a short synopsis of probably some of the *Nīti Śāstras* in his possession in the chapter on the various branches of learning cultivated by the people of Hindustan ruled by his master, the great Akbar. Besides giving an elaborate description of Hindu law under the heading *Beyhar* (*Sans. Vyavahāra*) and referring to "many other sensible books upon government" the compiler of this Moghul Gazetteer gives the following summary of *Rajneet*, "the art of governing a kingdom:"

"It is incumbent on a monarch to divest himself of avarice and anger by following the counsels of wisdom. * * * It is his indispensable duty to fear God * * * to pay particular respect to men of exalted rank and behave with kindness towards his subjects of every description. * * * He should be ambitious to extend his dominions. * * * No enemy is so insignificant as to be beneath his notice. * * * A wise prince will banish from his court all corrupt and designing men. * * *

"The king resembles a gardener, who plucks up the thorns and briers, and throws them on one side, whereby he beautifies his garden, and at the same time raises a fence which preserves his ground from the intrusion of strangers. * * *The king detaches from the nobles their too numerous friends, and dangerous dependents.* * *

"In affairs of moment it is not advisable to consult with many.* * * Some ancient monarchs made it a rule to consult men of a contrary description and to act diametrically opposite to their advice.* * * They found it the safest way to join with the prime minister a few wise and experienced men and to require each to deliver his opinion in writing. A prince, moreover, requires a learned astrologer and a skilful physician. ***If any monarch is more powerful than himself he continually strives to sow dissension among his troops; and if he is not able to effect this, prudently purchases his friendship.*** The prince whose territory adjoins to his, although he may be friendly in appearance, yet ought not to be trusted; he should always be prepared to oppose any sudden attack from that quarter. With him whose country lies next beyond the one last mentioned he should enter into alliance; but no connexion should be formed with those who are more remote. If he finds it necessary to attack his enemy, he should invade his country during the time of harvest."

Here we have from a non-Hindu source the traditional ideas of the Hindus regarding constitution, international morality, etc. as preserved in the Hindu literature of the 16th century. The student of comparative politics will be justified to go farther. In so far as the general, philosophical or theoretical ideas are concerned, the *Ain-i-Akbari* is to be treated virtually as a Persianized edition, so to say, of a Sanskrit *Nīti Śāstra.* It is within the philosophical framework of a Hindu treatise on politics that Abul Fazl has put in the statistics and administrative details of Akbar's Empire. It not only preserves the Hindu tradition by describing Sanskrit literature and Hindu philosophical ideas in Book IV, but is a document of the most profound assimilation of Hindu culture by a philosophically minded Mussalman.

Let us analyze a bit of his own philosophical synthesis. In the general preface to his *Ain-i-Akbari* Abul Fazl says about royalty as follows:

"If royalty did not exist, the storm of strife would never subside, nor selfish ambition disappear. Mankind, being under the burden of lawlessness and lust, would sink into the pit of destuction, the world, this great market place, would lose its prosperity, and the whole earth become a barren waste. But by the light of imperial justice some follow with cheerfulness the road of obedience, whilst others abstain from violence through fear of punishment; and out of necessity make choice of the path of rectitude."

In this political philosophy of Abul Fazl we have an adaptation from the Hindu doctrines of *mātsya nyāya* (logic of the fish) as well as of *daṇḍa* (punishment, sanction etc.). He is a first class writer and stylist and he has presented the Hindu philosophical "patents" in a most polished and dignified language, which only the Persianists of course can appreciate in the original.

Among the "excellent qualities" flowing from royalty as conceived by Abul Fazl we are told that the king "puts the reins of desire into the hands of reason; in the wide field of his desires he does not permit himself to be trodden by restlessness nor will he waste his precious time in seeking after that which is improper.****He is for ever searching after those who speak the truth and is not displeased with words that seem bitter but are in reality sweet." Here, again, we have but a paraphrase from the Hindu doctrine of *vyasanas* (vices) and *rājadoṣas* (faults or disqualifications of kings).

It is exceedingly interesting that even in regard to the professional structure of the people Abul Fazl cannot think of anything but the fourfold Hindu social stratification. He says that the political constitution becomes well tempered by a "proper division of ranks." The four classes into which according to him the world may be divided are (1) warriors, (2) artificers and merchants, (3) the learned and (4) husbandmen and labourers. We are taught also that it is obligatory for a king to "put each of these in its proper place, and by uniting personal ability with a due respect for others, to cause the world to flourish."

It does not take anybody acquainted even cursorily with the Hindu *Artha*, *Smriti* and *Nīti Śāstras* long to feel that Abul Fazl is reproducing the most fundamental concept of the king's functions *vis-à-vis chāturvarṇya* (the four-ordered social polity). It is curious that no modern scholar seems to have even suspected that the words, phrases and sentences of a philosophical, theoretical or general character in all these paragraphs are almost *verbatim* copies from the *Manu Samhitā*, ch. VIII (*Rājadharma*).

We shall now point to one or two other Sanskritisms or Hinduizings of the Persian text. In *Ain* 13 which discusses the origin of metals, Abul Fazl speaks of the "seven bodies" within quotation marks. According to some manuscripts the Hindus are referred to as giving the opinion that the metal called *ricac* is a "silver in the state of leprosy". One wonders if Abul Fazl is not dealing in this chapter with the Hindu doctrine of seven metals. And one may not be surprised if *zinc*, the seventh metal, which began to be recognized by the fourteenth century Hindu writers on medicine like Madanapāla, is Abul Fazl's "silver in the state of leprosy", for some of the Sanskrit names for zinc, namely, *rasaka*, *rūpyabhrātā* etc. connect it with silver.

In *Ain* 41 which deals with the imperial elephant stables the four kinds of elephants (namely, *bhaddar*, *mand*, *mirg* and *mir*) and their three dispositions (namely, *sat*, *raj* and *tam*) are derived from the Sanskrit treatises on elephants. Abul Fazl names also the eight *dig-gajas* or elephants as guardians of the quarters or points of the earth in the Hindu manner and gives likewise another Hindu classification of elephants. The entire chapter (pp. 117-124) points to a fine assimilation of Sanskrit *gajaśāstras* by Moslems in regard to other items as well. Abul Fazl quotes neither Varāhamihira's *Brihat Samhitā* nor Bhoja's *Yuktikalpataru* nor any treatise like the *Śukranīti*. He is, however, not a plagiarist, as he says explicitly that these ideas about elephants are Hindu.

Ain 72 describes the "manner in which His Majesty spends his time" (pp. 153-156). In such expressions as the "care with which His Majesty guards over his motives and watches over his emotions", "he listens to great and small", "he does not allow his desires or his wrath to renounce allegiance to wisdom", "his august nature cares but little for the pleasures of the world", etc. one may read the echoes or reminiscences of the "qualifications" and "vices" of kings with which the Hindu *Artha* and *Nīti Śāstras* deal as a matter of course. Some of these virtues are by all means but generalities and platitudes found in every treatise on ideal polity from Plato and Kauṭalya to Al Farabi (*c* 950), the great Arab encyclopaedist, who based his *Al-Madinat-Al-Fadila* (*Model City*) on Plato. Abul Fazl does not therefore have to copy such maxims from any specifically Hindu sources.

Such moralizings or ascriptions of moral qualities to a *Padshah* may also be expected of Abul Fazl quite independently. It should still be observed however that he is writing in a Hindu atmosphere about a monarch who is pro-Hindu with vengeance, nay, who is condemned as *Kafer* by orthodox Mussalmans.[1]

[1] For the pro-Hindu habits and laws of Akbar as described and condemned by Badaoni see Blochmann vol.I. pp.179-184, 193, 205.

Further, Abul Fazl is actually using Hindi words at every turn and referring to Hindu customs in the most familiar way. One may perhaps suggest, therefore, that the author of *Ain-i-Akbari* is not uninfluenced by the traditional (Kauṭalyan) Hindu conception of the *Rājarṣi*, the philosopher-king, while describing Akbar's daily routine, meals and other habits, as well as temperament etc. in *Ains* 72-75 (pp.153-160). The characteristic Muslim salutations (*taslim* and *kornish*) are, however, not included in these remarks. But Abul Fazl's *dicta* that "royalty is an emblem of the power of God and a light-shedding ray from this Sun of the Absolute" (p.159) or that "even spiritual progress would be impossible unless emanating from the king in whom the light of God dwells" (p.158) point perhaps to the fact that Abul Fazl is here making propaganda about his hero for a people that is used to the language of the *Manu Saṁhitā*. Not the least *tendencioes* item in all these statements is the one, as told by Abul Fazl, that "His Majesty abstains much from flesh so that whole months pass away without his touching any animal food". The author makes it a point to observe in this connection that the animal food, "though prized by most, is nothing thought of by the sage." This can be easily interpreted as an attempt on the part of Abul Fazl at "speaking to the gallery". But the fact that these statements about Akbar are truths and not mere propaganda furnishes all the more ground for believing that the Emperor, his court, as well as Abul Fazl were Hinduized in thought and form.

These suggestions about Abul Fazl's Hinduization of the *Ain-i-Akbari* will derive fresh strength from what is known about his personal character. According to the *Maasir-ul-Umara* quoted in Blochmann's *Ain-i-Akbari* (pp. xxvii-xxviii). Abul Fazl is reported to have been "an infidel". "Some say, he was a Hindu, or a fire-worshipper or a free-thinker, and some go still further and call him an atheist; but others pass a juster sentence, and say that he was a pantheist, and that like other Sufis he claimed for himself a position above the law of the prophet." All these descriptions, repugnant naturally as they are to an orthodox Mussalman, are however quite in keeping with an academically high placed or philosophically minded Hindu or Hinduized scholar. And since Prince Salim in his *Memoirs* describes Abul Fazl as a "Hindusthani Shaikh by birth, who was well-known for his learning and wisdom"[1] we may not be far from the truth when we surmise that this Indian-born Shaikh was well up in the Hindu *Smriti* and *Nīti Śāstras* and at any rate had grown up by assimilating the contributions of Hindu cultural tradition. It is interesting to have to observe that even as a profound student of Arabic literature Abul Fazl must have been introduced to the Hindu *vidyās* because, as is well-known, a considerable portion of Arabic texts was made up of translations from Sanskrit treatises in the eighth and ninth centuries. The amount of original researches in Hindu culture embodied in the work on India by Alberuni (973-1048), the great Arab mathematician and philosopher, was immense.

Had we known less than we actually do about Akbar's socio-religious pro-Hindu propaganda and the ultraliberal intellectual activities of Abul Fazl, his

[1] Blochmann, vol. I. (1873), Biography p. xxvi. For the translations from Sanskrit works into Arabic from 750 to 850 A.C. See E.C. Sachau : *Alberuni's India* (London 1916), Vol. I. pp. xxviii-xxxv. Alberuni's own translations or adaptations from Sanskrit may be seen *Ibid*, pp.xxxvi-xl.

elder brother Faizi and their father we might perhaps have been led to suspect that part of the idealism in Abul Fazl's work,—the general preface as well as the text—is to be ascribed to an acquaintance with Al Farabi's treatise on the model city (*c* 950). As a learned scholar Abul Fazl may certainly have studied the Arabic treatise on governmental statutes (*El-Akham es Soulthaniyah*) by Mawerdi (972-1058), Chief Justice of Bagdad, or derived profit from the Persian *Siassat Namah* (Treatise on Government) by Nizamoul Mulk (*c* 1063-1092). And of course the greatest philosophico-historical work of the "Middle Age," namely, the *Mokaddemah* in Arabic by Ibn Khaldun (1332-1406) the Egyptian judge, could not have failed to furnish this "Hindusthani Shaikh" with literary norms.[1]

But the borrowings, assimilations, reminiscences or adaptations from the Sanskrit texts are too direct and palpable as well as pronounced. The surroundings of Abul Fazl's daily life and the literary activities in which he took part while preparing the *Ain-i-Akbari* should appear to be Muslim only in name. The Hindu-Moslem camaraderies of his *Padshah* as well as of himself and his group are enough to explain that forces nearer home were responsible for

[1] For Al Farabi see the German translation (*Die Muster-Stadt*) by F.Dietrici, Leyden 1895, and Carra de Vaux: *Avicenne*, Paris 1900. The *El-Akham es Soulthaniyah* is available in French as *Les Status Gouvernementaux* by Fagnan, Paris 1915. The *Siasset Nameh* is available in French as *Traité du Gouvernement by* Schefer, Paris 1893. The *Mokaddemah* is available in French as *Prolegomènes Historiques* by de Slane, Paris 1862-68. See also T. Husein: *La Philosophie Sociale d' Ibn Khaldhoun*, Paris 1917. A study as to the nature of Abul Fazl's contacts with these and other Arabic and Persian "old masters" in politics, economics, history and sociology, etc. ought to be very interesting for an investigation into the achievements of Indo-Saracenic Renaissance.

the kind of idealism and political philosophy which found expression in his *Akbar-nīti*.

The translations from "Hindi" (Sanskrit)[1] into Persian of works like the *Mahābhārata*, the *Rāmāyaṇa*, the *Atharva Veda*, the *Harivamśa*, the *Nala Damayantī*, etc. such as are described in the *Ain* 34 indicate the Hindu atmosphere which could not fail to leave its impress upon the contributions of Abul Fazl. It is not quite clear, however, whether the translations were made direct from Sanskrit or from Hindi translations. But it is important to notice that he himself had a hand in the translations of the *Mahābhārata*, just as Faizi in that of *Nal Daman*.

In the special preface to the sections dealing with Hindu culture we learn from Abul Fazl's own statements that his studies in Hindu culture were commenced early. But he felt that his knowledge was not sufficient. So he renewed his former studies with the help of those who could guide him. He speaks of the painful researches undertaken in order to arrive at the truth about the Hindus, their sciences, philosophies and religions. This explains naturally the almost *verbatim* extracts from Hindu treatises on law and politics in this Muslim work.

It is interesting that at the very threshold of his study on Hindu culture, even in the introduction Abul Fazl makes the readers acquainted with his fundamental conclusion, namely, that the Hindus are

[1] Blochmann, Vol. I. (1873), Biography, pp. xvii, 104, 199-200. For the translations of Sanskrit works under Moslem auspices see also D. C. Sen: *History of Bengali Literature* (Calcutta 1911), N. N. Law: *Promotion of Learning in India during Muhammadan Rule by Muhammadans* (London 1916), B. K. Sarkar: *Folk Element in Hindu Culture* (London 1917), M. Z. Siddiqi: "Services of Muslims to Sanskrit Literature" (*Calcutta Review*, February 1932).

not polytheists but are worshippers of God and only one God. And this conclusion he poses against the popular tradition of his times to the effect that the Hindus are polytheists. He repeats his conclusion at the commencement of the lengthy section and remarks that the Hindus are no mere idolators, "as the ignorant suppose." The Hindu explanation of image-worship is reproduced by himself as his own conviction, namely, that the images are designed simply to prevent the thoughts of the people from wandering while at prayer. Abul Fazl should here appear to be a twin to Alberuni who preceded him by over five hundred years.

It is evident that Abul Fazl has taken his pen in the interest of a propaganda. It is a propaganda of inter-religious understanding and inter-racial peace. And in regard to his own race and religion this propaganda is nothing but fanatically pro-Hindu. Indeed he has made it a point to collect together all the good things that may be said about the people whom he wants to raise in the estimation of his co-religionists. Perhaps from Megasthenes to Nivedita the Hindus have never been flattered in such a dignified manner by any non-Hindu as has been done by Abul Fazl in the *Ain-i-Akbari*.[1]

In all essentials the *Ain-i-Akbari* has turned out to be a joint Hindu-Moslem literary work so characteristic of the Indo-Saracenic Renaissance of the sixteenth and seventeenth centuries. Nay, it is perhaps one of the first creative specimens of Hindu-Moslem cultural fusion such as have marked the evolution

[1] See in this connection Alberuni's sympathetic appreciation (although critical) of Hindu philosophy and general culture in the eleventh century (*c* 1017-1030); E. C. Sachau, Vol. I. pp. xvii-xix.

of Indian arts and sciences since then. And in his emphasis on goodness and moral life as the foundation of spirituality and the key to the kingdom of God he is an *avatāra* of positivism representing thereby the very spirit of the Renaissance. For, no student of *Nīti Śāstras*, Oriental or Occidental, can afford to forget that the statement "that every man of sense and understanding knows that the best way of worshipping God consists in allaying the distress of the times and in improving the condition of the poor" (*Ain* 2) came from the pen of the Indian Mussalman of the sixteenth century.

As a rationalist, as a "protestant", and as a humanist Abul Fazl has served to liberate the Moslem mind. The enfranchisement of the intelligence which was consummated in the Christian world by the Renaissance was accomplished in Moslem India by the author of the *Ain-i-Akbari*, the same enfranchisement which was to attack the Hindu mind two centuries later in and through Rammohun Roy (1774-1833). For the students of world culture in political philosophy it is of importance to observe that some of the formative forces in Abul Fazl's toleration, humanism, eclectic approach to the things of matter and spirit, as well as positivism were furnished by the Hindu *Manu Samhitā* and *Mahābhārata*.

SECTION 6

THE CULTURAL NATIONALISM OF ŚIVĀJI THE GREAT

The Anti-Foreign and Democratic Tradition

The Maratha positivism such as in politics took shape in the *Dharma-rājya* of Śivāji the Great is not an isolated phenomenon in the Hindu culture of

Southern India or of the Deccan. Among the formative forces of Śivāji's *Hindwi Swarājya* are to be detected from his mother's side the memories of the war of self-defence against the Moslems conducted by the Yādavas of Devagiri (*c* 1200-1318). And on account, again, of his father's experiences in Vijayanagara, the Empire (1346-1646) which successfully upheld Hindu liberty for several centuries although with vicissitudes of fortune, the ideas of Hindu statehood were imbibed by Śivāji as a matter of course.[1] Śivāji can then be regarded as but a continuator under Moghul conditions of the traditional Hindu spirit, the *dharma*, which is obstinate enough not to submit to foreign forces. In Śivāji's ambitions, exploits and achievements are further to be seen the embodiments of the same *parākrama* (prowess) and *digvijaya* (conquest of the quarters) which enabled Chandragupta Maurya to emancipate the north-western frontiers of India from the Hellenistic Seleukos (*c* 305 B.C.). In subsequent times the same assertion of the Hindu spirit against foreign domination had found expression in Skandagupta's expulsion of the Huns (*c* 455 A.C.),—furnishing thereby another precedent to Śivāji's triumphant service to Hindu culture. Historically, however, it is the South-Indian exploits of the Yādavas and of the Vijayanagara Rāyas that in point of time as well as region served to inspire Śivāji with direct examples.

Śivāji was a nationalist in culture. "Back to Hindu tradition" may be said to have been his war-cry. It is the language of the *Manu Samhitā* and the *Nīti Śāstras* that was on his lips on the most important problems of life. Speaking to a Bundella ("Rajput," "Kṣatriya") chieftain Śivāji gave

[1] G. S. Sardesai : *The Main Currents of Maratha History* (Bombay 1933) pp. 5-7.

a bit of his mind when he declared as follows:[1]

"Does not the Kṣatriya faith consist in protecting the cow and the Brāhmaṇa, in guarding the *Veda*, in showing skill and valor in battle? And if you lose your life, will you not through the solar orb enter the mansion of bliss, enjoying plenitude of happiness and repose?"

In this inspiring message of Śivāji the Rajput chief was introduced to the deliberate restoration of ancient ideals,—to the Renaissance of Hindu culture,—by which Śivāji's personality was fired. It is as an apostle and embodiment of *Hindwi Swarājya* (Hindu independence) and a *Dharmarājya* (kingdom of *Dharma*, i.e., Law, Duty and Justice as conceived in the *Nīti Śāstras*) that he wanted to hold forth.

There are other items in the Maratha *milieu* which point likewise to the strength of the Hindu tradition. It is out of tailors, carpenters, potters, gardeners, shopkeepers, barbers and even untouchable *Mahars* that the Maratha saints and prophets of the fifteenth and sixteenth centuries arose.[2] The rise of the lower tribes into the higher orders of the Hindu society,—"social mobility" of the vertical type—has been an eternal fact of Indian culture-history since the earliest epochs of the Vedic period. In the Marathi-speaking regions during the epoch of the Hindu Renaissance expressions of the same democratic social "metabolism" were witnessed as elsewhere in India as but regular phases of the dynamic "culture-contacts." To a certain extent this ascendancy of the underworld was partly a manifestation of the great *Bhakti* or *Vaiṣ*-

[1] W. R. Pogson: *A History of the Boondelas*, pp. 52-53 in S. N. Sen: *The Military System of the Marathas* (Calcutta 1928), p. 24.

[2] M. G. Ranade : *Rise of the Maratha Power* (Bombay 1900) pp. 10, 24, 146-147, 150.

ṇava movement which was almost universal during the fourteenth to the seventeenth century. Democracy and *Bhakti* (love or faith) went hand in hand as much in Northern India and Bengal as in South-western India and the Deccan.

It was therefore as an integral feature of the Hindu societal tradition that by following the profession of arms the Movres of Jawli, the Savants of Wari, the Ghorpādes of Mudhol, the Nimbalkārs of Phaltan, the Jādhavs of Sindkhed, the Jedhkes, the Mānes, the Dāfles, and others rose into prominence in the Maratha world.[1] Śivāji the Bhonsle himself is alleged to have belonged to a low caste (cultivator). And prior to coronation he had to be dubbed a Kṣatriya. Not only Śivāji but all his successors down to the last Peshwa had to recruit the army from the lower tribes or castes. Husbandmen, carpenters, shopkeepers, men of mean birth always constituted the backbone of the Maratha army, as says the *Tarikh-i-Ibrahim* towards the end of the eighteenth century. All through the ages in India as elsewhere the military profession has functioned as a most patent "social ladder".

In the matter of organizing his army from among the lower orders Śivāji was but following in the wake of the Hindu generals and statesmen of yore. He followed the Hindu tradition in other ways too, as we shall see later. Śivāji's life and work were some of the best specimens of creative India's contributions to human history.

[1] S. N. Sen: *The Military System of the Marathas* (Calcutta 1928) pp. 11, 26; J. N. Sarkar: *Shivaji* (Calcutta 1929), pp. 210, 212. The idea of the lowly origin of Śivāji is contested by Balkrishna : *Shivaji the Great* (Bombay) Vol. I. (1932) p. 4. See the discussion on the Paretian "circulation of *élites*" in the section on "Race-mixture", pp. 133-135.

The Positivism of the Dāsabodha

The *Dāsabodha* by Rāmdās (1608-1681) is a work in 20 Books. Each Book is furnished with 10 sections, and is therefore called a *Daśaka*. The sections are called *Samāsas*. So there are altogether 200 *Samāsas* in the entire treatise, each of which is furnished with a colophon. The *Samāsas* are of diverse sizes. The *Dāsabodha* is described in every colophon as *Gurūśiṣyasambāda* (conversation between the master and the disciple). It is, however, throughout composed in the form of the master's sayings rather than in that of interview, i.e., questions and answers.

The sayings[1] in these 200 *Samāsas* deal with such topics as *bhakti* (faith), *rajoguṇa* (activism), *tamoguṇa* (inertness), *dukkha* (pain), *mrityu* (death), *Brahma*, *mokṣa* (liberation), *ātmā* (self), *anātmā* (not-self), *yugadharma* (duties or *mores* of the Kali age), etc. It is necessary to observe that of politics there is hardly anything in this treatise. There are but just a few references to *raya karun* (king's functions) in this work, voluminous as it is. Its make-up is non-political.

The work is mainly made up of ideas relating to man as an animal and as a person. The verses are terse and epigrammatic and simple enough to pass from mouth to mouth becoming thereby the household words of the masses. Although the gods are mentioned once in a while, the *Dāsabodha* is not a treatise of god-lore. It is principally a work of psychology and morals, such as we get from the genuine saints and *sādhus* even of today. Its teachings are calculated to have a sober influence on the mind and character of individuals. As such its spiritual significance is considerable. Like the Sanskrit *Gītā* and the Tamil

[1] L. R. Pangarkar: *Sārtha Śrīdāsabodha* (Poona 1923).

Kurāl the *Dāsabodha* is one of the greatest classics of world literature. Not less important as a moral and spiritual force than the *Rāmāyaṇa* of Tulsīdas (1532-1624), the *Dāsabodha* of Rāmdās (1608-1681) has a special literary feature in so far as it is, unlike the former, entirely independent of a story but is a collection of precepts bearing on man's nature and goal. It was by such doses of positive philosophy that the moral atmosphere of the masses in the midst of which Śivāji had to live, move and have his being in order to organize invincible legions was impregnated. Whether Rāmdās was the guide-philosopher-friend to Śivāji is perhaps a controversial point.[1] But that he wielded the moral dynamo with which to energize the springs of action of the folk that Śivāji was destined to serve there is no doubt. Rāmdās can by all means then be treated as a colleague of Śivāji in the self-same mission of establishing the *dharmarājya* of the Marathas. The personal relations between Rāmdās and Śivāji are likely to be debated for some long time. Whether he had any finger in Śivāji's military plans and constructive statesmanship may always remain among the unsolved questions of Maratha archaeology. But as makers of Mahārāṣṭra and remakers of Hindustan Rāmdās and Śivāji will always go together as one ideological complex in the historical scholarship of future generations just as tradition has brought them together in a more direct and personal relationship.

Rāmdās's utopia of Ānanda-vana-bhūvana

It is possible to detect an utopistic futurism in Rāmdās's writings. That futurism took shape in his conception of *Ānanda-vana-bhūvana* (the happy

[1] J. N. Sarkar: *Shivaji* (Calcutta 1929), pp. 381-382.

world) such as he is said to have seen in a dream.[1] The contents of this dream introduce us to the kind of miseries which he saw removed from his people and the kind of relief, joy or happiness that he found brought or restored to the community. The hindrances to *svadharma* were, we are told, things of the past. The emergence of the *sureśa* (the hero) and the *śūra-senā* (the army of the hero) on the one hand, and the discomfiture of the *Mlechchha Daitya* (the barbarian devil), on the other, constituted two important features of the *Ānanda-vana-bhūvana* as envisaged in the dream. The *pāpī* (sinners and criminals) of all sorts as well as the *abhakta* (faithless) disappeared or diminished in number. The expansion of *dharma* was consummated. The *pāpī* (sinner) *Āurāngyā's* (Aurangzib's) "sinking" or decline was distinctly seen (*buḍālā āurāngyā pāpī*). On the positive side were noticed, again, the assured facilities for *snāna* (bath) and *sandhyā* (evening prayers), *japa-tapa* (sacrifices) etc., ceremonial items such as affected the Hindus of those days as of today. Then, again, love, fellow-feeling and sympathy were on the increase (*chaḍhatā baḍhatā premā*).

In Rāmdās's doctrine of *Ānanda-vana-bhūvana* which has been exquisitely put in as the fourth hemstitch in every verse we are indeed getting a seventeenth century (?) paraphrase, adaptation or application of the celebrated *Gītā* doctrine of *Yugāntara*. The great transformation, transvaluation of values, or remaking of epochs is initiated by God Kṛṣṇa, as declared to Arjuna, whenever corruption creeps in into *dharma* (law, order and justice) and ascendancy is enjoyed by *adharma* (disorder, vile practices, negation of law, justice and morals). Kṛṣṇa takes shape

[1] V. L. Bhave: *Mahārāṣṭra-Sārasvat* (Poona 1921) p. 224.

in human form under those calamitous conditions in order to protect the *sādhu* (the good, the just and the honest) and to annihilate the *duṣkrita* (the culprits, the evil-doers and the ruffians) as well as to re-establish *dharma*, i.e., law, order, justice, morality, virtue and humanity.

Rāmdās's dream saw *Kalpānta*, the end of a *Kalpa* i.e., the close of an era of *pāpī*, *mlechchha*, *Chandāla*, *abhakta* and others of the kind. And at the same time the establishment of *svadharma*, *premā*, *ānanda*, etc. was an item in the consummation achieved by the hero dreamt of. It is interesting that the *Gītā* doctrine of God's *sambhavāmi yuge yuge* (I appear age by age) was serviceable to the Maratha poet-saint of the seventeenth century in the formulation of his professedly futuristic politics.

In Rāmdās's ideology there is no vagueness about the particular *pāpī* who was responsible for the miseries and calamities and against whom it was necessary to raise the *śūrasenā* in order that *Ānanda-vana-bhūvana* (the kingdom of God, so to say) might flourish on earth. Aurangzib has been singled out in the verses as the butt of Rāmdas's wrath, and naturally the *sureśa*, the hero, who is responsible for the break-up of the old conditions and the inauguration of the new era is none other than Sivāji.

Evidently all this jubilation over the annihilation of the *pāpī* and the restoration of *dharma* and expansion of *premā* is to be attributed to a date after the *dharmarājya* of Sivāji has become a *fait accompli* (1674-80). But the material, as we have it, is of course regarded as a part of something dreamt of by Rāmdās in a period of national calamity, i.e., previous to Sivāji's exploits and successes. The dream is narrated in the form of a prophecy and as something that is to happen at some future date. This "futuristic" forecasting of Maratha glories is in keeping with the prophetic form of the *Bhaviṣya-purāṇa* dynastic history. One may naturally suspect as to whether the verses on *Ānanda-vana-bhūvana* may be ascribed to Rāmdās at all. Besides, one cannot be positive about their being composed even in the lifetime of Śivāji himself. There is no harm in believing that some Maratha author of the eighteenth century while studying the glorious origins of the *dharmarājya* which had been established by the veritable *Yugāvatāra* Śivāji and which maintained its career of *digvijaya* for quite a long time afterwards should have been inspired by the pious imagination to father such prophetic verses on the greatest patriot-poet of Śivāji's time, Rāmdās. In any case, we understand from almost contemporary sources how powerfully the imagination of the young Maratha was inspired by the epoch-making and *kalpānta*-consummating achievement of the Indian Frederick the Great, perhaps the greatest Hindu of all ages and one of the profoundest remakers of mankind. The fine lyrical verses on *Ānanda-vana-bhūvana* constitute a valuable document of Maratha history as much as a text of Maratha *Nīti Śāstra* or political philosophy. Such texts, be it observed *en passant*, are very rare in Indian literature.

The Pluralistic World of Śivāji

In the fifteenth, sixteenth and seventeenth centuries the Maratha masses and classes were used in daily life to the Mussalman institutions and practices. The Hindu tradition survived by all means in the more important items of personal, and domestic life.[1]

[1] M. G. Ranade: *Rise of the Maratha Power* (Bombay 1900) pp. 27-38, 44-45.

The social polity may in general be taken to have been still governed by the *Manu Samhitā*, and the general *mores* by the *Mahābhārata*. Certain branches of public law, i.e., political life, also e.g. the land revenue system, the law of property, and agricultural practice remained Hindu to the last, although somewhat Moslemized in a few items. But the other branches of public law, i.e. the executive and the judiciary, the army and the police had become Islamic in the main and did not possess more than mere traces of the Hindu institutions.[1] In the Moslem states of the Deccan and south India the Hindu *personnel* was however always a noticeable feature even in the higher rungs of service.

In Śivāji's politics are therefore to be seen both these strands, Hindu and Moslem. He is a representative not only of the tribal-contacts and caste-fusions so common to the Hindu culture of all ages, but at the same time a specimen and embodiment of Hindu-Moslem cultural *rapprochement*. Like Abul Fazl the Hinduized Moslem, Śivāji was to a certain extent a Moslemized Hindu, both being true indices to the Indo-Saracenic Renaissance of the times. Śivāji's sympathy with Moslems in the practice of their religion and patronage of Moslem mosques is worthy of mention in this connection.[2]

It is in the perspective of these Hindu-Moslem culture-contacts, extensive and profound as they were, that we are to appraise the attempts of Śivāji to hold forth as a Hindu monarch, nay, as a Hindu nationa-

[1] For Moslem contributions to Maratha polity see S. N. Sen: *Administrative System* etc. (Calcutta 1925) pp. 593-664 and J. N. Sarkar: *Shivaji* (Calcutta 1929), pp. 216, 386-387.

[2] Ranade: *Rise of the Maratha Power*, p. 277; J. N. Sarkar: *Shivaji*, p. 381.

list bent upon reviving or rather providing a fresh fillip to the institutions and *mores* of Hindu culture. An important item as well as evidence of Sivāji's cultural nationalism is to be found in the very coronation itself.[1]

This ceremony, administered as it was by the "Brahmadeva and Vyāsa" of those days, namely, Paṇḍit Viśveśvar Bhatta (nicknamed Gāgā Bhatta) of Benares, served to establish his *liaison* with the entire Hindu world of the time. On the other hand, it was by this ceremony that his *Hindwi Swarājya* was affiliated to the great pre-Moslem Hindu empires of antiquity.

The *Śukranīti* can very often be cited in illustration of the institutions and principles of the polity established by Sivāji and developed by the Peshwas.[2] The State Council of Eight (*aṣṭa pradhāna*), town-planning, land revenue, forced labour, agricultural policy, military ideas, punishments, legal procedure, etc. can be explained in terms of this *Nīti Śāstra*. Indeed, in the *Positive Background of Hindu Sociology* Vol. I. (1914, p.259) it was pointed out that Śivāji's war-cry about the inviolability of the cow might suggest a date for that line of the *Śukranīti* (IV, vii. 453) which declares the killing of cows to be one of the most serious *casus belli*. And the ideas of Manu, nay, of Kauṭalya can likewise be detected in the system of Śivāji and his successors.

[1] J. N. Sarkar: *Shivaji* (1929) pp. 208-219.

[2] S. N. Sen: *The Administrative System of Marathas* (Calcutta 1925), pp. 488, 489, 499-501, 527 531, 533, 534, 541, 543, 549, 551-552, 556, 570, 573, 577. It is to this author that I am indebted for most of the books in Marathi language utilized in the present work as well as for the meanings of some of the more difficult words and phrases such as are beyond the competence of my very limited knowledge of Marathi. He is, however, not responsible for any of the interpretations offered in this study.

The Linguistic Patriotism of Śivāji

Śivāji was fully conscious of his mission as a restorer of Hindu political dignity to its ancient or rather pre-Moslem conditions. Accordingly, he wanted to go back to the fountain of Hindu culture in the smallest details of his life. The very words and phrases of daily existence had become Persianized in his time on account of long-standing Moslem influence. His first and foremost ambition in this regard consisted in Sanskritizing these terms. He desired the old Hindu atmosphere to be reborn even in the commonplace conversations of the day. A veritable Renaissance (rebirth) of the ancient conditions has thus to be ascribed to the conscious patriotism of this Hindu *avatāra* of the seventeenth century. As a specimen of the linguistic remaking of his fatherland may be presented the *Rāja-vyavahārakoṣa*[1] (Dictionary of Royal Conduct) in Sanskrit prepared under his orders by Raghunāth Paṇḍit more or less in the form of *Amarakoṣa.*

It is a work complete in 386 verses and comprises the following *vargas* and groups:

1. *Rājavarga* (relating to the king).
2. *Kāryasthānavarga* (relating to the office).
3. *Bhogyavarga* (relating to foods and drinks).
4. *Śastravarga* (relating to arms and accoutrements).
5. *Chaturaṃgavarga* (relating to four parts of the army).
6. *Sāmantavarga* (relating to officers of the army).
7. *Durgavarga* (relating to forts).
8. *Lekhanavarga* (relating to writers).
9. *Janapadavarga* (relating to territory).
10. *Paṇyavarga* (relating to goods).

[1] Apte and Divekar: *Śiva-Charita-Pradīpa* (Poona, 1925), pp. 144-175.

The classification into *vargas* does not indicate any special respect for logic, however. There are some 1500 words in this lexicon.

Some of the words in the *Rāja-Varga* are given below:

Sanskrit		Persian
Rājā	=	*Pādshā*
Swāmi	=	*Sāheb*
Rājaputra	=	*Sāhajādā*
Pradhāna	=	*Peshwa*
Amātya	=	*Majumdār*
Senādhyakṣa	=	*Hukumat*
Sandeśa-lekha	=	*Chitnis*
Dūta	=	*Hejivā*
Dhanika	=	*Saudāgara*
Sannihita	=	*Huzuri*
Anuchara	=	*Mahaldār*
Sarvakarī	=	*Harkarā*
Parichāraka	=	*Afrada*

The second chapter describes some of the offices and things relating to them as follows:

Sanskrit		Persian
Kāryasthāna	=	*Kārkhānā*
Koṣāgāra	=	*Khājānā*
Koṣarakṣaka	=	*Jāmdār*
Nikṣepa	=	*Dāfunā*
Samchita	=	*Dastānā*
Srimkhalika	=	*Janjeriā*
Nupūra	=	*Puinjne*

In the third groups that on foods and drinks, we have the following synonyms:

Sanskrit		Persian
Dhūmayantra	=	*Guḍguḍi*
Dhūmapatraka	=	*Tāmākhu*
Sugandhidravya	=	*Khusavaya*

The section on forts commences in the following manner:

Durgam killeti vijneyam
giridurgo gaḍah smritah
Prākārah kota ityukto
Janjirā drīpa ucyate.

We get the following synonyms:

Sanskrit		Persian
Durga	=	*Killā*
Giridurga	=	*Gaḍ*
Prākāra	=	*Koṭ*
Dvīpa	=	*Janjirā*

It is as an expression of Śivāji's cultural nationalism that we have to watch his sedulous re-christening of old hill-forts in Sanskrit.[1] The names of such forts as Sinhagaḍ, Viṣālgaḍ, Rājgaḍ, Suvarṇadurg, Vijaydurg, Bhīmagaḍ, Pāndavagad, Sundargaḍ, Prachanḍagaḍ bespeak his interest in the age-long tradition of the Hindu states.

Students of modern nationalism or of the "nationality question" are aware of the rôle that has been played by language in the military history and "geo-politics" of nineteenth century Europe and is still being played in the "minorities" problems of post-war Europe. Evidently Śivāji was no mere dare-devil soldier, victorious general and successful statesman.

[1] Balkrishna: *Shivaji the Great* (Bombay, 1932) Vol. I. part II. p. 11.

He was a political and social philosopher too and a champion of culture. In his life's work are to be detected the influences of linguistic patriotism. As a nationalist, more precisely as an exponent of national language in politics Śivāji can claim recognition as one of the first among the modern makers of history, as a precursor of Herder (1744-1803) and Fichte (1762-1814).[1] No estimate of Śivāji's achievement in political action and thought can be adequate which ignores his great solicitude for emancipating his countrymen from the thraldom of a foreign tongue.

It is to be observed that his linguistic patriotism is not restricted to Sanskrit. His mother tongue Marathi also he rescued from Persianization and rendered more popular among the masses and the classes.

As a result of the linguistic nationalism initiated under Śivāji the Marathi language became Sanskritized. In the sixteenth century the great Marathi writer Eknāth had used Persian words to the extent of 75 per cent. But in the eighteenth century the amount of Persian words to be found in Moropant's Marathi is not more than 5 per cent.[2]

Śivāji as Avatāra in the Śiva-Bhārata

In the imagination of Maratha poet-patriots Śivāji was certainly a *Yugāvatāra*. In the Sanskrit epic *Śiva-Bhārata*,[3] complete as it is in thirty-two *adhyāyas*,

[1] R. R. Ergang: *Herder and the Foundations of German Nationalism* (New York, 1931); B. K. Sarkar: *From Herder to Hitler* (Calcutta, 1933).

[2] Sardesai, p. 23.

[3] Edited by S. M. Divekar with a lengthy Marathi introduction (Poona 1927); P. K. Gode: "Harikavi *alias* Bhānubhatta a Court-poet of King Sambhāji and His Works" (*Annals of the Bhandarkar Oriental Research Institute* Poona Vol. XVI, 1935).

Kavīndra Paramānanda has left no room for doubt on this point.

In the very first chapter this *Śiva-Bhārata* is described as a *purāṇamiva nūtanam*, i.e., something like a new *Purāṇa*. It is said to be known in all the worlds. The messages of *Dharamaśāstra* and *Arthaśāstra* are likewise referred to as inspiring the contents of this epic (I. 18).

In this work Śivāji has the reputation of being the protector of gods, Brāhmaṇas and cows (*devadvijagavāmgoptā*) and *durdāntayavanāntaka* (destroyer of the vehement Yavana). He is, besides, known to be an *amśa* (part) of God Viṣṇu and descended from the parts of the eight *Lokapālas*, gods of the quarters (I. 12, 15).

In chapter VI we are presented with the miracle of Śivāji's birth. He is none other than a child of God Viṣṇu himself (2-7). In order to favour the *devas* (gods) and suppress the *daityas* (evil-doers) the Lord of the worlds got himself born in the family of Bhonslas (VI, 38).

It is with the application of the six military attitudes or tactics (*ṣāḍguṇyasya prabhāvena*), we are told, that Śivāji's father Śāhāji reduced the whole of Karṇāta to submission (XI, 3). The author has a command over racy and vigorous style adapted to ballads and chronicles and has his *forte* in descriptions of wars and war-preparations. One may believe that Paramānanda had always with him Kālidāsa's *Raghuvamśa*. And as for some text book of *Nīti Śāstra*, the author was by all means familiar with its contents. At certain points the *Śiva-Bhārata* reads almost like a *nīti* treatise in motion or historic application. In the colophons it is called an *Anu-purāṇa*. We may call it a text book of applied politics in verse.

The story is given out in the form of questions from a number of *Paṇḍits* in Benares and the replies by Paramānanda. If one overlooks the interview character of this piece one will not fail to find in it the application of Kālidāsan fine frenzy to some of the objective facts of solid history. But most of this material is to be taken as pure poetry and enjoyed as such, without reference to history.

The work is said to have been composed in the lifetime of Śivāji. Nay, it is alleged to have originated in his express order to describe all his *charitra* (exploits) commencing with his grandfather Māloji (I, 36-37). But, curiously enough, the story comes down to Śivāji's conquest of Ratnāgiri (1661). Whatever be the historical basis, the work has grown into a treatise on *dharma*, *artha*, *kāma*, *mokṣa*, horses, elephants, forts and whatnot. The *Śiva-Bhārata* has turned out to be nothing short of a *Rājanīti śaśvatī*, i.e., a text of eternal politics (I, 40).

The *Śiva-Bhārata* appears to have been composed both in Tamil and Sanskrit. The Tamil text is said not to be very old.

Incidentally attention may be called to the Sanskrit *mahākāvya*, *Sambhurājacharita* (1685) by Harikavi, a Court-poet of Sambhāji. This is but another instance of the continuity and Renaissance of the Sanskritic tradition fostered by Śivāji the Great.

CHAPTER V

THE CREATIONS OF MODERN INDIA

SECTION I

INDIA TODAY AND THE EQUATIONS OF COMPARATIVE INDUSTRIALISM AND CULTURE-HISTORY

The Struggle for Equality between the East and the West

In connection with the creation of values by modern India it were well to observe at the outset that Asia has never been reconciled to the cultural and other backwardnesses in which she finds herself *visàvis* Eur-American in recent generations.[1]

The events in India, China and Persia have only served to convince leading Asians of the need for a more thorough preparedness in order to consummate the great achievement, namely, the realization under present-day conditions of the traditional equality between the East and the West. It is, therefore, as a period of long-drawn-out "mewing of might" that Asia has regarded the last few generations of her inferiority in diverse fields. Saiyad Jamaluddin of Persia, the organizer of Pan-Islam, and Kang Yu-wei, the John the Baptist of China's modernization are no greater or

[1] Consult *Congress Presidential Addresses.*

Vol. I. 1885 to 1910. (From the Foundation to the Silver Jubilee).

W. C. Bonnerji, Dadabhai Naoroji, Budruddin Tyabji, George Yule, William Wedderburn, Pherozeshah Metha, P. Ananda Charlu, W. C. Bonnerji, Dadabhai Naoroji, Alfred Webb, Surendranatha Banerjee, R. M. Sayani, C. Sankaran Nair, A. M. Bose,

less embodiments of creative reaction to Eur-American hegemony than are one and all of India's great men who have furnished for a whole century the intellectual and moral backbone of the movement which subsequently culminated in the "ideas of 1905" as well as in the industrial, scientific, literary, artistic, social and other developments since then.

The spirit of modern India is the spirit of constructive protest and assimilative challenge.[1] We may tell the story of Rammohun Roy (1772-1833) of Bengal, the first prince Ito of New Asia, of Jamshetji Tata (1839-1903), the Parsi, whose creative adventures in cotton mills, steel, hydro-electricity and industrial research have demonstrated to the world that the East is not different from the West even in modern spirit, or of Aurobindo Ghosh whose cult of service to India inspires people to "work that she may prosper and

R. C. Dutt, N. G. Chandavarkar, D. E. Wacha, Surendra Nath Banerjee, Lal Mohan Ghosh, Henry Cotton, G. K. Gokhale (1905), Dadabhai Naoroji (1906), Rash Behari Ghose (Surat), Rash Behari Ghose (Madras), Pandit Madan Mohan Malaviya, William Wedderburn.

Vol. II. 1911 to 1934. (From the Silver to the Golden Jubilee) Bishan Narayan Dhar, R. N. Mudholkar, Syed Mohammed, Bupendranath Basu, Satyendra Prasanna Sinha, Ambica Charan Mazumdar, Annie Besant, Madan Mohan Malaviya, Motilal Nehru, C. Vijayaraghavachariar, Ajmal Khan, Chittaranjan Das, Mohamed Ali, Gandhi, Sarojini Naidu, Srinivasa Iyengar, M. A. Ansari, Motilal Nehru, Jawaharlal Nehru, Vallabhai Patel, Rajendra Prasad. (Madras, 1935).

[1] Consult *Indian Nation Builders Series* (Madras), *Speeches of Dr. Rash Behary Ghose* (Calcutta 1915), A. C. Mazumdar: *Indian National Evolution* (Madras 1916), Lajpat Rai: *Young India* (New York 1918); S. N. Banerjee: *A Nation in Making* (London 1926); B. C. Pal: *Madras Speeches* 1907 (Madras), and *Memoirs of My Life Time* (Calcutta 1932); B. K. Sarkar: *Greetings to Young India* (Calcutta, 1927) and "Chittaranjan Das and Young Asia" in the *Political Philosophies Since* 1905 (Madras 1928).

suffer that she may rejoice" (1907), and Mohandas Karamchand Gandhi of Gujarat, in whose tactics of *Satyāgraha* (devotion to truth) or passive resistance the leaders of the world are discovering the pragmatic methodology of all weaker races and classes. The topic may be the biography of Syed Ahmad Khan (1817-1893) of the United Provinces, the energizer of Indian Islam, of Dadabhai Naoroji (1821-1917), the Parsi, who rediscovered *Svarāj* (self-determination) from ancient and medieval (e.g. Maratha) polity as the inspiring goal of modern India, of Bal Gangadhar Tilak (1856-1920) of the Deccan, who furnished Indian patriots with their moral philosophy by championing the "categorical imperative" of the *Gītā* (the Bible of mystical energism) for all and sundry, or of Lajpat Rai (1865-1928) of the Punjab, who has sought in Urdu to assimilate for his countrymen all the progressive elements in modern thought. Or, again, the story may have to do with Surendra Nath Banerjee (1848-1925), the indefatigable agitator in the interest of the people's constitutional and civic advance, Bipin Chandra Pal (1857-1932), the philosophical organizer of the "ideas of 1905", Chitta Ranjan Das (1870-1925), the stern realist who in order to promote the service of political ideals manufactured a party, or Asutosh Mookerjee (1864-1924), whose educational endeavours were impregnated with the ambition of establishing India's equality with the creators of modern civilisation. In every instance,—Bengali, Punjabi, Maratha, Gujarati, Hindu or Moslem,—it is the story of invincible will, of self-assertion and pride, and of competitive intelligence. And these features are but naturally to be expected of persons nurtured in the traditions of Tipu Sultan (*c* 1795), the Moslem monarch of Mysore, and Śivāji the Great (*c* 1674), the Frederick the Great of the Hindus, to mention two of the most patriotic personalities of creative India in somewhat recent times.

If some of modern India's great men have claims to be remembered more in the social, religious and literary fields than in the political, the spirit of self-conscious challenge and co-operative competition is none the less characteristic of their message and life-work. Consider, for example, Dayananda (1824-1893) with his militant call to Vedic spirituality and morals as well as declaration of war against the imperialistic and chauvinistic missionaries from Eur-America, and Vivekananda (1862-1902) with his gospel of *Upaniṣadic* manhood and world-conquest in triumphant defiance of the dehumanizing conditions of life. Consider, too, Kali Charan Banerji (1847-1902), the seer of an "Indian Christianity" emancipated from foreign ecclesiastical control. And Rabindranath Tagore, also, notwithstanding his occasional neo-Platonic public utterances, is in the deeper estimation of his countrymen but the singer of songs and writer of essays which are filled, like those of Whitman and Shelley, with the spirit of resistance against the tyranny of "defeatism" and "inferiority-complex" on the one hand and of colonialism and "white man's burthen" on the other.

In every phase of life in India today, political or cultural, economic or artistic, everybody who is anybody is a fighter, a fighter against some social obscurantism, whether Hindu or Moslem, some alien chauvinism, some vassalage in art, some industrial thraldom or some subjection in scientific, sociological, economic and philosophical theory. It is in such fights that the emancipation of his soul lies. Verily, today as ever in the past *śakti*, energy or force, is the very deity of creative India's men and women. And this energism (*sākti-yoga*) is but normal with the genius of the people. For, what else is Indian culture but the successful consummation of the Promethean strife, —from epoch to epoch? And of this, as the folk-mind learns it from Bhartrihari's (*c* 800) *Nītiśataka* (Century of Verses on Morals, stanza 80), the most typical landmark is bodied forth in the cosmic struggle of the gods for the acquisition of nectar, *amrita* (immortality or deathlessness).

Current Tendencies in Indian Life and Thought

With the new Government of India Act (1935) we are at the threshold of a cultural and social reconstruction.[1] The contributions made by Indian scholars in recent years to the diverse branches of science and learning should encourage us to invest more of our idealism, energy and resources in research and investigation. Attention may be drawn, among other things, to the growing number of publications, for instance, by Indian medical practitioners and researchers in the *British Medical Journal*, the *Lancet*, the *Transactions of the Royal Society of Tropical Medicine and Hygiene* and other European and American Journals. We cannot ignore in this connection the fact that journals like the *Indian Medical Gazette*, the *Indian Journal of Medical Research*, the *Journal of the Indian Medical Association* etc. indicate the large amount of original work in medical sciences for which Indian talent is responsible.

This is a new sign of the times, the spirit of research

[1] For political topics, not discussed in the present work, see B. G. Sapre: *The Growth of Indian Constitution and Administration* (Sangli, 1924), G. N. Singh: *Landmarks in Indian Constitutional and National Development* (1600-1919) Benares, 1933, and A. B. Keith: *Constitutional History of India* (1600-1935), Landon, 1936.

among Indian scholars. Even a few years ago Indians were hardly known in the world of modern culture as original thinkers and contributors. To-day, we find that every year there is some Indian author or artist,—man of science, philosophy or antiquities,—who is visiting Europe, America and Japan and taking part in teaching, lecturing or discussion at first class institutes of learning or in international congresses. The scholars of India are at present making a mark in all sciences from anthropology to zoology. This fact is to be stressed not only as an item of inspiration to the younger generation of our men and women, but also as a piece of solid information for our elders, the educators, statesmen and publicists, nay, for the larger world in Asia as well as Eur-America.

The world today is being enriched by India's creative work in the arts and sciences. The world is becoming more and more dependent on India's brains and exertions. India's claims to the world's recognition are thereby getting more and more justified. What India needs today is a more systematic and strenuous pursuit of the paths that she has been following. The post-graduate studies in Indian Universities have vindicated themselves. It is time to render them more efficient and heighten their standard. Nor is it less important to think of making them accessible to larger classes of students. Higher education ought not to remain a mere luxury of the well-to-do. India will have to find the means in order to democratize it as much as possible, both from the economic standpoint as well as from that of the diverse races.

We must not in any case minimize the progress that has already been achieved in India. The horizon of the Indian *intelligentsia* has been widened by the all-India Congresses and Conferences of the University men, such as are being held at different academic centres in regular succession. The work of the Inter-University Board as an agency in what may be described as "rationalization" in Indian academic life has also been noteworthy. A more direct and continuous contact between the different limbs of the Indian academic organism should now be attempted, for instance, by the regular exchange of students between Mysore and Lahore, Calcutta and Bombay, Osmania and Benares, Aligarh and Madras. The exchange of professors also between the diverse academic regions has been a desideratum for quite a long time.

The exchange may likewise be attempted with centres outside the Indian lands and waters. The British students who came out on debating tours were met on friendly terms by Indian students. The movement deserves careful and scientific nursing from the Indian side. In Germany and Italy organizations of high academic rank—e.g., the *Deutsche Akademie* (Munich) and *Istituto Italiano per il Medio ed Estremo Oriente* (Rome)—have been established with the object of coming into direct cultural and educational intercourse with the Indian seats of learning. The academic bodies of India ought to treat these friendly gestures from overseas as another new sign of the times and come forward to co-operate with the continental and other foreign Universities and academic bodies by returning in some suitable manner the courtesies offered by the latter to Indian professors and students. Thanks to the system of Readership lectures the University of Calcutta is in a position to invite almost every year eminent scholars from abroad for short public courses. But perhaps something more effective than these public lectures will have to be promoted in the near future in the interest of a really substantial impact on Indian scholarship from foreign sources.

While dealing with the subject of academic reconstruction let us touch on an important branch of discipline which has become well-established in recent years. We are thinking of "indology". For a long time indology has meant in India as in Europe and America,—and indeed in India because of the tradition in the Western world—the cultivation of *ancient* Sanskrit, Prakrit and Pali as well as Arabic and Persian. Modernists cannot afford to permit this interpretation of indology to continue in the future. It is certainly desirable that the philological, literary and cultural study of old documents in these languages should advance. One will, besides, have to admit that the researches about ancient and medieval India based on the evidences of these Oriental languages have constituted a special feature of Indian scholarship in recent years. But this interpretation of indology as a study exclusively of ancient things should not be allowed to persist for any length of time.

Indology must include the studies and researches into modern India also and therefore into modern Indian languages as well. The claims of the modern Indian languages, Bengali, Hindi, Urdu, Marathi, Gujarati, Tamil, Telugu, Kanarese and Malayalam should not be treated as of secondary importance in philological, historical or sociological studies. Modern and contemporary India deserves to be studied with at least as much enthusiasm and as much literary and linguistic equipment as ancient and medieval India. And from this standpoint it is necessary and desirable to cultivate a new orientation to the modern Indian languages. We should organize ourselves to utilize the modern languages of India as indispensable aids to every research about the economic, social, political and cultural developments of modern India. The Department of Indian Vernaculars at the Calcutta University has made important contributions in this field. Anthropology, literature, sociology and modern history are being enriched on account of the contacts of specialists with the researchers in the Indian vernaculars. But the work has to be conducted in a more conscious and systematic manner.

We should not ignore the very important consideration in this connection, namely, that the Bengali language is going to be made the medium of instruction at the Matriculation of the Calcutta University, as Urdu has always been at the Osmania. This is the result of a long-standing nationalist agitation since the National Education Movement in Bengal associated with the "ideas of 1905". It is a move in the right direction and deserves to be followed up everywhere. But what we are pleading for the vernaculars at the present moment is a more extensive appreciation by scholars in all fields bearing on modern India of the importance to be attached to the languages and literatures of today as the sources of information about the varied phases of contemporary life.

In regard to the physique of the rising generations as well as the promotion of hygienic habits the schools and colleges have been playing an important rôle. We need not be believers in the now very popular feats of muscular demonstration as examples of gymnastic prodigy. Such exhibitions of physical strength and endurance may have a scenic value and will always be enjoyed by people who want spectacular shows. Be it observed, however, that the interest in physical health and vigour has taken a different turn also. There is throughout India today a remarkable emergence of enthusiasm for physical training in the interest of health and efficiency. The people as well as the Government have been exhibiting their keenness on this health movement. Sports and games, football, cricket, hockey, tennis, long distance excursions on foot, cycling and motoring, swimming and rowing have been taken up by young men in right earnest. The University of Calcutta maintains a Student Welfare Department where the health and physical stamina of young intellectuals are attended to in a scientific manner. All this indicates that what is known as the "youth movement" in Europe is also represented in India although on a very modest scale.

While dealing with the new forces in the life and habits of Young India we cannot refrain from referring to a very important item in the social life of the young academicians. We are speaking of their great delight in amateur theatrical performances. School and college functions, especially in Bengal, are invariably attended with these plays, very often improvised for the occasion. These exercises of the youngsters in music and play have proved to be not only genuine sources of recreation and entertainment but valuable assets in the literary and artistic life of the Bengali people.

Altogether, one should have to admit that India has been advancing along right lines. Only, the rate of our advance requires to be quickened. And our national endeavours should be directed towards rendering all this advance as universal and country-wide as possible. Of late the Muslims have been putting forth laudable efforts to assimilate modern science and culture on a somewhat mentionable scale. The measures in behalf of the depressed classes in order to raise them to a higher cultural, economic and political status are also to be appreciated as activities calculated to bring the most diverse sections of the Indian people within a common orbit of progressive and liberal tendencies. Our aim should always be in the direction of helping forward the democratization of learning, culture and efficiency among all our races, tribes, castes, religions and regions. It should be a part of Indian political statesmanship also to hasten the progress of India along these lines of race-uplift and caste-uplift.

Technocracy and Capitalism in India[1]

As long as unemployment stares the "middle classes" in the face and economic depression continues to dominate India and the rest of the world it would be unreasonable to be too optimistic in the volume that is being prepared in 1935. But luckily the world-economic depression has commenced retreating inch by inch. It is gratifying to have to observe that in the process of reconstruction the Ottawa Agreement has already exhibited the potentialities of a beneficial agency.

There were misgivings in many quarters, both

[1] See the present author's "Die Industrialisierung Indiens" (V. D. I. *Nachrichten*, Berlin, 1924), *Economic Development* (Madras, 1926), "Aspetti *e* Problemi della Moderna Economia Indiana" (*Annali di Economia*, Milan, 1930), *Die Entwicklung und weltwirtschaftilche Bedeutung des modernen Indien* (Stuttgart, 1931), *Applied Economics* Vol. I. (Calcutta, 1932), *Nayā Bānglār Goḍā Pattan* (The Foundations of a New Bengal), Calcutta, 2 vols. (1932), *Indian Currency and Reserve Bank Problems* (Calcutta, 1934), *Imperial Preference visàvis World-Economy* (Calcutta, 1934), *Bāḍtir Pathe Bāānglī* (Bengalis in Progress), 1934, *Social Insurance Legislation and Statistics* (Calcutta, 1936), see also the footnote on p. 427.

theoretical and commercial. But the facts and figures have made it clear that the Imperial preferences have not proved detrimental to any Indian industry. The fact that the industrialization of India, which we take delight in describing as the *Swadeshi* Movement, is not likely to be hampered as a consequence of the Ottawa Agreement should prove to be a source of great encouragement to many. No less important is the consideration that the prices of goods have not risen on account of this arrangement. We understand, further, that the Indian revenues have not been adversely affected. The most valuable consideration from certain standpoints is perhaps the conclusion that the exports of India have a chance of steady expansion. This means that the agricultural classes of the diverse parts of India can look forward to a period of relative prosperity.

In the atmosphere of intellectuals we are indeed interested chiefly in the propagation of knowledge and the promotion of research as well as originality and leadership among scholars. But we cannot be blind to the measures such as are expected to add to the purchasing power of India's peasants and improve, however slightly, their standard of living.

The interests of cultivators lie nearest to the hearts not only of the people and publicists but also of the Government of India and the Indian princes and administrators throughout the Indian sub-continent. All constructive nationalists and patriotic social servants are fully aware of this. We should like to suggest that the problems of cultivators and agricultural indebtedness ought to demand the serious attention of the academic bodies, professors and students alike. The progress of co-operative credit societies is well-known. But it is only short period credits that can be offered by the co-operative credit societies as constituted at present. In order that agricultural improvements may be taken in hand, especially such as involve a good few years,—what the cultivators require in the line of finance is a long-period credit. It is time that the co-operative departments throughout India expand their functions by taking up the problems of long and intermediate credits. In France the co-operative system is elaborately developed. French agriculturists do not have to remain content with mere short-period credits. They can get loans for ten years. The period may be extended to twenty-five years also. It is to be doubted, however, whether such radical expansions of the co-operative credit system will be feasible in India at the present stage.

It is, however, noteworthy that the Governments in India have been initiating a new type of bank for cultivators, namely, the hypothec or land mortgage banks. These were badly needed. It is on the security of land mortgaged by the landholders or tenants that credit can be offered by the land mortgage banks. As a rule, fifty to sixty per cent of the value of the land can be rendered available to the borrower. He becomes also a shareholder of the bank by buying a number of shares. And in order to furnish themselves with money the land mortgage banks can issue debentures, generally twenty times the value of the share capital. The experiences of the Federal Farm Loan system of the U. S. A. as well as of the Hypothec Bank of Japan ought to be very instructive in this regard.

In this connection the establishment of the Reserve Bank should prove to be beneficial to cultivators. India has fought quite a strenuous fight over this institution. But now that this central bank has become a reality it is to be trusted that a strong foundation of economic stability and financial rationalization will be furnished thereby. As the ordinary functions of commercial banks lie outside the scope of this institution the currency and credit problems of India may be expected to be cared for in a sound manner. India has at last initiated an institution which, like the Bank of England, the mother of central banks throughout the world, or like the *Reichsbank* of Germany which in the midst of political vicissitudes has continued to function according to strict banking principles, will serve to place the financial and economic structure of India on autonomous, up-to-date and advanced lines. While admitting all this we should not fail to impress upon our scholars and publicists the importance of looking upon the Reserve Bank through the agriculturist's eyes. It should be the concern of the public men, economic experts and directors to utilize this instrument in such a manner that substantial loans and grants at favourable rates may be rendered available for the co-operative credit societies and land mortgage banks, etc. such as are directly interested in the welfare of cultivators.

Villages, peasants, handicrafts and cottage industries constitute indeed the dominant feature of Indian economic and social life,—even in 1935. But Indian statesmen and economists cannot afford to ignore or belittle the immense growth of large and medium industries as well as the concentration of men and women in towns such as characterize the Indian society of today. Machines, industrialization, factories as well as urbanization, expansion of cities etc., in other words, technocracy as well as capitalism have come to stay. The Indian *intelligentsia* cannot therefore fight shy of the problems of industrialism and city life. It would not do in season and out of season to idealize the virtues of village life and the blessings of agricultural civilization. The atmosphere of academic teaching and research and cultural life generally will have to be adequately adapted to the new conditions of the social environment and economic organization.

The problems of the industrial worker, the colliery labourer, the railway man, the plantation cooly and the factory hand ought to be implanted in the intellectual and moral consciousness of the world of culture. At the Tenth All-India Medical Conference held at Bombay in December 1933, the Central Council of Indian Medical Assocation in collaboration with the Standing Committee of the All-India Medical Licentiates' Association has drawn up a scheme of national health insurance on the lines of similar schemes in Germany, Great Britain and other countries. The subject is bound sooner or later to acquire prominence in the economic life as well as legislative activity of India. This is a field in which the medical man, the lawyer, the economist, the sociologist, and the social service worker like the members of the Ramakrishna Mission, can all work together on a common platform harnessed to the promotion of national efficiency and welfare.

Just at present India does not possess anything in this line more substantial than the Maternity Benefit Acts of Bombay and the Central Provinces. In regard to the vital questions bearing on the labourer's safety the Workmen's Compensation Act, especially in its enlarged form, bids fair to be an important landmark in Indian social legislation. But altogether the entire subject of labour protection, including the protection of female and child labour, in

India demands careful thinking over both from the points of view of the employee and the employer.

No topic should deserve more attention in Indian public life as a subject for research than the question of social assurance. The League of Nations has been serving as the friend of all and sundry by issuing valuable publications on the diverse branches of assurance as applicable to the working classes. A part of the idealism and research activities of the Indian *intelligentsia* ought certainly to be directed to the analysis and assimilation of the fine documents published by the League.

In connection with the labour problems and labour economics the Servants of India Society established by G. K. Gokhale at Poona (1905) has been functioning as an important centre of investigations. Under N. M. Joshi's guidance Bombay, nay, all India is today furnished with expert counsel in regard to labour legislation and movement.[1]

[1] *Statistical Abstract for British India*, *Large Industrial Establishments in India*, *Joint Stock Companies in British India and Indian States*, *Review of Agricultural Operations in India*, *Annual Reports of the Chief Inspector of Mines*, *Reports of the Controller of Currency*, *Indian Insurance Year-Book*, *Statistical Tables relating to Banks in India*, *Bombay Labour Gazette*,—all Government publications.

Consult M. G. Ranade: *Essays in Indian Economics* (1898-1906), R. C. Dutt: *Economic History of British India* (1901-03) D. Naoroji: *Poverty and Un-British Rule in British India*, 1901, S. C. Mukerjee: "Principles of the Swadeshi Movement" (*The Dawn*, Calcutta, 1905), D. E. Wacha: *Life and work of J. N. Tata* (1918), L. Fraser: *Iron and Steel in India* (1919), L. Rai: *England's Debt to India* (1920), R. K. Das: *Labour Movement in India* (1923), J. C. Coyajee: *India's Fiscal Problems* (1924) and *Indian Currency System* (1931), D. R. Gadgil: *The Industrial Evolution of India in Recent Times* (1924), P. P. Pillai: *Economic Conditions in India* (1925), P. A. Wadia and G. N. Joshi: *Money and the Money Market in India* (1926), Vakil and Muranjan: *Currency and Prices in India* (1927), Mehta and Subbaya: *The Co-operative Movement*

It would not be correct either to describe India as a purely agricultural sub-continent or to forecast her future sustaining power exclusively on the strength of her mechanical and biological progress in agriculture.[1] Slowly but steadily India has been growing into an industrial region also. In 1913-14 the total production of cotton piece goods in Indian mills was 1,164,300,000 yards. In 1933-34 it was 2,945,000,000 yards. The increase was 153 per cent in twenty years. During the same period the censused population rose from 315 millions to 352 millions only.

Even during the so-called depression period

in India (1927), S. C. Ghosh: *The Organization of Railways* (1927), B. Narain: *Eighty Years of Punjab Food Prices* (1927), L. C. Jain: *Indigenous Banking in India* (1929), K. T. Shah: *Federal Finance in India* (1929), B. Sanyal: *Development of Indian Railways* (1930), J. Hasan: "The Labourers and the Problem of the Standard of Living in India" (*Indian Journal of Economics*, (1932), V. G. Kale: *India's National Finance Since* 1921 (1932), R. K. Mukerjee: *Land Problems of India* (1933), S. C. Dutt: *Conflicting Tendencies in Indian Economic Thought* (1934). See also the footnote on p. 422 for the works by B. K. Sarkar.

Attention is likewise invited to the following papers at the *Bangiya Dhana-Vijnan Parjshat* (Bengali Institute of Economics): S. C. Dutt: "Colliery Labourers" and "Cottage Industries" *vs.* "Large scale production"; S. K. Dey: "The Cotton Tariff" and "India in International Trade"; K. C. Bose: "The Earnings and Expenses of Indian Workingmen"; G. C. Roy: "Forecasting Business Expansion"; R. K. Datta-Roy: "New Uses of Bengal Coal" (*Advance*, Calcutta, March 29, 1934); P. K. Mukerjee: "Indian Women Workers" (*Forward*, Calcutta, February 8, 1935); R. N. Ghose : "Indian Price Movements during Depression" (*Amrita Bazar Patrika*, May 24, 1935). See the volumes of *Arthik Unnati* (Economic progress), the monthly, for 1926-36.

[1] *Review of the Trade of India* 1928-29 (Calcutta) pp. 150, 151, 200-203, 1933-34 (Delhi), pp. 98, 179, 228-231, *Budget for* 1934-35 (Delhi, 1934) pp. 39, 230-231; *Census of India* 1931 Vol. I. Part I. (Delhi 1933) pp. 5, 37, 55-59.

(since 1929) the indices of industrialization in India have been quite noteworthy. With 1928=100 the index of production in the cotton mills of India rose to 141 in October 1933. In the output of steel the index rose during the same period to 175. It is worth while to observe that at the present moment (October 1936) a number of new steel mills is nearing completion or under project. The total capacity of steel output in India is likely to be just the double of the present in a few years, rising up to, say, a million tons.

In 1913-14 India imported iron and steel goods to the extent of 1,018,000 tons. The *quantum* of these imports rose to 1,169,000 tons in the pre-depression year. The pre-War average of imports in the line of *Produktionsmittel* (means or instruments of production), namely, machinery, mill work etc. was valued at Rs. 56,114,000. In the pre-depression year the value of this class of imports, calculated as it is to promote industrialization, rose to Rs.183,604,000.

In the pre-War year (1913-14) the export of "manufactures" from India constituted 23 per cent of her total exports. In 1933-34, i.e., at the end of the so-called depression period it was 27.2 per cent. The growth of India as a manufacturing or industrialized region is self-evident.

During the last few years India has been absorbing larger and larger quantities of metal, hardware, motor cars etc. The increasing trends in industrialization are marked features of the depression period. The production of electric lamps and all kinds of electrical apparatuses, rubber tyres, water softening plant, cooking stoves, asbestos, cement products, paints, enamels etc. as well as railway rolling stock, bridge work and other heavy structures points likewise to the expansion of industrialism. Last but not least ought to be mentioned the fact that the whole of the sugar that India used to import from Java is now being produced in Indian mills.

The spirit of Tata is abroad and Tataism has come to stay. The "tonic of machinery" has commenced functioning in no unmistakable manner. Today the Indian people is not only importing and consuming tools, implements, machineries etc. as, say, previous to the war of 1914-18 but is actually manufacturing them at home. The production of the *Produktionsmittel* is a mentionable feature in the industrial economy and technocracy of creative India at the present moment. The review for the year 1934-35 enables us to understand that industrial and domestic utility machinery such as litho-printing machines, paper perforators, tablet making machines, pulverizers, sewing machines, sanitary equipment, hospital requisites etc. are being manufactured in India.

The progress of industrialization can be watched even in regions like Bengal which in the main is known to be agricultural in economic morphology. While one watches the expansion and improvements of the metropolis, Calcutta, one should not ignore the economic and social changes that have come upon Japlaiguri, Serajganj, Narayanganj, Kharagpur, Chittagong, and other areas. During the last quarter of a century all these places have grown considerably, first, as "ports", secondly, as industrial centres, and thirdly, as commercial emporia for agricultural produce and manufactured goods. This growth has made itself felt in the houses, roads, water-works, schools, hospitals, motor conveyance, engineering repair-stations, etc. of the *Mofussil.* These items indicate not only transformations in the economic and social conditions of the people but at the same time some rise in the standard of living of the peasants and "middle classes". The rate of this rise is certainly not high but it is perceptible.

One of the main factors in the industrialization of Bengal is the jute crop. Bengal has naturally grown in acreage under jute. But the rate of expansion in jute *manufacture* has been higher than that of expansion in jute *cultivation*. And in foreign countries Bengal is known no less as an exporter of manufactured jute than of raw jute.

The expansion of capitalism is manifest in the amount of transactions conducted by the banking institutions including the saving banks as well as the "individual bankers". The progress of the insurance companies also during the last three decades furnishes another testimony to the growth of capital available for investment. In both these instances we have to visualize institutions run not only by foreigners but by Indians as well.

It is possible to discover some changes in the social structure such as have been generated on account of the progress of capitalism especially in and through the insurance companies. Today in every province of India there are in evidence thousands of insurance agents, and they constitute a class by themselves in the occupational morphology of the sub-continent. Like the *zamindars* (landholders)[1] who owe their status and position to the political revolution of the latter half of the eighteenth century ("permanent settlement", 1793), and the lawyer-schoolmaster-medical doctor group that has come into prominence on account of the cultural revolution and modernization movements

[1] P. K. Mukerjee: *The Economic Services of Zamindars to the Peasants and the Public as analyzed by Benoy Sarkar* (Calcutta, 1934).

of the middle of the nineteenth century (Calcutta University, 1856), the insurance agents embody the processes and consequences of the industrial revolution or transformation that has been going on in the twentieth-century.

As a new socio-economic group or professional class the insurance agents, in so far as the life branch is concerned, have succeeded in popularizing among the Hindus, and to a certain extent among the Mussalmans the idea of making provision for widows, orphans and old age. Their services in this regard have amounted in practical life to more than what tons of literature on social reform could produce in India during the last century.

Indian Economy visàvis West-European Economy

Notwithstanding the divergences of latitude and longitude and notwithstanding the differences in the make-up of the blood among the different races, anthropology as well as modern and contemporary history furnish us with what may be described as equations or identities and at any rate similarities in the ideals as well as technical and other attainments of the historic nations of the world.

It is necessary at this stage to invite the attention of scholars to some of these equations in the field of economic life and civilization. In the place of the traditional ideas regarding racial and geographical differences in the so-called types of culture we are presented with differences or distances in time only. The fundamental features of civilization, pragmatically considered, are found to be the same in the different peoples. It is only proceeding step by step or rather stage by stage from epoch to epoch: the differences between the peoples are in the main but differences in the stage or epoch. The equations that are being established here reveal but the distinctions between earlier and later, go-ahead and slow peoples. *More or less* the same features are appearing today in one race or region, tomorrow in a second, and the day after tomorrow in a third.

The "curves" of life in economic or political theory and practice as manifest in the modern East are more or less similar to those in the modern West. If one were to plot out these curves diagrammatically one would notice that the Asian series ran almost parallel to the Eur-American. The "trends" of evolution would appear to be nearly identical in the most significant particulars and incidents of thought and experience.

The "exactnesses" of the mathematical and "positive" sciences, are, however, not to be expected in the human and moral disciplines. But certain socio-philosophical "equations" may still be discovered in a comparative estimate of the East and West. By placing the Asian curve in the perspective of the Eur-American one might establish a number of identities for the modern period,—although, of course, not without 'buts' and 'ifs'.

But, in any case, taking Asia as a whole one would come to the conclusion that the economic, political and social philosophies and endeavours in the different regions of the Orient are mainly but repetitions of Eur-American developments in their earlier stages. The following socio-philosophical as well as economico-technocratic equations may be established on the strength of positive data:

(1) New Asia (*c* 1880-1890) = Modern Eur-America (*c* 1776-1832).

(2) Young India (*c* 1930-35) = Eur-America (*c* 1848-1870).

In the first equation, Asia comprises Turkey and Egypt, indicating that the entire Orient from Tokyo to Cairo was witnessing a technical and social transformation roughly corresponding to the remaking of the West during the epoch of the "Industrial Revolution".

The second equation has special reference to India, suggesting that Japan and Turkey as well as China, Persia and Egypt will have to be comprehended by separate, perhaps five different equations. There are likewise to be separate equations not only for Hedjaz, Palestine, Syria and Iraq but also for Afganistan which has for some time been enjoying lime-light as a somewhat serious and sincere youngster attempting the alphabet of modernism in technocracy, administration, economic life and general culture.

The modern East is about two generations behind the modern West in technocracy and socio-economic polity. New Asia is born through (1) contact with and example of modern Western progress, (2) industrialization, however slow and halting, and (3) dislike of foreign domination, intervention of concession.

The inspiration derived from the economic, political and cultural achievements of ancient and medieval Asia is another formative force in the New Orient. This "romantic" appreciation of the past is, however, intimately associated with modern historical, archaeological and anthropological scholarship. Nationalism, in so far as it is an aspect of romanticism, is ultimately to be traced, therefore, in the main to Western education such as began to bear fruit—among the pioneers of the new life and thought in Asia—between 1850 and 1886 and has been more or less democratised filtering down to the masses since then.

The process of Asia's rebirth may be said to have begun *c* 1850 and taken about one generation or so, thus:

1. Western Asia (Turkey, Egypt and Persia): 1857 (Crimean War) to 1876, 1882, 1890.

2. Southern Asia (India) : 1857 (Mutiny) to 1886.

3. Japan : 1853 (Commodore Perry) to 1867-1889.

4. China : 1842 (Nanking Treaty) to 1898.

Although modernization began to influence the Asian continent at different points more or less simultaneously during the decade from 1880 to 1890 the rate of growth for different regions since then has been different.

For instance, the distance of some fifty years that existed between Japan and Eur-America, say, about 1886, has been made up to a very considerable extent; so that for today the appropriate economico-sociological identity would perhaps be indicated by the following equation :

Japan (*c* 1930-35) = Eur-America (*c* 1910). That is, while India continues still to be some two generations or so behind the modern West in industrialism, constitution, social legislation etc. and the allied philosophies,—the distance that existed during the decade 1880-1890,—Japan has succeeded in "catching up to" the go-aheads by more than a generation. And to that extent Japan today is ahead of contemporary India.

It is not the place here to go into details about

the technocratic and economic transformations of the world. But these transformations may be indicated in four successive periods beginning with the new conquests of technocracy in which England commenced pioneering the world about 1760-85. The following scheme exhibits the West-European Economy and the Indian Economy in four periods of transformation, which however, from the nature of the case cannot be synchronous or identical. In regard to West-European Economy the British-German equations are being shown for each of these periods. The French equations with Germany or with England are being given for the first two periods only. In regard to India it is the equations with Germany as a "relatively late" comer and with England as the pioneer in the domain of technocracy and industrial revolution that are chiefly pointed out while the relations with France are indicated only incidentally. It is to be observed that the categories, "industrialization", "first industrial revolution", and "second industrial revolution" have reference to the different degrees in the intensity and extensity of the socio-economic transformation as measured by *per capita* or per sq. mile values. In any case they are vague and sociologically anything but definite. International statistics, besides, are very incomplete and very uncomparable, and therefore must not be made too much of. And yet some amount of precision for general purposes can be obtained,—provided we take care to guard ourselves against the monistic economic determinism of Karl Marx,—from an examination of the equations of comparative industrialism as tabled below:[1]

[1] In no instance should the equation be treated as possessing more than the value of "nearest approaches" or "approximate similarities", cf. H. Hauser: *Les Débuts du Capitalisme* (Paris,

West-European Economy	*Indian Economy*
I	I
1785-1830	1793-1853
"Industrial Revolution" is consummated in England. The age of technocracy commences its career. But France and Germany (1830) = England (1800).	From the Permanent Settlement in Bengal to the first cotton mill in Bombay. "Commercial Revolution" in India on account of contacts with Europe through England. No new "industries." India (1853) = England (1785) = almost France (1830) = almost Germany (1830).
II	II
1830-70	1854-85
"Industrial Revolution" progresses in France and somewhat later in Germany. But Germany (1870) = England (1830-48). Rising birth-rate in the West-European economy (1841-80).	"Industrialization" (but not industrial revolution) commences slowly and in a weak manner. India (1885) = France (1848) = Germany (1848) = England (1815).
III	III
1870-1905	1886-1905
In technocracy Germany catches up to England. Germany (1905) = England (1905). The epoch of "world-economy" in its most pronounced phases commences with the opening of the Suez Canal (1869).	"Industrialization" continues at a slow rate. The Indian *intelligentsia* is growing self-conscious and seeks to achieve a veritable "Industrial Revolution." The economic sentiments of the Indian National Congress (1885) lead upto the Swaraj-Boycott-Swadeshi complex (1905).

1931), pp. 42-44, 309-323, where the terms "industry", "industrial revolution", "capitalism" etc. have been subjected to careful sociological criticism. The strength and weakness of the economic interpretation of history have been examined at length in R. Michels: *Corso di Sociologia Politica* (Milan, 1927), pp. 15-17, 47-52, 81-85.

The decline commences in the birth-rate (1881-90).	India (1905) = Germany (1850-60) = England (1830) Rising birth-rate in India (1881-1910).
IV 1905-35	IV 1905-35
The "second" Industrial Revolution progresses in Germany, England, (the U. S. A. and some other countries). "Rationalization" and Technocracy paramount. The epoch of world-economy is intensified among other factors by the opening of the Panama Canal (1915). The decline in the birth-rate continues.	Industrialization somewhat accentuated on account of the Swadeshi-Movement and the Great War (1914-18) and yet hardly constitutes an "industrial revolution" in terms of *per capita* or per sq. mile values. In technocracy India (1935) = Germany (1865-75) = England (1848). The decline in the birth-rate commences (1910-20).

In the above *tableau économique* the processes of transformation are identical on both sides, the West-European and the Indian. The chronological backwardness of certain regions in the West-European economy in relation to England the pioneer is quite clear. Equally clear also is the chronological backwardness of economic India in relation not only to England but to the West-European economy as a whole. In technocracy India at 1905, i.e., when the *Swadeshi* Movement commences is about 45-55 years behind Germany and about 75 years behind England. The general economic and social conditions of the Indian people, as well as their material standard of life and efficiency are at this time on more or less the same level,—allowing for the differences in climate and manners,—as in these West-European countries between 1830 and 1860. There is nothing extra-ordinary, therefore, that the birth-rate tendencies, namely in the direction of ascent, which prevailed in these regions in those earlier years should manifest themselves along general lines in the Indian economy during this later period (1886-1910). It is under the more or less identical conditions of "temperature and pressure," to use a phrase from physics, that the more or less identical birth-phenomena namely, the rising birth-rates have taken place. Only the periods of time during which the conditions have developed are some three decades apart from each other, the third period of the Indian Economy corresponding with the second period of the West-European.

The next phase in both these economies is a declining birth-rate. The decline commences in the West-European in the third period but in the Indian in the fourth period. This decline, is however, quite a curious phenomenon.

The third and fourth periods of the West-European Economy are, if any thing, but continuations of the previous two periods in technocracy, industrial revolution etc. We have here indeed the beginning of real "world-economy" and what may be called the "second" industrial revolution, altogether an expansion and intensification of the economic prosperity which commenced about 1760-1830. And so far as the Indian Economy is concerned, the fourth period has likewise witnessed nothing but the accentuation of all the technical and financial forces which operated in the third. The progress of industrialization in India has certainly embodied itself during this period in such productive enterprises and items of consumption as sharply distinguish it from the third as moving on a higher plane. Material prosperity has grown in India as in Western Europe, although undoubtedly at different rates, in recent years.

Should the growing economic prosperity be a concomitant factor with the rising birth-rate in certain periods of West-European and Indian life-history, the birth-rate ought to continue to rise during succeeding periods which witness the continuity, nay, expansion of the economic prosperity. But the actual facts of international vital statistics happen to be the exact opposite of what is logically expected. Instead of the birth-rate rising higher or at any rate maintaining a high level with higher doses of industrialization, techno-cracy, world-economy, and material prosperity, it has actually fallen and has been going down lower and lower. And the decline is patent as much in the West-European Economy as in the Indian.[1]

India's Problems in Economic Statesmanship

Within the limitations to which all sociological equations as attempts at measuring magnitudes bearing on "un-exact" sciences are bound to be subject, it should be equally possible to indicate, for the purposes of comparative social statistics, the rates of growth in the line of modernization for different regions of Eur-America as well. The entire West is not one in industrialism, democracy or the corresponding philosophies. To take one instance, that of Germany, we should find the following equations :

(1) Germany (*c* 1870)=Great Britain (*c* 1830-48),

[1] The present author's "Quozienti di Natalità, di Mortalità e di Aumento Naturale nell'India Attuale nel Quadro della Demografia Comparata" in the *Proceedings of the International Congress for the Study of Population*, (Rome, 1931); "The Trend of Indian Birth Rates" (in the *Indian Journal of Economics*, Allahabad, April and July 1934); *Neu-Orientierungen in Optimum und wirtschaftlicher Leistungsfaehigkeit* (International Congress for the Study of Population Problems, Berlin, 1935), published in *Bevoelkerungsfragen* (Munich, 1936), pp. 256-267, edited by H. Harmsen and F. Lohse.

but (2) Germany (*c* 1905) = Great Britain (*c* 1905).

The first equation says that about 1870 Germany was tremendously behind Great Britain, say, by a whole generation. But by 1905, i.e., in 30 years she, first, made up the distance and, secondly, caught up to the latter. She was indeed on the point of crossing the equation-limit. The war of 1914-18 should appear socio-philosophically to be nothing more than the dramatic demonstration of this disturbance of the economico-technocratic equation or societal equilibrium in the international field.

The societal equations discussed here involve two fundamental considerations in the problem of human progress. The first has reference to the fact that during historic periods the evolution of mankind has been continuous,—although not without ups and downs, cuts and breaks. And the second invites us to note that the societal development has been in the main along uniform lines,—although not without diversities in regional and racial contexts.

For earlier periods the more or less approximate socio-philosophical identities or similarities may be roughly indicated as follows:

(1) East (down to *c* 1300) = West (down to *c* 1300) institutionally as well as ideologically.

(2) Renaissance in the East (*c* 1400-1600) = Renaissance in the West (*c* 1400-1600).

(3) *c* 1600-1750. The new physical or positive sciences in the West constitute a special feature of the European Renaissance. The Asian Renaissance produces fine arts but no new positive science worth mentioning. All the same, no genuine societal differentiations between the East and the West are perceptible as yet. We may then institute the following two equations:

(a) Asia in positive science (*c* 1600-1750) = Europe in positive science (*c* 1400-1600).

(b) Asia in socio-economic life (*c* 1600-1750) = Europe in socio-economic life (*c* 1600-1750).

(4) *c* 1750-1850. Industrial Revolution in the West creates a new civilization, the "modern world". East and West differ substantially for the first time. Thus,—Asia (*c* 1850) = Europe (*c* 1750).

About 1850 the "East" is behind the "West" by nearly a century,—in technocracy, economic institutions and general culture. (See the Table I above).

The previous stages of evolution may be left alone for the present. An analysis of economic life in the Balkans would lead to the result that Jugoslavia, Roumaina, Bulgaria, Greece, Turkey, etc. represent almost the same stages in technological evolution in which India finds herself at the present day. Almost each one of the new states that lies between the German and Russian spheres and between the Baltic Sea and the Eastern Mediterranean,—with the exception perhaps of Czechoslovakia,—is an India in miniature. Economically speaking, each of these states embodies the efforts of semi-developed and more or less chiefly agricultural peoples at imbibing the culture of the more advanced Western Europe and America. They represent the process by which Eastern Europe is tending to bid adieu finally to the lingering vestiges of the feudal-agrarian system, the mediæval economic organization and technique, which disappeared in England, the U. S., France and Germany between 1750 and 1850.

In point of industrialization, technocracy and capitalism the British, German and American standard is the highest in the world. Nearly two-thirds of the European continent are in the more or less undeveloped and mediæval conditions of Spain.[1] That is why the people of India should make it a point to study the methods and achievements of Spain and other second-rate and third-rate countries of Eur-America. It would be a wrong policy for young India always to talk of England, Germany and America while organizing industrial, literary, educational and library movements.

Modern civilization has been advancing from the West to the East. There is no region today more significant for the development of India than the Balkans, Central-Eastern Europe, the Baltic states and Russia. The problems that are being fought over and settled in these territories,—generally described as the "Balkan Complex" by the present author, are identical in many ways with the problems that await solution and are challenging the patriots, industrial experts and social workers of India.

The conclusion from an examination of the earlier stages of "modern" banking in France and Germany from the standpoint of comparative bank-statistics is equally significant with reference to the equations that are being discussed here. When one studies the European figures with special reference to Indian conditions one should suspect that in banking, as in other aspects of economic and social (perhaps also cultural) development, India has yet to commence mastering

[1] H. S. Suhrawardy: "Diversities of Spain", a lecture at the "*Āntarjātik Banga*" *Parishat* ("International Bengal" Institute), Calcutta, April 27, 1932; M. Deb-Ray: "Spain Today", a lecture at the "Malda in Calcutta" Society, July 5, 1935, reported in the *Amrita Bazar Patrika*, Calcutta, for July 12, 1935. See also the present author's *The Politics of Boundaries* (Calcutta, 1926), *Greetings to Young India* (Calcutta, 1927), and *The Political Philosophies Since 1905* (Madras, 1928).

the ideas of 1870 or thereabouts and traverse the ground covered by the moderns since then.

The cumulative effect of all these investigations may be embodied in the following futuristic equation: "Whatever has happened in the economic sphere in Eur-America during the past half-century is bound also to happen more or less on similar and even identical lines in Asia and, of course, in India during the next two generations or so." The problem before applied sociology and economic statesmanship, so far as India is concerned, consists in envisaging and hastening the working out of the "next stages" in technical progress as well as socio-economic and socio-political life.

The practical significance of the equations of applied economics as indicated here is not to be overlooked. Comparative industrialism discovers that in orientations to the "world-economy" economic India exhibits the features of an economically young, undeveloped or semi-developed people *visàvis* the industrial "adults" of the day. In the interest of economic legislation and other aids to economic development, it may perhaps be quite one's worth while in India to try to cultivate up-to-dateness in the world-statistics, world-techniques, and the world-ideals of economics. But for the more "practical" considerations of "realizable" ideals and methods of economic statesmanship India will have to devote special attention to assimilating intensively the achievements in theory and practice such as the economic adults were contributing to the world, say, a generation or two ago. It is easier for a certain number or rather a handful of intellectuals, considered as individuals, to advance "ideologically" than for an entire race or some substantially large sections of the population to grow in terms of institutions and get used to new techniques, habits and usages.

The banking situation in India today, to take an instance of current interest, can be aptly described in the words of the National Monetary Commission (1908), which sat to examine and report on the defects in the financial organization of the U. S. A. In 1911, we are told, the Americans exported about $650,000,000 in value of cotton. It was largely financed by 60 or 90 day bills drawn on Liverpool, London, Paris or Berlin. And this business was "practically all done by foreign banks or bankers." In regard to domestic trade also the American methods were "crude, expensive and unworthy an intelligent people." The Commission observed as follows:—"The man who raises cotton in Mississippi or cattle in Texas, or the farmer who raises wheat in the North-West cannot readily find a market in Chicago, New York or London for the obligations arising out of the transactions connected with the growth and movement of his products because the bankers of these cities have no knowledge of his character and responsibility."[1]

Factually, perhaps, from the standpoint of comparative development, in spite of the modest language of the Commission, the American conditions of two decades and a half ago were not literally as "crude" and "disgraceful" or "young" as the Indian conditions today. But "generically" speaking, the two conditions are similar, if not identical. And Indian bank-reformers have, therefore, more to learn of pre-war than of post-war America or the Rooseveltian "New Deal" of the hour. We should have to begin at, say, the American stage of 1908. It is to be observed, how-

[1] *Report of the National Monetary Commission* (Washington D. C.) 1912, pp. 27-29.

ever, in the interest of precision, that the American economic curve of 1908 or thereabout was already much too high, as representing quite an "adult" phenomenon,—for the Indian curve of 1930-35. Statistically, there are indeed reasons to believe that for all practical purposes, the present Indian conditions hardly register anything beyond the Western-European or American growth of the 70's of the last century. Altogether, when we in India speak of pre-War Eur-America as a general guide for our present purposes we should really have in our mind the second-half or rather the third-quarter of the nineteenth century.

That is why, with a view to the pressing requirements of Indian commerce, manufacture, agriculture, labour and economic legislation bearing on these practical aspects of life, we should often be at liberty to overlook or ignore the latest developments in the Western World. Indian studies in the twentieth-century and especially the post-War phases of Eur-American experience,—rationalization, trustification, "economic planning" etc.,—are mainly to be evaluated as academic investigations into the possiblities of mankind's economic evolution and as scientific researches into the "next stages" of the world's developments in technical and national lines. To that extent such investigations would possess indeed a dynamic value of no mean order, fraught as they are likely to be with suggestions of a practical character even for India.

On the other hand, the methods and policies of economic India today should appear to be almost akin to, nay, identical with those of the other industrial youngsters of the world,—in Southern or Eastern Europe, South America, Asia and Africa. The industrialization of India and other young regions can be appreciated at its proper worth,—technocratic, commercial, social and political,—only by those who are prepared not to overlook or minimize the importance of the "new industrial and commercial revolution" through which the adults have been passing for the last three decades, especially during and since the Great War. Once these perspectives of international economic life and the new world-order were grasped in their due proportions, it might perhaps be possible to discover the proper scientific approaches to the regulation of the economic and other conflicts between the "young ambitions" and the "vested interests."

The world-economy as patent today is the system of economic institutions and ideologies prominent since, say, 1919-20. In a concrete manner they may be said to be embodied in organizations like the League of Nations, the International Labour Office, the International Chamber of Commerce, International Cartels, "planned economy", etc. It is clear that India is already a part of this complex and willy-nilly has been trying to rise up to the methodology and technique of the new world-order. But the discrepancies lie no less on the surface. These consist in the attempts of a junior that is furnished, as it evolutionally is, with somewhat semi-medieval paraphernalia, but is compelled none the less to observe and follow the up-to-date standard of the comparatively advanced members in the society of nations. This compulsion perpetually to aim at the highest and attitudinize oneself to the *mores* and codes of the seniors may to a certain extent undoubtedly hasten the developmental processes in the junior. But the frictions due to actual maladjustment and absence of natural harmony in the economic *Realpolitik* cannot fail to be the source of internationally tragic situations. The lack of adaptation between the economics of youngsters and those of the adults constitutes the greatest stumbling block, technically considered, to international concord in the epoch of world-economy.[1]

SECTION 2

FROM RAMMOHUN TO GANDHI: THE QUEST OF WORLD-FORCES AND NATIONALISM

The Realism of Rammohun

The literary work of Rammohun Roy (1772-1833) belongs to the second and third decades of the nineteenth century. He is different from both Bālambhatta and Jagannātha in so far as although they came into contact with British scholars, jurists or administrators neither was a student of Western legal or social institutions. Rammohun was born almost at the time when Warren Hastings got the *Vivādārṇavasetu* compiled by several Pandits (1773), translated into Persian and then rendered from Persian into English as Halhed's *Gentoo Code* (1774). His early years were passed during the period of the expansion of Western administration in India. We may recall that the Asiatic Society of Bengal was founded in 1784 and the College of Fort William established at Calcutta with Carey as Principal in 1800.

He was experiencing the new all the time. And if he still appreciated the old it was because of its innate strength and utility. Besides, while Bālambhatta and Jagannātha wrote in Sanskrit, Rammohun wrote

[1] See the discussion on the relations between the "second" and the "first" industrial revolutions,—the "adults" and the "youngsters"—in connection with the analysis of the world-economic depression in the present author's *Applied Economics* (Calcutta), Vol. I. (1932); cf. also his *Pressure of Labour upon Constitution and Law 1776-1928* (Benares 1928).

in Persian, Bengali and English, and very little in Sanskrit. Last but not least, so far as the present times are concerned, he was convinced (1) of the greater utility of the modern knowledge, i.e., the culture developed in Europe since the appearance of Baconian[1] philosophy—"mathematics, natural philosophy, chemistry, anatomy and other useful sciences"—than of the Hindu *Vyākaraṇa*, *Vedānta*, *Mīmāṃsā* and *Nyāya* and (2) of the English language than of the Sanskrit as a medium of instruction and culture. To him Bacon was a veritable *Yugāvatāra* for Europe and for mankind, and the entire Hindu culture similar in value to the pre-Baconian achievements of Europe. It is the post-Baconian arts and sciences that he wanted to see introduced in India under British auspices. All this, of course, had been *ultima thule* to Bālambhatta and Jagannātha.

"During the last twenty years", says Rammohun[2] "a body of English gentlemen who are called missionaries, have been publicly endeavouring in several ways to convert Hindus and Mussulmans of this country into Christianity". One of the methods of the missionaries is described as that of distributing among the people various books, large and small, reviling both Hinduism and Islam, as well as of abusing and ridiculing the gods and saints of the former.

This attitude of the English missionaries is subjected by Rammohun to strong criticism, and here

[1] *A Letter on English Education* (Calcutta, 1823); *The English Works of Raja Rammohun Roy* (Panini Office, Allahabad, 1906) pp. 471-474.

[2] *The Brahmunical Magazine* (or the Missionary and the Brahman), being a Vindication of the Hindoo Religion against the attacks of Christian Missionaries, 1821 (*The English Works of Raja Rammohun Roy*), pp. 145-147.

we can encounter, first, his scientific contribution to comparative methodology, and secondly, his objective approach to the socio-religious realities of life. He begins by observing that if the missionaries were to preach the Gospel in countries not conquered by the English, such as Turkey, Persia etc. they would be esteemed a body of men truly zealous in propagating religion. But in his logic Bengal's case is entirely different, because "for a period of upwards of fifty years this country has been in exclusive possession of the English nation. Here the mere name of an Englishman is sufficient to frighten people." And, therefore, argues he, under such conditions of helplessness "an encroachment upon the rights of her poor, timid and humble inhabitants and upon their religion cannot be viewed in the eyes of God or the public as a justifiable act."

Rammohun is a hard-headed realist. His positivism does not allow him to remain blind to the inevitable disadvantage of a subject-race in regard to the scientific and philosophical controversy or discussion with representatives of its political masters. "It seems almost natural", says he, "that when one nation succeeds in conquering another the former, though their religion may be quite ridiculous, laugh at and despise the religion and manners of those that are fallen into their power. *** It is, therefore, not uncommon if the English missionaries, who are of the conquerors of this country, revile and mock at the religion of the natives."

It is interesting that nearly a century after these epoch-making passages were written the position of comparative sociology or culture-history with special reference to the relations between Asia and Eur-America remained virtually the same. And the present writer's criticism of the "century-old doctrine of superior races" as responsible for the pernicious fallacies in social science was published as "The Futurism of Young Asia" in the *International Journal of Ethics* (Chicago, July, 1918). Virtually the same situation obtains today also in the world of social science (1936).

Not less positive and realistic is the manner in which Rammohun accepts the challenge of the English missionaries *visàvis* the problems of Indian religions *vs.* Christianity. He knows the realities of the world too well to believe that arguments command respect solely as arguments. Naturally, he suspects that "the small huts in which Brahmans of learning generally reside, and the simple food such as vegetables, etc. which they are accustomed to eat, and the poverty which obliges them to live upon charity" are likely to be taken as evidences of intellectual inferiority by those who happen to be materially in prosperous circumstances. So at the threshold of accepting the challenge on behalf of Hindu India Rammohun hopes that "the missionary gentlemen may not abstain from controversy from contempt of the poor as the Brahman intellectuals generally are."

To the English missionaries, used as they are to political mastery and economic superiority, Rammohun's logic that "truth and true religion do not always belong to wealth and power, high names or lofty palaces" should appear to have been quite revolutionary or radical although expressed in a rather moderate and modest language. We understand, at any rate, that at the beginning of the nineteenth century the Hindu Brāhmaṇa was maintaining the same secular viewpoint and clear-headed grasp of the objective joys and sorrows of the world as everybody who had been anybody in Hindu culture-history from the earliest times on.

The problem of Hinduism *vs.* Christianity or rather

East *vs.* West, as it is called today, found in Rammohun the first great controversialist of modern Asia and the most redoubtable champion of Brahmanical culture. In his own field he was successfully accomplishing what had been likewise successfully accomplished by Śivāji the Great in another.

In the first number of the *Brahmunical Magazine*[1] he replied to the arguments that had been adduced against the *Śāstras* or immediate explanation of the *Vedas* by the Christian missionaries writing in the *Samāchāra Darpaṇa* of July 14, 1821. The objections against the *Purāṇas* and the *Tantras* were answered by him in the second number. Rammohun demonstrated (1) that the doctrines of the *Vedas* were "much more rational" than the religion which the missionaries professed, and (2) that the teachings of the *Purāṇas* and the *Tantras*, "if unreasonable, were not more so than their Christian faith."

Comparative religion and sociology were thus placed on new foundations, nay, as we have seen, the logic of the comparative social sciences, i.e., comparative methodology itself.[2] One will recall that almost the same foundations of the comparative method in religion had been laid by Abul Fazl in the *Ain-i-Akbari* although he was a member of the ruling race. It is the traditional objectivity, humanism, worldly wisdom and realistic sense of Hindu positivism that enabled Rammohun to encounter the new socio-economic

[1] *The English Works* etc., pp. 147-148.

[2] *Re.* the comparative methodology in Rammohun see the present author's *Vartamān Yuge Chīn Sāmrājya* (The Chinese Empire Today, 1921), pp.352-63; *The Futurism of Young Asia* (Berlin, 1922), pp. 83, 301, 303, 304; *Bāḍtir Pathe Bāngālī* (Bengalis in Progress), Calcutta, 1934, pp. 544-548. Cf *Rethinking Missions* (ed. Hocking), New York, 1932.

forces and the new *mores* on terms of equality. Thus was modern India once for all endowed with the doctrine of racial equality with which to carry on the subsequent tug-of-wars with the powers that be in fields of societal reconstruction and the remaking of man. The *Vedānta*, the *Purāṇa*, and the *Tantras*, those great documents of humanism and secular strength that had served the Indian millions through the ages with the perennial power to fight the battles of life, were once more assured the self-same status in connection with the new conjunctures of the nineteenth century. Indeed, the era dawned for a fresh career of *charaiveti* (march on) or *digvijaya* (world-conquest) for Hindu culture both in the East and the West.

The last word of Hindu culture as embodied in the qualifications, aptitudes and character of the Indian people was found by Rammohun to be eminently satisfactory. Writing in 1832 (Sept. 28) while in London Rammohun gave his opinion that the Hindus and Mussalmans had the "same capability of improvement as any other civilized people." In his judgment, the people about the courts of the Indian princes were not inferior in point of education and accomplishments to the respectable and well-bred classes in any other country.[1]

The passage is derived from Rammohun's paper on the "condition of India" submitted as a part of his communication to the Board of Control in connection with the enquiries instituted by the Select Committee of the House of Commons (1831) to consider the renewal of the Company's Charter. His communication dealt also with (1) the judicial system, (2) the revenue

[1] *The English Works* etc., p. 299.

system, and (3) the settlement of India by Europeans.[1]

Be it observed *en passant* that Rammohun, as author of this communication, is the "first" Indian economist of the modern type. It is by offering salutations to this pioneer of economic research and applied economics that every Indian economist of today ought to commence his investigations. Rammohun, the contemporary of Ricardo, is the Adam Smith, as it were, of modern Indian economic thought. And it is very interesting that the lines of thought laid out by him continue in the main to be followed up, unconsciously perhaps, by the Indian economists of our own times.

Rammohun's Respect for Hindu Law and Tradition

Like Hemādri (*c* 1300), Raghunandana (*c* 1550), Mitra-Miśra (*c* 1650) and others Rammohun is somewhat of an encyclopaedist. But his writings did not assume the systematic form of those stupendous encyclopaedists among his great predecessors. Like his works on the *Vedānta*, the *Upaniṣads*, the *Bible* etc., his works on economics, politics, law and sociology also are "occasional", i.e., dictated by the circumstances, occasions or needs of the day. He is a philosopher of action and his pragmatic philosophy has grown from need to need. Each one of his literary contributions owed its existence to a definite and precise purpose. His studies are nothing but "applied" and each one is therefore an essay. He is a propagandist, a pamphleteer and an essayist.

In the fields of applied sociology two items de-

[1] *Exposition of the Practical Operation of the Judicial and Revenue Systems of India and of the General Character and Condition of its Native Inhabitants* (London, 1832), see the *English Works etc.*, pp. 229-320.

manded his special attention. The first is the law of property affecting both men and women and the other is the doctrine of *sahamaraṇa* or concremation. It is in these two fields that he touches the ground of *Smriti* and *Nīti Śāstras* and represents the transition between the old and the new in modern India.

Rammohun's *Brief Remarks regarding Modern Encroachments on the Ancient Rights of Females According to the Hindu Law of Inheritance* came out in 1822. It was followed in 1830 by the *Essays on the Rights of Hindus over Ancestral Property According to the Law of Bengal*. It has to be added that eight letters on the Hindu law of inheritance were published in the *Bengal Hurkaru* from September 20 to November 23, 1830. Last but not least are to be mentioned his statements to the Select Committee of the House of Commons (1831-32) on the judicial, revenue and economic conditions of India.

Rommohun's appreciation of the Bengali jurists and social thinkers is marvellous. In his *Essays on the Rights of the Hindus over Ancestral Property* (1830) he agrees with Colebrooke in describing Raghunandana, the author of *Dāyatattva* (one of the eighteen sections of the *Aṣṭaviṁśatitattva*) based on Jīmūtavāhana's *Dāyabhāga* as the "greatest authority on Hindu law" in the province of Bengal. The description of Śrikriṣṇa Tarakālamkāra as the "author of the most celebrated of the glosses of the text of Jīmūtavāhana's *Dāyabhāga*" is also accepted by Rammohun as quite valid. And Jagannātha Tarkapanchānana is described by Rammohun himself as the "most learned", as the "first literary character of his day". "Jagannātha's authority has nearly as much weight as that of Raghunandana", says he.

The conservation of the Bengali Hindu tradition in property-law has found in Rammohun a staunch supporter. The "doctrine of free disposal by a father of his ancestral property" is alleged in certain quarters to be opposed to the authority of the medieval Bengali jurist Jīmūtavāhana. This allegation is not accepted as valid by Rammohun. For argument's sake he is prepared to concede this for a moment. But he points out at the same time that the three greatest *Smriti* writers of Bengal since Jīmūtavāhana have openly advocated this doctrine. Accordingly Rammohun would ask everybody to support at least the latter-day jurists even if necessary against Jīmūtavāhana and argues that "it would be generally considered as a most rash and injurious as well as ill-advised innovation for any administrator of Hindu law of the present day to set himself up as the corrector of successive expositions, admitted to have been received and acted upon as authoritative for a period extending to upwards of three centuries back".[1] Rammohun functions here as a continuator of the tradition established not only by Raghunandana but by the great starting-point of Bengali jurisprudence, namely, Jīmūtavāhana himself.

On *Suttee*, the burning of widows, called *sahamaraṇa* (concremation) Rammohun has three brochures published in 1818, 1820 and 1830. In regard to this question he analyses the *Smriti* texts from Manu to Raghunandana and finds that the practice has not been advocated by all. Among the ancients neither the *Vedas*, nor Manu nor Yājnavalkya can be cited in support, says he. On the other hand, Angirā, Viṣṇu, Hārīta and some other latter-day jurists recommend either concremation or a virtuous life. Rammohun argues, besides, that even when concremation is recom-

[1] *The English Works* etc., pp. 411-412. See also the present author's "Hindu Sociological Literature from Chandesvara to Rammohun 1300-1833" (*Calcutta Review*, October 1935).

mended as an alternative by a jurist it is done as a measure for obtaining "future carnal fruition." But measures like this are forbidden by the *Gītā*, Manu and Raghunandana. And Vijnāneśvara, the author of the *Mitākṣarā*, considers concremation as something inferior to virtuous life. Rammohun argues, further, that even Hārīta and other advocates of concremation do not support concremation if it is not free and voluntary and permits the widow to abstain from it if she desires. According to Rammohun, therefore, *Suttee* is nothing but suicide and female murder.[1]

We observe that Rammohun's logic is realistic enough not to condemn the Hindu *Smritiśāstras*. He examines the authorities one by one and finds that they cannot be reasonably held responsible for the *suttee*, inhuman as it is. His profound respect for the juristic and other achievements of Hindu culture is an element in his remarkable positivism. It is the objective *data* of Hindu legal literature that he ransacks and then he applies his reason to the elucidation and comparison of those texts. It is on the strength of Hindu law that he passes his final verdict against concremation[2] such as became associated with some latter-day self-seekers.

The old Hindu institutions of law and polity are in Rammohun's judgment useful and important enough to be preserved in modern times. "The principle of juries", says he, "under certain modifications has from the most remote periods been well-understood in this country under the name of the *panchayat*." In his days the system existed "on a very defective

[1] *The English Works* etc., pp.368, 370, 372.

[2] *Address to Lord William Bentinck on the Abolition of the Practice of Suttee*, January 14, 1830, see the *English Works* etc., pp. 475-476.

plan". "In former days", he observes, "it was much more important in its functions. It was resorted to by parties at their own option, or by the heads of tribes who assumed the right of investigation and decision of differences; or by the government, which handed over causes to a *panchayat*." He considers, therefore, that the *panchayat*-jury system would be beneficial and acceptable to the inhabitants. Only, as a realist, again, he would like to have it adapted to the circumstances of the times,[1] i.e., supplemented or enriched with the new British judicial institutions. It is necessary to observe that those Indian scholars who are studying ancient Hindu polity and economy will have to look up to Rammohun as the "first" Indian "indologist" in these fields.

In regard to the laws of inheritance,[2] again, Rammohun is convinced of the value of the Hindu and Moslem codes in use for generations. He wants them to be preserved. It is the *Dāyabhāga*, says he, that is generally followed by the Bengali Hindus "with occasional references to other authorities." But he observes that in the Western province and a great part of the Deccan, it is the *Mitākṣarā* that is chiefly followed. As for the Mussalmans, the majority is described by him as following the doctrines of Abu Hanifah and his disciples. Their chief authority is accordingly the *Hidaya*. He is aware also of the use of *Fatawae Alamgiri* and other books of decision or cases.

Rammohun does not believe that the diverse Hindu and Moslem laws of inheritance are in need of any change. They should "remain as at present", says he. That is, their diversity is not to be disturbed. But he is an advocate of standardization, and yet not

[1] *The English Works* etc., pp. 250-252.
[2] *The English Works* etc., pp. 265-266.

at once. He believes that "by the diffusion of intelligence the whole community may be prepared to adopt one uniform system." The vitality and utility of Indian institutions are to him the first postulates. But he is at the same time modernist enough to admit the importance of assimilations, modifications, uniformizations, codifications etc.

The Double Quest of Modern India

In these statements to the Select Committee Rammohun, the student of law, polity, finance, economics and culture, is functioning in a double capacity. First, he is a spokesman of the Indian tradition and is giving the Devil his due. He is not writing original *Smriti* and *Nīti Śāstras* or *Bhāṣyas* or *Nibandhas* on the same topics. But his short observations furnish us with the final estimate of all that he thinks about their societal "value". He is a votary of indology but not as a mere academician. He never loses sight of his propaganda, namely, that for the vindication of his fatherland. In the second place he is convinced of the importance of the new forces and their usefulness to the people of India. He wants the association of the European institutions with the Indian or of the Indian with the European in order that the needs of today may be satisfied.

Altogether, in Rammohun the jurist, economist, statesman and sociologist, we meet two personalities. We encounter, on the one hand, the last representative of the *Smriti-Nīti* (or Kauṭalya-Manu-Śukra-Abul Fazl-Mitra Miśra) tradition. On the other, the British socio-economic and politico-legal philosophies as embodied in the tradition of Bacon, Hume, Smith, Austin, Ricardo and Bentham have found in him an able exponent for the Indian people. While analyzing the mentality and achievements of Rammohun the economists, sociologists, statesmen and jurists of today will have to hark as much back to Āpastamba, Vaśīṣṭha, Kauṭalya and Manu as to the Europeans from Aristotle to Bacon and Bentham.[1]

Thus interpreted, Rammohun should appear to be the embodiment of or the very key to the entire trend in modern Indian history,—namely, the double quest of "world-forces" (*viśva-śakti*) on the one hand and "nationalism" on the other. The respect for the "tradition", the past, the "folk", the national lines and ideals is no less conspicuous a constituent of Indian life and thought in the nineteenth and twentieth centuries than the yearning after the "now", the "new", the forces far and near, the *Weltkultur*. Every man, institution and movement in India during the last three generations or so registers the synthesis of "the home" and "the world" in all thoughts and activities.

The progress of this double quest in Bengal during the nineteenth century may be followed in journals like the *Sambād-Kaumudī* established by Rammohun (1819), the *Sambād Prabhākara* by Ishwar Gupta (1830), the *Tattvavodhinī* by Akshaya Kumar Datta (1843), the *Vividhārthasamgraha* by Rajendra Lal Mitra (1851), the *Education Gazette* by Bhudev Mookerjce (1868), and the *Vamga-Darśana* by Bankim Chandra Chatterjee (1872). The dailies both in Bengali and English have likewise to be named. These and allied extra-academic sources of inspiration have grown in number, volume and quality during the last two generations.

During the *Swadeshi* period the double quest took

[1] The present author's *Ekāler Dhana-daulat O Arthaśāstra* (The Wealth and Economics of Our Own Times), Vol. II. (Calcutta, 1935), pp. 603, 604, 607, 646.

definite shape in the "ideas of 1905" and was fostered in Bengal by monthlies like *Navyabhārata*, *Sāhitya*, the *Prabāsī*, the *Grihastha* etc. Since the Great War (1914-1918) the dailies, the monthlies, and the weeklies have been functioning as some of the most influential moral and cultural agencies throughout India. They may be regarded virtually as constituting a large number of "unrecognized Universities."

Some of the journals are indeed ephemeral and many of the journalists, i.e., editors, sub-editors, news-reporters, para-writers or contributors to the dailies, weeklies, and monthlies may not often enjoy an enviable economic and social position. Yet it is these members of the journalistic profession rather than the successful lawyers, medical men, Congress leaders or "schoolmen" that are "creatively" serving the people as propagators, nay, at times seers of new ideas and as pioneers of new movements. Today it does not take India more than seven or ten years for certain groups of serious-minded intellectuals to get used to some of the latest international currents of thought as well as to the leading character-building forces of the age,—thanks to the educative work carried on by the journals as extra-academic sources of science and morality. The work of the schools, colleges and universities need not be ignored. But the dailies, weeklies, monthlies and quarterlies,—as well as the public libraries, small, medium and large,—will have to be appraised more and more as the organs and instruments of nationalism on the one hand as of world forces on the other.

The Futurism of Dayānanda

As the founder of the Ārya Samāj, Dayānanda (1824-83) is generally taken to be a Punjabi. But born as he was in Kathiawar, he is in reality a Gujarati, the same race to which Gandhi belongs. All the same, perhaps no single individual deserves the distinction of being the maker of the modern Punjab to the same extent and in the same sense as Dayānanda. Practically everything that is new in Punjabi life and thought can be traced to the energistic "futurism" of this remarkable personality, who, however, paradoxically enough is regarded as the pioneer of a "back to the past" movement. We shall point out one or two of the special features associated with this product of creative India in the nineteenth-century.[1]

Dayānanda, the author of *Satyārthaprakāśa* (1874), is known to be a religious reformer in so far as he is the enemy of images, rituals, the *Purāṇas*, the *Tantras*, etc. The Ārya Samāj (est. 1875) has some distinct religious views, based as they are exclusively on the *Vedas*, and these have been propagated with success. But another evidence to the effect that about modern or ancient India the religious scaffolding of an individual, institution or movement should not be made too much of by the student of culture is furnished by the fact that the Ārya Samāj has been the most powerful factor in Northern India, especially in the Punjab, in the propagation of Hindi language and literature. It is necessary to observe that Hindi is not the mother-tongue of the Punjabis. Equally characteristic of the Ārya Samāj activities is the spread of interest in Sanskrit language and literature. The cultivation of ancient Sanskrit as the key to Hindu culture is an item of modern civilization which the Punjab owes to Dayānanda. His achievement in this field bears apt comparison with that of the greatest Hindu of all ages, Sivāji the

[1] Lajpat Rai: *The Arya Samaj* (London, 1915).

Great, whose self-conscious nationalism succeeded in restoring Sanskritic studies among his people thereby helping forward the Sanskritization also of their mother-tongue, Marathi.

Then, there is the educational work (e.g., D. A.V. College, Lahore, 1886, Gurukul, Hardwar, 1902) carried on by the Ārya Samāj that alone would entitle any organization to the highest respect of mankind. And these schools and colleges are meant for boys as well as for girls. It is in the Ārya Samāj schools, again, that the "depressed classes" got some of their first tastes of literacy. Industrial schools have likewise been the handiwork of Dayānanda's followers. Although professedly he had his eyes pinned to the past, nobody was thus a greater "futurist" than this Gujarati remaker of the Punjab. His was the philosophy of Dewey's *Schools of Tomorrow*. It is the inculcation of modern values in which he was profoundly interested. The interest of the Ārya Samāj in science and technocracy is such an integral part of its faith that one might be tempted almost to ignore its formal religion and religious propaganda.

The modernism or futurism of Dayānanda has nowhere taken a more characteristic shape than in the movement for the re-conversion of such Hindus as for one reason or other have lost their Hindu moorings. This *śuddhi*, purification or re-initiation is a modern counterpart of the *Vrātyaṣṭoma* ceremony of the *Atharva Veda* by which such Aryans as had forsaken their Aryan *mores* could be taken back into the Aryan folds. The logic or the instrument of Dayānanda here is old, but he has shown the way towards a renewal of the Hindu society in flesh and blood. The application of the *śuddhi* principle in new fields and in diverse ways is likely today not only to help forward the *Harijan* (*Pariah*) uplift movement, conservatively conceived as it is, of Gandhi, but also the somewhat recalcitrant propaganda of Ambedkar, the apostle of the "untouchables".

It is by an extension of the Ārya Samāj system of *śuddhi* that the age-long *charaiveti* (march on) or expansion cult of the Hindus can be carried forward among the diverse races of India in a systematic and scientific manner. Dayānanda's rôle as a demographic statesman and as an architect of Indian manhood is bound to grow from more to more along with the progress of the interest in caste-fusions, race-mixture etc. as agencies in the expansion of the Hindu population.

Rāmakṛṣṇa as a Remaker of Man

The category, "from Rammohun to Gandhi," might imply that during the nineteenth and twentieth centuries creative India has perhaps taken interest solely or chiefly in matters economic, political, educational or social. It would be wrong to appraise the creations of modern India as having reference to these fields only. There are other aspects of life and other interests of culture, and to these also the Indian mind has addressed itself during the last four or five generations. The creations of modern Indian culture in these other fields are apt continuations of ancient and medieval, and by the world standard of today also they would be found to be as humane, as edifying and as ennobling as anything of *le monde des valeurs* in the two Hemispheres. We are talking of the contributions of modern India to inner life, morality and religious experience, and in this connection would like to single out Rāmakṛṣṇa (1836-86), the Bengali saint, who is now a world-figure as the preceptor and maker of Swāmi Vivekānanda.

At the outset it is necessary to observe that Rāmakṛṣṇa was a worshipper of Kālī and professionally a priest in a temple. His book learning was limited and he knew as little of geology or the binomial theorem as the man in the moon. Besides, he did not think in terms of social reform, political advancement, industrial reconstruction or things like that. Neither the category, "world-forces," nor the category, "nationalism," would have conveyed any meaning to his life. And yet his *Kathāmrita*, "the nectar of words" (1882-86), has turned out to be the most dynamic social philosophy of the age, and this has created for him a position of one of the greatest "remakers" of mankind.

It is in the language of the folk that Rāmakṛṣṇa[1] administers the following bit of folk-logic (No. 781): "My strength is all-sidedness. I would like to enjoy fish, for instance, in a variety of ways, fried and boiled, made into soup, pickled etc. I enjoy the Lord not only in His unconditioned state of Oneness, as unqualified Brahman in Samādhi, but also in his various blessed manifestations." The power of Rāmakṛṣṇa over the folk-mind can be easily guessed from such statements.

Rāmakṛṣṇa's messages are pervaded by the milk of human kindness. He has his own conception of personal and inner life. But he is realistic and shrewd enough to understand that not everybody is like himself. He makes distinctions between individuals, and his programme for the making of man knows how to adapt itself to the requirements of each. "The worship from fear, e.g., of hell fire," we are taught (No. 397), "is intended for the beginner. Some people look upon the sense of sin as the whole of religion. They

[1] *The Teachings of Sri Ramakrishna* (Advaita Ashrama, Calcutta, 1934).

forget that it marks only the earliest and lower stage of spirituality." In his judgment "there is yet a higher ideal, a higher stage of spirituality, viz. the love of God as our own Father or Mother." It is this personal nexus,—the human touch,—between God and the individual that Rāmakṛṣṇa emphasises in season and out of season. To be able to conceive such a direct *liaison* in these matters constitutes by itself a revolution of capital importance.

The teachings of Rāmakṛṣṇa are pregnant with catholicity and the spirit of universal freedom. "As you rest firmly on your own faith and opinion," runs his advice (No. 564), "so allow others also equal liberty to stand by theirs." A precept like this is intended especially perhaps for the "high-brows," the lover of *vitaṇḍā* (discussion), the disputants. And armed with a methodology like this his disciples can exercise their *charaiveti* (march on) undaunted and in a dare-devil manner. Here we have the doctrine of a self-conscious pluralism such as would afford "the other fellow" also an opportunity for self-assertion and create chances for an open-air intellectual tug-of-war at mutual convenience.

The respect for the "other fellow's" individuality is in Rāmakṛṣṇa's social ethics a cause as well as an effect of his "appreciation" of other faiths. *Yata mat tata path* (as many faiths, so many paths) is perpetually on his lips. The diversity of paths in the moral world does not frighten him. It is rather the fundamental ground-work of spirituality in his analysis of human behaviour. As a true servant of man he is profoundly convinced of the dignity of individual manhood and personality.

Each one of the thousand and one expressions of this personality and manhood is to him a sacred phenomenon. The multiplicity of *mores*, creeds, cults, manners and sentiments as prevailing in the social world—the "varieties of religious experience",—constitute in his psychology but an encyclopaedia of the manifold attempts made by the might of man to realize the *Brihadāraṇyaka-Upaniṣad* (I, iii, 28) ideal as embodied in the prayer, namely, *asato mā sadgamaya, tamaso mā jyotirgamaya, mrityor mā mritam gamaya* (from unreality lead me to reality, from darkness lead me to light, from death lead me to immortality). Rāmakṛṣṇa's faith in the dignity of man enables him thus to welcome the exponents of every faith as the builders of and travellers on roads to reality, light and immortality.

Every *cheminot* or wanderer on all these most heterogeneous roads is to him a colleague and fellow-priest in the temple of man's struggle towards higher and higher flights of freedom. And in this psychology we are furnished with the profoundest conceptions bearing on the toleration of and friendly orientations to the diverse religious systems of the world. A deeper foundation for inter-racial harmony and inter-religious concord it is hardly possible to conceive.

Rāmakṛṣṇa is a believer in the equality of faiths. He has established the democracy of religions. His conceptions of religious democracy and spiritual equality are organically linked up with his ideals of the fullness of life. It is not in any single groove,—the groove, the coterie, the sect or the community to which he and his kith and kin are used because of birth and domicile,—that he sees life functioning. His mind is bent on recognizing the claims of the not-self, the other I's or we's, and on establishing a harmony between the self and the not-self.

His philosophy of life's fullness, based as it is on

the sympathy with the urges and requirements of the not-self, the others, the duality or the plurality, is not confined to the reactions and demands of the individual personality alone. To him the doctrine that *cotesta dualità resta insopprimibile come legge immanente del nostro essere* (this duality remains irreducible as the immanent law of our being) goes much beyond the life and art of single individuals, as analyzed by the Italian social philosopher Giorgio del Vecchio.[1] Rāmakṛṣṇa would apply this maxim of dual, multiple or complex personality to each and every group of men as well as to all inter-group relations and inter-communal moralities.

Rāmakṛṣṇa's religion of life does not consider itself to be adequate and complete until it has granted a franchise of self-expression and self-direction to the creative urges, moral and spiritual experiences of the "other groups",—new races, strange faces, the minds of the great not-self. Monistic religiosity, spiritualitarian absolutism, or imperialistic autocracy in religion and morality is as the poles asunder to his socio-spiritual planning of the universe. Nobody in the world's culture-history and philosophical annals has been a more pronounced architect of the republic of religions than Rāmakṛṣṇa.

To Rāmakṛṣṇa vacillation is a sin, weakness is a sin, procrastination is a sin. In the very manner of Sākya the Buddha expounding the cult of *appamāda* and *viriya* Rāmakṛṣṇa teaches Young Bengal the value of great and noble thoughts as follows (No. 518): "Many with a show of humility say, 'I am like a low worm grovelling in the dust'. Thus always thinking themselves worms, in time they become weak in spirit like worms."

[1] *Etica, Djritto e Stato*, Rome, 1934, p. 6.

Rāmakṛṣṇa would not allow anybody to cultivate such dehumanizing, ignoble and demoralizing thoughts. "Let not despondency ever enter into thy heart", says he, "despair is the great enemy of progress in one's own path." His burden is as follows: "As a man thinks, so he becomes."

He is the enemy of cowardice-promoting humility, genuine or counterfeit. It is the mind on which he works. The objective of his spiritual conversations is the transformation of the mental processes along channels of strength, courage and hope.

"The bondage is of the mind", says he (No. 516), "freedom is also of the mind. If thou shouldst say,—'I am a free soul, I am the son of God, who can bind me?'—free thou shalt be." Rāmakṛṣṇa's pedagogics is nothing but a steady and comprehensive play upon the mind. As we have already observed, he does not talk much of social reforms, moral propaganda, plans of national reconstruction or the like. It is the transformation of the mind in which he is almost exclusively interested. For he is convinced (No. 514) that "the mind is everything. If the mind loses its liberty, you lose yours. If the mind is free, you are free too." In the *milieu* of such Kantian or Fichtean messages bearing on the mind and its freedom, coming as they did from the lips of a man whose school learning hardly went beyond the three R's one can easily understand why the "highbrow" Universitarians, equipped as they were with Kant, Fichte, Hegel and whatnot, felt like pigmies, and "fools who came to scoff remained to pray."

Fichte's attitudes are well-known. Writing in 1808[1] for Young Germany he said: "*Euch ist das*

[1] *Reden an die Deutsche Nation,* Address XIV.

groessere Geschick zuteil geworden, ueberhaupt das Reich des Geistes und der Vernunft zu begruenden (To you has been assigned the greater destiny, namely, that you have to establish the Empire of the spirit and reason), *und die rohe koerperliche Gewalt insgesamt als beherrschendes der Welt zu vernichten* (and that you have to annihilate the raw physical power as a determinant of the world)." It is this supremacy of the spirit and reason, and the emancipation of the mind from matter, or rather the mind's dominion over the world that constitutes the *Leitmotif* of Rāmakṛṣṇa's sayings.

Nothing but strong determination and doggedness can please Rāmakṛṣṇa's soul. It is the strenuous and tenacious young men that he would like to see around himself. And for them he has propagated one soul-inspiring motto. They are to say all the time (No. 504): "I must attain prefection in this life; yea, in three days I must find God, nay, with a single utterance of his name, I will draw Him to me." Such is the creed of individual self-discipline preached by Rāmakṛṣṇa in the interest of the remaking of youths.

Hollow formalism can have no place in Rāmakṛṣṇa's thought. "What is the good of merely repeating the word *Sivoham* (I am Śiva or God)?" he asks (No. 413), "It is only when one, by perfect meditation on the Lord in the temple of one's heart, has lost all idea of self and realized the Lord Śiva within that one is entitled to utter this sacred word. What good can the mere repetition of the formula do without the realization?" We are to understand that this attack on "words, words, words" is delivered as much against the Hindus of all denominations, as against Christianity, Islam, Buddhism and all other faiths, great or small. Rāmakṛṣṇa is a teacher of all mankind in the direction of sincerity and genuine spirituality.

Lectures on eternal verities like God and the soul, howsoever popularly delivered, or on the denunciation of *Kāma* (lust) and *Kānchana* (gold or wealth), howsoever well-meaning they be, may leave in the long run hardly any impression upon the worldly-minded man. He needs a definite prescription for his daily life. Everybody in the two hemispheres has often asked the question as to how it can be possible to harmonize God and the world. Rāmakṛṣṇa's homely recipe is as follows: "Look at the carpenter's wife", says he (No. 252), "how many things she is doing at once! With one hand she stirs the flattened rice in the mortar of a *Dhenki*, with the other hand she is nursing her child, and at the very same time she bargains with a purchaser about the rice. Thus though her occupations are many, her mind is fixed the while on one idea that the pestle of the *Dhenki* shall not fall on her hand and bruise it." The moral is self-evident. We are taught to "be in the world but always remember Him and never go astray from His path."

Rāmakṛṣṇa's messages do not therefore compel everybody to renounce house and home, family and property. His followers are not all *Sanyāsins*, *Sādhus* and *Swāmis*. He is the teacher of householders, businessmen, lawyers, clerks, cultivators and others as well. In spite of his perpetual emphasis on the soul and communion with God Rāmakṛṣṇa has thus succeeded in becoming one of the most influential expounders of positivism and secular endeavours. In this synthesis of the transcendental and the positive he is but a chip of the old Hindu block coming down from the Vedic times. And it is on the strength of this synthesis, again, that his Narendra the Vivekānanda thundered a Young India into being,—the India of economic energism as well as of spiritual creativeness, of material science and technocracy as well as self-control and social service.

Moslem Renaissance

During the last quarter of the nineteenth-century Bengali literature was enriched with contributions from Moslem authors. The poet Kaikobad is one of the pioneers of Moslem Renaissance in Bengal. His writings (*c* 1880) in Bengali, Sanskritized or "chaste" (*sādhu*) as it is, served to construct a bridge between Moslem and Hindu thought. To the same school belonged the poet Mozammel Huq. Ahmed Riazuddin used to be described as a "Paṇḍit". His *Agni-Kukkut* (Fire-Cock) is well-known. As the author of a biography of Syed Jamaluddin of Persia, the founder of Pan-Islam, Riazuddin helped the Hindus and Moslems to cast their eyes beyond the Indian boundaries in order to see fresh sources of light. Among the Moslem writers of this period in chaste Bengali Mir Mosharef Hosein has an important place.

Somewhat later (*c* 1890) came Munshi Sheikh Abdur Rahim to work in the same field. A special value is to be attached to the prose writings in Bengali by Tashimuddin Ahmed. His Bengali translation of the *Koran* has enriched Bengali thought (*c* 1890). As editor of *Islam* (Bengali Journal) he enabled Bengal to expand her intellectual and social consciousness in a systematic manner. Another great Moslem writer of this time, although junior, is Abdul Karim. He got the title of *Sāhitya-viśārada* in Sanskrit because of his researches and publications in Bengali. By the beginning of the present century he was a prominent figure of literary Bengal.

The twentieth century commenced with strong "reformist" tendencies among Bengali Mussalmans.

A powerful critic of Moslem life, who succeeded to a certain extent in inspiring divine discontent in the ranks of his co-religionists, is Imdadul Huq. The inspiration furnished by Kaikobad was operative still. Emdad Ali, who established the *Navanūr* (Bengali journal) was a Kaikobadian in his viewpoint. Bengali literature got an impetus likewise from the journal *Kohinur* edited by Roshan Ali and the *Nūr* edited by Ismail Hosein Shirazi.

The "ideas of 1905" found able exponents among the Mussalmans of Bengal. The contributions of Abdul Rasul to the popularization of ideas are immense although his literary work does not seem to be much. Abdullah Surhawardy's *Hablul Matin* may be mentioned in this connection. The self-sacrificing idealism of Liakut Hussain, the door to door preacher of *Swadeshi* and the friend of students and young men, deserves recognition among the achievements of Moslem India. He was not a Bengali but he adopted Bengal as his home, and although it was not possible for him to serve Bengali literature his place in Bengali ideology is considerable. Liakut Hussain is a figure that Young Bengal will not willingly let die.

During the first decade of the present century two powerful Bengali writers appeared on the scene among the Mussalmans and both developed in a large measure the critical and reformist tendencies of Imdadul Huq. The one is Maniruzzaman Islamabadi. His *Bhārate Mussalman Sabhyatā* invites attention to the religious, social and educational activities of the Mussalmans. His Bengali journal, *Al-Islam*, sought, among other things, to "rationalize" Islam. The other "rationalist" is Akram Khan, whose journal *Mohammadī* is to be counted as a great power in Bengali thought.

We have to call attention to the fact that conservatism or reactionarism is not, as is generally alleged, the sole feature of Moslem life and thought. Strong criticism of Moslem life, demand for new social and cultural conditions, at any rate, the desire not to remain satisfied with what is,—these traits have been in evidence in Moslem Bengal continuously for nearly two generations. Mrs. R. S. Hosein, the educationist, who died in 1932, was a stern critic of the conventional Moslem *mores*. The same tendency is manifest in Lutfur Rahaman. "Rationalism" is likewise prominent in the contributions of Abul Kalam Azad, who, however, writes in Urdu.

Among the lyric poets of Moslem Bengal Nazrul Islam, Abdul Kadir, Jasimuddin and Wazed Ali are endowed with creative gifts. No account of Bengali poetry since 1920 can be complete without reference to the contributions of these and other Mussalman authors.

The politics of Moslem Bengal are almost as varied as those of Hindu India. It is, therefore, not necessary to go into details about the "parties." In spite of the great improvements engendered as a result of the Government of India Act 1921 in economic standing and worldly esteem the Moslems *en masse* do not as yet happen to be socially as high as the Hindus. This fact explains as a rule the occasional absence of amity between the two wings of Bengali public life. But otherwise, so far as general ideas are concerned, the Bengali Mussalmans represent as many tendencies from the "extreme right" to the "extreme left" as do the Hindus. But the number of "higher intellectuals" among the Mussalmans in proportion to their populational strength is not as great as that among the Hindus. In social statistics Moslem progressivism is yet not much in evidence. The strands of progressive thought and liberal outlook do not therefore appear as prominently or voluminously and powerfully among the Mussalmans as among the Hindus.

It is necessary, however, to get oriented to an important fact in the modern cultural life of Bengali Mussalmans. We have observed that for the last two generations or so their authors and journalists have been awakening a desire among their co-religionists to study the achievements of "ancient" Islam, i.e., the contributions of Moslem culture to the medieval world. This tendency has got a fillip in recent years on account of the Bengali Moslem Literary Conferences (*c* 1932). The organizers of these Conferences are equipped with the modern spirit as well as international outlook. They represent the same double quest of modern India from Rammohun to Gandhi as do the Hindus, viz., the cultivation of nationalism on the one side and of *viśva-śakti* (world-forces) on the other. In their orientations to "ancient Islam", therefore, they are not raising the cry for "back to the past" in any manner. It is the spirit of Moslem positivism in science and historiography that they are trying to restore, and they are interpreting it in a way calculated to serve the requirements of modern life.

For the last two generations, therefore, we have been watching a genuine *Renaissance* or rebirth among the Mussalmans. It is not merely a Renaissance in the ordinary sense to the effect that Mussalmans are trying to accomplish something and thus exhibit signs of life and vigour of some sort or other. We see here a Renaissance in the original sense as well, i.e., the Moslem past is being re-born under new conditions, and the present is being reconstructed under the inspiration of past ideals to help forward the supply of the pressing wants of today. The past is thus being re-interpreted and transformed to serve as a plank for "futurism". The ideological foundations of a deeper solidarism between the Hindus and Mussalmans are thus being laid wide and deep in Bengal, and this notwithstanding the frictions of the "communal award" as sanctioned by the Government of India Act (1935).

Viśva-Śakti (World-Forces) in India Today[1]

Rammohun (1772-1833), the father of New India, was also like Herder and Comte one of the founders of the comparative method in social science. He was thus a maker of the modern world. Since then every movement with which the Indian nation-builders have been associated has been broad-based on world-culture. And Rammohun in inviting Western culture into Indian consciousness and according to it the rightful place it deserves in all human development was only continuing the historic tradition of India's old masters, e.g., of Varāhamihira (*c* 505-589 A.C.). This astronomer of the sixth century had frankly admitted that although the Greeks were *Mlechchhas* i.e., "unclean barbarians", they must have to be worshipped as *Riṣis* (sages) because the science of astronomy had made great progress among them (*Brihat Samhitā* II, 14). Openness of mind is not a new feature in Indian *Weltanschauung*.

[1] See the present author's "Doctrine of World-Forces" in the paper read at the Bengali Literary Conference at Mymensingh (April 1911), contributions to the *Grihastha* (Calcutta, 1912-1916), *The Science of History and the Hope of Mankind* (London, 1912), *Viśva-Śakti* (Calcutta, 1914), contributions to the "World of Culture" Section of the *Collegian* (Calcutta, 1920-24), "Die Soziale Philosophie Jung-Indiens" (*Deutsche Rundschau*, Berlin, April, 1922), *Arthik Unnati* (1926-36), the "Miscellany" Section of the *Calcutta Review* (1933-36), *Ekāler Dhana-Daulat O Arthaśāstra* (The Wealth and Economics of Our Own Times) 2 vols. (1930, 1935), as well as *Varttamān Jagat* (The Modern World) in twelve vols. (1914-35).

A veritable *Wanderlust* corresponding to the *charaiveti* (march on) of old (*Aitareya Brāhmaṇa* VII, 15) and desire to master the *viśva-śakti* (world-forces) is embodied in the memorable verse (*c* 1886) by Hem Chandra Banerji (1838-1903) as follows:

"Take thee to the ocean's deeps;
And crowns of mountains scramble bold;
Planets of the universe
Ransacked be merciless;
Tempests and meteors,
Flame of lightning fierce,
Grasp, man, audacious-firm,
Venture, then, on life's work."

And the comparative method foreshadowed in the life's work of Rammohun is so ingrained in India's *psyche* that the principle of boycott which has operated several times in the sphere of politics as a weapon for freedom and racial equality has hardly any application in the cultural enterprises of creative India.

The number of Indians who visit Japan, America, England, France, Germany and Italy for industrial, technocratic and economic investigations has been steadily on the increase, especially since the *Swadeshi* Movement of 1905. India does not study the advance of modern capitalism alone. The other side of the shield, namely, socialism in all its wings,—Godwin, St. Simon, Owen, Marx, Engels, Kautsky, Sorel, Lenin, Cole,—has been likewise receiving attention among the Indian path-finders.

In the appreciation of the world's celebrities, again, India does not make any distinction between nationalities. The Washington Day and the Goethe Day were celebrated at different centres in India in 1932. In 1933 Indian scholars in philosophy paid homage to the spirit of Spinoza. Firdausi's memory was honoured in

1934. And homage to Andrew Carnegie was paid in 1935.

Wanderlust has already had solid influence on thought. The methodology of Voltaire's *Lettres Philosophiques*, in which a foreign land is idealized as the depositary of all possible cultural and political bliss, has more or less been at work in the Indian journalism and travel literature such as comes from the pen of authors who have lived in Eur-America and Japan. Writers on foreign institutions and life are quite popular.

The painters and sculptors of Bombay, Calcutta and Madras do not seek their technique exclusively from old Buddhistic and medieval Indo-Persian sources. The great masters of Japan and China as well as of Europe have profoundly influenced the work of Abanindra Nath Tagore, Nanda Lal Bose, M. K. Mhatre and Phanindra Nath Bose.

Dante, Shakespeare, Goethe, Hugo, Whitman, Browning, Ibsen, Yeats, Dostoyevski, Gorki, Bojer, Hamsun, Galsworthy and Shaw call forth among Indians the same enthusiasm as among the Westerners. Helmholtz, Pasteur, John Stuart Mill, Bergson, Lombroso, James, Hobhouse, Wundt, Croce, Einstein—they all have admirers and followers in India. The great philosophers of Germany from Kant, Fichte and Hegel, to Haeckel and Eucken are as popular in India as her own masters. Indeed, there are hardly any world-currents to which modern India does not react in a creative manner.

For instance, the growth of a "Greater America" of culture and commerce on the Indian subcontinent may be appraised as a profound reality of contemporary civilization. And this expansion of America in India has been promoted by Americans and Indians alike. The beginnings of the Agricultural Institute at Pusa were laid with American money. The Rockefeller Institute of Hygiene at Calcutta as well as the Rāmakṛṣṇa Temple at Belur on the Ganges (near Calcutta) are embodiments of American idealism. Co-operation of Indian capital with American is to be found in the Tata Hydro-electric works. The origins of the Tata Iron and Steel Works likewise were to a certain extent due to Indo-American collaboration. The investment of American capital in jute and other enterprises is moreover an important factor in the Indian economy. Then there is to be noticed the work of American missionaries and educators in Indian hospitals and schools or colleges.

Indians themselves have not failed to appreciate and assimilate the contributions of American culture. It was our poet Hem Chandra Banerji who during the eighties of the last century was one of the first to draw our attention to the epoch-making energism of the American people. The activities of the Rāmakṛṣṇa-Vivekānanda Mission in the U.S.A. have enabled us to realize the value of American social ideals and institutions.

It is the American farms, factories, banks, business houses, industrial and commercial schools, and Universities on which Jogen Ghosh's Association for the Industrial and Scientific Education of Indians in foreign countries laid a special stress during the glorious *Swadeshi* period (1905-10). The National Council of Education, Bengal, likewise sought to Americanize Indian education, industry and business organization by importing American methods and ideals through its scholars educated in the U.S.A. (1910-14). Nor have the Indian Universities under the creative leadership of Asutosh Mookerjee lagged behind in deriving inspiration from American institutions, books and journals. In mathematics, physics, chemistry, medicine, biology, anthropology, philosophy, statistics, economics, politics, sociology, banking, insurance, transportation and what not,—American authors or translators from French and German have been permitted by the University authorities to invade the academic life. In so far as Young India's brain is nurtured on English thought it is today at least one-third Americanized in methodology and outlook. Emerson, O. W. Holmes, James, Boas, Stanley Hall, Dewey, Seligman, Taussig, Mitchell, Small, Giddings, Lowie, Goldenweiser, Ross, Sorokin, Max Weber (artist), Barnes, Hocking, Hankins, Parmelee, as well as Carnegie, Edison, Ford and other American names are to be counted among some of the enduring influences on Indian life and thought.[1] To this list have to be added the names of Hopkins, Lanman, Bloomfield, Jackson, Laufer, Ryder, Clark, Edgerton and other indologists, as well as Sunderland, J. H. Holmes and other publicists.

Among the formative forces of Young India (*c* 1905-10) nothing can be described as having been more constructive and solid than the Japanese artist

[1] See the present author's *Yankeestan or Europe Writ Large* (Calcutta, 1914-1923), "Types and Tendencies in American Banking" (*Journal of the Bengal National Chamber of Commerce*, June 1927), *The Political Philosophies Since 1905* (Madras, 1928); "America's Business Contacts with the People of India" (*India and the World*, Calcutta, January 1932), *Ekāler Dhana-Daulat O Arthaśāstra* (The Wealth and Economics of Our Own Times), 1930, 1935, Calcutta, 2 Vols.; D. C. Das Gupta: "Vocational Guidance in America", lecture at the Bangiya Dhana Vijnan Parishat (Bengali Institute of Economics), 8 July 1934, published in the *Insurance and Finance Review* (Calcutta) for August 1934, "Industrial Education in Dewey's Social Philosophy", lecture at the "Āntarjātik Banga" Parishat ("International Bengal" Institute), 29 July, 1934, published in the *Calcutta Review*, for September 1934.

Kakasu Okakura's two books, *Ideals of the East* and *The Awakening of Japan*. Okakura may even be regarded as perhaps the greatest single foreign influence in the life and thought of Indian intellectuals during the *Swadeshi* period in its first phases. Japan has taught India great lessons during the generation commencing with the Russo-Japanese War (1904). India's admiration for Japanese industry, efficiency and diplomacy has grown from more to more all this time.[1]

Since the end of the Great War, however, India has been encountering Japan more as a dangerous rival than as an inspiring guide. The glass, hosiery, porcelain and other industries of Bengal as well as the big textile industry of India have begun to experience a life-and-death struggle *vis-à-vis* the imports from Japan. But all the same, India is learning along with the world the old lesson over again, namely, that "peace hath her victories no less glorious than war." Even when the Great War came to an end (1918) neither Eur-America nor of course Asia could suspect that industrialization as well as technocracy were being

[1] See the present author's *The Futurism of Young Asia* (Berlin 1922), *Economic Development* (Madras, 1926), *Navīn Asiār Janmadātā* (The Parent of New Asia), Calcutta, 1915-1927, "The Strength and Limitations of Economic Japan" and "Business Organization as an Aid to the Economic Expansion of Japan" in the *Calcutta Review*, for November 1933 and January 1934;and "Japanese Expansion Through Bengali Eyes" (*Oriental Economist*, Tokyo, July 1936); P. K. Mukerjee: "The Economic Expansion of the Japanese People", lecture at the "Āntarjātik Banga" Parishat ("International Bengal" Institute) April 8, 1932; R. N. Ghose: "Labour and Wages in Japan", lecture at the "Malda in Calcutta" Society, Calcutta, 27 December 1934, reported in the *Commercial Gazette*, Calcutta, for 14 January 1935; S. M. Bose: "Business Organization in Japan", lecture at the Bangiya Dhana-Vijnan Parishat (Bengali Institute of Economics), Calcutta, 24 March 1935, reported in the *Amrita Bazar Patrika*, Calcutta, 29 March 1935.

mastered by Japan so adequately as to constitute in the near future a veritable "Japanese peril" in the estimation of commercial nations.

India understands, however, that with nothing more than three meals of rice and raw fish without milk and butter as the daily staple the Japanese people has demonstrated that it is possible to command the latest engines, machines, implements, and machine tools and challenge comparison with the pioneers of industrialism and capitalistic civilization. Japan is therefore still continuing to inspire the creative thinkers and organizers of the Indian people during the period of her new triumphs. Japan has influenced Indian thought not only by works like *Fifty Years of New Japan* edited by Okuma, Nitobe's *Bushido* and the indological researches of Anesaki, Takakusu, Hattori, Suzuki, Sugiara, Otani and others but also on account of the demographic investigations of Uyeda, the journals like the *Oriental Economist* (Tokyo) and the publications of the Bureau of Social Affairs (Home Office, Tokyo) in regard to "Social Work in Japan" (1934).

The civilization of France has had an abiding influence on the education and culture of Young India.[1] From Descartes to Henri Poincaré, from Lamarck to Pasteur, from Molière to Maupassant, from Montesquieu and Saint Simon to Jean Jaurès, Gide and Bou-

[1] See the present author's "A View of France" (*Modern Review*, Calcutta, October 1921), *Economic Development* (Madras 1926), *The Political Philosophies Since 1905* (Madras 1928), *Comparative Pedagogics in relation to Public Finance and National Wealth* (Calcutta 1929), *Parise Daś Mās* (Ten Months at Paris), Calcutta 1920-1932; D. C. Das Gupta: "Educational Ideals in France," lecture at the "Åntarjātik Banga" Parishat ("International Bengal" Institute), Calcutta, on February 17, 1935, reported in *Forward*, Calcutta, February 22, 1935. On Rabelais see his paper in *Prabuddha Bhārata*, Calcutta, January 1935.

glé, from Rousseau, Comte and Guizot to Bergson, Durkheim and Lévy-Bruhl, from Corot to Cezanne and Rodin, from Montaigne to Anatole France, Romain Rolland, and Henri Barbusse—the contributions of the French genius have conveyed to the Indian mind profound messages of creative value. And these are as varied and complex as are the different cross-sections of the Indian *intelligentsia* to which they are addressed. One can almost assert that after British thought no culture has left a greater impression upon the head and heart of Indian writers and scholars than have the creations of the French mind.

Then there are the French products in "indology." The indologists of Young India have derived immense benefit from the works of French savants relating to ancient India including "Greater India", especially China and Indo-China. The studies in *indianisme* of French antiquarians and philologists from Chézy, Bergaigne and Burnouf to Barth, Sénart, Lévi, Foucher, Pelliot, Bloch, Przyluski, Finot, Masson-Oursel, Renou, de la Vallée Poussin, Ph. Stern, and Grousset belong to the most substantial food of latterday Indian scholars in philology, Buddhism, archæology, etc.

With French civilization the direct contacts of Young India on a large scale have to be traced back of course to the "ideas of 1905", but especially to the happenings of the Great War when the Indian soldiers found themselves in Flanders and Northern France. Since then the intercourse has gone on expanding in diverse directions, cultural and social.

As representatives of *sciences morales et politiques* comprising, as they do, in French thought economics also Levasseur, Tarde, Worms, Yves-Guyot, R. G. Lévy, Rist, Henri Sée, Truchy, Bousquet, Aftalion, André Siegfried, Brunhes, Richard, Duprat, Hauser, Oualid,

Joseph-Barthélemy, Liesse, Nogaro, Gonnard, Bouthoul, Baudin and Lasbax have, it may be observed, already entered the domain of Indian research.

From the standpoint of technocracy and occupational structure Italy is not a "capitalistic" region but a land of "mixed" (i.e. agrar-industrial) and diversified economy, as Mussolini has made it clear in the speeches explaining the law of corporations (December, 1933). In other words, Italy is nearer to India socio-economically than are Germany, Great Britain and the U.S.A. This aspect of Italian economy and sociography has been gradually dawning upon the business world and economic thought in India.[1]

So far as the culture of Italy is concerned, Madhusudan Dutt, the greatest Bengali poet of the nineteenth century, was powerfully influenced by Italian creations. His *Meghanāda Vadha* bears the impress of Virgil and Dante. His sonnet to Petrarca is well-known. The Bengali prose-writer Jogindranath Vidyabhushan wrote the biographies of Mazzini and Garibaldi. These two Italian celebrities have formed the subject-matter of biography likewise in Marathi, Urdu, Hindi and other Indian languages. The painter Sasi Kumar Hesh and the sculptor Gopeswar Pal also have derived inspiration and guidance from Italy.

[1] See the present author's *Economic Development* (Madras 1926), "Contacts with Economic Italy" (*Journal of the Bengal National Chamber of Commerce*, June and December 1931), "Italo-Indian Intercourse" (*India and the World*, Calcutta, August 1932), *Itālite Bār-Kayek* (Several Times in Italy, Calcutta, 1924-1932); P. K. Mukerjee: "The Economic and Social Aspects of Fascist Italy", lecture at the "Āntarjātik Banga" Parishat ("International Bengal" Institute) Calcutta, April 8, 1934, published in the *Insurance and Finance Review*, Calcutta, June and July 1934; P. N. Roy: *Mussolini and Young Italy* (Calcutta 1933); U. Redano: *Lo Stato Etico* (Florence, 1927); R. Morandi: *Grande Industria in Italia* (Bari, 1931).

India's contacts with Italy since the middle of the nineteenth century, especially since the opening of the Suez canal in 1869, have been extensive. The visits of Indian scholars to Italian centres of art and science, during the twentieth century, especially since the end of the Great War (1914-18), have grown in number and frequency. It is during this the latest period that leaders of Italian life and thought such as Pantaleoni, Luzzatti, Croce, Formichi, Giorgio del Vecchio, Niceforo, Mortara, Gini, Gentile, Tucci, Graziani, Tivaroni and others have come forward to meet Indian scientists, poets, economists, philosophers, historians and educators halfway, so to say. The anti-malaria and anti-tuberculosis campaigns of Italy have been furnishing Indian social workers with constructive suggestions. Students of land-economics and rural reconstruction have been watching the Italian *bonifica integrale* movements with admiration and creative enthusiasm.

The contributions of "modern", i.e., Bismarckian and post-Bismarckian Germany to the economic and social welfare of mankind have been arresting the attention of the Indian *intelligentsia*. The German *Anerbenrecht* is the law relating to land by which equal partition among heirs (conceded as much by Roman as by Hindu jurisprudence) is forbidden. By its provisions the proprietor is authorized to "select" any one of his heirs (not necessarily the eldest son) to be the sole heir. At the same time the "selected" heir is compelled to pay off in cash or otherwise the other legal heirs. This German legislation is being appraised as eminently suitable for Indian conditions. *Sozialversicherung*, i.e. social insurance is another achievement of the German people to which Indian economists and statesmen are directing their attention. The *Berufs-und Fachschulwesen*, i.e., the system of professional and industrial "subject-schools" for which the Germad business world is so noted has equally appealed to the technical experts and educators of India. Attention is also being directed to the *Soziale Frauenschulen*, i.e., the Social Welfare Schools for Women, whose importance for India cannot be over-emphasised.

These are some of the latest counts on which German culture has been demanding the attention of Indian thinkers and practical men. As for pre-Bismarckian Germany it may be said that theie was no universitarian in India during the nineteenth century who did not come under Goethe's influence. Hegel contributed much to the mentality of the reformers of Hinduism constituted under the Brāhmo-Samāj. Not less influential were Kant and Schopenhauer. It is with the *Swadeshi* Movement (1905) that Young India began to take interest in the Germany of exact science, medicine, industry, technocracy and business organization. Since then German science and industry have been well represented in Indian life. To the "ideas of 1905" Young India may be said to owe its discovery of Germany as the land of Frederick List, author of *Das Nationale System der Politischen Oekonomie*, and of Fichte, the philosopher of the "youth movement".

Since the end of the Great War the firms like Krupp, Borsig, Demag, M. A. N., Siemens-Schuckert, I. G. Farbenindustrie, Leuna-Werke, Junkers etc. have become some of the engineering and chemical realities of Indian experience. In and through the Reichsverband der deutschen Industrie, Verein deutscher Ingenieure, Verein deutscher Maschinenbauanstalten and other organizations it has been possible for Indians to catch glimpses of "rationalization" and the "second industrial revolution". Today in

Indian thought German *Kultur* is a living stream of contributions to nationalism and the world-forces from Herder to Hitler. It should be observed that in India, generally speaking, Austria,—no matter what be the fortunes of the *Anschluss* (union) question,—is taken as a member of the German culture-system, and the influence of this system on Indian culture is as profound and comprehensive as on any other culture-system of the world.

Kālidāsa's *Śakuntalā* was translated into German by Forster in 1791, and Herder introduced this German rendering to Goethe and Schiller. Schlegel's *Weisheit der Indier* (The Wisdom of the Indians) was published in 1808 and Bopp's studies in comparative grammar between 1816 and 1852. Since then indology has been sedulously cultivated in very many of the twenty-three Universities of Germany, and the results of researches by German indologists have to a certain extent filtered down to the non-Sanskritists, general intellectuals and indeed the entire *Volk* of Germany. This reputation of Germany for indology was already a great force among the Indian intellectuals even previous to 1905. The Germans were regarded as in a somewhat special sense the Sanskritists, the *Paṇḍits* or *Brāhmaṇas* of Eur-America. This position was created for them, among other reasons, on account of the employment of a large number of German scholars,—Aufrecht, Hultzsch, Kielhorn, Oppert, etc.,—in the Archæological Department of the Government of India.

It is very interesting that when Kauṭalya's *Artha-śāstra* was discovered in 1905 the question of its authenticity was left with the German *Brāhmaṇas* to decide. This dependence on the German *Paṇḍits* in matters relating to Indian culture was a feature in the scholarship of the British indologist Vincent Smith. In the third edition of the *Early History of India* (Oxford, 1914, p. 153) his chief support in regard to the Kauṭalya question is found to be the "researches of German scholars", which have "clearly established", as he thought, "that the *Arthaśāstra* is *echt und alt* (genuine and old)". In A. B. Keith's *History of Sanskrit Literature* (Oxford, 1928), also, the influence of German indology is patent at almost every page. It is not strange, therefore, that even those Indians who do not know the German language and cannot read, for instance, a work like Windisch's entitled *Geschichte der Sanskrit-philologie und Indischen Altertumskunde*, Vol. I. (Strasburg, 1917) and Vol. II. (Berlin 1920) should cherish extraordinary conceptions about Germany's contributions to the study of Indian culture.

In recent years (1920-35) the intimate contacts between Indian and German indologists have served but to maintain those ideas intact. Equipped as some Indian indologists today are with a knowledge of the German language they are cultivating a first-hand acquaintance with the publications of Zimmer, Lassen, Deussen, Garbe, Hillebrandt, von LeCoq, Jolly, Jacobi, Lueders, Geiger, Wuest, Hauer, Schrader, Schubring, Nobel, Zimmer jun., Breloer, von Glasenapp and others. The interest of von Glasenapp and Reinhard Wagner in the topics of modern India is a new feature in German indology. The humanistic approach to and secularization of indology in the researches of Hillebrandt, Fick, J. J. Meyer, Goetz, Piper and Breloer have been attracting the notice of Indian scholars.

Among those interested in economics, statistics, and social science the publications of Sering, Toennies, Diehl, Eugen Fischer, Spranger, Sombart, Schumpeter, Herkner, Adolf Weber, von Wiese, Zahn, Wagemann, Zwiedineck, Matschoss, Spann, Haushofer, Schumacher, Burgdoerfer, Lotz, Manes, Aschaffenburg, Freud, Waffenschmidt, Freyer, Koellreutter, Ruedin, Baxa, and others are gradually getting known as contributions likely to introduce Indian scholars to fruitful methods of investigations.[1]

The most important cultural influences on India

[1] See the present author's *Economic Development* (Madras 1926), "Industrial Centres and Economic Institutions in Germany" (*Journal of the Bengal National Chamber of Commerce*, September 1931), "Goethe, Germany and the Indian People" (*India and the World*, Calcutta, March 1932), "Social Idealism in Goethe's Lyrics and Dramas" (*Prabuddha Bhārata*, Calcutta, July and August 1932), "The Hitler-State" (*Insurance and Finance Review*, Calcutta, October and November 1933), *Parājita Jārmāni* (Germany under Defeat) Calcutta, 1921-35. Attention may be drawn to the papers read at the Bangīya German Vidyā Samsad (Bengali Society of German Culture), namely, H. Richter: "New Germany" (September 12, 1933), S. C. Mitra: "Experimental Psychology in Germany" (Nov. 21, 1933), published in the *Calcutta Review* for February 1934; K. L. Ganguli: "Lessing and German Literature" (January 10, 1934), H. Nitzschke: "Three German Sociologists: Toennies, von Wiese and Freyer" (March 27, 1934) published in the *C. R.* for May 1934; B. K. Ghosh: "Recent German Researches in Linguistics" (April 20, 1934), J. N. Basu: "Engineering and Industrial Germany" (December 15, 1934) published in the *Journal of the College of Engineering and Technology*, Jadabpur, Calcutta, January 1935, H. L. Roy: "Chemistry in German Industry and Commerce" (May 3, 1935) published in the *J. C. E. T.* September 1935, H. Kabir: "Kant and Modern Thought" (Sept. 13, 1935), B. K. Sarkar: "German Winter Relief as a Form of Social Service" (May 14, 1936), published in *Prabuddha Bhārata* (October 1936), B. N. Roy: "Aviation in Germany" (July 18, 1936) and S. C. Mitra: "The Gestalt Theory in German Psychology" (September, 26, 1936).

See also D. C. Das Gupta: "Fichte and His Educational Philosophy" (*India and the World*, Calcutta, August 1934). For the contributions of German (as of other) scholars to indology see E. Windisch: *Geschichte der Sanskrit Philologie and Indischen Altertumskunde*, Vol. I. (Strassburg 1917), and Vol. II. (Berlin 1920).

from the Russian side have been in the fields of literature and social philosophy. Tolstoy was already a force among the Indian *intelligentsia* in the nineteenth century. The establishment of the Duma by the Czar as an aftermath of the first Russian revolution engendered by the failures in the war with Japan (1904-05) was synchronous with the *Swadeshi* Movement in India and could not fail to be a source of inspiration in the Indian constitutional struggle. The treatment of social questions as a feature of Russian literature was discussed through the pages of the monthly *Grihastha* or "Householder" (1912-14) in connection with Karamsin's (1766-1826) *Poor Louisa*. Dostoyevski and Turgenev were introduced through the same journal during the war of 1914-1918. The *Swadeshi* movement in India was characterized by the enthusiasm for industrialization on the one hand and by that for folk movements, rural service, village reconstruction and cottage industry on the other. In regard to this second aspect Kropotkin's *Fields, Factories and Workshops* was a formative force. Down to the end of the Great War, however, interest in Russia was confined to a handful of star-gazers and culture-pioneers in India.

Russia became a power in the world of culture in the two Hemispheres with the establishment of the Soviet regime in November 1917. But it was not before the American or rather the British translators, authors and publishers rendered the Russian revolution intelligible to the English-speaking world from diverse angles of vision that Indian journalists, undergraduates and school boys could assimilate its contents and utilize them for their own nourishment. By 1925 Russia was perhaps established in India as a culture-force. Post-Lenin Russia has drawn a number of Indian travellers to Moscow.

Curiously enough, the greatest single pro-Russian factor in contemporary India has been Gandhi's doctrine of non-co-operation. No matter what be his own views regarding communism, Bolshevism or Sovietism, his propaganda in favour of Tolstoy's non-violence and condemnation of the state during 1919-22 was synchronous with Lenin's *digvijaya* in Russia and thus served to render Leninism popular in India.

But as yet hardly any Indian contributions on Russia are based on a knowledge of the original Russian language.[1] However, today there are as many political or socialist parties in the different provinces of India among the Labourites, Congressmen and other publicists *vis-à-vis* Stalin and Trotzky as there are in the British Isles or indeed in other countries where freedom of opinion is more or less tolerated. Besides, the progress of the two *Gosplans* (Five Year Plans) is being watched by Indians, generally through Anglo-American eyes, with the greatest interest.

It has to be observed, further, that Indian researchers in medicine, mathematics and the other exact sciences have some contact with the scientific contributions of contemporary Russia. One must not overlook the Russian indologists who have continued to be a force among the intellectuals of India from the days of Oldenbourg and the St. Petersburg *Dictionary of Sanskrit* to Minayeff, Vostrikov, Ober-

[1] K. T. Shah: *The Russian Experiment* (Bombay 1927), J. L. Nehru: *Soviet Russia* (Allahabad 1929). The present author's *Navīn Rusiār Jīvan Prabhāt* (The Life's Dawn of New Russia) published in the *Śamkha* and *Bijolī* (Calcutta, 1923-24), is based on Trotzky's German. See also the Chapter on Russia in his *Politics of Boundaries* (Calcutta 1926), *Political Philosophies Since 1905* (Madras 1928), *Comparative Pedagogics* (Calcutta 1929) and *Ekaler Dhana-Daulat O Arthasastra* (The Wealth and Economics of Our Own Times), 2 vols. (1930, 1935).

miller, Stcherbatsky and Nicholas Roerich.

Czechoslovakia is a "new country" created by the surgeons of the Versailles Treaty (1918-19) out of the womb of Central Europe. But she was born almost like a Minerva equipped with all the paraphernalia of modernism. As the inheritor of all that Austrian (and German) technocracy, science and organization have to offer to mankind, Czechoslovakia has been accepted by Young India almost as a little Germany, or, in any case, something like a Switzerland of Mid-Eastern Europe. Prague is gradually being appreciated by the Indian *intelligentsia* as but second only to Vienna in the entire "Balkan Complex", so to say, between the Baltic and the Black Seas.

As the Indian mind today is predominantly industrial and scientific, Czechoslovakia among all the "new states" has happened to monopolize the attention of Indian publicists. This is perhaps the only new culture-area with which the post-War geography of Europe has enriched the mentality of intellectuals in India.

And India's interest in Czechoslovakia is likely to expand in the near future. The reasons are very objective and realistic. Following the example of America, Germany and other countries, Czechoslovakia has been offering facilities to dozens of Indians for training in workshops. Besides, within the boundaries of India itself Czechoslovak enterprises, like the Bata Shoe Company, have been meeting Indians in a spirit of constructive co-operation. In 1932 this Company established a factory at Konnagar on the Ganges, a few miles north of Calcutta. Today a large town is being built to the south of Calcutta,—to be called Batanagar—in order to accommodate much enlarged workshops, furnished with an employment capacity of 5,000 hands. From American concerns in

India likewise Indians have been deriving similar benefits.

Czechoslovakia is not exclusively a nation of shoe-makers or glass bangle manufacturers and armament-suppliers, nor are the Indians all materialists. There are other items in Czechoslovak culture from which India has been deriving considerable inspiration. The rural hygiene of Czechoslovakia, the physical exercises associated with the Sokol movement, and President Benes's previous activities at the League of Nations as well as in connection with the Little Entente, have not been without some influence on Indian thought. Lésny's interest in Bengali language and literature, Czech-Czechenherz's interpretation of Indian culture through stories, Hujer's lectures and writings on India are being followed by the Indian journalists and educators with attention. Among indologists, of course, Winternitz because of his *History of Indian Literature* in German (now available in English) and Stein because of his studies in Kauṭalya are two of the attractions in Prague.

The International Congress of Philosophy at Prague in 1934 did not fail to bring to India's notice the positivistic tendencies of J. B. Kozak and the critical realism of Em. Radl. *La Philosophie Tchécboslovaque Contemporaine* (1935), dealing as it does with the philosophical contributions of Czechoslovak thinkers since 1918, is likely to be the starting point of India's renewed and somewhat steady interest in this field.[1] As for the older items in Bohemian culture, the establishment of the Prague University in 1348, the martyrdom of Hus (1418), the educational philosophy of Komen-

[1] N. Losskij: *Die zeitgenoessische Philosophie in der Tschecho-slowakei* (Prague 1935).

sky (Comenius, 1592-1671), Drobavsky's revival of the Czech language (*c* 1805), Havlicek's enthusiasm for Mazzini in the movement of 1848, Kollar's interest in Herder (*c* 1850),—all these have some meaning in India today.

Last but not least, Indians are acquainted with the energism of the grand old man, ex-President Masaryk, the father of Czechoslovakia. Masaryk, the democrat and liberal statesman as well as the humane servant of his people, is well established in the affections of the Indian public as an idealist and a constructive social worker. In the story of his growth from the period of *The Czech Question* (1894) to *The Making of a State* (1925-27) Indians can follow the slow transformation of a mystical and non-political soul-philosophy into the most businesslike and realistic bargain emerging out of the "conjuncture of circumstances".

The most successful diplomat of the war-period from among the champions of the subject nationalities, Masaryk has known how to carry his head high in the interest of freedom and democracy down to 1935. India's interest in the psychology and social philosophy of Masaryk will grow from more to more, and his country bids fair to attract serious visitors from India in large numbers.[1]

[1] J. Herben: *Thos. G. Masaryk* (Prague 1919), Gruber: *Czechoslovakia* (New York 1924); the present author's *Politics of Boundaries and Tendencies in International Relations* (Calcutta 1926), *Economic Development* (Madras 1926), *Social Insurance Legislation and Statistics* (Calcutta 1936), "Masaryk's Mind in Growth" (*Calcutta Review*, February 1936); Pelc: *Rural Hygiene in Czechoslovakia* (Prague 1931), S. N. Chakravarti: "The Commerce and Industry of Czechoslovakia" (*Insurance and Finance Review*, Calcutta, 1934); D. C. Das Gupta: "Comenius and His Educational Philosophy" (*India and the World*, Calcutta, 1934), G. C. Ray: "Economic Developments in Czechoslovakia" (*Arthik Unnati*, Calcutta 1935).

In India's cultivation of *viśva-śakti* a distinct place has to be accorded to her relations with the countries of Asia. We have already touched upon the achievements of Japan since 1905 as formative forces in modern Indian life and thought. The developments in Persia since 1906, in Egypt—which although lying in Africa is treated by Indians as an Asian territory,—since 1908, in Turkey since 1908, in China since 1911-12, and in Afghanistan since 1919 are regarded in Indian public life and journalism almost as items of India's fortunes.

The Persian Medjlis, Enver Pasha, the Young Turk, Sun Yatsen, Zaghlul Pasha, Amanulla, Kemal Pasha, Riza Shah and Chiang Kaishek are almost household words among Indian intellectuals.[1] The work of the Pan-Asian Congress which held its first session at Nagasaki (Japan) in 1926 as well as that of the Pan-Oriental League which met for the first time in Odessa (Russia) during the same year have their bearings on the growth of views in India.

The relations are not all political, however. The paintings of Persia and China have had some solid influence on the work of modern Indian artists. In 1934 the International Buddhist Congress was held at Tokyo and the Asiatic Labour Congress at Colombo. India was well represented in both these functions. The same year the Firdausi millenary was celebrated in different centres of India. The growth of an Asian consciousness among the Indians as a part of their world-sense or internationalism is one of the outstanding features of Indian culture during the last three decades or so.

[1] The present author's *Politics of Boundaries* (Calcutta 1926) and T. N. Das: *Foreign Policy in the Far East* (New York 1936).

A great value has to be attached to the influences of the different countries of Asia on the antiquarian researches of Indian scholars with special reference to "Greater India", a part of which has already been described elsewhere (pp. 84-104). The movement in this direction commenced under the guidance of Satis Chandra Mukerjee of the Dawn Society (est. 1903, Calcutta) during 1906-10 and took the first concrete shape in Radha Kumud Mookerji's *History of Indian Shipping* (1911), sections of which were published in the *Dawn Society's Magazine*. Modern India's *liaison* with Asia of the past as well as of the present is thus being built up on extensive and deep foundations.[1]

It is not necessary to refer to the Indian Universities in connection with internationalism as they have been by all means among the pioneers in the establishment of India's contacts with the British and other forces in the arts and sciences. But the attention of scholars deserves to be drawn to the fact that the Universities in India, although run on British lines, are not exclusively British in ideology and spiritual outfit. The Universities of India have grown to be no less centres of universal culture than are the Universities of Great Britain and Ireland, nay, of entire Eur-America and Japan.

A special reference must however be made to the Readerships and Tagore Law Lectureships of the Calcutta University. For nearly half a century it is through these media that Young India has been brought into direct academic and social fellowship with

[1] The present author's *Chinese Religion Through Hindu Eyes* (Shanghai 1916), "The Futurism of Young Asia" in the *International Journal of Ethics* (Chicago, July 1918), *The Futurism of Young Asia* (Berlin 1922). See the publications of the Greater India Society (Calcutta).

a large number of foreign scholars. To mention some of the more recent imports, the American international jurist Garner, the French indologists Lévi and Foucher, the British Islamologist Margoliouth, historian Arthur Newton and town planning expert Harris, the German indologists Lueders, von Glasenapp and Goetz, the French jurist Solus, the Czechoslovak indologists Lesny and Winternitz, the Hungarian Turcologist Germanus, the German mathematician Blaschke and physicist Sommerfeld, the Italian indologists Formichi and Tucci, the Turkish feminist Mme. Halide Bey, the Japanese poet Yone Noguchi and the Dutch Javanist Kempers may be singled out as having been invited to co-operate with the Indian world of culture.

Internationalism has been promoted by private initiative also. In 1904 the Indian Association for the Scientific and Industrial Education of Indians in foreign countries was established by Jogen Ghosh and has been functioning still. The National Council of Education, Bengal, established in 1906, has made it a point to specialize in mechanical, electrical and chemical engineering through its scholars educated abroad. The industrialization of Bengal and to a certain extent of India has been rendered possible because, among other agencies, of the youngmen such as have been associated with these institutions.

The Bose Institute, established by Jagadis Chunder Bose in 1916, is a scientific laboratory. Under the auspices of this institution Hans Molisch, the botanist of Vienna, was invited to Calcutta for a semester.

Rabindranath Tagore's *Viśva-Bhāratī* (est. 1922) at Shanti-Niketan (Bolpur) has likewise been instrumental in importing scholars, especially indologists, from France (Lévi), Norway (Konow), Czechoslovakia (Winternitz) and Italy (Formichi) and rendering them available for Indian archæologists and culture-historians. Persian and Chinese scholars as well as Japanese artists have also been introduced to India through the same channel.

In regard to the promotion of internationalism in culture a special place belongs to the Mahabodhi Society at Calcutta. It was established in 1891 by Anagarika Dhammapala (1866-1933) of Ceylon, who may be described as another Vivekānanda of Young India. As true Buddhist, Dhammapala felt that Buddhism is neither exclusively Ceylonese nor exclusively Indian. For, in truth it is Tibetan, Burmese, Siamese, Chinese, Korean and Japanese as well at the same time. Hence as an embodiment of the traditional *appamāda* or energism of the Buddhists he sought to establish the intercourse of modern India with China, Japan and other countries of Asia. He is one of the pioneers of the Young Asia movement. The work started by him through the *Mahābodhi* journal (1892) and otherwise has contributed to the cementing of bonds between the diverse regions of the Buddhist world; and the beginnings of an International Buddhist University have recently been laid at Sarnath near Benares (1935).

The Research Fellows of the *Bangīya Dhana-Vijnān Pariṣat* (Bengali Institute of Economics), established in 1928, have been carrying on investigations in economics, theoretical and applied, in the perspective of "world-economy" and publishing the results of their studies in Bengali in the *Ārthik Unnati* (Economic Progress) monthly, which has been going on since 1926. Likewise in Bengali are being published the studies of the Research Fellows associated with the "*Āntarjātik Banga*" *Pariṣat* ("International Bengal" Institute), established in 1932, which is interested in researches in sociology, constitution, current history, law and pedagogics on the basis of international statistics and developments. Then there is the *Bangīya German-Vidyā Samsad* (Bengali Society of German Culture), established in 1933, which enables Indian scholars to communicate to the world of arts and sciences the results of their studies based on original German documents.

The work of the Indian dailies, weeklies and monthlies in the development of India's contact with the world-forces has already been referred to as substantial enough to entitle their being described as "unrecognised" Universities. It remains only to add that the Indian students in foreign countries, as well as merchants, travellers, workingmen, cultivators, preachers and others settled or sojourning abroad,—the Indians overseas,—have accomplished a great deal in the matter of destroying India's spiritual isolation and introducing the world-atmosphere into India's home affairs.

The impact on Mother India of the work of Indians residing temporarily or permanently in the two Hemispheres,—as "emigrants", "indentured" labourers, businessmen, culture-pioneers or otherwise,—is of tremendous importance and demands an independent thesis. No history of modern India can be complete which is indifferent to or overlooks the achievements —agricultural, industrial and cultural,—of this "Greater India" in the nineteenth and twentieth centuries.

The Dignity of The Mother-Tongues

The assimilation of world-forces from the most diverse nooks and corners has been paradoxically enough but catering to the promotion of nationalism itself, and this in a profoundly influential manner. Throughout India there is in evidence a strong movement in favour of Bengalicising, Hindicizing, Urduizing, Tamilizing, Marathicizing and so forth some of the best specimens of the thought-products originating in other countries. A great deal of Indian literary activity in diverse branches from journalism to metaphysics is manifest in adaptations, paraphrases or summaries from foreign sources. Formal translations also occupy a part of the contemporary literary output. In this development India is but repeating the attempts in every country of the world to render available to its nationals the literary treasures of foreign peoples. And this is all the more to be observed in India because here as in Japan, China, Java, Persia, Turkey and Egypt virtually the entire literature on higher science and philosophy has to be borrowed wholesale from the standard classics in the Western languages.

Perhaps the most advanced of all Indian languages in the direction of translation from foreign tongues is Urdu or Hindustani (as distinguished from Hindi). The Muslim University at Aligarh has its eyes in this direction. Solid progress has been made at Hyderabad. There at the Osmania University highest education is being imparted through the medium of Urdu. It is to be remembered, however, at the same time that Urdu is the only living language of India in which up till now such an experiment has been undertaken and deemed to be possible. The experiment has proved to be successful. All other Indian languages have still to play the "second fiddle" in India's educational system,—even in those which are conducted independently of the Government auspices by "National Councils" or "National Universities" under the influence of the "ideas of 1905".

But the desire to bring the mother-tongues up to the level of an adequate medium of higher culture suited to the modern requirements of a progressive life furnishes the *élan* of *Swarajist* activity in education. Translations, adaptations and compilations from foreign sources, whether by individual publishing houses or by collective efforts, are bidding fair to become prominent in the journalism and literary life of every important city.

Today in every province there are scholars who are competent enough to translate direct from French and German. The knowledge of Italian, Dutch, Spanish or Russian is not yet so widely distributed. But it should be possible to start a movement in each language-area of India for the translation of, say, a hundred works of science, philosophy, economics, history etc. from the leading European languages within the next decade. Indian publishers and authors may come to some understanding with the publishing houses abroad.

The cry was worded for Bengal[1] before the Literary Conferences at Malda and Mymensingh in 1911 to the following effect: "In what way and in how many years can our literature occupy the position of French, German and English for the study of science, philosophy, history and other serious subjects in the highest classes of a University? The efforts and activities of our men of letters will have to be regulated in such a manner as to focus our whole literary devotion on the realization of this single object".

[1] In the present author's *Sāhitya-Sevī* (The Man of Letters) published in Bengali, English, Hindi and Marathi. See the *Modern Review* for August 1911. See also his *Śikṣā-vijnāner Bhūmikā* (Calcutta, 1910) and *Introduction to the Science of Education* (London 1913).

In this as in other trends of literary growth Young India is exhibiting not only the nationalistic animus of the Poles, Czechs, Serbs, and Irish but also the Herderian and Fichtean romanticism for the linguistic or cultural soul, *Volksseele*, *Volksgeist* etc.[1] And it is from such a platform of cultural independence and not from the standpoint of a senseless anti-alienism that Gandhi's prejudice against the English language (1921-23) acquires a deep significance in the history of contemporary civilization. In this item as in many others Gandhism is but the "ideas of 1905" somewhat effectively propagated on a large scale throughout India, especially in Gujarat.

Urdu Translations

Translators from foreign works into Urdu are legion. The volume of translation-literature in Urdu has been growing from year to year. Even now most of the translations are from English. But the translations from Arabic and Persian are no less voluminous. Nay, Sanskrit, Bengali and Hindi texts also have been rendered into Urdu. It would be wrong, therefore, to suppose that the "borrowed" section of Urdu literature is Moslem in inspiration. Urdu is not a "Mussalman" language. One is struck by the catholicity and internationalism of the reading public in Urdu language when one goes through the list of authors such as have been rendered accessible to it in translations.

[1] Herder (1744-1803): *Saemmtliche Werke* (Berlin, 1877-1913) Vol. XIII, pp. 384-385; Fichte (1762-1814): *Reden an die Deutsche Nation*, Fourth Address; K. Francke: *A History of German Literature as Determined by Social Forces* (New York, 1911); J. Baxa: *Einfuehrung in die romantische Staatswissenschaft* (Jena, 1923); P. Kluckhohn: *Die deutsche Romantik* (Leipzig 1924); R. R. Ergang: *Herder and the Foundations of German Nationalism* (New York 1931).

A short list of the authors and translated books is being furnished below:

Science: Draper's *Conflict between Religion and Science*, Darwin, Wallace, Haeckel, Huxley, Lyall, Geikie, Tyndal, Bose, Kelvin, Maxwell, Crookes and Lodge.

Education: Spencer, Bain, Froebel, Pestalozzi, Herbart and Montessori.

General History and Biography: Plutarch's *Lives of Eminent Greeks and Romans*, Rollin's *Greece*, Bury's *History of Greece*, Thacker and Schwill's *General History of Europe*, Dozy's *Islamic Spain*, Wallace's *Russia*, Abbott's *Napoleon*, Green's *History of the English People*, Vincent Smith's *Early History of India*, Elphinstone's *History of India*, Malcolm's *History of Persia*, and portions of Gibbon's *Roman Empire*.

Politics and economics: Aristotle's *Politics*, Mill's *Liberty*, *Representative Government* and *Political Economy*; Bell's *Laws of Wealth*; Morley's *Machiavelli* and *Reminiscences;* Curzon's *Persia*; Mazzini's *Duties of Man;* Schuster's *Strangling of Persia;* Blunt's *Future of Islam;* Vanbery's *Future of Islam*; Seeley, Bluntschli, Wilson, Pollock, Sidgwick, Jevons, Marshall and Morison.

Philosophical History: Guizot's *History of Civilization*, Buckle's *Civilization in England;* Le Bon's *Civilization of the Arabs* and *Civilization of Hindustan;* Lecky's *European Morals*; Draper's *Intellectual Development of Europe* and Dutt's *Ancient Hindu Civilization.*

Philosophy: Plato, Aristotle, Chāṇakya's *Maxims*, Seneca's *Reflections*, Berkeley's *Principles* and *Dialogues;* Le Bon's *Crowd*, *The Psychology of the*

Evolution of Peoples and *The Psychology of the Great War;* Bacon, Hume, Kant, Mill, Spencer, James and Stout.

Poetry and Drama: Homer's *Iliad*, *The Mahābhārata*, *The Rāmāyaṇa* (Vālmiki's as well as Tulsidāsa's), Kālidāsa's *Sakuntalā and Meghaduta*, Milton's *Paradise Lost;* Tagore's *Gitanjali and Chitra;* Shakespeare's *Othello*, *Hamlet*, *King Lear*, *Tempest*, *Romeo and Juliet*, *Cymbeline*, *The Merchant of Venice*, *Winter's Tale*, *Measure for Measure*, *The Comedy of Errors*, and *As You Like It*; Sheridan's *Pizarro*; Sophocles, Sappho, Dante, Goethe, Longfellow, Southey, Shelley, Byron, Wordsworth and Tennyson.

Fiction: Reynolds, Scott, Marie Corelie, Conan Doyle, Bankim Chandra Chatterjee, Tagore, Stevenson, Rider Haggard, Oscar Wilde, Bernard Shaw, and Wells.

General Prose: Macaulay, Carlyle, Smiles and Lubbock.

In the present context we are not interested in the original literature in Urdu. A word may be added to say that it is not inconsiderable whether in poetry or prose.[1]

The Legacies of Lajpat Rai

Lajpat Rai (1865-1928) is one of those few publicists of modern India who without being a Bengali have their second home in Bengal. In this he is one of a trio which comprises Tilak and Gandhi. It is questionable if there is another non-Bengali maker of modern India except Gandhi, Tilak and Lajpat who may be regarded as having profoundly influenced the life and thought

[1] R. B. Saksena: *History of Urdu Literature* (Allahabad, 1927).

of the Bengali people as almost a Bengali. India is after all such a huge continent that in questions of deeper import to the problems of life the diverse provinces can be spiritually influenced almost exclusively by regional or provincial leaders. One may examine the situation among the Marathas, Madrasis or the Punjabis as among the Bengalis. It will perhaps be borne out from every region that in the long run extra-regional influences do not count for much in the making of its policies and trends. To say that the Bengalis look upon Lajpat as one of their own thereby behaving as but second only to the Punjabis is the highest recognition that an Indian can possibly win on account of services to the people of India.

Lajpat Rai's services to the Indian people are marked by several outstanding features. He is one of those far-sighted "publicists" of India who made it a point to "write" and contribute to the making of "thought". And in this field his writings and contributions to thought were confined almost exclusively to contemporary questions and current affairs. Every publicist is of course a "speaker" and by public addresses contributes to political, social and economic thought. In this sense there is nothing special about Lajpat. Then, again, almost every publicist is a journalist whether as editor or contributor. And since journalists also are writers and makers of thought it may not be possible to make any distinction between Lajpat and other publicists. We intend to emphasise the fact, however, that Lajpat went beyond speaking and journalism into what may be described as the sphere of writing proper or authorship. It is as one of those intellectuals who take to writing, as it were, for writing's sake under the inspiration of more or less purely inquisitive or studious habits, in other words, as a "scholar" that Lajpat the writer and contributor to thought has to be distinguished from many other writers and contributors to thought among the publicists.

In Indian public life it is not possible to mention many such "scholars". The first that deserves mention in this connection is Romesh Dutt and the second Tilak. It would be interesting to analyze the literary career of, say, all the Congress Presidents since 1885 (p. 412). Perhaps one should come to the conclusion that not even Gokhale who was eminently noted for his speeches on the budget at the Legislative Assembly might be described as an "author" in the sense in which Dutt, Tilak and Lajpat were authors. Lajpat's differences from Dutt and Tilak lie on the surface. Lajpat was a "self-made" man in scholarship as in other domains of life. His range, again, was not ambitious enough to cover the metaphysico-philosophical regions of Tilak. Nor was he an encyclopædist in scholarship and literary creativeness like Dutt.

If we ignore his Urdu "history of India" and contributions to Urdu journalism on topics of all sorts such as every editor or publicist is professionally compelled to touch we may say that Lajpat the scholar or "researcher" was a specialist in contemporary politics. His *forte* lay in the study of modern developments, political, economic, social, educational and what not. In Urdu he wrote on Mazzini, the maker of modern Italy, and an inspirer of modern India. The contents of his English works are very instructive in this regard. *The Ārya Samāj* (London 1915), *The Evolution of Japan* (Calcutta 1917), *Young India* (New York 1918), *National Education in India* (London 1918), *The United States of America* (Calcutta, 1919), *The Political Future of India* (New York, 1919), *England's*

Debt to India (New York 1920), *Unhappy India* (Calcutta, 1928), indicate in their very titles the characteristic make-up of Lajpat's brain.

It is applied politics, comparative in essence, with special reference to the India of today and tomorrow that commanded his attention, and it is on the elucidation of these problems that he bestowed his scholarship or researches. No other "publicist" in modern India has been a specialized author on these questions in the same sense as Lajpat. Had Naoroji's literary work been more continuous and steady than it actually is perhaps it would have been possible to treat Lajpat formally as his successor. Another near approach to Lajpat would have been Gokhale. But as we have already seen, Gokhale did not go beyond the occasional "speeches", howsoever meritorious they be.

Authorship and scholarship are time-killing agencies. The scholar has always to be at the desk and in the library. The fact that Lajpat has, among other things, to be remembered as a "scholar", as a researcher and as an author, is explained by another great fact of his life, as can be attested by many of his friends and visitors at London, New York and Tokyo, nay, in India also, namely, that he was wedded to the desk and wedded to the library. Notwithstanding his preoccupations with the party politics at home and abroad, Lajpat could not be beaten by any of the "professional" intellectuals or researchers in applied politics or other sciences on the score of devotion to bookshelves and sheets of writing paper. He took to political research, scholarship or authorship in a religious manner, so to say. His studious and literary habits raised him to the highest level attained by some of the busiest politician-authors of Eur-America. Without discussing his political, economic or social views we do not hesitate to mark

Lajpat's services to the Indian people in this field as some of the most signal contributions from the sphere of Congress leaders.

Here it may not be out of place to observe that Lajpat had no sympathy with Bipin Pal's philosophical comprehensiveness and synthetic presentations. The intellectual subtleties of the latter's *Soul of India* were the farthest removed from his matter of fact and prosaic view of things. And it is interesting that Bipin Pal is no less the maker of Young Bengal than Lajpat of the Young Punjab.

It is very characteristic of the man Lajpat that his ideology was not made by himself alone. Lajpat's mind was the result of co-operative discussions,—made by thousand and one *têle-à-têtes*. He was learning from others all the time. It is his career as a man of letters, as an intellectual that is perhaps somewhat responsible for his openness of mind and receptivity to ideas. It is this that rendered him so susceptible to "discussions". And in this he was greatly helped by his personal habits also. He was a man of the masses in mind and life. Nobody ever could notice any aloofness in his dealings with others. There are many publicists to whom, in spite of philanthropic disposition and charitable habits, aristocratic aloofness is almost a second nature. In Lajpat's life aloofness was entirely unthinkable. Nothing was more natural to him in social intercourse than democratic give and take even with loafers and vagabonds. His chummy and mobocratic tendencies brought within his range even more extensive circles than within Madan Mohan Malaviya's, who as a man of the people has all his life been a profound democrat in habits in spite of his being an orthodox Brāhmaṇ.

As a consequence it was possible for the young,

the liberal and the radical to find access to Lajpat's mind in the easiest manner. He was perpetually prepared to receive influences from all and sundry. He assimilated even words and phrases, nay, the titles of his writings from the young. None of the publicists of India were perhaps so much in contact with the youngsters, the rising, the new, the rebellious and the militant as Lajpat. His career bears the marks of influence from the Punjabi youth, the Madrasi youth, the U.P. youth, the Maratha youth, and last but not least, the Bengali youth. He *was* Young India.

No Indian politician of substantial importance could exhibit in his career the impress of so many novel urges and fresh adventures as Lajpat. His was the career of eternal youth, ever moving from idea to idea, always growing from movement to movement,—the constant journey from freshness to freshness. It is the youngsters that influenced him, the spirit of youth that conquered him. And his literature, his scholarship, his writings have served but to transmit this freshness and creativeness, the spirit of youth, into the public life of India.

It is the restlessness of spirit that accounted for Lajpat's interest in the new. His propaganda in favour of Dayānanda testifies as much to this spirit as that in favour of Mazzini. And subsequently it drove him into sympathy with the ideals of Leninism also.

Nothing is more characteristic of Lajpat's public life, be it repeated, than his constant association with the young and the new and his perpetual submission to their demands. In the company of the young and the new he hardly ever dictated, he almost invariably followed. His spirit was therefore always a going concern. He never ceased to grow. The philosophy of perpetual youth is the dominant characteristic of his contributions to Indian public life. A contribution like this, extending as it did over quite a long period, can hardly be attributed to any other Indian publicist. One may perhaps recall Chittaranjan Das's submission to the spirit of youth. But Chittaranjan's effective career as a publicist was too short for comparison with Lajpat in this regard.

Perhaps the most distinctive legacy of Lajpat as a "senior" publicist, or "*Genro*" (Elder Statesman), to use a Japanese expression,—to the people of India was his cultivation of *viśva-śakti* or world-forces. He is the first conscious internationalist among the "Elders" in modern Indian public life. There are, of course, very few political leaders of India who have not had first-hand experience of non-Indian, especially, Western, or rather British civilization. And yet it is a fact that with the exception of Naoroji no Indian leader cared to understand and assimilate the methodology of British public life. It is the urge for the new in Lajpat's life, the desire to renew and educate himself perpetually that took him to the West several times previous to 1914. During all these visits, however, his goal invariably was England. And although he was not a mere dilettante or pleasure-seeking tourist and although the object of these journeys was in the main the acquisition of political experience it is worth while to stress that he never cared to come into contact with any other country except England. So when in 1914 under the influence of the spirit of youth Lajpat determined for the first time,—although hesitantly,—to cross the Atlantic over to the New World it was for himself as well as for Indian public life a veritable rejuvenation.

The period of five or six years (1914-19) that he spent in the U.S.A. and Japan brought him into living contact with the creative forces in world-culture, world-economy and world-politics. For the first time he learnt that the politics and culture of modern India were being made as much outside India as within. His contacts with the young and the new forced upon him the experience that "Greater India" had been a reality of these world-forces for over a decade or so. And once again he yielded to the urges of youth. He became a convert to the cult of the youngsters in regard to the importance of India's foreign activities for India's regeneration. The utilization of world-forces in the interest of India's growth was discovered by him to be a question of practical politics. In quarrels, fights, jealousies and meannesses the men and women of the white races were likewise discovered to be not much different from those in Asia. He was thoroughly "humanized" and became convinced of India's strength from new angles of vision.

The new convictions as regards men, manners, social forces etc. did not dawn upon him as the result of any theoretical studies in the "science of history" and international movements or race-psychology and anthropology. Pragmatist and shrewdly business-like as he was, it took him months or even years of wear and tear among the men and women of the most diverse races, nationalities and professions to realize that he was growing into something really new and fruitful under the pressure of novel conditions.

American political and cultural life presented to Lajpat as to every non-American the spectacle of an eternal "League of Nations", so to say. In the United States Lajpat encountered not the Americans alone. All the European peoples from the Irish to the Portuguese, Italians, Rumanians, Czechs, Hungarians, Lithuanians, Poles and Russians were there. From the Asian side there were the Persians, the Chinese and the Japanese. Then there were the Jews, the Negroes, the Mormonists, the Greek Church Christians, the Syrians, the Armenians and so forth. It did not take the Americans, the Europeans, the Asians and the Africans of the New World long to realize that the precursors of Lajpat in the U.S.A. had prepared the ground for India in quite an efficient manner such as might do credit to the younger representatives of any nation. The "seniors" of all those peoples also felt that Lajpat the senior publicist of India, "moderate" as he was in political demands, might function as a senior anywhere on earth, and that men who later were destined to win celebrity as Masaryk were not made of other stuff than what the "Hindus", young and old, had brought with them from India.

It was during these years that Lajpat's manhood was remade. He rose to the full stature of his personality. The world-standard was injected into his intellectual consciousness, the comparative method became the integral part of his logic, and he mastered the A. B. C. of genuine political science and diplomacy. Thus were acquired for India the strategy and tactics of public life, the positive foundations of realistic internationalism.

One item deserves a special mention in this connection. Previous to 1914 among the senior publicists of India "labour" as a category was virtually unknown and socialism as a cult hardly existed even in ideology. Even the professional intellectuals and academicians were innocent of these categories. It is a special feature in the mentality of Lajpat that,—without troubling himself about the theories of the capitalistic economy,—he was drawn almost instinctively to the labour-leaders of the Western world. It is among the members of the British Labour Party that he felt at home. In the U.S.A. also the group that attracted him the most was the "crowd" associated with the Rand School of Social Science and the Civic Club in New York, both centres of socialistic intellectuals. In the evolution of socialism as a power in Indian public life Lajpat's associations with British and American labourites are to be appraised as a formative force. Among the many things with which Lajpat has enriched the Indian *intelligentsia* not the least significant are the doses of socialistic philosophy imported by him from his experience of the world-forces.

The virtually undivided attention to contemporary Indian politics as a subject of scholarship is a precious legacy bequeathed by Lajpat to the publicists of India. His constant preparedness to assimilate the spirit of the young and the new is a feature that everybody in India and abroad would appreciate as the key to progress as well as to mental and moral freedom. Finally, by cultivating intimacy with the world-forces he has opened up to Indian publicists and intellectuals the universal and world-tried methods of national growth and expansion. Altogether, Lajpat should be valued as the greatest contribution of the Punjab after Ranjit Singh and one of the most remarkable products of creative India in the twentieth century.

Asutosh's Cult of Cultural Equality

Asutosh Mookerji (1864—1924) was known chiefly and to a certain extent almost exclusively as a "schoolman." But he was first and foremost a nationalist and a patriot. Rather, it is the life's urges of Asutosh the nationalist and the patriot that found positive expression in the activities of Asutosh the "schoolman". He was not an educationalist in the conventional and stereotyped sense of the term. His educational policy and programme were but planks in a larger scheme of constructive statesmanship.

To him the one problem worth energizing for as the maker of schools and colleges and as the reformer of higher learning was nothing short of elevating the culture of the Bengali people to the rank of a creative world-force, original, assimilative and self-determined. The one ambition of his life as a schoolman and as a patriot was to see Young Bengal function as a power among the powers of the world, on terms of equality and in co-operation with the living spiritual, scientific, economic and social agencies in the two hemispheres. And in this ambition he has had but one colleague among the "Elders" of contemporary Bengal. This is none other than Rabindranath, who, however, be it said *en passant*, hardly ever came into official or close social intercourse with the great academician in any of his perambulations.

The reference to Rabindranath brings into the boldest relief a signal feature of Asutosh's personality. Of all the leading men of Bengal since the days of Rammohun, Asutosh is perhaps the only publicist of the front rank who never crossed the seas and never saw with his own eyes the structure and rhythm of the modern world. And yet of all the social reformers, politicians, culturists and educators nobody was more convinced than Asutosh as to the necessity of modernizing the life and institutions of the Indian people.

Nearly thirty years ago, in the year 1907 the present writer enjoyed the privilege, although yet within his teens, to enter into warm discussion with Asutosh on several occasions. The themes were "national education", *swaraj*, country's welfare, and the entire socio-economic complex. On one occasion the following sarcastic remarks fell from his lips:

"*Ekśo deḍśo bachhar āge āmāder ṭhākurdādārā ki korto jāniṣ? Tārā du pātā pharśī poḍto ār khaḍam pāye diye beḍāto! Eito chhilo sekāle āmāder dauḍ"!* (Do you know how our fathers and grandfathers used to live a century or a century and a half ago? They used to read a page or two of Persian and moved about with wooden sandals on! This was the limit of our life's interests and experiences in those days).

Asutosh was not the man to be bamboozled by idealistic and roseate pen-pictures of ancient Hindu or medieval Hindu-Moslem civilizations. His brain was that of a realist like that of Vidyāsāgara, for instance, who, in spite of his special interest in old Sanskritic culture, was not prepared to ignore its limitations as a discipline for the modern mind. And while the trend of discussion referred to above was neither anti-ancient nor anti-medieval,—while indeed the conversations turned on topics of scientific researches into and sympathetic approaches to India's past history,—Asutosh's whole spirit was fired by the enthusiasm of enriching the people of India with modern institutions and, what is more, with modern outlook in learning as well as in life.

The simple Bengali "Ashu Babu of Bhawanipur", as known in those days, keen as he was on modernism, was necessarily a serious student of world-forces. And so, as soon as opportunities presented themselves, Asutosh knew how to utilize for Young India the resources of Eur-Amerięa and Japan as available at Harvard, London, Paris, Berlin, Rome, and Tokyo. The foundations of the Indian culture of tomorrow he sought to lay broad and deep in the international discoveries and inventions of today. The emissaries of Asutosh, scientific as well as literary, were in evidence in every nook and corner of the academic world, so to say; and he did not neglect to invite the men of science and learning from here and there and everywhere to the banks of the Ganges.

The ambition of Asutosh went farther. It was not enough that the world-forces were being brought into contact with the creative spirits of Young India, and that the exchange of cultures was being established in a direct manner. He wanted to see all this intercourse established on a basis of equality. It is the insistence on equality in scientific and social dealings with the foreigners, both at home and abroad, that was an ingredient in his very life-blood and really furnished the spiritual foundations of his being.

A bit of another conversation of those early *Swadeshi* days will illustrate the mental and moral make-up of Asutosh. In one of his fighting moods he declared, as usual, again, in Bengali, in part as follows:—"It is your nationalist leaders, the *Swadeshiwallas* of today, who dare not appear in public in the streets of Simla and Darjeeling or even in Calcutta with their *dhoti* and slippers on in the fear lest they be observed by their foreign acquaintances. But I, the son of a Brāhmaṇa, have never in my life felt ashamed to expose my *paitā* (sacred thread) to the gaze of these foreigners. Cowards at heart as these leaders are, how can they command respect from foreigners or emancipate the mind of Young India and inculcate in young men the spirit of independence and equality in regard to the ruling forces of today?" These words contain a very bitter truth and exhibit the spirit which years later pervaded his epoch-making plan and measures in connection with the organization of higher education at Calcutta.

It was a part of his ambition to see the intellectuals of Young India spurn the attitude of *kowtow* and carry their heads high before the intellectuals of Europe, America and Japan. He wanted to exorcize the inferiority-complex out of Young India's mentality by a continuous series of first-class achievements in every sphere.

This was his ambition. But he was fully conscious of the intellectual and moral shortcomings of his countrymen. He knew that Indian youths and adults used to look upon foreign intellectuals as geniuses, as demi-gods, as *avatāras*, or what not, and behave with them as juniors to superiors and masters, of whom one ought only to beg for certificates and letters of recommendation. It was too well-known to him, besides, that Indian intellectuals generally considered their chief or exclusive function to be that of summarizing the publications of foreign book-makers. It did not take him long to realize that his ambition was yet too premature for the common run of Bengali and other Indian academicians, who, constituted as they were in brain stuff, were incompetent to emancipate themselves from their spiritual imbecility and hence incapable of asserting their claims to equality of treatment in the world's republic of sciences and arts. The same cowardice that he discovered among his peers in regard to *dhoti*, he found also in the more or less universal attitude of his countrymen in regard to their own intellectual worth. The measure of Asutosh's greatness is the height of his ambition or rather the depth of the country's degeneracy and diffidence.

Asutosh did not live long enough to take more than the preliminary first steps towards the fulfilment of his dream. His ambition in this direction was indeed shared by a few of his contemporaries like Rashbehari Ghosh, Taraknath Palit and some other founders and benefactors of the National Council of Education. But, on the whole, the sentiment was not more than vaguely felt and indistinctly realized by these contemporaries. The next step in the realization of Asutosh's dream about India's equality with the great powers of Eur-America and Japan, in so far at any rate as a large number of individual achievements is concerned, can become a reality of everyday only when the country is prepared to organize regular post-M.A. and post-M.Sc. studies and investigations on an extensive scale and in a systematic manner. The admirers of Asutosh and lovers of Young India will have to ponder over this question for quite a while.

Another serious shortcoming of his countrymen of which Asutosh was painfully conscious was the disrespect, nay, contempt with which our mother-tongues were treated in the institutions of higher learning and centres of social importance throughout India. This was another item in the inferiority-complex prevalent among his colleagues, high and low. It was therefore but a part of the measures calculated to strengthen the backbone of the people of India and compel the international recognition of Indian culture as a modern world-force when he fervently espoused the cause of the Indian languages like that of the Indian *dhoti* or of the Indian intellectuals. To set the ball rolling, the mother-tongue of the Bengali people was elevated by him to the dignity of a *subject* of highest instruction (M. A.) in Bengal.

The revolution was thereby only initiated. But in order that man-to-man relations of mutual respect might be established between the scholars and scientists of Bengal and those of other countries the Bengali language would have to be made the *medium* of highest instruction, research and publication in every science and every art in all the urban and rural nuclei of culture. That end of the revolution remains yet to be consummated. It is this aspect of the "ideas of 1905," as cherished by Young Bengal, that should appeal to every Indian in a powerful manner, because it is on the consummation of this revolution that the heightening of intellectual efficiency, the ecomony of time and energy in matters educational, and last but not least, the expansion of democracy in Indian life and thought would in a large measure depend.

In his noble ambitions for Young India Asutosh was marked by the loftiest idealism combined with the boldest will such as has characterized the nation-making enthusiasm and efforts of all great men of action from Epaminondas to Mussolini and Hitler. In the annals of the twentieth century he is destined to have a conspicuous place as a tremendous dynamic force, as an embodiment of revolutionary energism and as a mighty maker of modern mankind.[1]

Socio-Religious and Racial Reconstructions

The societal remaking of India in the religious sphere may be said to have commenced in 1830 with the establishment of the Brāhmo Samāj at Calcutta. It was not before 1864 that the religious reform movement more or less on Bengal lines touched Madras perhaps under the influence of Keshub Chandra Sen, and the Veda Samāj was established. The Prārthanā Samāj of Bombay came into existence in 1867 in order to respond to the same call. These reform movements served to cry halt to the early and temporary successes of Christianizing in India. But it is not clear as to

[1] See the Convocation Addresses by Asutosh Mookerjee at the Calcutta University (1907-14), Second Edition, 1936.

whether these efforts had any positive effect on the major problems of the traditional Hindu society, namely, those bearing on the caste, the Pariah and the woman. As embodying liberal ideas about caste and other social questions these movements were of course undoubtedly serving as aids to the quickening of unrest among the intellectuals. The same must be said about the radical Satyasodhak Samāj established at Poona in 1873, with the object of organizing a revolt against the caste-system. But perhaps somewhat greater success may be credited to the Ārya Samāj established by Dayānanda in the Punjab in 1875.

On the other hand, the story of the Rāmakṛṣṇa Maṭh, established by Vivekānanda at Belur near Calcutta in 1899, is entirely different. Be it observed *en passant* that the Rāmakṛṣṇa "Order" had been organized by Vivekānanda in 1886, the very year of the saint's death. Neither the Order nor the Maṭh had any definite social programme in connection with the castes or the position of women in society. It took the orthodox society as it was and its propaganda took the form of disseminating spiritual knowledge among the people without distinction of caste and creed. The problem before the Maṭh was not so much the remaking of institutions as the transformation of individual character. It was more a moral than a "social" work that the followers of Rāmakṛṣṇa placed before themselves. In so far as they had any "social" aims these were chiefly or rather exclusively in the domain of philanthropy, humanitarian work, in one word, "social service".

The reform movement among the Mussalmans obtained a tremendous fillip from the poetry of Altaf Hussain the "Hali" or Modern (1835-1914), who may be regarded as the most effective colleague of Syed

Ahmad, the Rammohun of Moslem India. The faults and shortcomings of the Mussalmans were laid bare by Hali in his *Musaddas* (Six-line stanzas on the Ebb and Flow of Islam) in 1879, just at the moment when Islam was under attack from the Christian side. At a time when the orthodox Maulavis were placing the study of the Bible by the Mussalmans under a ban Hali was inspiring his community to probe into its own defects and weaknesses. It was under the inspiration of Hali that the go-aheads of Moslem India learnt to flout the "long-bearded and flowing-robed gentry."[1] Constructive reformers soon rose with programmes calculated to promote the expansion of modern education among the Moslems as well as do away with the old and effete customs of the Moslem society and religion.

The first important manifestation of Moslem endeavour in the line of social or rather cultural remaking is to be attributed to Syed Ahmad (1817-1898). It took shape, however, not in any religious or social reform propaganda, but in an educational institution. The Anglo-Mohammadan College, established at Aligarh (U.P.) in 1875, has in any case turned out to be the nucleus of all types of "modernism" in Moslem India since then.

So far as the liberalization of the Hindu society is concerned, the work was not obstructed owing to the failure of direct attacks by the *Samājes* on caste and other questions. Rather, the establishment of the Indian National Congress in 1885 prepared the way for social reform propaganda among the Hindus on pan-Indian dimensions. The National Social Conference came into being as a virtual wing of the Con-

[1] Amin Jung: "Hali's Musaddas" (*Indian Review*, Madras, November, 1935); R. B. Saksena: *History of Urdu Literature* (Allahabad, 1927), pp. 210-219, 279-282.

gress in 1888, and the *Indian Social Reformer* was established at Bombay in 1890, as the organ of this movement under the editorship of K. Natarajan, the Madrasi exponent of social liberalism. This was the channel through which even persons not belonging to the *Samājes* were being inoculated to progressive ideas perhaps in homoeopathic doses.

In 1897 the Rāmakṛṣṇa Mission "Association" was established by Vivekānanda on his return from America and Europe. With the establishment of the Maṭh in 1899 the "Association" ceased to exist. But in 1909 the Rāmakṛṣṇa Mission was established seven years after Vivekānanda's death with an enlarged programme and it has been functioning separately from the Ramakṛṣṇa Maṭh all the time since then. The enlarged programme comprises extensive plans of social service of diverse categories in addition to spiritual propaganda on broadly moral lines. Social reform, as such, with special reference to caste or woman questions, does not as yet belong to the programme of the Maṭh or the Mission. *Prabuddha Bhārata* (Awakened India), established by Vivekānanda as the organ of the movement in 1895, has been running its career on the universal morality lines without any categorical social reform bias. It is more a general philosophico-cultural than a propaganda publication.

No definite social reform programme, be it observed carefully, was associated with the "ideas of 1905" in Bengal or in Mahārāṣṭra, the two leading centres of nationalism and world-culture in those days. Social liberalism as going on since the fourth quarter of the last century—especially under the auspices of the Indian Social Conference—was postulated to continue its course in its own way. But the 1905-ers were on the whole indifferent to caste or woman questions. The situation today is virtually the same among the "nationalists" as a generation ago. Political publicists as a rule are not deeply interested in social questions which therefore have to be taken care of by separate organizations. The separation of social reform from politics has been on the whole perhaps beneficial to both.

Those who watch the daily polemics, especially in their earlier phases, might perhaps be led to describe the Brāhmo Samāj movement as rather "anti-national" and the Ārya Samāj and the Rāmakṛṣṇa movements as "revivalist". From the viewpoint of long-range societal planning, however, it should appear that the exponents of the Brāhmo movement draw their inspiration as much from the old Hindu texts and ideals as the exponents of the other two. The Brāhmo Samāj has to be sociologically interpreted as being as "nationalistic" in cultural tradition as the other movements. It is certainly possible to fight, as propagandists or missionaries, over the individual items in the creed or the institution advocated by each. But neutral observers and students of science cannot overlook the great reality that the Brāhmo Samāj is drawing inspiration from certain phases of ancient Hindu culture and *mores*, of which certain other phases are being drawn upon by the Ārya Samāj and still others by the Rāmakṛṣṇa Mission. If the last two are "revivalists" the first one is not less so. Then, again, it is impossible to describe the Brāhmo Samāj as being in social morphology more oriented to "modern", i.e., Eur-American conditions and inspirations than the Ārya Samāj and the Rāmakṛṣṇa Mission. Flourishing as they all do under conditions of world-wide democratic, socialistic, scientific, international, and Christian movements and ideologies the impact of these on the Ārya Samāj and the Rāmakṛṣṇa Mission has been no less profound than on the Brāhmo Samāj. From Rammohun to Gandhi it is impossible to find any movement or institution of somewhat large size and substantial importance which is not Janus-like in its orientations, i.e., nationalist, traditionalist or revivalist on the one hand and at the same time internationalist, modernist and reformist on the other.[1]

The first important intervention of the state in social affairs in modern India is embodied perhaps in the Act of 1829 inspired by Rammohun relating to the abolition of the *suttee* or concremation of the widow along with the deceased husband. The problem of the woman was thereby raised into a political question.

The caste problem was likewise raised into a political issue along with the Act of 1850 (Caste Disabilites Removal Act). It declared that nobody forfeited one's ordinary rights of property owing to loss of caste or change of religion. Freedom of views and practices in social and religious matters was thus assured to the individual. This was followed by the Widow Remarriage Act of 1856, to the inception of which Ishwara Chandra Vidyasagara's contribution has to be recorded. Although meant specially for the Hindus, the legislation has up till now been attended with very little success. It is well known today that demographically the Hindus can hardly do without the remarriage of widows.

The problem of untouchables was touched by the Government of Bombay in 1858. The Government educational institutions were declared open to

[1] S. N. Sastri: *History of the Brahmo Samaj* (Calcutta), L. Rai: *The Arya Samaj* (London, 1915), *The Seventh General Report of the Ramakrishna Mission* (1931-33), issued by the Governing Body from Belur Math, Howrah, September 1934.

all castes, and those schools which refused to admit untouchables were declared ineligible to Government financial support.

Another major problem was attacked in 1872. By the Special Marriage Act "intercaste" marriages were permitted on condition that both parties declared themselves to be casteless or religionless, i.e. *konfessionslos* as in the German, Austrian and other continental laws.

The stigma attached to such "religionless" marriages was not removed until 1923 when the Special Marriage Amendment Act was passed under the agitation of Hari Singh Gour. It applies only to Hindus, including Jains, Sikhs and Brahmos. Marriage has thus been rendered free. That is, intercaste marriage is no longer "socially" or rather "emotionally" unpleasant. One does not have to declare oneself casteless or religionless. Legally, of course, it has been valid since 1872. Be it observed, however, that the Act of 1923 regulates the property affairs not according to the Hindu law but according to the Indian Succession Act.

From the angle of social reform it is important, finally, to observe that the "Sarda" Act was passed in 1929. It fixed the minimum marriage age for girls at 14 and for boys at 18. This constitutes a very big dose of reform administered to the Hindu social system, nay, the social organization of the Mussalmans also.

The rôle of the state in societal remaking during the century (1829 to 1929) cannot be considered to be trivial. Most of the major questions have been attacked. The *Samājes* established by the reformist groups, especially the Indian Social Conference, played their part as exponents of new and progressive views. But in the last analysis the *dictum* of Hindu political philosophy has been verified to the letter in so far as we see that it is the state that establishes the *dharma* (law, justice and duty) and that it is the *rājā* that makes the time or epoch (see the section on the doctrines of *Daṇḍa* and *Dharma*, pp. 250-272).

The question of the untouchables remains yet to be solved. To this as to the questions of caste, marriage and woman the "ideas of 1905" were indifferent. The social reform propaganda of those days was held in solution among the people but concentrated chiefly in the Indian Social Conference or bodies and individuals such as derived inspiration from it. The political ideology of 1905 was in the main innocent of these questions. It was not until Gandhi made his *début* in politics in 1919-20 that social questions, especially the problem of the untouchables, began to attract the direct attention of the politically minded people. The revolt of the untouchables in Travancore at Vaikom in 1924 took serious proportions as they were determined to pass through the "forbidden roads" at any cost. In 1925 the Government of Madras declared open all roads, streets, public offices, wells, tanks and places of public resort.

But it is questionable if even today (1936) the problem of the untouchables or "depressed" classes has succeeded in arousing the activity of the Hindus, whether politically-minded or otherwise. Gandhi's memorable determination to "fast unto death" in 1932 was indeed associated with the untouchability question. But enthusiastic idealism in favour of the depressed is hardly yet in evidence on a large scale in the villages, nay, towns of India. The *Harijan* (God's men) movement initiated by Gandhi (1934) in order to enfranchise the Pariahs and other socially submerged classes is yet in its non-age.

The experiences of the caste-people under the new Government of India Act (1935) which has politically enfranchised the "scheduled castes" are likely to solve the untouchability question to a mentionable extent. From the standpoint of the evolution of individuality, manhood, economic efficiency, social worth and political power of the teeming millions the preferential treatment accorded to the depressed or scheduled castes according to the clauses of this new Act[1] is likely to be as beneficial to the entire Hindu society as the preferential treatment accorded to the Mussalmans by the Act of 1919 has been to India as a whole. Such preferential awards may be found to be unnecessary in no distant future.

Some substantial social legislation or reform has been carried through in the State of Travancore. K Ramakrishna Pillai's journalism has been a source of education in public life to his readers. In Malayalam, Varghese Mapella has written in favour of marriage reform. The removal of untouchability was advocated by Dewan Kesava Pillai. He succeeded also in affording scope to the depressed classes. Public roads were opened to untouchables by Dewan K. Rajagopalachariar. The disabilities of the Syrian Christians were removed by Dewan V. P. Madhava Rao. Married boys were removed from schools by K. V. Sesha Iyer.

In Madras the propaganda against early marriage as well as caste disabilities found a strong champion

[1] *Report of the Joint Committee on Indian Constitutional Reform* Vol I. Part I. (London, 1934) Paras 118-120; G. S. Ghurye: *Race and Caste in India* (London, 1932). See the present author's "Hindu Dharmer Digvijaya O Rāmakṛṣṇa Sāmrājya" (The World-Conquest of Hinduism and the Rāmakṛṣṇa Empire) in *Udbodhana* (Calcutta, July and August 1936).

in T. Sadasiva Iyer. A. K. Kumaraswamy is known for his work against the dowry system. Viresalingam of Rajamundry likewise has fought against early marriage. The free education of the boys and girls as well as training in the handicrafts have been championed by him in an effective manner.

Constituted as the Hindu societies in Northern India and the Moslem communities happen to be, "feminism" in its very first stages means that the "higher classes" (or castes) should permit their adult women to appear in public. As for the alleged lower classes or castes, in other words, ninety-nine per cent of the population feminism in this sense has always been a fact of social polity. Nearly 30 per cent of the women of India are reported as "gainfully employed" and this percentage is higher than that of Italy, England, Wales, U.S.A., Japan and so forth. With the exception of Bulgaria, Poland, France, Norway, Germany, Switzerland and a few other countries India's percentage of female "actives" is the highest in the world (p. 555). We understand that women in India are not lazy and that the *purdah* (the veil or the screen) is not important enough to be counted as a force in socio-economic statistics.

The *purdah* was a social problem of Nothern India in the nineteenth century and continues still to be a problem in certain parts of the country. Historically, perhaps it is possible to trace the beginnings of feminism as thus defined in its elementary sense, i.e., emancipation from the *mores* of the *purdah*, to the middle of the last century. But the instances of such emancipation were few and far between and the enthusiasm in its favour did hardly manifest itself in anything but a few isolated cases of journalism. It is questionable if the professed social reform movements such as those associated with the Brāhmo Samāj, in so far as their membership did not go beyond a few thousand in the nineteenth century, and was by all means confined to the *élites*, could factually exhibit instances of substantial success except in select "family circles", so to say. The establishment of the Bethune College (Calcutta) for girls was the only positive embodiment of progress in this regard.

Excluding a few individuals we may say that the persons associated with the "ideas of 1905" were almost entirely masculine. It is the post-War politics (1919-22) that brought Indian women into public life and even prisons. The emancipation from the *purdah* became then a social reality for the first time. Today it is possible to speak of women's societies and clubs of all denominations not only in big cities but in the district headquarters as well. And these organizations address themselves as much to the questions relating to maternity, "better babies", women's and children's health, music, literature, handicrafts, as to "non-co-operation", suffrage, property laws, equality with men, and what not. It is possible to assert that hardly any institution, organization, or movement in India today is exclusively masculine. Then the special Provincial Women's Conferences as well as All-Indian Women's Conference have become the order of the day. The tenth session of the All-India Women's Conference was held at Trivandrum (Travancore) in December 1935. Naturally the number of girls at schools and colleges has enormously increased during the last decade. Journals conducted by women for women's interest as well as for general culture are important limbs of contemporary literature and social thought. The establishment of the Indian Women's University by D. K. Karve at Poona in 1916 is specially to be noted. The position of women in the constitution has been assured by the Government of India Act (1935).[1] Feminism has then gone beyond the elementary stage and reached the world standard, if not in institutions, at any rate, in ideology (pp. 552-558).

All these developments of the feminist movement in India must have to be seen in the background of Eur-America, where, also, it has to be admitted, the recognition of women's rights is not older than just a few decades.

The world-process in group "metabolism" is visible under our very eyes in Bengal. In the social economy of Bengal there are some thirty tribes known as "aboriginals" constituting a diversified group of a million and a quarter, and representing some 3 per cent of the total population.[2] The "big three" of these "primitives", namely, the Santhals, the Oraons, and the Mundas, are statistically responsible for nearly two-thirds of this number.[3] But while the "big three" higher "castes", the Kāyasthas, Brāhmaṇs and Vaiśyas, numbering something over three millions, have during the last forty years grown 37 per cent, the "aboriginals" have grown 219 per cent. The rate of growth is phenomenal, pointing, as it does, to extraordinary "differential fertility".

This numerical growth, important in itself as it is, acquires a fresh significance when one observes that

[1] *Report of the Joint Committee on Indian Constitutional Reform* Vol. I. Part I, (London, 1934), paras 122, 128, 132, 133, 136, 196; E. A. Hecker: *A Short History of Woman's Rights with reference to England and the United States* (New York, 1911).

[2] The present author's *Les Races, les Classes et les Forces Transformatrices au point de vue du Métabolisme Social* (International Congress of Sociology, Brussels, August 1935).

[3] *Census of India* 1931. Vol. V. *Bengal and Sikkim.* Part I. (1933) pp. 441, 444, 448, 454, 480-484.

the "aboriginals" are today more "Hindu" than "tribal" or animistic in religion. Nearly sixty-six per cent of the "big three" primitives is Hindu. As a qualitative transformation the Hinduization of the "aboriginals" is further interesting in another regard. The Hinduized aboriginals form a part, nearly 12 per cent, of what are generally called the "depressed classes" of the Hindu society.[1] We understand, then, that the "aboriginals" of yesterday constitute the "depressed" classes of today. In other words, the social metabolism, which acts as a force in Hinduization hides the facts of, or prepares the way to race-fusion and race-assimilation.

Nor does the "qualitative" aspect of social metabolism stop here. Among the "big three higher castes", the Kāyasthas were during the last four decades just below the Brāhmaṇs in number. But they were rising until today they have outnumbered the latter. In forty years while the Brāhmaṇ has grown 24 per cent, the Kāyastha has grown 58 per cent.[2] What is this growth of Kāyasthas due to? Not all to "relative" fecundity or "natural increment", i.e., surplus of births over deaths as embodied in "differential fertility". A great deal is to be accounted for by invasions from other castes whose upward trends have been manifest for some long time. The non-Kāyastha, perhaps one of the "depressed" of yesterday, has grown into the high caste of today. And in this, again, we have to register not only a vertical social or class mobility but a racial transformation as well. From the "aboriginal" to the "high caste" Hindu the gap may be great, but the bridges are sure, although slow, and quite

[1] *Census etc.* pp. 480, 482, 485, 497, 498, 502.

[2] *Ibid.* pp. 454, 492.

solid. Social "stratification" is not as rigid as Ammon believes.[1]

Altogether, the Bengali people is expanding although it is undergoing a profound social metabolism, i.e., a radical change in "class" character and "racial" make-up. The transformations that have been going on in Eur-America today on account of the pressure of the Slavs upon the other races should appear to belong almost to the same category as those in India. As for the "quality" of "hybrids" or their capacity for carrying forward the torch of civilization eugenics is still discreetly inconclusive unless the exponent happens to have a conservative reform scheme on the anvil. But history announces that, notwithstanding the doctrine of Lapouge,[2] races may come and races may go but that civilization goes on for ever.

Hinduizing the non-Hindus

The Rāmakṛṣṇa Mission is not directly interested in social reform although its thoughts and activities have by all means served to liberalize the Hindu mind in regard to social and caste observances, the gods and goddesses, the forms of worship etc. The ideology of social reform generated by the Brāhmo Samāj, the Rāmakṛṣṇa Mission and general culture as well as world-forces has been utilized by a special movement which has grown around the Hindu Mission in recent years. The Hindu Mission can be singled

[1] *Die Gesellschaftsordnung und ihre natuerliche Grundlagen* (1895).

[2] *Les Sélections Sociales*, pp. 65-70, 442-444. See the criticism of certain aspects of Lapouge's doctrine in A. Niceforo: *Les Classes Pauvres* (Paris, 1905), F. Hankins: *The Racial Basis of Civilization* (New York, 1924), Sorokin: *Contemporary Sociological Theories* (New York, 1928) p. 308.

out as an organization that has been marked with striking success in this field.

Social reform among the Hindus is the principal objective of the Hindu Mission and this reform activity is to be seen in two prominent directions. One consists in Hinduizing the non-Hindus, the un-Hindus, the *Vrātyas*, so to say, the aboriginals, the tribals, the Christians, the Mussalmans, as well as the Hindus converted to Christianity or Islam. This is *Suddhi* (purification, conversion or assimilation) as understood by the Hindu Mission. The other direction of the Hindu Mission's social reform work lies in the field of service now well-known throughout India, as people have been talking it over and trying to carry it out for some long time, namely, the removal of untouchability. This has constituted, be it observed *en passant*, the core of the *Harijan* (God's men) movement started by Gandhi in 1934.

The Hindu Mission was established by Swami Satyānanda at Calcutta in 1925 but in the course of three years succeeded in Hinduizing some 60,000 Santhals, Oraons, Khasis and other tribals. According to the Census of 1931 we notice a decrease in the number of tribals in Bengal and Assam and a corresponding increase in the number of Hindus. "The figures for tribal *religions* show a pronounced decline since 1921, although a comparison with the total figures of selected groups of primitive peoples shows a marked increase during the last decade. And it is therefore clear that there has been a considerable access to the *Hindu* community of persons who by birth belong to the primitive tribes" (*Census of India* 1931, Vol. V. *Bengal and Sikkim*, Part I., p. 395). The conversion of large numbers of aboriginals or tribals to Hinduism on account of the proselytizing activities of the

Hindu Mission is testified to also in the Census volumes on Bihar and Assam for 1931. The Census reporters are not in a position to give the exact figure. The Hindu Mission claims on the whole about 1,000,000 converts in Bengal and Assam and about 300,000 in Bihar.

We have observed in our previous discussions that even the earliest specimens of Hindu life, society, culture and religion were signalized by the *Aitareya Brāhmaṇa* (VII, 15) cult of *charaiveti* (march on). Hinduism has all through the ages been a very proselytizing, all-conquering and aggressive religion, a religion of world-conquest. It has moved from village to village conquering province after province, and country after country. In its career of restless wanderings it has established its dominion over myriads of tribes, races and nations. It is but a continuation of the same millennium-long world-conquest that during the nineteenth and twentieth centuries we see in the establishment of a new Hindu empire, as it were, on account of the philosophico-cultural and religious activities of the Rāmakṛṣṇa-Vivekānanda group (1893-1936) in the two Hemispheres. When, therefore, since 1925 we have been finding that non-Hindus are being Hinduized in large numbers through the propaganda of the Hindu Mission we are encountering but new specimens of aggressivism such as ever constituted the life-blood of Hindu faith and culture. The cultural and spiritual transformation of tribes, races, communities and nations that is being consummated on account of the "social metabolism" engineered by the Rāmakṛṣṇa Mission and the Hindu Mission is to be regarded as one of the most virile world-forces set in operation by Creative India in modern times. Today as during the previous six thousand years Hindu energism or

Buddhist *appamāda* (strenuousness) has been functioning as a vital agency in the remaking of human civilization and the promotion of world-progress.

Along with this Hinduization commonly known as *śuddhi* (purification, conversion or reconversion), i.e., assimilation of tribals to the Hindu social organism the Hindu Mission concentrated its attack on the social evil of "untouchability" as prevalent among the Hindus themselves. As long as untouchability obtains in Hindu society it is self-evident that the assimilation of outsiders, externals, the *Vrātyas* etc. is bound to be ineffective or superficial. Untouchables remain to all intents and purposes unassimilables. The removal of untouchability was therefore considered by the Hindu Mission to be as important a plank as assimilation, reconversion or Hinduization itself.

In the group-psychology of the tribals and aboriginals as of the Hindus *śuddhi* or Hinduization alone does not imply automatically social mobility of the vertical type. Without vertical mobility, however, the converted or Hinduized tribals would but swell the ranks of the depressed classes or *Harijans* of the Hindu society. For all practical purposes, indeed, they have served but to constitute another group of untouchables or depressed castes.

The removal of untouchability need not therefore be treated as logically linked up with *śuddhi* or Hinduization as such. It is an independent item of social reform necessary for the Hindus and it is worth while to observe that the Hindu Mission directs its propaganda towards this objective in an organized manner. A number of high class priests was engaged to minister to the religious ceremonies of the untouchables comprising as they did the converted tribals. Another instrument in this direction was the organization of worship and religious service in such a manner that "all classes and castes" might take part in it. These *sārvajanīn* (all-class or all-caste) *Pūjābs* (adorations), especially in connection with the most popular goddess, Durgā, have succeeded in removing untouchability to a considerable extent and breaking the social barriers.

The Hindu Mission has nearly four dozen branches in different parts of Bengal, Bihar and Assam. And it is reported that its workers and preachers are "active from the border of China in the East to the Arabian Sea in the West, in the hills and plains, among peoples speaking different languages and professing different faiths."

During eight months of 1934-35 Satyānanda and his group carried through a propaganda tour of Bihar, Orissa, the United Provinces, the Punjab, Delhi, the Central Provinces and Central India. They did 52 centres holding 208 meetings addressing the audiences in English, Bengali and Hindi. Among the lecture-themes we find such topics as the expansion of Hindu culture in Greater India, social malady and its cure, Hindu civilization in Java, Bali, Indo-China and other Eastern countries.[1]

It is interesting to observe that the conclusions of researches in ancient and medieval Indian history are being utilized by the missionaries of the new Hindu religion of the twentieth century. Archæology has thus grown into an applied science. Applied archæology is being appreciated as a powerful ally by exponents of applied sociology, interested as they are in the remaking of personality and in societal reconstruc-

[1] *The First Decennial Report of the Hindu Mission* 1925-1935 (Calcutta), pp. 9, 12, 15, 24, 27, 28.

tion as well as in the transformation of classes and castes, races and nations.

Dhammapāla's New Buddhism and Young Asia

Numerically speaking, Buddhism is not a prominent faith in India today. But its hold on the cultured classes has begun to grow. This growth of Buddhism as a cultural and spiritual factor is a phenomenon of creative India during the *Swadeshi* period; and it is to be traced in the main to the activities of Devamitta Dhammapāla (1864-1933). Dhammapāla was born in Ceylon, travelled in the two Hemispheres and worked in India. He was a world-man and it so happens that his life has a message which is not meant exclusively for the Ceylonese or the Indian but for every man and woman of flesh and blood. One of the most appropriate descriptions about Dhammapāla's thoughts and activities is to be found in the almost untranslatable although very elaborately explained Pali word, *sammādiṭṭhi* (right, correct, comprehensive or complete view, observation, seeing or understanding), which constitutes the very foundation of Sākya the Buddha's teachings (*Majjhima Nikāya*).

Dhammapāla gave concrete evidence of his right observation or proper understanding of the realities of the world when he discovered the truths, first, that Ceylon is today a part of Greater India, and secondly, that India, Ceylon and Burma are integrally associated with the rest of Buddhist Asia. The old Sākyan cult of right observation was thus applied by Dhammapāla to modern conditions and practical problems of the day. Thereby he has succeeded in revivifying Buddhism and becoming virtually an architect of new Buddhism. This new Buddhism is not the Buddhism that is to be discovered in old Pali, Sanskrit, Tibetan, Chinese,

Burmese and other texts or archæological monuments but the Buddhism as an instrument of daily life and the actual realities.

Another evidence of *samāddiṭṭhi* or right observation was furnished by Dhammapāla while travelling in Japan, Korea, Manchuria and China (1915). In that *milieu* it became a part of his social philosophy to preach, as it was my experience to observe on the spot, that India, Ceylon and Burma needed the spirit of Japan or Japanese Buddhism. For a Ceylonese Hīnayāna Buddhist, as he was, to invite Japanese Mahāyāna Buddhism into regions in which Buddhism is either alleged to be extinct or prevalent mainly in the Hīnayāna form is a tremendous psychological or spiritual revolution. Incidentally it is worth while to emphasize that the Mahāyānic Buddhism of Japan as of China, equipped as it is with its gods, goddesses, saints, votive offerings etc. is to all intents and purposes identical with the Pauranic-Tantric neo-Hinduism, say, of Hindu Bengal as of other regions of Hindu India, as analyzed in my *Chinese Religion through Hindu Eyes* (Shanghai 1916). Dhammapāla perhaps was not interested in this aspect of the identity between Japanese Buddhism and modern Hinduism. But his *sammāddiṭṭhi* was profound enough to counsel him to believe that if Buddhism was living anywhere in the world, it was in Japan. He wanted for India, Burma and Ceylon a living Buddhism, the cult that obtained in ancient and medieval times in the land of its origin, namely, the system of devotion to life in the now and the here, the pursuit of *appamāda* (energism) as well as indifference to *anāgatam* (the future) and *atītam* (the past), combined with genuine appreciation of the "life beyond" (*Dhammapāda* and *Bhaddekaratta-Sutta*). Dhammapāla's discovery of these features of ancient Indian Buddhism in the Japan of his days has enabled him to function as a maker and exponent of Young Asia.

Today a part of this Young Asia movement is seen to be realized in the Mahābodhi Society of Calcutta, which, established as it was by the Ceylonese go-aheads under the inspiration of Dhammapāla himself, has been serving to bring under one roof the Chinese, the Japanese, the Burmese, the Tibetans, the Ceylonese, the Bengalis and other Indians several times a year. Then the foundations have been laid (1935) at Sarnath, Benares, of the International Buddhist University, which, again, is growing into a centre of co-operative cultural creations of the Buddhists of all Asia, nay, of Eur-American as well.

While analyzing Dhammapāla's contributions to the intellectual life and social philosophy of Ceylon, India, as well as the rest of Asia and the world we cannot remain indifferent to the fact that he was first and foremost a hero of action. In this regard,—like his great Bengali contemporary, Vivekānanda,—he may be compared to the Japanese energist of the sixteenth century, Nichiren. Indeed both Dhammapāla and Vivekānanda have continued for our own times the age-long tradition of *charaiveti* (march on) and *nānāśrāntāya śrīrasti* (prosperity is not for the preson who is not tired by travels), of which the *Aitareya Brāhmaṇa* (VII, 15), the oldest Vedic book, speaks so eloquently as the ideal of the Hindus.

Young Asia is today self-conscious enough, thanks to the activities of men like Vivekānanda and Dhammapāla at home and abroad, to lead Eur-America to acquire some of the *sammāddiṭṭhi* and to feel that, after all, a new age has made its appearance. It is an age in which domination of one race by another is to be a thing of the past but in which the diverse races, cults, faiths and cultures are to meet on a platform of equality, freedom, and mutual respect. Dhammapāla has then like Vivekānanda to be appraised as one of the apostles of international peace and world-wide brotherhood.

Benefactions and Charities

In India the Carnegie spirit as embodied in educational and humanitarian benefactions may be virtually as old as Indian culture itself. The first hospitals of the world, established in the main by private charities go back to the Gupta, nay, the Maurya times. In the first century the Gujarati General, Uśavadāta,[1] made endowments for gardens, tanks, ferry boats, bathing places, rest-houses, seats of learning etc. in dimensions such as might appeal to the imagination even of the Andrew Carnegie of modern times. Charities, both individual and organized, have constituted the topic of a most important section (that on *Dānas* or gifts) in the socio-legal literature of India known as the *Smriti-śāstras*. A classic in this line is the *Dānakhaṇḍa* of the *Chaturvarga-Chintāmaṇi* by the South Indian sociologist Hemādri (*c* 1300).

Educational benefactions constitute an important item in the social ethics and collective conscience of the modern Indian people. As long as India's national dividend is modest it is not possible for our donors to deal in gifts of hundreds of millions. But the million mark in Rupees has been exceeded by dozens of Indian idealists in recent years. The charities of the Parsis are proverbial in the Bombay Presidency. Not less so are the Gujarati benefactions. Vithaldas Thackersay's gifts in support of the Indian Women's University at Poona and Govardhandas's in connection with the

[1] The present author's *Political Institutions and Theories of the Hindus* (Leipzig, 1922), pp. 34-36, 51, 62, 120.

new Medical College at Bombay have gone beyond the million Rupee level. The Gujarati Premchand Roychand's Studentship at the University of Calcutta is a household word in Bengal. The Madrasi educational benefactor, Pachaiyappa, is likewise one of the quite a few donors whom South India can never forget. In the United Provinces the *Prem Mahāvidyālaya* of Brindaban is a technical institution which owes its origin to the single-handed gifts of Mahendra Pratap. Not below the million mark, again, is Shiva Prasad Gupta's grant for the *Kāshī-Vidyāpīṭha* at Benares. It is Mohsin's educational gifts of the early nineteenth century that have enabled untold Mussalmans in Bengal to rise in life both culturally and socially. The Hindu University of Benares and the Muslim University of Aligarh point likewise to large scale charities towards educational expansion in the U.P. The socio-religious institutions of the traditional type such as are maintained by Hindu or Moslem endowments throughout India are also to be listed in this connection.

The benefactions of Ganga Ram, the Punjabi philanthropist, like those of other "Indian Carnegies", deserve to be narrated in detail. The sum of five million Rupees was donated by him to the Sir Ganga Ram Trust Society with the object of attending to the welfare of the widows. He started Hindu Widows' Homes for such widows as would not care to remarry. A central industrial workshop was also started by him in Lahore for widows. A free hospital as well as a college of commerce likewise owe their origins to his philanthropy. Stipends were instituted by him in order to enable young men to take to industrial or other business studies. One hundred non-refundable stipends were announced by his Hindu Students' Career Society for 1936. Last but not least, Ganga Ram has, like Carnegie, considered it worth while to endow a free public library.[1]

Coming to Bengal[2] we may recall that the gifts from Subodh Mallik, Brajendra Kishore Roy-Chowdhury, Maharaja Surya Kanta Acharya-Chowdhury, Maharaja Manindra Chandra Nandy and others on which the National Council of Education made its start (1905-07) were worth not less than a million. The University of Calcutta, likewise, which is rich in the supply of prizes, medals, scholarships, fellowships and lectureships donated by educationally minded philanthropists, owes the beginnings of its post-Graduate Department in the diverse sciences, theoretical and applied, entirely to private benefactions. In this connection have to be named not only Prosonno Coomar Tagore, who instituted the Tagore Law Lectureship but also two men who gave away the entire earnings of their lifetime, Tarak Nath Palit and Rash Behari Ghosh. It is to Palit that the University is indebted for a million and a half and to Ghosh for two millions and a half. The total charities of Ghosh, which comprise also the National Council of Education and other institutions among the beneficiaries, amount to something over four millions.

It is indeed impossible to think of schools, colleges, and libraries in the different regions of India,—district headquarters, sub-divisions or villages,—without reference to the help derived from the zamindars, landholders and others in a relatively prosperous position. As for the promotion of literature in the Indian languages, researches in antiquities, folklore, manuscripts, archæo-

[1] M. C. Mohan: "Sir Ganga Ram" (*The People*, Lahore, 11 July 1936).

[2] The present author's *Bāḍtir Pathe Bāngālī* (Bengalis in Progress), Calcutta (1934), pp. 496-512.

logy etc., no small part is to be ascribed to the financial patronage of the landed aristocracy. For instance, in Bengal, modern Bengali literature has had patrons like Radhakanta Dev and Manindra Chandra Nandy. Every institution can cite its own benefactors in this regard, e.g., the *Bangīya Sāhitya Pariṣat* (Bengali Academy of Literature) of Calcutta, the Varendra Research Society of Rajshahi, the District Council of National Education (*Maldaha Jātīya Śikṣā Samiti*) in Malda, the *Sāhitya Pariṣat* of Rangpur, and so forth.

It is not the place to go into a lengthy catalogue. But we must mention the Institute of Science at Bangalore which was rendered possible because of the pioneering enthusiasm of Tata in regard to scientific and industrial research. It is likewise necessary to call attention to the fact that over a thousand Bengali scholars whose technical and commercial education in Eur-America and Japan has been facilitated by Jogen Ghosh's Association for the Scientific and Industrial Education of Indians are the products of benefactions from the zamindars and others. In the course of nearly one generation this Association has been instrumental in collecting and disbursing over a million. Reference may be made also to the collections from the people worth nearly half a million Rupees per annum, made by the Ramakṛṣṇa Mission for educational and philanthropic work through its nearly hundred centres in different parts of India.

Altogether, the Carnegie spirit will be found to be well represented throughout the length and breadth of India in so far as educational, literary, scientific and research patronage by the wealthier classes is concerned. India undoubtedly has her Carnegies, big, medium, and small. While doing homage to the great American philanthropist it behoves his Indian admirers to get oriented to the great reality that the East is qualitatively, if not quantitatively, at one with the West in this matter of gifts in the interest of cultural expansion and progress. It is this identity in ideals and character that should, pragmatically speaking, facilitate intellectual and social co-operation between the peoples of Eur-America and India with a view to the remaking of the world.

Indian Workingmen

At the most liberal computation the total "industrial" workers of India in 1931 were not more than 5,000,000 constituting nearly 1.4 per cent of the population (353,000,000). The percentages would be nearly 2.5-3.0 in Japan, 10.7 in the United Kingdom and 15.5 in Germany.[1] The relative strength or weakness of Indian labour is manifest in these proportions.

In 1927 not more than 407,000 working men were unionized. This included some 100,000 members of the All-India Trade Union Congress. We get, therefore, 13 per 10,000 of the total population as against, say, 38 in Japan, 594 in Russia, 1051 in the U. K. and 1295 in Germany. Indian workingmen, then, whether individually or unionally, cannot be regarded as constituting a "great power" in Indian societal economy or polity.

The labour movement strictly so-called is a post-War phenomenon in India. It can be traced back to the eighties of the last century among the cotton workers

[1] The present author's *Social Insurance Legislation and Statistics: A Study in the Labour Economics and Business Organization of Neo-Capitalism* (Calcutta, 1936), pp. 16, 18, 48, 56. See the *Bombay Labour Gazette* for February 1936, pp. 421-462 (Trade Unions in Bombay, Labour in Indian Mines).

of Bombay. But the first All-India Trade Union Congress was not held before 1920 (Bombay).

The First Trade Union Act was passed in India in 1926. For the purposes of socio-economic equation as established in this treatise it is worth while to observe that the first corresponding Act was passed in Italy in 1890, in France in 1884, in England during 1871-76 and in Germany in 1869. We must not, however, overlook the consideration that in Europe much preparatory and transitional work in trade union legislation had been gone through during the first half of the nineteenth century. These circumstances enable us to visualize the "social distance" between India and the more advanced sections of Europe as registered in the chronology of labour legislation.[1]

In India the first Factory Act was passed in 1881. For England the corresponding date is 1801. The latest Indian Act is that of 1934, which, thanks among other things to constant association with the International Labour Conference (Geneva) since 1919, has been equipped with large doses of liberalizing features.

The present status of Indian labour may be seen from an examination of some of the clauses of the Indian Factories Act of 1934 especially in regard to women workers and child labour.[2]

The number of women employed in factories, however, is not high. But the importance of factory population, both male and female, lies in the fact that

[1] Freedom of Association (Geneva), Vol. II, (1927) pp. 10-13, 92-96, Vol. III, (1928) pp. 2, 11; Foignet: *Legislation Industrielle* (Paris, 1925), p. 30.

[2] Discussion on P. K. Mukherjee's papers at the *Bangiya Dhana-Vijnan Parishat* (Bengali Institute of Economics, Calcutta), reported in *Forward*, 8 February 1935, and *Advance*, 16 July 1936. See *Arthik Unnati* (Economic Progress), February-March 1935.

it is partly through this section that India is becoming industrialized and rising in the scale of modern technocracy and culture.

Legislation regarding female labour commenced in the year 1891 and subsequently it was improved by the Acts of 1911 and 1922 and then by the amended Acts of 1926, 1928 and 1934. The Mines Acts of 1923 and 1928 have attempted to improve the condition considerably. Generally the Factories Acts have tried to minimise the period of labour and to assure hours of rest as well as to control the abuse of labour by prohibiting night work. The Act of 1928 has tried to eliminate female labour from mines altogether. The principle is being enforced gradually. It is to be adopted completely by the year 1939.

Regarding the fixing of age, it may be emphasised that the minimum age for the employment of female labour ought to be statutory. This should not be left to be governed by the general provision of the children and young persons clause. The minimum age for female labour should perhaps be fixed at the seventeenth year.

The condition of female labour is not very secure anywhere in the world, especially in India. Legislation as to the minimum wage is an imperative necessity. In determining the minimum wage, the living wage is to be calculated after considering various circumstances like the standard of living, skill of labour etc. From the viewpoints of morality and health women should be protected from dangerous work. We may instance the prohibition of female labour in some more poison manufacturing works than those which are already forbidden. The prohibition of female labour under certain age in outdoor enterprises is absolutely necessary. We have to observe, in any case, that a social problem is created automatically because the men workers come, as a rule, from outside the province for their employment and without their wives. It is important to observe that heavy work, load-lifting and the like, as done by the Chinese and Japanese women, are not allowed in the U.S.A.

The Act of 1934 is not only a consolidating one but provides also some additional measures for the protection of labour. Chapter III which relates to health and safety is especially valuable. The powers conferred on the Local Government, especially those in connexion with "hazardous occupations", have bearings on women and may prove to be beneficial. But the immediate need of the country is the enactment of Maternity Benefit Acts on the Bombay plan throughout India. Besides, a larger dose of protection both for men and women is required such as may be rendered available only when Health Insurance legislation is enacted.

According to the Act of 1934 the Government is authorized to require the factories to reserve a room for the use of women employees' children under six years of age. This is good so far as it goes. But the standard of child welfare has risen very high in the world.

In modern morality and legislation the care of the child belongs not so much to the parents and the family as to the community and the country. The Hindu poet Kālidāsa's (fifth century A. C.) conception of "the king being the real father, the parents being simply the causes of birth" (*sa pitā pitarastāsām kevalam janmahetavaḥ*) has thus become an institution of positive law.

Modern legislation is as old as the industrial revolution, factory system and capitalism (*c* 1785-1800). It is in and through diverse Acts bearing on education, health, punishment, and factories that this modernism involving as it does state control of or communism in children has been brought about. The British Children's Act of 1908 has been followed by several such Acts in India, for example, the Bengal Children's Act of 1922. The Indian Factories Act of 1934 also has certain measures, as already hinted at, quite favourable to children.

The number of factories has increased from 3,000 in 1922 to over 8,000 but the employment of children has gone down from 68,000 to 22,000. This is a desirable consummation.

According to the latest Factory Act in India the child is a boy or girl under 15. But children can be employed at the commencement of the 13th year. Night work has been forbidden as well as double employment. The British legislation is more restrictive as it forbids employment under 14. But in regard to delivery of newspapers, milk, parcels etc. employment is permitted in the U.K. to boys and girls between 12 and 14. In Egypt, on the other hand, employment is permitted to boys and girls even between 9 and 12.

In spite of improvements effected in children's lot by legislation double employment still persists in certain areas. Besides, the pledging of children by parents continues to some extent to be a reality of economic India. Stricter legislation as well as more effective enforcement of the Acts would be required to remove this kind of child-slavery, mild or otherwise, where-ever it exists (pp. 557-558).

Unless elementary education is rendered compulsory it would not be possible to control child labour successfully. But in the meantime some of the tea plantations in Assam have made provisions for the care of children and of workingmen in general.

Attention has to be invited to the problems of leisure and recreation such as would be necessitated by the removal of children from mills, mines and workshops as well as by the adoption of shorter hours in industrial establishments. In this connection we have to note the activities of the International Congress for Leisure and Recreation (*Weltkongress fuer Freizeit und Erholung*) which held its second session in July 1936 at Hamburg (First session, Los Angeles, U.S.A., 1932). The problem has not arrested India's serious notice up till now.

It is necessary to repeat that per head of population and per square mile of territory Indian labour is not yet a considerable power in economic or social relations. In politics also it cannot function as yet in a remarkable manner. But some of the *modernisms* in "ideology" have already established themselves among the labour *intelligentsia*. A section of Indian labour leaders has affiliations with the Second International ("moderate", socialistic) of Amsterdam. The "communistic" or radical ("extremist") Third International (Moscow), the Comintern, seems likewise to have influence with a wing of the Indian workers and their champions. These circumstances have contributed to the diversification and enrichment of politics with fresh categories not only in connection with the Indian National Congress and other "private" political bodies but even with the Government politics as embodied in the Legislative Assemblies and Councils as well as municipal, district board, union board and corporation politics.

The affiliations of labour to Indian politics are at any rate not clear. Something like a Labour Swarajaya Party was established in 1925. Two years later the Peasants and Workers' Party made its appearance. As "organizations" these so-called parties perhaps do not possess substantial value. But they furnish factual indices to the new currents such as inspire the mentality and activity of growing sections of the *intelligentsia* as well as of the working men.

The growth of the working men in self-consciousness, no matter how small their number in absolute or relative statistics and how backward in comparative or international socialism, is an outstanding reality of the last decade or so. In the meantime has grown up such a thing as factual or positive democracy and socialism in and through the Government of India Act (1935). The Lower Houses of the Provinces as well as the Lower Chamber of the Federal Government have provided for the representation of labour through its own representatives.

When even under Government auspices socialism of some type or other is becoming a constitutional reality it is but inevitable that ideologists like Jawaharlal Nehru, Subhas Chandra Bose and other political leaders such as in the main stay away from the official atmosphere should pitch their ambitions much higher and sigh for the highest that is yet to come.

The establishment in 1936 of a Labour Party or rather of a socialistic wing in the *milieux* of the Indian National Congress as well as the Indian Legislative Assembly is but in keeping with all these consummations, positive, constitutional and idealistic. For India's chronological distance from the pioneers of labour-democracy and socialism it is worth while to recall that the British Labour Party was formally established in 1906, the *Fédération Nationale des Syndicats* of France in 1886 (growing finally into the *Confédération Générale du Travail* 1895), the American Federation of Labour in 1881, and the *Sozialdemokratische Partei* of Germany in 1875.[1] It is at least by two generations that the economics and politics of Indian labour as of other Indian classes are behind the "adults" of the modern world.

The ideals and realities of socialism as developed in India since the Great War have to be envisaged in the background of some concrete and objective facts of the socio-economic world. Developments in techno-cracy, industrialism, capitalistic enterprises, joint stock concerns, banking and insurance institutions constitute some of the great forces of the day. Strikes and agitation on the part of the workingmen, judicial trials bearing on the violation of law and so forth have grown into common occurrences. The five amendments of the Factories Acts (1922, 1923, 1926, 1931, 1934) point inevitably to the rising tide of socialism on the one hand as of capitalism on the other.[2] Then there are the thousand and one contacts of Indian leaders,—cultural, political, economic and labour,—with the world-forces in Eur-America and Japan, such as have succeeded in injecting ideas of neo-capitalism and neo-socialism, not to speak of radical labour ideology,

[1] The present author's *Political Philosophies Since* 1905 (Madras, 1928), pp. 71-85, 204-213 and

[2] The present author's *The Pressure of Labour upon Constitution and Law*, 1776-1928 (Jnanmandal, Benares, 1928); S. C. Dutt: "Colliery Labourers in the Jharia Field" (*Journal of the Bengal National Chamber of Commerce*, 1929), "Tea Industry in Assam" (*Arthik Unnati*, Calcutta 1929), "Unemployment Problem in Great Britain" (*J.B.N.C.*, 1930), *Dhana-Vijnāne Sākreti* (Apprenticeship in Economic Science, Calcutta 1932) and *Conflicting Tendencies in Indian Economic Thought* (Calcutta 1934); K. C. Basu : "Workingmen's Compensation" (*Arthik Unnati*, 1930), and "The Earnings and Expenses of Indian Workingmen" (*A.U.*, 1933); P. K. Mukherji : "International Labour Legislation" (*A.U.*, 1934); R. N. Ghose: "Labour and Wages in Japan", a lecture at the "Malda in Calcutta" Society, December 27, 1934 (*A.U.* 1935).

into the mentality of India and her journalistic and academic complex. Last but not least have to be singled out the world-propaganda carried on by the International Labour Office of Geneva since 1919 as well as the deliberations and Report of the Royal Commission on Labour in India (1929-31) which have served as powerful formative forces in the establishment of the Indian labour-mind.

The Aims and Methods of Indian Feminism

We have observed in a previous connexion (pp. 528-29) that the establishment of the Indian Women's University at Poona by D. G. Karve in 1916 is an important landmark in the progress of womanhood in India. Another landmark is to be seen in the enactment of the Sarda Act in 1929 which fixes the minimum age of marriage for girls at 14 and of boys at 18. Child marriage has thus been restrained to some extent by positive legislation. Women's societies, clubs, schools and journals conducted in the main by women themselves have grown into the principal features of Indian society since the end of the Great War (1914-18).

For certain purposes the All-India Women's Conference which held its first session at Poona in 1927 may be taken as the sample of women's creative endeavours in India at the present moment. Not all the activities of the women are directly or indirectly associated with this Conference, equipped although it is with 39 constituent and 49 subconstituent associations. But it can by all means be used as an index to the quality, quantity and variety of life's urges to which Indian womanhood, especially among the economically favoured classes, has been reacting in a conspicuous manner.

The ten sessions[1] held up till now are enumerated below with the names of the Presidents:

1. 1927. Poona. Her Highness the Maharani of Baroda.

2. 1928. Delhi. Her Highness the Begum Mother of Bhopal.

3. 1929. Patna. Her Highness the Dowager Rani of Mandi.

4. 1930. Bombay. Mrs. Sarojini Naidu of Bombay.

5. 1931. Lahore. Dr. (Mrs.) Muthulakshmi Reddi of Madras.

6. 1932. Madras. Mrs. P. K. Ray of Calcutta.

7. 1933. Lucknow. Lady Ramanbhai Nilkanth of Ahmedabad.

8. 1934. Calcutta. Lady Abdul Quadir of the Punjab.

9. 1935. Karachi. Mrs. Rustomji Faridoonji of Bombay.

10. 1935. Dec. 25-1936 Jan. 4. Travancore. Her Highness the Maharani of Travancore.

Feminism, as organized in the All-India Women's Conference is in its ideals and achievements a noteworthy specimen of contemporary creative India. It is indeed a chip of the world-feminism of today and furnishes but another link in the chain of modern values,

[1] *All-India Women's Conference Tenth Session* (Trivandrum, 1936) pp. 13, 243-253.

See also the Memorandum on the Status of Women in India submitted to the League of Nations by the All-India Women's Conference and the Women's Indian Association (Secretary, Mrs. Ammu Swaminadhan, Madras, 1936).

social and spiritual, such as serve to establish a *liaison* between the East and the West. The lines of evolution embodied in Indian feminism, young as it is, are but following at some chronological distance those traversed by the adult Eur-American feminism during the previous decades. And this is but in keeping with the other socio-cultural equations between India and the pioneers of modernism in the West.

The very fact that feminism like many other modernisms has arisen in Eur-America is an index to the great reality that the womanhood of the West was not used to equality or identity of rights and obligations with the other sex. And the age of Western feminism also can be told within precise limits. The publication of the *Subjection of Women* by John Stuart Mill places the female suffrage movement towards the beginning of the fourth quarter of the nineteenth century. Joseph-Barthélemy's *Le Vote des Femmes* (Paris, 1920), as an anti-feminist treatise, serves to point out that feminism has not yet been able to conquer a great part of the Western world. *La Vita Femminile* of Rome is a monthly organ which establishes in an emphatic manner the absence of universal or even somewhat general appreciation of the ideals and methods of feminists in Eur-America. France, Italy and Spain, to mention a few countries, do not see eye to eye with England in regard to the claims of feminism. Teutonic (Anglo-Saxon) America, again, cannot be taken as the representative of Latin America in this regard. The latter follows France, Spain and Italy in the main. Nay, in the U.S.A. there are many States, say, like Alabama, where guardianship of children belongs by law exclusively to the father. The mother cannot there become the guardian of children. In the New England States the wife's earnings belong by law not to herself but to her husband.[1]

That the Indian women, especially among the intelligentsia, bourgeoisie or upper ten thousands, have already succeeded in assimilating the categories of world-feminism shows only that the womanhood of India, in part at any rate as in Eur-America, can be depended upon as constructive workers and thinkers in schemes of world-wide importance for mankind. We need not overlook the consideration that women in India have perhaps some special disabilities. But it is entirely wrong to believe that the total womanhood of India lives in seclusion, behind the veil (*purdah*). In reality, Indian women are active as economic agents as their sisters anywhere on earth. Indeed, thirty per cent of total Indian womanhood is "gainfully employed." This is a much higher percentage than in Italy, Hungary, Sweden, England, Czechoslovakia, Denmark, Belgium, Holland, Austria, U.S.A., Japan, Canada, Spain and many other countries. Just a few countries like Switzerland, Germany, Finland, Norway, France, Poland and Bulgaria yield a higher percentage in this field than India (p. 528).[2]

Women in India, economically speaking, are not idlers. Nor is the *purdah* important enough,—for the masses of the population—to be counted as a factor

[1] The present author's *Ekāler Dhana-Daulat O Arthashāstra* (The Wealth and Economics of Our Own Times), Vol. I. (1930), pp. 66-68, *Nayā Bānglār Goḍā Pattan* (The Foundations of a New Bengal), Vol. I. (1932), pp. 153-157.

[2] *Statistisches Jahrbuch fuer das Deutsche Reich* (Berlin, 1928), p. 26,* *Statistical Abstract for British India*, 1927-1932 (Delhi, 1934), pp. 40-44; cf. the American situation in H.A. Phelps: *Contemporary Social Problems* (New York, 1932), pp. 511-513, 517-519.

in the employment market. In certain parts of Northern India, and especially among the Mussalmans,—the *purdah* is a social evil and deserves to be condemned as militating against physical health and moral personality. Altogether, the *purdah* may be taken to affect a very small section of the population. The movement to get it abolished belongs, as it should rightly do, to the irreducible minimum of social reform as championed by the womanhood of India.

As may be naturally expected, the attack on *purdah* has been a regular feature of the sessions of the Conference. Some of the other items in which the Conference has been interested during the decade are being detailed in following statement, based in the main, as it is on the *Report* of the tenth session (Trivandrum, 1936).

A special committee was appointed to inquire into and suggest adequate remedies for the legal disabilities of women. These disabilities refer in the main to marriage and inheritance. The Marriage Dissolution Bill as proposed by Hari Singh Gour has received in the main the support of the Conference. They consider the practice of divorce as prevalent among the Mussalmans to be inequitable in so far as it enables the husband to divorce his wife arbitrarily at his sweet will. It is also considered by them to be not in accord with the principles of Islam.

In regard to the establishment of equality between the sexes, so far as inheritance and control of property are concerned, the Conference supports the Jogiah Bill to make better provision for Hindu women heirs as well as the Sarda Bill to secure share for Hindu widows in their husband's family property. As regards Muslim women the inheritance laws of Islam are considered by the Conference to be reasonable enough for preservation, and the Government is advised to declare null and void the customary practices such as violate the Koranic injunctions.

The student of comparative jurisprudence and sociology is not entitled, however, to make too much of the disabilities of Indian women. Western tradition in regard to women's property rights is not something enviable. The Hindu law of *Strīdhana* (woman's special property) was not surpassed in its liberal features by the Institutes of Justinian, the Code Napoleon and other European laws until the Married Woman's Property Act was passed in England in 1886.[1]

Birth control has been considered by the Conference to be an imperative necessity on account of the "low physique of women, high infant mortality and increasing poverty of the country." The opinion has been propagated that men and women should be instructed in methods of birth control and the suggestion has been made that municipalities and local bodies ought to open proper clinics (*Report*, pp. 150, 170). It is to be observed that the Conference has not cared to associate the birth control propaganda with the conventional scare of over-population.

In politics the Conference stands for "perfect sex equality" and has demanded that women should possess the citizen rights of men. One resolution runs to the effect that "no disability either legal or social shall be attached to women on account of sex, or in regard to public employment, office, power or honour and in the exercise of any trade or calling".

So far as the legislative bodies of the Indian constitution are concerned, the "communal award" has been

[1] The present author's *Political Institutions and Theories of the Hindus* (Leipzig 1922) pp. 28-29.

condemned by the Conference which is strong in its demand for a system of joint electorates. At Trivandrum (1935-36) the Conference condemned the clauses of the Government of India Act relating to "wifehood qualification" and "application condition". It condemned likewise the electoral clauses and reiterated its demands for (*i*) direct election and (*ii*) non-reservation of seats on a communal basis as well as (*iii*) the rejection of separate electorates for women (*Report*, pp. 152, 172).

The passing of a Maternity Benefit Act for the whole of India on the lines of the Bombay, C.P. and Madras Acts is to be found among the resolutions of the Conference. The appointment of at least one woman factory inspector for every large industrial area is another of its objectives. The Bill prohibiting the pledging of child labour in regulated and unregulated industries has received the full support of the Conference, and it has likewise resolved that persons besides guardians amd parents who pledge child labour or act in collusion with parents and guardians should be penalized. Altogether the Conference is in general sympathy with the more liberal suggestions or recommendations of the Royal Commission on Labour in India (1929-31).[1]

In its tenth session, namely, that at Trivandrum the Conference supported the Bakhale Bill introduced in the Bombay Legislative Council to prohibit the employment of children under 12 in shops. It was also urged that All-India legislation on similar lines limiting the hours of work and fixing a minimum age of employment for children in non-industrial under-

[1] The present author's *Social Insurance Legislation and Statistics* (Calcutta, 1936) pp. 219-230, 286.

takings generally be introduced (*Supra* pp. 545-548).[1]

The Eternal in Gandhi

The creations of Gujarat in modern times have been mainly her company-promoters, businessmen and financiers. She has, besides, contributed a handsome number of philanthropists whose charities are not confined to their race. But otherwise Gujarat should appear to have left no conspicuous mark on West-Indian, not to speak of Indian culture. By the side of their redoubtable neighbours, the Marathas (i.e., the Deccanis), the Gujaratis of the nineteenth century would perhaps be nothing more than second-rate in the diverse walks of life.

Unluckily for the Gujaratis, two remarkable personalities of modern India, Dadabhai Naoroji, the statesman and economist, and Jamshedji Tata, the *avatar* of industrialism and technocratic efficiency, are generally overlooked in the catalogue of Gujarat's contributions, because they happen to be Parsi by faith. This is a wrong attitude. The Parsis are Gujaratis by all means. Besides, Dayānanda, although Gujarati, is lost to Gujarat because his field of activity was associated with the Punjab. Be this as it may, the rôle of Gujarat was revolutionized as soon as Mohandas Karamchand Gandhi appeared on the scene during 1919-22. In the first place, the death of Tilak (1920) happened to create a gap in the Bombay Presidency but it was at once filled up by the personality of Gandhi. "It was a splendid sunset and a splendid dawn". The hegemony of the Marathas in Western India came to

[1] P. K. Mukherjee's papers at the *Bangiya Dhana-Vijnan Parishat* (Bengali Institute of Economics) on "Indian Women Workers" and "Child Labour in India and Abroad" (*Amrita Bazar Patrika*, February 1, 1935, and July 20, 1936).

an abrupt end and was replaced by the *de facto* ascendancy of the Gujaratis.

In the second place, Gandhi has succeeded in establishing Gujarat's *liaison* with the main currents in All-Indian culture and assuring to the land of his birth a position and respect such as it had never enjoyed since the dawn of history. And finally, Gandhi has enabled Gujarat to function as a "great power" in Indian politics so much so that for the last decade and a half entire India may be said to have been witnessing to a certain extent a "Gujarati period," as it were, of her modern developments. It is these Gujarati aspects of Gandhism that require to be thoroughly understood in an analysis of creative India's present-day contributions.

But once we are adequately oriented to the "local" phenomenon, namely, the Gujarati *milieu* there should not be any difficulty in realizing that Gandhism is nothing but the eternal double quest of modern India. Like every other movement the *Swadeshi* movement also brought with it the urge for world-forces and the urge for nationalism. It is the "ideas of 1905", developed as they were chiefly by the Bengalis and Marathas in alliance, and to a certain extent also by the Madrasis and Punjabis, that Gandhi has sought to render current coin throughout the length and breadth of India and especially among the masses. From Rammohun to Gandhi the movement has been broadening down from precedent to precedent.

The pan-Indianization and massification (so to say) or democratization of the "ideas of 1905" under the auspices of Gandhi must not be taken to be the work exclusively of Indians. The Great War of 1914-18 stood between the "ideas of 1905" and Gandhi (1919-22). In India the mind of the folk, the masses, the peasants, workingmen, depressed classes and what not had all been warmed up by the newspapers of the war-period. And the rise and fall of states, the overthrow of dynasties, the upheaval of the proletariat, the self-assertion of the masses here and there and everywhere in Europe were the main items in the news in India as elsewhere during 1918-22. The impact of these *viśva-śakti* (world-forces) on the Indian masses was tremendous. It was Gandhi's rôle to organize the power that had already been generated. Gandhism (1919-22) is inconceivable without the repercussion of world-events since 1914 on India. Neither the "ideas of 1905" nor the mass-forces of 1914-22 were the creations of the Gandhian categories. It is as an instrument of the world-forces on the one hand and of nationalism on the other that Gandhi was functioning.

It is further of interest to observe that a very important category which Gandhi contributed to creative India, namely, non-co-operation, was derived by him from abroad. Neither Kauṭalya nor Manu nor Abul Fazl nor Śukrāchārya nor Śivāji could ever counsel him to condemn the state and declare non-co-operation with it. They were all *statists*, exponents of the state as the instrument of national welfare. The message of "away from the state" and glorification of statelessness was imbibed by him from his Russian *guru*, Tolstoy. We may recall, also, that in Rabindranath's *Swadeshī Samāj* (1904) the philosophy of indifferentism to state was inspired by the *laissez faire* of British individualists, especially, the anti-statalism or anarchism of Spencer.

Another important contribution of creative India through Gandhi is the condemnation of industrialism. This category also could not have been possibly derived by him from ancient and medieval India because neither the *Dharmaśāstras* nor the *Arthasāstras*, nor the *Vārttāśāstras*, nor the *Śilpaśāstras* knew anything of technocracy or capitalism such as might be condemned. It is from his British *guru*, Ruskin, that Gandhi imbibed this denunciation of some of the aberrations of modern economy.

The impact of world-forces on Gandhi's head and heart, nay, on the Gandhian "soul-force" is, then, as powerful as that on everybody who has been anybody in India from Rammohun to the present-day. The other side of the shield, namely, nationalism and reverence for things Indian is equally bright in the Gandhi-complex. His cult of *charkhā*, the spinning wheel, brought his world-forces into contact with the Indian masses. Gandhi could thereby feel that he was a real leader of the Indian people. Nobody before him had risen to that position. He functioned therefore almost as a second Lenin or a second Mussolini during 1919-22.

In this philosophy of cottage spinning there was something "romantic", however,—a *quasi*-proletarian element, a *quasi*-philanthropic factor. Gandhi was thus more of a St. Simon than of a Karl Marx. But in any case, outsiders who had no orientation to the development of Indian public life since the "ideas of 1905" might be misled into believing that Gandhism implied perhaps some denomination of present-day socialism.

The inspiration of Gandhi and the Gandhian *entourage* was quite otherwise. India had not grown during fifteen years to be a proper field for real socialistic experiments on a continental scale. For the cultivating masses the cottage spinning meant perhaps a few meals more per month. But to the nationalists, to the political leaders, to the Swarajists, to the champions of the "ideas of 1905" this cottage spinning, as propagated by Gandhi, meant the universalization of the propaganda against the import of foreign goods. The cry of 1905 was at last being *factually carried from door to door*.

And it is at this point that Gandhi was hailed by the Gujaratis as the maker, the saint and the *avatāra* of modern Gujarat. The hard-headed businessmen, the Gujarati mill-owners, found in this anti-foreign-cloth movement just the very big doses of protective tariff that they had always been looking for. It was to them a God-send because the fall of the foreign currencies during this period rendered the imported goods rather too cheap in India. The *Swadeshi* mill cloth found it impossible to compete with the foreign cloth in the Indian bazars. Gandhi's anti-machinism or *charkhā*-cult was therefore financed by the Gujarati businessmen, especially the mill-owners, in the most enthusiastic manner conceivable. It is as Gujarati leader and supported by Gujarati finance in the interest of Gujarati capitalism that Gandhi held forth throughout India ostensibly for *charkhā* and the soul-force but essentially for the *Swadeshi* cotton industry and boycott of foreign goods, in other words, for industrialism and nationalism.

The "ideas of 1905" found therefore in Gandhism a remarkable embodiment and expansion. He turned out to be a worthy successor of Bipin Chandra Pal, Bal Gangadhar Tilak and Lajpat Rai. As a specimen of creative India's output in modern personality Gandhi can then go down to posterity as one who succeeded in continuing the tradition of her best servants, expanding, democratizing and "massifying" it as well as advancing her claim to equality with the rest of the world on the strength of solid self-sacrifice and positive achievements.

It is not necessary to go into details about the diverse phases of nationalism as developed in the Gandhi-complex. Today in 1936 one must not in any case overlook that in espousing the cause of the *Harijan*, the depressed classes or the *pariah*, Gandhi has but linked himself up with the thousand and one champions of race-uplift, Aryanization, colonizing and *charaiveti* (march on) such as have characterized creative India's annals from the Mohenjo Daro and Vedic ages to the age of Rāmakṛṣṇa-Vivekānanda.

Leadership in public life is essentially an ephemeral phenomenon. So Gandhi (1919-22) has virtually ceased to exist. But today it is possible to see in this specimen of creative India's modern products the more permanent features of his contributions. The distinction between the ephemeral and the permanent is equally patent in other countries of the world. The Japanese Cabinets and French ministries rise and fall like mushrooms. Even in Great Britain there are very few statesmen who have enjoyed real popularity for more than one term. In social affairs, especially in the political arena, it is almost an exception for any person to be lionized for more than six months to a year and a half. In the temporary character of Gandhism as an effective political power the student of philosophy or sociology does not therefore have to read anything exceptional, Oriental or Indian.

But there is another Gandhi, even as a man of politics. This is Gandhi the permanent, the eternal, unconditioned by the local and temporal circumstances of 1919-22. We are not talking of Gandhi's post-1922 or post-1925 career in diverse, especially non-political, fields. The Gandhian complex of 1919-22 itself contains values that are endowed with permanence and universality. It is those eternal and absolute elements in his thought that render him so different from the hundreds of political leaders in the East and the West. Most political leaders of the world have their day and cease to be. But one of the few that have a claim to rank as a leader of mankind for all ages is Gandhi.

Let us begin, however, by clearing away certain misconceptions that have grown about or around the Gandhi-cult. We are quite far today from the political controversies in the midst of which the Gandhi-complex was flourishing. In Gandhi the controversialist's day to day utterances people of all shades of opinion, sentiment and emotion were reading their own propagandas, *pro* or *contra*. And once in a while it was necessary for Gandhi himself to stress or over-emphasize certain aspects of his programme or creed. Students of social or political philosophy and economics all the world over were in this way introduced to a Gandhi who looked bizarre, queer, weird, incomprehensible. And since in the traditional philosophy developed by Eur-Americans in the nineteenth and twentieth centuries the Orient is alleged to be mysterious and the Indian mind to be mystical, Gandhism was automatically linked up by them with what they were pleased to regard as the characteristic products of Asia. Today it should be possible to go back to the original Gandhi, so to say, rescue him from the dusts of controversy and see what the Gandhi texts themselves have to say about the exact cultural, economic and political realities of India, and the methods of constructive statesmanship suggested by him.

Gandhi has been generally taken to be an enemy of modern civilization and a pessimist. But even in the dog-days of 1920 (October 6) he declared his *credo* as follows: " I believe that in the midst of all the bloodshed, chicane, and fraud being resorted to on a colossal scale in the West, the whole humanity is silently and surely making progress towards a better age". This is "futurism" or progressivism with vengeance and it would have delighted the soul even of a Walt Whitman to see the creed of optimism presented in such a bold and powerful manner. The Gandhi-myth is in any case at poles asunder from Gandhi himself.

Another commonplace idea about Gandhi finds in him an inveterate enemy of everything non-Indian or foreign. But in this regard also his own declarations are entirely opposite to what the Gandhi-cult happens to be. In 1921 (June 1) he said: "I do not want my house to be walled in on all sides and my windows to be stuffed. I want the cultures of all lands to be blown about my house as freely as possible. * * * Mine is not a religion of the prison-house." Gandhi is thus a conscious exponent of *viśva-śakti*, i.e., world-forces or world-culture as everybody in India has been since the days of Rammohun.

Gandhi's faith in culture-contacts and in the utilization of world-forces in the interest of India can be seen in another passage, which, however, happens to be rather recent. In the *Amrita Bazar Patrika* (Calcutta) for September 17, 1933 he says: "India cannot stand in isolation and unaffected by what is going on in other parts of the world. We should therefore range ourselves with the progressive forces of the world." Internationalism is thus an important ingredient in the genuine Gandhi-complex. It is perhaps unknown to the Gandhi-myth.

Nobody has been considered to be a greater antimachinist than Gandhi. In contemporary Eur-American thought, indeed, Gandhism = antimachinism. This is perhaps the most salient feature of the Gandhi-myth. Let us then discover in his own words what his article of faith in this field is. Writing in 1924 (November 20) he said: "Machines will remain because, like the body, they are inevitable". Another statement of his is as follows (November 5, 1925): "Machinery has its place, it has come to stay." Be it observed, however, that all this is much later than the Gandhism of 1919-22.

What, then, is there in the machinery-complex which Gandhi would like to oppose? "Machinery," says he, "must not be allowed to displace necessary human labour." If we carefully underline the word "necessary" in this Gandhi creed we shall see that no protagonist of machinism in the West or the East since the advent of the "first industrial revolution" (c 1785-1800) would object to being described as a Gandhist. "What I object to", says he again (November 13, 1924), "is the craze for machinery as such. The craze is for what they call labour-saving machinery. Men go on 'saving labour' till thousands are without work and thrown on the open streets to die of starvation". Such an article of faith is not that of an anti-machinist. It cannot be described as the vague idealism of Orientals, Buddhists or Hindus who are alleged to be unpractical mystics and pessimists. Every industrialist, machinist and economist of today as of yesterday and of tomorrow would find in this *dictum* of Gandhi nothing but the rational anxiety of all practical statesmen and serious students of the unemployment question. When, therefore, Gandhi declares in 1926 (June 17) that he is against the "indiscriminate multiplication" of machinery he is voicing the sentiment as well as the reasoning of every expert in "standardization", "rationalization" and so forth down to Adolf Hitler.

It is then by going back to the original Gandhi that we can emancipate ourselves from the tyranny of the Gandhi-myth. Let us now dive deep into the Gandhi-complex. It is not unreasonable to forget for the time being that Gandhi ever was a lion. We can then discover that the "eternal" in Gandhi is made up of such stuff as the following. In 1920 (August 25) he declared as follows: "A nation that is capable of limitless sacrifice is capable of rising to limitless heights.

The purer the sacrifice, the quicker the progress." A motto like this is independent of space and time.

The idealism of Gandhi is of the loftiest type and it has an universal appeal. "We should be ashamed of resting or having a square meal", says he (October 6, 1921), "so long as there is one able-bodied man or woman without work or food". Here is a message which establishes the kinship of this Gujarati Vaiśya or *Bania* of the twentieth century with the Bodhisattvas of old.

And yet Gandhi's philanthropy is not of the emotional type. He is not misled by hysterical ideas of charity or help to the poor. "To a people famishing and idle", says he (October 13, 1920), "the only acceptable form in which God can dare appear is work and promise of food as wages." Gandhism is here nothing but hard-headed economics. It is not in sentimental outbursts of the "human heart" that Gandhi indulges in connection with the poverty problem. He is brutally sincere when he admits as follows: "I have found it impossible to soothe suffering patients with a song from Kabir. The hungry millions ask for one poem,—invigorating food. They cannot be given that. They must earn it. And they can earn only by the sweat of their brow." It is this logic, this realism and this positivism that will enable Gandhian idealism to endure through the ages.

Internationalism as a craze is the farthest removed from his objective orientation to the realities of life. Gandhi's realism is quite definite about the "duty that lies nearest thee." He is absolutely convinced (October 13, 1921) and teaches senseless idealists to remember that "India must learn to live before she can aspire to die for humanity." He is not the man to be dazzled by the will-o'-the-wisp of an alleged world-peace or international world-order.

Gandhi has a place as a maker of character. Of universal import is a passage like the following with its emphasis on firmness in conviction: "It is poor faith", we are told, "that needs fair weather for standing firm. That alone is true faith that stands the foulest weather." No less human and energizing is his teaching to the effect that "strength lies in absence of fear, not in the quantity of flesh and muscle we may have in our bodies." These are some of the messages with which men and women of the world will like to be familiar in order to acquire strength and courage.

Nothing, again, can be more heartening and re-assuring than for a young man to be told that "true morality consists not in following the beaten track, but in finding out the true path for ourselves and in fearlessly following it." Individuality is the keynote of Gandhian ethics and it is on this basis that men and women are taught to obey the call of duty. Not the gang-morality, not the crowd-psychology, but individual conscience, the sense of one's own responsibility as a "moral person" is what Gandhi inculcates. The philosophy which teaches that the "strength of numbers is the delight of the timid" and that "the valiant in spirit glory in fighting alone" is the philosophy neither of the East alone nor of the West alone, neither for yesterday alone nor for today alone nor for tomorrow alone. It is the ethics of manhood, timeless, spaceless, unconditioned, absolute. Gandhism is destined to be immortal, as immortal as the categorical imperative of Immanuel Kant or the *karmaṇyevādhikāraste mā phaleṣu kadāchana* (It is to work alone that thou hast a right but never to the result) of India's glorious *Gītā*.

One will perhaps remark that in all these philosophizings or moralizings there is more of ethics than of politics. Such a criticism can come only from those who by politics understand solely or chiefly the constitution-making, programme-planning or party-bossing. But in this kind of ethics of politics Gandhi is in very good company with Fichte, as author of *Reden an die Deutsche Nation*, and Śukrāchārya as author of the *Nītisāra*, nay, with Plato, as author of the *Republic*. Gandhi is quite conscious of his position in political philosophy. Writing in 1925 (January 8) he makes it clear that his "duty lies in discovering and employing means by which the nation may evolve the strength to enforce its will. When once the nation is conscious of its strength it will find its own way or make it". Gandhi is, therefore, not the last term of Creative India's modern achievements.[1]

SECTION 3

THE LITERATURE AND ART OF MODERN INDIA

A George Brandes attempting to make a survey of the tendencies in the literature of Young India will have to begin with the statement that there is, strictly speaking, no "Indian literature" but that the literatures in India are as varied as those in Europe. The languages in which the mind of India speaks are as different from

[1] N. K. Bose: "*Selections from Gandhi* (Calcutta, 1934), pp 201, 199, 90-91, 58-60, 99, 47, 45-46, 90, 149, 38, 152, 36. Consult the Gandhi literature in the following publications: M. K. Gandhi: *The Story of My Experience with Truth* (Ahmedabad) Vol. I. (1921), Vol. II. (1929), *Ethical Religion* (Madras) *Speeches and Writings* (Madras, 1918), *A Guide to Health* (Madras 1930), *India's Case for Swaraj* (Bombay, 1932), *Hind Swaraj or Indian Home Rule* (Madras), *My Soul's Agony* (Bombay), *The Nation's Voice* (Ahmedabad, 1932), *Satyagraha in South Africa* (Madras, 1928),

one another as is Portuguese from Russian or Czech from Danish. And yet it would not take long to touch the bottom and find that what the Indian mind speaks through all these diverse media,—Tamil, Telugu, Bengali, Urdu, Marathi or Hindi—is invariably the same. The literature of Young India is intrinsically one. When life is so complex and pluralistic as today it is difficult to classify the "themes" of art. But several leading sources of inspiration for creative literature may here be indicated.

The characters, situations, plots and motives in modern Indian prose and poetry have been profoundly influenced by the study of antiquities, translations from ancient Hindu and Mohammedan literature as well as general archæological scholarship. A "real" *Renaissance* has thus set in in Indian thought, i.e., a re-interpretation of the past in the light of modern viewpoints and techniques. In this transvaluation of values there has been working the all-too familiar "romantic" spirit.

In the second place, the folk movements in public life, the anthropological investigations of scholars and learned societies, the cult of social service which has become popular among the educated classes, the statistical studies in regard to peasants and working men's budgets, the cry of rural reconstruction, these and allied activities have served to enrich the novels, songs and short stories not only with folk-lore material

Self-Restraint vs. *Self-Indulgence* (Ahmedabad, 1930), *From Yervada Mandir* (Ahmedabad), *Young India* 1919-22, 1924-26 (Madras). See also M. Desai: *Gandhiji in Indian Villages* (Madras, 1927) and *With Gandhiji in Ceylon* (Madras, 1928); B. Sen Gupta and R. Chowdhury: *Mahatma Gandhi and India's Swaraj* (Calcutta) as well as Romain Rolland: *Mahatma Gandhi* (London, 1926) and R. Fueloep-Miller: *Lenin und Gandhi* (Vienna, 1927). For the economic ideas of Gandhi see S. C. Dutt: *Conflicting Tendencies in Indian Economic Thought* (Calcutta, 1934).

but also with the heroic and the tragic in the life and labour of the masses, the *pariahs*, the workingmen and the villagers. The democratic experience of Young India has here its literary counterpart.

Thirdly, as might naturally be expected, Western fiction and drama have furnished Indian authors with many new subjects for conscious imitation or adaptation. And of course the indirect suggestive value of these foreign creations in regard to the treatment of legends, the analysis of attitudes, and creation of types is immense. The sway of the world-spirit or the cosmopolitan element in Indian literature is hereby assured.[1]

Hindi Literature

In medieval times the contacts between Hindi literature and Bengali literature were intimate. In modern times Hindi got an impetus in Bengali culture through the curriculum of studies introduced by the National Council of Education in 1906. Baburao Paradkar, at present editor of *Āj* (Benares) and Ambika Prasad Vajpeyi, editor of *Bhārata-mitra* (Calcutta) were the first official teachers of Hindi for Young Bengal. Since then the importance of Hindi has been very well recognized at the Calcutta University on account of the idealism of Asutosh. Hindi is being studied by Bengali scholars today both from the standpoint of philology as well as from that of creative thought.

Among the contemporary writers[2] Sumitrānan-

[1] R. P. Yajnik: *Indian Drama* (London).

[2] L. P. Sukul's lecture on "Contemporary Hindi Literature" at the "Antarjatik Banga" Parishat ("International Bengal" Institute), Calcutta, Feb. 23, 1934. See the *Calcutta Review* July, 1934. See also works on the history of Hindi Literature (in Hindi) by the Misra Brothers (Misra-Vandhu) of Lucknow and by R. C. Sukul, Benares 1931).

dan Panth's poems, entitled *Chhāyā* (Shadow) and *Nakṣatra* (Star), indicate command over imagery, sometimes for its own sake. In Śrīmatī Mahādevī Varma's poems on "Dream" and "Answer" we can touch the pessimistic strains of Urdu poetry. In novels the attempts of authors like Premchand appear to have followed the classic examples in the matter of supernatural and mythological themes. But Kausik's *Mā* (Mother) and *Bhikhāriṇī* (Beggar Woman) are born of the experiences of daily life. In short stories Śrīmatī Sudhā Kumārī Chauhan has been leading off. The writers have learned to deal with social and current topics.

The drama is of recent growth. Jaishankar Prasad's *Ajātaśatru* and *Skandagupta* are the results of modern historical studies. Kālidāsa's influence is to be seen in Govind Das. Hindi dramatists have adopted Bengali technique and are under the influence of English playwrights like, say, Galsworthy.

Mahavir Prasad Dvivedi's appreciative criticisms of Surdās and Tulsīdās as well as works like those of Bakshi entitled *Viśva-Sāhitya* (World-Literature) have served to enrich the language with serious thought and dignified prose. The public speeches of Madan Mohan Malaviya, Purushottamdas Tandon and Shiva Prasad Gupta have served to render the language flexible and powerful. The *Prithvī-Pradakṣiṇā* (Tour Round the World) by Shivaprasad Gupta, published in 1925, is an extensive work on modern civilization (1914-16), embracing as it does Egypt, America, China and Japan. Hindi literature owes a number of scholarly and educational works to the Jnan-mandal (publishing office) and the Kashi Vidyapitha ("national school"), both established as a result of Shivaprasad's financial idealism.

It requires to be observed that a great impetus

has been furnished to Hindi language and literature through Gandhi's speeches as well as writings in Hindi. Gandhi is rightly known as a maker of modern Gujarati literature. He is to be regarded as a powerful foster-parent of Hindi also. His propaganda in favour of Hindi has borne fruit even in South India where the mother tongues of the people are known to be the least allied to the Hindi, Bengali and other North-Indian languages.

Gujarati Literature

We shall now describe some of the features in the modern literature produced in Gandhi's mother-tongue, namely, Gujarati.[1] In Bengali scholarship Gujarati has been very little cultivated. Hardly anything was known about Gujarati literature until a few years ago. But it will be noticed that all the characteristics of modern Bengali literature are observable in this literature of Western India.

Karan Ghelo is a historical novel in Gujarati by Navalram. It deals with the exploits of the last Rajput (Hindu) king, Karan, who challenged Alauddin, the Moslem. The motif and treatment make this Gujarati work essentially akin to the numerous Marathi novels in which Hari Narayan Apte has brought before his compatriots the life and activities of Sivāji or to the novels in Bengali by Bankim Chandra Chatterjee, which have for their theme the political and military enterprises of energists in medieval India.

The romantic handling of the past with a leavening of nationalism, love of individuality, and the sturdy

[1] Based to a considerable extent on the discussions with Mr. Ambalal Bapalal Mehta and other Gujarati merchants at Paris (1921).

spirit of freedom which characterize the robber-stories of Goethe and Schiller and the romances of Scott has certainly been a common feature in India's modern fiction, saturated with idealism as it is. In this sense *Vande Mātaram* (Hail Motherland) is the message not only of Chatterjee's *Ānanda Maṭha* ("Abbey of Bliss") but virtually of every literary work, novel or drama conceived in the back-ground of mediæval history.

On the other side, the spirit of Gustav Freytag, Victor Hugo or Dickens is represented by the author of *Sarasvatī-Chandra*, Govardhanram Madhavaram Tripathi, who is reputed to have contributed to the Gujarati people their "nineteenth *Purāṇa*". In this novel dealing, as it does, with the life of modern Gujarat we are presented with a realistic picture of men and manners such as the eighteen *Purāṇas* of old India have perpetuated for us in Sanskrit in regard to previous ages.

The *Gujarati Sāhitya Pariṣat* (Academy of Gujarati Literature) owes its origin to Tripathi. Academies of literature together with *Sammelans* i.e. congresses (generally annual) of the men of letters are a regular feature in the cultural life of every language-zone in India. The institution is as popular among the Telugu-speaking Andhras of Madras as among the Oriyas of Orissa. The subjects discussed in these assemblies of authors and journalists are throughout uniform. They range from philological, anthropological and archæological investigations to dramatic criticism, the discussion of scientific and technical terminology, as well as philosophical dissertations, oriental and occidental.

An author who like Tripathi has interested himself in the same problems of present-day life, but whose *modus operandi* is the instrument of satire is Ramanbhai

Nilkanth. His *Bhadram Bhadra* is enjoyed by the Gujaratis as an Indian *Don Quixote*. Nilkanth is, besides, a reformer not only in social organization, but also in linguistic taste. In the controversy between the erudite Sanskritized diction and popular vocabulary he has thrown in his lot with the masses.

The poet "Kalāpī" is well known for his translations from Wordsworth. But his place in Gujarati literature is assured by his *Kekārava* (The Peacock's Notes). The technique of Kālidāsa's *Meghadūta* (Cloud Messenger) has been brilliantly employed by the author, who, by the by, is prince of Lathi in Kathiawar, with a most wonderful sense of rhythm.

To a "migrant bird" Kalāpī addresses the following song:[1]

"To the land of Kashmir, of sweet springs and balmy breezes!
Dear traveller ! linger there in a land that is dear to me—
In a land of uttermost delight and honey-flowing groves
Where shadows of clustered grapes are cast on crystal streams.

* * * *

"At eventide the Himalayan peaks are dyed with the colour of roses
Then vale after vale, and countless fountains and lakes grow fairer yet,
And the trees in the mountains above the clouds converse with the stars—
They are bathed in the light of heaven and smile in a happy trance.

[1] Translated by A. K. Coomaraswamy and P. V. Vaishya for the *Modern Review* (Calcutta) for March 1920.

* * * *

"Bethink thee then of the love of thy Master and friend—
My child, my darling, alas ! thy tears are falling still, my grief !
But perch in the crown of a mighty tree I have reared for thee,
And I shall recite to thee, my dear, this little song I have made."

But the poet-patriot who has equipped Young Gujarat with its soul-stirring cry is Narmada-Shamkar Lal-Shamkar, in whose songs much of the spirit that is agitating India's mind today was anticipated. His refrain, *Jaya Jaya Garavī Gujarāta* (Victory to Great Gujarat) has earned for him a pan-Indian reputation. Among his scholarly works the *Dictionary of the Gujarati Language* is a solid testimony to his capacity for labour.

Gandhi's contributions to modern Gujarati prose are considerable. His weekly *Navajīvan* (New Life) has perhaps succeeded in accomplishing for Gujarat and her literature as well as language what Tilak's *Kesarī* has done for the Marathas (Deccanis) and the Marathi language and literature. The people of Gujarat consider themselves revolutionized by Gandhi's literary output since, say, 1920.

Marathi Literature

The *Svadeshī-Swarāj* movement (1905-14) has automatically been associated among the Marathas (Deccanis) with the revival of Śivāji-cult both as cause and effect. Around this worship of the Frederick the Great of India the best brains of the Deccan grouped themselves as explorers and novelists, as historians and artists towards the end of the nineteenth century. The influence of Marathi language and literature was already apparent in Bengal when Dharmananda Kosambi of Poona was appointed by the National Council of Education in 1907 to teach Marathi as well as Pali to the students of Indian history at the Bengal National College.

Among the most signal contributors to the songs of latter-day Mahārāṣṭra is to be mentioned Vināyak Savarkar. Śivāji is the hero of his historical lyrics. His *Sinha-gaḍchā Pāwāḍā* (The Ballad of Sinhagad) depicts one of the pioneering achievements of the Hindu nationalist of the seventeenth century. The ballad narrating the devotion of Baji Prabhu Deshpande to the duty set by his master is likewise a soul-inspiring execution in the Śivaji-legend.

Besides these "national" lyrics modern Marathi possesses a host of songs which the theatre has contributed to the man in the street and made part of the people's folk-literature. The melodies sung by "Bāl-Gandharva" on the stage have served to set the musical taste and standard of the Marathas. He plays invariably the female part, since in Bombay, perhaps in every cultural region outside of Bengal, actresses are yet unknown.

The dramatist whom "Bāl Gandharva" has thus succeeded in making a popular figure is Krisṇāji Prabhākar Khadilkar. This playwright made his *début* with prose-dramas like *Kīchaka-vadha* (The Slaying of Kīchaka), which is based on a legend in the *Mahābhārata*. Khadilkar has several other plays in prose of which the themes are derived from the Maratha history of

[1] Based to some extent on discussions with the late Shyamakant Govind Sardesai, son of the historian G. S. Sardesai, at Berlin (1922); See also Nadkarni: *A Short History of Marathi Literature* (Baroda).

the eighteenth century. *Bhao Bandki* (Family Quarrel) deals with the murder of Narayan Rao through the machinations of his aunt Ānandī Bāi. *Kānchangaḍchi Mohanā* (Lady of Kanchangad) is another piece from the same quarry. Khadilkar's genius is versatile. He has created several types of womanhood in some of his dramas in verse. He has laid under contribution the ancient story of Kacha coming to Śukra for education and wooing his daughter Devajāni. The play is called *Vidyāharaṇa* (The Stealing of Learning) and will be found to be more complex in the treatment of the relations between the sexes than is Tagore's *Chitrā* which is equally based on ancient legends. In Khadilkar's two other woman-pieces, *Rukminī-svayamvara* (The Choosing of her Husband by Rukminī) and *Draupadī*, the Marathas can see the female sex in its atmosphere of freedom, individualism and self-assertion. Khadilkar has taken part in politics, belonging to the extremist group of patriots. His daily, *Lokamānya* (Respected by the People), is the organ of the *Swarajists*.

The founder of the Marathi theatre is Anna Kirloskar. His plays like *Sakuntalā* and *Saubhadra* were adapted from the old Sanskrit treatises. Although he did not originate any theme he is the creator of the new drama of the Marathas. He was, besides, a genuine poet in whose songs the people find the flow of the soul which as a rule is not characteristic of Khadilkar's compositions. In the work of adapting ancient classics for the modern stage Kirloskar found a colleague and follower in Deval. This latter's *Mrichchhakatika*, *Sāpa-sambhrama* (based on the *Kādambarī* of old) and *Mukanāyaka* have served to bring home to the present generation the literary and cultural tradition of the past on which the contemporary revaluation is erected.

Altogether, in these literary achievements of the

Maratha playhouse Bengal will remember the work accomplished for it by Girish Chandra Ghosh, and the Western students of drama will notice the counterpart of the movement by which the Greek and the Latin sources have been exploited for the modern stage in Europe.

A brilliant poet has been cut off in his prime at the age of 32. This was Ram Ganesh Gaḍkarī. His poetry breathes the atmosphere of undiluted natural sentiment. The elegies composed by him touch the tenderest chord in the human heart. His poems on nature and love possess an originality in the handling of emotion. Gaḍkarī was strongest in the treatment of pathos. Perhaps no composition in Marathi has excited so much universal pity among the people as this sad young author's *Ekach Pyālā* (Just One Glass) acted on the stage. The drama is a study in the drink-evil and domestic misery, and can always be used in propaganda for prohibitionism.

While Khadilkar, because of his many-sided dramatic productions and feverish fecundity, is almost a household word to the literary public, a playwright of exceptional merit whose popularity is no less patent is Narsingh Chintamon Kelkar, the present editor of the *Kesarī*, the Marathi weekly. His *Totāyāche Bāndā* (Revolt of the Pretender) has for its theme the problems of double personality akin to many of the theses in psychology and fiction which the Great War (1914-18) has contributed to literature through the unrecorded deaths of many soldiers. In 1761 at the Battle of Panipat (near Delhi) Sadāsiva Rāo Bhāo, the chief of the Marathas, was killed in action. But as no trace was found of his body, a pretender came back from the front and claimed to be the ruler of the territory as well as the husband of the widow.

While reading Kelkar's story based on this incident one is easily reminded somewhat of Madame Borel's novel, *Le Survivant* (The Survivor), in which is presented the study of a strange personality constituted of the physical body of one man and the soul of another who is dead. The Maratha author has tried moreover to visualize the folk-India of the latter half of the eighteenth century. His characterizations are lively and his treatment has the grace of natural humour.

In the field of romance Hari Narayan Apte was until his death (1920) the most prominent figure. As an exponent of social reform and social service and as director of the *Ānandāśrama* publications of old Sanskrit texts he was also one of the most influential makers of modern Mahārāṣṭra. As a man of letters he has naturally been attracted by that rich mine of legends and hearsays, namely, Maratha history. And nobody has made use of this valuable source of fiction more artistically than Apte. Among his historical novels, the *Uṣaḥkkāl* (Dawn) deals with the exploits of the early Marathas. *Gaḍ Ālā Paṇ Sinha Gelā* (The Castle Came, but the Lion is Gone) is based on the statement of Śivāji to his followers who had stormed the fort of Sinhagad to the effect that although they had achieved their aim their triumph was eclipsed by the death of their commander, "the lion" Tānāji. Apte's description of the manner in which people of the lowest class were organized into a mighty army and bands of young patriots used to form themselves into associations for political purposes has become a classic among the Marathas. Although in his personal views Apte happened to be an associate of the "moderate" leaders of nationalist India his artistic creations have furnished Mahārāṣṭra with the tenets of radical politics.

Apte has selected his theme from Rajput annals

also, the source so popular in modern Bengali drama, poetry and fiction. His *Rūpa-nagarchi Rājkanyā* (The Princess of Rupnagar) has curiously enough the same plot as Bankim Chandra Chatterjee's *Rājsimha*.

One of Apte's last pieces is *Paṇ lakṣāt kon gheto* (But who cares for it?). In it the novelist holds the mirror up to the modern Maratha society,—and has a chance to expose the current abuses in domestic and public life.

Tilak and the Kesarī

Khadilkar and Apte are unforgettable names in Marathi literature. Equally or rather more so is Bāl-Gangādhar Tilak. His claims to mankind's recognition in other, non-literary lines are of course unparalleled. For a whole generation Tilak was the "uncrowned king" of Mahārāṣṭra in the estimation alike of the *intelligentsia* as of the workingmen and women. His moral persuasion was eminently successful among the masses in combating alcoholism. Unnumbered families of mill-hands in Bombay and the Deccan loved and worshipped him as father, friend and benefactor.

Vedic scholarship counted Tilak among its veterans of the premier rank. He was one of the brilliant pioneers of modern education in his province, a cause to which he devoted himself at immense personal sacrifice. In the world of science he was a keen seeker of truth, and as a human being he was an indefatigable energist in the service of freedom and democracy.

Prince among journalists, Napoleon among fellow-men, propagandist among philosophers, mathematician, lawyer, orator, this apostle of liberty was the very sun of the social system among the Marathas—the Goethe of Poona as much in the radiation of influences as in the bringing together of world-forces.

A towering personality that he was both in thought and deed, in idealism, organizing capacity, and constructive statesmanship, Tilak's life-long persistence in self-expression has rendered to Marathi language and literature a service which is monumental, such indeed, as very few men of letters individually have been able to accomplish in the world.

And yet authorship was hardly a vocation with Tilak. His two books in English are entitled *The Arctic Home in the Vedas* and *Orion*. The only book which he has left for his readers in Marathi is the *Gītā Rahasya* (The *Meaning* or Philosophy of the *Gītā*). This was written during his second imprisonment and published shortly before his death (1920). It embodies the maturest experience of his fully-lived life and reinterprets the traditional soul-metaphysics, optimistic as it is, in the interest of a vigorous energism. This Marathi introduction to the *Gītā* will appear to students of comparative philosophy to be another Voltaire's *Essai sur les Moeurs* (Essay on Morals), the analogy being confined chiefly to logic and language.

But the entire Tilak literature bearing as it does the stamp of a mighty intellect is to be found in the columns of the weekly *Kesarī*, the journal which he founded (1881) and which has furnished the "whole duty of man" to thousands of its regular readers on every question of life, social, religious moral, political, literary. Under his guidance the *Kesarī* remained the real "national university" of the Marathas. To it the young men of letters looked for suggestions in diction, the historian for judgment and criticism, the scientist for the language of the laboratory, and the patriot for inspiration in self-sacrifice and social service.

Tilak was not a poet, novelist or dramatist. His medium was the essay, conversation, lecture written or *extempore*. His writings are the compositions of a man of action, pithy, pointed, precise, popular, addressed to the man in the street, to the woman in the home. Supremely a journalist and a lecturer, first and last an essayist and a popularizer, Tilak has imparted to his mother-tongue a vocabulary, style and range for which a parallel is to be sought only in the epoch-making achievements of French prose in the eighteenth century through the writings of Montesquieu, the sociologist, and Diderot, the director of the *Encyclopédie*. Nay, if one should look ahead and try to envisage the future career of the new Maratha in its historical perspective one should have to appraise the literary output of Tilak, the prophet, preacher, patriot, as a tremendous dynamic force no less vitalizing and momentous for his race than was that of Voltaire for France during the last and the greatest period of his devotion to "reason" and "humanity" through journalistic pamphleteering manipulated, as it was, from Ferney on the Swiss side of the Lake of Geneva.

The Poetry and Paintings of Rabindranath

The Vaiṣṇava poets of our Middle Ages had their Rādhā; the Italian Dante had his Beatrice; and Rabindranath Tagore has his Mānasa-Sundarī or Jīvana-Devatā as his Inspiration-Deity. Living as we do under modern conditions, pre-eminently businesslike, unsentimental and prosaic, it is perhaps difficult to envisage the medieval atmosphere of Eur-Asia and to realize concretely what it means for such authors as those of the *Padāvalī* and the *Divine Comedy* to be possessed by the demon of genius,—the godlike madness of creators, or to be born as the chosen children of "fine frenzy". But here we have in our very midst one who as "Fancy's child" will always rank among the world's greatest, blest with an address in Creation Avenue, so to say, and it should be possible for us by taking a plunge into the Tagore encyclopædia to catch a glimpse of the creative spirit such as moves under the magic wand of an Inspiration-Deity.

Mānasa-Sundarī or Jīvana-Devatā has compelled Rabindranath to express himself in diverse forms and through diverse media. Many of us will remember Robert Browning's lines in this connection, such as the following:

> "Dante once prepared to paint an angel:
> Whom to please? You whisper Beatrice.
> Rafael made a century of sonnets,
> Made and wrote them in a certain volume
> Dinted with the silver-pointed pencil;
> Else he only used to draw Madonnas,
> These the world might view,—but one, the volume.
> Who that one, you ask? Your heart instructs you."

So Rabindranath the poet has become a painter. In him we have, as it were, a Dante Rafaelizing. For,

> "Ay, of all the artists living, loving,
> None but would forego his proper dowry,—
> Does he paint? He fain would write a poem,
> Does he write? He fain would paint a picture;
> * * * * * *
> Put to proof art alien to the artist's
> Once and only once, and for One only,
> So to be the man and leave the artist."

The poet Rabi has presumably been trying to "put to proof art alien to the artist's" perhaps in order "to be the man and leave the artist". All the same, it is at the beck and call of "one only", the same Mānasa-Sundarī of his literary inspiration. In that world of "art alien to the artist's", therefore, Rabi has not been going about as an alien, as one who has to "forego his proper dowry". The alphabet and language of painting should appear to be nothing foreign to him. The lyrical designs, the rhythmic shapes, and plastic colours created by Rabi's brush are already so multiform and so extensive and at the same time so youthful, so warm and so enthusiastic that one need not be surprised if a generation or two later some connoisseur, perchance unfamiliar with the poet Rabi, should seriously remark:

"Does he paint? He fain would write a poem."

The workmanship embodied in these paintings is not that of a junior commencing his career. It is already ripe art. Place them in a gallery of the pure "futurists" in Eur-America, and the visitors will not fail to be struck by the liquid flow of original forms to which both the drawing and the colour-technique of the artist, conceived in the latest style as they are, have contributed. The boldness with which he has executed the systematically weird but none the less expressive figures may have been imbibed by him, if at all, from only one Indian painter, and this by no means from Abanindra but from Gogonendra, who has already some following at Calcutta.

In any case, Rabi is adequately at home in the phrases and idioms of painting. The morphology of the painter's world is his own. But, be it observed, this morphology is not the conventional structure of the too familiar anatomy, physiognomy and architecture. In Rabi's paintings we obtain the compositions with which the most radical post-War experimenters in art-forms have enriched our visual sense. He is one of the world's most advanced "moderns" in the sphere of painting.

In Eur-America the latest discoverers of shades and colours have consciously placed themselves under the inspiration of African, American-Indian and other "primitives" derived from archæological excavations or anthropological researches. In Rabi's creations there is a conscious attempt up till now at modernizing the possibilites of the Javanese or Indonesian art-structures. No doubt he has been tapping other sources as well.

The geometry of Rabi's art can already pass as a household commodity in the show-rooms, salons and museums of the West. There the eyes and tastes of a large section of the art-public have got trained in the new forms invented, discovered or rediscovered during the last two generations or so under the pioneering inspiration of Gaugin, Van Goch, Cezanne and others. But in India it has taken us some two decades to appreciate on a somewhat large scale the creations even of Abanindra. Naturally it will be long before Rabi's works in painting can pass beyond the range of curios in colour and design. For, it is necessary to observe that the experiments of Gogon and his followers are not yet numerous enough to constitute a smooth and easy transition, a firm and dependable bridge to the juxtaposition of masses and motions conceived by Rabi's revolutionary vision. But as painter he is destined to pioneer a new world of artists and art-critics in India.

It is clear at any rate that Rabi is a citizen of two worlds in the sphere of art. And this double nationality of his artistic self should appear to be so genuine and natural that very often one is tempted to believe that as painter Rabi has been but translating or paraphrasing his literary songs, poems, dramas and stories, of course, with modifications adapted to the changed circumstances of the day. The divine madness of paintings has seized him and is not likely to let him loose, it seems, until his forms and tints have become the replicas of his words and vocal expressions,—until indeed the Tagore encyclopædia doubles itself in volume and weight.

The name of themes already attempted in these paintings is legion. Purely descriptive and realistic scenes have not been neglected. The joy of life, the mere living, the fulness of activity is patent everywhere. But idealism furnishes the fundamental atmosphere of these creations. The laughing, the humorous Rabi is also to be encountered in this society. One piece criticises, another caricatures, and a third satirizes,—and all through runs the vein of interpretation. Many of the diverse moods and attitudes of the poet are already in evidence in this world of forms and colours.

It may shrewdly be suspected, moreover, that Rabi the painter is going beyond Rabi the poet and that the painter is not a mere translator or paraphraser of the poet. The painter has commenced where perhaps the poet left off. In the aquarelles of Rabindranath we are getting new men and women, new ideas of nature and society, new criticisms of life and art, new moral and spiritual values such as were hardly dreamt of in the entire gamut of Tagore literature. These newnesses, these additions have been serving but to expand Rabi and furnish some more indices to his devotion to the mistress of his being and to his constant responsiveness to the call of the Inspiration-Deity. The intellectual and social revolution through which Rabi was growing as author during the last few years he has accepted as an accomplished fact at the very threshold of his experience as painter. Young India is in for another *Vita Nuova*, this one in keeping with the "storm and stress" of 1930-31. The art-connoisseur as well as the student of social forces are sure to feel that we have moved far, very far away from the "ideas of 1905" in fine arts and societal reconstruction, and that we are now ready for a big jump. The social message is unmistakable.

The vital urges of the Tagore creations in literature as in painting are as elemental and profound, as vast and world-embracing as life itself. But it is *élan vital* in motion, it is life such as is ever awake and ever growing, such as knows no bounds of age and clime. To associate oneself with the Tagore creations is but to enjoy so many sips out of living streams, as well as to move as a limb of the very vital process, as an energized being among active and expanding energies.

Let us catch one of the moods of the poet when in 1892 he is about thirty years old. One evening he is arrested by the song of a cowherd boy while the latter "homeward plods his weary way". Rabi forthwith remembers his own childhood as well as

> "*kata śata nadītīre kata āmrabane*
> *kāmsyaghanṭāmukharita mandirer dhāre*
> *kata śasyakṣetraprānte pukurer pāre*
> *grihe grihe jāgitechhe naba hāsimukh*
> *kata asambhav kathā apūrba kalpanā*
> *kata amūlak aśā aśes kāmanā*
> *ananta biśvas Dānḍāiye andhakāre*
> *dekhinu nakṣatrāloke asīm samsāre*
> *rayechhe prithivī bhari bālikā bālak*
> *sandhyā śajyā, mār mukh, dīper ālok.*"

Rabi's *Saiśav Sandhyā* (Evening in Infancy) is an exquisite study in the scenes of child-life and the sundry happinesses of infancy. The picture is one of movements and activities associated with

> "Many hundreds of riverbanks,
> Many forests of mango trees,

And the neighbourhoods of temples
Resounding with the music of bronze bells;
The edges of many corn fields
And the slopes of tanks,—
Where in house after house
Flourish new smiling faces,
New joys that fill fresh hearts,
Impossible tales, strange fancies,
Hopes without base, endless longings
And faith infinite."[1]

All these child-sentiments and child-surroundings are recollected from the poet's own personal experience. But they serve to carry his imagination up to the entire world of children in the human race. And his vision expresses itself as follows:

"Standing in the dark
I saw in the light of the stars
In the limitless universe
The world full of boys and girls,
Evening beds, mothers' faces,
And the lights of lamps."

Verily, the poet grasps the real kernel of the world's life as we encounter him admiring:

"*Ekhano ki briddha haye jāy ni samsār*!"
(Even yet is the world not grown aged!)

The perennial infancy, childhood or youth of mankind is a leading *motif* of the Rabindric creations. The world has not grown old, mankind has always been enjoying spring, and along with it Rabi as well as his mind and art have been preserving their freshness.

[1] All the English renderings of Tagore in this section are by the present author.

About the same time Rabi is interesting himself in the alleged "divine love" of Vaiṣṇava poetry. Sceptically he asks

> "*Sudhu Vaikuṇṭher tare tabe Vaiśṇaver gān!*"
> (Are then the songs of the Vaiṣṇavas
> Solely for the ends of Heaven?)

Rabi is too sincere, too human to be bamboozled by mediæval metaphorizings or allegories and modern mediævalisms. A front attack is, therefore, delivered by him in a thoroughly vitalistic manner on the Bastille of other-worldliness in the Rādha-Kriṣṇa relations. He poses the straight question in a straight way, as follows:

> "Tell me truly, oh Vaiṣṇav poet!
> Where you got this picture of love?
> *** *** whose eyes
> Led you to remember Rādhā's
> Tearful eyes? *** **** ****
> *** *** From whose face
> And eyes have you stolen
> The bitter pangs of Rādhā's rent-up heart?"

It is genuine, flesh-and-blood, human experience that Rabi postulates in the Rādhā-songs of the Vaiṣṇava poets. The same rights of human, earthly experience, the same rights of flesh-and-blood truth he demands, therefore, for the men and women of today. True as he is to life's urges, his natural challenge to the modern mediævalists and contemporary spiritualitarians finds an humanistic expression in the following query:

> "And today no right does the same person
> Possess to those songs?"

In a more positive vein the poet asserts:

> "*** *** It is in our cottages and groves

That blossom flowers. Certain persons offer
Them to the gods, others preserve them for
The beloved. The gods do not take it
Amiss. This garland of love-songs
Is woven in the intercourse of men and
Women. It is offered to the gods by some,
By others to the necks of their beloved.
Whatever we can offer to the gods we
Offer also to the dear ones, what to the
Dear ones likewise to the gods. What else
Can we obtain? We make the gods
Our dear ones and the dear ones gods.

This is how the alleged god-lore, the "soul"-metaphysics of Vaiṣṇava poets is secularized in the poetry of Rabindranath and their "ends of Heaven" are discovered to be but such stuff as man and woman are made of. The bounds of life and art have been expanded by Rabi's humanism and he presents us with an extensive range of joys and sorrows.

The prophet of a larger and greater life, of a really humane and sincere art, as Rabi appears here to be, he is not to rest anywhere, to enjoy standstill at any particular point in the journey. In *Nirjharer Svapna-bhaṃga* (The Fountain's Break of Dream) he has admitted us into the laboratory of his soul and we taste a bit of his mind, mobile, racy and elastic as it is. Says he:

"*Śikhar haite śikhare chhutiba,*
Bhūdhar haite bhūdhare lutiba,
Hese khalakhal geye kalakal
Kare kare diba tāli
Tatinī haiyā jāiba bahiyā
Jāiba bahiyā, jāiba bahiyā,
Hridayer kathā kahiyā kahiyā

Gābiyā gābiyā gān.
*** *** ***

Jata diba prān, baye jābe prān
Phurābe nāka ār prāṇ."
"I would run from peak to peak
And roll from hill to hill,
Laughing, giggling, singing, prattling,
I would clap the hands to time.
I would flow in rivulet's self,
Would flow and flow onward,
And speak and speak heart's longing out,
And sing and sing my songs.
*** ***

The more of life I give
The more would it flow on,
And life would never cease.

This restlessness of Rabi's, his perpetual dynamism, his constant desire to be flowing on and generating a continuous stream of values for mankind makes him akin to Goethe's *Weltgeist*, the Earth-Spirit, in *Faust*, who declares:

"In floods of being, in action's storm,
Up and down I wave,
To and fro I flee,
Birth and the grave,
An infinite sea,
A changeful weaving,
An ardent living;
The ringing loom of Time is my care,
And I weave God's living garment there".

This chip from the German poetic studio can indeed serve as a preamble or a conclusion to the lengthy, magnificent and soul-enfranchising ode of Rabindranath on *Vasundharā* (The Earth) composed in 1893 at the age of thirty-one. It begins as follows:

> "Take me back to thee, oh Earth!
> The child of thy arms into thy arms,
> Under the cover of thy vast garment.
> O Mother Earth! how would I
> Remain spread out on the soil,
> In directions far and wide,
> Have myself scattered like the joys
> Of the spring. ** ***
> *** *** How I wish to make myself
> Into whatever exists anywhere
> *** *** how I long in my mind
> To be kinsman with all races,
> In diverse lands."

Once more do we remember Browning whose "principle of restlessness" "would be all, have, see, know, taste, feel all." This passion of Rabi's "to be all",—

> " **** *ichchhā kare āpanāre kari*
> *jekhāne jā kichhu āchhe*",

"to make myself into whatever exists anywhere",

> "**** *ichchhā kare mane mane*
> *Svajāti haiyā thāki sarbalok sane*
> *Deśe deśāntare*"

"to be kinsman with all races in diverse lands",—is the keynote of the two encyclopædias,—in poetry and in paintings, with which he has enriched mankind.

Nay, the very source of life he would like to possess so that he may be at one with the processes of creation itself. His wish is thus worded:

> "*** *** *Āmāre phirāye laha*
> *sei sarva mājhe, jethā hate aharaha*

aṇkurichhe mukulichhe munjarichhe prāṇ
śatek sahasra rūpe etc.,"

He says—

"   ***Take me back
Into the midst of that All, from whence,
Day and night sprout blossoms and flowers,
Life in hundreds and thousands of forms,—
Music vibrates in million melodies,
Dance enthuses in unnumbered poses,
And the heart flows on in emotion's streams.
*** *** ***
*** *** Those varied joys
Of the World-All would I partake
Even in one moment, at one
With all others."

The self-expression of Rabindranath has turned out to be the self-expression of the very muses of poetry and painting in all their moods in growth and attitudes in motion. It should be possible, therefore, for lovers of artistic inspiration in all ages and regions to quench their thirst at this living fountain-head of art.[1]

Art Exhibitions and Artists

The exhibitions organized by the Indian Society of Oriental Art (Calcutta) enable us to watch the tendencies of modern Bengali and other Indian artists.[2] It

[1] For other phases see the present author's *Rabīndra-Sāhitye Bhārater Vāṇī* (The Message of India in Rabindra Literature), Calcutta, 1913 composed on the occasion of the award of the Nobel Prize for literature to Rabindra Nath Tagore, *Viśva-Sakti* (Calcutta, 1914), pp. 275-280, and *Love in Hindu Literature* (Tokyo, 1916).

[2] The present author's "Aesthetics of Young India" and "Social Philosophy in Aesthetics" (*Rupam*, Calcutta, 1922 and 1924).

appears that, practically speaking, those workers who are bound by old conventions have not been able to display much creative spirit. For instance, Durga-shankar Bhattacharya's *Story of the Unseen Land* is only an execution in the conventional spirit although the legend is original and fresh. The central piece consists of four figures in different corners of a square form made of bamboo rafts. The pose in the act of catching fish is quite noteworthy. The forms of the two boats have added to the piece some amount of colour and have served also to contribute a contrast to the yellow rafts. But the artist has deliberately attempted a number of what he seems to consider to be "mystic" lines. To the observers, however, these attempts appear to be vague and meaningless. The total absence of the background of any sort is a technique that can hardly excite one's interest under ordinary conditions of treatment. Perhaps the painter believes that by placing the central piece in such an unoccupied and empty space he is continuing the "tradition" of ancient and medieval Oriental artists. And perhaps this is why he calls his work "Unseen Land".

It is clear of course that Bhattacharya has not taken the subject-matter from anything known in Indian art-history. To that extent he is undoubtedly free and unhampered. But although not handicapped in theme he has chosen to experiment with the so-called mystical handling. The result is disappointing. He has failed to create the atmosphere of the infinite in spite of the negation of the background. It must be admitted, however, that the artist has skill in drawing and possesses the sense of colour.

The pieces which deal with Paurāṇic story and mythological or religious history are invariably defective. The artists have tried to be true to the tradition but have succeeded in becoming mere imitators without a vital message. Thus whether the treatment of the subject be traditional or not, the result is in both cases unencouraging. But the Indian art exhibitions of today are not mainly collections of ancient and medieval subjects or styles. And this is a happy sign of the times. A change in out-look is noticeable among the artists.

Now let us see some of those workers who deal with things in which they themselves happen to be interested in their daily lives and who have cared to be true to themselves instead of trying to "reproduce" the "ancient spirit," as it is called. We shall take the *Joy of Rains* by A. K. Majumdar. It has been executed in a very dexterous manner. In the first place, the colour-scheme in it is made up of different shades of blue, secondly, the peculiar form of the bungalow cottages of Bengal, the oblique sides of its thatched roofs as well as its angularities have been enriched with the round concave of an umbrella shape over the bent figure of a young boy. The whitish figures of moving ducks have brought into relief the dusky atmosphere of a rainy day. There is no conscious effort on the part of this artist to "play" the Indian or the Bengali. But all the same, he has succeeded in contributing a nice quota to our form-sense. He has been able to create a plastic joy, so to say. It is a piece of "sincere" art.

In the like manner is another piece by the same artist to be appreciated. Here, again, we have a really creative composition. To begin with, the piece is not monotonous. The uniformity of the blue has been broken in upon by dots of whitish flower forms as well as swarms of flying birds. Further, the artistic effect is heightened by an expanse of greenish surface which cuts the background in an uneven rough manner. Two boat-forms we see in parallel positions, and the human figures, erect as they are, form transverse parallels to the former. And their combined effect on the entire grouping is that of wealth in heterogeneity. The boats, again, have acquired prominence on account of the red streaks. These latter, moreover, are to be seen distributed in different sections. Altogether, we have here all the delights that the juxtaposition of varied forms and colours can offer to the eye. The success of this artist as contrasted with the failure of the two mentioned above is chiefly to be attributed to the absolute repudiation of the "ancients".

One may enquire as to whether it is impossible to achieve greatness when a painter deals with ancient subjects or attempts to follow the methods of the old masters. The answer would be that it is not impossible. If the artist knows how to divide the space, which colours to mix and in what proportions, how to distribute the forms, and what use to make of the background, he can be a great artist even although he borrows his theme from the ancients or even although he deliberately tries to catch their technique. An instance of such success is a piece by Abanindra Nath Tagore.

Probably it is a Christian scene,—the figure of some saint, may be, Christ himself. The artist has sought to call up the atmosphere of monasticism which one may even call Buddhist or Christian at random. The influence of the ancients is quite palpable. But,—and this is a speciality,—the artist's workmanship does not consist in a mere attempt to be true to what older mystics have drawn. The author of this piece is not a copyist. He has command over the *methodology* of the makers of the old frescoes. At the very first glance, indeed, every observer will notice in it the marks of the great "primitives". You have the bold arms and the vigorous human figure. By the by, this is rather exceptional with the present artist whose brush, as a rule, is used to the softer, more delicate, gentler touches.

The halo is not wanting in the background. The staff, a long, almost vertical piece, seized with the right hand bent in a lifted posture, has delightfully broken the space and added to the majesty of the composition. A dignity characteristic of the 'heroic ages' is perceptible.

But wherein, outside of these elements, lies the grandeur of this composition? The basic dignity in this work lies in the manner in which the artist has filled up three-fourths of the entire surface from top to bottom, with the bulky yet simple figure of a human being. The very height and weight of the shape as apparent in the *milieu* of the space constitute the marvel of the workmanship. The artist is an expert in space management.

Deep brown drapery flowing from the neck in a magnificent manner covers, properly speaking, the entire space. This indeed is the very soul of the present technique. There remains but slight uncovered surface to the right and the left. The not very loud grey of the face has been placed in an environment of equally mild tints of colour. The three or four touches of bold blue in the halo have served to offer a pleasing contrast to the generally soft colour-scheme of the entire work.

The gentleness of the hues does not fail to tell a significant story to the eyes. We do not wait to inquire how the figure has been named by the artist. A piece like this might have a natural place in a collection of the Tang and Sung masterpieces of medieval China.

The pictures drawn by Sunayanī Devī are some of the new forms with which our art-world is being enriched. There are four or five human forms in different poses. The artist has got an admirable conception of structure. The shapes perhaps would not be enjoyed by those who form their aesthetic sense on the strength of the experiences of physiognomy culled from their everyday life. Sunayani Devi's faces might have been described as outlandish or archaic by persons used to the normal standard. But the figures display in their workmanship a sculptural solidity of remarkable character. And this has been produced by the manipulation of different degrees of whitish or black and white colour. The artist's brush has manufactured a liquid flow of grey marble, as it were. A soft, idyllic, lyrical quality is the characteristic charm of her studies in the plastic possibilities of colour.

The *Deserted House tells its Owner's Fate* and *Captive Light* have mysterious titles. The artist Gogonendra Nath Tagore has chosen to be frankly mystical, at any rate, in description. But there is hardly anything mystifying in the works themselves.

Ostensibly, the painter has given us some houses. But nobody would be prepared to believe that these are houseforms at all. One may not object to believing at the utmost that one is perhaps here in the presence of brick or stone structures. No stereotyped architectural design is there, nothing to connect it with the familar forms of masonry work, much to the discomfiture of the contractors and engineers. From this standpoint one would not be wrong if one were to believe that a mystical something is in sight. Indeed, one might go to the extreme and remark that there does not seem to be anything in the line of conventional forms except only a few touches at different points.

And yet a lover of art will find in these "formless forms" of absolutely no historical or racial context some of the most vitalizing colour-compositions and architectonic expressions. The blue and white of the one piece and the red and blue of the other exhibit delightful varieties of structural colour-design of moderately large size. There is plenty of nourishing food here for the student of aesthetics.

Even without being able fully to understand what forms lie before our eyes according to the recognized canons of the objective world we feel that the shapes have been placed alongside of one another in symmetrical and harmonious groups. We can invite all art-critics and lovers of art to begin with such specimens as object lessons in "pure art".

It is in such compositions, thoroughly futuristic as they are, that we begin to appreciate, without the scaffolding of legends, stories, messages and moralizings, the foundations of genuine artistic sense. This artist certainly is a creator of new forms which no doubt have a great message to the souls that thirst for new creation.

Some other tendencies of modern Indian artists are to be observed, e.g., at the Exhibitions organized by the Government School of Art (Calcutta). In Art Exhibitions as a rule we come into contact with the work of professional artists. But here it is possible to see the work of artists in the making. Practically the entire collection is the work of students.

The Commercial Section is as a rule rich and diversified both in themes as well as art forms. Posters and illustrations constitute a special feature. There are some illustrations exhibiting the activities of the Health Week. The circus as well as other entertainments have been finding able exponents. Perhaps a great service is being done to the Railway Companies in so far as the artists try to prepare blocks in advertisement of some of the prominent stations in the country. Manufacturing houses likewise are interested to see that the painters have prepared designs illustrating the goods which are generally to be found in the market. A point of interest to publishers and booksellers should appear to be in the number of exhibits, such as seek to give shape, in colour or black and white, to persons and objects as well as geographical and social items such as occupy the attention of boys and girls in primary and secondary schools.

Etchings, also, generally of a high order in finish are observed in these exhibitions. In these pieces of etchwork one notices the treatment of landscapes, harbour scenes, as well as social life. This new form of art was until a few years ago hardly known among Indian artists. Mukul Dey, as I have had the occasion to mention elsewhere, is the first Bengali to cultivate etching as a mode of artistic expression.

Extensive mural works are being done. Command over colour combination as well as the spacing of the background are noticeable. Such works are beginning to have their markets in the prominent public buildings of the country. Municipal, sanitary, educational and other establishments might gradually learn to interest themselves in getting at least some of their walls painted in the manner indicated in these pieces.

The figures in bronze as well as in clay appear to be the work of men endowed with the sense of proportion as well as movement. Bronzing was not practised until a few years ago. The same may be said of the wood-engraving work. This also is a line of applied art along which Indian talent has not previously taken much interest. In the field of designs one is agreeably struck by a variety which is certainly a sign of wealth in aesthetics as much as mechanical drawing. The mills in the textile line can draw upon such artists in order to man their departments for border print-work and so forth. The jewellers as well as potters who for a long time have been used to stereotyped ornamental work can also find able co-operation in the authors of these objects.

The exhibitions are not all commercial and modern. The students are undoubtedly showing assimilation of European art methods as well as orientation to the requirements of daily life. But it should be added that their work is at the same time the result of their acquaintance with old Indian art techniques. They are attempting to catch the spirit of our "old masters" and they know also how to interpret our traditions according to modern needs.

For some long time art as a rule has implied more or less what is known as "fine art", i.e., something which generally is taken to be a luxury. But in the exhibitions of the Government School of Art it appears that the institution has been able to indicate to businessmen, industrialists as well as educators how art education can also be a handmaid to industry and commerce.

The art exhibitions in India are not all obsessed by devotion to the alleged national ideals in inspiration and technique or by the considerations of illustrative, decorative or industrial art. In Calcutta, for instance, there is the Indian Academy of Fine Arts which, thanks to the enthusiasm of Maharaja Sir Prodyot Coomar Tagore, addresses itself every year to the exhibition of paintings and sculptures of all schools, old and new, Indian and foreign. The exhibitors also represent all nationalities. In art appreciation, then, as in other items of life India has been pursuing a synthetic and comprehensive ideal.

The Reading Public

Publishing has of late been growing into an independent business in Bengal as in other parts of India. And this marks, on the one hand, the expansion of capitalism and industrial economy among the Indian people, and on the other, the development of an intellectual democracy and literary freedom throughout the length and breadth of the country. Even during the second half of the nineteenth century as during the first half the literature, arts and sciences, and academic culture of Bengal grew and developed virtually under the exclusive patronage of the landed aristocracy, the Zamindars. Indeed for all practical purposes, it was the Zamindars in whom as financiers and promoters was concentrated almost the entire public life of the country. From Raja Radha Kanta Deb to Maharaja Manindra Chandra Nandi the tradition of Bengali Zamindars as patrons of learning, education, literature and science is continuous.

It is perhaps in the "ideas of 1905" with which the glorious *Swadeshi* Movement of Young Bengal made its *début* that we have to see the beginnings of a new era in our publishing industry and trade. Authors began to discover new patrons,—and these patrons were found among the men and women of the villages, subdivisions, district head-quarters, in one word, the great Bengali reading public of the *Mofussil.* Not that Calcutta as the metropolitan centre failed to furnish a growing number of readers such as might constitute the expanding market for the goods produced by poets, novelists, dramatists, essayists, orators, journalists and others. But the upheaval of the *Mofussil*—the rural centres, the lower hundred thousands of the Bengali society, so to say,—was the most signal feature of the tremendous outburst of Bengali vitalism in 1905. It is with that epoch-making revolution in morals, manners and sentiments, nay, in the very outlook on life, that the new publishing business of Bengal is materially and spiritually associated.

Since 1905 authors have been finding it possible to depend more and more on the men and women who read books, pamphlets, and journals as well as are ready and in a position to pay for them. The patronage from Zamindars has been functioning still but it is the expansion of the reading public that has led to the enfranchisement of authors to a certain extent because of the intensification, universalization or democratization of effective demand for literary goods. And this has automatically led to the emergence of the middlemen, the booksellers, the publishers, the book market, and publishing as an independent business.

The expansion of democratization may be seen in a nutshell as follows. In 1901 there were altogether 37,733 educational institutions of all sorts with 1,133,896 scholars on the rolls. Today 67,639 institutions educate more than double the number of the first period of the *Swadeshi* Movement, namely 2,712,553. In 1901 there were less than one hundred thousand scholars in some 400 high schools. Today the number of scholars is 275,000 and the number of high schools is nearly 1,100. In the Arts and Science Colleges the number of scholars has grown from some 7,300 of those days to over 18,000 of today.

The demand for printed stuff has naturally grown more than double. Along with this growth, and as a mark of this expansion of demand for books and journals among the masses is to be noticed the growth of libraries during the last generation. There are today nearly 1200 libraries of all sizes in Bengal, serving sometimes even the meanest villages of the country.

The growth has not been merely a quantitative one.

The readers have grown not merely in number but in quality and variety as well. Their tastes have been multiplied and diversified. Literary stuff, aesthetic canons, intellectual entertainments, social philosophies, economic ideas, political views are being demanded by them not in one uniform mode or according to some stereotyped pattern. Readers have grown in their selective functions. We can notice already the beginnings of "classes" of readers. Like the general social economy the structure of the reading public is becoming differentiated on the "class-basis." Naturally, therefore, publishing business in Bengal is getting richly diversified in technique, methodology and substance.

Perhaps some of the publishing houses themselves have consciously and deliberately served to create untried tastes and new demands. The publishers must certainly be credited with having succeeded to some extent in enriching the intellectual life and expanding the academic horizon of Young India. Of all the new agencies that are operative today in the modernizing and uptodatizing of Indian culture none have played a more educative rôle than the publishing houses. These publishing houses are indeed the symbols as well as embodiments of uptodatized and modernized Indian culture. It may be trusted that the publishers of today and tomorrow will continue to maintain their tradition of serving Young India with "evolutive" publications of all sorts and inspiring the personality of Indian men and women by manufacturing books and journals such as furnish life's futureward urges. The publishing houses may be expected to function more and more systematically as the employers of research scholars, statisticians, authors and journalists in the interest of the remaking of our literature, arts and sciences adapted to the growing demands of the new Indian democracy. They will have to rise more and more consciously to their legitimate position as peers of the Universities in the cultural and social life of the people.

Aurobindo's Pluralism

Aurobindo Ghosh made his *début* as an architect of the "ideas of 1905". But since 1918 he has been known almost exclusively as the "sage of Pondicherry". As the author of works like *Life Divine* he is indeed destined to play a leading rôle in the evolution of modern mysticism. But it is interesting to watch how during this entire period of some thirty years it is in the service of life, man, personality, the awakening of *śakti* and *la renaissance de l'ésprit* that his intelligence and intuition have been functioning. Aurobindo's humanism is superb and of the intensest type, and his spirituality is encyclopædic as life itself.

One of his oldest works is the English drama, *Perseus the Deliverer* (*c* 1907). This is perhaps the first specimen of creative India enthusing over a Greek theme. Students of world-literature will not fail to find in it the assimilation of the Aeschylean spirit by a Bengali poet of the twentieth century. Aurobindo's hand is equally skilled in the handling of Kālidāsa. One of the finest renderings of ancient Hindu poetry in English or any other modern language is that of Kālidāsa's *Vikramovasī* by Aurobindo under the title of the *Hero and the Nymph*.

In this piece we have a situation in which Pururavas is confident about the fitness of his young son to take charge of his empire because he is a "ruler born". We read:

"The ichorous elephant

Not yet full-grown tames all the trumpetings
Of older rivals. * * *

So is it with the ruler born.

His boyish hand inarms the sceptred world.
The force that rises with its task, springs not
From years, but is a self-and in-born greatness".

In such passages we encounter a command over English prosody such as happens to be but another mark of Aurobindo's extraordinary spiritual elasticity and attempts to taste life in its manifold *līlā* (phases). We shall now see some of Aurobindo's observations on literary appreciation.

"Both Dante and Shakespeare", says he,[1] "stand at the summit of poetic fame, but each with so different a way of genius that comparison is unprofitable. Shakespeare has powers that Dante cannot rival; Dante has heights which Shakespeare could not reach; but in essence they stand as mighty equals. As for Blake and Shakespeare, that is more a personal fantasy than anything else. Purity and greatness are not the same thing; Blake's may be pure poetry, and Shakespeare's not, except in a few passages; but nobody can contend that Blake's genius had the width and volume and richness of Shakespeare's. If you say that Blake as a mystic poet was greater than Shakespeare,—of course he was, for Shakespeare was not a mystic poet at all. But as a poet of the play of life Shakespeare is everywhere and Blake nowhere. One has to put each thing in its place without confusing issues".

The reaction as exhibited above has been caused by Housman's over-estimation of Blake. Aurobindo is too human, too well up in the things of the personality,

[1] *Forward* (Calcutta) October 20, 1935.

too familiar with the inner recesses of the spirit to be carried away by exaggerations one way or the other. It does not take Aurobindo's intellectual sanity to detect the excesses in Goethe's judgment on the authors of the eighteenth century. Such excesses he discovers in our Bankim Chandra Chatterjee's literary likes and dislikes also.

According to Aurobindo the errors of great poets in judging their contemporaries are personal freaks—that is to say, failures in intuition due to the mind's temporary movements getting in the way of the intuition. "The errors of Goethe and Bankim were only an over-estimation of a genius or a talent that was new and therefore attractive at the time. Richardson's *Pamela* was, after all, the beginning of modern fiction. Over-estimation of a contemporary is frequent, under-estimation also."

With Aurobindo, as with John Dewey in *Human Nature and Conduct*, *Democracy and Education* and other works, the standard or authority in literature and art is set by life. The greatest unreality is a "fixed self", a fixed individual, or the like. It is the diversity of expectations, the diversity of ends, the diversity of norms that would correspond to the requirements of life. Accordingly there is the life Dantesque and there is the life Shakespearean. As a philosopher of life Aurobindo has thrown in his lot, therefore, with the pluralist. Then, again, the self is moving from moment to moment, the individual of today is already a thing of the past when the individual of to-morrow is flourishing. In the language of Croce's *Philosophy of the Practical*, every individual is different at every moment of his life. Man wills always in a new and different way, not comparable with the other modes of his or of others willing. The Italian neo-

Hegelian is here in the same boat with the American pragmatist. No less striking is the fact that the Bengali mystic explains the exaggerations of Goethe as of Bankim by reference to the plurality of personality.

Some of the difficulties that arise in the correct evaluation of foreign poetry are attributed by Aurobindo to the absence of command over the language in which the original is composed. He says: "As for the verdict of Englishmen upon a French poet or *vice versa*, that is due to a difficulty in entering into the finer spirit and subtleties of a foreign language. It is difficult for a Frenchman to get a proper appreciation of Keats or Shelley or for an Englishman to judge Racine, for this reason. But a Frenchman like Maurois, who knows English as an Englishman knows it, can get the full estimation of a poet like Shelley all right. These variations must be allowed for; the human mind is not a perfect instrument, its best intuitions are much veiled by irrelevant mental formations; but in these matters the truth asserts itself and stands fairly firm and clear in essence through all changes of mental weather."

In Aurobindo the literary critic one can have profound confidence. Although he deals very often with intuition his observations are based fundamentally on facts, experience and life. He is a philosopher of the "practical", i.e., of serviceableness to life's interests, and of freedom of the will to choose its norms and to experience novelties.

SECTION 4

EDUCATION AND RESEARCH IN SCIENCE[1]

The Bose-Ray Landmark

The beginnings of modern Indian researches in exact science are not older than the last decade of the nineteenth century, when Young India made its *début* with the successful experiments in wireless telegraphy of Jagadis Chunder Bose and in mercurous nitrite of Prafulla Chandra Ray. For nearly a quarter of a century Bose and Ray happened to remain two solitary figures, and it was hardly worth while for the learned societies of the extra-Indian world to pry into the mysteries of the academic atmosphere in India and reassure themselves as to whether these "single swallows" were at all destined to harbinger a summer.

It was not without reason that Bose and Ray were treated as curios in the international world of science. For, after the mathematical investigations of Bhāskarāchārya in the twelfth century and the contributions of Madanapāla to materia medica in the fourteenth the *corpus* of mankind's exact science could not legitimately claim a single creative thinker or researcher as belonging to the Indian sub-continent.

The Bose-Ray landmark in the Indian pursuit of science and scientific research embodies, however, the end of a long period of the people's strenuous and steady efforts in the assimilation of modern knowledge. While taking note of the successes achieved in

[1] The present author's *Śikṣā-Vijnaner Bhūmikā* (Calcutta, 1910), *Introduction to the Science of Education* (London, 1913), *Hindu Achievements in Exact Science* (New York, 1918), *The Futurism of Young Asia* (Berlin, 1922), *Comparative Pedagogics in Relation to Public Finance and National Wealth* (Calcutta 1929).

our own times it should be appropriate to call to mind the perseverance and patriotism of our forefathers, who during the nineteenth century strove by every means to popularize positive science in India and build up a scientific tradition among the Indian intelligentsia.

The Age of Rammohun (1772-1833)

As in many other fields of intellectual and social activity, in positive science also Rammohun (1772-1833) was the pioneer, not of course as a man, strictly speaking, of "science", but as an organizer of national education and culture. It was through the journal *Sambād Kaumudī*, established in 1819, and other channels, that Rammohun in the midst of his multifarious interests found scope to direct his countrymen's attention to the scientific discoveries and inventions of the day.

It is well known that in connection with the establishment of the Hindu College (1832), it was Rammohun whose cry was raised more for modern physics, chemistry, anatomy, physiology, etc., than for ancient Sanskrit and Persian lore, a subject in which he himself as "Maulavi-*cum*-Pandit" happened to be an expert. And in this he may be said to have been guided by the principle of Varāhamihira, Hindu mathematician of the sixteenth century, namely, that even the Yavanas ("Barbarians", Greeks) were to be respected when they were known to be superior in intellect.

From 1833 *to the Establishment of the University of Calcutta*

From the death of Rammohun to the establishment of the University at Calcutta in 1856 the popularization of science was taken up as the life's mission by a large number of Indian culture-propagandists. The scientific education of the people of those days was catered for by some first class reviews founded by scholar-organizer-educationists.

The *Sambād-Prabhākara* (1830-50) was established by Rammohun's junior contemporary, Ishwara Gupta, *par excellence*, a man of *belles lettres*. In 1843 was established the *Tattva-bodhinī* by Akshaya Kumar Datta, who proved to be a formative force among his contemporaries as much because of his *Bāhya bastur sahit mānava prakritir sambandha vichāra* (Examination of the relations between man and nature) as of his other scientific essays published in the journal. Rajendralal Mitra, the archæologist and historian, founded *Vividhārtha-Samgraha* in 1851.

All these journals, whatever be their names and whatever the special fields of the editors, had the common objective of "Indianizing Western science," as Akshaya Kumar used to say. The editors, each with his own circle of "young lions"—the cultural "general staff", so to say,—were all inspired, on the one hand, by robust patriotism such as knew how to serve the fatherland in spite of discouraging circumstances, and on the other hand, by the spirit of modernism which sought to uptodatize the masses and classes in every sphere including the exact sciences. The linguist Krishna Mohan Banerji's *Vidyā-Kalpadruma* (or Bengali Encyclopædia) was published between 1846 and 1849.

It was during this period, likewise, that Ishwara Chandra Vidyāsāgara, the apostle of Sanskrit learning though he was, interested himself with great zest in the work of promoting the cultivation of modern science and philosophy. In keeping with all these modernist intellectual currents was organized in 1856 the *Vidyotsāhinī Sabhā* (Association for the Encouragement of Learning) by Kaliprasanna Sinha, Bengali translator of the *Mahābhārata*. But down to the end of this period actual investigation in modern experimental science does not appear to have been undertaken by anybody. In the domain of positive science and technology India continued to remain a blank as during the later Middle Ages.

Fifty Years of the University (1858-1907)

The establishment of the Calcutta University in 1856 may be regarded as an event in modern Indian culture not so much in the line of exact sciences as in that of the "humanities". For, it was not until 1902 that a special degree in science was offered, namely B.Sc. and not until 1908 that M.Sc. was instituted. The positive sciences were thus for more than half a century but subsidiary subjects of instruction. It is, besides, notorious that down to the end of this period laboratory equipment and practice in colleges were all but unknown even in regard to elementary teaching work. Another shortcoming of the University during this period of half a century is to be found in the very poor number of scholars who passed out in the "arts" (including the sciences), in medicine and surgery as well as in engineering.

The first decennium yields the following figures[1] for passes:

[1] Adapted from the figures published by the Calcutta University Organization Committee, 1924.

	B. A.	M. A.	L. M. S. Medicine.	M. B. Medicine.	L. C. E. Engineering.
1858	2	...	...	...	...
1859	10	...	...	...	...
1860	13	...	...	...	...
1861	15	...	14	...	6
1862	24	...	7	...	14
1863	25	6	14	...	...
1864	30	3	11	...	5
1865	45	11	18	...	2
1866	79	15	20	...	...
1867	60	22	15	2	6
Total	303	57	99	2	33

For the second decennium we have the following figures:

	B.A.	M.A.	L.M.S.	M.B.	L.C.E.	B.C.E.
1868	99	15	11	3	2	...
1869	77	18	19	2	4	1
1870	98	24	5	1	3	...
1871	84	35	27	1	2	...
1872	100	24	27	3	7	1
1873	126	20	23	2	2	1
1874	92	32	36	1	2	...
1875	90	18	13	...	6	3
1876	73	24	9	3	5	3
1877	144	31	28	7	8	3
Total	983	241	198	23	41	12

For the third decennium the passes are registered in the following table:

	B.A.	M.A.	L.M.S.	M.B.	L.C.E.	B.C.E.
1878	68	28	34	7	5	1
1879	91	28	19	7	...	...
1880	112	32	65	7	10	3
1881	155	37	17	9	6	...
1882	105	32	10	10	2	...
1883	197	44	4	7	3	2
1884	356	64	1	9	...	...
1885	307	34	3	11	3	...
1886	452	70	5	23	1	1
1887	449	56	18	10	...	1
Total	2,292	425	176	100	30	8

The fourth decade may be scheduled as follows:

	B.A.	M.A.	L.M.S.	M.B.	L.E. and B.E.
1888	378	69	9	6	5
1889	409	64	15	7	9
1890	435	58	12	6	11
1891	240	52	13	5	5
1892	303	56	19	4	6
1893	315	59	15	2	5
1894	497	54	12	4	6
1895	443	84	25	5	6
1896	326	87	30	3	11
1897	403	85	24	4	6
Total	3,749	668	174	46	70

The statistical situation for the fifth and for our present purpose the last decade may be envisaged in the following table:

	B.A.	M.A.	L.M.S.	M.B.	B.E.
1898	326	70	56	3	4
1899	463	93	44	3	14
1900	529	94	40	2	10
1901	378	87	80	3	9
1902	487+2	71	67	2	13
1903	430+8	74	54	2	12
1904	331+5	54	56	3	7
1905	518+3	71	65	3	9
1906	497+12	92	86	6	14
1907	426+9	97	62	4	11
Total	4,424	803	610	31	103

N.B. The second entry under B.A. has reference to the newly introduced B.Sc.

The University passes described above may now be summarized for the five decades (1858-1907) as follows in the perspective of the total population as numbered at different censuses:

	1858-67	1868-77	1878-87	1888-97	1898-1907
I. "Arts" (including sciences) B.A. and M.A. combined	360	1,224	2,717	4,417	5,227
I. (*a*) Sciences					
i. B.A. and M.A. combined ..	72	245	543	883	1,045
ii. M.A. alone	11	48	85	133	160

II. Medicine and Surgery L.M.S. and M.B. combined ..	101	221	276	220	641
III. Engineering all denominations combined ..	33	53	38	70	103
Total Population	34,687,000 (1871)	37,014,000 (1881)	39,805,000 (1891)	42,881,000 (1901)	

In order to measure the growth in the total academic strength of the people during the first half a century of the University's life-history it would be necessary also to mark the progress in the number of passes in the law faculty. But as we are interested, for the time being, in exact sciences only, we have excluded the B.L.'s from our survey. It is now necessary to analyze the figures in I. "Arts" (above) in order to isolate the "Science" element in the make-up of the B.A.'s and M.A.'s. On the strength of the relative proportion between B.A.'s and B.Sc.'s as well as between M.A.'s and M.Sc.'s as observable in recent years it is not possible to figure out the science passes of those fifty years at anything more than 15 to 20 per cent of the combined B.A.'s and M.A.'s. Should this conjecture be correct, we should find a growth in the number of science men at Calcutta from 1858 to 1907 as marked I (*a*) i. and ii. For the present we are excluding from our consideration the fact that the proportion must have varied from decade to decade.

The comparatively large number of passes in medicine and surgery is noteworthy, although really negligible when considered per 10,000 of the population. During the first decade of the University medical men were 101 in the background of 72 men of general science (B.A. and M.A. combined) and 33 engineers. Down to 1907 the number of medical men was always larger than that of science M.A.'s and engineers put together. The steep ascent in the curve from 1888-97 to 1898-1907 is by all means extraordinary. Altogether, one understands why all through the history of modern Bengal, especially during the present epoch, that of the *Swadeshi* Movement, the medical men, like the lawyers and the schoolmasters, have played a leading part in the nationalistic, educational, scientific and technological efforts of the people.

On the other hand, the unusually low number of engineers from decade to decade can escape nobody's notice. We see that the people's tastes and aptitudes were not being trained along directions of modern industry and applied science. It is to be observed, besides, that the few engineers that were sent forth by the University knew only how to survey lands, construct roads and build houses. The technological utilization of the country's resources was not promoted. And naturally, practical ideas in regard to economic reconstruction were conspicuous by their absence in the academic and social atmosphere.

Engineers,—the heroes of the "Industrial Revolution" in Eur-America and Japan,—were therefore virtually unknown among the leading men of India in the nineteenth century even during the latter half. With fifty years of University education the people failed to grasp the A.B.C. of the momentous industrial revolution such as had already engendered a social and philosophical transformation in the rest of the world. The mind of India was shunted off from the main tracks of the new spirituality as embodied in modern materialism. Nay, when the movement for industrialization was started in and through the fruitful "ideas of 1905" Young Bengal had to begin to all intents and purposes on a clean slate, so far as technology and applied economics are concerned. Perhaps the first prominent engineer among Bengali leaders is Ramakanta Roy (1873-1906), who about this time came back as mining engineer from Japan.

Scientists under Conditions of Discouragement (1858-1907)

The patriotic work of the culture-pioneers was not rendered superfluous when the University was established. Rather, the movement in favour of "mass-education" in science obtained a fillip through the acquisition of fresh blood in the propaganda *corps*.

A colleague of Vidyāsāgara's and a great enthusiast for modern science and culture was the educator and sociologist Bhudev Mookerji, who started the *Sikśā Darpaṇa* monthly in 1864 and in 1868 took up the Bengali weekly *Education Gazette*. The propagation of science was no less promoted by Bankim Chandra Chatterjee, novelist and social philosopher, whose monthly *Bamga-darśana* (The Philosophy of Bengal) came out in 1872. This review functioned during the last quarter of the nineteenth century as a genuine organ of modernism and positive thinking.

In 1876 the Indian Association for the Cultivation of Science was established by Mahendralal Sircar (1833-1904), homoeopathic practitioner. It was his patriotism and love of experimental science that stood by the side of his professional success and social position in the matter of placing this institution on a secure footing. This Association was a regular Science College and for more than a quarter of a century served to offer some practical training in physics, chemistry and botany to the students of Calcutta, who in their own colleges had hardly any facilities for demonstrations and laboratory experiments. It may be said to have supplemented to a considerable extent the work of the University and thus pointed the way to genuine University reform which, be it observed, has been undertaken in certain respects in subsequent years. India's debt to Mahendralal Sircar's institution is inestimable.

As for contributions to science and scientific literature during this period, we may begin with the medical men as being numerically and chronologically the most prominent in social life. Madhusudan Gupta is the first Bengali (and perhaps Indian) Hindu who undertook dissections on the human body thereby pioneering modern medical education in Bengal. Kanny Lal Dey wrote *Indigenous Drugs of India* in 1867 and *Padārtha-Vijnān* (physics) in 1872-73. He was the author also of *Vaidyik Vyavahāra* (medical jurisprudence) and *Rasāyana-Vijnān* (chemistry). Dey did some original research work also, for instance, in indigenous medicines. Altogether, he can be regarded as the father of medical and chemical investigations in modern Bengal. Udoy Chand Dutt's *Materia Medica of the Hindus* was published in 1877 and helped, like the investigations of Rajendra lal Mitra in other fields, to call the attention of Indian researchers to the secular, scientific and materialistic achievements of the Hindus of ancient and medieval times.

A popularizer of modern anatomy, medicine and pharmacopoeia through the medium of Bengali on the lines of Kanny Lal Dey was Radha Govinda Kar. But he is chiefly known today as being one of the pioneers, like Suresh Prasad Sarvadhikary, in the establishment of medical schools. Kar's work has taken a final form in the Carmichael Medical College of today (est. 1914). Another author of modern anatomy in Bengali was Zahiruddin Ahmed.

In 1892 Baman Das Basu may be said to have made a start with his paper on the study of indigenous drugs (in the *Indian Medical Gazette*), part of a subject on which later he produced an epoch-making work (in collaboration with others). While Basu was thus following to a certain extent Dutt's lines, Dey had a successor in Chunilal Bose, chemist, to whose credit belong some researches in the medicinal and poisonous plants of India.

Medicine of the old Hindu tradition, namely, *Āyurveda*, continued as of yore to be the subject of study as well as of profession and industry. And so the *tols* or home-schools of Gangadhar Sen, Dwaraka Nath Sen and others did not fail to prosper in spite of the progress of the Western system of medicine introduced through the University. Rather, towards the end of the period something like the beginning of a *Renaissance* of Ayurvedic science and practice was observable in the translations of old texts and in historical essays bearing thereon as well as in the institution of Ayurvedic congresses. Bengali Kavirajes took their proper place in the development of this all-India movement.

In other branches of scientific knowledge also

modern methods were at work. Girish Chandra Bose wrote on botany and Bhopal Chandra Bose on agriculture. Nritya Gopal Mukerji's agricultural investigations had a fruitful bearing on silkworm rearing and sericulture, as the people of Malda and Murshidabad recall it even today with gratitude.

During the latter half of this period the enthusiasm of Aghore Nath Chatterji, domiciled long in the Nizam's Dominions, for industrial chemistry embodied itself not only in investigations but in practical ventures as well. Among the industrial pioneers of the Indian people in the field of chemistry a great place has to be accorded to Chandra Bhushan Bhaduri, who, along with Prafulla Chandra Ray, Kartik Chandra Bose and others, may be regarded as one of the founders of the Bengal Chemical & Pharmaceutical Works Ltd. (est. 1892-95).

It is in the *milieu* of the organizing activities of the pioneers like Mahendralal Sircar and Radha Govinda Kar and the research activities of their junior contemporaries, Baman Das Basu, Chunilal Bose and others that the earlier phases of the Bose-Ray landmark (*c* 1890-1900) mentioned at the outset have to be placed for the proper sociological orientation in the field of modern Indian pursuit of science. In 1902 Jagadis Chunder Bose made his communication to the *Académie des Sciences* of Paris and his work in the field of plant response was getting well-known. The same year saw the publication of Prafulla Chandra Ray's *History of Hindu Chemistry*, Vol. I. which was followed in 1907 by Vol. II. It is obvious that Ray's work lay as much in modern science and industry as in the antiquarian exploration of ancient knowledge. At this stage it is appropriate to mention the monographs by Brajendra

Nath Seal on the physical, chemical and mechanical theories of the Hindus as well as on their scientific methodology which were incorporated in Ray's book on Hindu Chemistry.

The University and the institutions affiliated to it were during this entire period of five decades poor in laboratory facilities as well as in the number of scholars. And naturally, scientific investigation and research as such were not even talked of within the four walls of the college buildings, general, medical or engineering. The official academic world in India was thoroughly innocent of the categories, applied science and technology, except in so far as medicine and civil engineering may be said to belong to this group. Under these conditions it is to the traditional patriotism, love of learning for its own sake, and devotion to positive science of the Indian *intelligentsia* that we have to ascribe, in the first place, the popularization of science through the journals, schools and associations, as well as in the second place, the carrying on of researches by isolated scholars. In those days researchers could not dream of any encouragement, financial or otherwise, from the side of the state or from that of the institutions they served. The entire work in the fields of science that India succeeded in putting in from 1858 to 1907, no matter what be its absolute worth,—whether in the direction of propaganda or in that of creative research, must be pronounced to have been heroic by all standards.

The Epoch of Swadeshism (*c.* 1905-35)

Young Bengal was not to remain content with the popularizing work of Bankim Chandra Chatterjee's *Bamgadarśana* or the school laboratories of Mahendralal

Sircar's Indian Association for the Cultivation of Science or even the original investigation of some half a dozen stray researchers in medicine, chemistry and physics. Young Bengal could not be blind to the fact that in 1901 when the Bengali people was numbered at 42,881,000 the University turned out only 93 graduates in science as B.A. and M.A. (20% of 465), 83 medical men (L.M.S. and M.B.) and 9 engineers! The almost non-scientific and thoroughly untechnical character of the University's educational system stood self-condemned.

The Bengali people was, therefore, bent on a super-heroic endeavour, and this took shape in the glorious *Swadeshi* Movement of 1905. The situation called forth the noblest spiritual energies and self-sacrificing idealism of which the men and women of India are capable. Stripped of the political activities and philosophies, the "ideas of 1905" conveyed to India and the world the determination of the people in two different fields: (1) the promotion of education along national lines and under national control with special reference to the exact sciences and technology, and (2) the industrialization of the country and advancement of modern materialism (the *Swadeshi* movement proper).

And so the National Council of Education was established in 1906 not, however, as an institution like the Indian Association for the Cultivation of Science calculated merely to play the second fiddle to the University's institutions and supplement their work in a subsidiary capacity, but as an independent and all-round teaching University by itself with scientific and technological as well as literary faculties. Funds were contributed by landowners like Subodh Chandra Mallik of Calcutta, Brajendra

Kishore Roy Chowdhury and Surya Kanta Acharya Chowdhury of Mymensingh, and lawyers like Rash Behari Ghosh, Tarak Nath Palit, and others.[1] Two colleges were set up in Calcutta, namely, Bengal National College and Bengal Technical Institute. In due course an amalgamation of these institutions took place and their combined continuity is being kept up by the College of Engineering and Technology located at Jadavpur near Calcutta. With a staff of over forty teachers, some of whom are graduates of Michigan, Illinois, Harvard, Berlin and Edinburgh this College offers today a five-year training in the three departments of mechanical, electrical and chemical engineering to some 550-600 scholars of the post-Matriculation or rather post-Intermediate standard.

The young engineers turned out of this College have been instrumental in the industrialization of Bengal, to a certain extent, in a responsible capacity. Industrial concerns in different parts of India, like, say, Tata Iron & Steel Company, have likewise drawn a part of their man-power from this institution. Among the promoters of this national engineering University we find the names, along with those of the financiers mentioned above, of Satis Chandra Mukerjee, a maker of Young Bengal through his Dawn Society (1903-7) and social philosopher, Judge Gooroodas Banerji, Barrister Abdul Rasul, Bipin Chandra Pal, and Aurobindo Ghosh, political philosophers, Ambika Charan Ukil, economist, co-operator, and founder of banking and insurance companies, Hirendra Nath Datta, writer of philosophical essays, Ramendra Sundar Trivedi, author of scientific treatises, Devaprasad Sarvadhikary, lawyer, and Satya-

[1] See the present author's "The Carnegie Spirit through Indian Eyes" in *India and the World* (Calcutta, December 1935).

nanda Bose, publicist. Some of the professors of the College of Engineering and Technology have published the results of their researches in the journals of science and commerce.

While the National Council of Education was coming into being, or rather a year or two previous to 1905, Jogendra Chandra Ghosh, lawyer, established the Association for the Scientific and Industrial Education of Indians in Foreign Countries. Not less than some five hundred young Bengalis have enjoyed the fellowship, travelling and other facilities for training in Japan, America, Germany, France, Italy and Great Britain placed at their disposal by this institution. Jogen Ghosh's Association is almost a household word among the Bengali middle classes. It is as much to the foreign-educated engineers, chemists, bankers, businessmen etc. brought into existence by this Association as to the alumni of the National Council of Education that the experiments, failures and successes of Bengal in the industrialization aspects of the *Swadeshi* Movement are in the main due.

The University could not long remain impervious to the impacts of the National Council and Jogen Ghosh's Association or indeed of the all-embracing *Swadeshi* outburst. The reform scheme of 1901-3 which should have reconstructed the University at snail's pace and in homoeopathic doses was already much too antiquated for the demands of the people. Here, again, as in other instances throughout the history of the Bengali pursuit of science from the time of Rammohun, a robust patriot and an idealistic *Realpolitiker* came to the rescue. Judge Asutosh Mookerjee, who has a name also in mathematical researches, knew how to coax a part of the nationalist fervour on towards the University campus, state-controlled although it was.

Tarak Nath Palit and Rash Behari Ghosh, two of the biggest financiers of the National Council of Education, felt eventually inspired to come forward with donations in favour of the University. Thus were laid in 1914 the beginnings of the College of Science as a limb of the University of Calcutta. For the first time in the University atmosphere people learnt officially how to spell the word "research". With Palit and Ghosh as with Ashutosh research in science, theoretical and applied, was a veritable passion.

The next event of scientific importance in the chronological order is the establishment of the Bose Institute at Calcutta in 1916 by Jagadish Chunder Bose. This Institute has acquired an international reputation especially for the fine precision-instruments prepared in its workshops by Bengali mechanicians. The plant-physiological and other researches in electrical response of the Institute are published regularly in its *Annals*.

Prafulla Chandra Ray has no special Institute of his own. His nitrogen researches at the University College Science Laboratory have all the time been pursuing their steady career notwithstanding his numerous public functions of nationalistic character and newly acquired enthusiasm in the propagation of *Khaddar* (home-spun). His spirit, moreover, lives today and is represented by dozens of his pupils who, employed as they are in different culture and industrial centres from Dacca to Madras and Allahabad, have won respect for the Bengali school of chemistry by investigations of international importance.

In 1920 was established the first Indian Dental College at Calcutta by Rafiddin Ahmed, who is the author also of papers on the treatment of teeth in American journals. Asanulla's munificence was about this time responsible for the nucleus of a modest but very useful and practical school of engineering at Dacca.

The progress of Western medicine and surgery has not been able to kill our old Ayurvedic science and profession. It has, on the contrary, but contributed to stimulate the people's scientific and industrial interest in the Hindu system of medicine and medicinal drugs. Under the impulse of the *Swadeshi* Movement, further, Kavirajes like Jamini Mohan Sen, Gana Nath Sen, Syamadas Vachaspati and others in Calcutta have been inspired to establish colleges, clinics and hospitals on modern lines for *Ayurveda*. The old medical system seems destined to acquire a fresh lease of life as the result of intimate co-operation in research and industrial ventures between M.B.'s and Kavirajes.

So far as the University College of Science is concerned it did not take more than half a dozen years of just a little financial assistance and some modest laboratory facilities for Young India to demonstrate to the world that there is nothing mysterious in scientific research, and that scientific research is not the monopoly of non-Indian or extra-Asian climate, region or race. By 1920-21 the learned societies of Eur-America as well as their journals and the scientists of Berlin, Paris, London, New York and Stockholm were talking of the achievements of several Indian scientists. And in 1930 a physicist maintained by the Palit Fund at the Calcutta University, Chandrasekhara Venkata Raman, was the recipient of the Noble Prize. Even a decade and a half of Young India's creative contacts with the exact sciences served to revolutionize the world's mentality in regard to the men and women of Asia.

Science Students and Researchers of the Swadeshi Period (c 1905-35)

We shall now proceed to watch the developments of the people's interest in science and technology as a result of or as an index to the growth of *Swadeshism*. Let us take the figures of the University in science passes from 1909 to 1928. The figures of the National Council of Education are to be seen in the Appendices. Unfortunately the figures for medical passes as published by the Calcutta University Organization Committee are so complicated that it is difficult to make use of them for the purposes of the present paper. The medical figures, such as they are, have been collected for the chart from the University Calendars and are to be taken tentatively[1].

For the first decade the progress of scientific education at Calcutta since 1909 can be envisaged below:

	I.Sc.	B.Sc.	M.Sc.	B.E.
1909	143	45	..	10
1910	326	75	11	12
1911	566	139	21	13
1912	554	168	35	16
1913	728	266	47	10
1914	597	231	55	10
1915	612	241	57	22
1916	694	366	88	6
1917	848	304	81	14
1918	935	302	96	13
Total	6,003	2,137	491	126

[1] I am indebted to Dr. K. C. Chaudhuri for the interpretation of some of the figures relating to the medical examinations.

In 1909 specialization in science was introduced at the Intermediate stage, i.e., previous to graduation. Hence a new entry. It is to be observed that the standard was likewise raised at the same time so that I. Sc. students had to master nearly as much science as the B. A.'s of the previous decade.

For the next decennium, the post-War decade, we have the following figures:

	I.Sc.	B.Sc.	M.Sc.	B.E.
1919	1,179	334	85	34
1920	1,190	409	63	36
1921	1,406	466	56	35
1922	1,426	346	63	29
1923	1,924	480	74	28
1924	2,431	575	61	39
1925	2,426	558	75	47
1926	2,360	684	72	59
1927	2,114	593	93	51
1928	2,002	589	117	54
Total	18,458	5,034	759	412

For subsequent years the figures may be seen in the following statement derived from the table in the *Report of the Syndicate* (University of Calcutta 1935):

	I.Sc.	B.Sc.	M.Sc.	B.E.	M.B.
1929	1,846	652	101	63	252
1930	1,555	437	120	58	152
1931	1,745	536	117	60	151
1932	1,488	439	90	65	156
1933	1,923	497	106	85	115
1934	1,948	477	122	89	134
1935	1,855	580	112	80	...

A comparative estimate of the two decades in regard to the science passes is given below in the background of the decade 1898-1907:

	1909-18	1919-28	1898-1907
I. General Science B.Sc. and M.Sc. combined ..	2,628	5,793	(Science M.A. & B.A.) 1,045
I. (*a*) I.Sc. alone..	6,003	18,458	...
I. (*b*) I.Sc., B.Sc. and M.Sc. combined	8,637	24,251	...
I. (*c*) M.Sc. alone	491	759	160 (Science M.A.)
II. Medicine ..	648	1,767	641
III. Engineering ...	126	412	103
Total Population	46,305,000 (1911)	47,592,000 (1921)	42,881,000 (1901)

As the I.Sc.'s of today command the scientific knowledge of the science B. A.'s of 1898-1907, so to say, one may take the I. Sc., B. Sc. and M. Sc. together for the purpose of comparison with that decade's combined strength in B. A. and M. A. in science. So far as University passes in general science are concerned, one can see that

Bengal (1919-28) 24,251 = 23.2 Bengal (1898-1907) 1,045.

In general scientific knowledge and in interest in the topics of science the post-War Bengali people is 23.2 times as equipped as previous to the *Swadeshi* Movement.

But in the meanwhile there has been an increase of population as indicated below:

Bengal (1921) 47,592,000 = 1.1 Bengal (1901) 42,881,000.

In twenty years the population has grown 1.1 time. The real increment in scientific knowledge is therefore 21 times.

Excluding the I. Sc.' s the equation of progress would be as follows:

Bengal (1919-1928) 5,793 = 5.5 Bengal (1898-1907) 1,045.

The interest of Young Bengal in "higher science"—as measured by the B. Sc. and M. Sc. standard—has grown 5.5 times compared to the situation in pre-*Swadeshi* days. As the growth in population (1.1 time) has to be considered as in the previous calculation, the real increment is 5 times.

In higher science (M. Sc. or science M. A. standard)

Bengal (1919-1928) 759 = 4.7 Bengal (1898-1907) 160.

The real increment in knowledge of higher science is, then, 4.2 times.

The progress in medical knowledge is registered by the following equation:

Bengal (1919-1928), 1,767 2.7 Bengal (1898-1907) 641. The real increment is 2.45 times.

In regard to engineering we have the following equation:

Bengal (1919-1928) 412 = 4 Bengal (1898-1907) 103.

Here, again, the real increment in engineering knowledge is not 4 times but 3.6 times. In subjects bearing on civil engineering also the Bengali people has thus made progress but the rate is lower than in general scientific equipment. Evidently, the University has been powerfully influenced by the enthusiasm for industrialization incorporated in the "ideas of 1905" as well as in the events of the Great War period.[1]

The original researches of Indian mathematicians, physicists, meteorologists, chemists, geologists, botanists, zoologists, and physiologists from 1915 - 1916 on have constituted a feature in the scientific journalism of Eur-America even in non-English languages. It is generally admitted that in the expansion of the world's modern science Indian co-operation has been playing an increasing part. It would be quite worth while for some student of exact science to prepare in the near future an objective monograph on these researches and publications somewhat along the lines of the different chapters in the two volumes of *La Science Française* (1916) or in Charles Moureu's *La Chimie et la Guerre* (1920) or, again, in the French author Caullery's *Universities and Scientific Life in the United States* (1922).

In connection with the Indian work in medical research, which as a rule is ignored in a survey of scientific investigations, a number of names may be listed here. Baman Das Basu and Chunilal B sc, who had been active previous to 1905, later strengthened their claims to recognition in the fields of medicinal plants and drug chemistry. Upendra Nath Brahmachari's researches in Kala-azhar, Gopal Chandra Chatterji's in bacteriology and Kedar Nath Das's in midwifery have crossed the frontiers of India. Hem Chandra Sen is known for his investigations in therapeutics and Bidhan Chandra Roy for those in asthma, diabetes etc.

[1] On war-industrialism in India see the present author's *Economic Development* (Madras, 1926).

Haran Chandra Mukerji has been working in the diseases of blood, Biraj Mohan Das Gupta in the parasitology of tropical medicine, Manindra Nath De in the pathology of spleens, Jyotiprakas Basu in diabetes, Umaprasanna Basu in heart diseases, Sivapada Bhattacharya in infantile liver, Amulya Chandra Ukil in cholera, dysentery, tuberculosis etc., Susil Kumar Mukerjee in eye diseases, Charubrata Roy in diabetes, Subodh Chandra Mitra in the cancer of uterus, anæmia of pregnancy etc. and Kshirod Chandra Chaudhuri in the brain tumour, megacolon etc. of children. Ekendra Nath Ghosh's researches in zoology and Sahay Ram Bose's in botany may be listed as lying within the domain of biologico-medical research.

Among important publications as books may be mentioned those of Karuna Kumar Chatterji on tropical surgery, of Dhirendra Nath Banerjee on pathology, of Akhil Ranjan Majumdar on clinical medicine, of Susil Kumar Mukerji on infantile liver, of Rafi Ahmed on operative dentistry, of Birendranath Ghosh on materia medica besides those of Brahmachari and Das. Girindra Nath Mukerji has published a work on ancient Hindu surgery. Hari Nath Ghosh has written on hygiene in Bengali.

The *Calcutta Medical Journal* has been running for nearly a quarter of a century. It is the medium of publication for a part of the researches by Indian scholars. Substantial portions have been published in All-India journals like the *Indian Medical Gazette*, *Journal of the Indian Research Fund Association*, *Journal of the Indian Medical Association*, etc. as well as in the journals of Great Britain, Germany and France.

In certain branches of industry, chemical, medical and metallurgical, some names are mentionable. The industrial inspiration derived partly from Chandra

Bhushan Bhaduri is being done into life by Biraj Mohan Das in tannery works and Satya Sundar Deb in potteries. The *Institut Pasteur* of Paris has got a scholar in Hemendra Nath Ghosh who is active in immunology and immunity industry. In the domain of vegetable oils and hydrogenation Baneswar Dass is applying his experience derived from the American Edison works and the German Krupp and Borsig. Ali Karim is doing work in the chemistry of forest produce, drugs and paints. Prafulla Kumar Mukerji, has long been associated with the Carnegie Steel Corporation at Pittsburg in a responsible position and was chief metallur ist of the steel works at Magnitogorsk on the Ural in Russia. Obeidulla's services as a mining engineer have been requisitioned in Afghanistan for a part of the pioneering work.

Researches are being conducted at the Bengal Chemical and Pharmaceutical Works Ltd., which is today an industrial concern of world-wide commercial importance. Its laboratories maintain a number of investigators as also does Kartick Bose's Laboratory, another successful manufacturing establishment specially in the field of acids and instruments. To this group likewise belongs the firm of Butto Kristo Paul, importers of scientific apparatus and manufacturers of chemicals.

Attention may here be invited to the historical work entitled *The Positive Sciences of the Ancient Hindus* (1915) by Brajendra Nath Seal, which is made up, in part, as already noted, of his monographs contributed to Ray's book on Hindu Chemistry (1902-1907), as well as in part, of his other monographs, namely, those relating to Hindu ideas on plants and plant-life, Hindu classification of animals, Hindu ideas about the nervous system, heredity, vital forces etc., as well as Hindu acoustics and Hindu kinetics, contributed to the present author's

Positive Background of Hindu Sociology, Vol. I. (1914). Nalin Bihari Mitra's studies in Hindu mathematics (1916) deserve likewise a special mention in this context. The main body of all these investigations was epitomised and appraised for the researchers in social science and comparative culture-history by the present writer in his *Hindu Achievements in Exact Science* (1918). Investigations in Hindu mathematics have since then been followed up in an intensive manner by Bibhuti Bhusan Datta and Sukumar Ranjan Das.

The scientific essays in Bengali by Ramendra Sundar Trivedi, Jagadananda Roy (of Rabindranath Tagore's *Viśva-bhāratī* at Bolpur), Jogesh Chandra Roy, Sundari Mohan Das and others have been continuing the tradition of the previous generation of the Bengali men of letters. The ornithologist Satya Churn Law has been editing a special scientific review, *Prakriti* (Nature).

The *Bangīya Sāhitya Pariṣat* (Bengali Academy of Literature) of Calcutta has, somewhat like the *Institut de France*, a science section, which addresses itself especially to the preparation of scientific terminology in Bengali, an item on which the University has been bestowing attention in recent years (1934). There is likewise a Science Division in all the annual congresses, known as *Sāhitya Sammelan*, convened under the auspices of this *Pariṣat* in different districts of Bengal as well as Greater Bengal (comprising domiciled Bengalis in diverse parts of India). The Science Division invites papers in Bengali on the latest scientific researches and discoveries and is thus instrumental in the propagation of higher science among the people and the stimulation of research among the scholars. Finally, as embodiments of the Bengali pursuit of science and scientific research must be mentioned the large number of monthly and other reviews which have set before themselves the educative and modernizing mission of Bankim Chandra Chatterjee's *Baṁga-darśana* and Rajendralal Mitra's *Viridhārtha Saṁgraha*.

It is the simultaneous activity on diverse fronts of a large number of men and institutions functioning independently of one another that has characterised and helped forward the progress of science and scientific research among the Bengali people. When all has been told it is necessary to observe that neither the number of students under the Universities of Calcutta and Dacca as well as under the National Council of Education nor the number of researchers in the diverse sciences throughout the Indian sub-continent is adequate to meet the requirements and ambitions of the Bengali people, numbering today, as it does, over fifty-one million men and women. The world-standard in regard to the number of students and researchers in science per 10,000 of the population is very high,—especially among the "great powers."[1] It is, besides, to be remembered carefully that the highest science graduates of India (M.Sc.'s) are in academic worth somewhere near the second year students of continental Universities. As a rule, Indian M.A.'s and M.Sc.'s require, therefore, nearly two or three years[1] to complete the regular degree course,—doctorate—, say, of a German University or *Technische Hochschule* (Technological University).

No matter what the proportion of scholars per 10,000 of the population or the real academic standing of the B.Sc.'s and M.Sc.'s, the century's record has proven that Young India is capable of the highest idealism,

[1] In regard to the academic equations between Indian Universities and those of the Great Powers as well as the proportion of scholars per 10,000 of the population see the present author's *Comparative Pedagogics in Relation to Public Finance and National Wealth* (Calcutta, 1929).

constructive self-sacrifice and persistent devotion to the exact sciences, as well as of the most tenacious pursuit of science and learning in the teeth of tremendous financial and other handicaps. The world is waiting for another high jump in India's conquest of difficulties, similar to the epoch-making endeavours which took shape in the industrial-*cum*-scientific materialism of the *Swadeshi* Movement. While appeals to the state for research grants have undoubtedly to become incessant and cumulative, the demands on the people's patriotism itself will have to grow from more to more. It is time for the Indian people to unfold another chapter of its energism by pushing forward the existing institutions along their higher flights as well as by organizing new seats of creative learning and research in science and technology.

The contributions in technically equipped youths from the National Council of Education (College of Engineering and Technology) during the last two decades or so are considerable. Many of the industrial and commercial enterprises of the Bengali people,—however modest be their dimensions or success,—are associated with the mechanical, electrical and chemical engineering as embodied in the scholars turned out of this College. This is naturally to be expected of an educational institution of a formally industrial character.

The College of Science maintained by the University of Calcutta might from the nature of the case be considered to be an institution for the pursuit of theoretical studies and researches in the sciences. But the Bengali ideology of the *Swadeshi* period is so technocratic and Young Bengal is so industrial-or machine-minded that even in this college the bearings of the laboratories on the applied sciences and industries also are too valuable to be overlooked. For instance, in connection with the Bengal State Aid to Industries Bill 1931, discussed in the Bengal Legislative Council, the achievements of the Calcutta University in regard to the training of technical experts were discussed by Senator (now Vice-Chancellor, 1934-36) Syama Prasad Mookerjee, in a lengthy speech delivered on July 22, 1931.

"Amongst the various problems which have been worked out in the laboratories of the Science College," said Senator Mookerjee, "are some vital problems which have a direct connection with the industries of the Province. * * * The Clyde fan is the first electric fan which was designed in Bengal, if not in India. It was actually designed in the laboratory of the Applied Physics Department. * * * Among the other problems which they have taken up are the manufacture of telephones, of dry cells for torch, storage cells for automobiles, designs for suitable lamps for street illumination, and suitable engines for use of vegetable oil as fuel. * * * All this work is being done by Indian professors in collaboration with Indian students." The department of Applied Chemistry was described as working on diverse problems, such as the manufacture of paints and pigments, manufacture of alkaloids, of drugs and of rectified spirit, of glass and enamel manufacture, introduction of oil firing in glass manufacture, paste boards and cardboards, soaps, oil and perfumery.

As for the career of the alumni turned out of the University College of Science, they were reported as working as experts in the Customs laboratories in Calcutta, Bombay, Madras and Karachi. "We find them," observed Mookerjee further, "in the Public Health Laboratory in Calcutta, in the Government Stationery Office in the Alipur Test House, we find them employed in the Science Department at Jubbulpore, in the Explosive Research Institution at Rawalpindi, and last but not least, we find one of the M. Sc. s recently appointed Inspector in the Explosives Department under the Government of Bengal."

Appendix I

THE NATIONAL COUNCIL OF EDUCATION BENGAL

Number of the Successful Candidates at the Final Examinations
(1906-19)

Year	Secondary Tech. M.E. & E.E.	Primary Tech.	Survey and Draftsmanship
1906	5	10	x
1907	2	15	x
1908	3	10	x
1909	13	11	x
1910	11	13	x
1911	8	19	x
1912	10	17	x
1913	2	6	1
1914	1	3	2
1915	3	8	x
1916	1	10	4
1917	2	10	5
1918	3	12	3
1919	2	11	8

APPENDIX II

THE NATIONAL COUNCIL OF EDUCATION BENGAL

Number of the Successful Candidates at the Final Examinations

(1920-35)

Year	M.E.		E.E.	Ch. E.	Primary Tech.	Survey & Drafts-manship
1920	3	4 *	4 (3)	x	13	8
1921	5	7 *	4 (3)	x	11	3
1922	10	11*	3 (2)	x	5	2
1923	15	27*	15 (3)	x	13	4
1924	12	..	25	x	25	5
1925	14	..	44	9	jr. 23	7
1926	9	..	51	7	13	9
1927	19	..	37	8	15	5
1928	8	..	14	4	11	11
1929	6	..	18	8	13	8
1930	11	..	16	6	12	5
1931	21	..	32	5	18	7
1932	16	..	18	3	9	8
1933	7	..	15	5	9	16
1934	10	..	17	3	23	12
1935	27	..	21	9	15	5

Figures within brackets show the number of students passed, both M.E. and E.E.

*Shows the actual number of students passed during the year.

Jr.= Junior Technical instead of Primary Technical
M.E.= Mechanical Engineering
E.E.= Electrical Engineering
Ch. E.= Chemical Engineering

SECTION 5

THE CULTIVATION OF POLITICAL SCIENCE AND SOCIOLOGY

Political science and sociology as developed at the Calcutta University today are at once humanistic and practical. That is, on the one hand, the cultural objectives of liberal pedagogics are strongly in evidence. On the other hand, equally influential is the impact of the demands of modern and contemporary requirements of life on the discussions of political and sociological topics.

And in both these directions each of these two disciplines follows a universal, comparative or comprehensive trend. Neither in the academic or cultural aspects nor in the realistic, practical or applied does political science or sociology submit to a monistic obsession or one-track methodology. The theories and practices as investigated at Calcutta are multiform and pluralistic.

Political Science

To begin with, let us visualize the humble status of political science as it was previous to 1917. The importance that this science has acquired at Calcutta is inextricably bound up with the "new regulations" of the University as well as the establishment of the Post-Graduate Department for which Asutosh is justly celebrated.

During the first decade of the twentieth century this science as cultivated at the Calcutta University was a very primitive commodity. The entire encyclopaedia of political science down to almost the beginnings of the Great War comprised Mill's *Representative Government*, Bluntschli's *Theory of the State*, Wheaton's *Inter-*

national Law and Strachey's *Government of India*. Political science was in those days a part of the comprehensive domain of history. The treatment also was defective since it used to be in the main abstract, speculative, divorced from the social and economic realities as well as untouched by the vital concerns of life.

Today the studies and investigations in political science have emancipated themselves from domination by speculations into the fundamental origins and ends of morality, law and the state. The requirements of daily life that is being lived at the present moment are given their due. Constitutional and administrative questions have risen to the forefront in the discussions. Naturally, therefore, the problems of public finance on the one hand and party organization on the other have been demanding considerable attention. While in regard to these items the historical treatment is accorded its proper place, the emphasis is directed towards the actualities and events of the day.

Some of the most pressing political problems of our own times in Eur-America as well as in India are to be found in the questions bearing on races, classes, religions, social groups, "communities," minorities, nationalities etc. The lectures and investigations are quite oriented to the reality that the "nationalistic" questions are no less acute in India than, say, in the Balkan complex and Central Europe. Among the publications of the Calcutta University or of its staff are to be found works given over to this and allied topics.

Never was the contact between nations more extensive and profound in daily life than in post-War years. Developments in international law and usage, the League of Nations, the little Entente, the Danubian Federation, the expansion of Japan, the rejuvenation of Turkey, air-transport and oversea phone, "world-economy" and so forth have not failed therefore to influence the handling of political science at Calcutta. The constitutional and social experiments or achievements associated with Russia, Italy and Germany as well as the rise into prominence of new states like Czechoslovakia and Poland belong likewise to the same complex as a matter of course.

In India today as in other countries of the world the consciousness of the people about the economic considerations is a powerful ingredient in public life. The "contents" of such categories as freedom, equality and democracy have therefore been getting tremendously transformed on account of contact with the realities of poverty and prosperity. The impact of the middle classes as contrasted with the propertied (landowning, commercial or industrial), as well as of the workingmen, and to a certain extent, of the peasants has made itself felt in social institutions and ideologies. The University could not escape this impact, and political science as developed in this atmosphere has been seeking to do justice to the evolution of new ideals from Godwin, St. Simon and Owen to Marx, Bakunin, Kautsky, Jaurès, Hobson, and Stalin. The achievements of constructive socialism as embodied in Factory Acts, labour legislation, trade unions, social insurance etc. have grown into integral parts of studies in political experience and speculation.

The parliaments and national assemblies or legislative councils of today have entered the social field in a conscious and deliberate manner in Eur-America as in Asia. The questions of race-uplift, caste elevation, sterilization, miscegenation etc. such as are intimately mixed up with the problems of societal evolution, human development and progress have in India as elsewhere grown into the normal problems of states. The treatment of political science at the University has accordingly been oriented to the needs of this aspect of statesmanship as well.

The rôle of general philosophy in the evolution of political science is well recognized in the academic *milieu*. The contributions of Croce, Gentile, Dewey, Hobhouse, Russell, Meinecke, Jhering, Vierkandt, Joseph-Barthélemy, Charmont, Faguet, Masaryk and others have therefore a chance to enrich the atmosphere.

It is a realistic and matter of fact age no doubt in Bengal as in other parts of the world. But care is taken to cultivate still the idealistic strands of political thought as embodied, for instance, in Herder, Fichte, Renouvier, Mazzini and Green among the "moderns". More recent expressions of the idealistic or neo-idealistic tradition are equally appreciated, for instance, the tendencies represented by Bosanquet, Watson, Giorgio del Vecchio, Hocking, Kohler, Jellinek, Spann, Koellreutter, Redanò, and others.

The ancients and medievals of the East and the West are likewise admitted into the intellectual complex. And in this connection it is worth while to observe that the creations of India in the field of political institutions and theories from the earliest times have been demanding considerable attention on the part of the University's researchers. This is a new feature in Indian academic life and cannot be taken to be older than a generation. The bearings of these researches in what may generally be described as the Kauṭalya-Śukra tradition on contemporary political life and thought receive due recognition.

The influence of the University studies and investigations in political science may be watched on the extra-academic institutions of the country, namely, on the clubs, societies, institutes, conferences etc. as well as on the journalism and literary output of Bengal in English and Bengali. The dailies, weeklies as well as monthlies are publishing papers on international events, civic and municipal affairs, labour questions, contemporary politics and topics of representation, election, suffrage etc. in a manner that undoubtedly does credit to the authors and can somewhat be attributed to the spirit imbibed in their academic career.

In comparison with the Bengali thought of a decade or a decade and a half ago in regard to corresponding problems the Bengali thought of today would be found to be more realistic and factual, more comprehensive and international, more uptodate and informative, more practical and precise. A part of this consummation may easily be ascribed to the studies and investigations at the University. At any rate, the University may be said to have succeeded in trying to respond to the new and growing demands of the people for effective introduction to the world-forces and the requirements of practical life.

The work in political science done at the University is known to a certain extent in the academic circles of the world on account of publications in the *Séances et Travaux de l'Académie des Sciences Morales et Politiques* (Paris), *Geopolitik* (Berlin), *Annali di Economia* (Milan), the *American Political Science Review* and other journals of international importance, as well as in the *Calcutta Review* and in books and brochures issued in India and abroad. The incorporation of the results of these studies in the publications of Eur-American authors may also be referred to.

It would have been clear that as for the data, institutional or ideological, they are derived from America, Britain, France, Germany, Italy, Japan and Russia as well as, of course, from India. So far as the students are concerned, however, the lack of a knowledge of French, German or Italian is to be treated as a great handicap. A long-felt want can be removed in case a modern language be rendered obligatory for every student of political science.

Another desideratum in the interest of students of political science is an obligatory course of some twenty-five lectures on the constitutional, political and international developments in the world since 1919.

The intimate contact with economics such as the students of political science are required to cultivate at Calcutta is a very happy feature and should be considered to be stimulating as much to the alumni as to the teaching corps.

It is desirable, however, that the University authorities should attach importance to the use of statistical reports, charts, maps as well as journals as an integral element in the teaching of politics. The creation of adequate facilities in an effective manner ought to be striven after. Some amount of personal contact with the functioning of governmental bodies, corporations, municipalities, union boards etc., by travels and visits to important centres may also be suggested for further advance along the channels of realistic and applied politics.

Among the social forces that have contributed to the expansion and enrichment of political science at the Calcutta University may be mentioned the Great War, the Government of India Acts 1919 and 1935, the Indian National Congress and Trade Union activities since 1919, the newspapers and journals, and last but not least, the investigations and experiences of Indians settled or travelling in foreign countries from China to Peru as reported in journals or published in books.

Thanks to the elastic character of the Post-Graduate Department it has been possible for the University to assimilate the new tendencies and uptodatize itself in regard to studies in politics as much as in sociology and economics. The *liaison* between the University and the social life or the world at large has functioned to mutual advantage.

Sociology

Sociology as an independent discipline was unknown at the Calcutta University or for that matter in the Indian academic world down to 1917. During the first decade and a half of the present century ethics and the philosophy of religion may be said to have comprised, if at all, the topics of sociology, especially in so far as Spencer's *First Principles* was recommended as a text book.

Even in those days, however, the Indian Universities were not entirely innocent of the sociological atmosphere, specially if we consider the diverse faculties and manifold courses offered. Much of the topics included in the rather vague category, sociology, used to be dealt with in one form or other in the academic *milieu*.

The hodge-podge like character of sociology is apparent even in the most recent publications. The *Fields and Methods of Sociology* (edited by L. L. Bernard New York, 1934) describes the centrifugal movement in sociology since 1890 by furnishing the following list of its present-day sub-divisions : (1) historical sociology, (2) biological sociology, (3) demography, (4) social geography, (5) human ecology, (6) study of the community, (7) rural sociology, (8) urban sociology, (9) folk sociology, (10) cultural sociology, (11) sociology of art, (12) social psychology, (13) social psychiatry,

(14) educational sociology, (15) sociology of religion, (16) sociology of law, (17) study of the family, (18) political sociology, (19) social ethics, (20) sociology of institutions, (21) social organization, (22) social control, (23) sociology of economic relations, (24) social pathology, (25) criminology and delinquency, (26) penology, (27) social work, (28) social investigation, (29) social statistics. Evidently there is no logic in this classification. (cf. Bogardus: *Contemporary Sociology*, 1932).

A schedule like this furnishes hardly any clue to the province and boundaries of sociology and serves but to indicate its extremely uncertain and indefinite character as a system of scientific discipline. Many of the categories used above with the adjective "social" are but new words without describing any new things and used to and actually do deal with topics generally known to belong to other sciences. Hardly any one of these categories is precise enough to convey its scope and limits.

It is apparent that without professionally being known as students of or researchers in sociology many intellectuals have in the past been and continue in the present to be genuine sociologists,—although not of course in the radical view of Leopold von Wiese. In the India of those days students of history, philosophy, psychology, ethics, metaphysics, law, marriage, property, aesthetics, myths, civilization, literature and what not were therefore dealing with sociology or rather its *data* in a more or less unconscious manner. These were, however, primitive conditions,—a state of things in which sociology was not yet differentiated in category or content from the sister disciplines. Such conditions obtained in other countries as well, albeit no doubt decades earlier.

Writing on "Science and Learning in Young India"

for the *Collegian* (Calcutta) in 1920 the present author observed among other things as follows:[1]

"Thanks to the activities of the folk-lorists and collectors of legends and manuscripts[2] associated with the *Sāhitya Pariṣats* and *Sammelans* (literary academies and conferences) much useful work on anthropological topics has been done in India during the last quarter of a century. One or two publications by Indian ethnologists have also been able to draw the attention of Western experts to the merits of their work. But on the whole the scientific study of anthropology cannot be said to have begun in India. Nay, this branch of learning was officially unrecognized by the Universities until a year or two ago. But time has come when the undergraduates should be taught to regard the investigations into the life and institutions of the Africans, American-Indians and the aboriginal tribes of India, Australia and the Polynesian Islands as an integral part of "general culture." For, the impact of anthropological researches on the approach to the problems of the human *psyche*, morals, religion, criminology, social behaviour, and inter-racial justice, in one word, on the entire science of civilization has been nothing short of revolutionary.

"Everybody is aware of the tremendous influence that the social forces of the last fifteen years have exerted on University curriculum and administration in India. But we have still to remark that sociology is a science that remains yet to take its place as an independent course of instruction along with the other arts and sciences. The very fact that in India today there are

[1] The present author's *The Futurism of Young Asia* (Berlin, 1922), p. 332.

[2] *cf.* H. D. Palit: *Adyer Gambhira: A Socio-religious History of Bengal* (Calcutta, 1912), on which the present author's *Folk-Element in Hindu Culture* (London, 1917) is in the main based.

at least one hundred propagandas from the Andhra library movement and Malabar women's association to temperance conference and depressed classes mission, each with its regular congresses, publicity journals and lectures, should challenge the authorities of higher learning to create opportunities for the scientific study not only of Indian institutions and *mores* but of all facts and theories bearing on social progress, social inheritance, social control and social service."

It is in 1917 that the category "sociology" officially invaded the academic atmosphere at Calcutta and it came to stay. It is therefore much younger than economics as well as politics. At the end of some two decades it continues still to be in a rather infantile condition. The studies in sociology have not yet been organized as adequately as they ought to be. The Post-Graduate Department is, however, comprehensive and elastic enough to admit of a scientific organization of sociological studies in the near future.

At the outset it is proper to observe that at Calcutta sociology has been placed on broad foundations. Both economics and political science are compulsory for the sociology course. This is an item of capital importance for the development of sociological discipline. The factual, institutional and materialistic basis of social forms, processes, movements and ideologies has thereby been automatically assured. It has therefore been possible for sociology to get relieved of the exclusive attention to the conventional atmosphere associated with speculative categories like social philosophy, ideals of civilization, the destiny of mankind etc.

The background of sociological studies and researches at Calcutta deserves more than a passing notice. The historical growth, decline and progress of India in societal institutions, economic, political, religious and social,—have constituted the theme of somewhat extensive investigations for over a quarter of a century. The publications on these topics in books and journals both at home and abroad form a noteworthy feature of the University's post-graduate work. They have won recognition also in the standard Eur-American treatises.

The ancient, medieval and early modern developments in the societal organization as well as the social, political and economic thought of India have succeeded in injecting into the *milieu* of modern sociological discipline strong doses of the historic sense and Asian data as well as genuine comparative methodology. It may be observed *en passant* that, generally speaking, these items are virtually ignored or marked by non-observation, mal-observation as well as misrepresentation or inadequate and erroneous understanding in the Eur-American seminars of sociology. The references to Indian or for that matter to Oriental society or social ideology with which we are familiar in the researches of Eur-American sociologists of the highest standing do not, as a rule, indicate more than a conventional estimate such as they imbibe almost with their mothers' milk or in their kindergarten atmosphere. At Calcutta, thanks to the keen and intensive interest in antiquarian and archæological researches based on the first hand knowledge of the original sources in the manifold languages of India, living and dead, the students of modernism and the latest disciplines in the societal sciences are easily furnished with the opportunities of doing justice both to the East and the West.

The progress of sociological discipline may be expected to move along relatively more sound lines at Calcutta than elsewhere in India or abroad. The impact of sound and scientific *indianisme* or indology and *orientalisme* on the growth of sociology in Asia as well as Eur-America is bound to be more profound than has yet been the case. This consciousness is a prominent feature of the studies and investigations in modern sociology at Calcutta. It was brought to the notice of the *Société Asiatique* of Paris in 1921 by the present author's paper entitled *L'Indianisme et les Sciences Sociales* as well as of the *Deutsche Morgenlaendische Gesellschaft* (Berlin) in 1922 by his paper on *Die soziale Philosophie Jung-Indiens*.

Of equal, although not fully recognized, importance to the eventual and prospective progress of modern sociology at Calcutta is the anthropological factor in the background as furnished by the Post-Graduate Department. The researches of the Calcutta anthropologists, both physical and cultural, into the races and castes of India are very often utilized in the discussions of sociological problems. Care is being taken to emphasize the *liaison* between anthropology and sociology on as many fronts as possible.

Not less valuable for the future of sociological studies and researches at Calcutta is the existence of the department of experimental psychology as a section of the Post-Graduate system. There is as yet no official link between this section and that of sociology. But in the treatment of sociological topics the data of experimental, and especially, of social and comparative psychology are accorded a significant place.

The concrete factual data of societal life receive a comprehensive treatment. In regard to family, property, state, myth, arts and crafts, sciences, *mores* etc. the discussions have bearings as much on the primitive, undeveloped or semi-developed conditions as on the developed and hyper-developed stages. Indian sociography naturally occupies a prominent position on all counts. The diversities prevailing in the varied regions of Europe,—Balkan, Slavic, Teutonic, Southern, Latin, Anglo-Saxon etc.—as well as of the two Americas are always kept before the mind's eye historically as well as statistically. The sociographic data of the two Hemispheres, ancient, medieval and modern, primitive as well as futuristic, are placed on a common platform of objective and analytical investigation. The races, castes, gilds, villages, towns, parties and other group formations of India obtain thereby their world-wide perspective and the traditional conception about the alleged distinction between the East and the West can therefore be appraised at its proper worth.

The Calcutta school of sociology is known by its researches to the sociological circles of the world. Journals like the *Revue de Synthèse Historique* (Paris), the *Revue Internationale de Sociologie* (Paris), the *Koelner Vierteljahrshefte fuer Soziologie* (Cologne), the *Deutsche Rundschau* (Berlin), the *Giornale degli Economisti e Rivista di Statistica* (Rome), the *International Journal of Ethics* (Chicago), the *Journal of International Relations* (U. S. A.) etc. have rendered the conclusions of these researches accessible to the scholars in Eur-America. Publications in books have likewise to be mentioned.

The analysis of the mind as operating in the economic, political, religious, social and other societal institutions has likewise been a feature of the sociological studies conducted at Calcutta. The categories like instinct, intelligence, behaviour, society-making process, folk-ways, public opinion, leadership, the *élites*, social mobility and so forth are examined in their bearings on the social man. Perhaps one might desire a more detailed and intensive investigation into these topics of social psychology than has yet been attempted.

Great stress is laid on the problems relating to the remaking of personality, the transformation of tradition, and societal reconstruction. The treatment is comprehensive enough to include societal planning of all sorts including religion such as are calculated to promote "social metabolism" along the most varied channels. Broadly speaking, these items of what for general purposes may be described as Applied Sociology can be grouped under the following disciplines:

1. The Control of Poverty. This study involves, among other things, a discussion of the occupational structure of India and the world as well as the problems of national wealth and income. Rural reconstruction, labour questions, wages and earnings, unemployment, social insurance etc. are dealt with in this section.

2. Population Questions. The treatment is both demographic and eugenic. Light is thrown on the one hand on the problems of vital statistics, optimum, standard of living, dietary, migration, "Greater India", old and new, "internal colonizing," rural-urban relations, the rôle of the woman etc., and on the other on the problems of race-betterment or race-degeneration engendered by the rise of the alleged lower, inferior and poorer classes or castes and so forth. The experiences of Japan, America and the European countries form the permanent background in these quantitative and qualitative studies.

3. Public health and Sanitation. Special attention is bestowed on the progress of hygienic measures in the more advanced countries of Eur-America and Japan during the last two generations or so as well as on the work that is being done in the villages and towns of India in recent years.

4. Crime and Punishment. The study is conduct-

ed not only as a psychological investigation in behaviour and reaction. The statistical, regional, climatic and racial (anthropologico-biological) aspects are also emphasized. The evolution of modern penology in Eur-America as well as the problems of penal reform in India receive simultaneous attention.

5. Pedagogics. The statistics of schools, colleges, teaching staff, financial equipment etc. form the chief feature of educational sociology as dealt with in this section. Attention is directed especially to the systems of school hygiene and physical training.

Applied sociology in all these branches is essentially a discipline in comparative statistics. The data are Indian, Japanese as well as Eur-American. The object consists in appraising India by the world standard and raising the Indian peoples to the "next higher" level in efficiency. India is presented as in the main belonging to the Balkan and East-European socio-economic system. The societal "relativities" constitute the fundamental bed-rock of these discussions in comparative social statistics. The way has been opened to the establishment of equations between regions or between epochs in the fields of societal development.

At the International Congress of Population in Rome (1931) and Berlin (1935) as well as that of Sociology at Brussels (1935) and of Orientalists at Rome (1935) the researches of the Calcutta school were in evidence on account of the present author's contributions in Italian, German and French. These and other works have been noticed in British and American circles as well. Scientific contacts with the larger world have been maintained on account of honorary membership of the *Comitato Italiano per lo Studio dei Problemi della Popolazione* (Rome) as well as association with the *Institut International de Sociologie* (Geneva), the American Sociological Society, the Royal Economic Society (London), the *Société d'Economie Politique* (Paris), the *Deutsche Akademie* (Munich), and the Royal Asiatic Society (Shanghai).

In Eur-America the studies in the history of sociological theories ignore as a rule the contributions from the Asian mind. Sorokin's *Contemporary Sociological Theories* (New York, 1927) may be cited as an exception in view of the fact that the treatise has made it a point to refer to ancient Hindu and Chinese sources on various occasions. At the Calcutta school attempts are being made to be thoroughly comprehensive. The evolution from the *Aitareya Brāhmaṇa* to Kauṭalya, from Kauṭalya to Hemādri, from Hemādri to Śukra and Abul Fazl, from Abul Fazl to Rammohun and from Rammohun to Dayananda, Saiyed Ahmad, Vivekananda, Ranade, Tilak, Asutosh, Lajpat Rai, Dhammapala, Gandhi and Rabindranath cannot be ignored anywhere in the world's academic atmosphere while dealing with the "encyclopædia of the social sciences". This aspect of the question receives proper attention at Calcutta in connection with the progress of social thought in the West from Homer, Hesiod and Pythagoras to Vico, Montesquieu, Beccaria and Herder, and from Herder to Comte, Spencer, Schaeffle, Galton and Lombroso. It is not overlooked, of course, that intensive studies and specialization have proceeded far in the contemporary Eur-American world, represented by such workers as Tarde, Durkheim, Toennies, Giddings, Pareto, Lapouge, Ammon, Aschaffenburg, Bonger, Ross, Hobhouse, Freud, Bouglé, Westermarck, Lévy-Bruhl, Carr-Saunders, Goldenweiser, Pearson, von Wiese, Sorokin, Gaston Richard, Gini, Haushofer, Lasbax, Hankins, Michels, Niceforo, Thurnwald, Duprat, Barnes, Bogardus and others. The publications in the *Indian Historical Quarterly*, *Prabuddha Bhārata*, the *Calcutta Review* and other journals have served to indicate to a certain extent the scope and contents of sociological thought as developed in India through the ages without reference to which, be it observed once more, no history of sociology can be worth its name.

The sociological studies at the University have had some influence on the scientific output of the Bengali *intelligentsia*. At literary conferences and in journals well-written papers on the topics of criminology, population, caste-mixture, co-education, marriage-customs, vocational guidance, pedagogic history, feminism, folk-festivals, rural arts, Hinduization, library organization, radio, cinema, educational finance, food reform and so forth constitute a mentionable feature. Much of these extra-academic publications in Bengali or English can be traced for inspiration and guidance to the University investigations or the institutes associated with the academic world. It is not to be ignored, on the other hand, that the youth movement, the literary and other conferences, labour congresses, communal disturbances, the Harijan and depressed class movements, the health weeks, the prison-seeking tendencies associated with the non-cooperation and civil disobedience agitation, the library associations, municipal and union board activities, women's conferences, the work of the Ramakrishna Mission, the Hindu Mission, the Mahabodhi Society, and the Moslem League, the constitutional experiences of the people since 1919, the American immigration legislation, the exclusion of the Oriental races in the British Dominions, the participation of the Indians in the functions of the League of Nations and the "Geneva complex" as well as in many other international institutions in an official or personal capacity, the race-problems of Eastern and Balkanic Europe,—these have all contributed to the expansion of the scope of sociological studies at the Calcutta University. Sociology like political science has been growing by responding to the thousand and stimuli of the practical world. It is intensely alive to the requirements of expanding life and the satisfaction of daily social needs.

We must not overlook the fact that sociology is still in the making at Calcutta. The raw materials or brick and mortar and the scaffoldings alone may be said to be in evidence. But as has been observed at the outset, an adequate organization is wanting. In the first place, due emphasis has to be placed on the anthropological groundwork. Secondly, the psychological investigation into the *soziale Beziehungen*, the social relations, processes and forms, has to be accorded a special, nay, a very fundamental place in the entire scheme. Thirdly, the comparative-historical treatment of the sociological doctrines deserves to be established on a sound and secure footing.

Finally, what has been suggested about political science holds equally good of sociology also. Visits to prominent institutions of social service, excursions to areas of anthropological importance, contacts with the workers in the anthropological and psychological laboratories, mental hospitals, Borstal institutions, after-care associations, experimental schools etc. will have to be promoted in the interest of concrete grasp over the realities of societal development.

Then there is the question of a modern language, French, German or Italian, to which the attention has likewise to be directed.

The establishment of a number of Research Fellowships may be recommended as a measure calculated to remove some of the hindrances to the proper progress of the sociological sciences at Calcutta.

Academic or professional sociology has in India as in Eur-America and Japan been chronologically preceded as well as supplemented by extra-University sociological output. Sociology, as cultivated in Bengal today, has a number of extra-academic and pre-academic sources to thank for its background and development.

The *Bangīya Sāhitya Pariṣat* (Bengali Academy of Literature), established during the last decade of the nineteenth century, is to be regarded as one of the most influential pre-academic institutions of sociology along with other research. The *Patrikā* (Journal) of this *Pariṣat* has been functioning for over forty years as the organ of first hand investigations in folk-lore, social *mores*, cultural institutions, historical developments etc. The work of Hara Prasad Sastri, Ramendra Sundar Trivedi, Rakhal Das Banerji, Nagendra Nath Basu, Dines Chandra Sen, Amulya Charan Vidyabhushan, Haridas Palit and others has contributed much to the awakening of sociological sense among the Bengali intellectuals. Trivedi's (1864-1922) researches in Vedic socio-religious institutions as well as in characterology, personality, activism and so forth deserve a special mention. For the first two decades of the twentieth century Trivedi's work may be appraised as of the same value in extra-academic sociology as that of Bhudev Mookerji, founder of the *Sikṣā-Darpaṇa* (Mirror of Education, 1864) and editor of the *Education Gazette* (1868) and author of works on family, society, customs and so forth during the last generation of the nineteenth century. Trivedi's importance as a pioneer sociologist bids fair to grow during the next generation.

Another pre-academic and extra-University source of sociological research in Bengal was the *Dawn* (1897), the monthly edited by Satis Chandra Mukerjee.[1] Among

[1] S. C. Dutt: *Conflicting Tendencies in Indian Economic Thought* (Calcutta 1934), pp. 3, 8, 9, 10, 11; the present author's *Badtir Pathe Bangali* (Bengalis in Progress), 1934, pp. xvi, xlvii-xlix,

other topics of socio-cultural and philosophical interest the problem of relations between the East and the West as engendered by culture-contacts used to arrest Mukerjee's special attention. The journal became the nucleus of the Dawn Society established by Mukerjee in 1903 and was known as the *Dawn Society's Magazine* for three years. When as a result of Mukerjee's activities in collaboration with those of others the National Council of Education was established in 1906 during the epoch of the *Swadeshi* Movement, the *Magazine* became the organ of the national education institutions and ideals until it ceased to exist in 1913.

Investigations based on statistical reports, especially of the Government of India Census Department, constituted a chief feature of the Dawn Society's publications. Much attention was bestowed on the rural society, the arts and crafts, the professional groups, the races and the castes. The papers directed the eyes of the *intelligentsia* to the anthropological topics of cultural, social and economic character as well as to the historical developments of institutions and ideas.

It is as pupils and colleagues of Mukerjee that Haran Chandra Chakladar (Calcutta University), Radha Kumud Mookerji (Lucknow University), Rabindra Narayan Ghosh (Calcutta), the present author and others made their *début* in sociological, economical and historical investigations. Because of family and friendly relationships Radha Kamal Mukerjee (Lucknow) also has to be linked up with the Dawn Society group.

Under the influence of the "ideas of 1905" the National Council of Education and the *Bangīya Sāhitya*

Ekaler Dhana-Daulat O Arthashastra (The Wealth and Economics of Our Own Times), Vol. II (1935), pp. 604-606; P. K. Sarkar: "Satis Mukerjee the Economist and Sociologist of the Swadeshi Period" (*Arthik Unnati*, November 1936).

Parișat became the nuclei of several research societies in the districts of Bengal. The *Sāhitya Parișats* at Rangpur, Dacca, Gauhati, etc. and the Varendra Research Society of Rajshahi may be mentioned in this connection. The Literary Conferences held under the auspices of these *Parișats*, central or local, were instrumental in evoking some first-hand and field-work socio-cultural and anthropological studies in the rural centres. One of such societies, the *Maldaha Jātīya Śikșā Samiti* (Malda District Council of National Education), established by the present author in 1907, used to maintain a special research department for investigations into folk-lore, folk-arts, folk-festivals and the like. Radhes Chandra Seth, Bipin Bihari Ghosh, Haridas Palit, Kumud Nath Lahiri, Vidhu Sekhara Sastri, Krishna Charan Sarkar, Nagendra Nath Chaudhury and others made some valuable contributions. Palit's *Ādyer Gambhīrā* (1911) formed the basis of the present author's *Folk-Element in Hindu Culture* (London 1917). Palit and Chaudhury have been associated with the *Ārthik Unnati* (Economic Progress) group since 1926 and the *Āntarjātik Banga Parișat* since 1932.

The third prominent extra-academic and pre-academic centre of sociological research is to be seen in the Ramakrishna Mission which has been in existence in one shape or other since Vivekānanda's return from Eur-America in 1897 but was formally established in its present form in 1909. The monthly journal of this movement, *Prabuddha Bhārata* (Awakened India), was started in 1895. This journal, philosophical as it is, addresses itself not only to the topics of *Vedānta*, the *Upanișads*, the *Gītā* and so forth as well as to professional religion and morality of all types but to every item of social relations and reconstructions. Topics of psychological, pedagogic, economic, socio-cultural and inter-racial interest have always been studied with attention by the editors and contributors, among whom are to be counted writers representing the most diverse sciences and arts. The impact of this journal on the social thinking and practice of the intellectuals and the middle classes is immense.[1] The Mission has also been conducting a monthly journal in Bengali entitled *Udbodhana* (Awakening) since 1898.

It is worthwhile to observe also that the first anthropological journal established by the Bengalis, commenced under extra-academic auspices. In 1920 *Man in India* was brought into being at Ranchi (Bihar) by Sarat Chandra Roy, then known chiefly as author of investigations relating to the Oraons and the Mundas. In recent years, thanks to the investigations of Panchanan Mitra and other Calcutta University researchers, it has grown into an organ of the academicians as well.

From the Calcutta University's side patronage for sociological research is to be seen in the establishment of the *Indian Journal of Psychology* in 1926. The Department of Experimental Psychology is responsible for the initiation of this enterprise. The work of researchers from all University centres in India finds place in this journal. The contributions of Narendra Nath Sen-Gupta, Girindra Sekhar Bose, Manindra Nath Banerji, Suhrit Chandra Mitra, Gopeswar Pal and others have direct bearings on educational, industrial

[1] A short statement about the work of Indian sociologists is to be seen in L. von Wiese's paper "Der gegenwaertige internationale Entwicklungsstand der Allgemeinen Soziologie" in *Reine und Angewandte Soziologie, eine Festagabe fuer Ferdinand Toennies* (Leipzig 1936, p.14). The author invites attention to *Prabuddha Bhārata* and Vivekānanda's philosophy and observes that the Indian sociologists of today are attempting to establish a bridge between the Brahmanical culture of the old *Vedas* and modern sociology.

and other sociological research, both qualitative and quantitative.

Sociology is one of the topics of investigation and research at the "*Āntarjātik Banga*" *Pariṣat* ("International Bengal" Institute) established by the present author in 1932. Bengali is used as the medium for these studies and investigations, and the monthly *Ārthik Unnati* (Economic Progress), est. 1926, as the organ, which, otherwise, publishes chiefly the contributions of the *Bangīya Dhana-Vijnān Pariṣat* (Bengali Institute of Economics) conducted along the same lines and under the same auspices as the "*Āntarjātik Banga*" *Pariṣat*.

The expansion of Japan, social life in Gujarat, the prisons of today, the economic and social aspects of Fascist Italy, the aboriginal tribes of West Bengal, social conditions in Persia and Spain, Indians in South-East Asia, industrial education in Dewey's social philosophy, the anthropology of animal sacrifice, social ideals in British education, the castes of Bengal, municipal administration at home and abroad, Freud, crimes and punishments etc. are some of the items which have engaged the discussions of the Sociological Division of the "*Āntarjātik Banga*" *Pariṣat*. Haridas Palit, Bhupendra Nath Datta, Pankaj Kumar Mukherjee, Shib Chandra Datta, Debendra Chandra Das Gupta, Sarasi Lal Sarkar and others have contributed to the research output of this Institute.

Likewise does sociology come in for treatment among the themes discussed at the *Bangīya German-Vidyā Samsad* (Bengali Society of German Culture), established by the present author in 1933. The work of Toennies, von Wiese and Freyer, the *Gestalt* theory, and *Winterhilfswerk* (winter relief) as a form of social service may be mentioned as some of the topics investigated.

Some sociological material is to be found, it may be mentioned in this connection, in the *Teacher's Journal* published by the All-Bengal Teachers' Association. This monthly Journal has in recent years been improving in the form and matter of its output.

The *Mahābodhi* (est. 1892), conducted by the Mahābodhi Society as a journal of international Buddhism, and the *Hindu Review*, the organ of the Hindu Mission (est. 1925), furnish valuable data for sociological research. Antiquarian journals like the *Indian Historical Quarterly* edited by Narendra Nath Law (1926) and *Indian Culture* established by Bimala Charan Law (1934) deserve likewise to be mentioned in the sociological inventory of contemporary Bengal.

The castes began to be self-conscious towards the beginning of the twentieth century. The Census publications of 1901 served to give a fillip to this caste-consciousness. The lead was taken by the Brahmans and Kayasthas, each group equipping itself with an association and a journal of its own. The movement acquired strength as a result of the Government of India Act 1921 and the social reform ideology and legislation of the last two decades. Today, the Mahisyas, the Sadgops, the Tilis, the Suvarnavaniks, the Kaivarttas, the Vaisya-Sahas and many other caste-groups are fortified each with its own organ. Social mobility of the vertical type and of course of the horizontal type is the chief feature of the ideology pervading these caste-journals. The contents of these journals furnish valuable indices to the economic and political as well as cultural dynamics associated with the *groupements professionnels* such as cannot fail to be of tremendous importance to scientific sociology.

The sociology of socialism and feminism is to be watched, in the first instance, in the journals run by or for the workingmen as well as by women. In the second place, the general dailies, weeklies and monthlies are rich in the sociological topics bearing on these classes. The special *Pujah* (Autumn) numbers of the *Ananda Bazar Patrika*, the *Pānchajanya* (Chittagong), *Sonār Bānglā* (Dacca), the *Amrita Bazar Patrika*, *Advance*, *Forward*, etc. can also be counted among the organs calculated to promote sociology, theoretical and applied.

Statistics and statistical methods have to be requisitioned by sociology as by many other sciences. The establishment of the Indian Statistical Society at Calcutta as well as its quarterly organ, *Sankhyā* (Number), by Prasanta Chandra Mahalanobis has to be listed in the *milieu* of sociological investigations.

Sociological theories, both Indian and Eur-American, constitute a substantial part of the contents of the *Calcutta Review*, the monthly organ of the Calcutta University. Short, introductory and bibliographical reports about modern Eur-American sociologists from Herder to Sorokin have been a feature of this *Review* since 1926. Among the exponents of recent sociology many of the names mentioned above have been admitted thereby into the domain of sociological knowledge in India. From the Indian side the contributions of the *Aitareya Brāhmaṇa*, Kauṭalya, Manu, Śukra, Chandeśvara, Mitra-Miśra, Nīlakaṇṭha, Abul Fazl, Ramdas and Rammohun among the ancients and medievals have been the themes of some of the papers in the *Calcutta Review*. It addresses itself likewise to the anthropological, demographic, eugenic, psychological, criminological and pedagogic topics of sociology.

The time has come when Bengali scholars should establish an exclusive but comprehensive Institute of Sociology on the lines, say, of the American Sociological Society. A journal in Bengali, given over, again exclusively, to sociology in all its phases and branches is also a necessity for the Bengali world of culture.

SECTION 6

VIVEKĀNANDA AS "WORLD-CONQUEROR"

As a student of world-culture and the creations of modern India it is possible to call the attention of scholars to Vivekānanda (1862-1902) as one of the "world-conquerors" of our own times. More than two decades ago (1912-13), even when the Vivekānanda movement was in its infancy, the present writer[1] ventured to foresee that the moral and spiritual values in the transcendental experiences of Rāmakṛṣṇa and the self-control, self-sacrifice and social service personified in the men and institutions of the Rāmakṛṣṇa-Vivekānanda *Gestalt* or socio-cultural complex were destined to constitute the living religion of our country, of our masses and classes, during the present century. I have often called Vivekānanda the Carlyle of Young India and have also credited him with the gospel of Napoleonic energism and triumphant defiance of the Western chauvinists.[2]

It is indeed possible to talk an entire encyclopædia about Vivekānanda's messages and activities. Physically of athletic build, healthy and strong as a mere man, he knew, let us begin by saying, how to do justice to the daily meals. He was a lover of art, a poet, a

[1] *Viśva-Śakti* (World-Forces), Calcutta 1914 (first published in the *Gribastha*, Calcutta 1913).

[2] *The Complete Works of Swami Vivekananda* in seven volumes (1907-1927), Mayavati Memorial Edition; *The Life of Swami Vivekananda* by his Eastern and Western Disciples in two volumes (1933), all published by the Advaita Ashrama, Mayavati and Calcutta.

musician and a singer. *Wanderlust* was in his very blood. He knew every province of India by travel, and he was a world-tourist. Men and things he knew how to observe shrewdly.

A first-rate orator, he was a writer of the same rank. Bengali literature he has enriched with vigour and Bengali language with expressions picked up from the streets. A researcher and a translator, he was no less a commentator and a propagandist. He knew the Islamic teachings and the Christian Gospels as much as he knew his Hindu and Buddhist texts. His knowledge of Western institutions and ideals was no less extensive than that of Oriental. He studied the antiquities as much as he came into contact with the modern realities.

He was deeply absorbed in religious preaching and social reform. But his patriotism also was perennial and of the loftiest type. Nay, he was a socialist too. His socialism, however, was not Marxian, but rather romantic like that of, say, the Frenchman, St. Simon[1]. Or rather like Fichte, the father of the German *Jugendbewegung* (youth movement), nationalism and socialism, Vivekānanda initiated in India the cult of *Daridra-Nārāyaṇa* (God as the Poor). He was emphatically a nationalist and yet a fervent internationalist. His comparative methodology served to establish the universalistic, cosmopolitan and humane basis of all religious and social values.

As one dying at the age of forty and accomplishing so much for his fatherland and the world, Vivekānanda was certainly an *avatāra* of youth force. One may

[1] C. Bouglé: *Socialismes Français* (Paris, 1933); J. Baxa: *Einfuehrung in die romantische Staatswissenschaft* (Jena, 1923); Bonar: *Philosophy and Political Economy* (London, 1893).

worship him as a man of action, as a man of self-sacrifice, as a man of devotion, as a man of learning, as a man of *Yoga*. He was a hundred per cent idealist, a thoroughgoing mystic, and yet he was a foremost realist and a stern objectivist.

If we look upon Rāmakṛṣṇa as the Buddha of our times, Vivekānanda may pass for one or other of the great apostles of yore, say, the scholar Rāhula, the constitutional authority Upāli, the devoted lieutenant Ānanda, the sage Sāriputta, or that master of discourses, Mahākachchāyana. One can almost say that Vivekānanda was all these great Buddhist preacher-organizers boiled down into one personality.

And yet when this whole encyclopædia has been said about Vivekānanda, we have not said all or enough. He was much more than a mere exponent of Vedānta, or Rāmakṛṣṇa, or Hinduism, or Indian culture. Antiquarian lore, translation of other persons' thoughts, past or present, popularization of some Hindu ideals did not constitute the main function of his life. In all his thoughts and activities he was expressing only himself. He always preached his own experiences. It is the truths discovered by him in his own life that he propagated through his literature and institutions. As a modern philosopher he can be properly evaluated solely if one places him by the side of Dewey, Russell, Croce, Spranger, and Bergson. It would be doing Vivekānanda injustice and misinterpreting him hopelessly if he were placed in the perspective of scholars whose chief or sole merit consists in editing, translating, paraphrasing or popularizing the teachings of Plato, Aśvaghoṣa, Plotinus, Nāgārjuna, Aquinas, Śaṃkarāchārya and others.

Vivekānanda's lecture at Chicago (1893) is a profound masterpiece of modern philosophy. Before the

Parliament of Religions this young Bengali of thirty stood as an intellectual facing intellectuals, or rather as a whole personality face to face with the combined intelligence of the entire world. And the impression left by him was that of a man who told certain things that were likely to satisfy some great human wants, as one who thus had a message for all mankind. There he shone not as the propagator of Vedānta or Hinduism or any other "ism" but as a creative thinker whose thoughts were bound to prevail.

What, then, is Vivekānanda's self? What is the personality that he expressed in this speech? The kernel can be discovered in just five words. With five words he conquered the world when he addressed men and women as "Ye divinities on earth,—Sinners?" The first four words thundered into being the gospel of joy, hope, virility, energy and freedom for the races of men, and yet with the last word, embodying as it did a sarcastic question, he demolished the whole structure of soul-degenerating, cowardice-promoting, negative, pessimistic thoughts. On the astonished world the little five-word formula fell like a bomb-shell. The first four words he brought from the East, and the last word he brought from the West. All these are oft-repeated expressions, copy-book phrases both in the East and the West. And yet never in the annals of human thought was the juxtaposition accomplished before Vivekānanda did it in this dynamic manner and obtained instantaneous recognition as a world's champion.

Vivekānanda's gospel here is that of energism, of mastery over the world, of *élan vital* subduing conditions that surround life, of creative intelligence and will, of courage trampling down cowardice, of world-conquest. And those who are acquainted with the trends of world-thought since the middle of the nineteenth century are aware that it was just along these lines that the West was groping in the dark to find a solution. A most formidable exponent of these wants and shortcomings was the German man of letters and critic, Nietzsche, whose *Als sprach Zarathustra* or "The Sayings of Zoroaster" (1885) and other works had awakened mankind to the need of a more positive, humane and joyous life's philosophy than that of the *New Testament*. This joy of life for which the religious, philosophical and social thought was anxiously waiting came suddenly from an unexpected quarter, from this unknown young man of India. And Vivekānanda was acclaimed as a tremendous creative power, as the pioneer of a revolution,—the positive and constructive counterpart to the destructive criticism of Nietzsche.

There are very few men who have promulgated this doctrine of energism, moral freedom, individual liberty and man's mastery over the circumstances of life. One was the German philosopher, Immanuel Kant, another was Vivekānanda's senior English contemporary, the poet Robert Browning. And among the ancients we have our great intellectual giants, the thinkers of the *Upaniṣads* and the *Gītā*.

The key to Vivekānanda's entire life, his decade-long preparation down to 1893 and his decade-long work down to his death in 1902, is to be found in this *śakti-yoga*, energism, the vigour and strength of freedom. All his thoughts and activities are expressions of this energism. Like our Paurāṇic Viśvāmitra or the Aeschylean Prometheus he wanted to create new worlds and distribute the fire of freedom, happiness, divinity and immortality among men and women.

In his life-work there is to be found another very striking characteristic. This consists in his emphasis on individuals, on persons, and in his attempt to harness energism and *la renaissance de l'ésprit* to their thoughts and activities. Vivekānanda may have ostensibly preached religious reform, social reconstruction as well as crusade against poverty. But it is the making of individuals, the training for manhood, the awakening of creativeness and individuality on which his whole soul was focussed. Everywhere he wanted to see men and women who were energistic, freedom-loving, courageous and endowed with creative manhood. The objective of his diverse treatises on *Yoga* is none other than the "chiselling forth" of such individuals as may be depended upon as "divinities on earth," as persons who are determined to master the adverse conditions of life and conquer the world.

Vivekānanda's gospel is that of *śakti-yoga*, human energism. It is above the region, the climate, the space, the environment, in one word, Nature that he places man and his destiny. "Man is man," says he in London (1896),[1] "so long as he is struggling to rise above Nature." Again, "Man is born to conquer Nature and not to follow it." According to his "*sociologie des valeurs*," therefore, the whole history of humanity is a continuous fight against the so-called laws of Nature, and man gains in the end. * * * He, as it were, cuts his way out of Nature to freedom. It is to his ceaseless strivings, his continuous fights, the unbroken display of his energy that man owes his achievements, *vidyās*, *kalās*, arts, sciences, civilization, culture.

The words that are constantly on Vivekānanda's lips are the *Upaniṣads* and the *Vedānta*. These philosophical documents of ancient India appeal to him simply be-

[1] *The Complete Works*, Vol. II. (1924) pp. 65, 104, Vol. V. (1924) p. 323.

cause they can be utilized as texts of his own cult of *śakti*, energy, individuality and manhood.

Lecturing at Madras in 1897 on "Vedānta and Indian Life" on his return from America and Europe, Vivekānanda held forth on energism as follows :[1]

"Strength, strength is what the *Upaniṣads* speak to me from every page * * * Strength, O man, strength, say the *Upaniṣads*, stand up and be strong; aye, it is the only literature in the world where you find the word *abhīḥ*, fearless, used again and again * * * The *Upaniṣads* are the great mine of strength. Therein lies strength enough to invigorate the whole world. They will call with trumpet voice upon the weak, the miserable, and the down-trodden of all races, all creeds and sects to stand on their feet and be free; freedom, physical freedom, mental freedom, and spiritual freedom are the watchwords of the *Upaniṣads*. * * * * Aye, this is the one scripture in the world, of all others, that does not talk of salvation but of freedom. Be free from the bonds of Nature, be free from weakness."

The philosophy of Vivekānanda is, therefore, for the declaration of war against the "bonds of Nature," against the weaknesses engendered by geography,—the science of space and environment, regionalism and what not. And since "tradition," again, is nothing but environment in *time*, i.e., the despotism of the region or the space solidified in *history* his doctrine of continuous fights against Nature makes of man a permanent soldier against the tyrānny of tradition, history, established norms, usages and popular ideas or ideals.

Nowhere can we *pākḍāo* or catch this radical Man-above-Naturism or Man-born-to-conquer-Naturism of Vivekānanda more effectively than in the following

[1] *The Complete Works*, Vol. III, pp. 237-238.

words of his "Plan of Campaign" described at Madras (1897): "For centuries," says he, "people have been taught theories of degradation. They have been told that they are nothing. The masses have been told all over the world that they are not human beings. They have been so frightened for centuries till they have nearly become animals." And again, "you have been told and taught that you can do nothing, and non-entities you are becoming every day." This is the tradition, the history, the custom, the environment, the social *milieu* that he condemns. Defeatism is not to find a place in his intellectual and moral system. As against this psychology, logic or ethics of decay, degeneration, downfall, his societal planning introduces the cult of courage, energy and hope, of life, conquest and expansion. "What we want is strength, so believe in yourselves," thus runs his recipe. "Make your nerves strong," he tells us, "what we want is muscles, muscles of iron and nerves of steel. We have wept long enough. No more weeping, but stand on your feet and be men." It is the man above Nature, of the *Puruṣa* over *Prakriti* that he understands. Accordingly, in his words, "it is a man-making religion that we want. It is man-making theories that we want. It is man-making education all round that we want."[1]

Vivekānanda is not the man to appreciate his great French contemporary, the sociologist Durkheim to whom *la morale est pour nous un système de faits realisés* (morality is for us a system of facts already realized). According to Durkheim the life of the individual is almost tyranically "determined" by the "society," the *groupement professionnel*, the social *milieu*. He has, therefore, no interest in the question of *valeurs respectifs des états sociaux* (respective or relative values of the different

[1] *The Complete Works*, Vol. III, pp. 223-224.

social conditions).[1] Vivekānanda is the farthest removed from the man of "closed systems" or of settled facts. He is the man to open the questions closed and unsettle the settled conventions, dogmas, doctrines and norms.

It is to the ideas of another great French contemporary, the philosopher Bergson, that Vivekānanda's creative spirit would find a natural affinity. No single person in modern India has given rise to so many categories calculated to awaken the *renaissance de l'ésprit*, which serves to combat the domination of the region, the age, the *milieu*, and the time as Vivekānanda. He is the prophet of what Lasbax calls the *médecine sociale* and the doctor of social health. To him life is action and science is nothing but "social art." It is not the Durkheimian domination of the individual by the society and the social *mores* but the Bergsonian *élan vital*, the urge of life, *l'impulsion vitale* of Espinas[2], which creates the stir and turmoil in the individual, which sets the forces of "social metabolism" in motion, that best expresses the dynamic philosophy of Vivekānanda. His is the *Gītā* of social mobility.

It is in Vivekānanda's activism, the doctrine of creative reactions against the data of Nature and society

[1] E.Lasbax: *La Cité Humaine* (Paris, 1927), Vol. II., pp. 5-13.

In *Lecons de Sociologie sur l' Evolution des Valeurs* (Paris, 1929) C. Bouglé discusses the limits within which and the sense in which Durkheim's doctrine of the society as the creator of ideals is valid, pp. 27-37. For the formulation of this doctrine see Durkheim: *Formes élémentaires de la vie religieuse* (Paris, 1912), as well as *Règles de la Methode Sociologique* (Paris, 1904) in connection with the doctrine of *contrainte* (force or compulsion) as the formative factor in social phenomena.

[2] *La Philosophie Sociale du* XVIII *e Siécle et la Revolution* (Paris, 1898), pp. 13-17.

that we see one of the latest illustrations of the *Aitareya Brāhmaṇa* (VII, 15) cult of *charaiveti* (march on). His perpetual fights are nothing but being eternally on the go, uninterrupted wanderings and movements, both physical and spiritual. In his cult of life's urges and expansion we see embodied the Vedic dictum that *nānāśrāntāya śrīrastīti* (there is no prosperity to a man who does not weary himself with movements) and that *pāpo nriṣadvaro jano indra ichcharatah sakhā* (evil is who stayeth among men and Indra is the comrade of the wanderer).

Vivekānanda is not a statistical fact. He is a going concern. His philosophy compels one to move not only from village to village and region to region but from idea to idea, *mores* to *mores*, custom to custom, ideal to ideal. He is to move out of the shackles of the degrading and dehumanizing theories to the theories of man-making, or, rather, the transformation of nature and man by manhood, the remaking of man. It is such "social mobility," vertical and horizontal, in space as well as time, whose blessings are adumbrated in the *Aitareya Brāhmaṇa*[1] as follows:

> "Wandering one findeth honey,
> Wandering the sweet *udumbara* fruit,
> Consider the pre-eminence of the sun,
> Who wearieth never of wandering."

It is the example of the sun (*sūryasya paśya śremāṇam yo no tandrayate charan*), whose eternal movements inspired the Vedic philosophers to the doctrine of *charaiveti* or *Wanderlust*. In Vivekānanda's declaration of war against the contemporary theories and in his call for an ideal which transcends the existing customs and

[1] Eng. transl. by A. B. Keith (*Rigveda Brahmanas*, Cambridge, Mass. 1920), Harvard Oriental Series.

breaks the "bonds of Nature" we encounter once again the same age-long Hindu philosophy of mobility and vital dynamics.

Vivekānanda's doctrine of creative manhood, Nature-conquering personality, man in eternal fights or movements, is but an expression of the modern ontology of life. In his vitalism he shakes hands, on the one hand, with Espinas and Bergson. On the other, he meets the Italian philosopher Benedotto Croce, who in his *Theory and History of Historiography* (1916-19) teaches that "reality does not stay still" but that its "true being" is to be found in the "perpetual increment of itself upon itself, the ever new history". These remakings, creations of the "ever new history", the constant conquests of Nature by man enable us to place Vivekānandism likewise by the side of the progress-cult of Oswald Spengler, who in spite of the pessimistic title of his *Untergang des Abendlandes* (1918-22) is interested not so much in the world's declines, deaths and ends as in the transformation of epochs, in what Hindus would call *Yugāntara*, in the "culture yet to be". In so far as Spengler is looking for the "new element of inwardness" such as can sponsor the regeneration of life for the "world-historical phase of several centuries upon which we ourselves are entering" he is echoing the Vivekānandist doctrine of Man-born-to-conquer-Naturism. It is characteristic of Spengler's judgment that modern degeneracy is manifest in the absence of an Immanuel Kant such as should command the problems of all the exact sciences. The regeneration will be possible, according to Spenglerian philosophy[1], when a new Kant arises

[1] See the present author's *Political Philosophies Since* 1905 (Madras 1928), pp. 280-286; J. Dewey: *German Philosophy and Politics* (New York, 1915).

who because of his command over the exact sciences will know how to overthrow their will to victory. In Spengler's "back to Kant" as in Vivekānanda's "back to the *Upaniṣads*" we have one and the same message delivered to modern man, viz., that of the need for Nature-conquest or world-conquest by the strength of manhood, the overthrow of dehumanizing theories by man-making philosophies.

Creative idealism,—the conception of Espinas that *l'ideal a sa part dans la genèse de la realité* (the ideal has its part in the origin of the reality),—is Vivekānanda's life-blood. At Calcutta in 1897 in reply to the address of welcome on his return from the West, Vivekānanda reminds Young Bengal of the story of Nachiketā in the *Kaṭhopaniṣad*. "I am superior to many", said Nachiketā, as we are aware,[1] "I am inferior to few, but nowhere am I the last. I can also do something". It is the religion of self-confidence in the interest of action that Vivekānanda inculcates, and he reminds the audience also that this creativeness of man is not conditioned by the circumstances, the social situations. He energizes the humblest and the poorest to the creative enthusiasm of Nachiketā. It is above Nature and social surroundings that man has to rise in keeping with Vivekānanda's general philosophy. "The whole world has been made by the energy of man," says he, "by the power of enthusiasm, by the power of faith."

The glorification of the individual, the deification of the personality, which enables the man of the *Atharva Veda* (XII, i, 54) to declare to Nature, "Mighty am I, Superior by name, upon the Earth, conquering am I, all-conquering, completely conquering every region," is the "ideal that creates the reality" in Vivekānanda's

[1] *The Complete Works*, Vol. III. (1932) pp. 316, 319.

psychology. His doctrine of Man-born-to-conquer-Naturism finds therefore its natural paraphrase in the message he delivers to Young Bengal at that epoch-making Calcutta meeting. "We have to conquer the world," he declares, "That we have to! India must conquer the world, and nothing less than that is my ideal. It may be very big, it may astonish many of you, but it is so. We must conquer the world or die. There is no other alternative. The sign of life is expansion; we must go out, expand, show life or degrade, fester and die. There is no other alternative."

Let us remember the year. It is 1897, seven or eight years before the Indian "ideas of 1905" take a definite shape. Today in 1936 it is possible to observe objectively that among all the agencies that are contributing to the expansion of the intellectual horizon both in the East and the West, and the establishment of international *rapprochement*, none is more substantial and profound as a world-force than the Vedānta Centres in the U.S.A., which, as is well known, have served to bring the men and women of America into friendly contacts with the men and women of India. Vivekānanda's selection of New York as the nucleus of Vedānta propaganda in Eur-America nearly a generation ago, possesses almost the same significance in the history of inter-racial relations as St. Paul's selection of the capital of the Roman Empire as the seat of his missionizing activity. Vedānta has been tending to break down the distinction between the modern peoples, and at the present moment, Americans and our countrymen are working hand in hand in diverse fields of social endeavour both at home and abroad. It has proved to be a powerful unifying force calculated to strengthen the foundations of world-peace.

The movement was pioneered by Vivekānanda

but it did not die with him. He has been lucky enough to be succeeded by a band of brilliant colleagues and disciples who have known how to continue and foster his work with whole-hearted devotion and energy. Until Vivekānanda came upon the scene India's relations in cultural trade with the rest of the world were almost exclusively "passive". We were virtually mere importers. But with Vivekānanda begins an epoch in which the men and women of India have been functioning also as active partners in the spiritual commerce of mankind. Since then India has been not only importing but also exporting modern culture-goods of all kinds: literature, art, science, philosophy and religion.

This new gospel of energism, individuality and freedom is being propagated today by deed and by word in over a hundred centres throughout India, of which nearly a third is to be found in Bengal. There are twelve centres in the U.S.A. In 1932 a call came from Buenos Aires (Argentina) and a centre has been established there by one of the missionaries of the Rāmakṛṣṇa-Vivekānanda *Gestalt* (Swami Vijayānanda) as the nucleus of neo-Vedantic culture in Latin America.

Recently Europe also has been annexed to the movement. At Wiesbaden in Germany in response to an invitation from a group of German Nordics interested in philosophy a study circle has been established in 1933. In the work done by Swami Yatiśvarānanda, the missionary who has been deputed by the movement from Belur (near Calcutta) German intellectuals can detect the family likeness of the philosophical idealism such as is embodied in the greatest thinkers of their race, namely, Kant, Fichte and Hegel.

In 1934 the British Isles came likewise to be interested in study circles conducted by a missionary of the movement,—Swami Avyaktānanda. At the moment of writing, it is possible to announce the preparation of Czech, Spanish, German, Polish and French editions of some of the works of and about Rāmakṛṣṇa and Vivekānanda.

It is necessary to add that in Indian centres this neo-Vedantism manifests itself, among other things, in the social service activities of all sorts from the *ārogyadānam* (health-gifts), i.e., dispensary and hospital work of Hemādri's *Chaturvarga-chintāmaṇi* (*c* 1300 A.C.) down to night schools, industrial training, farming, girls' homes, rest houses, refuges for invalids, as well as famine, flood, fire and tornado relief, etc. Preaching and publication belong to the system as a matter of course.

From the Mohenjo Daro culture of the Indus Valley to the neo-Vedantic positivism of the Gangetic Delta of today world-culture and humanity have been experiencing the *charaiveti* (march on), i.e., *l'exubérance de vitalité*[1] of Hindu energism. It is but the five-thousand year old Indian tradition of *digvijaya*, world-conquest, and elevation of the most diverse races and classes to soul-enfranchising ideals and activities that Vivekānanda and after him the Swāmis of the Rāmakṛṣṇa Order have been pursuing under modern conditions, thereby exhibiting the virility and strenuousness of Hindu humanism and spirituality.[2]

[1] E. Lasbax: *La Cité Humaine* (Paris), Vol. II. (1927), p. 219.

[2] *Life of Sri Ramakrishna* edited by the Advaita Asrama, Mayavati and Calcutta (1929), 2 Vols.; *The Teachings of Sri Ramakrishna* (Calcutta 1934); Romain Rolland: *Ramakrishna and the Universal Gospel of Vivekananda* (London), 2 Vols; *The Seventh General Report of the Ramakrishna Mission* (1931-33) issued by the Governing Body, Belur Math, Howrah, September 1934.

Rāmakṛṣṇa-Vivekānanda as a New Category

The strenuousness and tenacity of the Rāmakṛṣṇa movement deserve by all means to be emphasized. The categories of Rāmakṛṣṇa might have become things of the past with his passing away in 1886 had there been no Vivekānanda to take them up and make them current coin for the East and the West. Humanly speaking, again, in 1902 with Vivekānanda's death the world might have heard no more either of himself or of his master. Both might have been drowned, further, in the epoch-making "ideas of 1905". But Vivekānanda's colleagues and followers have succeeded in accomplishing a miracle, as it were, by assuring immortality to their Prophet and their Leader.

Many of them were born of the "ideas of 1905", or reborn with those ideas, and all of them knew how to utilise those ideas in order to build up the Order left by their Great Exemplar, Vivekānanda. They have grown to be the architects of the third stage, so to say, of the Rāmakṛṣṇa philosophy of life and the universe. It is indeed questionable if Rāmakṛṣṇa or Vivekānanda could become the power that they are today without the sincerity and doggedness of their successors and torch-bearers. Some of them specialize in *jnāna* (intellectualism), others in *karma* (activism), while all are inspired by the common cult of *bhakti* or devotion to the great ideals of self-sacrifice and social service.

At this phase the Swamis may be described as the result of Rāmakṛṣṇa multiplied by Vivekānanda. This joint product is to be called Rāmakṛṣṇa-Vivekānanda. What Rāmakṛṣṇa had dreamt of in regard to the prospects of his message, if he had dreamt at all, is not known to us. So far as Vivekānanda's dreams are concerned, he would perhaps have felt today, had he lived up till now, that they have been realized to a great extent. Thanks to the activities of Rāmakṛṣṇa-Vivekānanda, Vivekānanda is today one of the great world-forces in the East and the West. It is because of the energism of Rāmakṛṣṇa-Vivekānanda that Rāmakṛṣṇa has become almost a household divinity in Bengal and even parts of India within fifty years of his passing away. It is worth while to recall that Śākya the Buddha's influence could not assume these proportions in such a short period.

Not the least mentionable fact about the character, intelligence and organizing ability of the Rāmakṛṣṇa-Vivekānanda Order is the item that the first birth-centenary of Rāmakṛṣṇa (1936) has called forth the widest support and co-operation from the intellectuals, academicians and social workers in the most diverse regions of the world. For instance, Burma, Ceylon, Straits Settlements, China, Japan, England, France, Germany, Italy, Poland, Czechoslovakia, East and South Africa, South America, U.S.A. and Australia have cared to join in the centenary celebration and contributed to its character as an international spiritual event of the year.

The Rāmakṛṣṇa-Vivekānanda Order is, besides, equipped with a *Weltanschauung* or world-view which is eminently calculated to render it durable and capable of expansion. In connection with the centenary and indeed as its last item the Order is organizing a Parliament of Religions to be held at Calcutta in March 1937. The Order has asked the participators to note that no direct or indirect reference to India or Indian religions and philosophical systems, ancient, medieval or modern, is obligatory. The Parliament is to address itself to every faith and every system of moral and spiritual tenets, old and new; and participators are at liberty to expound their own views and ideals in a scientific and philosophical manner without any spirit of intolerance. The Order attaches great importance to rendering the Parliament as universal in its contentual or topical make-up and as world-wide in race as possible. And this would be but a realization, as the Order understands it, of Rāmakṛṣṇa's teachings to the effect, *yata mat tata path* (every faith is a path to God).

It is in this world-view of Rāmakṛṣṇa-Vivekānanda that we find embodied for the twentieth century the millennium-old tenets of *sanātana-dharma* (eternal or universal religion), as Hinduism is popularly known. The Rāmakṛṣṇa-Vivekānanda Order is thereby carrying forward the *Aitareya Brāhmaṇa* (VII, 15) cult of *charaiveti* (march on) or world-conquest among "fresh fields and pastures new" of humanity. It is in keeping with the same *Weltanschauung*, again, that the Rāmakṛṣṇa Institute of Culture is being organized by the Order.

This Institute will have for its object the carrying out and realization of the teachings of Rāmakṛṣṇa through the study and promotion of the creative achievements and spiritual experiences of the diverse races, castes, classes and communities of mankind on a scientific, comparative and cosmopolitan basis. On the one hand, the proposed Institute will seek to furnish platforms and centres of intellectual and moral co-operation as well as social solidarity on terms of equality and mutual respect between the representatives of the East and the West. And on the other hand, the philosophies, religions, moralities, arts and crafts, sciences, literatures, industries, economic developments, measures for the control of poverty, health and educational organizations, economic developments etc. of the four quarters of the globe will form the theme of appreciative and rational discussion under the auspices of this Institute. Through these processes of broad, international and world-embracing approach to the problems and requirements of human life, the Institute will attempt to supply the cultural and spiritual foundations of a new personality among the men and women of the world, thereby equipping them as proper and adequate instruments for the establishment of world-peace, genuine internationalism, and a really humane culture on earth.

In the *milieu* of such achievements, ideas and projects we feel that Vivekānanda was not the last word of *Rāmakṛṣṇa Kathāmrita* (The Nectar of Rāmakṛṣṇa's Sayings). Vivekānanda's colleagues and followers have succeeded in carrying both Rāmakṛṣṇa and Vivekānanda forward to their farthest logical consequences. They are already in sight of new domains and they are preparing the soil for fresh adventures in world-conquest, spirituality and human welfare. Ramākṛṣṇa-Vivekānanda (1936) is not to be understood in terms of Rāmakṛṣṇa (1836-86) and Vivekānanda (1862-1902) alone.

Rāmakṛṣṇa-Vivekānanda does not merely copy, translate or paraphrase Rāmakṛṣṇa or Vivekānanda. It is not to be confounded wholesale with either the Prophet or the Leader. It is to be appraised as a new and distinct product of Creative India.

The Rāmakṛṣṇa-Vivekānanda amalgam is endowed with a virility and creativeness all its own. Like all its precursors from the days of Mohenjo Daro on, it is not content with the achievements of today and yesterday but is ever prayerful for tomorrow with a view to the acquisition of more *sat* (truth), more *jyoti* (light), and more *amrita* (immortality) for itself, for India and for mankind. The creativeness of Creative India is then assured for the future.

At the present moment it is possible to say that

mankind has something like a Rāmakṛṣṇa Empire. It is the new Hindu Empire of the twentieth century, furnished as it is with colonies of Hindu culture and spirituality in Asia, Europe, Africa and the two Americas. The ideals that inspire these colonies of the Greater India of today are none other than those of humanity and brotherhood. The *Leitmotif* of this spiritual empire is to be seen in *yata mat tata path* (as many faiths, so many paths), freedom of conscience, and inter-racial concord. A world-wide republic of religion and morality is in this manner coming into existence.

The Rāmakṛṣṇa Empire has been seeking to establish under modern conditions the traditional Hindu *Pax Sārvabhaumica* (peace of the world-state or universal kingdom). And this is being rendered possible not with material possessions and the ways and means such as are accessible to persons favourably placed in the diplomatic perspectives but by methods natural to those who have renounced the world and do not possess bank-accounts. It is the poor, the penniless and the self-sacrificing band of Swamis, men whose sole capital is the name of Rāmakṛṣṇa and sole captainship the example of Vivekānanda, that are responsible for the platform of equality, harmony and mutual appreciation between the nations that has been established in this world-wide *chakravartti-kṣetra* (territory of the universal sovereign). The work of this "Spiritual General Staff" in the world's inter-racial relations is of the most substantial importance. The five hundred Swamis of today, the architects of this Empire, have altogether a new place in the scale of modern values as distinguished from the place of Rāmakṛṣṇa as well as from that of Vivekānanda.

The Social Service Activities of the Rāmakṛṣṇa Mission

Excluding the hundreds of "unaffiliated" institutions

in Bengal conducted according to the ideals of the Ramakrishna Mission, which may be aptly described as the "Indian Spiritual Service", the total number of centres including those in Burma, Ceylon and Straits Settlements as well as in North and South America, and Europe was 102 at the end of 1935. The number of centres of the Mission in India, exclusive of the Ramakrishna Maṭh and its branches, was 42. A new educational centre in the Coimbatore district was added in the year.

The Mission conducted two kinds of work: temporary and permanent. Temporary relief work was done in times of distress caused by floods, famine, fire, tornado or epidemics during the year in Bankura, Hooghly and Burdwan Districts, as well as in Abdelpur, Dhalla, Manbhum and Tamluk. The total expenditure for the works was more than Rs. 16,000, the most important of them being the Damodar Flood Relief.

The permanent work was of three kinds, viz., philanthropic, educational and missionary. Each of the centres conducted one or more of these.

Philanthropic Activities

The philanthropic activities include three types of work, viz. (1) Indoor Hospital work, (2) Outdoor Dispensary work, and (3) Regular and Occasional Service of various kinds. In India 32 centres conducted one or more of these types of work.

In all there are 7 Indoor Hospitals including the Child Welfare Centre with its attached Maternity Hospital at Bhawanipore, Calcutta, which does both pre-natal and post-natal work along with its other activities and also trains midwives. There are 31 Outdoor Dispensaries including a Tuberculosis Dispensary at Delhi. The centres doing philanthropic work are widely distributed in different parts of India, and many of them are situated in Benares, Hardwar, Brindaban, Allahabad and other places of pilgrimage, as well as in cosmopolitan cities such as Rangoon, Bombay, Cawnpore, and Lucknow. The Sevashram at Benares is the largest philanthropic institution of the Mission, and the Hospital at Rangoon holds the highest record in outdoor and indoor work. The latter treated nearly 200,000 patients in 1935.

Philanthropic work is done also by such rural centres of the Mission as Bhubaneswar in Orissa, Jayrambati in Bankura, Sargachi in Murshidabad and Sonargaon in Dacca.

The Indoor Hospitals of the Mission treated more than 6800 cases in 1935 as against 6500 in 1934, and the Outdoor Dispensaries treated over 900,000 in 1935 as against nearly 830,000 in 1934. The number of new cases and the number of repeated ones were in the proportion of 10 : 17.

Educational Activities

The Educational work of the Mission falls mainly into two divisions, viz., (1) Boys' Schools, Girls' Schools, Mixed Schools (the classes ranging from the Matriculation Standard down to the Primary), and (2) Students' Homes and Orphanages.

Mass education for adults and juveniles through day and night schools forms a feature.

Twenty-nine centres conducted some type of educational work or other. In all there were 15 Students' Homes, 3 Orphanages, 3 Residential High Schools, 4 High Schools, 2 Middle English Schools, 33 Primary Schools, 7 Night Schools and 3 Industrial Schools.

Some of these institutions are situated in or near

the University Centres of Calcutta, Madras and Bombay and in the towns of Jamshedpur, Deoghar and Barisal. Physical, cultural, moral and religious training was imparted to the inmates or pupils.

Rural educational work was done as usual by some of the centres such as Sarisha near Diamond Harbour, Contai in Midnapore, Habiganj and Sylhet in Assam. The Centre at Sarisha has nearly 500 boys and girls in its schools, and spends over Rs. 12,000 every year.

The Industrial Schools taught one or more of the arts, crafts and industries such as may be grouped under the following heads: (1) Mechanical and Automobile Engineering, (2) Spinning, weaving, dyeing, calico-printing and tailoring, (3) Cane-work and (4) Shoe-making. In the Industrial School at Madras, the mechanical and automobile engineering course covers a period of 5 years, and a certificate issued by the Mission is recognised by the Government. The centre at Habiganj conducts two shoe factories to provide better training ground for the cobbler boys of the locality, and runs two co-operative credit societies for the benefit of the cobblers.

The Students' Homes at Madras and Calcutta, the Vidyapith at Deoghar, the Sister Nivedita School at Calcutta and the centre at Sarisha are a few of the most prominent educational institutions of the Mission. The educational centre at Madras is the largest. It had 925 pupils in 1935. It spends over Rs. 40,000 annually for its work.

In the 70 educational institutions of the Mission in India there were over 3900 students in 1935 as against 3050 in 1934.

In Ceylon there are 12 schools conducted by the Mission with over 2200 boys and girls, and in Singapore two schools with over two hundred students.

In all there were over 6300 students in all the centres and of these more than 4800 were boys and 1500 girls.

Expenditure

The disbursements of the Mission in India and Burma may be roughly computed to be over Rs. 200,000 for philanthropic work, and over Rs. 300,000 for educational activities, the total approximate expenditure being over Rs. 525,000 for its permanent work.

Libraries and Reading Rooms

There were 60 Libraries and as many Reading Rooms, each centre having one or more. The Mission Society at Rangoon did excellent work and had a daily average attendance of nearly 100 in its Reading Room. The Students' Home at Madras had more than 17,000 volumes in its libraries.

Missionary Activities

The monastic members of the Mission went on propaganda tours in India and abroad. The teachings of the *Vedanta* as interpreted by Rāmakṛṣṇa and Vivekānanda were disseminated chiefly through the English monthlies—*Prabuddha Bhārata* (Mayavati), *Vedanta Kesari* (Madras) and *The Message of the East* (Boston), and the *Udbodhan* in Bengali and the *Ramakrishna Vijayam* in Tamil, as well as through the publications of the Rāmakṛṣṇa and Vivekānanda literature and similar works. Classes were held and lectures and sometimes radio-talks were given at or near the various centres, associations, Universities and other bodies. A member of the Order (Swami Yatiswarananda) formed the nucleus of a Vedanta centre in

Switzerland and another (Swami Avyaktananda) started a centre in London, during the year under review.

There are colonies for the Harijans and other backward classes in some centres, those at Trichur (Cochin State) and Shella in Khassia Hills being two of the important ones. At these colonies the monks of the Mission have been conducting for over a dozen years educational and other work for the uplift of these neglected communities.[1]

Rāmakṛṣṇa the Prophet of the Young and the New

In 1936 while watching the activities of the Rāmakṛṣṇa-Vivekānanda movement at home and abroad it is almost superfluous to inquire as to whether in this epoch of technocracy, industrialism, exact sciences and machine-mindedness, the teachings of Rāmakṛṣṇa are likely to be useful to the men and women of India and the world.

There is no doubt that Rāmakṛṣṇa's spiritual experiences combined with the self-control, self-sacrifice and social service activities of the Swamis of the Rāmakṛṣṇa-Vivekānanda movement constitute the living religion of India in the twentieth century. Besides, Rāmakṛṣṇa is being honoured by the most diverse races of mankind and in the highest intellectual centres in Asia, Europe, Africa and America.

And yet be it observed, Rāmakṛṣṇa cannot be identified with the movement for any particular Hindu gods, rituals, religious scriptures or institutions. Rāmakṛṣṇa did not promulgate a religion. Rāmakṛṣṇa was not the exponent of any ethical code or system of morals either. No set of commandments and duties

[1] Adapted from the annual report published from Belur Math, Howrah 1936.

or virtues and vices can be discovered in Rāmakṛṣṇa's *Kathāmrita*, the nectar of his words. It would be difficult also to discover in Rāmakṛṣṇa's teachings any advocacy or propaganda in regard to caste-reforms, race-uplift and other social questions. And as for the questions of constitutional progress, nationality, provincial autonomy, federation or the like, Rāmakṛṣṇa had no message whatsoever.

Where then lie Rāmakṛṣṇa's claims to recognition by the East and the West as a world-teacher, as an *avatār?* They are to be found in some very elemental characteristics.

Rāmakṛṣṇa functioned as the guide and the friend to all and sundry in regard to the most fundamental questions of daily life. He spoke to the individual man and woman of flesh and blood and tried to evoke in their personalities just those human qualities which enable persons to flourish in the world. In the East as well as the West, human beings,—the richest and the the poorest, the expert and the layman, the businessman, the scholar, the lawyer, the peasant and the workingman, all are subject to diffidence in the concerns of the day to day round of duties. Rāmakṛṣṇa's teachings enable the meanest of human beings as well as the mightiest to combat diffidence and acquire self-confidence in the pursuit of life. Cowardice is another vice which attacks human nature under certain conditions both in the East and the West. In the atmosphere of Rāmakṛṣṇa men and women, no matter what be the race, profession or earnings, learn to pick up courage and advance boldly in their walks of life.

Rāmakṛṣṇa has delivered the gospel of strength with which a human being can overpower the thousand and one frailties of worldly existence. That is why Rāmakṛṣṇa has been accepted as a Teacher by the merchants, industrialists, lawyers, medical men, scholars, as well as by other persons belonging to the most varied economic professions. Rāmakṛṣṇa has, therefore, been a prophet for every corner of the globe, and as long as there is human nature with its tendencies to diffidence, cowardice, and weakness his teachings are destined to be the energiser of human souls. He is thus in a special sense a prophet of the young and the new individuals, groups as well as races. Everybody and every community that is trying to start a new concern, business or other enterprise, cultural or social, is likely to find in Rāmakṛṣṇa the most appropriate guide, philosopher and friend. His messages of self-confidence, courage and power are just adapted to the requirements of those individuals or groups that have no past and no history, nay, indeed, are submerged and repressed,—in order that they may commence their careers of world-conquest.

It is the householders, the men and women who have to live on earthly earth and make their homes prosperous, healthy and dignified, for whom Rāmakṛṣṇa spoke his words of nectar. In his sociology or metaphysics of values *Jīva* (man) = *Śiva* (God). The formulation of this equation by Rāmakṛṣṇa enables us to establish an identity between service to man and service to or worship of God. We are again and again rendered conscious that he was not constructing a "kingdom that is not of this world." This is the most marked characteristic in the "sayings" of Rāmakṛṣṇa. He was a positivist, a teacher of the worldly duties in the most emphatic sense. On the other hand, Rāmakrsṇa's perpetual emphasis on the spirit and the soul is epoch-making. He has taught mankind that with this instrument men and women can demolish the discouraging conditions of the surrounding world and transform them in the interest of the expansion of life. And we are enabled to feel all the time that Rāmakṛṣṇa's idealism and transcendentalism were of the highest order. The freedom of personality is a concept by which Rāmakṛṣṇa has succeeded in electrifying the mentality of the middle classes, the higher classes and the lower classes of the human society.

Altogether, as embodying the synthesis of the positive and the idealistic, Rāmakṛṣṇa has furnished the young and the new with the tremendous psychology of world-conquest, of supremacy over the bonds of nature, of emancipation from the fetters of society. And it is under the inspiration of this synthesis that an India of secular activities and cultural adventures, an India of material prosperity and idealistic social service,—has been absorbing the interest of constructive thinkers and statesmen of Young India[1].

[1] *Supra*, pp. 360-361, 464-472; based to a certain extent on the author's presidential addresses at the Conventions of Religion (under the auspices of the Ramakrishna Birth Centenary) held at Rangoon (8-10 April 1936), and at Karachi (1-8 November 1936).

INDEX

I. SUBJECTS

A

J

K

L

M

N

T

U

II. PERSONS

A

B

C

D

E

F